THE CAMBRIDGE HANDBOOK OF
LAW AND POLICY FOR NFTS

As blockchains in general and NFTs in particular reshape operation logistics, data creation, and data management, these technologies bring forth many legal and ethical dilemmas. This handbook offers a comprehensive exploration of the impact of these technologies in different industries and sectors, including finance, anti-money laundering, taxation, campaign-finance, and more. The book specifically provides insights and potential solutions for cutting-edge issues related to intellectual property rights, data privacy and strategy, information management, and ethical blockchain use, simultaneously presenting insights, case studies, and recommendations to help anyone seeking to shape effective, balanced regulation to foster innovation while safeguarding the interests of all stakeholders. This handbook sets out an invaluable roadmap for navigating the dynamic and evolving landscape of these new technologies.

Nizan Geslevich Packin is Professor of Law at the Baruch College Zicklin School of Business and University of Haifa. Her corporate law background, public-sector work, and academic contributions provide a unique perspective on tech policy and business law.

The Cambridge Handbook of Law and Policy for NFTs

Edited by

NIZAN GESLEVICH PACKIN

Baruch College Zicklin School of Business and University of Haifa

CAMBRIDGE
UNIVERSITY PRESS

Shaftesbury Road, Cambridge CB2 8EA, United Kingdom

One Liberty Plaza, 20th Floor, New York, NY 10006, USA

477 Williamstown Road, Port Melbourne, VIC 3207, Australia

314–321, 3rd Floor, Plot 3, Splendor Forum, Jasola District Centre, New Delhi – 110025, India

103 Penang Road, #05–06/07, Visioncrest Commercial, Singapore 238467

Cambridge University Press is part of Cambridge University Press & Assessment,
a department of the University of Cambridge.

We share the University's mission to contribute to society through the pursuit of
education, learning and research at the highest international levels of excellence.

www.cambridge.org
Information on this title: www.cambridge.org/9781009279178

DOI: 10.1017/9781009279215

First published 2024

A catalogue record for this publication is available from the British Library

A Cataloging-in-Publication data record for this book is available from the Library of Congress

ISBN 978-1-009-27917-8 Hardback

To Tamir, Yoel, and Lea, who make everything possible, and to Hadas, Liam, Adar, and Carmel, who are the future, and make it all worth the while

Contents

Figures

Tables

Contributors

Eric C. Chaffee, Case Western Reserve University School of Law.

Chris Draper, Third Coast Commodities, LLC.

Brian L. Frye, College of Law, University of Kentucky.

Jon M. Garon, Shepard Broad College of Law, Nova Southeastern University.

Yuliya Guseva, Fintech and Blockchain Research Program, Rutgers Law School.

Esfan Haghverdi, School of Informatics, Computing, and Engineering, Indiana University.

Lital Helman, School of Law, Ono Academic College.

Joan MacLeod Heminway, College of Law, University of Tennessee.

Jiaying Jiang, Levin College of Law, University of Florida.

Kristof Lommers, HashCurve.

Juliet M. Moringiello, Commonwealth Law School, Widener University.

Tyler T. Ochoa, Santa Clara University School of Law.

Christopher K. Odinet, College of Law, University of Iowa.

Moran Ofir, Harry Radzyner Law School, Reichman University (Interdisciplinary Center Herzliya).

Nizan Geslevich Packin, Baruch College Zicklin School of Business and University of Haifa.

Anjanette H. Raymond, Kelley School of Business and Maurer Law School, Indiana University.

Carla L. Reyes, Dedman School of Law, Southern Methodist University.

Ido Sadeh, Desmarais LLP.

Hamutal Schieber, Schieber Research, LLC.

Amy J. Schmitz, Moritz College of Law, Ohio State University.

Scott J. Shackelford, Kelley School of Business, Indiana University.

Jamiel Sheikh, Chainhaus; Columbia Business School; Zhejiang International Business School; and Baruch College Zicklin School of Business, City University of New York.

Sean Stein Smith, Lehman College, City University of New York.

Lawrence J. Trautman, College of Business, Prairie View A&M University.

Ofer Tur-Sinai, School of Law, Ono Academic College.

Uri Volovelsky, Bar Ilan University; and Ministry of Justice, Israel.

Kevin Werbach, Wharton School of Business, University of Pennsylvania.

Acknowledgments

I would like to express my heartfelt gratitude to Ido Sadeh, the Editing Assistant whose unwavering support, contributions, and invaluable expertise in the area of financial and technology regulation have greatly enriched this book and made it possible.

PART I

Introduction and Background

Introduction

Nizan Geslevich Packin

In the vast expanse of the digital age, technological innovations seem to burgeon with every passing day. Among these novelties, blockchain technology has solidified its position as a transformative force, paving the way for novel applications that transcend the boundaries of traditional digital paradigms. The ascent of blockchain has not only metamorphosed how we perceive and understand financial systems and transactions but has also ushered in a wave of possibilities in myriad sectors, most notably in the domain of digital assets – enter Non-Fungible Tokens (NFTs).

NFTs represent a radical shift from traditional conceptions of ownership, value, and originality in the digital world. This distinctiveness has garnered immense attention from artists, creators, collectors, investors, gamers, digital platform developers, realtors, marketers, community managers, and many others. But as with any groundbreaking technology, the law must evolve in tandem with it. The intertwining of blockchain and legal realms brings forth a plethora of complexities warranting an in-depth exploration of law and policy surrounding NFTs.

This Handbook comes at a pivotal juncture when the blockchain technology in general, and the cryptocurrency market in particular, is maturing and specific applications and tokens,[1] including such that are based on or powered by NFTs, are undergoing transformative developments. With the blockchain technology establishing roots in everything from supply chain management to voting systems, the relevance of its most vibrant offspring, NFTs, cannot be understated. But what becomes vital is understanding its implications, not just from technical, financial, and business perspectives, but also from legal and public policy standpoints, which have seen very little development.

---

[1] *See, for example,* Krisztian Sandor, *OpenTrade Unveils Tokenized U.S. Treasuries Offering as Tokenization Race Gains Steam,* CoinDesk (September 29, 2023), www.coindesk.com/business/2023/09/29/opentrade-unveils-tokenized-us-treasuries-offering-as-tokenization-race-gains-steam/; Ezra Reguerra, *Swiss Bank UBS Launches Tokenized Money Market Fund on Ethereum,* CoinTelegraph (October 2, 2023), https://cointelegraph.com/news/ethereum-ubs-tokenize-money-market-fund-launch.

THE LAW AND POLICY LANDSCAPE

NFTs – and cryptoassets more broadly – present a wide range of legal, regulatory, and policy challenges.

The years 2021 through 2024 were significant in the cryptoasset world, particularly in the realm of NFTs. The year 2021 witnessed an unprecedented surge in institutional adoption, with many large-scale corporations and financial institutions integrating or investing in cryptocurrencies. This era also saw the proliferation of decentralized finance (DeFi) platforms which aimed to replicate traditional financial services without intermediaries, offering novel ways of earning, borrowing, and lending. Concurrently, the NFT concept embarked on an extraordinary journey into the mainstream. Starting with rather unconventional use cases like virtual cats and monkeys, it gradually expanded into various aspects of our daily lives, from marketing to fashion to gaming, and saw massive institutional adoptions.

Against this background, by 2022, regulatory bodies around the world began to grapple more seriously with the crypto ecosystem. A notable development was the Executive Order the White House released in March 2022,[2] seeking to safely regulate the crypto industry in the near future. Although no US regulator has formally asserted jurisdiction over NFTs following the Executive Order, many regulators asserted oversight over different aspects of it, manifesting the challenge of categorizing this novel asset class, which may embody a variety of rights to digital or physical assets.

Illustrative examples include the Securities and Exchange Commission's (SEC's) first NFT-related enforcement action against Impact Theory, LLC, applying the *Howey* analysis,[3] which helped determine that NFTs are securities;[4] the Lummis-Gillibrand Responsible Financial Innovation Act,[5] which proposed that the majority of cryptoassets (including NFTs) be classified as commodities, which are primarily regulated by the Commodity Futures Trading Commission (CFTC); the FinCEN's comprehensive report on the money laundering (ML) and terrorist financing (TF) risks involved in the use of NFTs in art markets;[6] and the Biden administration's proposed tax framework for NFTs and other cryptoassets.[7]

Aside from the categorization challenge, the creation, use, transfer, and purpose of NFTs raise novel legal and policy questions. Lawsuits related to copyright and trademarks in the context of NFTs are progressively making their way into the

---

[2] Exec. Order No. 14,067, 87 Fed. Reg. 14,143 (Mar. 9, 2022).

[3] *SEC v. W.J. Howey Co.*, 328 U.S. 293, 298 (1946).

[4] In the Matter of Impact Theory, LLC, Securities Act Release No. 11226 (Aug. 28, 2023).

[5] S. 4356, 117th Cong. (2022).

[6] Press Release, US Dep't of the Treasury, Treasury Releases Study on Illicit Finance in the High-Value Art Market (February 4, 2022), https://home.treasury.gov/news/press-releases/jy0588.

[7] Hannah Lang, *Biden Administration Unveils New Crypto Tax Reporting Rules*, REUTERS (August 25, 2023), www.reuters.com/markets/us/biden-administration-unveils-new-crypto-tax-reporting-rules-2023-08-25/.

courtroom, introducing cutting-edge questions.[8] New privacy and cybersecurity challenges, as well as reimagined manifestations of existing challenges, are also emerging in this evolving landscape, posing the challenges of aligning existing regulatory frameworks with the novel concept of NFTs and striking a balance between innovation and security.

MOVING FORWARD PAST THE "CRYPTO WINTER"

The increasing efforts to establish a regulatory framework for crypto sparked a variety of responses from the crypto community, ranging from staunch resistance to adaptive compliance. The industry responded with increased lobbying and sophistication but also experienced significant value drops as several major and widely known crypto players collapsed due to various reasons which resulted in what has been termed a "crypto winter."

Then, in 2023, a more realistic (and somewhat hesitant) adoption of blockchain technology started taking place in various sectors, including the financial industry,[9] while leading cryptocurrencies made a formidable comeback in the first half of 2023 and 2024.[10] The NFT markets, however, painted a starkly contrasting picture. While some cryptocurrency giants soared, the NFT realm grappled with a downturn. The trading volume of NFTs plunged and the total number of NFT sales also witnessed a drop. In fact, reports accentuated this decline by revealing a staggering 79 percent drop in NFTs minted on the Ethereum network in the first eight months of 2023.[11]

This unexpected downturn in the NFT market is arguably a confluence of several factors. An upsurge in competition owing to other blockchain networks making inroads into the NFT space played a role. Furthermore, the unpredictable volatility in cryptocurrency prices fostered an ambiance of market uncertainty. Another significant aspect was the saturation of the NFT supply which arguably surpassed the demand, leading to a market imbalance.

---

[8] *See, for example, Hermès Int'l v. Rothschild*, 590 F. Supp. 3d 647, 650 (S.D.N.Y. 2022); *Yuga Labs, Inc. v. Ripps*, 2023 WL 3316478 (C.D. Cal. Apr. 21, 2023).

[9] Jordan Smith, *Why Big Banks Like JP Morgan and Citi Want to Put Wall Street on a Blockchain*, CNBC (July 26, 2023), www.cnbc-com.cdn.ampproject.org/c/s/www.cnbc.com/amp/2023/07/26/why-big-banks-like-jpmorgan-want-put-wall-street-on-a-blockchain.html (discussing how U.S. financial institutions want to use blockchain to speed up trades on Wall Street, and $5 trillion in assets could be tokenized on blockchains in the next five years, according to reports).

[10] Wayne Duggan, *The 10 Best-Performing Cryptocurrencies of 2023*, U.S. NEWS & WORLD REPORT (July 18, 2023), https://money.usnews.com/investing/articles/the-10-best-performing-cryptocurrencies-of-2023 (describing how "[t]he 'crypto winter' has transitioned into summer in 2023, as investor concerns about a hard landing for the U.S. economy have somewhat subsided and appetite for risk assets has returned").

[11] *See, for example*, Edith Muthoni, *NFTs Minted on the Ethereum Network Down 79% Since the Year Began*, TRADING PLATFORMS (August 7, 2023, updated), https://tradingplatforms.com/blog/2023/08/07/nfts-minted-on-the-ethereum-network-down-79-since-the-year-began/.

However, the future of NFTs remains intriguing for several reasons. First, while their popularity may be waning in certain sectors, places like museums are showing a growing interest in these assets and embracing them more than ever. Second, there is a strong belief in the potential of NFTs, which have diverse and relevant applications across various industries. The crux of the challenge is to pinpoint the genuine value NFTs can provide beyond just community access and perks. What is pressing now is a shift toward tangible applications. While many perceive NFTs primarily as investments, their true potential might be found in other realms. For example, in the art world, artists can tokenize their work, providing a mechanism for collectors to verify the authenticity and provenance of their acquisitions. In the gaming industry, NFTs represent in-game assets like weapons or outfits and enable players to buy, sell, collect, or even trade these assets across different platforms. In education, NFTs have the potential to play a transformative role in credential certification and authentication as they can bring more trust, efficiency, and flexibility to the processes of learning recognition and skill verification. For musicians, NFTs can open up the realm of tokenized albums, tickets, or unique experiences, paving the way for direct sales to fans and potential royalties from secondary transactions and possibly simplifying royalty distributions and transfer rights. In addition, NFTs are being considered for representing one's digital identity, creating a more secure online environment. For fashion enthusiasts, digital clothing can become a valuable asset, especially in immersive virtual realities. In the luxury sector, with goods that have always grappled with authenticity issues, NFTs can help ensure provenance and counter counterfeits. In real estate, while it is ambitious to fully transform transactions using NFTs, aspects like title deeds can arguably benefit from some innovation. Lastly, the DeFi sector is eyeing NFTs as potential collateral or even using them for crypto-native and decentralized credit scoring, recordkeeping, and lending protocols' purposes.[12]

As technology progresses, the horizon for NFT applications is likely to broaden. This potential is particularly evident if NFTs can successfully establish a non-tech native audience, as such an achievement would further foster their growth and acceptance.

AN OVERVIEW OF THE HANDBOOK

Aimed at law enthusiasts, public policy advocates, computer technologists, finance aficionados, and business professionals, this Handbook serves as a beacon of knowledge, guiding readers through the intricate labyrinth of NFTs. Moving beyond the hype, the Handbook bridges the myriad gaps in understanding associated with

---

[12] *See, for example,* Nizan Geslevich Packin & Yafit Lev-Aretz, *Decentralized Credit Scoring: Black Box 3.0,* ABLJ (forthcoming 2024); Nizan Geslevich Packin & Yafit Lev-Aretz, *Crypto Native Credit Score: Between Financial Inclusion and Predatory Lending,* 45:3 Cardozo L. Rev. 845 (2024).

NFTs and critically assesses their implications in diverse contexts, separating true value from hype. Recognizing the novelty and interdisciplinary nature of NFTs, this Handbook offers an expansive yet thorough exploration of their intersections with the world of law and policy, encompassing not only the relevant legal frameworks, regulations, and established norms but also providing a guiding path for future policymaking within this dynamic domain.

Part I provides an introductory overview of NFTs, exploring the genesis of blockchain and NFTs, and the terminology underlying this ecosystem. In Chapter 1, Brian L. Frye offers a brief history of NFTs and the NFT market, beginning with the invention of blockchain technology, through the creation of the Bitcoin, Namecoin, and Ethereum blockchains, and the NFT phenomenon. In Chapter 2, Carla L. Reyes addresses the linguistic inaccuracies and misunderstandings that permeate discussions on blockchain technology and NFTs. Too often commentators employ inconsistent terminology and provide inaccurate definitions and descriptions, revealing a lack of understanding of how blockchain and NFTs function, which can hinder policymaking in this domain. Reyes discusses language landmines prevalent in blockchain and NFT discussions, helping to bridge this understanding gap.

Having understood what NFTs are – and more importantly, what they are not – as well as their historical context, Part II shifts to focus on the interactions of NFTs with financial regulation and the intricate task regulators face when trying to categorize NFTs: Are they commodities, securities, cryptocurrencies, or an entirely different class? In Chapter 3, Yuliya Guseva analyzes the economic reality of the rights, assets, and transactions associated with NFTs to help decision-makers to ascertain to which market an NFT belongs and which corresponding legal regime should govern. A special emphasis is given to the questions of whether and when federal securities laws may, and should, apply. In Chapter 4, Nizan Geslevich Packin and Uri Volovelsky focus on the ML and TF risks within the NFT market and survey global regulatory developments, compliance challenges, technological solutions, enforcement actions, collaborative efforts, and future trends. In Chapter 5, Eric C. Chaffee delves into the often overlooked promising role that state regulation – particularly in the areas of securities and virtual currency and money transmission – may play in addressing the prominent concerns posed by NFTs. In Chapter 6, Sean Stein Smith explores the complexities of taxing cryptocurrencies, examining factors such as classifying tax liabilities for various digital assets and the implications of crypto transactions on taxable events. Combined, these chapters provide a through overview of the interactions between NFTs and financial regulations, their associated challenges, and the implications for practitioners and policymakers.

Part III delves into the multifaceted world of marketing, branding, social platforms, fundraising, donations, and crowdfunding within the NFT landscape. In Chapter 7, Joan MacLeod Heminway examines the use of NFTs in financing nonprofits and political campaigns and offers guidance on core issues under applicable laws and regulations. Chapter 8, authored by Ido Sadeh and Moran Ofir, supplements this examination by focusing more broadly on blockchain-based fund-raising mechanisms – ranging from Initial Coin Offerings to Initial NFT Offerings – and on the asymmetric information problem in this context. In Chapter 9, Hamutal Schieber delves into the challenges and opportunities surrounding the use of NFTs as a marketing tool, highlighting the potential of NFTs as groundbreaking branding tools, but also raises concerns about their resemblance to controversial multilevel marketing schemes. Finally, in Chapter 10, Nizan Geslevich Packin explores the impact of NFTs on digital gaming, including innovative business models and their role in altering how users use, acquire, exchange, and sell virtual assets.

Part IV encompasses discussions on the intersection of NFTs and property rights – real property and intangible property – the minting of NFTs, the effect of NFTs on the concept of ownership, and their influence on the music, art, collectibles, and profile pictures (PFPs) sectors. In Chapter 11, Tyler T. Ochoa explores copyright implications associated with NFTs, with a focus on the concept of ownership and the question whether unauthorized minting of Non-Fungible Tokens (NFTs) is copyright violation under US, EU, and UK laws. Chapter 12, authored by Lital Helman and Ofer Tur-Sinai, supplements this discussion with a normative exploration of whether copyright law *should* forbid unauthorized minting of NFTs. They analyze this question under key theories that underly copyright law and conclude that the right to mint an NFT should be awarded to the author of the work that underlies the NFT. Against this background, in Chapter 13, Lawrence J. Trautman turns to examine the impact of NFTs on the art market and surveys recent developments in this context. Lastly, in Chapter 14, Juliet M. Moringiello and Christopher K. Odinet move to question one of the most frequently cited promises of NFTs – their use in real property transactions. Going beyond the hype, they argue that NFTs provide few, if any, benefits in this context, and explain why the potential use case for NFTs in the realm of property rights lies in the world of intangible property instead.

Part V explores data protection, privacy, and cybersecurity issues associated with blockchain and NFTs. A special focus is given to the processes and mechanisms in which information can be collected and transferred in the context of NFTs, data integrity and cybersecurity risks, and the policy issues. In Chapter 15, Jamiel Sheikh and Jiaying Jiang begin with a much needed technical analysis of NFT transactions work, highlighting vulnerabilities for creators' and users' data, and discussing the policy challenge of balancing between privacy interests and the need for transparency in the realm of NFTs. Chapter 16, authored by Scott J. Shackelford and Esfan Haghverdi, supplements the discussion by focusing on the cybersecurity perspective. It delves into the inherent risks and challenges associated with NFTs, and examines how existing laws and policies have addressed these issues and speculates on how they may evolve in the future. Having understood the potential risks and benefits associated with the use of NFTs in terms of data integrity and data security, in Chapter 17, Anjanette H. Raymond and Chris Draper move to analyze applications of NFTs and blockchain-based solutions within the supply chain context.

Recognizing the rapid advancements in NFT applications, Part VI offers insights into the emerging trajectories in the world of NFTs and their potential legal implications, encompassing fervor around the metaverse and the aspirational vision of Web 3.0 (or Web3).[13] In Chapter 18, Jon M. Garon examines the role of NFTs in the metaverse's emergence, emphasizing their part in enabling interoperability and consumer trust and reshaping various aspects of public life, ranging from work to education to entertainment. In Chapter 19, Amy J. Schmitz examines the resolution of disputes involving NFTs and smart contracts and proposing that parties turn to online dispute resolution (ODR) to efficiently and fairly resolve such disputes.

Finally, in Part VII, Kevin Werbach and Kristof Lommers, the authors of Chapter 20, culminate with a synthesized overview, presenting a potential prediction for the business, legal, regulatory, and policy dimensions of NFTs in the future.

* * *

This Handbook embarks on an enlightening journey which seeks to understand the potential of NFTs, and delves deep into the different complexities associated with them, dissecting and understanding them, not just as digital assets or more specifically, cryptoassets but as a fusion of technology, art, finance, community, policy, and law. Through this exploration, the Handbook seeks to provide clarity, insight, and a comprehensive roadmap for the ever-evolving world of NFTs. Welcome to the intersection of the future!

---

[13] The term has been used to describe a futuristic Web in which the Internet would be more intelligent, semantically rich, and interconnected. As such, many envision it to offer a decentralized digital experience and users operating without intermediaries thereby enhancing their autonomy and privacy. Julia Y. Lee, *Trust and Social Commerce*, 77 U. Pitt. L. Rev. 137, 142 n. 21 (2015) (explaining that "[s]ome have begun referring to Web 3.0, a third generation of the Web, characterized by use of semantic web technologies, natural language processing, machine learning, and artificial intelligence technologies"); Zoe Niesel, *#personaljurisdiction: A New Age of Internet Contacts*, 94 Ind. L.J. 103, 137 (2019) (describing the goal of Web 3.0 applications). However, "[b]ecause it remains a collection of ideas more than anything else, it's challenging to nail down a precise definition of Web3" (ibid.).

1

A Brief History of NFTs

Brian L. Frye

I INTRODUCTION

In the second millennium of the Common Era, the Internet comprehended just about all the known works of humankind and made them available to anyone with a computer. Its domains and protocols were governed by international organizations, and the image of neutrality and decentralized authority was decently preserved. But then, for better or worse, the blockchain revolution called it all into question. The purpose of this chapter is to describe one small part of that revolution, to deduce its role in challenging the prevailing order, and to speculate on whether it will be remembered or forgotten.

Of course, I am speaking of non-fungible tokens or "NFTs," a novel medium that seems at once ridiculous and inevitable. NFTs are cryptographic tokens that usually represent ownership of something, typically a digital artwork. They were conceived in 2014, and after a long gestation, suddenly expanded into a global bubble, which eventually popped, leaving a humbled, but functioning market.

It may seem premature to write a history of a medium that has only existed for about a decade. But time moves fast in the Internet Age, and yesterday is history before you know it. In a few short years, NFTs went from obscurity, to ubiquity, to catastrophe, to cliche. Who's to say where they will go next?

II WHAT IS AN NFT?

Essentially, an NFT is a blockchain entry that represents something other than a quantity of cryptocurrency. NFTs are "non-fungible" because each NFT is unique, unlike blockchain entries that represent a quantity of cryptocurrency. And NFTs are "tokens" because they typically represent ownership of something other than just the NFT.

Thanks to Tyler T. Ochoa, Michael Assis, Robness, Dmitri Cherniak, and Kevin McCoy for helpful comments and suggestions.

In theory, an NFT can consist of any kind or amount of data and can represent literally anything or nothing. However, most NFTs consist of as little data as possible and represent ownership of a digital artwork. Writing data onto a blockchain is costly, and the more data you write, the more it costs. Accordingly, NFT creators have an incentive to minimize the quantity of data included in their NFTs. Typically, an NFT consists of nothing more than the name of the NFT, the date it was created, the wallet address of the creator, and a URL pointing to a copy of the digital artwork the NFT represents. Each NFT is tracked by a "smart contract" that defines ownership of the NFT, usually written in the ERC-721 token standard.

NFTs have many potential uses. Businesses already use NFTs to track shipments and settle transactions, among other things, and are developing new uses all the time. But the primary use of NFTs is currently to represent ownership of digital artworks. The NFT market is essentially the cryptographic equivalent of the art market. So, to understand the NFT market, we have to understand the art market. But I think the NFT market can also help us better understand the economic realities of the art market.

As Walter Benjamin famously observed, the essence of art is authenticity, and the art market is a market for authenticity.[1] In the art market, collectors buy and sell unique physical objects such as paintings and sculptures. But it is not really the object that matters; it is what the object represents. An object is valuable in the art market only if it is authentic. In other words, the object is a physical token that represents ownership of an artwork. The art market does not actually value the object itself; it values the object's provenance, or the object's connection to the artist who created it. Without this connection, the object is worthless.

The NFT market is just a cryptographic version of the art market, in which collectors buy and sell NFTs that represent ownership of a digital artwork. The art market is a market for unique physical tokens, and the NFT market is a market for unique cryptographic tokens. Otherwise, they are identical.

It is no wonder the art market accepted NFTs so readily. They made perfect sense. In fact, NFTs are merely the cryptographic equivalent of the certificates of authenticity that conceptual artists and digital artists have been using for decades, with varying degrees of success. The only problem was that art collectors did not really understand certificates. Or, rather, they did not believe other collectors would want to buy them. So no one bought certificates because no one thought there was a market for them. And then it turned out there was, because conceptual art became cool and everyone thought they needed the permission of a certificate owner to show a work of conceptual art. They were wrong, but it was understandable, and it would have been awkward to show conceptual artworks without asking permission.[2]

---

[1] WALTER BENJAMIN, THE WORK OF ART IN THE AGE OF MECHANICAL REPRODUCTION (1936).
[2] *See generally* Guy A. Rub, *Owning Nothingness: Between the Legal and the Social Norms of the Art World*, 2019 BYU L. REV. 1147 (2020); and Peter Karol, *Permissive Certificates: Collectors of Art as Collectors of Permissions*, 94 WASH. L. REV. 1175 (2019).

And yet collectors still had a question: What do you get when you buy an NFT? This is best answered by another question: What do you get when you buy an artwork? In both cases, the real answer is "nothing" (aside from the actual material from which the artwork is made), other than the right to say you own an artwork created by a particular artist. An artwork is valuable because of what it represents, not because of what it is. And a cryptographic token such as an NFT can represent ownership just as well as a physical token such as a painting, sculpture, or certificate. Or, rather, NFTs and objects can both represent ownership of an artwork, so long as we believe they represent ownership of an artwork.

When you buy an artwork in the conventional art market, all you get is ownership of an object, the right to publicly display that object or the artwork it represents, and the right to transfer ownership of that object to someone else.[3] The same is true of NFTs. When you buy an NFT in the NFT market, all you get is ownership of the NFT, the right to publicly display the artwork the NFT represents, and the right to transfer ownership of the NFT to someone else.[4]

III THE GENESIS OF BLOCKCHAIN AND NFTS

This section of the chapter provides a brief overview of the birth of blockchain and cryptocurrencies, spanning from the inception of bitcoin to the introduction of Ethereum and the invention of NFTs. This introductory part is essential for understanding the historical context underlying this ecosystem.

A *The Birth of the Blockchain*

Let us start at the very beginning. The concept of a ledger has existed since time immemorial. Indeed, many of the earliest preserved writings are ledger entries recording transactions, dating to about 2600 BCE.[5] But blockchain requires both digital computers and advanced cryptography, which were not invented until many millennia later.[6]

So we will fast forward a few thousand years to 1972, when Ralph Merkle explained how to use a cryptographic hash to immutably link blocks of data to each other, and 1974, when he explained how to implement a form of public-key

---

[3] Under 17 U.S.C. 109(c), the owner of a particular lawfully made copy of a work has the right to publicly display that copy.

[4] Under the Copyright Act of 1976, it is not entirely clear that an NFT owner is necessarily an owner of a particular lawfully made copy of the artwork the NFT represents under 17 U.S.C. 109(s). However, selling an NFT of an artwork is universally understood to convey the right to publicly display that artwork, so even if the Copyright Act does not explicitly give NFT owners the right to publicly display the artwork represented by their NFT, courts are certain to imply a license to publicly display the artwork.

[5] For example, Assyrians, Babylonians, and Egyptians recorded ledgers on cuneiform tablets and papyrus scrolls.

[6] *See, for example,* Alan Turing, *Computing Machinery and Intelligence,* 236 MIND 433 (1950).

cryptography.[7] While Merkle provided the building blocks, David Chaum invented blockchain in 1979, although he never created one, and did not even know its name.[8] Chaum explained how to use cryptographic "vaults" to create a distributed ledger that could be established, maintained, and trusted by mutually suspicious groups.[9] While Chaum's system included most of the essential elements of a blockchain, it was different from and more complicated than modern blockchains. And, in any case, soon after describing what eventually became blockchain, he abandoned the project.[10]

Blockchain was born in 2007, when a pseudonymous coder or group of coders known as Satoshi Nakamoto began working on what became bitcoin. On August 18, 2008, Nakamoto registered the domain name bitcoin.org and created a website. On October 31, 2008, Nakamoto published a white paper titled "Bitcoin: A Peer-to-Peer Electronic Cash System" on a cryptography mailing list.[11] And on January 9, 2009, Nakamoto created the bitcoin blockchain by publishing the bitcoin software and defining the "genesis block" of the blockchain (Figure 1.1).

Essentially, a blockchain is a method of using cryptography to enable mutually distrustful parties to reach a consensus of the state of a ledger. The bitcoin blockchain is a remarkably simple demonstration of how a blockchain can be used to create a decentralized currency. The bitcoin blockchain is a public ledger that records bitcoin transactions. It consists of a series of blocks of data, which are maintained by a vast network of independent nodes. Each block of the bitcoin blockchain includes a cryptographic hash of the previous block, which enables the nodes to instantly determine whether a block is valid. As a consequence, the bitcoin blockchain is effectively immutable, and bitcoin transactions are irrevocable.

Bitcoins are registered to a bitcoin address or "wallet," which is protected by a cryptographic "key." The owner of a bitcoin wallet can transfer any bitcoins in their wallet to any other wallet by "signing" the transfer with their key. The Bitcoin network is the gatekeeper that ensures only the keymaster can access a wallet. The network will recognize any signed transfer and will only recognize signed transfers. Therefore, anyone who obtains the key to a bitcoin wallet can "steal" all of the bitcoins in that wallet by irrevocably transferring them to another wallet, and if the owner of a bitcoin wallet loses their key, they cannot transfer the bitcoins in their wallet, which are irretrievably "lost."

---

7 *See* David Lee Chaum, *Computer Systems Established, Maintained, and Trusted by Mutually Suspicious Groups* (unpublished manuscript) (22 February 1979), https://chaum.com/wp-content/uploads/2022/02/techrep.pdf.

8 *Cf.* The Weakerthans, *Virtute the Cat Explains Her Departure*, BANDCAMP (2003), https://theweakerthans.bandcamp.com/track/virtute-the-cat-explains-her-departure ("I can't remember the sound that you found for me").

9 *See* Chaum, *Computer Systems Established.*

10 *See generally* Alan T. Sherman, Farid Javani, Haibin Zhang, & Enis Golaszewski, *On the Origins and Variations of Blockchain Technologies* (2018), https://arxiv.org/ftp/arxiv/papers/1810/1810.06130.pdf.

11 *See* SATOSHI NAKAMOTO, BITCOIN: A PEER-TO-PEER ELECTRONIC CASH SYSTEM (2008), https://bitcoin.org/en/bitcoin-paper.

```
             Bitcoin Genesis Block
                   Raw Hex Version

00000000   01 00 00 00 00 00 00 00   00 00 00 00 00 00 00 00   ................
00000010   00 00 00 00 00 00 00 00   00 00 00 00 00 00 00 00   ................
00000020   00 00 00 00 3B A3 ED FD   7A 7B 12 B2 7A C7 2C 3E   ....;£íýz{.²zÇ,>
00000030   67 76 8F 61 7F C8 1B C3   88 8A 51 32 3A 9F B8 AA   gv.a.È.Â^ŠQ2:Ÿ¸ª
00000040   4B 1E 5E 4A 29 AB 5F 49   FF FF 00 1D 1D AC 2B 7C   K.^J)« Iÿÿ...¬+|
00000050   01 01 00 00 00 01 00 00   00 00 00 00 00 00 00 00   ................
00000060   00 00 00 00 00 00 00 00   00 00 00 00 00 00 00 00   ................
00000070   00 00 00 00 00 00 FF FF   FF FF 4D 04 FF FF 00 1D   ......ÿÿÿÿM.ÿÿ..
00000080   01 04 45 54 68 65 20 54   69 6D 65 73 20 30 33 2F   ..EThe Times 03/
00000090   4A 61 6E 2F 32 30 30 39   20 43 68 61 6E 63 65 6C   Jan/2009 Chancel
000000A0   6C 6F 72 20 6F 6E 20 62   72 69 6E 6B 20 6F 66 20   lor on brink of
000000B0   73 65 63 6F 6E 64 20 62   61 69 6C 6F 75 74 20 66   second bailout f
000000C0   6F 72 20 62 61 6E 6B 73   FF FF FF FF 01 00 F2 05   or banksÿÿÿÿ..ò.
000000D0   2A 01 00 00 00 43 41 04   67 8A FD B0 FE 55 48 27   *....CA.gŠý°þUH'
000000E0   19 67 F1 A6 71 30 B7 10   5C D6 A8 28 E0 39 09 A6   .gñ¦q0·.\Ö¨(à9.¦
000000F0   79 62 E0 EA 1F 61 DE B6   49 F6 BC 3F 4C EF 38 C4   ybàê.aÞ¶Iö¼?Lï8Ä
00000100   F3 55 04 E5 1E C1 12 DE   5C 38 4D F7 BA 0B 8D 57   óU.å.Á.Þ\8M÷º..W
00000110   8A 4C 70 2B 6B F1 1D 5F   AC 00 00 00 00            ŠLp+kñ._¬....
```

FIGURE 1.1 Bitcoin genesis block
Source: https://en.wikipedia.org/wiki/Satoshi_Nakamoto#/media/File:Bitcoin-Genesis-
block.svg.

B *The Early Days of Bitcoin*

At least initially, bitcoin was primarily a proof of concept for a decentralized crypto-currency rather than an actually viable currency. A few days after creating the bitcoin blockchain, Nakamoto proved that it could be used for transactions by transferring ten bitcoins to Hal Finney, a computer programmer who created a proof-of-work sys-tem similar to bitcoin in 2004. And in 2010 Laszlo Hanyecs completed the first known commercial bitcoin transaction, paying 10,000 bitcoins for two Papa John's pizzas.

Later that year, after mining about 1 million bitcoins, Nakamoto handed control of the bitcoin blockchain over to Gavin Andresen and then disappeared. Andresen focused on decentralizing control of the bitcoin blockchain, which gradually devel-oped into a truly viable cryptocurrency. Initially, the primary users of bitcoin were people engaging in criminal activity, who wanted to make anonymous transactions in order to avoid detection. For example, the short-lived black market website Silk Road only allowed payment in bitcoins, and in 2011 alone processed 9.9 million in bitcoin transactions, worth about $214 million.

While cryptocurrency has always been a volatile asset, the initial price of bitcoin was particularly unstable. In 2011, it seesawed from $0.30 to $31, then back down to $5. But by 2013, bitcoin prices began to rise, hitting $770 by the start of 2014.

However, technical problems bedeviled bitcoin, causing frequent and unexpected price collapses whenever they hit. Between 2017 and 2020, the average price of bitcoin gradually rose, even as it hit highs of almost $20,000 and lows of $4,000 or less.

C It's a Gas

If bitcoin laid the foundational blockchain technology, Ethereum represents its significant evolution and expansion. Everything bitcoin could do, Ethereum could do better – except maybe convince true believers of its authority. The old regulars cling to bitcoin because it never changes, but the "degens" love Ethereum and its progeny because they are designed to change.[12]

In any case, Vitalik Buterin invented Ethereum in 2013.[13] In a nutshell, Buterin realized that bitcoin was a tool, but blockchain could be a method. Bitcoin was designed to do one thing: record cryptographic transactions. But blockchain can do so much more. While you can use bitcoin off-label, the results are unpredictable and inefficient. You need a flexible blockchain.

That is what Buterin developed. The purpose of Ethereum was flexibility. He wanted Ethereum to focus on goals rather than methods. Ethereum does not tell you what to do; it tells you the rules and invites you to make your own. Coders call them "smart contracts," but they are really ways of telling the blockchain how to manage transactions, without human input. We want to eliminate transaction costs in order to increase efficiency, but the reality is that we are the biggest transaction cost, and Ethereum offers a solution: just do not ask people anymore.

Obviously, some people do not like it. Probably most of them. Does it really matter? Maybe if they are getting hurt. But what if they are just standing in the way because they find it all distasteful? If people like using the blockchain, why not let them? It might turn out to be useful. After all, the Internet was controversial in the 1990s, but everyone seems to have come around and realized they like it.

D The Invention of NFTs

Often, the most important inventions are accidental. While the jury is still out on whether NFTs are important, there is no question they were an accident. After all, an NFT is just a blockchain entry that represents something – essentially anything – other than a quantity of cryptocurrency. In other words, cryptocurrency traders inadvertently

---

[12] "Degen" is an abbreviation of "degenerate," coined as a derogatory term for inexperienced gamblers who make large bets. Cryptocurrency traders adopted the term as an ironic self-description. *See, for example,* Thom Waite, *Degens: The High-Risk Crypto Traders Making Millions from Nothing,* Dazed (January 19, 2022), www.dazeddigital.com/art-photography/article/55263/1/degens-the-high-risk-crypto-traders-making-millions-from-nothing.

[13] *See generally* Laura Shin, The Cryptopians: Idealism, Greed, Lies, and the Making of the First Big Cryptocurrency Craze (2022).

FIGURE 1.2 Dan Kaminsky, *Len Sassaman Tribute* (2011)
Source: https://cirosantilli.com/cool-data-embedded-in-the-bitcoin-blockchain.

created NFTs without even realizing it, simply by adding unnecessary data to their transactions. The additional data made the transaction unique, transforming it into an NFT.

So the first NFTs were bitcoin transactions accompanied by unnecessary data, usually describing the nature of the transaction. While a bitcoin transaction consists of the
transfer of a quantity of bitcoin from one wallet to another, the bitcoin blockchain's
data space enables the person executing a bitcoin transaction to record additional
information as part of the transaction, much like people use the memo line on a paper
check to document the subject or purpose of the transaction. That additional information transforms the transaction into an NFT because it is recorded on the blockchain.

Of course, those bitcoin transactions were NFTs in name only. They were not
intended as NFTs, did not represent anything interesting, and could not easily be
transferred. But coders are clever, and coders of Web 3.0 – the latest evolution of the
internet, which includes more decentralized and distributed networks – are especially clever, so they soon figured out how to use the bitcoin data space to record
simple artworks on the blockchain. Among the first was an ASCII tribute to the
cypherpunk programmer Len Sassaman created on July 30, 2011, by computer security expert Dan Kaminsky (Figure 1.2).[14]

---

[14] *See* Ciro Santilli, *Cool Data Embedded in the Bitcoin Blockchain*, CIRO SANTILLI, https://cirosantilli
.com/cool-data-embedded-in-the-bitcoin-blockchain.

Some programmers saw even more potential in the bitcoin data space. In 2012, the business entrepreneur Yoni Asia proposed the creation of "colored coins," or bitcoins paired with metadata that could represent something other than bitcoin.[15] Essentially, Assia observed that the metadata associated with a bitcoin transaction could be used like a "watermark" to differentiate it from other bitcoins. Those watermarks or "colors" could be used to represent something other than bitcoin, and color-sensitive wallets would enable users to use and trade bitcoins based on their color rather than their value.

But the most ambitious early efforts to record data on a blockchain was the creation of the Namecoin blockchain, a fork of the bitcoin blockchain designed to record data rather than cryptocurrency transactions. The primary purpose of the Namecoin blockchain was to manage .bit, a decentralized and censorship-resistant top-level internet domain. A Namecoin transaction created a "Name" or unique .bit domain name only the wallet owner could access. In order to prevent congestion of the Namecoin blockchain, all Names eventually expired, unless renewed.

Obviously, every Name recorded on the Namecoin blockchain was an NFT because it represented a domain name rather than a quantity of cryptocurrency. But the concept of an NFT did not exist yet, so no one noticed. Instead, people observed that the Namecoin blockchain was a cool idea, and started asking themselves what they could do with it. Digital artist Kevin McCoy had an especially innovative and impactful idea: use blockchain to sell digital art.

E *The Demosthenes of NFTs*

While there is considerable disagreement about who created the first NFT, McCoy is a plausible contender. Before the NFT market, it was hard for digital artists to sell their artworks to collectors. Why? There is no such thing as an original because every copy of a digital artwork is identical. Paintings and sculptures are unique objects, but digital images are not. Of course, digital artists could sell certificates of authenticity, but collectors were not biting. Maybe certificates of authenticity did not feel like "real" ownership, or maybe digital artists selling pieces of paper was a little too ironic even for art collectors.

McCoy wanted to sell his digital artworks and was looking for a digital alternative to certificates of authenticity. In 2014, he realized that he could use the Namecoin blockchain to create a transferrable cryptographic record of the provenance of an artwork. While the purpose of the Namecoin blockchain was to register .bit domain names and create a decentralized domain name system, it could be used to record any kind of data, including information about the ownership of an artwork. So McCoy registered a Name on the Namecoin blockchain and stated that ownership of "this blockchain entry" constituted ownership of his digital artwork *Quantum*. In other words, he created

---

[15] Yoni Assia, *Bitcoin 2.X (aka Colored Bitcoin) – Initial Specs*, YONI ASSIA (March 27, 2013), https://yoniassia.com/coloredbitcoin/.

a cryptographic certificate of authenticity. It was the "first NFT," because it was the first time someone had used a blockchain entry to represent ownership of a work of art.

Excited by the potential of cryptographic certificates of authenticity, McCoy founded Monegraph (a portmanteau of "monetized graphics"), a company dedicated to helping artists create and sell cryptographic certificates of authenticity.[16] Unfortunately, he was ahead of his time, and his concept did not immediately catch on. Part of the problem was that it relied on the Namecoin blockchain, which provided that Name registrations would automatically expire after about a year, unless they were renewed. You can lose a paper certificate of authenticity, but at least they are not written in disappearing ink. Ironically, the Name McCoy registered for *Quantum* expired when he failed to renew it, which became an issue when the NFT market took off, and Free Holdings Inc. registered the same Name. McCoy created a new NFT of *Quantum* on the Ethereum blockchain, which was intended to represent both ownership of the artwork and the expired Namecoin NFT. The new owner of the Name claimed to own *Quantum* and sued McCoy for slander of title, among other things. While the district court dismissed the action, the plaintiff intends to appeal.[17]

In any case, the dispute subtly presents a question everyone is avoiding. When an artist sells an artwork, what is the artist actually selling? Or, rather, what makes provenance "real"? Free Holdings and McCoy do not dispute the facts, only what those facts mean. There is no question that McCoy registered the Name that Free Holdings now owns and said "this blockchain entry" represented ownership of *Quantum*. The question is whether the "blockchain entry" that represented ownership of Quantum was the Name or McCoy's registration. In other words, the question is whether McCoy should be compelled to endorse ownership of the Name as meaning ownership of *Quantum*, whatever that means.

The district court dismissed Free Holdings's complaint, stating that there was no real dispute because Free Holdings claims to own one blockchain entry and McCoy sold a different blockchain entry. But that misses the point. The question is what it means to "own" an artwork, what it means for a blockchain entry to represent ownership of an artwork, and what it means for a blockchain entry to remain the "same" entry. None of these questions have easy answers. Maybe they are unanswerable. Or maybe we are asking the wrong questions. In any case, it is time to move on.

IV POP! GOES THE NFT MARKET

Initially, NFTs looked like a dead end, or at best a niche medium for digital artists focused on coding and blockchain. But then, in about 2017, interest in NFTs began to grow. Several different companies released large collections of NFTs representing algorithmically generated images like *CryptoPunks* and *CryptoKitties*. These NFT

---

[16] *See* MONEGRAPH, www.monegraph.com/.
[17] *See* Free Holdings Inc. v. McCoy, 22-CV-881 (JLC), 2023 WL 2561576 (S.D.N.Y. March 17, 2023).

collections eventually became known as "profile picture" or "PFP" NFTs because owners used the image associated with their NFT as their profile picture on social media platforms such as Twitter and Discord.[18]

PFP NFTs were important because they provided an easy way for people not only to express their interest in NFTs but also to brag about owning a particular NFT. As a practical matter, anyone can use any image as their social media profile picture, subject to the theoretical possibility of a takedown notice or copyright infringement claim under the Digital Millennium Copyright Act (DMCA), which protects online service providers from secondary liability for copyright infringement arising from works posted by their users. But NFT collectors created a social norm prohibiting the use of an image associated with an NFT unless you owned the NFT. So you can use any image you want, but you are a tool if you use the image associated with an NFT you do not own. While NFT artists and collectors gleefully ignore copyright law, violating their own social norms is a bridge too far. Sticking it to the man is cool, but looking like a fool is a drag.

A few years later, the NFT market suddenly and unexpectedly exploded in popularity, and PFP NFTs were at the epicenter of it.

A *Punks not Dead*

You have to start somewhere. When it comes to PFP NFTs, the *Cryptopunks* collection created the genre. *CryptoPunks* is a collection of 10,000 Ethereum NFTs, created in June 2017 by Matt Hall and John Watkinson, each of which is associated with an algorithmically generated image. It was a game changer. Arguably the first PFP NFT collection, *CryptoPunks* helped inspire not only the creation of the term NFT but also the ERC-721 standard commonly used to create NFTs on the Ethereum blockchain.[19] Even more importantly, *CryptoPunks* was the first NFT collection to really take off.[20]

When Hall and Watkinson released *CryptoPunks* on June 12, 2017, anyone could claim a *CryptoPunks* NFT for free by paying the transaction cost or "gas fee" to mint it on the Ethereum blockchain, which at the time was about eleven cents. Initially, no one was interested, and only a few dozen NFTs were claimed. But when *Mashable* published an article about *CryptoPunks* on June 16, suddenly everyone wanted one, and the entire collection was claimed in only a few hours.[21]

---

[18] *See* Benedict George, *What Are PFP NFTs?*, CoinDesk (April 27, 2022), www.coindesk.com/learn/what-are-pfp-nfts/.

[19] *See* William Entriken, Dieter Shirley, Jacob Evans, & Nastassia Sachs, *EIP-721: Non-Fungible Token Standard*, Ethereum Improvement Proposals (January 24, 2018), https://eips.ethereum.org/EIPS/eip-721.

[20] For more details on the style, attributes, and traits of the *CryptoPunks* NFTs, *see* Chapter 13 of this Handbook; *10 Things to Know about CryptoPunks, the Original NFTs*, Christie's (April 8, 2021), www.christies.com/features/10-things-to-know-about-CryptoPunks-11569-1.aspx?sc_lang=en#FID-11569.

[21] Jason Abbruzzese, *This Ethereum-Based Project Could Change How We Think about Digital Art*, Mashable (June 16, 2017), https://mashable.com/article/cryptopunks-ethereum-art-collectibles. Apparently, Hall and Watkinson of LarvaLabs minted about 1,000 *CryptoPunks* NFTs for themselves.

A secondary market in *CryptoPunks* NFTs emerged almost immediately. The day after the *CryptoPunks* collection was fully claimed, one *CryptoPunks* NFT sold for about $3,500, and by a year later, an unusual alien *CryptoPunk* NFT had sold for about $16,000.[22] When it became obvious that *CryptoPunks* was a hit, Hall and Wilkinson created Larva Labs to manage their creation. For a time, the market for *CryptoPunks* NFTs was volatile, but gradually trended upward. Then, in early 2021, the market exploded, and the price of a typical *CryptoPunks* NFT shot up to about $30,000. That was when auction houses like Sotheby's and Christie's really got interested.[23] On May 11, 2021, Christie's auctioned a lot of nine rare *CryptoPunks* NFTs for almost $17 million.[24] Suddenly, *CryptoPunks* were art.

CryptoPunks has attracted many imitators. The funniest is probably the *CryptoPhunks* NFT collection, which was created by Not Larva Labs in July 2021.[25] The *CryptoPhunks* collection consists of 10,000 NFTs, each of which is associated with a *CryptoPunks* image facing left rather than right. Yes, Not Larva Labs copied the entire collection of 10,000 *CryptoPunks* images, flipped them, and sold NFTs associated with those flipped images.

B V1 CryptoPunks *NFTs*

A reason *CryptoPunks* NFTs are especially popular among NFT collectors is that *CryptoPunks* was one of the first NFT collections on the Ethereum blockchain. Many NFT collectors highly value "historical" NFTs that represent "firsts" in the NFT marketplace. Accordingly, "NFT archeologists" are always looking for forgotten NFT projects they can rescue from oblivion and sell.

Before Larva Labs created the *CryptoPunks* NFT collection it released on June 12, 2017, it released a collection of 10,000 *CryptoPunks* NFTs with a defective contract that allowed the buyer of the NFT to withdraw the funds deposited in the contract, but not the seller. When Larva Labs realized there was a defect in the contract, they created a new collection of 10,000 *CryptoPunks* NFTs and disowned the original, defective NFTs.[26]

Eventually, NFT archeologists discovered the original collection of *CryptoPunks* NFTs and devised a way to transact in them despite the defective contract, by "wrapping" them

---

[22] Chloe Cornish, *CryptoKitties, CryptoPunks and the Birth of a Cottage Industry*, Fin. Times (June 5, 2018), www.ft.com/content/f9c1422a-47c9-11e8-8c77-ff51caedcde6.

[23] Lucas Matney, *The Cult of CryptoPunks*, TechCrunch (April 8, 2021), https://techcrunch.com/2021/04/08/the-cult-of-cryptopunks/.

[24] Larva Labs, *9 Cryptopunks: 2, 532, 58, 30, 635, 602, 768, 603 and 757*, Christie's (2021), www.christies.com/lot/lot–6316969/. *See also 10 Things to Know*, Christie's.

[25] *CryptoPhunks*, Not Larva Labs (2021), https://notlarvalabs.com/cryptophunks. Unsurprisingly, Larva Labs is unhappy about the CryptoPhunks. *See generally* BowTied SizeLord, *Let's Get Phunky: CryptoPhunks and Web3 Censorship*, Bowtied Island (December 27, 2021), https://bowtiedisland.com/lets-get-phunky-cryptophunks-and-web3-censorship/.

[26] *See* Jon Torrey, *Breaking Down V1 CryptoPunks: The First CryptoPunks Release*, Start With NFTs (January 15, 2022), www.startwithnfts.com/posts/breaking-down-v1-cryptopunks-the-first-cryptopunks-release.

in a new ERC-721 smart contract.[27] These wrapped NFTs from the original *CryptoPunks* NFT release became known as "V1 Punks," and were associated with *CryptoPunks* images on a purple background, to distinguish them from so-called "V2 Punks."[28]

Reportedly, Larva Labs continued to disown the V1 Punks, and objected to their sale.[29] In response to Larva Labs's objections, OpenSea, the largest NFT marketplace, prohibited the sale of wrapped V1 *CryptoPunks* NFTs. However, LooksRare, a smaller NFT marketplace, welcomed the sale of the V1 Punks NFTs, which were quite popular with NFT collectors.[30]

On January 25, 2022, Larva Labs made the controversial decision to both reiterate its disapproval of the V1 Punks NFTs and announce its intention to sell some or all of the 1,000 V1 Punks NFTs it still owned.[31] NFT collectors were allegedly confused and upset by this announcement. Soon afterward, Larva Labs explained that it regretted the decision to sell its V1 Punks NFTs and suggested that it might pursue legal action against future sales.[32] But nothing came of it and V1 Punks NFTs are still listed on OpenSea and other NFT marketplaces.

C CryptoKitties

The Internet has always loved cats, and blockchain is no different. So it should come as no surprise that the NFT craze began with *CryptoKitties*, a game based on the Ethereum blockchain, in which players buy, breed, and sell NFTs of virtual cats. Each *CryptoKitties* NFT represents "ownership" of a unique digital image of a cartoon cat, which has a unique "genome" and twelve "cattributes," many of which are "inheritable." Players can buy *CryptoKitties* NFTs, or "breed" them, which essentially consists of creating a new *CryptoKitties* NFT that is similar to its "parents."

In November 2017, the Canadian software company Axiom Zen released *CryptoKitties*, a game based on the Ethereum blockchain that enables players to buy, breed, and sell virtual cats. Each CryptoKitty is represented by an Ethereum NFT, and consists of a unique digital image of a cartoon cat with a unique "genome" and 12 "cattributes," many of which are "inheritable." Players use Ether to buy new *CryptoKitties* NFTs, and also to "breed" CryptoKitties, which essentially consists of creating a new *CryptoKitties* NFT that is similar to its "parents."

[27] *See* Andrew Hayward, *CryptoPunks Controversy: Creators Apologize for 'V1' Ethereum NFT Sales*, Decrypt (February 24, 2022), https://decrypt.co/92155/cryptopunks-controversy-creators-apologize-v1-ethereum-nft.

[28] *See* V1 Punks, https://v1punks.io/.

[29] *See* Hayward, *CryptoPunks Controversy*.

[30] Eduardo Próspero, *What Are the CryptoPunks V1? And, How Can They Disrupt the Market?*, NewsBTC (February 3, 2022), www.newsbtc.com/news/ethereum/what-are-the-cryptopunks-v1-and-how-can-they-disrupt-the-market/.

[31] *@larva labs*, Twitter (January 25, 2022), https://twitter.com/larvalabs/status/1486092138534387712?s=20&t=dVrMoeRLarzOmGgEMdGGcw.

[32] *See* Hayward, *CryptoPunks Controversy*; Próspero, *What Are the CryptoPunks V1?*.

Axiom Zen first publicly presented CryptoKitties at ETH Waterloo on October 19, 2017, and released the game a couple of weeks later. It was a hit. By December 2017, *CryptoKitties* transactions were overwhelming the Ethereum network, at one point accounting for about 25 percent of network activity.

CryptoKitties used the new ERC-721 standard, which avoided most of the technical problems that affected *CryptoPunks*. But *CryptoKitties* had a problem with their business model, which was much worse. There are only 10,000 *CryptoPunks* NFTs, which makes all of them reasonably scarce. But the number of *CryptoKitties* NFTs is effectively unlimited, which makes scarcity harder to establish. Unsurprisingly, the lack of scarcity ultimately killed the market for *CryptoKitties* NFT.

D *Monkey Business*

For better or worse, one of the most popular NFT collections is the Bored Ape Yacht Club (BAYC) NFT collection created by Yuga Labs in 2021. The BAYC collection is similar to the *CryptoPunks* collection in that it consists of 10,000 NFTs, each of which represents "ownership" of an algorithmically generated image of a cartoon ape. Yuga Labs launched BAYC for presale on April 21, 2021, selling the NFTs for 0.08 ETH, which was about $190 at the time. Initially, sales were slow because collectors did not know what the images would look like. But when they released the BAYC images on April 30, the entire collection sold out in about twelve hours.[33] Prices on the secondary market started rising almost immediately, and some BAYC NFTs have sold for millions. What is more, many celebrities (and at least one law professor) became BAYC NFT owners.[34]

Like the *CryptoPunks*, knockoff projects proliferated, two of the most prominent being the PHAYC and Phunky Ape Yacht Club collections.[35] Yuga Labs was less open-minded about copycats than Larva Labs, sending some takedown notices.[36] But when it comes to NFTs, "all press is good press," and unauthorized replicas arguably increase the visibility and desirability of an NFT collection.

---

[33] Corporate Trash, *What is Bored Ape Yacht Club? The Ape NFT Transforming NFTs*, COLLECTIVE (June 18, 2021), https://collective.xyz/blog/what-is-bored-ape-yacht-club-the-ape-nft-transforming-nfts?action=welcome.

[34] *See* Edward Lee, *The Bored Ape Business Model: Decentralized Collaboration via Blockchain and NFTs* (November 16, 2021) (unpublished manuscript), https://papers.ssrn.com/sol3/papers.cfm?abstract_id=3963881.

[35] Adi Robertson, *Two NFT Copycats Are Fighting over Which Is the Real Fake Bored Ape Yacht Club*, THE VERGE (December 30, 2021), www.theverge.com/2021/12/30/22860010/bored-ape-yacht-club-payc-phayc-copycat-nft.

[36] *See, for example*, Michael Bodley, *Yuga Labs' Intensifying IP Takedowns Spur CryptoPunk Backlash*, BLOCKWORKS (July 18, 2023), https://blockworks.co/news/yuga-labs-nft-takedowns; Justin Doom, *Yuga Labs Lawsuit Accuses Ryder Ripps of 'Scamming Consumers' With Fake Bored Apes*, DECRYPT (June 25, 2022), https://decrypt.co/103824/yuga-labs-lawsuit-accuses-ryder-ripps-of-scamming-consumers-with-fake-bored-apes (Reporting that, "Ripps first began minting his RR/BAYC NFTs on May 13 on Foundation, and after Yuga sent him an initial DMCA takedown claim, it quickly rescinded the claim when Ripps fought it").

So is BAYC just CryptoPunks with different pictures? Not exactly. For one thing, the pictures matter. Many NFT collectors love CryptoPunks and hate BAYC or vice versa. And there are plenty of other NFT projects competing for their attention, which they might like better. For another, Larva Labs and Yuga Labs took very different approaches to their intellectual property rights, whatever those rights might be.

Larva Labs was in the business of selling NFTs and that is it.[37] When you bought an NFT, that is what you got, whatever it is, nothing more. You did not get any copyright interest in the image associated with your NFT, and you certainly did not get any trademark interest in the CryptoPunks brand.

Yuga Labs took the opposite approach. It gave BAYC NFT owners certain rights to use the image associated with their NFT, including limited "commercial rights."[38] What does that mean? One may understand it to mean a copyright license to use the image associated with the NFT and a trademark license to promote one's own brand.[39] Presumably, Yuga Labs gave BAYC NFT owners "commercial rights" in the images associated with their NFTs to encourage them to use the BAYC brand as much as possible. Yuga Labs was clever. It realized that the value of BAYC was the brand. Why not let NFT owners use the BAYC brand to sell their own brand? At least in theory, it was all upside for BAYC. It is impossible for your licensee to compete with your market when you are not selling anything but your brand.

But, there was a problem. What if people dislike the brand or consider it toxic? From the beginning, many people had criticisms about the BAYC images and branding.[40] In particular, conceptual artist Ryder Ripps alleged that the BAYC logo resembles the Nazi Totenkopf logo and that the BAYC images use many racially coded elements.[41] And I mean, come on. It is a bunch of monkey cartoons.

---

[37] *See* Edward Lee, *The Cryptic Case of the CryptoPunks Licenses: The Mystery Over the Licenses for CryptoPunks NFTs* (unpublished manuscript) (February 7, 2022), https://papers.ssrn.com/sol3/papers .cfm?abstract_id=3978963.

[38] *See* Yuga Labs, *Cryptopunks Terms*, https://licenseterms.cryptopunks.app/ (Section 2(a)). *See also* Alfred David Steiner, *Bored Apes & Monkey Selfies: Copyright & PFP NFTs* (unpublished manuscript) (December 16, 2022), https://nysba.org/bored-apes-and-monkey-selfies-copyright-and-pfp-nfts/. *See generally* Tyler T. Ochoa, *Non-Fungible Tokens (NFTs) and Copyright Law*, Santa Clara High Tech L. J. (forthcoming 2024); and Michael D. Murray, *Transfers and Licensing of Copyrights to NFT Purchasers*, 6 Stan. J. of Blockchain L. & Pol'y. 119 (2023).

[39] *See, for example*, Rosie Perper, *See You on the Otherside: How Yuga Labs Is Bringing Its Billion-Dollar Business Into the Metaverse*, CoinDesk (December 21, 2022), www.coindesk.com/web3/2022/12/21/see-you-on-the-otherside-how-yuga-labs-is-bringing-its-billion-dollar-business-into-the-metaverse/ ("Yuga Labs has released the IP rights of its collections to its holders, allowing NFT characters to be used on branding for food trucks, TV shows and music groups. This has created new revenue streams for holders and has fostered more brand loyalty").

[40] Noor Al-Sibai, *Anonymous Declares War on Bored Ape Yacht Club Over Alleged Nazi Symbolism*, Futurism (September 28, 2023), https://futurism.com/anonymous-bayc-hate-group-claims.

[41] *See* Motion to Strike Complaint, 11–4, *Yuga Labs* v. *Ryder Ripps Et Al.*, 2:22-cv-04355 (C.D. Cal. Filed 15 August, 2022) (claiming that "Yuga Systematically Embedded Racist Messages and Imagery in Its Trademarks and Products"); Daniel Kuhn, *Bored Apes, a Troll and a Conspiracy Walk Into a Courtroom …*, CoinDesk (January 10, 2023), www.coindesk.com/consensus-magazine/2023/01/10/bored-apes-a-troll-and-a-conspiracy-walk-into-a-courtroom/.

Whatever. People can disagree about what images mean and about what is or should be offensive. Yuga Labs dismissed Ripps's criticisms of the BAYC images and many NFT collectors accepted their explanations. But Ripps refused to give up and escalated his attacks on Yuga Labs. If criticism did not get as much attention as he wanted, maybe competition would.

Therefore, Ripps created his own collection of BAYC NFTs, Ryder Ripps Bored Ape Yacht Club (RR/BAYC), and used them to highlight his argument that the BAYC images are antisemitic and racist.[42] In the tradition of good pranks Ripps's fake BAYC collection was remarkably successful. Many people bought the RR/BAYC NFTs, maybe because they believed in the project or maybe just because they wanted to make money.[43] According to Ripps, it was expressive conduct either way. Of course, it was also profitable. And it got Ripps's criticisms of BAYC lots of attention.

Eventually, Yuga decided it could not keep ignoring Ripps. On 24 June 2022, Yuga Labs sued Ripps for trademark infringement.[44] Why trademark infringement rather than copyright? I suspect because Yuga cares about its brand, not its ability to control the use of individual BAYC images. From Yuga's perspective, copyright infringement is great. The more people who see the BAYC images, the better it is for the BAYC brand. But Ripps's criticisms of the BAYC images were hurting the brand and hurting it badly. At least some celebrity owners of BAYC NFTs were concerned by Ripps's allegations and reconsidered their association with the BAYC brand.[45] Nobody wants to be associated with neo-Nazi racism, even unproven allegations.

Not so fast. According to Ripps, the entire RR/BAYC collection is a work of conceptual art, and the only way to realize the concept is to copy the BAYC NFTs.[46] In other words, Ripps characterizes his use of the BAYC brand as an expressive use, not an infringing use. On his telling, no one was confused about the source of the RR/BAYC NFTs, and NFT technology ensures that buyers know the RR/BAYC NFTs are not "real" BAYC NFTs.

Unfortunately, for Ripps, the district court effectively rejected all of his arguments. First, it denied Ripps's anti-SLAPP motion, finding that Yuga Labs's claims were based on Ripps's misappropriation of the BAYC images and that his use lacked expressive

---

[42] *See* Jackson Lanier, *The Ninth Circuit's Split Personality: How NFTs Highlight A Concerning Split in the Court's Application of Trademark Law to Web 3.0*, DARTMOUTH L.J. (forthcoming 2023), https:// dx.doi.org/10.2139/ssrn.4411021 ("Ripps, among others, believes that Yuga Labs has intentionally hidden Nazi symbols and racial stereotypes in their trademark and NFTs and he seeks to call them out on it").

[43] *See* Daniel Kuhn, *Ryder Ripps, Bored Apes and 'Owning' an NFT*, COINDESK (May 19, 2022), www .coindesk.com/layer2/2022/05/19/ryder-ripps-bored-apes-and-owning-an-nft/.

[44] *Yuga Labs Inc. v. Ripps*, 223CV00010APGNJK, 2023 WL 2021142 (D. Nev. February 14, 2023). *See also* Chapter 11 of this Handbook.

[45] Elle Reeve & Samantha Guff, *A Twisted Tale of Celebrity Promotion, Opaque Transactions and Allegations of Racist Tropes*, CNN (February 10, 2023), www.cnn.com/2023/02/10/business/crypto-nft-bored-ape-moonpay-lawsuits/index.html.

[46] Yuga Labs, *Inc.* v. *Ripps*, 2:22-cv-04355, at *26 (C.D. Cal. June 24, 2022) ("Mr. Ripps's appropriation art project would not be readily identifiable, or even possible, without using Yuga's marks to conjure up the BAYC collection – the subject of Mr. Ripps's critique. As discussed above, the Complaint includes Mr. Ripps's explanation that his project uses BAYC marks in his conceptual appropriation art as a 'provocation' that serves to 'show bayc for what it really is'").

content.[47] And then it granted Yuga Labs's motion for summary judgment on its trademark infringement and cybersquatting claims, at the same time rejecting Ripps's affirmative defenses of expressive conduct and fair use.[48] Essentially, the court found that Yuga Labs owns a valid trademark in the BAYC marks and that Ripps used those marks to sell an effectively identical product. The case went to trial on Yuga's remaining claims and Ripps vows to appeal but he is unlikely to fare any better before the Ninth Circuit.

Courts have taken to heart Justice Holmes's observation, "It would be a dangerous undertaking for persons trained only to the law to constitute themselves final judges of the worth of pictorial illustrations."[49] It goes in spades for conceptual art. The court did not care what Ripps intended the RR/BAYC NFTs to mean or what RR/BAYC collectors understand them to mean. The question before the court was whether Ripps infringed Yuga's trademarks, not whether he created conceptual art. Or at least that is how the court saw it. Like a joke, conceptual art is not amusing if you have to explain it.

However, Yuga Labs may have won a Pyrrhic victory. It is possible that the damage to its BAYC brand is done and cannot be undone. If anything, Yuga arguably made it worse by suing Ripps who has used the lawsuit to amplify his criticisms of BAYC.[50] It is a perfect example of the Streisand Effect. If Yuga had only kept ignoring Ripps, fewer people would have noticed him and he might eventually have moved on. By suing him Yuga arguably only amplified his criticisms by turning them into news.

V THE ART OF CODING

Contrary to conventional wisdom, NFTs are not just PFP collections like CryptoPunks, CryptoKitties, Bored Apes. The original purpose of NFTs was to enable digital artists to sell their work and that is exactly how many digital artists use NFTs. From the beginning, artists were devising new ways to use NFTs to sell their art, new ways to use NFTs as art, and new ways to use NFTs as an expressive medium. While there are already far too many important NFT artists to provide a comprehensive survey in this chapter, I will discuss some representative examples.

A *Everyday Seems a Little Longer*

For better or worse, the best-known NFT artist is indisputably Mike "Beeple" Winkelman because, in March 2021, Christie's sold an NFT of his digital artwork

---

47 Yuga Labs, *Inc.* v. *Ripps*, 2:22-cv-04355, Order Denying Defendant's Anti-SLAPP Motion (C.D. Cal. December 16, 2022).

48 Yuga Labs, *Inc.* v. *Ripps*, 2:22-cv-04355, Order Granting in Part and Denying in Part Plaintiff Yuga Labs, Inc.'s Motion for Summary Judgment (C.D. Cal. April 21, 2023).

49 Bleistein *v.* Donaldson Lithographing Co., 188 U.S. 239 (1903).

50 *See, for example,* @ani-alexander, *Yuga Labs Sues Ryder Ripps, Jeremy Cahen, and DOES 1-10: This is not Monkey Business,* HACKERNOON (August 8, 2023), https://hackernoon.com/yuga-labs-sues-ryder-ripps-jeremy-cahen-and-does-1-10-this-is-not-monkey-business (Reporting that "[p]eople had traveled from Washington, Miami, and Arizona" to personally support Ripps on the trial, in addition to expressing their support on social media).

Everydays: the First 5000 Days (2021) for $69.3 million, the third-highest price ever paid at auction for an artwork created by a living artist.[51] *Everydays* was based on an artistic project Beeple started on May 1, 2007, in which he created a digital artwork every day. He created *Everydays* by combining 5,000 of those digital artworks into a single digital image at least in part because Christie's suggested that a single work would be easier to sell than 5,000 works.

Everydays was the first NFT sold at a major auction house. Before the auction, the art world and mainstream press were indifferent. After the sale of *Everydays* for $69.3 million, everyone took notice. Suddenly, everyone was interested in NFTs. But Beeple was far from the first digital artist to sell artwork as NFTs. McCoy invented NFTs as a way of selling digital art and many other digital artists followed his lead before Beeple discovered the medium. Indeed, Beeple himself allegedly credits the digital artist Pak with introducing him to NFTs.

B *Nobody's Killing Me Now*

Every contemporary art movement needs a Duchamp and Pak is the Duchamp of NFTs. Also known as Murat Pak or The Nothing, Pak is an anonymous digital artist, cryptocurrency investor, and coder. Or maybe Pak is a group of people, who knows?

In any case, Pak claims to have started creating digital art in the mid-1990s and is probably best known for *Archillect*, an AI bot created in 2014 that functions as a curator of digital art.[52] Superficially, *Archillect* looks like a generic internet "mood board," just another collection of things someone likes. But the "curator" of *Archillect* is not one person but the entire internet.[53] *Archillect* uses keywords and other information about what people like to determine which images to curate, in an endlessly recursive loop of giving people more and more of what they like.

That is all. Pak is not only a curator of images but also excels in selling and promoting NFTs. Pak's first NFT collection was *Cloud Monument Dark* released on February 3, 2020. In August 2020, Pak released X, an NFT collection that relied on time rather than volume to create scarcity. Anyone could mint any number of Pak's 13 X NFTs for 24 hours, at which point the edition closed.

Unsurprisingly, when Beeple made NFTs cool, or at least potentially valuable, the art world looked to impresarios like Pak for guidance. In March 2021, Pak helped

---

[51] *See* Beeple, *Everydays: The First 5000 Days* (2021), CHRISTIE'S, https://onlineonly.christies.com/s/ beeple-first-5000-days/beeple-b-1981-1/112924. *See* also Jacqui Palumbo, *First NFT artwork at Auction Sells for Staggering $69 Million*, CNN (March 12, 2021), www.cnn.com/style/article/beeple-first-nft-artwork-at-auction-sale-result/index.html (observing that Jeff Koons's sculpture *Rabbit* sold for $91.1 million in 2019 and David Hockney's painting *Portrait of an Artist (Pool with Two Figures)* sold for $90.3 million in 2018); and Chapter 13 of this Handbook.

[52] The word *Archillect* is a portmanteau of the words "archive" and "intellect."

[53] *See* M. W. Bowman, *The Most Interesting Curator on the Internet Knows Exactly What You Want to See*, VICE (October 23, 2015), www.vice.com/en/article/3daz8j/the-most-interesting-curator-on-tumblr-knows-exactly-what-you-want-to-see.

Sotheby's with its first NFT auction, *The Fungible*, which resulted in $16.8 million in sales, including Pak's *The Pixel* which sold for $1.36 million and Pak's *The Switch* which sold for $1.4 million.

Pak's biggest financial success was the *Merge* NFT collection released on December 2, 2021. Rather than selling individual NFTs, Pak sold "mass units" represented by a single NFT. Collectors could buy as many mass units as they wanted and received an NFT that recorded the number of mass units they bought. In any event, Pak sold 312,686 mass units of *Merge* to 28,983 buyers for a total of $91.8 million, one of the most lucrative NFT sales to date.

In February 2022, Pak released the *Censored* collection of NFTs and sold them as a benefit for the Julian Assange legal defense fund. One NFT in the collection, titled *The Clock*, was purchased for about $52.8 million by AssangeDAO, a group of 10,000 people. Reportedly, Pak has also sold NFTs to benefit other causes, including the government of Ukraine.[54]

C *The Pixel and the Glitch*

One of the earliest and most popular NFT artists is XCOPY, an anonymous, London-based digital artist. XCOPY started selling NFTs in about 2018, and has developed a distinctive style that consists of crudely drawn digital images with pulsating, glitchy digital grain. XCOPY's best-known artwork is *Right-Click and Save As Guy*, a satirical reference to the common criticism that anyone can download the image associated with an NFT. XCOPY minted an NFT of *Right-Click and Save As Guy* on December 6, 2018, and sold it on December 10 for 1 ETH or about $90 at the time. It was sold again on February 16, 2021, for 99 ETH, or about $174,000 at the time. And on December 8, 2021, it was purchased by notable NFT collector and impresario Cozomo de Medici for 1,600 ETH, or about $7 million at the time, among the highest prices paid for a single NFT (Figure 1.3).

Among other things, XCOPY is known for using and popularizing the Creative Commons CC0/Public Domain tool, which is designed to help authors place their works in the public domain.[55] As a consequence, XCOPY's artworks are not protected by copyright and can be used by anyone in any way they like, including without attribution to XCOPY. Of course, XCOPY's artworks are sufficiently distinctive that anyone familiar with them would immediately know the source of the works, even without attribution. In any case, many other NFT artists have followed XCOPY's lead and adopted the CC0 tool for their own artwork.[56]

---

[54] *See Live Updates: Ukraine Government Turns to Crypto to Crowdfund Millions of Dollars*, Elliptic (March 11, 2023), www.elliptic.co/blog/live-updates-millions-in-crypto-crowdfunded-for-the-ukrainian-military.

[55] *See CC0*, Creative Commons, https://creativecommons.org/public-domain/cc0/. *See also* Dave Fagundes & Aaron Perzanowski, *Abandoning Copyright*, 62 Wm. & Mary L. Rev. 487 (2020).

[56] For what it is worth, I commissioned a "plagiarism tool" modeled on the CC0 tool, which explicitly authorizes plagiarism, in case authors want to divest themselves of the extra-legal attribution rights created by plagiarism norms. *See* Brian L. Frye, *A License to Plagiarize*, 43 U. Ark. Little Rock L. Rev. 51 (2021).

FIGURE 1.3 XCOPY, Right-Click and Save As Guy (2018)
Source: www.glitchmarfa.com/e30dgallery/right-click-and-save-as-guy/.

D *Anarchy Means That I Litter*

The NFT market is large. It contains multitudes. In particular, it contains multitudes of artists emulating Duchamp in a variety of different ways. One of the most amusing and provocative is the American artist Robness, the progenitor of the NFT art movement known as "trash art." Robness first became interested in cryptocurrency in 2014 when he was living in his car by the beach, doing odd jobs to get by. Eventually, he started creating and selling NFTs. His breakthrough hit was *64 Gallon Toter* which consists of an image of a trash can taken from the Home Depot website, turned into a GIF with glitch effects. When Robness listed *64 Gallon Toter* on the popular NFT platform SuperRare, it removed the listing for fear of copyright infringement. But after considerable objection from Robness and others, SuperRare eventually relisted the NFT, presumably because the copyright in a conventional photograph of a conventional trash can is exceptionally thin, and in any case, Robness's use of the image was almost certainly a transformative fair use.[57]

---

[57] On the story of Robness, *see generally NFT Art World in a Tizzy: Robness, an American Artist, Sells an Image of a Trash Can at $252K*, ECON. TIMES (February 3, 2022), https://

FIGURE 1.4 ROBNESS, 64 Gallon Toter (2020)
Source: ROBNESS.

Anyway, the copyright controversy got a lot of attention. While Robness still owns the *64 Gallon Toter* NFT, he sold his *Brute Trash Can* NFT to prolific collector Vincent Van Dough for $252,000 (Figure 1.4).[58]

Incidentally, *64 Gallon Toter* gave rise to what became known as the "trash art" movement among NFT artists, which consists of artists using recycled images to create digital artworks with a new and distinctive style. It is a little bit Duchamp and a little bit Warhol with a big dose of cryptobro to make it new and different, for better or worse. While Robness and his work are not to everyone's taste, there is no denying his impact on the aesthetics of NFT art. Unsurprisingly, Robness also believes art should be in the public domain, and encourages people to use the artworks he creates in any way they like.

economictimes.indiatimes.com/magazines/panache/nft-art-world-in-a-tizzy-robness-an-american-artist-sells-an-image-of-a-trashcan-at-252k/articleshow/89319733.cms. *See also Ets-Hokin* v. *Skyy Spirits, Inc.*, No. C 96-3690, 1998 WL 690856 (N.D. Cal., September 28, 1998), *rev'd*, 225 F.3d 1068 (9th Cir. 2000); The Andy Warhol Found. for the *Visual Arts, Inc.* v. *Goldsmith*, 212 L. Ed. 2d 402 (2022) (holding that competing uses are non-transformative).

[58] Ian Dean, *An NFT of a Trashcan Sold for $252k*, CREATIVE BLOQ (February 2022), www .creativebloq.com/news/nft-bin-sells-for-252k.

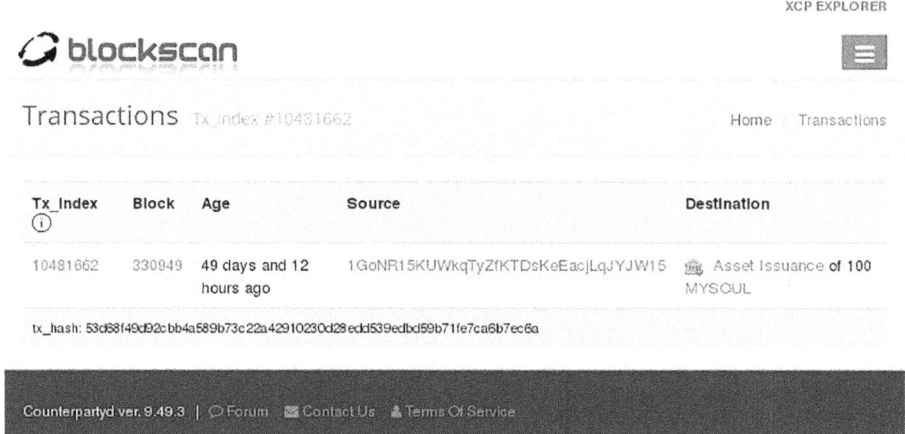

FIGURE 1.5 Rhea Myers, *My Soul* (2014)
Source: https://rhea.art/mysoul/.

E *Money for Nothing and Art for Free*

Some of the most interesting and important NFT artists create conceptual artworks that reflect on the nature of the NFT market, the history of the art market, and the nature of artistic practice. The NFT market has always been an art market although the art is often camouflaged by commerce. What else is new? In any case, conceptual artists were among the first people to recognize blockchain's potential as an artistic medium. After all, the first person to intentionally create an NFT was Kevin McCoy, a conceptual artist asking whether blockchain could enable the art market to accept digital art by making it artificially scarce.

One of the first and most provocative NFT artists was Rhea Myers who saw the blockchain as a medium for conceptual art long before anyone else, with the possible exception of Satoshi Nakamoto whoever he might be. Myers is an artist, writer, and hacker originally from the UK who currently lives in Canada. Myers created many of the first NFTs representing works of conceptual art, including *MYSOUL* (2014), which consisted of representing her soul as an NFT on the Dogecoin blockchain as a Dogeparty asset.[59] Myers continues to use NFTs as a medium for conceptual art and writes about digital art and NFTs (Figure 1.5).

Another pioneer of NFT conceptual art was Sarah Meyohas who created her own cryptocurrency in order to sell her art as NFTs. In 2014, Meyohas created *Speculations*, a series of photographs. She also created a cryptocurrency she called "Bitchcoins." Each Bitchcoin represented ownership of 25 square inches of a photograph, and you could exchange 25 Bitchcoins for a physical copy of one of her photographs. But it

---

[59] *See MYSOUL, 2014, Counterparty and Dogeparty Assets*, RHEA MYERS, rhea.art/mysoul.

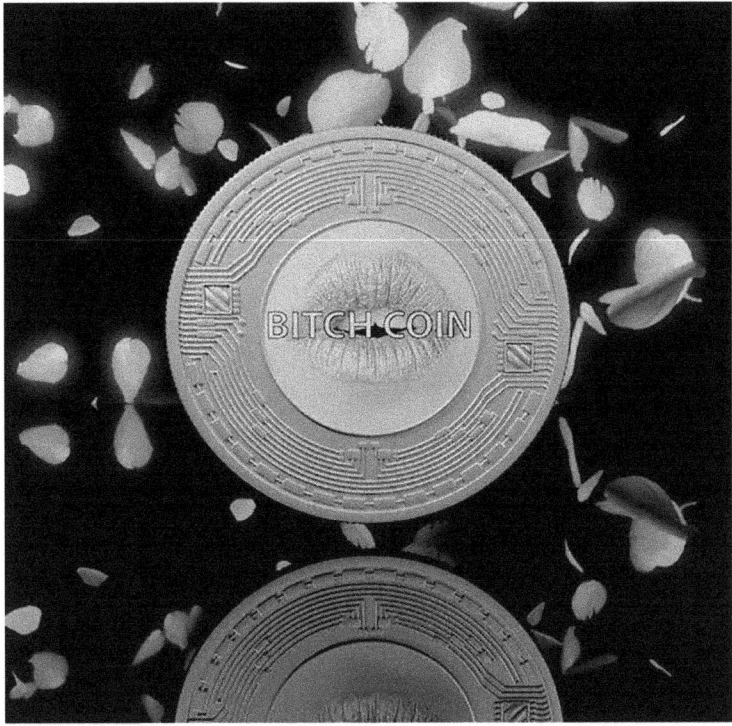

FIGURE 1.6 Sarah Meyohas, Bitchcoin token image (2014)
Source: Sarah Meyohas.

turned out that the NFTs were every bit as important as the photographs they represented. In 2023, the Centre Pompidou acquired two Bitchcoin NFTs recognizing Meyohas's role in establishing NFTs as an artistic medium (Figure 1.6).

One of the first artists to move from the conventional art market to the NFT market was Mitchell F. Chan, a Canadian conceptual artist who shifted from installation art to NFTs. Chan was inspired by French painter and conceptual artist Yves Klein whose work *Zone of Immaterial Pictorial Sensibility* (1959) encouraged art collectors, critics, and consumers to ask themselves why they value art and what they value. Klein is best known for his "ownership" of a particular shade of blue, "International Klein Blue" or "IKB" which he used to create monochrome paintings. But Klein also sold ideas. For example, he "sold" a check representing an "immaterial space" and the buyer decided whether to consummate the sale by burning the check, in which case they got only art. Chan created and sold "digital reproductions" of Klein's immaterial spaces which he described as "empty digital spaces imbued with an immaterial artistic sensibility." He also wrote a "blue paper" explaining the project which was quite influential (Figure 1.7).[60]

---

[60] *NFT Notes 5: Mitchell F. Chan on Conceptualizing the Blockchain*, Ipse Dixit (October 28, 2021), https://shows.acast.com/ipse-dixit/episodes/nft-notes-5-mitchell-f-chan-on-conceptualizing-the-blockchai.

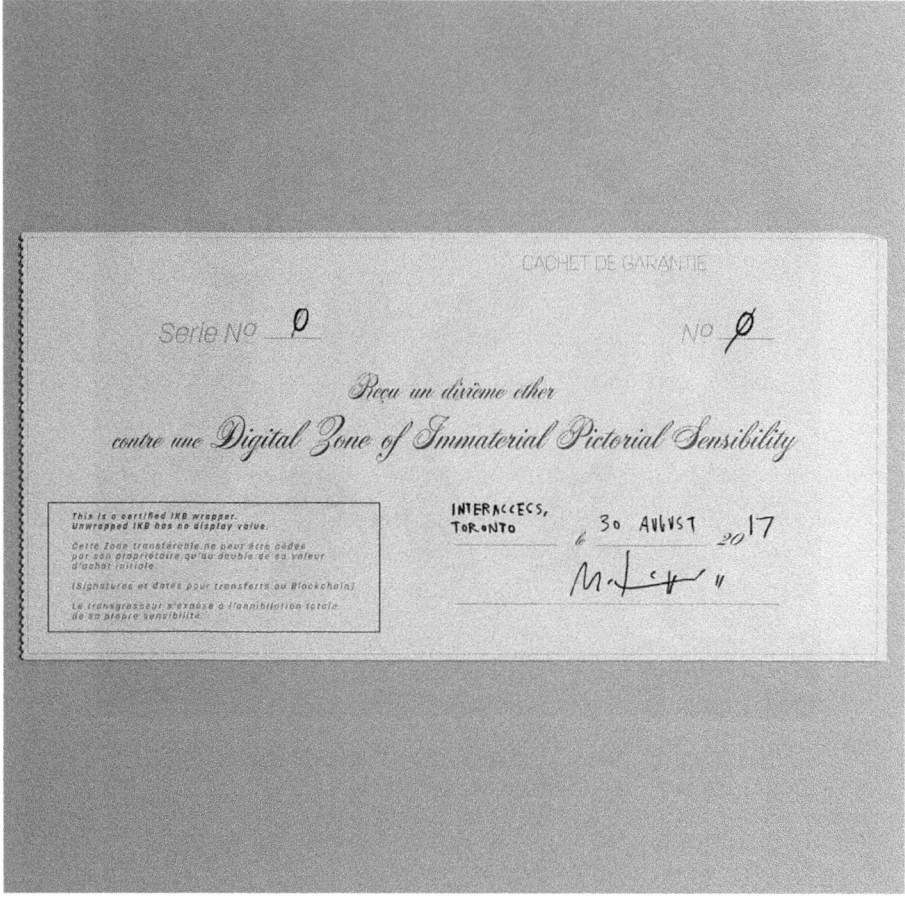

FIGURE 1.7 Mitchell F. Chan, *Digital Zone of Immaterial Pictorial Sensibility* (2017)
Source: https://chan.gallery/ikb/.

VI GENERATIVE ART NFTS

Many NFT collectors are primarily interested in "generative art" or art generated by algorithms. What is generative art? Essentially, an artist creates an algorithm that produces artwork automatically, usually digital images. The results can be quite distinctive depending on the algorithm. Typically, generative artists use the algorithm they create to produce a limited number of images which they sell in limited editions of NFTs.[61]

Generative NFT art draws from many different styles and schools of modern and contemporary art, including cubism, futurism, abstraction, minimalism, and

---

[61] *See generally* Jason Bailey, *Why Love Generative Art?*, Artnome (August 26, 2018), www.artnome .com/news/2018/8/8/why-love-generative-art.

FIGURE 1.8 Tyler Hobbs, *Fidenza #612*
Source: https://tylerxhobbs.com/fidenza.

conceptual art, among other things. Two of the most popular generative artists are Tyler Hobbs, best known for his *Fidenza* series, and Dmitri Cherniak, best known for his *Ringers* series.[62] Generative NFT art was popularized and promoted in considerable part by Art Blocks, a company that commissions and sells generative art by a wide range of different digital artists. Art Blocks was founded in November 2020 by Erick "Snowfro" Calderon with his *Chromie Squiggle* collection of generative art NFTs.[63] By 2023, Art Blocks had released about 400 collections of generative art NFTs by hundreds of different artists (Figure 1.8).[64]

[62] *See* TYLER HOBBS, *Fidenza*, https://tylerxhobbs.com/fidenza; Dimitri Cherniak, *Ringers*, OPENSEA, https://opensea.io/collection/ringers-by-dmitri-cherniak.

[63] *See* CHROMIE SQUIGGLES EXPLORER, https://chromie-squiggles.com/. *See also* Jex Exmundo, *How Chromie Squiggles Pioneered Generative NFT Art*, NFT NOW (November 28, 2022), https://nftnow .com/art/how-chromie-squiggles-pioneered-generative-nft-art/.

[64] *See* Cripco, *NFT Project Research: ART BLOCKS*, MEDIUM (February 15, 2023), https://medium .com/@cripco/nft-project-research-art-blocks-db77e02f8be0; *Interview with Erick Calderon*, EDGE OF NFT (May 18, 2022), www.edgeofnft.com/podcasts/erick-calderon-of-art-blocks-the-first-interactive- nft-generative-art-platform-and-more.

VII THE ECONOMIC REALITY OF THE NFT MARKET

Why are NFTs valuable? Obviously because people want to own them. The interesting question is why people want to own them. After all, as NFT skeptics never tire of reminding anyone who will listen, NFTs make no sense. Why would anyone want to own a digital receipt for a digital artwork you can download for free? Just "right-click save" and the artwork is yours, or at least a copy of it is, and a copy is all you need. When it comes to digital artworks, there is no such thing as an "original" because every copy is identical.

Why NFTs? They create scarcity out of abundance by enabling artists to designate NFTs as representing "ownership" of their artworks. Anyone and everyone can own a copy of a digital artwork, if they want one, but you cannot "own" the artwork itself unless the artist says you do. So artists create NFTs that represent "ownership" of their artworks and buying an authentic NFT makes you an "owner" of the artwork it represents.

What does that mean? It is a little hard to say. On one level, it depends. The only thing an NFT owner necessarily owns is the exclusive right to transfer their NFT from their wallet to another wallet. In other words, if you own an NFT you can sell it or give it away. In some cases, NFTs also give their owners certain rights to use the artwork the NFT represents. For example, some NFTs give their owner a license to use the artwork they represent in certain ways, or even transfer copyright ownership to the NFT owner. Other NFTs place the artworks they represent in the public domain. But most NFTs do not explicitly give their owner anything more than the right to transfer their NFT. Of course, if the author of an artwork creates an NFT intended to represent ownership of their artwork, ownership of the NFT at least implies a limited right to display and use the artwork consistent with art world norms.

But what about the NFT itself? Most NFT collectors just buy and sell NFTs and do not care how the artwork associated with their NFT is used. In fact, they often encourage people to distribute the artwork their NFT represents in the belief that it will make their NFT more valuable. After all, "The only thing worse than being talked about is not being talked about," and the NFT market is all about being talked about. Buzz builds brands and silence is deafening.

So what gives? Why do people want to own NFTs? Maybe NFT collectors are just degen speculators looking to make a quick buck by fleecing the suckers who "diamond hand" rather than flip. But some legal scholars have advanced property-based theories of the NFT market. For example, Fairfield argues that NFTs are a form of virtual property, and Lee argues that NFTs are a form of decentralized intellectual property.[65] But there is a problem. As Moringiello and Odinet observe, in this book,

---

[65] *See* Joshua A. T. Fairfield, *Tokenized: The Law of Non-Fungible Tokens and Unique Digital Property*, 97 IND. L.J. 1261 (2022); Edward Lee, *NFTs as Decentralized Intellectual Property*, 2023 U. ILL. L. REV. 1049 (2023).

property doctrine largely ignores NFTs.[66] Sure you could use an NFT as the vehicle for a property transaction. But why? You do not need it and it only makes the transaction needlessly more complicated.

I think Moringiello and Odinet are right. NFTs have nothing to offer property doctrine, and property doctrine has nothing to offer NFTs. Understandably, when legal scholars learned about NFTs, they assumed property law would explain the NFT market. When people are buying and selling things, it always looks like property. But looks can be deceiving. What exactly are people buying and selling in the NFT market and why does the market exist in the first place?

I believe that the answer is simple: the NFT market is a securities market in clout. Artists create NFTs that represent ownership of their artworks and sell them to collectors. What are the collectors buying? An investment in the artist's career. If the artist becomes famous, then the value of their artwork will increase and the NFT collector can sell for a profit. If the artist does not become famous, oh well, you win some and you lose some.

VIII THIS IS NOT A TOKEN

The art market has always been a securities market, we just could not see it because objects got in the way.[67] The art market is the market for art as an investment rather than as a consumption good. When people buy an artwork as a decoration, they are not participating in the art market, because they are buying a consumption good, not an investment. Art collectors participate in the art market only when they buy an artwork as an investment with a reasonable belief that it might be more valuable in the future.

Why is the art market a securities market? When art collectors buy an artwork, they are effectively buying an investment in an artist's career.[68] According to the Supreme Court, an investment is a security if it is an investment of money in a common enterprise with the expectation of generating a profit from the efforts of someone else. That describes the art market to a tee. Art collectors invest in artworks because they believe the artist will become more famous and their artworks will be worth more money.

I should be more specific. The art market is the market for art as an investment rather than as a consumption good. Of course, there is considerable overlap. When people buy artworks in order to consume them, they often hope those artworks will increase in value over time. They are usually disappointed. Likewise, when people

---

[66] Juliet M. Moringiello & Christopher K. Odinet, *Property Law of Tokens*, 74 Fla. L. Rev. 607 (2022).

[67] *See generally* Brian L. Frye, *The Uncanny Token*, *in* NFTs and Metaverses versus Law (Oreste Pollicino & Fabiana Di Porta, eds., forthcoming 2023); Brian L. Frye, *The Value of Art*, *in* The Cultural History of Collecting (Robert Jensen, ed., forthcoming 2023).

[68] *See generally* Brian L. Frye, *After Copyright: Pwning NFTs in a Clout Economy*, 45 Colum. J.L. & Arts 341 (2022).

invest in artwork, they usually buy things they actually like or at least think other people will like. After all, if you're buying an artwork, you might as well like it. And nothing makes an artwork more appealing than the prospect of profit.

Anyway, the point is that people buy artworks in the art market because they hope to sell them for a profit. Yes, people also buy artworks as consumption goods. But the art market exists because people reasonably believe it is an investment market, not just a market for consumption goods. No one would pay tens of thousands of dollars for an artwork, let alone millions, unless they thought it was an investment.

So why is the art market an investment market and what are art collectors actually buying? Everyone assumes art collectors are buying objects, like paintings and sculptures. Superficially that is true. But they are not really buying objects, they are buying provenance.[69] And the objects are just physical tokens that represent provenance.

Realistically, the art market is really a market for ledger entries. When art collectors buy an artwork, what they are really buying is an entry on an artist's catalogue raisonnée. The artwork is just a token that represents ownership of the ledger entry. When the collector sells the work, everyone looks to the catalogue raisonée to see whether it is authentic. If the answer is yes, the artwork is valuable. If the answer is no, the artwork is worthless.

It is the same artwork. But the facts do not matter. Or rather, the facts matter only if the authentication committee thinks they matter. In other words, whoever controls the artist's brand decides what counts as an original artwork and what is a knockoff or copy.

Artists have always sold artworks for money, and art collectors have always bought artworks in order to sell them for a profit. Big surprise, everyone wants to make money.

There is a problem. What are they selling? It seems obvious. Artists sell objects. Give me a break. Some artists sell objects, but the artists selling objects in the art market are really selling their brand. When you buy a painting or sculpture by a promising artist, you are not just buying a decoration, you're buying an object you can sell for a profit in the future when the artist gets more famous. Or rather you're buying an investment in the artist's career. The artwork is just a physical token that represents your investment.

The NFT market works exactly the same way, it just eliminates the need for objects by allowing artists to sell and collectors to trade the ledger entries directly. While many artists and collectors have a sentimental attraction to physical objects, there is lots to like about the shift to NFTs. For one thing, they eliminate the need to transport, store, and insure immensely valuable and often fragile objects. For another, they make the art market wildly more efficient by drastically reducing transaction costs on sales. Historically, artists relied on galleries and collectors relied on

---

[69] *See generally* Amy Adler, *Artificial Authenticity*, 98 NYU L. REV. 706 (2023).

auction houses, both of which are highly selective and expensive. NFTs are easily and quickly listed and sold on marketplaces like OpenSea, Rarible, and SuperRare.

But eliminating the object does something else that is immensely important. It forces us to see the economic reality of both the NFT market and the art market. It forces us to see that the art market has always been a securities market in which artists effectively sell investments in their future commercial goodwill – their celebrity or "clout." As long as the art market relied on objects, that was hard to see because the objects got in the way. But now that the objects are unnecessary, it is painfully obvious, even though no one wants to admit it.

IX CONCLUSION

While NFTs and the NFT market seemingly came into existence out of nowhere, almost overnight, in reality it was a long time coming and probably inevitable. Why? Because NFTs are effectively demanded by the logic of the art market itself. After all, the art market long ago invented analog NFTs in the form of certificates of authenticity. All the NFT market did was make the market for those certificates more efficient. In so doing, it showed us that markets in clout like the art market are far more versatile and attractive than we had previously realized. Whether NFTs themselves are here to stay or on their way out, something like NFTs and the NFT market are inescapable. Once you can see the potential of a market for information goods that does not need scarcity of anything but clout, there is no going back.

2

The Language Landmines of Blockchain Technology and Cryptocurrency

Carla L. Reyes

I INTRODUCTION

As a highly interdisciplinary area of inquiry, researchers, law-makers, software developers, engineers, and the public often use the same words but mean different things.[1] Indeed, some inaccurate terminology and hype-phrases are used so frequently that the discourse begins to assume their accuracy.[2] Adopting such commonly misused terminology without questioning its technical accuracy can result in detrimental policy and legal outcomes. These commonly used but inaccurate words and phrases lay dormant within law and policy discussions, threatening to explode and derail efforts at reform – they act as a type of language landmine.

Two particularly explosive language failures result in the creation of legal regimes that are neither clear nor, more basically, fit for purpose: (1) failure to understand the technical nuances of blockchain technology and (2) failure to recognize the links between the terminology employed to craft law and policy for blockchain-related products and services and the technical nuances of varying blockchain protocols.[3] Using misappropriated or ill-understood technical terms in law and policy-making can also heighten the risk of discouraging useful innovation in emerging applications of the technology.[4] To avoid such pitfalls, those researching and articulating the law and policy of blockchain technology must avoid various language landmines and ensure that the technical attributes, functions, and limitations of blockchain protocols feature prominently in law-making and policy discussions.

---

[1] *See* Carla L. Reyes, *Emerging Technology's Language Wars: Cryptocurrency*, 64 WM. & MARY L. REV. 1193, 1197–1198 (2023); Carla L. Reyes, *Emerging Technology's Language Wars: Smart Contacts*, 2022 WISC. L. REV. FWD. 85, 88 (2022).

[2] Reyes, *Language Wars: Cryptocurrency*, 1210.

[3] *Written Testimony of Carla L. Reyes Before the U.S. House of Reps. Innovation, Data & Commerce Subcommittee, Energy & Commerce Committee* (June 7, 2023), https://d1dth6e84htgma .cloudfront.net/IDC_Reyes_Testimony_Blockchain_Hearing_2023_06_07_d0d6c4bf9a .pdf?updated_at=2023-06-05T15:59:42.558Z.

[4] Ibid.

This volume explores, in particular, the role of law and policy in the governance of non-fungible tokens (NFTs). NFTs exist as a second layer of software built on top of a blockchain protocol. As such, the language landmines that threaten to impede sound law and policy for blockchain technology also threaten more specific efforts aimed at NFTs. With this in mind, the current chapter explores six distinct blockchain, cryptocurrency and NFT-related language landmines – terminology errors made so frequently in blockchain law and policy discussions that they threaten to obliterate well-intended policy reforms. If interdisciplinary discussion cannot bridge the understanding gap related to – at the very least – these six language landmines, then the law should expect to continue to lag behind blockchain technology and its use cases, including NFTs.

II LANDMINE 1: THE TERMS "BLOCKCHAIN TECHNOLOGY" AND "DISTRIBUTED LEDGER TECHNOLOGY" MEAN THE SAME THING

Too often, commentators use the terms "blockchain technology" and "distributed ledger technology" (DLT) interchangeably. Doing so perpetuates the idea that one archetypal blockchain technical architecture (often the Bitcoin network or Ethereum network) predominates.[5] Holding out one archetypal blockchain technical architecture and treating the rest of the industry as monolithic can result in legal frameworks that underperform their intended function, at best, and actively damage stakeholders and consumers by sewing market confusion, at worst. For example, a DLT operated by a consortium of banks, such as R3 and its Corda DLT, boasts different features and higher levels of centralization than, say, the Bitcoin network. If legal analysis uses DLT and blockchain technology as interchangeable synonyms and keeps a vision of the Bitcoin protocol in mind when doing so, the legal analysis may miss key issues that arise from the differences in centralization and features offered in a permissioned DLT like Corda as opposed to a decentralized permissionless blockchain protocol like bitcoin. This section seeks to expose the most basic of language landmines – the myth that the terms blockchain technology and DLT mean the same thing – and expose the potential policy-making harm that can ensue from failure to avoid it.

Researchers define DLT as a "type of distributed database that assumes the possible presence of malicious users (nodes)."[6] In other words, where a distributed database builds data redundancy by distributing storage of database contents among many trusted nodes, a distributed ledger also guards against attempts by one or more nodes to proactively alter the database's contents.[7] Blockchain technology, for its part, refers to a subset of distributed ledgers that structure their data in a literal

---

[5] Reyes, *Language Wars: Cryptocurrency*, 1224.

[6] *See* GARRICK HILEMAN & MICHEL RAUCHS, GLOBAL BLOCKCHAIN BENCHMARKING STUDY 13 (2017).

[7] Ibid.

"chain of blocks" by linking blocks of validated transactions together using one-way cryptographic hashes.[8] The combination and implementation of the specific features creating that chain of blocks, such as the type of consensus mechanism used to verify transactions, vary widely among blockchain protocols.[9]

Importantly, blockchain technology is a protocol technology.[10] A protocol is "a set of instructions for the compilation and interaction of objects."[11] Blockchain technology is a protocol that sets the rules that enable networked computers to track transitions in the global state of recorded data without a centralized third-party intermediary.[12] Evidence suggests that the archetypal blockchain protocols used in law and policy-making discussions to craft new legal frameworks for blockchain technology and its use cases are the Bitcoin protocol and the Ethereum protocol.[13] A quick review of the differences between even these two prominent protocols reveals why holding on too tightly to a technical archetype without considering other variations can result in deeply flawed legal responses to the technology.

The Bitcoin protocol tracks transactions in unspent transaction outputs (UTXOs),[14] while the Ethereum protocol constructs and operates a global virtual computer (the EVM).[15] This core architectural difference leads to different use cases and triggers different legal questions in certain circumstances. For example, the Bitcoin protocol locks UTXOs using a small computer program that says, "this can be redeemed by a public key that hashes to X, along with a signature from the owner of that public key."[16] However, building more complex programs on the bitcoin blockchain usually requires implementing the program off-chain and "anchoring" the program outputs to the bitcoin blockchain periodically.[17] Meanwhile, the Ethereum virtual machine enables developers to build a variety of applications and other programs fully or partially on-chain using the programming language Solidity.[18] In particular, the Ethereum protocol ushered in experimentation with smart contracts that the Bitcoin protocol simply was not designed to support. Such smart contract experimentation included, of course, the creation of

---

[8] Ibid., 11.

[9] Carla L. Reyes, *Creating Cryptolaw for the Uniform Commercial Code*, 78 WASH. & LEE L. REV. 1520, 1537–1538 (2021).

[10] Ibid., 1538.

[11] ALEXANDER R. GALLOWAY, PROTOCOL: HOW CONTROL EXISTS AFTER DECENTRALIZATION 75 (2004).

[12] Reyes, *Creating Cryptolaw*, 1538.

[13] Reyes, *Language Wars: Cryptocurrency*, 1224.

[14] ARVIND NARAYANAN ET AL., BITCOIN AND CRYPTOCURRENCY TECHNOLOGIES: A COMPREHENSIVE INTRODUCTION 51–52 (2016).

[15] ANDREAS M. ANTONOPOULOS & GAVIN WOOD, MASTERING ETHEREUM: BUILDING SMART CONTRACTS AND DAPPS 2 (2018).

[16] Ibid., 55.

[17] Ibid., 58–59.

[18] ANTONOPOULOS & WOOD, MASTERING ETHEREUM, 4.

NFTs and, later, the development of technical standards, ERC-721 and ERC 1155, to support adoption of NFTs.[19]

Just as assuming the technical architecture of these two blockchain protocols operate similarly when in reality they boast strikingly different features and functionality can lead to mistakes in crafting legal rules related to the industry, so too can assuming that all NFTs exist only on the Ethereum protocol cause difficulty for the law related to NFTs. A variety of other protocols support NFTs, including Flow, Polygon, and Cardano, among others.[20] Flow uses a proof-of-stake consensus mechanism and a purportedly easier-to-learn programming language called Cadence to support NFTs for gaming, the metaverse, and digital collectibles.[21] One of Flow's core selling points is that it does not require its nodes to complete all the tasks required to operate the protocol.[22] Rather, nodes can specialize in collection, consensus, execution, or verification in order to increase efficiencies and throughput, and decrease transactions costs.[23] Polygon does not operate its own blockchain protocol; rather, the Polygon Network is a Layer 2 blockchain, meaning that it is built on top of the Ethereum protocol.[24] Operating as a Layer 2, blockchain enables high throughput, lower fees, and easy interaction with other Layer 2 applications.[25] Cardano offers a Layer 1 blockchain that uses proof-of-stake consensus and remains compatible with the Ethereum network.[26]

Even without exploring the technical details of each protocol in radical depth, it remains clear that the differences between a proof of work (bitcoin)[27] and proof of stake (Ethereum, Cardano)[28] consensus mechanism may have an impact on how

---

[19] For more on the standards *see* Tonya M. Evans, *Cryptokitties, Cryptography, and Copyright*, 47 AIPLA Q.J. 219, 248 (2019) (explaining the inspiration for the standards and comparing them); and Michael D. Murray, *NFTs and the Art World – What's Real, and What's Not*, 29 UCLA ENT. L. REV. 25, 50–51 (2022) (explaining how it "allowed NFTs to be created as 'non-fungible' (i.e., unique) bundles of data").

[20] Crypto APIs Team, *Which Blockchain Protocols Are the Best for NFTs?*, CRYPTO APIS BLOG (May 10, 2022), https://cryptoapis.io/blog/79-which-blockchain-protocols-are-the-best-for-nfts.

[21] Ibid.

[22] Ibid.

[23] Ibid.

[24] Ibid.

[25] Ibid.

[26] Ibid.

[27] Proof of Work (PoW) consensus, such as in the Bitcoin network uses a technical consensus rule – the longest proposed chain and the requirement to expend effort to solve a very difficult math problem (finding the correct nonce) – together with two mechanisms to incentivize honest transaction validation by nodes: block rewards, whereby block validators get a fixed number of bitcoin for creating a successfully proposed and accepted block of transactions, and transaction fees. NARAYANAN ET AL., BITCOIN AND CRYPTOCURRENCY TECHNOLOGIES, 30–39; *see also* ANTONOPOULOS & WOOD, BITCOIN AND CRYPTOCURRENCY TECHNOLOGIES, 2 (explaining proof of work as a "game-theoretically sound incentivization scheme (e.g., proof-of-work costs plus block rewards) to economically secure the state machine in an open environment").

[28] "Instead of miners, proof-of-stake systems employ vast numbers of 'validators.' To become a validator, you have to deposit, or 'stake,' a set amount in coins – 32 ether, in the case of Ethereum. Staking

the law applies to transactions on the protocol.[29] The difference between a Layer 1 protocol and a Layer 2 protocol may also impact the legal analysis in unforeseen ways. Ultimately, those engaging in law and policy debates around blockchain technology, cryptocurrency, and the NFTs built upon blockchain technology, must understand the technical attributes of the protocol and how the functionality resulting from those attributes may impact the legal analysis. Often, understanding the differences leads to the realization that a one-size-fits-all approach is untenable in the blockchain arena.

III LANDMINE 2: A BLOCKCHAIN PROTOCOL PRODUCES A LEDGER OF AUDITABLE DATA THAT CAN NEVER BE CHANGED

The myth that a blockchain protocol produces a ledger of auditable data that can never be changed suffers from three potentially explosive trigger points. First, many blockchain protocols only nominally produce something that resembles a "ledger" in the commonly understood meaning of that term. Next, a blockchain protocol does produce auditable data, but the actual ability to audit depends upon the sophistication of the auditor. Lastly, a blockchain protocol commonly relies upon an append-only data structure that remains highly tamper-resistant, but blockchain protocols are not immutable in the sense that, under certain circumstances the records can in fact be changed. This section unpacks how failure to avoid even just one of these three bundled explosive aspects of the second language landmine can obliterate well-intentioned law and policy-making.

When explaining what a blockchain protocol does, people commonly use the term "ledger."[30] Indeed, frequent use of the term ledger to explain a blockchain protocol's function partially underlies the persistence of the first language landmine – using blockchain protocol and distributed ledger interchangeably when they actually feature important and distinct technical architectures. But a blockchain protocol docs not typically produce the type of double-entry bookkeeping ledger that likely serves as the most familiar reference point when the term ledger is used.[31]

---

gives validators a chance to check new blocks of transactions and add them to the blockchain so they can earn rewards on top of their staked coins. The more coins you stake the better your odds of getting picked to add the next block of transactions to the chain." Amy Castor, *Ethereum Moved to Proof of Stake. Why Can't Bitcoin*, MIT Tech Rev. (February 28, 2023), www.technologyreview .com/2023/02/28/1069190/ethereum-moved-to-proof-of-stake-why-cant-bitcoin/.

[29] *See, for example*, James Grimmelmann & A. Jason Windawi, *Blockchains As Infrastructure and Semicommons*, 64 Wm & Mary L. Rev. 1097 (2023) (examining the ways governance choices such as consensus architecture may intersect with the law).

[30] *See, for example*, Jenny Cieplak & Simon Leefatt, *Smart Contracts: A Way to Automate Performance*, 1 Geo L. Tech. Rev. 417, 420–421 (2017).

[31] Kevin Werbach, *Trust but Verify: Why Blockchain Needs the Law*, 33 Berkeley Tech. L.J. 487, 499 (2018).

At its most basic, "[a] ledger is a record of accounts."[32] Blockchain protocols track transitions in state – they track changes to the global data recorded by the computer software.[33] Tracking transitions in state does produce a record of accounts in so far as with some tracing and investigation a person can identify how much cryptocurrency is associated with a certain wallet. However, not all blockchain track transactions use an account-based method that produces an easy-to-read balance at the end – at least not on its own.[34] Rather, commonly used wallet software often displays a balance to users for ease of asset management.[35]

Ultimately, a blockchain protocol offers a ledger of transactions in so far as it ultimately produces a cryptographically linked list of verified transactions.[36] However, in light of the commonly used ledger metaphor, certain assumptions about the accessibility and usability of a blockchain protocol's data persist and not all of them reflect reality. For example, the second explosive element of this language landmine: that blockchain protocol data is openly readable, auditable, and understandable to anyone. Although public open source blockchain protocols enable anyone to see every transaction ever made using the protocol, to do so without an intermediary requires maintaining a copy of the full transaction history of the protocol. If a person is unable to operate a full node that maintains a full copy of a blockchain protocol's transaction history, the only way to see transaction data is through a block explorer.[37] While block explorers allow anyone to look up details of any transaction, those details amount to little more than metadata: the transaction ID, the sending and receiving address, the amount of the transaction, the associated fees, and the transactions status.[38] To make sense of such metadata, which all appear as strings of letters and numbers, requires a certain amount of user sophistication. Thus, while transaction history of public blockchain protocols may be available for everyone to see, it may only be available through an intermediary and even then, it may only be useful to those who know how to use the metadata made available. Legal and policy discussions that place too much emphasis on the idea that a blockchain protocol

---

[32] Ibid.

[33] Reyes, *Creating Cryptolaw*, 1539.

[34] Jordan Clifford, *Intro to Blockchain: UTXO vs Account Based*, MEDIUM (September 20, 2019), https://jcliff.medium.com/intro-to-blockchain-utxo-vs-account-based-89b9a01cd4f5.

[35] Jake Frankenfield, *Cyrptocurrency Wallet: What It Is, How It Works, Types, Security*, INVESTOPEDIA (May 27, 2022), www.investopedia.com/terms/b/bitcoin-wallet.asp ("Cyrptocurrencies are not 'stored' anywhere – they are bits of data stored in a database. These bits of data are scattered all over the database; the wallet finds all of the bits associated with your public address and sums up the amount for you in the app's interface").

[36] Clifford, *Intro to Blockchain*; NARAYANAN ET AL., BITCOIN AND CRYPTOCURRENCY TECHNOLOGIES.

[37] Kristy Moreland, *How to Read a Blockchain Transaction History*, LEDGER ACADEMY (May 22, 2023), www.ledger.com/academy/how-to-read-a-blockchains-transaction-history#:~:text=%E2%80%94%20 Blockchains%20are%20public%20ledgers%2C%20meaning,search%20your%20blockchain %20transaction%20history; Luit Hollander, *Understanding Event Logs on the Ethereum Blockchain*, MYCYRPTO (March 4, 2020), https://medium.com/mycrypto/understanding-event-logs-on-the-ethereum-blockchain-f4ae7ba50378.

[38] Moreland, *How to Read a Blockchain Transaction History*.

can be read, audited, and understood by anyone will create frameworks that do not map well to the technological reality of blockchain protocols.

Lastly, the all too common misuse of the word "immutable" to describe a blockchain protocol as data records that can never be changed may represent the most explosive aspect of this language landmine. Immutability, when used with reference to blockchain protocols, means very difficult to change, not impossible to change.[39] Indeed, the term immutable never appeared in Satoshi Nakamoto's Bitcoin White Paper; rather, Satoshi Nakamoto described blockchain protocols as "computationally impractical to reverse."[40] To unpack the difference between immutable – as in can never be changed – and "computationally impractical to reverse" recall that blockchain transactions are verified by consensus.[41] Each consensus protocol is designed to incentivize honest behavior of the protocol's nodes, however, circumstances exist in which the incentive to behave honestly does not outweigh the temptation to maliciously alter the protocol's transaction history.[42] Even when such circumstances exist, and even if a node or group of nodes takes advantage of such circumstances to attempt to alter the transaction history, blockchain protocols remain highly tamper-resistant in so far as the cryptographic links between blocks of data will allow users to identify when transaction tampering has occurred.[43] Failure to understand the nuance of blockchain protocol immutability can lead law and policy discussions to combat nonexistent threats while allowing real concerns to go unabated. Failure to understand the technical realities of blockchain protocols can also compound misunderstandings of second-layer applications, such as NFTs.

IV LANDMINE 3: THE TERMS "CRYPTOASSETS," "CRYPTOCURRENCY," "DIGITAL ASSETS," AND "VIRTUAL CURRENCY" CAN BE USED INTERCHANGEABLY

In 2013, the U.S. Treasury's Financial Crimes and Enforcement Network (FinCEN) stepped squarely onto blockchain and cryptocurrency's third common language landmine, setting off an explosion of misunderstandings that reverberate to this

---

[39] Gideon Greenspan, *The Blockchain Immutability Myth*, CoinDesk (May 9, 2017), www.coindesk .com/markets/2017/05/09/the-blockchain-immutability-myth/ ("In blockchains, there is no such thing as perfect immutability. The real question is: What are the conditions under which a particular blockchain can and cannot be changed? And do those conditions match the problem we're trying to solve?").

[40] Satoshi Nakamoto, Bitcoin: A Peer-to-Peer Electronic Cash System 1 (2008), https:// bitcoin.org/bitcoin.pdf.

[41] Narayanan et al, Bitcoin and Cryptocurrency Technologies.

[42] For example, Ethereum Classic, which operated on a proof of work consensus mechanism, suffered a 51 percent attack. Gareth Jenkinson, *Ethereum Classic 51% Attack – The Reality of Proof of Work*, CoinTelegraph (January 10, 2019), https://cointelegraph.com/news/ ethereum-classic-51-attack-the-reality-of-proof-of-work.

[43] Narayanan et al, Bitcoin and Cryptocurrency Technologies.

day.[44] FinCEN issued guidance on what it referred to as "virtual currency" for the first time in March 2013, relying upon terminology such as "administrator" and "centralized repository" to apply regulation to newly created terms "centralized convertible virtual currency" and "decentralized convertible virtual currency."[45] Few understood the terms or their application to existing industry business models and companies incurred significant legal fees trying to determine whether the guidance applied to their business.[46] The terminology used in the law and policy space to refer to cryptocurrency has varied widely ever since. In particular, law and policy discussions continue to use the terms "cryptoassets," "cryptocurrency," "digital assets," and "virtual currency" interchangeably, sowing confusion and misunderstanding into legal frameworks and guidance.[47]

Importantly, failure to recognize the distinctions between the terms cryptoassets, cryptocurrency, digital assets, and virtual currency reflects at least three separate opportunities for explosive miscommunication between law and industry.[48] First, these terms hold technical meaning that many fail to recognize.[49] Second, even when the technical meaning of these terms are known, many cannot take technical definitions and conceptualize the functional importance they hold – an underappreciation of the impact of technical differences on functionality leads to mis-attribution of problems and the creation of one-size-fits all legal solutions with no chance of success.[50] Third, even when an appreciation of the functional impact of technical nuances exist, law and policy discussions sometimes fail to grasp that the trade-offs reflected in different technical architectures grow out of deeply held values and goals.[51] Failure to understand the root of design choices lead to faulty assumptions about when and whether one technical architecture can be substituted for another. For example, some policy discussions suggest that in order to save the environment from the alleged energy-intensive nature of proof-of-work consensus, proof-of-work protocols should switch to proof-of-stake consensus.[52] Such suggestions ignore, or simply reflect unawareness of, debates in the technical community about the appropriate trade-offs between security of the protocol and throughput.[53]

---

[44] Fin. Crimes Enf't Network, U.S. Dep't of the Treasury, Guidance FIN-2013-G001: Application of FinCEN's Regulations to Persons Administering, Exchanging, or Using Virtual Currencies (2013).

[45] Ibid., 2, 4.

[46] Reyes, *Language Wars: Cryptocurrency*, 197.

[47] Ibid.

[48] Ibid., 1198.

[49] Ibid.

[50] Ibid.

[51] Ibid.

[52] *See, for example*, Hearing, Energy & Commerce Committee Innovation, Data, and Commerce Subcommittee Hearing: "Building Blockchains: Exploring Web3 and Other Applications for Distributed Ledger Technologies" (June 7, 2023), www.youtube.com/live/optrUUCNKNs?feature=share.

[53] *Proof-of-Stake vs. Proof-of-Work: Pros, Cons, and Differences Explained*, CoinTelegraph (2022), https://cointelegraph.com/learn/proof-of-stake-vs-proof-of-work:-differences-explained.

Protocols that use a proof-of-work consensus mechanism aim to provide exceptional security to the transaction history recorded by the blockchain protocol, while protocols that use a proof-of-stake consensus mechanism prioritize increasing transaction volume.[54] Meanwhile, others undertake extensive research to try variations in between these two extremes – searching for a consensus mechanism that preserves a highly secure protocol while also improving scalability.[55]

All that is to say that the terms cryptoasset, cryptocurrency, digital asset, and virtual currency should not be used interchangeably.[56] Although commentators often use any one of these four terms to refer to the broadest set of cryptocurrency,[57] they each reflect subsets of a digital asset class. Considering these terms from the most general to the most specific, the order should appear as follows: Digital asset, virtual currency, cryptoasset, and cryptocurrency. The term digital asset refers to a wide variety of digital items that might be treated as property by the law.[58] For example, the term digital asset might refer to emails, social media accounts, pictures, or databases.[59] Within that broad class of potential assets, virtual currency tends to refer to the definition offered by FinCEN:[60] "[a] medium of exchange that operates like a currency in some environments, but does not have all the attributes of real currency. In particular, virtual currency does not have legal tender status in any jurisdiction."[61] A cryptoasset, for its part, seems to refer to virtual currency that is created and transacted using some type of cryptographic system.[62]

Cryptocurrency should be understood to refer to one type of cryptoasset that is often called "native cryptocurrency"[63] or "intrinsic tokens," or "protocol tokens."[64] Blockchain protocols rely upon native cryptocurrency to incentivize the operation of the protocol's consensus mechanism and act as a security tool.[65] Native cryptocurrencies are those that play a key role in the proper functioning of the blockchain

---

[54] Ibid.

[55] Ibid.

[56] Reyes, *Language Wars: Cryptocurrency*, 1249–1250.

[57] Ibid.

[58] Revised Uniform Fiduciary Access to Digital Assets Act § 2(10) (2015) ("'Digital asset' means an electronic record in which an individual has a right or interest. The term does not include an underlying asset or liability unless the asset or liability is itself an electronic record").

[59] Natalie M. Banta, *Electronic Wills and Digital Assets: Reassessing Formality in the Digital Age*, 71 Baylor L. Rev. 547, 549 (2019); *see also* Reyes, *Language Wars: Cryptocurrency*, 1224 (explaining "the term 'digital asset' is used broadly to refer to information held in a password-protected online account, such as Facebook and mobile banking applications") (citing Suzanne Brown Walsh, Naomi Cahn, & Christina L. Kunz, Digital Assets and Fiduciaries, *in* Research Handbook on Electronic Commerce Law 91, 107 (John A. Rothchild, ed., 2016)).

[60] Reyes, *Language Wars: Cryptocurrency*, 1225.

[61] FinCEN.

[62] Reyes, *Language Wars: Cryptocurrency*, 1248.

[63] Werbach, Trust but Verify, 498.

[64] Reyes, *Language Wars: Cryptocurrency*, 1212.

[65] Narayanan et al., Bitcoin and Cryptocurrency Technologies, 51.

protocol – without bitcoin, the Bitcoin network does not function correctly, and without ether, the Ethereum protocol cannot prevent the deployment and call of an unwieldy smart contract that could unintentionally use all of the network's computing power.[66] The term cryptocurrency, then, refers to the subset of cryptoassets that are inseparable from the protocol in which they exist; without the native cryptocurrency, the protocol does not properly function.

Many blockchain protocols allow the creation of non-intrinsic tokens which can be transacted via a blockchain network.[67] Such tokens might be created using a smart contract, and similar smart contract-created tokens are what the world colloquially refers to as non-fungible tokens, or NFTs. Understanding how different classes of cryptoassets are created and transacted and whether they serve any fundamental purpose for the proper functioning of the protocol neutralizes the three potential types of language explosions that can occur when using these terms carelessly. Being precise in naming a specific cryptoasset class can also help avoid several other language landmines that often plague discussions around smart contracts and NFTs.

V LANDMINE 4: SMART CONTRACTS ARE ARTIFICIALLY INTELLIGENT, SELF-EXECUTING, AND AUTOMATICALLY ENFORCING

Despite many attempts by academics,[68] lawyers,[69] and software developers[70] to explain that smart contracts are just computer programs that say "if event x happens, then execute result y,"[71] confusion as to the nature of and use cases for smart contracts remain common.[72] Commentary often depicts smart contracts as either a new technology capable for revolutionizing everything,[73] or a danger that threatens core aspects of consumer protection and investor protections.[74] Such hyperbole

---

[66] Reyes, *Language Wars: Cyrptocurrency*, 1213.

[67] Ibid.

[68] Carla L. Reyes, *A Unified Theory of Code Connected Contracts*, 46 J. CORP. L. 981 (2021); Primavera De Filippi, Chris Wray, & Giovanni Sileno, *Smart Contracts*, 10 INTERNET POL'Y REV. (2021); Rafal Tomasz Prabucki, *Self-Executing Contracts from the Perspective of the Selected Polish Regulations and the Future Potential Prevalence of 'Smarter' Contracts*, 3 J. BRITISH BLOCKCHAIN ASSOCIATION (2020).

[69] J. Dax Hansen, Laurie Rosini, & Carla L. Reyes, *More Legal Aspects of Smart Contract Applications*, PERKINS COIE WHITE PAPER (2018), www.perkinscoie.com/images/content/1/9/v3/199672/2018-More-Legal-Aspects-of-Smart-Contract-Applications-White-Pa.pdf.

[70] Shuai Wang, Yong Yuan, Xiao Wang, Juanjuan Li, Rui Qin, & Fei-Yue Wang, *An Overview of Smart Contract: Architecture, Applications, and Future Trends*, 4 IEEE INTELLIGENT VEHICLES SYMPOSIUM 108 (2018).

[71] Reyes, *Code Connected Contracts*, 987.

[72] Reyes, *Language Wars: Smart Contracts*.

[73] Silas Nzuva, *Smart Contracts Implementation, Applications, Benefits and Limitations*, 9 J. INFO ENGINEERING & APPLICATIONS (2019).

[74] Lucas Forbes, *Consumer Protection in the Face of Smart Contracts*, 34 LOYOLA CONSUMER L. REV. 45 (2022); Marina Kasatkina, *Consumer Protection in the Light of Smart Contracts*, ELTE L.J. 95 (2021); Shaanan Cohney, David A. Hoffman, Jeremy Sklaroff, & David A. Wishnick, *Coin-Operated Capitalism*, 119 COLUM. L. REV. 591 (2019).

often occurs because law and policy discussions around smart contracts fall victim to three language landmines – namely, that smart contracts are artificially intelligent, self-executing, and automatically enforcing.

First, many imagine smart contracts as capable of sensing outside data and acting on their own accord.[75] Smart contracts, however, are quite passive.[76] Smart contracts do not actively mine data on an unsupervised basis like an advanced machine learning algorithm. Indeed, smart contracts cannot reach out to find data evidencing an event "x" has occurred.[77] Rather, the smart contract must be told that an event "x" has occurred.[78] A smart contract can be triggered by an outside source, or by other smart contracts operating on the same blockchain protocol.[79] Industry often refers to such sources as "oracles," which sounds very mysterious, but in reality the oracle could simply be a designated person, a data feed, an algorithm, or another smart contract.[80] The point is that conceptions of smart contracts as automated agents that can contract on their own, or perform obligations automatically without oversight misunderstand the way the technology functions and, more importantly, those misunderstandings seep into law as governments, organizations, and legal scholars race to "accommodate" smart contracts.[81]

Many commentators also focus on the so-called "self-executing" nature of smart contracts, reading any number of legal implications into the idea that, essentially, a smart contract goes into effect after creation without requiring any further action by anyone.[82] As just discussed, however, that understanding of "self-executing" in reference to smart contracts cannot possibly be accurate given how these software programs work as a technical matter. Rather, a more precise understanding of what

---

[75] *Smart Contract*, Corp. Fin. Inst. (January 15, 2023), https://corporatefinanceinstitute.com/resources/valuation/smart-contract/ ("Essentially, a smart contract is a digital version of the standard paper contract that automatically verifies fulfillment and enforces and performs the terms of the contract").

[76] Antonopoulos & Wood, Mastering Ethereum, 128–129 ("All smart contracts in Ethereum are executed, ultimately, because a transaction initiated from an EOA. A contract can call another contract that can call another contract and so on, but the first contract in such a chain of execution will always have been called by a transaction for an EOA").

[77] Ibid., 129 ("Contracts never run 'on their own' or 'in the background'").

[78] Ibid. ("Contracts effectively lie dormant until a transaction triggers execution, either directly or indirectly as part of a chain of contract calls").

[79] Ibid.

[80] Nizan Geslevich Packin & Yafit Lev-Aretz, *Decentralized Credit Scoring: Black Box 3.0*, Am. Bus. L.J. at 8 (forthcoming 2024), https://papers.ssrn.com/sol3/papers.cfm?abstract_id=4375920 (defining an oracle as "a service or agent that acquires and confirms real-world data for a smart contract on a blockchain").

[81] Reyes, *Language Wars: Smart Contracts* (discussing government attempts to "accommodate" smart contracts in law); Kristian Lauslahti, Juri Mattila, & Tim Seppala, *Smart Contracts – How Will Blockchain Technology Affect Contractual Practices?*, Rsch Inst. of the Finish Econ. Rprt. No. 68, at 4 (2017) (discussing the need to determine if Finnish law must "accommodate" smart contracts).

[82] Marsha Simone Cadogan, *Enforcing Smart Legal Contracts: Prospects and Challenges*, Centre for Int'l Gov. Innovation, CIGI Papers No. 271, at 5 (2023).

"self-executing" means in the context of smart contracts narrows in on the ability of smart contracts to cause something to happen (execute "y") after the fulfillment of certain coded conditions (triggering the contract when "x" occurs).[83] Take, for example, the smart contract that makes each bitcoin transaction work. The Bitcoin network uses a locking script (a smart contract) that says, "this can be redeemed by a public key that hashes to X, along with a signature from the owner of that public key."[84] When the public key hashes to X and the owner of the public key signs the transaction, the preconditions of the smart contract have been fulfilled, and the smart contract "self-executes" by unlocking the bitcoin and executing the transaction.

Similarly, commentary often falls victim to the idea of smart contracts as "automatically enforcing" – capable of enforcing contract terms autonomously and without any human intervention.[85] These misunderstandings stem from the same linguistic imprecision as assumptions about smart contracts being artificially intelligent and self-executing. If we take these three language errors and consider them in the context of NFTs, the potential for explosive damage to the law and policy landscape becomes apparent. An NFT is created by a smart contract.[86] The process commonly referred to as "minting" an NFT refers to the process of designing the smart contract that creates the NFT.[87] The NFT smart contract also sets the preconditions for allowing transfer of an NFT from one person to another.[88] When those conditions are met, the transfer will automatically enforce or self-execute.

Commentators, however, commonly merge these technical functions of the NFT smart contract with legal concepts.[89] For example, one explanation of NFTs asserts that "[w]hen an NFT is minted (published) on the blockchain, the smart contract automatically assigns ownership of the digital token to the purchaser."[90] Another commentator claims that "[s]mart contracts are used for

---

[83] Henning Diedrich, Ethereum: Blockchain, Digital Assets, Smart Contracts, Decentralized Autonomous Organizations 167 (2016); Narayanan et al., Bitcoin and Cryptocurrency Technologies, 264–265.

[84] Narayanan et al, Bitcoin and Cryptocurrency Technologies, 55.

[85] Cadogan, *Enforcing Smart Legal Contracts*, 5.

[86] *What is an NFT Smart Contract*, Hedera, https://hedera.com/learning/smart-contracts/nft-smart-contract (last visited July 16, 2023).

[87] *All You Need to Know about NFT Smart Contracts*, Binance (August 4, 2022), www.binance.com/en/blog/nft/all-you-need-to-know-about-nft-smart-contracts-568745413587703085.

[88] William Entriken et al., *EIP-165: ERC-721: Non-Fungible Token Standard*, Ethereum Improvement Proposals (January 24, 2018), https://eips.ethereum.org/EIPS/eip-721.

[89] Megan E. Noh, Sarah C. Odenkirk, & Yayoi Shionoiri, *GM! Time to Wake Up and Address Copyright and Other Legal Issues Impacting Visual Art NFTs*, 45 Colum. J.L. & Arts 315, 317 (2022) ("Thus, at a very basic level, the NFT is simply the underlying code written to evidence an associated asset's existence and non-fungibility. The code also records the transfer of ownership of that asset or rights in or to the asset (which may include custodial rights and/or intellectual property rights)").

[90] Alex Gomez, *What is an NFT Smart Contract? A Complete Beginners Guide*, CyberScrilla (March 8, 2023), https://cyberscrilla.com/nft-smart-contracts-explained/#:~:text=An%20NFT%20smart%20contract%20is,an%20intermediary%20or%20central%20authority.

NFTs' minting process (creation) and to assign ownership of the token. When a new non-fungible token is minted, the smart contract automatically sets the creator as the owner. NFT smart contracts can transfer the token to new owners when a sale is made."[91] This merging of technical attributes with legal implications due to imprecise language leads to confusion in the market.[92] Technical capability does not confer substantive legal rights.[93] A smart contract that mints an NFT cannot "assign ownership" to anyone, and it cannot transfer ownership to a downstream purchaser. Ownership is a legal concept that depends upon substantive legal rules which may apply to technologically created assets like NFTs but ownership cannot be determined by technical architecture alone. NFTs, standing alone as a technical artifact, do not convey property rights to anything.

VI LANDMINE 5: ALL CRYPTOASSETS, INCLUDING TOKENS AND NFTS, ARE EITHER ALL DECENTRALIZED OR ALL CENTRALIZED ASSETS

Some commenters seem to assume either that all cryptoassets, including non-intrinsic tokens and NFTs operate on an entirely decentralized basis, or that all cryptoassets operate on an entirely centralized basis.[94] An assumption that all cryptoassets are decentralized might stem from the common practice of holding out bitcoin or ether – both native cryptocurrencies – as the archetypal cryptoasset. Meanwhile, an assumption that all cryptoassets are centralized might stem from a hyper-focus on industry actors that provide intermediary services or that offer services via a permissioned system. Recall, however, that many creators of non-intrinsic tokens and NFTs build those assets using smart contracts on top of a blockchain protocol – at Layer 2 of the blockchain technology stack.[95] While it is possible to create a decentralized non-intrinsic token,[96] it is more common that a person or entity initiates a non-intrinsic token or NFT mint and maintains some measure of ongoing input, control, or interest in the token or NFT.[97] Notably, such non-intrinsic tokens and NFTs may continue to transact

---

[91] *What is an NFT Smart Contract*, HEDERA.

[92] Juliet M. Moringiello & Christopher K. Odinet, *The Property Law of Tokens*, 74 FL. L. REV. 607 (2022).

[93] Carla L. Reyes, Andrea Tosato, & Andrew Hinkes, *Digital Assets Have Legal Significance If Recognized by Substantive Law* (July 30, 2021) (unpublished manuscript), https://papers.ssrn.com/sol3/cf_dev/AbsByAuth.cfm?per_id=2370103.

[94] *See, for example*, LEE REINERS, HILARY ALLEN, & MARKY HAYS, STATEMENT OF OPPOSITION TO HFSC's DIGITAL ASSET REGULATION DISCUSSION DRAFT (June 27, 2023), https://sites.duke.edu/thefinregblog/2023/06/27/statement-of-opposition-to-hfscs-digital-asset-regulation-discussion-draft/.

[95] Mason Marcobello, *What Are Layer 2s and Why Are They Important?*, COINDESK (May 11, 2023), www.coindesk.com/learn/what-are-layer-2s-and-why-are-they-important/.

[96] Reyes, *Language Wars: Cryptocurrency*, 1216–1217.

[97] Ibid., 1213–1214.

on decentralized payment rails such as the Ethereum, Flow, or Cardano protocols, or they may transact within a more centralized, permissioned protocol such as NBA TopShot or Polygon.[98] Occasionally, law and policy discussions attribute whatever measure of centralization that exists in the non-intrinsic token or NFT to the decentralized protocol through which transactions occur.[99] The reverse also occurs – with law and policy discussions inappropriately attributing the level of decentralization present in the underlying protocol to the non-intrinsic tokens and NFTs.

Imprecision in such discussions can lead to the misidentification of problems or the mis-attribution of fault in relation to the source of a problem.[100] Misidentifying problems or the source of problems can, in turn, cause the creation of legal frameworks that impose unnecessary costly compliance obligations or that impose compliance obligations on actors that cannot comply as required.[101] For example, some emerging legal discussions suggest holding those engaging in Layer 1 protocol consensus-building responsible for activities undertaken by actors creating smart contracts, tokens, and NFTs at Layer 2 of the blockchain technology stack.[102] Such proposals make little legal or technical sense and, worse yet, are doomed to be unfit for purpose.

---

[98] Cheyenne Ligon & Cam Thompson, *Dapper Labs Ruling Could Spell Trouble for Other Centralized NFT Projects, Experts Say*, CoinDesk (February 23, 2023), www.coindesk.com/policy/2023/02/23/dapper-labs-ruling-could-spell-trouble-for-other-centralized-nft-projects-experts-say/; Oluapelumi Adejumo, *Crypto Investments Fund Founder Says Polygon Is 'Highly Insecure and Centralized,'* CryptoSlate (August 16, 2022); https://cryptoslate.com/crypto-investments-fund-founder-says-polygon-is-highly-insecure-centralized/.

[99] *See, for example*, Hillary Allen, *Congress Should Stop Trying to Make Crypto Happen*, Fin. Times (June 8, 2023), www.ft.com/content/3c84c0f1-ade5-49d9-bd81-a844cafec86d (alleging that all crypto is doomed to fail just like the centralized offerings of Terra/Luna, Celsius and FTX); Written Testimony of Hillary J. Allen, *Hearing on Crypto Crash: Why the FTX Bubble Burst and the Harm to Consumers*, Before the U.S. Senate Committee on Banking, Housing, and Urban Affairs (December 14, 2022), www.banking.senate.gov/imo/media/doc/Allen%20Testimony%2012-14-22.pdf (proposing a ban on all of crypto because a centralized intermediary cheated customers).

[100] *See, for example*, Angela Walch, *In Code(rs) We Trust: Software Developers as Fiduciaries in Public Blockchains, in* Regulating Blockchain: Techno-Social and Legal Challenges (Philipp Hacker et al., eds., 2019) (arguing core developers of Layer 1 protocols should have fiduciary duties); Raina S. Haque, Rodrigo Seira Silva-Herzog, Brent A. Plummer, & Nelson M. Rosario, *Blockchain Development and Fiduciary Duty*, 2 Stan. J. Blockchain L. & Pol'y 139 (2019) (arguing that the proposal to impose fiduciary duties on core developers of Layer 1 protocols stems from a misunderstanding of the layered blockchain technology stack and the roles various developers play in creating different types of software).

[101] *See, for example*, John Rizzo, *Elizabeth Warren's Bill Won't Stop Money Laundering, but It Could Ban Crypto*, CoinDesk (May 18, 2023), www.coindesk.com/consensus-magazine/2023/05/18/elizabeth-warrens-bill-wont-stop-money-laundering-but-it-could-ban-crypto/ (discussing legislation that would treat software developers and transaction validators as financial institutions, imposing obligations upon such actors with which it would be impossible to comply).

[102] *See, for example*, Law Commission of England & Wales, Law Com No. 412, Digital Assets: Final Report 179–181 (June 2023), https://s3-eu-west-2.amazonaws.com/lawcom-prod-storage-11jsxou24uy7q/uploads/2023/06/Final-digital-assets-report-FOR-WEBSITE-2.pdf.

VII LANDMINE 6: NON-FUNGIBLE TOKENS ARE IRREVOCABLY TIED TO THE THING THEY PURPORT TO TOKENIZE

The sixth language landmine focuses on the use of the term "tokenization" to describe the value of the NFT use case. Two inaccuracies often lurk behind the use of the term "tokenization" in the context of NFTs. The first inaccuracy lies in the belief that "tokenizing" things is a new digital technique first enabled by blockchain technology generally and NFTs specifically. The second inaccuracy boiled down to talk about the power of NFTs to "tokenize" assets lies in the idea that NFTs are irrevocably tied to the thing they purport to tokenize. Neither of these beliefs, both often imbued with the use of the term NFTs and descriptions of their economic uses, represent an accurate understanding of NFTs, the technology they are built on, or their intrinsic limits.

First, NFTs are not the first common use of digital tokenization. Indeed, when software developers and technical researchers use the term tokenization, they do not associate the term with NFTs or blockchain technology at all.[103] Rather, a token can be created using any number of computational techniques and can be employed without any use of a blockchain protocol at all.[104] In fact, it is quite likely that every time you use your credit or debit card, the merchant's payment processor "tokenizes" your card's primary account number (PAN) data and only transmits the token across the payment card rails to verify your payment information.[105] For payment processors, tokenization represents a technical mechanism to increase the security of personal identifying information and to reduce the processor's cybersecurity liability risk.[106] Similarly, the law uses "tokens" and the concept of "tokenization" in a variety of contexts,[107] most of which long predate the existence of blockchain technology.[108] As a result, the first step to eliminating the risk to law and policy-making posed by misunderstandings of NFTs and their uses is to simply recognize that the concept of tokenization is neither new to law nor a novel technological discovery.

---

[103] Reyes, *Language Wars: Cryptocurrency*, 1228, 1230 (exploring the results of a corpus linguistics study in which technical science researchers use the term "token" with reference to a wide variety of technical concepts, none of which relate to cryptocurrency or NFTs).

[104] Tim Winston, Kristine Harper, & Michael Guzman, *How to Use Tokenization to Improve Data Security and Reduce Audit Scope*, AWS SECURITY BLOG (January 25, 2022), https://aws.amazon.com/blogs/security/how-to-use-tokenization-to-improve-data-security-and-reduce-audit-scope/ (explaining that, for example, in the context of cybersecurity, "[t]okenization is the process of replacing actual sensitive data elements with non-sensitive data elements that have no exploitable value for data security purposes. Security-sensitive applications use tokenization to replace sensitive data, such as personally identifiable information (PII) or protected health information (PHI), with tokens to reduce security risks").

[105] Square, *Payment Tokenization Explained*, THE BOTTOM LINE (October 8, 2014), https://squareup.com/us/en/the-bottom-line/managing-your-finances/what-does-tokenization-actually-mean.

[106] Ibid.

[107] Reyes, *Language Wars: Cryptocurrency*, 1231–1238.

[108] Moringiello & Odinet, *The Property Law of Tokens*, 615.

Second, and likely more problematic, discussions around NFTs commonly zero in on the uniqueness of the NFT and transpose that uniqueness to the asset the NFT purports to "tokenize."[109] In other words, NFTs are often portrayed as irrevocably tied to another asset – sometimes a digital asset and sometimes a real-world asset (RWA).[110] As a technical matter, it is simply not the case that NFTs are always irrevocably tied to the asset that the NFT purports to tokenize. Although this reality is probably more self-evident for RWAs, it also remains true for digital assets that NFTs purportedly tokenize. For example, on the Ethereum Network, an NFT is a smart contract created under the ERC-721 technical standard.[111] Under that standard, every NFT smart contract contains "a unique unit256 ID" which does "not change for the life of the contract."[112] The unit256 tokenID and the smart contract address function together to create the digital uniqueness for which NFTs are popularly known.[113]

The ERC-721 standard also provides a way to associate an NFT smart contract with a Uniform Resource Identifier (URI) that points to the digital file that the NFT purports to "tokenize."[114] That is all an NFT is: a few lines of code that contain a unique ID and a link to a file that contains information about an off-chain asset that the line of code purport to "tokenize."[115] Notably, the very ERC-721 technical standard that popularized NFTs notes that it was designed so that the "URI MAY be mutable (i.e., it changes from time to time)."[116]

Indeed, in February 2021, a crypto-artist known as "Neitherconfirm," exposed the depth of the error embedded in this language landmine through a public demonstration.[117] Neitherconfirm sold 26 NFTs linked to digital stained-glass art featuring people and animal portraits.[118] At some point after the sale of the NFTs, Neitherconfirm swapped the image out, replacing the digital art with images of rugs.[119] Notably,

---

[109] Noh et al., *GM!*, 317 ("Thus, at a very basic level, the NFT is simply the underlying code written to evidence an associated asset's existence and non-fungibility … In common parlance, however, collectors, speculators, enthusiasts, the popular media, and even developers use the term "NFT" to refer not just to the token itself, but also to the asset to which the token relates (particularly when that asset is a digital artwork)").

[110] Noh et al., *GM!*, 316–317; Amy Adler, *Artificial Authenticity*, 98 N.Y.U. L. Rev. 706, 760 (2023); R. Wilson Freyermuth, Christopher K. Odinet, & Andrea Tosato, Crypto in Real Estate Finance, 75 Ala. L. Rev. (2023).

[111] Erik Khun, *NFT Misconception: JPEG Aren't on the Blockchain*, Eric Khun (October 31, 2021), https://erickhun.com/posts/nft-misconception-image-arent-on-blockchains/.

[112] Entriken et al., *EIP-165: ERC-721*, 88.

[113] Ibid.

[114] Ibid.; Khun, *NFT Misconception*, 111.

[115] Entriken et al., *EIP-165: ERC-721*, 88; Khun, *NFT Misconception*, 111.

[116] Entriken et al., *EIP-165: ERC-721*, 88.

[117] Turner Wright, *OpenSea Collector 'Pulls the Rug' on NFTs to Highlight Arbitrary Value*, Cointelegraph (March 9, 2021), https://cointelegraph.com/news/opensea-collector-pulls-the-rug-on-nfts-to-highlight-arbitrary-value.

[118] Ibid.

[119] Ibid.

Neitherconfirm did not create many of the rug images but, rather, scraped some of them from publicly available images on the Internet.[120] Neitherconfirm's image swap itself acted as a type of conceptual art performance – the artist made a statement about what purchasers of NFTs actually own most of the time by "pulling the rug" on his purchasers.[121] He made plain an often misunderstood fact about NFTs. Due to the size of the digital file an NFT purports to tokenize, much of the time, NFTs only point to the digital file but the NFT and the digital file it purports to represent are not irrevocably connected to one another. As Neitherconfirm explained, "All discussions about the value of NFTs are meaningless as long as the token is not inseparable from the artwork itself ... What is the meaning of creating an unforgeable token on a highly secured network if somebody can alter, relink or destroy your [off-chain] possession?"[122]

Neitherconfirm's stunt highlighted the fact that NFTs can make use of two distinct technical architectures. In one technical architecture, the NFT is simply a smart contract that contains: (1) a unique identification number and (2) a pointer to a digital or other object that exists off-chain.[123] If the off-chain object is a digital object, it may be hosted in decentralized file storage, or it may be hosted on a centralized server.[124] In either case, the image to which the pointer embedded in the NFT resolves can be altered, removed, or replaced by the person, persons, or entity who either controls access to the decentralized file storage or controls the data stored on the centralized server.[125] Thus, your NFT could resolve to digital stained-glass art of a wolf one day and the next day resolve to a picture of a rug sold at your local department store. The second technical architecture available to NFTs is to embed the digital object in the NFT smart contract itself instead of using a pointer to link the NFT to an asset stored off-chain.[126] When NFTs use this technical architecture the NFT and the digital asset that it "tokenizes" literally form one inseparable digital unit, just like popular discussion of NFTs assumes is true for all NFTs.

If technically possible to embed the digital object into the NFT smart contract, why do some NFTs only use a pointer to an off-chain image? In fact, many members

---

[120] Ibid. ("Neitherconfirm told CoinTelegraph that rather than making unique computer-generated rug images, they simply found pictures of carpets in a web search – some with watermarks included – and turned them into NFTs").

[121] Ibid. A reference to a "rug pull" is a reference to a scam. Valerio Puggioni, *Crypto Rug Pulls: What Is a Rug Pull in Crypto and 6 Ways to Spot It*, COINTELEGRAPH (February 6, 2022), https://cointelegraph.com/explained/crypto-rug-pulls-what-is-a-rug-pull-in-crypto-and-6-ways-to-spot-it ("A rug pull is a type of crypto scam that occurs when a team pumps their project's token before disappearing with the funds, leaving their investors with a valueless asset").

[122] Wright, *OpenSea Collector*, 117.

[123] Entriken et al., *EIP-165: ERC-721*, 88; Khun, *NFT Misconception*, 111.

[124] moreReese, *How Are NFTs Stored? On-Chain, Off-Chain and Decentralized Storage*, DECRYPT (August 25, 2022), https://decrypt.co/resources/how-are-nfts-stored-on-chain-off-chain-and-decentralized-storag.

[125] Ibid.

[126] Ibid.

of the public may be dismayed to learn that NFTs using a pointer to an off-chain object represent the lion's share of existing NFTs and NFTs with embedded assets remain less common.[127] This, too, reflects a technical reality. Often, the image, video, or other linked asset requires too much file storage to embed in an NFT as a fully on-chain object.[128] Commonly purchased NFTs that use a pointer to link the token to an off-chain asset include powerhouses such as Bored Ape Yacht Club.[129] NFTs that embed the digital image within the token contract include lesser known names, such as Autoglyphs, On-Chain Monkey's Genesis collection, Chainrunners, and Nouns WTF.[130] The famous Cryptopunks, for their part, began as off-chain NFTs and migrated to fully on-chain NFTs.[131]

Ultimately, with respect to NFTs, as with the rest of blockchain technology and cryptocurrency, the technical architecture is what mainly impacts the way substantive law applies to delineate users' legal rights. The technical nuances matter – a user who thought their rights in a digital object linked to an NFT were governed by property law may find that, rather, their NFT points to an off-chain asset and the link between the token and the asset is governed by a contract they may not have even bothered to read.[132] Ultimately, failure to uncover and defuse the common language landmine that NFTs are always irrevocably tied to the asset they purport to tokenize perpetuates confusion in the market and in legal and policy discussions. Those engaging in such discussions shoulder a duty of technical accuracy.

VIII CONCLUSION

Uncovering these six language landmines and taking a deep dive into the kernel of technical truth within them serves an important purpose for those working in the law and policy arena related to blockchain protocols, cryptocurrency, NFTs, and other related applications of the technology. Ultimately, the path to clear law and policy-making in the realm of blockchain technology and cryptocurrency – including NFTs – requires understanding how the technology works, right down to the very important but highly technical details. Without understanding the nuances of the technology, its variations, and its limits, attempts to create new legal frameworks will result in law that underperforms its intended function, and application of existing laws may be clunky and inefficient. The fact that the language landmines discussed in this chapter continue to be sources of confusion for law and policy-makers evidences a systematic failure to consider

---

[127] Ibid.
[128] Entriken et al., *EIP-165: ERC-721*, 88.
[129] moreReese, *How Are NFTs Stored?*, 124.
[130] AUTOGLYPHS, LARVA LABS, www.larvalabs.com/autoglyphs; *On-Chain NFTs and Why They're Better*, GNARS, https://gnars.com/on-chain-nfts-and-why-theyre-better/.
[131] *On-Chain NFTs and Why They're Better*, GNARS.
[132] Moringiello & Odinet, *The Property Law of Tokens*, 634–639.

the socio-technical context of blockchain technology and its many different use cases. Without deeper investigation into the socio-technical context of cryptocurrency, NFTs, and other applications of blockchain protocols, policy approaches and legal frameworks risk continuing generalizations and perpetuating myths that exacerbate the extent to which law lags behind, or worse, compounding the risks related to technology.[133]

---

[133] This lesson applies to everyone involved in the law and policy-making process: federal legislators, Reyes, *Written House Testimony*; state legislators, Reyes, *Language Wars: Smart Contracts*; and legal academics producing scholarship on blockchain-related legal topics, Reyes, *Language Wars: Cryptocurrency*.

PART II

Financial Regulation and Investor Protection

3

The Economic Reality of NFT Securities

Yuliya Guseva

I INTRODUCTION

The word "crypto" has acquired a negative connotation in 2022, following several notable collapses of crypto-related entities, arrests of their founders, and instances of blatant fraud.[1] These negative developments, however, do not prove that cryptography as a technology or assets secured through cryptography and transferred via distributed ledgers ("cryptoassets" and "digital assets") have neither place nor value in modern markets.[2] The scandals merely demonstrate that countries need a better legal regime to incorporate productive technological innovations into modern economic transactions. As technologies evolve, policy-makers face an endless challenge of designing new rules or applying existing regulations to emerging technology-enabled markets and assets.

One of the technology-based assets that can generate economic value but is tricky to regulate is non-fungible tokens (NFTs).[3] NFTs are a technology-enabled innovation that ensures digital uniqueness of tokens which may be used to represent bundles of rights with respect to assets and services in the virtual or non-virtual environment.[4] For the purposes of this chapter, the most relevant use of this technology

---

[1] *See, for example,* Eric Wallerstein, *FTX and Sam Bankman-Fried: Your Guide to the Crypto Crash,* Wall St. J. (January 19, 2023), www.wsj.com/articles/ftx-and-sam-bankman-fried-your-guide-to-the-crypto-crash-11669375609.

[2] Relevant definitions of the standard terms, including "blockchain," "tokens," "cryptoassets," and "distributed ledger technology," are discussed throughout this Handbook, particularly in the Introduction and Chapters 1 and 2.

[3] "[A]n NFT as an individually numbered crypto-token which contains an internal dataset and/or is linked to an external dataset. That individually numbered crypto-token can also be linked to legal rights (including in relation to the use of the internally or externally linked information) external to the crypto-token system." *See* UK Law Comm'n, Digital Assets: Consultation Paper, Consultation Paper 256, 318 (2022), https://s3-eu-west-2.amazonaws.com/lawcom-prod-storage-11jsxou24uy7q/uploads/2022/07/Digital-Assets-Consultation-Paper-Law-Commission-1.pdf.

[4] *See, for example,* Kristen E. Busch, *Non-Fungible Tokens (NFTs),* Cong. Rsch. Serv., R47189 1, 12–17 (July 20, 2022), https://crsreports.congress.gov/product/pdf/R/R47189 (defining the concept of NFTs and discussing legal implications, including copyright issues, consumer fraud, and other concerns that undermine the value of this technology); Michael Dowling, *Fertile Land: Pricing*

is in financial markets: NFTs may, theoretically, be used to record transfers of ownership of assets such as commodities and securities and/or be tethered to the bundles of rights associated with commodities and securities.[5]

The very concept that transfers can be accomplished through, and rights and assets represented by, some form of tokens goes back centuries. These technologies naturally evolved from one period to another, with the tokenization practices involving first pieces of paper and later on digital records.[6] "Tokenized" payment obligations (negotiable instruments) have been in use for hundreds of years and become part of *lex mercatoria*; tokenized (originally "certificated") securities have been known for centuries.[7] Similar uses of blockchain technology and assets such as NFTs continue these market practices.

NFTs can be used in a somewhat eclectic congeries of markets, including collectibles, art, securities, commodities, and others. As such, these are different markets

---

Non-Fungible Tokens, 44 Fin. Rsch. Letters 1, 1 (2022) ("An NFT is a blockchain-recorded right to a digital asset. This can be anything digital; an image, a video, a song, a digital trading card of your favourite baseball player, a coded piece of virtual land, or a virtual tunic for your virtual character to wear while he explores his virtual land"); Joshua A.T. Fairfield, *Tokenized: The Law of Non-Fungible Tokens and Unique Digital Property*, 97 Ind. L.J. 1261, 1266, 1273 (2022) ("Non-fungible tokens can be used to create digital artwork that can be bought, sold, and owned like a physical sculpture, or a database of real estate in which ownership is managed by electronic deeds that can be passed from one person to another with low or no transaction costs"). *See also* Juliet M. Moringiello & Christopher K. Odinet, *The Property Law of Tokens*, 74 Fla. L. Rev. 607 (2022) (discussing tokenization and questioning the value of NFTs); Nizan Geslevich Packin, *Financial Inclusion Gone Wrong: Securities and Cryptoassets Trading for Children*, 74 Hastings L.J. 349, 381–382 (2023) (discussing NFT uses).

5   Fairfield, Tokenized, 1272–1273

     ("Often, an NFT stands for ownership of something not directly stored on the blockchain–
     a piece of digital art, for example. So a token representing digital art might contain a URL
     pointing to the art and a hash of the art file. In this way, an NFT might convey an ownership
     interest in a piece of digital art, an asset in an online game, a card in a collectible trading card
     game (think rare baseball cards here), or a plot of land in a virtual world. Or, a token might
     convey rights in a real-world asset, in an RFID-linked consumer good, or a car that only unlocks
     and drives for the token owner").

     See also ibid., 1284; Carol R. Goforth, *How Nifty! But Are NFTs Securities, Commodities, or Something Else?*, 90 UMKC L. Rev. 775, 777 (2022) ("NFTs can be based on all kinds of things. These can include an image (or collage of images), a video, a highlight, a meme, a tweet, a piece of music or anything else – particularly creations that can be digitized"); Andres Guadamuz, *The Treachery of Images: Non-Fungible Tokens and Copyright*, 16 J. of Intell. Prop. L. & Prac. 1367 (2021) (examining the UK perspective and underscoring uncertainties of using NFTs for the transfer of rights); David Yermack, *Corporate Governance and Blockchains*, 21 Rev. Fin. 7, 8 (2017) (observing that blockchain technology can accommodate securities markets).

6   *See, for example*, Moringiello & Odinet, The Property Law of Tokens, 618–621 ("The tokenization of securities also has a long history, and, like negotiable instruments, developed to address a particular economic problem … [I]n the early 1600s, the Dutch East India Company issued (for what is believed to be the first time ever) true equity shares to the public … [Today t]his concept – the idea of being the ultimate beneficial owner of a token through the indirect holding of that token via an account with a securities broker – is memorialized in the UCC through Article 8's rules on securities entitlements, and this system dominates public securities trading to this day").

7   Ibid.

and there is no regulatory regime for all NFTs. Various jurisdictions struggle with classifying NFTs. As of this writing, for example, congressional bills either exclude non-fungible assets and/or call for an inquiry into NFTs[8] and the European Union has adopted a special cryptoassets regime that largely excludes NFTs.[9]

As I argued elsewhere, to determine a suitable legal regime it is essential to locate the market to which an NFT belongs.[10] This task requires a deep understanding of the economic realities of the associated rights, assets, and transactions. In securities markets, US courts have been successfully applying such economic reality test to establish whether cryptoassets are securities.[11] The test was honed by the Supreme Court in *SEC v. W.J. Howey Co.* about 80 years ago.[12] *Howey* aims to provide a systematic foundation for offerings of financial instruments under different labels and establishes when transactions and schemes in effect involve securities (namely, "investment contracts").[13] As I will demonstrate in this chapter, *Howey* compellingly establishes the economics of transactions.[14]

Admittedly, the application of the *Howey* test to crypto has been criticized as far-reaching and uncertain.[15] These criticisms of the test's *application* may be explained

---

[8] *See, for example,* The Financial Innovation and Technology for the 21st Century Act, H.R. 4763, 118th Congress (2023).

[9] Regulation (EU) 2023/1114 of the European Parliament and of the Council of 31 May 2023 on markets in crypto-assets, and amending Regulations (EU) No 1093/2010 and (EU) No 1095/2010 and Directives 2013/36/EU and (EU) 2019/1937, 2023 O.J. (L150/40) 42–43 [hereinafter MiCA] (the Preamble states,

"[t]his Regulation should not apply to crypto-assets that are unique and not fungible with other crypto-assets, including digital art and collectibles. The value of such unique and non-fungible crypto-assets is attributable to each crypto-asset's unique characteristics and the utility it gives to the token holder. Nor should this Regulation apply to crypto-assets representing services or physical assets that are unique and non-fungible, such as product guarantees or real estate. While unique and non-fungible crypto-assets might be traded on the marketplace and be accumulated speculatively, they are not readily interchangeable and the relative value of one such crypto-asset in relation to another, each being unique, cannot be ascertained by means of comparison to an existing market or equivalent asset. Such features limit the extent to which those crypto-assets can have a financial use, thus limiting risks to holders and the financial system, and justifying their exclusion from the scope of this Regulation").

[10] Yuliya Guseva, *Less Is More: Why NFTs Don't Need a New Regulatory Regime* (September 24, 2023) (unpublished manuscript) (on file with author).

[11] *See generally* Yuliya Guseva, *The SEC, Digital Assets, and Game Theory*, 46 J. OF CORP. LAW 629 (2021) (discussing the application of the *Howey* test in crypto-related enforcement actions).

[12] *SEC v. W.J. Howey Co.*, 328 U.S. 293, 298–99 (1946).

[13] Ibid. ("[A]n investment contract for purposes of the Securities Act means a contract, transaction or scheme whereby a person invests his money in a common enterprise and is led to expect profits solely from the efforts of the promoter or a third party"). *See also* Carol R. Goforth, *Regulation of Crypto: Who Is the SEC Protecting?*, 58 AM. BUS. L.J. 643, 649–53 (2021) (examining the meaning and application of *Howey* to crypto markets).

[14] In a recent cease-and-desist order and a decision on a motion to dismiss, the Securities and Exchange Commission (SEC) and a US district court, respectively, applied this economic reality test to examine schemes involving offers and sales of NFTs. *See Friel* v. *Dapper Labs, Inc.*, No. 21-CV-5837, 2023 WL 2162747 (S.D.N.Y. 2023); In the Matter of Impact Theory, LLC, Securities Act Release No. 11226 (Aug. 28, 2023). Both will be examined in this chapter.

[15] *See, for example,* Brief for The Chamber of Digital Commerce as Amici Curiae, p. 8, *SEC v. Ripple Labs, Inc.*, 2023 WL 3477552 (S.D.N.Y. 2023) ("[T]he dynamic nature of the *Howey* analysis makes it a

by the lack of a comprehensive regulatory regime tailored to all forms of cryptoassets and by the flaws of what has been described as "regulation by enforcement" in the crypto space.[16] By no means do these arguments prove that the *Howey* framework is inapplicable to all cryptoassets and NFT markets, particularly without any guidance from the US Congress.

There is no inconsistency here: the test *per se* may be fundamentally sound and courts may apply *Howey* to assay the economics of transactions involving novel assets, including cryptoassets. By way of explanation, as I argued in other work, NFTs should not be viewed as an independent asset class but as assets accompanying other assets that I called the *anchor*. In this framework, the main issue for courts and market participants is to determine the law governing the anchor assets and transactions: if the anchor is a security, securities law should apply; if the anchor is art, other relevant legal regimes are applicable.[17] This is precisely what *Howey* does by providing a framework for ascertaining what a promoter offers and promises to investors. Note also that the test has proven to be durable over the decades and can be modernized. Henderson and Raskin, for example, proposed tools of construction to operationalize *Howey* in the context of cryptoassets.[18]

particularly challenging framework to apply to secondary transactions involving fast-moving and ever changing technology businesses, especially those that incorporate the native digital asset essential to the operation of the blockchain network. The lack of clarity regarding secondary transactions in digital assets also impacts the blockchain industry as a whole"); Goforth, *Regulation of Crypto*, 649; Lewis Rinaudo Cohen et al., *The Ineluctable Modality of Securities Law: Why Fungible Crypto Assets Are Not Securities* 107 (Nov. 10, 2022) (unpublished manuscript), https://dx.doi.org/10.2139/ssrn.4282385.

[16] For a general discussion of this approach, see Chris Brummer, Yesha Yadav, & David Zaring, *Regulation by Enforcement* (2023) (unpublished manuscript), https://papers.ssrn.com/sol3/papers.cfm?abstract_id=4405036; Carol R. Goforth, *Regulation by Enforcement: Problems with the SEC's Approach to Cryptoasset Regulation*, 82 Md. L. Rev. 107 (2022); Guseva, The SEC, Digital Assets, and *Game Theory*.

[17] Guseva, *Less Is More*, 2

("It is appropriate to conceptualize NFTs as 'complementary goods' (or 'complements') that may be sold separately but exhibit a positive interaction with some underlying assets or rights. The logic of complements suggests that possessing both increases their consumption value. An oft cited example is computers and software. Yet, NFTs are more than simple cross-category complements like hardware and software. NFTs are lines of code that may have no intrinsic value *per se* but mainly derive value from their complements and, simultaneously, provide additional utility to the complements. Their complements thus become their anchors, and NFTs *accompany* various *anchor* assets across industries and markets. For example, a digital picture could be the anchor, and an NFT would be the accompanying asset. NFTs help users interact with the anchor assets, facilitate ownership transfers, and/or serve as evidence of transfers and instructions to transfer the anchor from one party to another. Purchasers value NFTs, i.e., lines of code, for these uses. In the end, the NFTs enhance the utility of the anchor itself. Clearly, as accompanying assets, NFTs should follow the laws of their anchor markets. If it is a market for securities, relevant NFTs should be regulated as securities; if it is a market for digital baseball cards, the associated NFTs would fall under the laws applied to transactions in collectibles").

[18] M. Todd Henderson & Max Raskin, *A Regulatory Classification of Digital Assets: Toward an Operational Howey Test for Cryptocurrencies, ICOs, and Other Digital Assets*, 2019 Colum. Bus. L. Rev. 443, 460–469 (2019).

Self-evidently, US Congress and regulators such as the SEC, which has broad exemptive authority,[19] may determine how the new asset classes and technologies should be regulated. Until that happens, the *Howey* test will continue to guide fact-finders and market participants in examining whether NFTs are securities under conventional securities regulation.

With these principles in the background (namely, the need for an economic reality analysis applied to NFTs as assets accompanying other assets, rights, and transactions), this chapter will first delineate the legal framework that broadly applies to NFTs. The chapter will then proceed to NFTs in securities markets. The analysis will conclude by reviewing a 2023 federal district court ruling that applied the *Howey* analysis to NFTs.

II THE OVERARCHING LEGAL FRAMEWORK

Different functionalities of NFTs are tailored to a variety of marketplaces and trigger diverse legal regimes.[20] The markets for collectibles and art touch upon intellectual property law, property law, contract law, and sales law, among others.[21] In transactions with assets that are deemed securities, securities law should control.

---

[19] Securities Exchange Act of 1934, 15 U.S.C. § 78mm (1934).

[20] UK Law Comm'n, Digital Assets, 319

("So NFTs are as variable in the rights they provide as any other thing that may be bought. NFTs as crypto-tokens have a reasonably straightforward and simple structure. But NFTs as 'cryptoassets' – a crypto-token linked to some thing or rights external to the crypto-token system – are incredibly varied and diverse. We consider that conceptualising NFTs in this way means that the design principles and legal structuring possibilities for the medium become much clearer. NFTs can become a powerful technological structure that can be used to link to – and to transfer – other legal rights to things external to crypto-token systems. This is not necessarily a problem for the NFT marketplace or for market participants or for the law. Instead, NFTs present an opportunity to iterate an experiment on novel legal structures within the online world").

[21] *See, for example,* Stacey M. Lantagne, *Of Disaster Girl and Everydays: How NFTs Invite Challenging Copyright Assumptions Around Creator Support,* 13 Harv. J. Sports & Ent. L. 265 (2022) (applying the copyright framework to NFT minting and auctioning); Tonya M. Evans, *CryptoKitties, Cryptography, and Copyright,* 47 Am. Intell. Prop. L. Ass'n Q.J. 219, 262 (2019)

("Beyond obvious common services like birth, death, marriage, and real property records, the power of NFTs to tokenize copyright interests (including fractional interests), encoded with immutable instructions, would be of great use to the Copyright Office, for example. In addition to the basic information collected during the registration process, use of the NFT standard for both pure UGAs and tokenized copyright interests could streamline registration, remove barriers to the registration process, aid in proof of ownership, provide evidence of relevant dates, automate and facilitate chain-of-ownership (and other interests), and downstream licensing and other transfers"); Fairfield, Tokenized, 1299–1306 (discussing the application of sales law, contract law, licensing, and copyright law); UK Law Comm'n, Digital Assets, 311 ("It seems likely that NFTs will play an increasingly important role in modern online interactions. In particular, we think that NFTs will take a leading, exploratory role in establishing property rights in data objects in mainstream and retail use. Beyond that, perhaps the most radical legal development that NFTs could bring about is a change in how the market, market participants, and the legal system operate and transact with respect to intellectual property rights").

In determining a legal regime, one starting point is whether to consider NFTs (and other tokens) as a form of personal property. These views are developing in both the US and Europe.[22] The Uniform Law Commission and the American Law Institute in the US have already embraced this approach: a token, including an NFT, is a line of code that can be deemed property.[23] The Uniform Commercial Code (UCC) covers NFTs (as a form of a "controllable electronic record" defined as "a record stored in an electronic medium that can be subjected to control").[24] Although it is hard to predict how fast these approaches to tokens as a form of property could be fully adopted, ten US states have already enacted the 2022 amendments to the UCC and about twenty states have introduced the amendments as of this writing.[25] The rate of adoptions suggests that the process is gathering steam.

With respect to securities markets, the drafters of the UCC have concluded that the term "security" under Article 8 of the UCC and the term "controllable electronic record" are different animals.[26] Nevertheless, controllable electronic records "might play a role in the facilitating transactions in Article 8 securities."[27] For example, the records may be used and operate as instructions to issuers of securities. The drafters of the UCC provide the following pertinent example:

> A Delaware corporation (D Corp) issues shares of stock and maintains books and records evidencing the registered ownership of the shares. Because the shares are not represented by security certificates, they are uncertificated securities. Pursuant to the applicable law and the organic documentation of D Corp, D Corp creates,

[22] *See, for example*, UK Law Commission, Digital Assets: Final Report, HC 1486, 44 (2023) ("Courts have consistently concluded that certain things (often digital assets) are capable of being objects of personal property rights, even where the thing in question does not neatly fit within either of the traditionally recognised categories of thing to which personal property rights can relate. The courts have done so, either expressly or impliedly, in respect of milk quotas, European Union carbon emission allowances ('EUAs'), export quotas, waste management licences, and a wide variety of crypto-tokens, including NFTs"); ibid., 2 ("We demonstrate in this report that the law of England and Wales has proven itself sufficiently resilient and flexible to recognise some digital assets as capable of being things to which personal property rights can relate. We conclude that the law in this respect is now relatively certain and that most areas of residual legal uncertainty are highly nuanced and complex"); ibid., 12 ("Our first recommendation for statutory intervention seeks merely to confirm and support what we consider to be the existing position at law. That is, that being neither a thing in possession nor a thing in action does not prevent a digital asset from being capable of being a thing to which personal property rights can relate").

[23] Guseva, *Less Is More*, 10.

[24] U.C.C. § 12-102(a) (Am. L. Inst. & Unif. L. Comm'n 2022).

[25] *UCC, 2022 Amendments*, Unif. L. Comm'n (2022), www.uniformlaws.org/committees/community-home?communitykey=1457c422-ddb7-40b0-8c76-39a1991651ac.

[26] U.C.C. § 12-102 cmt. 2 (Am. L. Inst. & Unif. L. Comm'n 2022) ("A controllable electronic record is not itself a 'security,' defined in part in Section 8102(a)(15) as 'an obligation of an issuer or a share, participation, or other interest in an issuer or in property or an enterprise of an issuer.' It also is not 'a share or similar equity interest,' an 'investment company security,' or 'an interest in a partnership or limited liability company.' See Section 8-103(a), (b), and (c)").

[27] U.C.C. § 8-102 cmt. 18 (Am. L. Inst. & Unif. L. Comm'n 2022).

or causes to be created, controllable electronic records (CERs) – "tokens" – to facilitate transfers of the shares. Also pursuant to that law and documentation, the transfer of control of a token on the platform on which the token is recorded constitutes an instruction to D Corp, as issuer, for the transfer of registration of the share(s) represented by the token to the transferee of control. Following receipt of the instruction upon transfer of control of a token, D Corp transfers registration of the share(s) on its books and records ... Although Article 12 governs the tokens (as CERs) and the transfer of control thereof, other law, including Delaware corporate law and Delaware Article 8 (and Article 9 of the relevant jurisdiction, if applicable) governs rights in the uncertificated securities and the transfer of registration.[28]

The outcome (e.g., whether and how transfers of controllable electronic records would represent transfers on the issuer's books) "would depend on the terms of ... the underlying organic laws,"[29] Article 8, and other relevant legal regimes. These examples illustrate how the UCC aims to bifurcate the treatment of tokens into property law *and* other legal regimes whose application is embedded into or triggered by the tokens and transactions with tokens.

Note that the drafters have achieved this result in a technology-agnostic way. The technology-neutral and future-oriented UCC does not mandate whether ERC-20 (the fungible token standard on Ethereum) should be preferred to ERC-721 (the traditional NFT standard on Ethereum).[30] The only constant variable in technology is change, and separating out changeable technologies from the underlying assets and relevant legal regimes may enable digital assets ("controllable electronic records") to be used in different markets, including securities and commodity markets.

III NFTS AS SECURITIES AND COMMODITIES

The current infrastructure for NFT creation ("minting"), listing, and trading differs from the infrastructure of legacy markets for commodities and securities.[31] NFT markets may also suffer from relatively low liquidity and efficiency compared with securities exchanges. None of these factors, however, should exclude NFTs from the scope of securities or commodity regulation.

In the US, commodity markets and derivatives on commodities fall within the ambit of the Commodity Exchange Act.[32] The Act defines the term "commodity" by providing a list of articles and goods, including "wheat, cotton,

---

[28] Ibid.

[29] Ibid.

[30] *See generally Token Standards*, ETHEREUM (August 1, 2023), https://ethereum.org/en/developers/docs/standards/tokens/.

[31] *See, for example, What Fees Do I Pay on OpenSea?*, OPENSEA, https://support.opensea.io/hc/en-us/articles/14068991090067-What-fees-do-I-pay-on-OpenSea-; Ollie Leech, *How to Make, Buy and Sell NFTs*, COINDESK (February 9, 2023), www.coindesk.com/learn/how-to-create-buy-and-sell-nfts/.

[32] Commodity Exchange Act of 1936, 7 U.S.C. § 1 et seq.

rice," etc., "in which contracts for future delivery are presently or in the future dealt in."[33] In theory, since futures on NFTs may be created (and it is certainly a possibility),[34] this definition covers NFTs.[35] The agency in charge of administering and enforcing the Commodity Exchange Act is the US Commodity Futures Trading Commission (CFTC). Bringing NFTs within the scope of the Act means that the CFTC will have antifraud and anti-manipulation enforcement authority in spot markets and regulatory authority in NFT derivatives markets.[36]

In fact, commodities are already tokenized with NFTs. The Mattereum Asset Passport NFT is a helpful example of tokenization: the "Passport NFT … aims to tokenise gold bars and includes a set of contractual warranties about the gold bar associated with the NFT. The NFT specifically identifies the gold bar to which it is linked, the vault location, the custodian, the insurance details and certificate, a dispute resolution mechanism, and a carbon-offsetting certificate in relation to the gold bar."[37]

When an NFT is a security, however, it will be within the remit of securities law and the SEC will claim jurisdiction. Two scenarios are theoretically possible here. First, the way an NFT is offered and sold to investors may fall under securities law even though the NFT itself may be related to non-securities. Second, an NFT *per se* may represent or be tethered to a security.

The first option presents crucial doctrinal challenges and calls for an analysis of the economic realities of transactions, the result that the *Howey* test aims to

---

[33] 7 U.S.C. § 1a (9).

[34] Futures on NFTs are not mainstream but possible. *See, for example,* Jack Kim et al., *NFT Perpetual Futures* (August 4, 2023) (unpublished manuscript), https://papers.ssrn.com/sol3/papers.cfm?abstract_id=4525785 (suggesting that perpetual futures could improve NFT market liquidity and market efficiency); for a specific example, *see Trade Perps, Any Asset, Anytime,* SynFutures (2024), www.synfutures.com/.

[35] *But see* Goforth, *How Nifty!,* 793–794

> ("Given that NFTs have value and can be sold, and therefore converted into, other currencies, they could easily be classified as commodities. There is, however, an argument that NFTs are outside scope of the CFTC's authority. This depends on the meaning of the phrase 'services, rights, and interests … in which contracts for future delivery are presently or in the future dealt in' … Unfortunately, it is not at all clear that NFTs will be lumped in with fungible cryptoassets, because they work so differently. If NFTs are treated as a distinct kind of asset, there are certainly no futures being traded in NFTs at this time, meaning that the CFTC would have no jurisdiction over fraud related to NFTs").

[36] Commodity Futures Trading Comm'n, Div. of Enf't, Enforcement Manual 2 (2020)

> ("[T]he CFTC has exclusive jurisdiction over futures, commodity options, and leverage contracts, with certain exceptions. The CFTC also has exclusive jurisdiction over certain swaps contracts and broad-based security index products. Certain anti-fraud and other specified provisions of the CEA apply to retail forex transactions and retail commodity transactions entered into on a leveraged, margined, or financed basis. In addition, the CFTC has authority to prosecute fraud and manipulation in connection with commodities in interstate commerce").

[37] UK Law Comm'n, Digital Assets, 295.

achieve.[38] The SEC used *Howey* in its first cease-and-desist order issued in August 2023 against Impact Theory, LLC.[39] In the order, the SEC concluded that the respondent *offered* and *sold* its NFTs as securities. The SEC did not examine the technical aspects of non-fungibility and generally referenced the *Howey* test without providing a detailed doctrinal analysis.[40] The order effectively described the transactions at issue as a capital raise through a sale of NFTs. According to the SEC, investors in those transactions expected to obtain profit from the managerial efforts of the respondent. For example, in light of the company's statements "numerous prospective and actual purchasers of KeyNFTs stated on Impact Theory's Discord channels that they viewed KeyNFTs as investments into the company and understood Impact Theory's statements to mean that the company's development of its projects could translate to appreciation of the KeyNFTs' value over time."[41]

Given the fact-specific nature of the analysis of the order, attempts at generalizing its conclusions in relation to the whole market for diverse and variegated NFTs may be futile.[42] In this sense, SEC enforcement targeting NFT firms illustrates why the application of the *Howey* test may generate uncertainty and send mixed signals to the market, even though the test *per se* remains valid. Interpretational issues matter greatly in these cases and so do the attitude and policies of the SEC.

---

[38] A more detailed discussion of *Howey* will follow in Part IV. *See also* Goforth, *How Nifty!*, 790

("For NFTs accompanied by an exclusive license or transfer of intellectual property rights in the underlying digital asset, where the purchase is for personal enjoyment or appreciation and there is no further promotion or activity by the creator, it seems unlikely that the transaction will be classified as having involved the sale of a security. On the other hand, where multiple purchasers acquire non-exclusive licenses and limited rights in the underlying asset, and particularly where the creator or a promoter works to increase the value of or interest in the creator's work, and the purchasers are motivated by the hope that their NFT will increase in value, the SEC could conclude that the NFTs in question are securities").

[39] In the Matter of Impact Theory, LLC, Securities Act Release No. 11226 (August 28, 2023).

[40] Ibid.

[41] Ibid., 4.

[42] The two dissenting SEC Commissioners commented, for example, that the SEC does not "routinely bring enforcement actions against people that sell watches, paintings, or collectibles along with vague promises to build the brand and thus increase the resale value of those tangible items." Hester M. Peirce & Mark T. Uyeda, Comm'rs, U.S. Sec. & Exch. Comm'n, NFTs & the SEC: Statement on Impact Theory, LLC (August 28, 2023), www.sec.gov/news/statement/peirce-uyeda-statement-nft-082823 (also observing that

"[e]ven though we believe strongly that adults should be able to spend their money as they choose, we share our colleagues' worry about the type of hype that entices people to spend almost $30 million for NFTs seemingly without having a clear idea about how they will use, enjoy, or profit from them. This legitimate concern, however, is not a sufficient basis to pull the matter into our jurisdiction. The handful of company and purchaser statements cited by the order are not the kinds of promises that form an investment contract").

On the one hand, the Impact Theory order does not appear to overclassify all NFTs as securities but focuses on the relevant facts and transactional analysis. This may suggest that the SEC recognizes that some NFTs are offered and sold as securities, while others are not. On the other hand, two weeks after the Impact Theory order, the SEC charged Stoner Cats 2 LLC, an NFT company, with violations of securities law and offering unregistered securities.[43] Just like in the order against Impact Theory, the SEC relied on the *Howey* analysis. Two Commissioners dissented from the orders and observed, inter alia, that "[t]he application of the *Howey* investment contract analysis in this matter lacks any meaningful limiting principle."[44]

All in all, the application of *Howey* in NFT enforcement may be ambiguous: enforcement actions produce settlements, and cease-and-desist orders offer arguments and analyses that are less detailed than those in court decisions. It becomes hard to generalize the lessons from enforcement actions when NFTs are linked to web series such as Stoner Cats or other artistic projects.

In comparison to this scenario, a situation where an NFT itself may be a security (more precisely, an asset tethered to a particular security) is simpler. Creating NFT securities is an option recognized by scholars,[45] and there is no reason why the technology behind NFTs cannot be used for issuing securities. NFT security offerings can be done through bespoke arrangements, massive distributions of tokens of the same class, or issuances of fractional NFTs. Firms can retrofit specific technical standards to suit their business and financial needs.

For example, on Ethereum, firms may use ERC-20 for fungible tokens,[46] and ERC-721 for NFTs,[47] as well as ERC-1155 (a multi-token standard which "allows for each token ID to represent a new configurable token type").[48] The fungible token ERC-20 standard could be applied to tokenize shares of stock or other financial instruments.[49] ERC-721 and ERC-1155 standards, however, might also be used for

[43] In the Matter of Stoner Cats 2, LLC, Securities Act Release No. 11233 (September 13, 2023).

[44] Hester M. Peirce & Mark T. Uyeda, Comm'rs, U.S. Sec. & Exch. Comm'n, Collecting Enforcement Actions: Statement on Stoner Cats 2, LLC (September 13, 2023), www.sec.gov/news/statement/peirce-uyeda-statement-stonercats-091323#_ftn1.

[45] Kimberly A. Houser & John T. Holden, *Navigating the Non-Fungible Token*, 2022 UTAH L. REV. 891, 919 (2022) ("Where an NFT is created to represent ownership in a business or other entity with an expectation of profit from the efforts of that business or other entity, it would likely meet the *Howey* test. Another way the sale of NFTs could implicate and violate securities laws is through the selling of fractional shares of ownership in an asset").

[46] Fabian Vogelsteller & Vitalik Buterin, *ERC-20: Token Standard*, ETHEREUM IMPROVEMENT PROPOSALS (November 19, 2015), https://eips.ethereum.org/EIPS/eip-20.

[47] William Entriken et al., *ERC-721: Non-Fungible Token Standard*, ETHEREUM IMPROVEMENT PROPOSALS (January 24, 2018), https://eips.ethereum.org/EIPS/eip-721.

[48] Witek Radomski et al., *ERC-1155: Multi Token Standard*, ETHEREUM IMPROVEMENT PROPOSALS (June 17, 2018), https://eips.ethereum.org/EIPS/eip-1155.

[49] Corwin Smith, *ERC-20 Token Standard*, ETHEREUM (May 30, 2023), https://ethereum.org/en/developers/docs/standards/tokens/erc-20/.

issuing securities, such as equity, bonds, and warrants, or for fractionalizing NFTs to create securities.[50]

Markets can adapt various token standards to different uses, transforming assets in the process and moving them from one legal regime to another. In this environment, technical standards remain relevant but not dispositive. As Kappos and co-authors emphasized in this respect, "while fungibility is a useful technical concept, it is not an adequate lodestar for classifying tokens for the purpose of applying legal mechanics."[51]

Looking past fungibility, however, is not an approach that has garnered uniform acceptance. Recall, for instance, that in 2023 the EU created a new regime (MiCA) that effectively performs a gap-filling function addressing cryptoassets that the EU financial regulation does not explicitly encompass – utility tokens and stablecoins.[52] Roughly generalizing, the MiCA and EU financial regulation are coterminous with the US commodity and securities laws, although, of course, there is no analog to the MiCA in the US yet.

The MiCA excludes from its ambit unique NFTs linked to art, collectibles, or real estate, among others. Understandably, the laws applicable to these examples would hardly be on all fours with the laws for stablecoins, for instance. The MiCA drafters recognized that fact. The resulting interpretation is that truly non-fungible tokens should fall outside the scope of the EU directives.[53] If, however, an NFT is fractionalized, the new fungible tokens would be covered by the EU directives.[54]

The Preamble to the MiCA also contains a general statement suggesting that fungibility represents grounds for regulation:

[50] *See, for example,* Houser & Holden, *Navigating the Non-Fungible Token*; Guseva, *Less is More* (discussing bond offerings); Will Gottsegen, *Some NFT Sales Could Be Illegal: SEC Commissioner Hester Peirce*, DECRYPT (March 26, 2021), https://decrypt.co/62989/sec-hester-peirce-nfts; Brian Elzweig & Lawrence J. Trautman, *When Does a Nonfungible Token (NFT) Become a Security?*, 39 GA. ST. U. L. REV. 295, 328–329 (2023)

("Fractionalizing ownership brings an element of fungibility to f-NFTs. By the nature of f-NFTs, investors are likely engaged in a common enterprise because of their investment in a single token. By selling shards of an f-NFT, both horizontal and vertical commonality may be met. Horizontal commonality may be met because there would be a pool of investors (other shard owners) whose investments are tied to each other in the underlying NFT. Vertical commonality may also be met because the seller of the shard may retain control of the NFT, and therefore, the investor and the seller's fortunes become intertwined");

Ekin Genç, *How Can You Share an NFT? Fractional NFTs Explained*, COINDESK (May 11, 2023), www.coindesk.com/learn/how-can-you-share-an-nft-fractional-nfts-explained/.
[51] David J. Kappos et al., *Fuzzy Tokens: Thinking Carefully about Technical Classification Versus Legal Classification of Cryptoassets*, BERKELEY TECH. L. J. 1, 2 (2023).
[52] MiCA. MiCA's ambit encompasses only assets that fall outside traditional financial regulation.
[53] *See, for example,* Claudia Di Bernardino et al., *NFT – Legal Token Classification*, EUR. UNION BLOCKCHAIN OBSERVATORY & F. NFT REPS. (July 24, 2021), www.eublockchainforum.eu/sites/default/files/research-paper/EUBOF%20-%20NFT%20-%20Token%20Classification%20Latam.pdf.
[54] Ibid.

[T]his Regulation should also apply to crypto-assets that appear to be unique and non-fungible, but whose de facto features or whose features that are linked to their de facto uses, would make them either fungible or not unique. In that regard, when assessing and classifying crypto-assets, competent authorities should adopt a substance over form approach whereby the features of the crypto-asset in question determine the classification and not its designation by the issuer.[55]

Fungibility, thus, is turned into a pivotal criterion similar to that of the conventional markets where transferable securities are routinely issued in classes.[56] From a market perspective, this disjunctive approach focusing on fungibility *may* (and let me emphasize *may*) fragment the market by placing existing and future assets into either one bucket or the other. This fragmentation could be exploited by firms using NFTs in some cases and fungible tokens in others primarily to evade regulation. From a legal perspective, the approach *may* create a future loophole in the generally comprehensive regulation of the EU. As a result, preventing a strategic lapse of judgment on fungibility becomes paramount.[57]

I emphasized *may* above to show that my concerns could be mitigated by the safeguards embedded in the MiCA. First, the EU left the door open to future NFT regulation. The European Commission is required to submit a report to the European Council and European Parliament. The report must include, among other items, "an assessment of the development of markets in unique and non-fungible crypto-assets and of the appropriate regulatory treatment of such crypto-assets, including an assessment of the necessity and feasibility of regulating offerors of unique and non-fungible crypto-assets as well as providers of services related to such crypto-assets."[58] Second, there is a chance that in some cases traditional financial regulation may apply even if MiCA does not cover NFTs.[59] Finally (and more importantly), in the passage cited above, the drafters of the

---

[55] MiCA, 43.
[56] *See, for example*, Directive 2014/65/EU of the European Parliament and of the Council of 15 May 2014 on markets in financial Instruments and amending Directive 2022/92/EC and Directive 2011/61/EU, 2014 O.J. (L173/349) 385

  ("'[T]ransferable securities' means those classes of securities which are negotiable on the capital market, with the exception of instruments of payment, such as: (a) shares in companies and other securities equivalent to shares in companies, partnerships or other entities, and depositary receipts in respect of shares; (b) bonds or other forms of securitised debt, including depositary receipts in respect of such securities; (c) any other securities giving the right to acquire or sell any such transferable securities or giving rise to a cash settlement determined by reference to transferable securities, currencies, interest rates or yields, commodities or other indices or measures").

[57] *See, for example*, Kappos et al., *Fuzzy Tokens*, 21 ("Dichotomies such as fungible and non-fungible are admittedly convenient shorthand to describe the technical classification of a digital asset. However, these simplifications are ultimately insufficient to give full color to the nature of a token").
[58] MiCA, art. 142.
[59] Ibid., 43 ("The exclusion of crypto-assets that are unique and non-fungible from the scope of this Regulation is without prejudice to the qualification of such crypto-assets as financial instruments").

MiCA emphasized a broad "substance over form approach." Reflected in the Preamble to the MiCA, this principle should serve as a safeguard against blatant mislabeling of NFTs.

To the extent that this principle focuses on the importance of the economic reality of assets and transactions, it represents a junction where the EU and US regulatory predicates meet. One of the US Supreme Court's edicts in securities law, for example, was to make sure that the definition of securities be based on "a flexible rather than a static principle, one that is capable of adaptation to meet the countless and variable schemes devised by those who seek the use of the money of others on the promise of profits."[60] It is possible that both the US and the EU could apply similarly panoramic analyses to the economic realities of NFTs and transactions with NFTs to address potential regulatory loopholes. The following section demonstrates this approach.

IV THE ECONOMIC REALITY ANALYSIS AND NFTS

At the heart of the economic reality test applied by US courts lies the *Howey* test. The test provides the foundational definition of securities that are unusual and do not fit within conventional categories – "investment contracts." An investment contract is "a contract, transaction or scheme whereby a person invests [their] money in a common enterprise and is led to expect profits solely from the efforts of the promoter or a third party."[61] This broad interpretation adequately captures the substance of future market developments and classes of securities after almost a century following the passage of the original securities statutes.[62] It also does not hinge on criteria such as "fungibility" of assets and instead provides a functional approach.[63]

In 2023, this functional approach to securities found its way into NFT markets through the SEC orders discussed in Section III and a decision of the Federal Court of the Southern District of New York. In February 2023, Judge Marrero denied Dapper Labs's motion to dismiss a securities law complaint concerning NFTs called "NBA Top Shot Moments" and provided a detailed analysis of Howey.[64] As of the time of writing, the court adopted a case management plan and plaintiffs were preparing to file a motion for class certification.[65] The ruling on motion to dismiss presents a unique opportunity to review the application of the economic reality analysis

---

[60] *SEC v. W.J. Howey Co.*, 328 U.S. 293, 299 (1946).

[61] Ibid., 298–299.

[62] *Tcherepnin v. Knight*, 389 U.S. 332, 336 (1967) ("[I]n searching for the meaning and scope of the word 'security' in the Act, form should be disregarded for substance and the emphasis should be on economic reality" (citing to *Howey*, 328 U.S. at 298)).

[63] For a description of a functional approach in securities law, see, *for example*, Howell E. Jackson, *Regulation in a Multisectored Financial Services Industry*, 77 Wash. U. L.Q. 319, 367 (1999).

[64] *Friel v. Dapper Labs, Inc.*, No. 21-CV-5837, 2023 WL 2162747 (S.D.N.Y. Feb. 22, 2023).

[65] Civ. Case Mgmt. Plan & Scheduling Ord., *Friel v. Dapper Labs, Inc.*, No. 21-CV-5837, 2023 WL 2162747 (S.D.N.Y. Feb. 22, 2023).

to NFTs. It provides a holistic review of transactional economics in light of "the totality of circumstances."[66]

The pertinent facts of the case are as follows: Dapper Labs is one of the major NFT firms. Domiciled in Canada, it had acquired an international reputation as the creator of CryptoKitties and NBA Top Shot Moments.[67] The defendant rose to fame on launching CryptoKitties – a game to collect and breed digital cats – on Ethereum.

Ethereum, however, struggled with scalability problems at the time. To improve scaling, Defendants built their own blockchain called "Flow." The NBA Top Shot Moments at issue in this case were built on Flow. (This move from Ethereum to Flow would become the crux of this case.) Ethereum is a public blockchain that is not controlled by any single authority, while Flow according to the Southern District of New York was a private blockchain.

Often, in a private blockchain, either a single authority or group administers it, may limit access to the blockchain, and even edits transactions. While still being distributed, a private blockchain is not fully decentralized and fewer nodes may participate in the consensus mechanism. Nevertheless, a private blockchain may offer better scalability and faster transaction processing. Alas, it may be more vulnerable to cybercrime and hacks than well-decentralized public blockchains.

The court referred to Flow as a "private blockchain" although Flow became more decentralized as of 2021.[68] Note that, at least allegedly, Flow's design targeted the blockchain trilemma (a conflict between scalability, security, and decentralization) making it more secure than some other private blockchains.[69] Crucial to this case, however, is that Flow was built and controlled by Dapper Labs when the assets at issue were offered and traded.

Flow was built on a "proof-of-stake" protocol, meaning that validators would stake the native tokens on this blockchain to be selected to validate incoming transactions. The native token of Flow was also called "Flow" and functioned somewhat similarly to Ethereum's Eth – Flow tokens could be used as payment for validation services, a currency, collateral, and in blockchain governance.[70]

Flow tokens were distributed to investors outside the US, with a certain number reserved by Dapper Labs for project development and other purposes. As of this writing, Flow tokens traded on cryptoassets exchanges, such as Binance, at approximately 0.857337.[71] The distribution of Flow tokens was not at issue in this class action; the NFTs called "NBA Top Shot Moments" were.

---

[66] *Glen-Arden Commodities, Inc. v. Costantino*, 493 F.2d 1027, 1034 (2d Cir. 1974).
[67] DAPPER LABS: THE NFT COMPANY, www.dapperlabs.com/.
[68] *Friel v. Dapper Labs, Inc.*, No. 21-CV-5837, 2023 WL 2162747, *4 (S.D.N.Y. Feb. 22, 2023). *See also Frequently Asked Questions*, FLOW, https://flow.com/faq ("Is Flow decentralized? Yes, as of October 2021, less than 1/3 of consensus nodes, the nodes responsible for the security of the network, are run by any single entity").
[69] *Road to Permissionless Deployment*, FLOW DOCS (2022), https://permissionless.onflow.org/.
[70] *Friel v. Dapper Labs, Inc.*, No. 21-CV-5837, 2023 WL 2162747, at *4 (S.D.N.Y. Feb. 22, 2023).
[71] *Flow Price*, BINANCE (January 14, 2024), www.binance.com/en/price/flow.

The NBA Top Shot Moments were released in partnership with the National Basketball Association (NBA) and NBA Payers Association (NBAPA) through an application built on the Flow blockchain. The Moments may be described as clips of highlights from basketball games. The three partners controlled which packs of highlights would be sold and how the highlights would be categorized. Just as the UCC Article 12 distinguished between the ownership of a controllable electronic record (the NFT in this case) and the underlying rights linked to the token, so did Dapper Labs, NBA, and NBAPA. Owners of the NFTs did not acquire "any rights to the basketball highlight" or any intellectual property rights.[72]

Dapper Labs facilitated the primary sales and secondary market transactions through its application built on its own blockchain. The Flow blockchain provided record keeping, transfer recording, ownership verification, and other "back-office" functions. Dapper Labs also did not recognize trading in the NFTs outside its own platform.

In short, Dapper Labs created a full-cycle business model. First, it sold its primary products (i.e., the NFTs) generated through the partnership with the NBA and booked revenue from the sales. Second, it ensured that transfers and sales were recorded on the Flow blockchain. Third, Dapper Labs generated profit from charging transaction fees on trading on its own market platform. Finally, it offered a digital wallet that served as the point of ingress and egress for the application and in this sense controlled the inflow of currency into NFTs and the outflow back to purchasers' bank accounts. The project proved exceptionally successful, with more than 800,000 users purchasing the NFTs.

In 2021, a plaintiff filed a class action complaint against Dapper Labs and its CEO alleging that Dapper Labs NFTs were securities. Since the defendant did not file a registration statement with respect to the alleged securities, the defendant violated the Securities Act that requires such registration unless an exemption is available.[73] The Securities Act has an accompanying strict liability provision that allows purchasers of such unregistered securities to recover consideration or rescissory damages.[74] The punishment for not complying with US securities statutes is harsh.

But are NFTs securities? As discussed in the previous sections, many NFTs are not. The test applied by US courts, however, does not follow a bright line analysis, which could be either overinclusive or underinclusive. Instead, as the Court in Howey remarked, traditionally, "[f]orm [i.e., the non-fungible nature of the assets in this case,] was disregarded for substance and emphasis was placed upon economic reality."[75] With this precept in mind, the *Dapper Labs* court decision began by acknowledging that "it is a close call and the Court's decision is narrow. If there

---

[72] *Friel v. Dapper Labs, Inc.*, No. 21-CV-5837, 2023 WL 2162747, at *5 (S.D.N.Y. Feb. 22, 2023).

[73] 15 U.S.C.A. § 77e.

[74] 15 U.S.C.A. § 77l(a).

[75] *SEC v. W.J. Howey Co.*, 328 U.S. 293, 298 (1946).

is a defining line separating those offerings that are securities from those that are not, whether Moments qualify toes that line intimately."[76]

The court's analysis transcends the NFTs and emphasizes the totality of the facts and circumstances. One of the key circumstances was that the Flow blockchain was built by the defendant. It was part and parcel of the economic realities of how the NFTs were traded. Flow tokens were used by validators to record prices and ownership of the NFTs, Flow tokens incentivized parties such as Dapper Labs and other validators to validate transactions on the Flow blockchain, and the blockchain itself was private according to the court.

The court essentially linked the value of and demand for two separate assets – the NFTs and the fungible Flow tokens of the underlying blockchain. Taken alone, this observation would not be probative, let alone determinative. The value of native tokens is generally dependent on the demand and value of the applications and cryptoassets built atop any blockchain.[77] The more developed an ecosystem is, the higher the value of the native assets ensuring that system's functionality. Blockchains compete for apps and developers and the network effect features prominently in digital asset ecosystems.

The court, however, distinguished Dapper Labs's Flow blockchain from other blockchains by classifying it as private. It was a "privatized" ledger "making the purchasers reliant upon the promoter for the asset's value."[78] The marketplace for trading the NFTs at issue was also controlled by Dapper Labs. A functioning marketplace for primary transactions and resales is indispensable to all markets in goods and services. This is particularly true if a platform reserves the right to deny access to users.[79] But even if there is no such right, investors depend on the liquidity and reliability of a marketplace, particularly when a party is the sole source and administrator of a trading platform.[80]

In the present case, the marketplace could not exist without the underlying technology (the Flow blockchain). Taken by themselves, the NFTs as lines of code had "no intrinsic or inherent value outside the Flow Blockchain."[81] Their value depended on the ecosystem and the underlying rights. Once this economic reality was ascertained, the Howey test cinched the conclusion that the scheme through which defendant offered the NBA Top Shot Moments produced a *relationship* "establish[ing] an investment contract, and thus a security."[82]

---

[76] *Friel* v. *Dapper Labs, Inc.*, No. 21-CV-5837, 2023 WL 2162747, at *8 (S.D.N.Y. Feb. 22, 2023).

[77] *See, for example*, Yuliya Guseva, *When the Means Undermine the End: The Leviathan of Securities Law and Enforcement in Digital-Asset Markets*, 5 STAN. J. OF BLOCKCHAIN L. & POL. 1, 39 (2022) ("[T]he value of cryptoassets may depend on the network effect, adoption by users, developer activity, network and product functionality, decentralization, listing and liquidity, scalability, and other factors").

[78] *Friel* v. *Dapper Labs, Inc.*, No. 21-CV-5837, 2023 WL 2162747, at *9 (S.D.N.Y. Feb. 22, 2023).

[79] Practitioners have underscored these issues in NFT markets. *See, for example, Busch, Non-Fungible Tokens*, 14.

[80] *See, for example, Gary Plastic Packaging Corp.* v. *Merrill Lynch, Pierce, Fenner & Smith, Inc.*, 756 F.2d 230, 240 (2d Cir. 1985).

[81] *Friel* v. *Dapper Labs, Inc.*, No. 21-CV-5837, 2023 WL 2162747, at *13 (S.D.N.Y. Feb. 22, 2023).

[82] Ibid., 22.

The first prong of the Howey test is "investment of money." The parties did not dispute that there was consideration (i.e., an "investment of money"). The court then examined whether there was a common enterprise, which is the second requirement of the Howey analysis.[83] This is not only the linchpin of the economic reality analysis of NFTs (which are digitally unique and may be minted in multiple markets) but also a doctrinal challenge.[84]

Crucial to this part of the court's analysis is a finding that the funds from the NFT sales were "pooled," meaning that they were received by Dapper Labs and reinvested into its business to increase the value of the investments.[85] The success of these pooled investments was related to the firm's revenue, including transaction fees and revenue from NFT sales, as well as success of the Flow blockchain.[86]

The digital uniqueness of the NFTs did not undercut the conclusion that the funds were pooled. This conclusion suggests that the technological differences between fungible and non-fungible tokens should not be dispositive. It also emphasizes the nature of the economic reality analysis: the unique Moments were functionally distinguishable from many NFTs of digital art or collectibles because the whole scheme, value, and viability of the tokens at issue were tied to the promoter. Had Dapper Labs declared bankruptcy, the NFTs represented by lines of code on its blockchain would lose value entirely.

The court proceeded with the Howey analysis and found that investors contributed funds into a common enterprise expecting profits from the efforts of others, "the undeniably significant [efforts], those essential managerial efforts which affect the failure or success of the enterprise."[87] The question whether NFT purchasers expected profits from Dapper Labs's efforts entailed an analysis of objective expectations of reasonable investors.[88] One relevant issue here was whether the promoters had promised financial return to investors. The court answered in the affirmative, concluding that Dapper Labs "objectively led purchasers to expect that they would

---

[83] The court focused mainly on horizontal commonality and strict vertical commonality. Ibid., 10–15.

[84] *See, for example,* Goforth, *How Nifty!,* 787–790; Elzweig & Trautman, Nonfungible Token, 327–328

> ("If an NFT that is purchased is a collectible, there are no further ties between the buyer and the seller in that transaction. These type[s] of NFTs are essentially one-of-a-kind products being sold on the market, albeit through blockchain. This is no different than the sale of a traditional painting. Horizontal commonality is not met because the value is not tied to other investors and there is no pro-rata share of investments. There is no pooling of investors whose fortunes depend on the profitability of the enterprise. Also, there is no vertical commonality because there are no promoter's efforts that would impact the investment past the point of purchase").

[85] *Friel* v. *Dapper Labs, Inc.,* No. 21-CV-5837, 2023 WL 2162747, at *10–12 (S.D.N.Y. Feb. 22, 2023).

[86] Ibid., 12–14.

[87] Ibid., 16 (citing *Balestra* v. *ATBCOIN LLC,* 380 F. Supp. 3d 340, 355 (S.D.N.Y. 2019)).

[88] *See, for example,* Elzweig & Trautman, Nonfungible Token, 330 (discussing the expectation of profit prong).

realize the same gains."[89] Incidentally, any consumptive intent investors might have had was commingled with the expectation of profit.[90] And that expectation was linked to the efforts of Dapper Labs.

It was Dapper Labs which controlled and operated the Flow blockchain that was vital to the operation of the trading application, provided a functioning marketplace, and thus bolstered the value of the NFTs.[91] According to the court, the defendant made an "implicit promise" to continue their operations,[92] and purchasers relied on their "managerial efforts" and managerial control to ensure investments are viable and profitable.[93] Under the circumstances, it was clear that securities laws should apply to the transactions and scheme at issue.

V CONCLUSION

The economic reality approach applied in Dapper Labs demonstrates why and how the legal regime that works in securities markets built on asset fungibility could be relevant in relation to transactions in non-fungible assets. Although the rich factual analysis done by the *Dapper Labs* court suggests that the court's conclusions may be specific to the facts of the case, the decision provides an illustrative example of how to look past the concepts of fungibility and non-fungibility. The *Dapper Labs* court's decision transcends the functionalities and utility of NFTs (namely, providing access to the underlying NBA Top Shots). Instead, the decision focuses on the legal relationship, including the overarching transactional scheme run by the issuer, as well as the expectations of purchasers and sellers of the NFTs.

Each NFT of an NBA game could be functionally similar to a digital baseball card and provide access to a digital file containing an NBA shot. Furthermore, the business objectives of promoters could be far from offering securities. Yet, the way Dapper Labs implemented its business strategy by offering and selling the NFTs and the totality of transactional circumstances tipped the balance in favor of applying securities law.

---

[89] *Friel* v. *Dapper Labs, Inc.*, No. 21-CV-5837, 2023 WL 2162747, at *17 (S.D.N.Y. Feb. 22, 2023).

[90] Ibid., 18 (the court observed that *Forman* left open the possibility that "[i]n some transactions the investor is offered both a commodity … for use and an expectation of profits' and noted 'the application of the federal securities laws to these transactions may raise difficult questions that are not present in this case'" (citing *United Hous. Found., Inc.* v. *Forman*, 421 U.S. 837, 853 n.17 (1975)); the court also declined to consider relevant factual questions at the motion to dismiss stage).

[91] "Dapper Labs's continued management and efforts to develop the ecosystem, both technologically and as a matter of promotion, are crucial to Moments retaining and increasing in value." Ibid., 19.

[92] Ibid., 20.

[93] Ibid., 20–22 ("By privatizing the blockchain on which Moments' value depends and restricting the trade of Moments to only the Flow Blockchain, purchasers must rely on Dapper Labs's expertise and managerial efforts, as well as its continued success and existence. As Plaintiffs allege, this is unlike public blockchains").

To summarize, tests like the one in the Howey decision focus on economic realities of markets and transactions and help decision-makers ascertain to which market an NFT belongs and which corresponding legal regime should govern. These holistic frameworks may equip courts and regulators with a thorough understanding of the economics of technology-based assets and transactions and provide a solid footing for better regulation.

4

Digital Assets, Anti-Money Laundering, and Counter Financing of Terrorism

An Analysis of Evolving Regulations and Enforcement in the Era of NFTs

Nizan Geslevich Packin and Uri Volovelsky

I INTRODUCTION

The analysis of digital assets, particularly non-fungible tokens (NFTs), in the context of anti-money laundering (AML) and counter financing of terrorism (CFT) is of utmost importance.[1] As the digital asset ecosystem continues to expand rapidly, new challenges and opportunities emerge in terms of financial crime prevention.[2] Understanding and addressing the evolving regulatory frameworks and enforcement measures associated with digital assets, in the context of AML and CFT, is essential to mitigate risks and foster a secure and compliant environment. This is especially because digital assets have gained immense popularity due to their decentralized nature, ease of transacting, and potential for value appreciation. NFTs, in particular, arguably attempt to revolutionize the concept of digital ownership and provenance by providing unique digital representations of assets. However, the inherent features and characteristics of NFTs can also present risks for illicit activities, including money laundering (ML) and terrorist financing (TF).

The regulatory landscape aims to ensure compliance in the digital asset space in general and in connection with NFTs in particular, addressing associated risks. Global regulators are developing comprehensive frameworks to prevent financial crimes linked to digital assets, covering areas like customer due diligence, transaction monitoring, record-keeping, and reporting suspicious activities. In parallel,

---

[1] For a detailed explanation of how NFT works, *see* Robyn Conti, *What Is an NFT? Non-Fungible Tokens Explained*, FORBES ADVISOR (May 17, 2023) www.forbes.com/advisor/investing/cryptocurrency/nft-non-fungible-token/.

[2] For example, the value sent to NFT marketplaces associated with illicit addresses substantially increased in the third and fourth quarters of 2021. *See* CHAINALYSIS, THE 2022 CRYPTO CRIME REPORT (February 2022), https://go.chainalysis.com/2022-Crypto-Crime-Report.html (last accessed June 30, 2023) [hereinafter CRYPTO CRIME REPORT].

regulatory bodies are actively monitoring and investigating suspicious activities, taking necessary actions against offenders. High-level enforcement actions increase awareness of non-compliance consequences while analyzing digital assets, in the context of AML and CFT, helping reveal vulnerabilities, and emerging risks, aiding the development of targeted preventive measures. Together, these evolving regulations and enforcement actions play a crucial role in maintaining the integrity of the digital asset ecosystem. Collaboration between the public and private sectors is essential to combat financial crime effectively.

This chapter explores these issues and emphasizes the significance of analyzing digital assets, particularly NFTs, to ensure a secure and compliant ecosystem. Understanding evolving regulations and enforcement efforts provides insights into associated risks, vulnerabilities, and emerging typologies. Addressing these challenges fosters a resistant environment against financial crime, safeguarding the integrity of the digital asset space.

II CONCEPTS, SIGNIFICANCE, AND THE ROLE OF NFTS

NFTs are unique digital assets stored on the blockchain. Unlike cryptocurrencies like Bitcoin or Ether, NFTs are non-interchangeable tokens with distinct signatures, making each one different. They represent digital assets like photos, movies, videos, audio, books, trading cards, and arguably even physical assets.[3] NFTs may be traded and transferred from one owner to another through designated digital markets.[4] To acquire NFTs, purchasers must open a crypto account and wallet on a platform or exchange. The wallet holds the private key to access the digital asset. If the wallet is on an exchange and gets hacked, the NFT can be stolen. Managing the asset independently reduces hacking risk but losing the private key means permanent loss of access. These technical choices have implications for individuals, entities, and organizations in the context of AML and CFT, as discussed in this chapter.

In recent years, the NFT market has seen significant interest.[5] Unlike relatively consistent demand for cryptocurrencies like Bitcoin and Ether, the NFT market volume is highly inconsistent and NFT prices are speculative. This volatility can present challenges in the context of AML and CFT, as described in this chapter. Criminals and terrorists may find the potential price fluctuations appealing for their illicit activities involving NFTs.

Furthermore, NFTs offer unique characteristics that allow for authentication in the digital assets context. This ability enables owners to declare their ownership of

---

[3] For examples of NFT-based businesses, *see* Nizan Geslevich Packin, *Financial Inclusion Gone Wrong: Securities and Cryptoassets Trading for Children*, 74 HASTINGS L.J. 349, 366 (2023).

[4] Such marketplaces include, inter alia: OpenSea, Rarible, and Nifty Gateway.

[5] *NFTs Hit $17B in Trading in 2021, Up 21,000%*, PYMNTS (March 10, 2022), www.pymnts.com/nfts/2022/nfts-hit-17b-in-trading-in-2021-up-21000.

the asset, distinguishing it from mere possession of a copy. Understanding these implications is crucial in the context of AML and CFT.

III AML AND CFT REGIMES: FRAMEWORK AND KEY PRINCIPLES

A *The Evolution of AML and CFT Regulations*

The evolution of AML and CFT regulations spans several decades and is driven by the increasing global recognition of the need to combat financial crimes and protect the integrity of the financial system. The history of AML and CFT regulations can be traced through key milestones, initiatives, and significant events that have shaped the frameworks we see today.

The first earlier initiatives in this space and the foundation for AML and CFT regulations were laid in the 1970s and 1980s, mainly in response to concerns about the increasing volumes of illicit funds flowing through the financial system.[6] The Financial Action Task Force (FATF) was established in 1989 by the G7 nations to promote international cooperation in combating ML and almost immediately afterwards released a set of recommendations which provided a framework for countries to develop their AML regime (Recommendations).[7] The Recommendations focused on criminalizing ML, implementing customer identification procedures, and establishing mechanisms for international cooperation.

However, the FATF was not the only relevant force in implementing such norms and standards. More than a decade before the FATF was established, the Basel Committee (initially named the Committee on Banking Regulations and Supervisory Practices on Banking Supervision), established in 1974, played a significant role in shaping AML and CFT regulations in the banking sector.[8] The Basel Committee later also issued the "Customer Due Diligence for Banks" paper in 2001, which emphasized the importance of customer identification, risk management, and ongoing monitoring.[9]

Around the same time, in the early 2000s, the scope of AML and CFT regulations started expanding beyond traditional financial institutions. Non-bank financial institutions, such as money services businesses and casinos, were then brought under

---

[6]   Norm Keith, *Anti-Money Laundering: A Comprehensive Review of Legislative Development*, 19 BLI 245 (2018); Sue Turner and Jonathan Bainbridge, *An Anti-Money Laundering Timeline and the Relentless Regulatory Response*, 82 JCL 215 (2018).

[7]   *History of the FATF*, FIN. ACTION TASK FORCE (November 2023), www.fatf-gafi.org/en/the-fatf/history-of-the-fatf.html (last accessed January 13, 2024). The FATF later revised the Recommendation and published the revision in February 2012. *See* (February 16, 2012) www.fatf-gafi.org/recommendations for the 2012 FATF Recommendations.

[8]   *See History of the Basel Committee*, BANK FOR INT'L SETTLEMENTS, www.bis.org/bcbs/history.htm.

[9]   BASEL COMM. ON BANKING SUPERVISION, CUSTOMER DUE DILIGENCE FOR BANKS (January 2001), www.bis.org/publ/bcbs85.pdf.

regulatory oversight, recognizing their vulnerability to ML and TF.[10] That era was also the beginning of a new age which was characterized by repeated Recommendations that the FATF released as it kept releasing updates in 1996, 2003, 2012, and 2019 that refined and strengthened global AML and CFT standards.[11] These Recommendations provided a comprehensive framework covering areas such as customer due diligence, reporting of suspicious transactions, international cooperation, and supervision of financial institutions. In order to ensure compliance, the FATF conducts mutual evaluations, during which the assessed country must demonstrate that it has an effective framework to protect its financial system from abuse. In order to do so, the assessed country must show it implemented effective measures to combat ML, TF, and proliferation financing.[12]

Simultaneously, in the late 1990s and early 2000s, regional and international organizations increased their efforts to combat ML and TF. The United Nations Convention against Transnational Organized Crime (UNTOC) was adopted in 2000,[13] followed by the United Nation (UN) Security Council Resolution 1373, which mandated member states to criminalize the financing of terrorism.[14] Likewise, the European Union (EU) has also been at the forefront of AML and CFT regulation, issuing multiple directives to harmonize and enhance efforts across member states. The Third, Fourth, Fifth and Sixth EU Anti-Money Laundering Directives (collectively "AMLDs") have expanded the scope of regulated entities, strengthened customer due diligence requirements, and emphasized risk-based approaches.[15] Finally, the International Convention for the Suppression of the Financing of Terrorism, was adopted in 1999.[16] The Convention is designed to strengthen international

---

[10] *Vulnerabilities of Casinos & Gaming Sector*, FIN. ACTION TASK FORCE (March 2009), www.fatf-gafi.org/en/publications/Methodsandtrends/Vulnerabilitiesofcasinosandgamingsector.html.

[11] For an overview of the Recommendations, *see The FATF Recommendations*, FIN. ACTION TASK FORCE (November 2023), www.fatf-gafi.org/en/home.html.

[12] *Mutual Evaluations*, FIN. ACTION TASK FORCE (November 2023), www.fatf-gafi.org/en/topics/mutual-evaluations.html.

[13] 2255 U.N.T.S. 209 (Dec. 12, 2020). The FATF mandates countries to join the Convention as a prerequisite condition for becoming a member of the organization.

[14] Sec. Res. 1373 (Sep. 28, 2001).

[15] Directive 2005/60/EC of the European Parliament and the Council of 26 Oct. 2005 on the Prevention of the use of the Financial System for the Purpose of Money Laundering and Terrorist Financing, 2005 O.J. (L 309), 15; Directive 2015/849/EC of the European Parliament and the Council of 20 May 2015 on the Prevention of the Use of the Financial System for the Purposes of Money Laundering or Terrorist Financing, Amending Regulation (EU) No 648/2012 of the European Parliament and of the Council, and repealing Directive 2005/60/EC of the European Parliament and of the Council and Commission Directive 2006/70/EC, 2015 O.J. (L 141), 73; Directive (EU) 2018/843 of the European Parliament and the Council of 30 May amending Directive (EU) 2015/849 on the Prevention of the Use of the Financial System for the Purposes of Money Laundering or Terrorist Financing, and Amending Directives 2009/138/EC and 2013/36/EU, 2018 O.J. (L 156), 43; Directive 2019/1153 of the European Parliament and of the Council of 20 June 2019 Laying Down Rules Facilitating the Use of Financial and Other Information for the Prevention, Detection, Investigation or Prosecution of Certain Criminal Offences, and Repealing Council Decision 2000/642/JHA, 2019 O.J. (L 186), 122.

[16] G.A. Res. 54/109, U.N. Doc. A/RES/54/109 (Dec. 9, 1999).

cooperation in establishing and adopting effective measures designed to prevent terror financing and its suppression (through indictments and punishment).

In recent years, technological advances, including in the area of virtual currencies
like cryptocurrencies, posed new AML and CFT challenges. Blockchain technology
and the pseudonymity of these assets required regulators to adapt and provide guidance for regulation and monitoring. This led to a stronger focus on the effectiveness
of AML and CFT measures. Regulators and international bodies aimed to ensure
countries and financial institutions achieve concrete outcomes in preventing financial crimes. To attain this, in 2018, FATF updated its Standards, extending AML and
CFT Recommendations to virtual asset service providers (VASPs) and virtual assets
(VAs).[17] This was done through the introduction of Recommendation 15 in 2018 and
the adoption in 2019 of the Interpretive Note to Recommendation 15 which outlines
how the Recommendation should be applied with respect to VASPs and VA.[18]

As a result of adopting Recommendation 15, privately owned VASP are obligated
to adopt and implement the FATF Travel Rule as part of their internal ongoing business procedure. The practical outcome of such requirement is that VASPs must obtain,
hold, and exchange information relating to the originators and beneficiaries of virtual
asset transfers. The premise is that by obtaining such information, financial institutions
and VASPs will be able to conduct sanctions screening and detect red flag transactions.
The adoption of Recommendation 15 reflects the FATF risk-based approach to VASPs
and VA. Countries, authorities, banks, and VASPs must comprehend ML and TF risks
related to virtual assets and apply suitable mitigation measures based on identified risks.[19]

However, as of the current date, the implementation of Recommendation 15,
with a focus on the Travel Rule, is still ongoing. This ongoing effort, which ideally
should have already been concluded, is partly the result of the complexity of some
of the new financial products and services that are currently available and the fact
that technology is not static but rather continuously changes and evolves. According
to information published by the FATF, the vast majority of jurisdictions have yet to
fully implement FATF Recommendation 15 to VASPs and VA.[20] In fact, out of the

[17] *Outcome FATF Plenary, 17–19 October 2018*, Fin. Action Task Force (October 19, 2018), www
      .fatf-gafi.org/en/publications/Fatfgeneral/Outcomes-plenary-october-2018.html.
[18] The Interpretive Note is included as part of the FATF Recommendations publications. *See also*
      FATF Guidance for a Risk-Based Approach to Virtual Assets and Virtual Asset
      Service Providers, Fin. Action Task Force (October 28, 2021), www.fatf-gafi.org/content/
      dam/fatf-gafi/guidance/Updated-Guidance-VA-VASP.pdf.coredownload.pdf. The Guidance provides
      practical insights which are designed to assist the effective implementation of Recommendation 15
      and the Interpretive Note.
[19] *See Risk-Based Approach for the Banking Sector*, Fin. Action Task Force (October 2014),
      www.fatf-gafi.org/en/publications/Fatfrecommendations/Risk-based-approach-banking-sector.html.
      The FATF has listed specific Recommendations with regards to VASP.
[20] *See* Targeted Update on Implementation of the FATF Standards on Virtual Assets
      and Virtual Asset Services Providers 2, Fin. Action Task Force (June 2022), www.fatf-
      gafi.org/en/publications/Fatfrecommendations/Targeted-update-virtual-assets-vasps.html [hereinafter
      FATF Standards Update].

fifty-three jurisdictions that have been assessed by the FATF's Global Network since June 2021, the majority still require major or moderate improvements with special emphasis on assessing applicable ML and TF risks and the applications of AML and CFT preventing measures.

In particular, significant work is still needed in implementing and enforcing the Travel Rule in the various jurisdictions. According to the FATF's Global Network, less than one third of the jurisdictions (29 out of 98) have passed Travel Rule legislation and only eleven have commenced enforcement and supervisory measures.[21] This implementation problem, which results from the fact that some jurisdictions have passed Travel Rule legislation while other jurisdictions have yet to move forward with the implementation of Recommendation 15 with regards to VASP and VA, is often referred to as the "sunrise problem."[22]

To summarize, AML and CFT regulations evolved globally to counter risks and criminal tactics in financial markets. The evolution of these regulations was driven by the global recognition of the significant impact of money laundering and financial terrorism on the financial markets. The recognition of the increasing sophistication and cross-border nature of financial crimes have led regulators and policymakers around the world to realize the importance of international cooperation in combating financial crimes.

B *Key Components of AML and CFT Regulations*

AML and CFT regulations encompass several key components designed to prevent and detect illicit activities. These components mainly include the following four.

  i. *Customer Due Diligence (CDD):*[23] CDD measures ensure that financial institutions identify and verify, in real time, the identities of their customers, assess the nature of their business relationships, and understand the purpose of their transactions. CDD can be simplified, standard, or enhanced based on the risk associated with customers and transactions.
  ii. *Transaction Monitoring and Reporting:*[24] Financial institutions are required to monitor customer transactions and report any suspicious activities to the appropriate authorities. Transaction monitoring systems help identify and investigate potentially illicit transactions, aiding in the prevention and detection of ML and TF.

---

[21] Ibid.
[22] Ibid., 13. In the context of NFTs, it is also important to mention Recommendation 16 of the FATF that implements the Travel Rule requirements with regards to cross-border wire transfers, as well as domestic wire transfers. It applies to financial institutions engaged in virtual asset transfers and VASP.
[23] FATF Recommendations No. 10.
[24] FATF Recommendations No. 10(d) (ongoing due diligence of businesses); No. 12(d) (monitoring of politically exposed persons); and No. 16 (financial institutions obligation to monitor wire transfers in order to identify wire transfers that lack required originator and/or beneficiary).

iii. *Record-keeping and retention:*[25] AML and CFT regulations mandate the main-tenance of comprehensive records related to customer transactions, account activities, and due diligence measures. These records serve as a vital source of information for regulatory authorities during investigations and audits.

iv. *Risk-based approaches:*[26] These approaches involve assessing the inherent risks associated with customers, products, services, and geographic locations. Financial institutions allocate resources and implement controls according to the identified risks, enabling more effective risk management and AML/CFT measures.

C *Relevant Regulatory Bodies and Oversight*

National regulatory authorities play a central role in overseeing compliance with AML and CFT regulations within their jurisdictions. These bodies are responsible for issuing guidance, setting standards, and supervising financial institutions. They monitor and enforce compliance, conduct inspections, and have the power to impose penalties for non-compliance as well as the power to bring criminal indictments. Additionally, central banks and monetary authorities contribute to AML and CFT efforts by coordinating with other regulatory bodies, providing guidance, and ensuring the stability and integrity of the financial system.

In the US, several regulatory authorities play a central role in overseeing compliance with AML and CFT regulations. These include:

i. *The Financial Crimes Enforcement Network (FinCEN):*[27] FinCEN is a bureau of the U.S. Department of the Treasury and is responsible for safeguarding the financial system against ML and other financial crimes. FinCEN administers and enforces the Bank Secrecy Act (BSA),[28] which includes all its implementing regulations such as the AML and CFT provisions.[29] It also serves as the U.S. Financial Intelligence Unit (FIU) and collects, analyzes, and disseminates financial intelligence to support law enforcement and regulatory efforts.[30]

---

[25] Ibid., No. 11 (Record Keeping).
[26] *See* GUIDANCE FOR A RISK-BASED APPROACH: THE BANKING SECTOR, FIN. ACTION TASK FORCE (October 2014), www.fatf-gafi.org/content/dam/fatf-gafi/guidance/Risk-Based-Approach-Banking-Sector.pdf.coredownload.pdf.
[27] Established in accordance with 31 U.S.C 310 (2023).
[28] 31 U.S.C. § 5311 (2023).
[29] In addition to the BSA, FinCEN's authority results from: (i) the Uniting and Strengthening America by Providing Appropriate Tools Required to Intercept and Obstruct Terrorism Act of 2001 (the USA Patriot Act), Pub. L. No. 107-56, § 411(c), 155 Stat. 272; (ii) The Anti-Money Laundering Act of 2020, Pub. L. No. 116-283, §§ 6001-6511 (Anti-Money Act); and (iii) the Corporate Transparency Act, 2019, H.R. 2513.
[30] *See FinCEN's Legal Authorities, Fin. Crimes Enforcement Network,* FinCEN (2023), www.fincen.gov/fincens-legal-authorities.

ii. *The Office of Foreign Assets Control (OFAC):* OFAC is also part of the U.S. Department of the Treasury and administers and enforces economic and trade sanctions based on U.S. foreign policy and national security goals.[31] Financial institutions are required to comply with OFAC regulations, which aim to prevent prohibited transactions with designated entities, countries, or individuals associated with terrorism, narcotics trafficking, and other illicit activities.

iii. *The Securities and Exchange Commission (SEC):*[32] The SEC is an independent federal agency responsible for regulating the securities industry, including broker-dealers, investment advisors, and securities exchanges. The SEC has implemented AML regulations that require registered entities to establish AML programs, conduct customer due diligence, and report suspicious activities.[33]

iv. *The Commodity Futures Trading Commission (CFTC):*[34] The CFTC is an independent agency that regulates commodity futures and options markets in the U.S. The CFTC has implemented AML regulations for futures commission merchants, commodity trading advisors, and other entities under its jurisdiction.[35]

Globally, various regulatory authorities oversee compliance with AML and CFT regulations. One prominent example is the FATF, which serves as the global standard-setter for AML/CFT, conducts evaluations of countries' regulatory regimes, and issues recommendations and guidance. Another is the EU, which has implemented several directives and regulations that establish AML and CFT obligations for member states, including the AMLDs that harmonize AML/CFT rules across the EU and enhance transparency and cooperation among member states, and has recently passed a comprehensive regulation designed to further synchronize regimes.[36]

Other prominent regulatory authorities in this area include the Financial Conduct Authority (FCA), which is responsible for overseeing financial services firms in the UK,[37] sets AML and CFT regulations, and supervises compliance for various sectors, and the Australian Transaction Reports and Analysis Centre (AUSTRAC),

---

[31] OFAC acts under the Presidential national emergency powers and specific legislation, including the International Emergency Economic Powers Act (IPEA), 50 U.S.C § 170; and the Trading with the Enemy Act, 50 U.S.C. § 4301.

[32] The Securities Exchange Act of 1934, 15 U.S.C. § 78.

[33] Rule 17a-8. *See also Anti-Money Laundering (AML) Source Tool for Broker-Dealers,* www.sec.gov/about/offices/ocie/amlsourcetool.

[34] The Commodity Exchange Act (CEA), U.S.C. 7.

[35] www.cftc.gov/IndustryOversight/AntiMoneyLaundering/index.htm.

[36] Regulation (EU) 2021/515 of the European Parliament and of the Council of 24 March 2021 on Markets in Crypto-Assets (MICA).

[37] Established according to the Financial Services Act, 2012, c. 21.

which monitors and enforces compliance with AML/CFT obligations for entities such as banks, remittance providers, and cryptocurrency exchanges in Australia.[38]

D *International Standards and Guidelines*

Other key component in the regulation of ML and FT are international standards and guidelines adopted. The FATF sets global AML/CFT standards, developing and updating comprehensive recommendations for combating financial crimes. These standards cover customer due diligence, record-keeping, reporting, and international cooperation. The G-20 also recognizes and encourages the FATF's work, incorporating its products into yearly reports. Additionally, the Egmont Group of Financial Intelligence Units (EGMONT), comprising 166 units, plays a significant role in sharing financial information per AML/CFT standards.[39] Other international organizations and initiatives also contribute to the development of AML and CFT frameworks, including regional bodies, such as the EU's AMLDs, the recent EU Regulation on Markets in Crypto-Assets (MICA).[40] Finally, Moneyval – a monitoring body of the Council of Europe with forty-seven states – is designated with the task of assessing compliance with principal international standards to counter ML and TF and the effectiveness of their implementation.

E *Cross-Border Regulatory Cooperation and Harmonization Efforts*

ML and TF crimes highlight the importance of cross-border regulatory cooperation in AML and CFT. Efficient cross-border collaboration requires information exchange between regulatory bodies and law enforcement agencies. Collaboration and harmonization is important because it fosters a more unified global AML/CFT system that could offer more predictability to the involved stakeholders.

One way by which such a collaboration can be achieved is through the FATF's mutual evaluation process, which foster international cooperation and regulatory convergence. Further, tools like Memorandum of Understandings (MOUs) and agreements, coupled with the EGMONT's aid in transferring financial intelligence and detecting transnational financial crimes, also help in achieving harmonization. Moreover, international standards may foster harmonization. For example, many countries have adopted the International Standards, including the FATF Recommendations and guidance, and aligned their AML and CFT regulatory frameworks with them.[41]

Regional organizations also play a vital role in promoting cross-border regulatory cooperation and harmonization. One example is the EU, which has implemented

---

[38] Established according to the Financial Transaction Reports Act 1988 (Cth.), s 1.
[39] *About*, Egmont Group of Fin. Intell. Units (2023), https://egmontgroup.org/about/.
[40] *See* above, note 36.
[41] *See* above, notes 19–20 and accompanying text.

various directives,[42] as well as regulations, such as MICA,[43] to harmonize AML and CFT measures across its member states. These directives and regulations establish common standards, the exchange of information between authorities, and the creation of centralized databases for suspicious transaction reporting. Similarly, different FIUs around the world promote collaboration and information sharing and facilitate the exchange of financial intelligence to support investigations and enforcement actions across borders.

Other key entities that contribute to the harmonization of the oversight of ML and FT are the regional bodies that serve as observers within the FATF. These regional bodies include, among others, the Asia/Pacific Group on Money Laundering (APG),[44] the Caribbean Financial Action Task Force (CFATF),[45] and the Financial Action Task Force on Money Laundering in South America (GAFISUD).[46] These bodies have proven themselves to be effective in working towards harmonizing AML/CFT standards within their respective regions through the adoption of a risk-based approaches.

Entities that contribute to harmonization exist also at the state level. An illustrative example here is the UK Joint Money Laundering Intelligence Taskforce (JMLIT), which also brings together regulators, law enforcement agencies, and private sector stakeholders to promote coordination and consistency in AML/CFT efforts.[47]

Finally, cross-border regulatory cooperation includes capacity building and technical assistance for countries with less developed AML/CFT frameworks. The World Bank and the International Monetary Fund (IMF) provide support to strengthen regulatory capabilities and align systems with international standards. These efforts are crucial in addressing the transnational nature of financial crimes. By promoting collaboration, information sharing, and common standards adoption, they create a stronger global AML/CFT regime, reducing vulnerabilities and enhancing the ability to detect and deter illicit financial activities.

F *Industry Initiatives and Public–Private Partnerships*

An effective AML/CFT system relies on both regulatory mechanisms and implementation of strategies uniting public and private stakeholders in the digital asset sector's fight against financial crime. Public–private partnerships, involving participants from finance, businesses, and civil society professionals and academics,

---

[42] *See* different directives, above, note 15.
[43] *See* MICA, above, note 36.
[44] ASIA/PACIFIC GROUP ON MONEY LAUNDERING, https://apgml.org/.
[45] CARIBBEAN FIN. ACTION TASK FORCE (2023), www.cfatf-gafic.org/.
[46] FIN. ACTION TASK FORCE ON MONEY LAUNDERING IN S. AM. (2023), www.imolin.org/imolin/GAFISUDintro.html.
[47] For a detailed explanation of the important work done by the JMLIT, *see* below, note 50 and accompanying text.

play a crucial role in the battle against financial crimes. These partnerships utilize expertise and resources to share information, thereby enhancing the effectiveness of AML/CFT measures. There are four prominent examples of public–private partnerships in this context.

i. *The FATF Private Sector Consultative Forum*: This forum brings representatives from public and private sectors together to exchange information and shape global AML/CFT standards, including banks, financial institutions, and industry associations that contributed expertise and insights during the review process of the Recommendations.[48]

ii. *The JMLIT*: This organization facilitates the sharing of intelligence and information on suspicious activities, enabling early detection and prevention of ML and TF, and promotes collaboration and understanding of emerging risks by facilitating the development of effective responses to financial crime.[49]

iii. *EGMONT and FIUs*: As discussed, these organizations act as the national centers for receiving, analyzing and disseminating financial intelligence, and collaborate with the private sector to share suspicious transaction reports (STRs) and engage in joint investigations, thereby strengthening the overall effectiveness of AML/CFT efforts.

iv. *The Wolfsberg Group*:[50] An association of thirteen global banks that focuses on developing industry standards and best practices to combat financial crime, and collaborates with various stakeholders to address emerging AML/CFT challenges.

By fostering collaboration, knowledge sharing, and joint action, these partnerships strengthen the collective response to AML and CFT risks, leading to more effective prevention, detection, and enforcement efforts.

IV AML AND CFT RISKS IN THE NFT MARKET

The rise of NFTs presents AML and CFT challenges within the market. While NFTs offer opportunities for artists and collectors, their unique attributes can be exploited for illegal activities. Understanding and addressing these risks are crucial to preserve the NFT ecosystem's integrity and prevent financial crimes. This discussion is important because the NFT market continues to evolve despite reduced initial enthusiasm.[51] Therefore, instances of NFTs being used in money laundering and terrorist financing schemes do happen and have already been observed.

---

[48] *FATF Meets with the Private Sector*, FIN. ACTION TASK FORCE (2023), www.fatf-gafi.org/en/documents/fatfmeetswiththeprivatesector.html.

[49] *The National Economic Crime Centre*, NAT'L CRIME AGENCY (2023), www.nationalcrimeagency.gov.uk/what-we-do/national-economic-crime-centre.

[50] *About*, THE WOLFSBERG GROUP (2023), https://wolfsberg-group.org/about.

[51] US DEP'T OF THE TREASURY, STUDY OF THE FACILITATION OF MONEY LAUNDERING AND TERROR FINANCE THROUGH THE TRADE IN WORKS OF ART (February 2022), https://home.treasury.gov/system/files/136/Treasury_Study_WoA.pdf.

A *ML Typologies and Risks Associated with NFTs*

In the context of ML and financial crime, there are various methods, techniques, or patterns that criminals use to conduct illicit activities. These can entail a wide range of activities and scenarios, from basic to complex structures, involving different types of transactions, financial products, sectors, and jurisdictions. Understanding these typologies, which include the following ones, is critical for law enforcement, regulatory bodies, and financial institutions to detect, prevent, and combat ML, especially in the evolving digital landscape.

i.   *Layering*: Criminals may use NFTs to layer their illicit funds by conducting multiple transactions, making it challenging to trace the original source of funds.

ii. *Pseudonymity*: NFT transactions often involve pseudonymous or a high volume of anonymous participants, making it difficult to identify the individuals involved and perform proper due diligence.

iii. *Complex Transaction Structures*: Criminals can create complex networks of transactions involving NFTs to obscure the origin and movement of illicit funds.

iv. *Offshore Platforms*: Some NFT marketplaces and platforms may operate in jurisdictions with lax AML regulations, making it easier for criminals to launder money through NFT transactions.

v.   *Wash Trading*: Criminals may execute transactions in which the seller is on both sides of the trade for the purpose of creating a misleading presentation as to the value of the asset and liquidity. In a wash trading transaction, the original owner of the NFT will send the NFT to a new wallet controlled by the original owner, thus creating the misrepresentation of the value of the sold NFT.[52]

B *TF Risks Associated with NFTs*

The diverse landscape of NFTs presents a range of potential risks associated with terror financing, as the unique properties of NFTs could be exploited for funding illicit activities while evading traditional financial controls and detection mechanisms.

1 Financing through Art

NFTs linked to artworks can potentially be used as a means to finance terrorist activities, allowing terrorists to raise and move funds covertly, due to several factors that

---

[52] *See* Crypto Crime Report, above, note 2.

allow for the covert movement and raising of funds.[53] At the present time, the scale and prevalence of such illicit financing-related activities within the NFT market is uncertain.[54] However, regulatory bodies, law enforcement agencies, and industry stakeholders are increasingly recognizing the following risks and working towards implementing stronger AML/CFT measures within the NFT ecosystem to ensure the integrity of the market.[55]

First, *anonymity and pseudonymity*. As mentioned above, NFT transactions often involve pseudonymous or anonymous participants, making it challenging to identify the individuals involved. Terrorist organizations may exploit this anonymity to conceal their true identities/goals and facilitate covert transactions, thereby raising and moving funds without detection.

Second, *the ease of transfer and global reach*. NFTs can be transferred digitally across borders with relative ease and speed without the need to physically transfer the art.[56] This global reach allows terrorists to access a wide range of potential buyers and supporters, increasing the likelihood of successful fundraising, and movement of funds across different jurisdictions.

Third, *not enough regulation and monitoring*. The NFT market is still relatively nascent and lacks comprehensive regulatory oversight.[57] This can create opportunities for terrorists to exploit loopholes and engage in illicit activities, as the market may not have established robust AML/CFT measures. The lack of effective monitoring and regulation can make it easier for terrorist / terrorist organizations to finance their operations covertly.

Fourth, *value transfer and laundering*. NFTs linked to artworks can provide a vehicle for value transfer. Terrorists could potentially use NFTs to transfer funds or assets between members of their networks without attracting attention. By leveraging the perceived value of artworks, they can create a cover for their financial activities

---

[53] Money Laundering and Terror Financing in the Art and Antiquities Market, Fin. Action Task Force 6 (February 2023), www.fatf-gafi.org/content/dam/fatf-gafi/reports/Money-Laundering-Terrorist-Financing-Art-Antiquities-Market.pdf.coredownload.pdf. The study was mandated by Congress in the Anti-Money Act, which included significant changes. *See Congress Passes the Anti-Money Laundering Act of 2020, Significant Changes to the Bank Secrecy Act Ahead,* Crowell (January 19, 2021) www.crowell.com/en/insights/client-alerts/congress-passes-the-anti-money-laundering-act-of-2020-significant-changes-to-the-bank-secrecy-act-ahead. *See also* Press Release, *US Dep't of the Treasury, Treasury Releases Study on Illicit Finance in the High-Value Art Market* (February 4, 2022), https://home.treasury.gov/news/press-releases/jy0588.

[54] Although it is not possible at this time to quantify ML and TF done through NFTs, feedbacks from FATF jurisdictions, alongside open-source data, indicates that NFTs may be used for illicit financial activities, including money laundering and terror financing. *See* FATF Standards Update, above, note 20, at 20.

[55] FATF has called jurisdictions to apply FATF's Standards on Vas to NFTs in case they perform the same function as VAs (i.e., payment or investment purposes). In addition, the FATF has stated that it will follow market development, hinting that additional regulation will be adopted based on additional data and information collected. Ibid.

[56] Ibid., 19.

[57] *See* ibid., Annex A.

and use NFT transactions as a layer in the process of laundering illicit funds. In this context and as mentioned above, the NFT market price is very speculative.

Fifth, *difficulties in provenance verification*.[58] Verifying the authenticity and provenance of artworks can be challenging in the NFT space. Terrorist organizations may exploit this ambiguity to create and sell NFTs associated with stolen or forged artworks, using the proceeds to finance their activities. The lack of a centralized authority overseeing provenance can make it difficult to track the legitimacy of NFT-linked artworks.

2 Exploiting Digital Wallets

Terrorist organizations could potentially leverage NFTs to transfer funds or assets between members by capitalizing on the relative anonymity and borderless nature of digital wallets. This could occur in light of the following issues.

First, as mentioned above, *pseudonymity and anonymity* elements that are often associated with the participants in NFT transactions makes things more challenging for regulators. Terrorist organizations could exploit this feature by creating multiple digital wallets under different pseudonyms, making it difficult to trace the real identities of those involved in the scheme / tracking the suspicious transactions. The pseudonymity allows the true owners of the wallets to operate covertly and conduct transactions without revealing their true affiliations. This was the case with the seizure of three terrorist financing cyber-enabled campaigns involving al-Qassam Brigades, Hamas's military wing, and al-Qaeda. These three terror finance campaigns all relied on sophisticated cyber-tools, including the solicitation of cryptocurrency donations from around the world.[59]

Second, *the global and instantaneous nature of NFT transactions*, facilitated by blockchain technology, presents a significant challenge in terms of TF. This borderless nature enables terrorist organizations to transfer funds or assets seamlessly across regions or countries, circumventing traditional financial intermediaries and cross-border regulations.[60] The absence of geographical limitations simplifies fund movement within NFT networks.

Third, *the facilitation of direct peer-to-peer trading of NFTs by decentralized exchanges* (DEXs) poses difficulties for oversight. Terrorist organizations might exploit DEXs for private transactions, evading scrutiny from centralized platforms and regulators.

Fourth, the *technique of layering and obfuscation* complicates tracing fund origins, creating intricate networks challenging for law enforcement to track.

---

[58] *See* Money Laundering and Terror Financing in the Art Market, 14.

[59] See *Global Disruption of Three Terror Finance Cyber-Enabled Campaigns*, Office of Public Affairs: U.S. Department of Justice (August 13, 2020), www.justice.gov/opa/pr/global-disruption-three-terror-finance-cyber-enabled-campaigns. Dylan Tokar, *U.S. Seizes Fake Website, Cryptocurrency Assets from Terrorist Groups*, Wall St. J. (August 13, 2020), www.wsj.com/articles/u-s-seizes-fake-website-cryptocurrency-assets-from-terrorist-groups-11597343549.

[60] Cynthia D. Schwarz et al., Terrorist Use of Cryptocurrencies: Technical and Organizational Barriers and Future Threats (2019).

Fifth, *laundering illicit funds*, which can be done by NFTs that have proven themselves to be as something that can provide a vehicle for such purposes. An example is the NFT named IS-NEWS#01, created and shared by a "terrorist sympathizer."[61] They can then transfer these NFTs to other members or sell them on marketplaces, effectively cleansing the funds and making it challenging for authorities to trace the proceeds back to their illegal origins. Therefore, these actions and the ever-evolving landscape of digital assets demands ongoing vigilance, regulatory initiatives, and collaboration between law enforcement agencies, financial institutions, and NFT market platforms to detect and curb any misuse of NFTs for illicit activities.

C *Regulatory Compliance Challenges and Vulnerabilities in NFT Transactions*

Navigating the rapidly evolving world of NFTs brings forth a unique set of regulatory compliance challenges and vulnerabilities, making it critical for stakeholders to understand and address these complexities to ensure the integrity of NFT transactions. Such challenges include the following:

 i. *Identification and verification*: The pseudonymous nature of NFT transactions poses challenges in verifying the identities of participants, conducting proper Know Your Customer (KYC) procedures and assessing the associated risks.
 ii. *Transaction monitoring*: The fast-paced and decentralized nature of NFT transactions can make it challenging for financial institutions and regulators to effectively monitor and detect suspicious activities in real-time.
 iii. *Cross-border transactions*: NFT transactions can occur across borders, involving different regulatory jurisdictions, which can complicate enforcement and regulatory coordination efforts.
 iv. *Lack of standardized due diligence, which leads to inconsistent AML/CFT procedures*: NFT marketplaces and platforms may vary in their adoption and implementation of AML/CFT measures, leading to inconsistencies and potential gaps in due diligence procedures.
 v. *Third-party risks (also associated with lack of standardization)*: AML/CFT risks can arise from third-party actors such as custodians, intermediaries, and digital wallet providers involved in NFT transactions.

V EVOLVING REGULATORY APPROACHES FOR NFTS

This section in the chapter explores regulatory responses to NFT-based risks and challenges through case studies and analysis. It highlights key regulatory bodies and

---

[61] *See above*, note 69 and accompanying text.

initiatives aimed at addressing AML and CFT risks in the context of NFTs and discusses cross-border regulatory cooperation and harmonization efforts.

A *Key Regulatory Bodies' Initiatives*

The regulatory landscape surrounding NFTs is still evolving and specific initiatives by regulatory bodies regarding NFTs may be subject to change. FinCEN's authority over financial institutions, including money services businesses, may include certain NFT marketplaces, platforms, or custodial services, depending on the specific activities they engage in. As such, FinCEN's existing AML/CFT framework, which includes requirements for customer due diligence, suspicious activity reporting, and record-keeping, may apply to relevant entities involved in NFT transactions. Under the BSA, FinCEN requires financial institutions to establish AML programs, conduct customer due diligence, monitor transactions for suspicious activity, and report suspicious transactions to the appropriate authorities.[62] While NFTs are not explicitly mentioned in the regulations, FinCEN is considering how to enforce its AML/CFT framework with regards to NFT. FinCEN's interest in the NFT market grew in light of a study conducted with regards to ML and TF through the trade in works of high-value art.[63] In the EU, somewhat similarly to the US, the recent MICA regulation adopted does not directly apply to NFTs unless they meet prerequisite definitions classifying the assets as a security token.[64]

B *Regulatory Responses to NFTs: Case Studies and Analysis of ML and TF Risks in NFT Transactions*

Despite how recent the interest and usage of NFTs are, there are at least six indictments in four separate criminal cases currently ongoing in US courts involving alleged ML or TF using NFTs.[65] First, in a pending case in the matter of *United States* v. *Le Ahn Tuan*,[66] a Vietnamese national in her twenties, was charged with

---

[62] *Information on Complying with the Customer Due Diligence (CDD) Final Rule*, FIN. CRIME ENFORCEMENT NETWORK (2023), www.fincen.gov/resources/statutes-and-regulations/cdd-final-rule.

[63] MONEY LAUNDERING AND TERROR FINANCING IN THE ART MARKET. *SEE ALSO FINCEN INFORMS FINANCIAL INSTITUTIONS OF EFFORTS RELATED TO TRADE IN ANTIQUITIES AND ART*, FIN. CRIME ENFORCEMENT NETWORK (March 9, 2021), www.fincen.gov/sites/default/files/2021-03/FinCEN%20Notice%20on%20Antiquities%20and%20Art_508C.pdf.

[64] Alys Key, *What Is MICA? The European Union Landmark Crypto Regulation Explained*, DECRYPT (May 10, 2023) https://decrypt.co/138713/what-is-mica-eu-crypto-regulation-explained.

[65] *See* Press Release, US Dep't Just., *Justice Department Announces Enforcement Action Charging Six Individuals with Cryptocurrency Fraud Offenses in Cases Involving Over $100 Million in Intended Losses* (June 30, 2022), www.justice.gov/opa/pr/justice-department-announces-enforcement-action-charging-six-individuals-cryptocurrency-fraud.

[66] *United States* v. *Le Ahn Tuan*, No. 2:20-cr-00385-JC, 2023 WL 1028293 (C.D. Cal. Mar. 8, 2023).

conspiracy to commit wire fraud and international ML related to a scheme in connection with the Baller Ape Club NFT. Tuan was implicated in the Baller Ape
Club, an NFT investment endeavor. Following the initial public sale of Baller Ape
Club NFTs, Tuan and his accomplices executed a deceitful maneuver – known as
a "rug pull" – abruptly terminating the project, erasing its website and absconding
with investors' funds. It is alleged that the defendants laundered the stolen money
through a technique called "chain-hopping," involving the conversion of one cryptocurrency into another and the transfer of funds across various blockchain networks. Tuan and his co-conspirators managed to obtain approximately $2.6 million
from unsuspecting investors.

Second, and somewhat relatedly, in *United States* v. *Emerson Pires, Flavio
Goncalves and Joshua David Nicholas*,[67] Emerson Pires and Flavio Goncalves,
who were both Brazilian nationals, and Joshua David Nicholas from Florida, were
charged with conspiracy to commit wire fraud and securities fraud in connection with a global cryptocurrency-based Ponzi scheme, which generated close to
US$100 million from investors. Pires and Goncalves faced charges of conspiring
to commit international ML. Alongside another individual, they were accused
of engaging in fraudulent activities to promote EmpiresX, an unregistered securities offering and cryptocurrency investment platform. Their fraudulent actions
allegedly involved making multiple false statements about a supposed proprietary
trading bot and deceitfully guaranteeing returns to investors.

Third, and an example of a potential TF activity, is related to a particular
NFT, IS-NEWS #01, which praised Islamic militants for an attack on a mosque
in Afghanistan. This NFT became known after it was publicized on pro-ISIS
social media accounts. The unavailability of this particular NFT for sale does
not negate its presence on an immutable network like IPFS, which utilizes multiple nodes to store and retrieve data. This characteristic presents challenges in
terms of censorship or eradication. Furthermore, the privacy and anonymity
associated with NFT transactions have raised concerns about the potential misuse of NFTs for TF.[68]

Fourth, the case of criminal charges involving ML financing and NFT that was
brought against Ethan Nguyen and Andre Llacuna for conspiracy to commit wire
fraud and ML also illustrates well how NFTs could be used for criminal purposes.
Indeed, in the case of Nguyen and Llacuna, the two men allegedly created the
Frosties NFT project and promoted it on social media. They promised investors
that the Frosties would be valuable and that they would receive rewards, giveaways,
and exclusive opportunities. However, after selling out the Frosties, the defendants

---

[67] *United States v. Joshua David Nicholas*, No. 2:20-cr-00385-JC, 2023 WL 1028293 (C.D. Cal. Mar. 8,
2023).

[68] *See* Ian Talley, *Islamic State Turns to NFTs to Spread Terror Message*, Wall St. J. (September 6,
2022), www.wsj.com/articles/islamic-state-turns-to-nfts-to-spread-terror-message-11662292800.

allegedly abandoned the project and transferred the cryptocurrency proceeds to cryptocurrency wallets under their control instead of to the purchasers.[69]

Fifth, illustrating the wash trading ML scheme mentioned in the previous paragraphs relates to a wallet holder who, in 2021, sold a single NFT from a popular collection and purchased that same NFT and resold it back to the original seller. According to the allegations, these activities were designed on purpose by the seller in order to inflate the price of the specific NFT.[70]

Finally, an interesting ML case involves a digital artist who transferred several millions euros from this virtual asset account to a personal bank account, alleging that the source of the funds was money received by the artist from the sale of digital art. However, the authorities suspected that the funds were the result of an illegal activity, based on the artist's criminal history, links to organized crime leads, and the surprising steep rise in the popularity of the artist that was followed by a rapid decline.[71]

While these examples may not encompass all potential illicit activities, manipulations, and schemes associated with NFT transactions, they certainly provide insight into the complexities that regulators and enforcement agencies need to consider. Moreover, the global nature of the use of NFT means that ML and TF cases involving NFTs are not limited to the US but are applicable to other countries as well. For example, in Latvia, a local developer and artist by the name of Ilya Borisov was indicted after the authorities claimed that the 8.7 million euros earnings from an NFT were in reality the proceeds of ML and criminal wrongdoing via a complex scheme of transactions.[72]

C *International Organizations' Approach towards ML and TF Risks Associated with NFTs*

As highlighted above, ML and TF are inherently cross-border crimes. This truth also extends to the illicit use of NFTs for ML and TF purposes. Therefore, cross-border regulatory cooperation and harmonization are critical in the sphere of AML and CFT to counteract ML and TF through NFTs. This section commences by articulating the detrimental consequences of inconsistent AML/CFT regulation. Following that, we delve into the strategies endorsed by international organizations in tackling the ML and TF risks associated with NFTs.

---

[69] Press Release, *United States Attorney's Office: Southern District of New York, Two Defendants Charged in Non-Fungible Token (NFT) Fraud and Money Laundering Scheme* (March 24, 2022), www.justice.gov/usao-sdny/pr/two-defendants-charged-non-fungible-token-nft-fraud-and-money-laundering-scheme-0.

[70] *See* MONEY LAUNDERING AND TERROR FINANCING IN THE ART MARKET, 21.

[71] Ibid.

[72] Justinas Baltrusaitis, *Latvian NFT Artist Faces 12 Years in Jail over 'Money Laundering,' €8.7 Million Art Earnings Frozen*, FIBBOLD NEWS IN BOLS (July 24, 2022), https://finbold.com/latvian-nft-artist-faces-12-years-in-jail-over-money-laundering-e8-7-million-art-earnings-frozen/.

The discordance in AML/CFT regulation across countries may potentially be exploited by criminals to bypass these rules. By pinpointing regulatory gaps, male-factors and terrorists may partake in activities that are disallowed in one jurisdiction but permitted in another. For instance, they can redirect their illicit activities to nations where regulations are laxer, less mature, or where AML/CFT laws are less stringently enforced or penalized. Additionally, as described earlier, the APG, CFATF, and GAFISUD have adopted a risk-based approach with regards to ML and TF. The result of such adoption is that such regional bodies will require their respective member countries to identify and take the appropriate measures needed in order to mitigate such risks according to the discussed four-step analysis.

Lastly, although the IMF has not formally addressed the potential risks of ML and TF through NFTs, the organization did refer to the risks associated with stablecoins. Such risks are, to some extent, similar in nature to those posed by NFTs. According to a 2021 IMF blog article,[73] the inherent anonymity of cryptoassets may leave regulatory blind spots, inadvertently paving the way for ML and TF. Moreover, the varied regulatory landscapes encompassing crypto ecosystems pose challenges for enforcement. The blog article argues that such complications underscore the need for international collaboration to effectively navigate these issues. In the same vein, the World Bank has expressed concerns about the absence of a universally accepted conduct code or tokenization standard for handling digital assets, specifically pointing to ML and KYC requirements.[74] The same concerns are also applicable with regards to NFTs.

VI COLLABORATIVE EFFORTS AND INDUSTRY INITIATIVES CONCERNING NFTS

A *Self-Regulatory Organizations and Industry-Led Initiatives*

Addressing AML and CFT risks in the NFT market requires a multi-stakeholder approach that involves regulators, NFT platforms, financial institutions, and other industry players for the purpose of implementing a robust AML/CFT measures that foster transparency and compliance. To mitigate AML and CFT risks in the NFT market, industry players and stakeholders need to take proactive measures, including:

  i. *Strengthening Regulatory Oversight*: This can be done through the adaptation of existing AML/CFT regulations to encompass NFT transactions and establish clear guidelines for market participants to ensure compliance.

[73] Dimitris Drakopoulos et al., *Crypto Boom Poses New Challenges to Financial Stability: As Crypto Assets Take Hold, Regulators Need to Step Up*, IMF BLOG (October 1, 2021), www.imf.org/en/Blogs/Articles/2021/10/01/blog-gfsr-ch2-crypto-boom-poses-new-challenges-to-financial-stability.
[74] THE WORLD BANK, INFRASTRUCTURE TOKENIZATION: DOES BLOCKCHAIN HAVE A ROLE IN THE FINANCING OF INFRASTRUCTURE? (2023), https://documents1.worldbank.org/curated/en/099200503082329768/pdf/P17425408f3aa00580a2620810813ed0370.pdf.

Implementation of this recommendation may lead to regulatory certainty, which as explained in the preceding paragraphs is a crucial element with regards to the digital assets including NFT.

ii. *Enhanced Customer Due Diligence*: NFT platforms and marketplaces should implement robust KYC procedures to verify the identities of participants and assess the associated risks.

iii. *Transaction Monitoring and Reporting*: Adequate transaction monitoring systems should be employed to detect and report suspicious activities in NFT transactions.

iv. *Collaboration and Information Sharing*: Industry collaboration, knowledge sharing, and cooperation between regulators, financial institutions, and NFT market participants are crucial for effectively addressing AML/CFT risks.

v. *Technological Solutions*: The use of advanced technologies such as blockchain analytics, data analysis, and artificial intelligence (AI) can aid in identifying patterns and detecting suspicious activities in NFT transactions.

B *Role of Exchanges, Marketplaces, and Custodial Services*

To bolster the effectiveness of an AML/CFT regime applicable to digital assets, including NFTs, particular attention should be given to exchanges, marketplaces, and custodial services. These entities share a common feature: they serve as vital intermediaries in facilitating transactions involving digital assets, including NFTs. Essentially, implementing robust AML/CFT measures for these gateway keepers can significantly improve the chances of reducing ML and TF activities. In the following paragraphs, we delve deeper into some entities, market designs, techniques, and measures that can enhance the AML/CFT effectiveness of such intermediaries.

i. *Exchanges*: The platforms that facilitate the trading of digital assets, including cryptocurrencies and NFTs. Exchanges enable buyers and sellers to interact and conduct transactions. In the context of AML/CFT regulation and enforcement, exchanges have several important legal requirements that need to be enforced by regulators in the context of digital assets and NFT. These requirements include: (a) *CDD*: Exchanges should apply CDD procedures to verify the identity of NFT transactions, assess their risk profiles, and ensure compliance with AML/CFT regulations. This includes conducting KYC checks and maintaining up-to-date customer information. (b) *Transaction Monitoring*: Exchanges should monitor NFT transactions conducted on their platforms to detect any suspicious activities. As part of said monitoring, the exchanges should have in place transaction monitoring systems to identify patterns, anomalies, and red flags that may indicate potential ML or TF financing activities. (c) *Reporting Suspicious Activities*: Exchanges should be obligated to report suspicious transactions or activities to the applicable regulatory authorities or FIU. This includes filing Suspicious Activity Reports (SARs) or other prescribed reports, which provide essential information to aid in investigations and enforcement actions. (d) *Compliance with Regulatory Requirements*: Exchanges must adhere to AML/CFT regulations set forth by relevant authorities. In the context of NFT, the exchanges should be expected to establish and have in place robust AML/CFT compliance programs, maintain appropriate record-keeping, and undergo regular audits and inspections to ensure regulatory compliance.

ii. *Marketplaces*: Similarly to exchanges, these are platforms where NFTs are bought, sold, and traded that also play a role in AML/CFT regulation and enforcement in the context of digital assets including NFTs, in the following ways: (a) *AML/CFT Compliance Policies*: Marketplaces should establish comprehensive AML/CFT policies and guidelines to ensure that sellers and buyers of digital assets including NFTs comply with regulatory requirements. These policies may include KYC procedures, transaction monitoring, and reporting suspicious activities. (b) *Verification of NFT Authenticity*: Marketplaces should take measures to verify the authenticity and provenance of NFTs being listed for sale. This will reduce the risk of fraudulent or illicitly obtained NFTs entering the market. (c) *Collaboration with Exchanges and Regulators*: Marketplaces should collaborate with exchanges and regulatory authorities to share information, insights, and best practices, subject to specific predefined conditions (i.e., threshold evidence, etc.) to be set forth in the requisite law. This collaboration will enhance the overall effectiveness of AML/CFT efforts and promotes a more secure marketplace for NFT transactions.

iii. *Custodial Services*: Services that involve the safe storage and management of digital assets, including NFTs, the secure holding of private keys and the offering of a secure infrastructure for the storage and transfer of digital assets. In connection with custodial services, it is important to consider the following: (a) *Secure storage of assets*: Custodial services play a crucial role in safeguarding digital assets, including NFTs, from theft, loss, or unauthorized access. They implement robust security measures to protect against potential AML/CFT risks, ensuring the integrity and confidentiality of customer assets. (b) *Compliance with regulatory standards*: Custodial services are expected to comply with AML/CFT regulations applicable to their jurisdiction. This involves implementing appropriate AML/CFT controls, conducting due diligence on customers, and reporting suspicious activities. (c) *Enhanced transaction monitoring*: Custodians may implement transaction monitoring systems to identify and report any suspicious transactions or patterns associated with the assets they hold. This contributes to the overall AML/CFT efforts and assists in mitigating risks, with respect to the assets to which they provide custodian services.

VII FUTURE TRENDS AND OUTLOOK

A *Anticipated Regulatory Developments in the Digital Asset Space Affecting NFTs*

Expected regulatory advancements indicate the growing awareness of the necessity for efficient supervision and protection of investors in this rapidly evolving market. As the regulatory landscape continues to develop, we anticipate key areas of regulatory progression which encompass the following six aspects:

i. *AML/CFT Regulations*: Strengthening AML/CFT regulations is expected to be a priority, targeting potential risks associated with NFTs. This could extend AML/CFT obligations to NFT marketplaces, platforms, and custodial services, introduce more rigorous KYC procedures and boost transaction monitoring and reporting requirements to prevent illicit financing through NFT transactions.

ii. *Investor Protection*: Given the cyclical popularity of NFTs, as seen during 2020–2021, regulatory bodies are likely to concentrate on enhancing protective measures for investors. This could include transparency promotion in NFT transactions, mandates for clear disclosures on underlying assets, and rights associated with NFTs and the establishment of dispute resolution and consumer recourse mechanisms in cases of fraud or misrepresentation.

iii. *Securities Regulation*: NFTs that bear similarities to investment contracts or securities may face increased regulatory scrutiny. A recent case in a New York court implies that NFTs may, in certain instances, be categorized as securities. If so, additional requirements such as registration, licensing, and adherence to disclosure and reporting obligations could be imposed to safeguard investors and uphold market integrity, which could indirectly influence the AML/CFT regime.[75]

iv. *Market Infrastructure*: The anticipated regulatory developments will likely address the infrastructure supporting NFTs, including exchanges, custodians, and wallet providers. This could involve implementing licensing requirements, capital adequacy standards, cybersecurity protocols, and operational safeguards to ensure the infrastructure's stability and integrity. In this context, we can expect a revised or supplemental version of MICA, directly applicable to NFT activities.[76]

v. *Taxation*: NFT taxation is a focal point for regulators as the market matures. Potential developments could clarify tax obligations relating to NFT creation,

---

[75] In *Friel v. Dapper Labs, Inc.*, 2023 U.S. Dist. LEXIS 29176, the court rejected a motion to dismiss that TopShot Moments are not securities. A final decision is still pending. Jonathan Stempel, *U.S. Judge Permits Lawsuit Claiming NBA Top Shot NFTs Are Securities*, REUTERS (February 22, 2023), www .reuters.com/legal/us-judge-permits-lawsuit-claiming-nba-top-shot-nfts-are-securities-2023-02-22/.

[76] Ledger Insight, *Crypto Regulation: Lagarde Proposes EU Mica 2*, LEDGER INSIGHTS: BLOCKCHAIN FOR BUSINESS (June 22, 2023), www.ledgerinsights.com/crypto-regulation-lagarde-proposes-eu-mica-2/.

sale, and transfer, and establish guidelines for the treatment of taxes on NFT transactions, including issues like capital gains tax and VAT. Progress in NFT taxation could indirectly enhance the efficacy of the AML/CFT regime for NFTs.

vi. *Cross-Border Regulatory Coordination*: The global nature of the NFT market necessitates enhanced cross-border regulatory coordination and harmonization. Expected developments could involve promoting international cooperation, information sharing, and alignment of regulatory frameworks to address cross-border risks, improve regulatory consistency, and facilitate enforcement actions. In this context, the FATF, as the leading international organization for AML/CFT, will continue to play a significant role in shaping and enforcing applicable guidelines and standards.

As the regulatory landscape continues to evolve, it is important to caution that future developments differ across jurisdictions, subject to each jurisdiction's unique characteristics, legal frameworks and prioritized agenda. Furthermore, a decision to adopt a stricter approach towards NFTs could potentially inhibit innovation. Thus, like with other emerging technologies, a balance must be struck – ensuring effective AML/CFT while fostering innovation.

B *Technological Advancements' Impact on AML/ CFT Compliance in the Context of NFTs*

Technological advancements in the area of blockchain, digital assets, and NFTs have a significant impact on AML and CFT compliance. However, these advancements present challenges and offer potential solutions in enhancing AML/CFT efforts. Key technological advancements and their impact include the following:

i. *Blockchain Transparency*: Blockchain technology, which underlies many digital assets including NFTs, offers transparency and immutability. All transactions recorded on the blockchain are accessible to the public, enabling enhanced visibility and traceability. This transparency can facilitate the identification and tracking of suspicious transactions, aiding AML/CFT compliance efforts.[77]

ii. *Smart contracts and programmable compliance*: Smart contracts, which automate and self-execute predefined terms and conditions, can be utilized to embed compliance requirements directly into transactions. This includes incorporating AML/CFT checks, such as verifying the identity of involved

---

[77] *See* Diksha Malhotra et al., *How Blockchain Can Automate KYC: Systematic Review*, 122 WIRELESS PERSONAL COMMUNICATION 1987 (2022); *How to use Blockchain to Prevent Money Laundering*, THE WORLD FIN. REV. (December 30, 2020), https://worldfinancialreview.com/how-to-use-blockchain-to-prevent-money-laundering/; Jason C.T Chuah, *Money Laundering Considerations in Blockchain-Based Maritime and Commerce*, 14 EUR. J. RISK REG. 49 (2023).

parties or assessing transaction patterns, into the smart contract code. By auto-mating compliance processes, smart contracts can reduce the risk of human error and ensure real-time adherence to regulatory requirements.[78]

iii. *Data analytics and AI*: Technological advancements in AI have revolution-ized various industries, including the field of natural language processing. ChatGPT, a generative AI model powered by OpenAI's advanced AI models, is an example of a significant breakthrough in AI-driven language generation. It leverages deep learning techniques, large-scale training data, and sophisti-cated algorithms to generate human-like responses and engage in interactive conversations. ChatGPT's ability to understand context, generate coherent and contextually relevant responses, and learn from user interactions show-cases the advancements made in AI. These developments in AI language models have the potential to enhance customer service, improve information retrieval, support creative writing, and drive innovations in a wide range of applications across industries. Big data analytics and AI technologies can be employed to analyze large volumes of transactional data and identify patterns indicative of potential ML or TF.[79] These technologies can help financial institutions and regulatory bodies identify high-risk activities, detect anom-alies, and generate alerts for further investigation. AI-powered algorithms can continuously learn and adapt, enhancing the effectiveness of AML/CFT monitoring and compliance efforts.

iv. *KYC solutions*: Technological advancements have led to the development of digital identity verification and KYC solutions. These solutions leverage bio-metrics, document verification and data analytics to establish the identity of individuals involved in digital asset transactions. Automated KYC processes enable efficient customer onboarding, enhanced due diligence, and real-time identity verification, contributing to AML/CFT compliance.[80] (v) *Blockchain analytics*. Specialized blockchain analytics tools enable the monitoring and analysis of blockchain transactions. These tools can trace the movement of funds, identify suspicious patterns, and map the flow of digital assets across the blockchain. By leveraging blockchain analytics, financial institutions and reg-ulatory bodies can gain insights into illicit activities and improve their AML/ CFT compliance efforts. (vi) *Collaborative platforms and information shar-ing*: Technological advancements enable secure and efficient information

---

[78] *See 3 Reasons Why the Future of Anti-Money Laundering Rests on Blockchain*, MERKLE SCIENCE, www.merklescience.com/3-reasons-why-the-future-of-anti-money-laundering-rests-on-blockchain.

[79] Several commercial companies offer financial institutions big data analytics with automated crypto-transaction monitoring for the purpose of AML/KYC compliance obligations, including Chainalysis and CipherTrace.

[80] The private sector has a relatively high number of companies and startups that have developed prod-ucts and services designed to facilitate the enforcement of AML and CTF. Among others, said com-panies and startups include Sumsub, Source, and Trulioo.

sharing between financial institutions, regulatory bodies, and other stakeholders. Collaborative platforms facilitate the exchange of AML/CFT-related
data, alerts, and intelligence, enhancing coordination and improving detection capabilities across jurisdictions. By sharing information in real-time, the
collective ability to identify and combat financial crimes is strengthened.

While these technological breakthroughs offer substantial benefits, they also
bring along challenges. Miscreants may seek to leverage the intricacies of the technology or discover innovative ways to launder funds using digital assets, including
NFTs. Therefore, regulatory bodies and industry players must continually refine
their AML/CFT frameworks to stay in line with the evolving technological risks
posed by criminals and terrorists exploiting technology for nefarious purposes. By
doing so, regulators can ensure that technology is deployed in compliance with
changing regulatory norms. It is crucial for regulators to remember that technology is a multifaceted domain. The effectiveness of technological advancements
necessitates considering various factors, including ethical, security, privacy, and the
capacity to foster long-term collaboration among various stakeholders (i.e., industry
participants, regulators, and technology providers).

VIII CONCLUSION

Despite substantial strides in AML and CFT regimes over the years, existing regulations do not adequately cover NFTs. To attain the necessary effectiveness, a con-
certed, proactive effort is required from all relevant stakeholders. Such measures
should include regulatory initiatives actively advanced by the FATF as the premier
international organization. In terms of regulation, the preliminary discussions of
revisions and supplements to MICA regulation to ensure direct application to NFTs
are undoubtedly a positive advancement. However, due to the cross-border nature
of NFTs, an efficient AML/CFT regime must be rooted in globally agreed principles. Lastly, for effectiveness, regulators and governmental authorities must maintain ongoing collaboration with private sector entities and organizations from the
third sector. The capacity to learn from one another's experiences and knowledge,
and to understand the challenges and difficulties to achieve cross-fertilization is crucial in building a truly effective AML/CFT regime while safeguarding the positive
economic and societal benefits associated with NFTs.

5

NFTs and State Laws Governing Securities Regulation, Virtual Currency, and Money Transmission

Eric C. Chaffee

I INTRODUCTION

Based on the meteoric rise in popularity of non-fungible tokens (NFTs), a "regulatory gap" has emerged between existing regulation and token-based distributed ledger technology,[1] or perhaps better put, the gap has widened even further because of the struggle to create a coherent regulatory scheme for cryptocurrencies.[2] Financial regulators have consistently struggled to keep up with financial technology (FinTech).[3] This has produced and continues to produce regulatory lag (RegLag), which is created when a gap emerges between existing regulation and effective regulation of innovation.[4] This gap can occur for numerous reasons.[5]

---

[1] *See* Lawrence J. Trautman, *Virtual Art and Non-Fungible Tokens*, 50 HOFSTRA L. REV. 361, 422 (2022) ("Rapid adoption of novel technologies, such as NFTs, vividly illustrate the struggle for our laws and regulations to keep pace").

[2] *See* Stephen T. Middlebrook & Sarah Jane Hughes, *Regulating Cryptocurrencies in the United States: Current Issues and Future Directions*, 40 WM. MITCHELL L. REV. 813, 814 (2014)

> ("Since virtual currencies first came into the marketplace in the 1990s, those responsible for monetary policy, federal anti-money-laundering and economic sanctions programs, along with federal and state consumer protection regulators, payment systems operators, businesses, and consumers have grappled with understanding how these 'currencies' work, whether they should be deemed 'lawful' payment methods in the United States, and, if so, the manner and extent to which they should be regulated").

[3] *See* William Magnuson, *Regulating Fintech*, 71 VAND. L. REV. 1167, 1215 (2018) ("[R]egulators currently struggle to understand and monitor fintech's behavior").

[4] *See* John W. Bagby & Nizan G. Packin, *Regulatory Technology Shortens Regulatory Lag with Predictive Regulation Targeting Disruptive Technology*, 41 BANKING & FIN. SERVICES POL'Y REP. 1, 1 (2022) ("Regulation persistently suffers delay starting at the initial detection of a 'regulable activity' until its deployment of effective regulatory response. This is regulatory lag (RegLag)").

[5] *See* John W. Bagby & Nizan G. Packin, *RegTech and Predictive Lawmaking: Closing the RegLag between Prospective Regulated Activity and Regulation*, 10 MICH. BUS. & ENTREPRENEURIAL L. REV. 127, 129–130 (2021) (reporting that RegLag occurs when "regulators … are … hamstrung in defining regulable activity by one or more of the following: (i) strict constructionism; (ii) opacity; (iii) narrowly defined wrongs too often resulting from political compromise; (iv) wrongdoer stealth; and/ or (v) limited investigatory and enforcement budgets or agency expertise").

Because regulation can kill innovation the existence of this regulatory gap is not necessarily a bad thing.[6] NFTs, for example, are an emerging technology and, as a result, all of the potential uses of this technology have not even been discovered yet.[7] Regulating too quickly could prevent these uses from being discovered and effectively deployed.[8]

With that said, an effective regulatory regime for NFTs will eventually need to be developed and certain risks posed by this emerging technology should be regulated relatively quickly. One useful model for developing efficient and effective regulation is through regulatory competition.[9] Because of the system of federalism established by the United States Constitution, one place where regulatory competition exists is between and among the states.[10] The 10th Amendment to the Constitution suggests that state law solutions ought to be favored generally and, regardless, through competition, better regulatory solutions are likely to emerge.[11] A complete laying out of the ways in which NFTs can or should be regulated under state law is obviously beyond the scope of this work. Consequently, the remainder of this chapter will focus on the application of state law to NFTs in two important contexts: securities regulation and the regulation of virtual currency and money transmission. After a discussion of what is an NFT, each of these topics will be explored. Ultimately, this chapter asserts that at least for now regulation of NFTs should occur sparingly and, to the extent that it does occur, regulatory experimentation and competition offers the best approach to creating a regulatory scheme.

---

[6] *See* Larry Downes & John W. Mayo, *The Evolution of Innovation and the Evolution of Regulation: Emerging Tensions and Emerging Opportunities in Communications*, 23 COMMLAW CONSPECTUS 10, 31 n.119 (2014) ("Heavy regulation and the regulatory machinery cannot keep pace with advances and often kills innovation").

[7] *See* Katya Fisher, *Once Upon a Time in NFT: Blockchain, Copyright, and the Right of First Sale Doctrine*, 37 CARDOZO ARTS & ENT. L.J. 629, 631 (2019) ("NFTs are new and the best uses cases for them likely have yet to be developed").

[8] *See* Yafit Lev-Aretz & Katherine J. Strandburg, *Regulation and Innovation: Approaching Market Failure from Both Sides*, 38 YALE J. ON REG. BULL. 1, 2 (2020) ("From pharmaceuticals and environmental markets to DNA testing and big tech, the argument that regulation can 'stifle' innovation has a long pedigree. Simply put, regulation is said to inhibit innovation by limiting potentially innovative paths and/or increasing innovation costs").

[9] *See* Sean J. Griffith, *Substituted Compliance and Systemic Risk: How to Make a Global Market in Derivatives Regulation*, 98 MINN. L. REV. 1291, 1328 (2014)

> ("[R]egulatory competition provides an incentive for regulators in different jurisdictions to innovate in search of more efficient regulation. More efficient regulation may either achieve the same regulatory result at a lower cost or a better regulatory result at the same cost. Regulators have an incentive to seek efficient regulatory solutions in order to maintain their authority over regulated entities that may otherwise have an incentive to move elsewhere").

[10] *See* William Magnuson, *The Race to the Middle*, 95 NOTRE DAME L. REV. 1183, 1190 (2020) ("[S]tates are free to compete with one another through their legislation as well.... In other words, federalism potentially leads to regulatory competition among the states").

[11] U.S. CONST. amend. X ("The powers not delegated to the United States by the Constitution, nor prohibited by it to the States, are reserved to the States respectively, or to the people").

II WHAT IS AN NFT?

An NFT, which stands for non-fungible token, is a cryptographic tool that employs blockchain or other distributive ledger technology to record and evidence the ownership in a digital or real world asset.[12] The term "token" refers to the fact that NFTs are assets that have been tokenized via blockchain technology, which allows an owner of the NFT to acquire title in the asset.[13] NFTs can be created from any digital asset – such as images, videos, or music – or to record an ownership interest in a real-world asset.[14] To date, the use of NFTs has largely focused on selling artwork and other collectibles.[15] Marketplaces have been created that focus on the trading of NFTs.[16] Similar to cryptocurrencies, access to and storage of NFTs is provided through digital wallets.[17]

The term "non-fungible" refers to the fact that NFTs are one-of-a-kind, which allows for exclusive ownership.[18] They are assigned identification codes and metadata that render them unique.[19] Unlike bitcoin, for example, which is fungible because one bitcoin is identical and interchangeable with another bitcoin, NFTs are non-fungible because they are unique and not interchangeable.[20] The distributed

[12] *See* Michael D. Murray, *NFTs and the Artworld: What's Real, and What's Not*, 29 UCLA ENT. L. REV. 25, 27 (2022) ("[NFTs] are a cryptography tool that uses blockchain technology to verify and secure a record of the existence and ownership of digital and real-world assets").

[13] *See* Juliet M. Moringiello & Christopher K. Odinet, *The Property Law of Tokens*, 74 FLA. L. REV. 607, 611 (2022)

("The idea behind the tokenization of a tangible or intangible asset is that the owner of the asset creates a digital item (essentially, an entry in a blockchain ledger) that is to be identified with the asset itself.… The purchaser of the token then ostensibly also owns the underlying asset, or at least that's the whole idea behind tokenization – hat the owner of the token acquires authentic title to the reference asset").

[14] *See* Murray, NFTs and the Artworld, 34 ("After being immutably linked or coded into an NFT, a digital or real-world item is now uniquely tied to a single block on a blockchain by what is understood to be an immutable and transparently traceable bond").

[15] *See* Joshua A.T. Fairfield, *Tokenized: The Law of Non-Fungible Tokens and Unique Digital Property*, 97 IND. L.J. 1261, 1274 (2022) ("Digital art was one of the first applications of NFT technology … NFTs now allow for ownership in digital art to be proven and for the owner to use their token in various online social spaces").

[16] *See* Stephanie L. Tang, *Cryptocurrency, NFTs, and the "Metaverse": Addressing the Expanding World of Virtual Assets in Divorce Proceedings*, 127 PENN ST. L. REV. 1, 33 (2022) ("Like cryptocurrency, every NFT transaction is permanently recorded and often available on marketplace websites").

[17] *See* Kimberly A. Houser & John T. Holden, *Navigating the Non-Fungible Token*, 2022 UTAH L. REV. 891, 896 ("Access to the NFT is provided through a 'wallet,' which also enables the holding of cryptocurrencies").

[18] *See* Fisher, Once Upon a Time in NFT, 631 ("An NFT represents something unique and, along with providing verifiable authenticity and ownership, creates digital scarcity").

[19] *See* Jon M. Garon, *Legal Implications of a Ubiquitous Metaverse and a Web3 Future*, 106 MARQ. L. REV. 163, 180–181 (2022) ("The use of NFTs creates a mechanism for digital assets to be uniquely identified, provided a nearly unforgeable provenance, and be available for trading, largely without the need for large, centralized intermediaries").

[20] *See* Tonya M. Evans, *De-Gentrified Black Genius: Blockchain, Copyright, and the Disintermediation of Creativity*, 49 PEPP. L. REV. 649, 677–78 (2022) ("Unlike their fungible cryptocurrency counterparts, NFTs are verifiably unique").

ledger technology of blockchain helps to ensure that the uniqueness and non-interchangeability of NTFs are maintained, which allows for the establishment of ownership.[21]

As of the writing of this chapter, the existence of NFTs has been relatively brief, although the history of NFTs extends beyond their dramatic rise in popularity in the early 2020s.[22] Some assert that the first NFT sold was *Quantum*, which was minted by Kevin McKoy in 2014 on the NameCoin blockchain and then preserved again on a token on the Ethereum blockchain in 2021.[23]

III STATE SECURITIES REGULATION

Securities regulation in the United States is expansive in scope.[24] Federal securities law covers a broad variety of investment instruments.[25] This breadth is expanded further by states securities regulation because states can maintain their own systems of securities law.[26] Notably, although the federal securities law in the United States is a disclosure-based system of regulation,[27] a number of states maintain merit-based

---

[21] *See* Houser & Holden, *Navigating the Non-Fungible Token*, 900

> ("By operating on the blockchain, all transactions and metadata that run the network are recorded, and this data is verifiable by any user with internet access. As a result, proof of authenticity can be created for digital assets such as NFTs…. Thus, an NFT has the advantage of demonstrating to others that a user has authentic and unerasable ownership over an asset").

[22] *See* Joel Seligman, *The Rise and Fall of Cryptocurrency: The Three Paths Forward*, 19 N.Y.U. J.L. & Bus. 93, 111 (2022) ("Growth on the NFT market … was meteoric, from $95 million in 2020 to $25 billion in 2021, led by the Bored Ape Yacht Club, a series of 10,000 digital images of languid simians in various shades").

[23] *See* Brian L. Frye, *Are Cryptopunks Copyrightable?*, 2022 Pepp. L. Rev. 105, 136 ("In 2014, digital artist Kevin McCoy created a token on the NameCoin blockchain that represented ownership of his work *Quantum*, but he failed to renew the token, so it expired. In 2020, McCoy created an NFT of *Quantum*, which he sold at Sotheby's for $1.47 million").

[24] *See* James C. Spindler, *How Private Is Private Equity, and at What Cost?*, 76 U. Chi. L. Rev. 311, 320 (2009) ("The federal securities laws regulate virtually any financing activity; the scope of what may be a 'security' for purposes of the securities laws is broad enough to encompass almost any investment vehicle").

[25] *See Reves v. Ernst & Young*, 494 U.S. 56, 61 (1990) ("[Congress] enacted a definition of 'security' sufficiently broad to encompass virtually any instrument that might be sold as an investment").

[26] *See* Joel Seligman, *The Obsolescence of Wall Street: A Contextual Approach to the Evolving Structure of Federal Securities Regulation*, 93 Mich. L. Rev. 649, 678 (1995) ("[T]he most significant augmentative aspect of the state blue sky laws may well be in providing broader private relief in many instances than do the federal securities laws").

[27] *See* Sean M. O'Connor, *Crowdfunding's Impact on Start-Up IP Strategy*, 21 Geo. Mason L. Rev. 895, 902 (2014) ("The core premise of the federal securities laws is that the government should not review the merits of investments represented by offers of securities, but rather simply mandate disclosures from the issuers of these securities so that investors can make reasonably informed decisions").

systems of regulation.[28] In these jurisdictions, regulators assess whether securities sold within their states are appropriate for investment.[29] As a consequence, when and how NFTs interact with state securities law is a big deal in regard to their regulation.

NFTs can interact with state securities regulation in at least four different ways. First, a business that creates or engages in transactions involving NFTs could issue securities that are subject to state securities law. The application of state securities law in this context is relatively uncontroversial because real-world businesses that engage in virtual activity are covered by state securities law in a similar way to all other businesses.[30] Well-known issuers of securities have already begun to engage in activities involving NFTs.[31] The application of state securities law would be the same as it would be regarding other types of businesses.

Second, NFTs could be used as a means of payment in securities transactions that would normally be subject to state securities regulation. This context is also relatively uncontroversial. For example, in *The Securities and Exchange Commission (SEC)* v. *Shavers*,[32] the United States District Court for the Eastern District of Texas held that an allegedly fraudulent investment scheme was covered by federal securities regulation, even though payments to invest in the scheme were made entirely in bitcoin, a type of cryptocurrency.[33] Although cryptocurrencies are different than NFTs because cryptocurrencies are fungible, little reason exists to doubt that payment in NFTs would be treated differently because NFTs can be exchanged for various currencies and payments in NFTs would represent an investment of money.[34] As a result, securities transactions with payment in NFTs would be covered as usual by state securities law.

---

[28] *See* Roberta S. Karmel, *Blue-Sky Merit Regulation: Benefit to Investors or Burden on Commerce?*, 53 BROOK. L. REV. 105, 105 (1987)

> ("All fifty states, the District of Columbia, and Puerto Rico have a securities regulation statute, called a blue-sky statute. Some are merit regulation statutes, and some are not. Merit regulation gives a state, through its blue-sky commissioner, the authority to prevent an issuer from selling its securities in that state when the offering or the issuer's capital structure is substantively unfair or presents excessive risk to the investor").

[29] *See* Thomas Lee Hazen, *Disparate Regulatory Schemes for Parallel Activities: Securities Regulation, Derivatives Regulation, Gambling, and Insurance*, 24 ANN. REV. BANKING & FIN. L. 375, 382 n.19 (2005) ("Merit regulation is a regulatory system under which a securities administrator has the power to evaluate the merits of an investment before allowing it to be sold").

[30] *See* Eric C. Chaffee, *Securities Regulation in Virtual Space*, 74 WASH. & LEE L. REV. 1387, 1429 (2017) ("Securities purchased and sold in real world transactions based upon virtual activity are also covered by federal securities law, except in extraordinary situations. Easy examples of this include companies such as Facebook, Snap, and Twitter").

[31] *See* Fairfield, Tokenized, 1277 ("Following the success of brands that first rose alongside NFT technology, more traditional intellectual property rights holders have begun to follow suit").

[32] No. 4:13-CV-416, 2013 U.S. Dist. LEXIS 110018 (E.D. Tex. Aug. 6, 2013).

[33] Ibid., 6.

[34] *See* ibid., 5 ("[Bitcoin can] be exchanged for conventional currencies, such as the U.S. dollar, Euro, Yen, and Yuan. Therefore, Bitcoin is a currency or form of money, and investors wishing to invest … provided an investment of money").

Third, NFTs could be used as a means of recording securities transactions. NFTs are a device to record and evidence the ownership in a digital or real-world asset.[35] Although NFTs have mainly been used as a means to evidence ownership of digital artwork and collectibles,[36] they could be used to evidence the ownership of securities as well.[37] Notably, tokenizing property occurs regularly in law and stock certificates already serve as real-world tokens of ownership of securities.[38] At the time of writing this chapter, NFTs are not commonly being used for such a purpose. If NFTs began to be used as a securities ownership system, existing state securities law could be applicable to such an ownership system and additional regulation might need to be developed. Having said that, without knowing how such a system would work, speculating on how it might be and ought to be regulated is extraordinarily difficult. In addition, questions would also likely emerge as to the division between the recording system and the securities themselves, which would need to be explored prior to considering a regulatory regime.

Fourth, under certain circumstances, NFTs could be securities for purposes of state securities regulation. Although variation exists among the definitions, "security" is a defined term in all systems of state securities regulation.[39] These definitions share many common features and section 102(28) of the Uniform Securities Act embodies many of these features, especially because at the time of writing this chapter, the 2002 revision of the Act had been adopted in twenty-one states and prior versions of the Act had been adopted in a number of other additional jurisdictions.[40] In relevant part, section 102(28) provides:

> 'Security' means a note; stock; treasury stock; security future; bond; debenture; evidence of indebtedness; certificate of interest or participation in a profit-sharing agreement; collateral trust certificate; preorganization certificate or subscription; transferable share; investment contract; voting trust certificate; certificate of deposit for a security; fractional undivided interest in oil, gas, or other mineral rights; put, call, straddle, option, or privilege on a security, certificate of deposit, or group or

[35] *See* above, note 12 and accompanying text.
[36] *See* Stacey M. Lantagne, *Of Disaster Girl and Everydays: How NFTs Invite Challenging Copyright Assumptions Around Creator Support*, 13 HARV. J. SPORTS & ENT. L. 265, 274 (2022) ("NFTs are often associated with digital artwork").
[37] *See* Katayoon Beshkardana, *Reversing the Irreversible: Mitigating Legal Risks of Blockchain-Based Data Breach through Corporate Governance*, 14 HASTINGS SCI. & TECH. L.J. 175, 185 n.36 (2023) ("From stocks and bonds to luxury handbags, and works of art, recording ownership of variety of assets on blockchain is being investigated by firms").
[38] *See* Joshua A. T. Fairfield, *Bitproperty*, 88 S. CAL. L. REV. 805, 826–827 (2015) ("Tying a token to a legal right is common in property law ... [A] stock certificate has no intrinsic value. The certificate serves as a token that conveys certain rights; for example, the right to vote or the right to receive dividends").
[39] *See* 1 ROBERT N. RAPP, *BLUE SKY REGULATION* § 2.01 (2d ed. 2023) ("'Security' is a defined term in all state securities laws").
[40] *Securities Act*, UNIF. L. COMM'N (2022), www.uniformlaws.org/committees/community-home?CommunityKey=8c3c2581-0fea-4e91-8a50-27eee58da1cf (providing a map of the jurisdictions adopting the 2002 and prior versions of the Uniform Securities Act).

index of securities, including an interest therein or based on the value thereof; put, call, straddle, option, or privilege entered into on a national securities exchange relating to foreign currency; or, in general, an interest or instrument commonly known as a 'security'; or a certificate of interest or participation in, temporary or 20 interim certificate for, receipt for, guarantee of, or warrant or right to subscribe to or purchase, any of the foregoing.

(A) includes both a certificated and an uncertificated security;

(B) does not include an insurance or endowment policy or annuity contract under which an insurance company promises to pay a fixed [or variable] sum of money either in a lump sum or periodically for life or other specified period;

(C) does not include an interest in a contributory or noncontributory pension or welfare plan subject to the Employee Retirement Income Security Act of 1974;

(D) includes as an 'investment contract' an investment in a common enterprise with the expectation of profits to be derived primarily from the efforts of a person other than the investor and a 'common enterprise' means an enterprise in which the fortunes of the investor are interwoven with those of either the person offering the investment, a third party, or other investors; and

(E) includes as an 'investment contract,' among other contracts, an interest in a limited partnership and a limited liability company and an investment in a viatical settlement or similar agreement.[41]

This definition is representative of how securities are commonly defined within state systems of securities regulation and for purposes of this chapter, it evidences a number of shared attributes. Within systems of state securities law, the definition of a security is similarly broad as to how a security is defined within the federal system of securities regulation in the United States. In addition, section 102(28) shows that investment contracts are commonly considered securities within state systems of securities regulation in the United States.[42] Finally, section 102(28) evidences that investment contracts are defined within state systems of securities regulation in a similar manner as they are under federal law.[43] Section 102(28)(D) provides in relevant part that "an 'investment contract' [is] an investment in a common enterprise with the expectation of profits to be derived primarily from the efforts of a person other than the investor."[44] In *SEC v. W.J. Howey Co.*, the Supreme Court of the United States provided the definition of investment contract in the federal system of securities law.[45] Writing for the majority, Justice Frank Murphy stated that to determine the existence of an investment contract, "[t]he test is whether the scheme involves an investment of money in a common enterprise with profits to come solely from the efforts of others."[46]

---

[41] Unif. Sec. Act § 102(28)(D) (Unif. L. Comm'n 2002) (amended 2005).

[42] Ibid.

[43] Ibid.

[44] Ibid.

[45] *SEC v. W.J. Howey Co.*, 328 U.S. 293 (1946).

[46] Ibid., 301.

Digital tokens can be investment contracts for purposes of state and federal securities law. This issue has been extensively explored on the federal level and the analysis is relevant to state systems of securities regulation as well. The SEC issued a report in July 2017 based upon potential securities violations, which the SEC did not ultimately pursue, related to The DAO, an unincorporated organization.[47] The DAO was a decentralized autonomous organization, which is a "virtual" organization that exists via computer code and blockchain technology. As conceived, investors would purchase DAO Tokens, and the proceeds from the sales would be used to fund various "projects" with holders of the tokens sharing in the profits from the projects. Online platforms were also to be employed to allow for secondary trading in DAO Tokens. A hacker stole roughly one-third of The DAO's assets prior to any projects being funded.[48] By applying the test for an investment contract found in *Howey*, the SEC concluded that The DAO Tokens qualified as securities under federal securities law because investors invested money to purchase The DAO Tokens in a common enterprise, that is, The DAO, with an expectation of profit, that is, the profits from The DAO projects.[49] Importantly, the SEC did not take a definitive position on whether all digital tokens are securities. The report provides, "Whether or not a particular transaction involves the offer and sale of a security – regardless of the terminology used – will depend on the facts and circumstances, including the economic realities of the transaction."[50] As a result, a bright line test does not exist whether a digital token will constitute an investment contract and, as a result a security, for purposes of state and federal law, but certain tokens, including NFTs, can qualify depending on their attributes and surrounding facts.[51]

Although investment contracts are commonly included within state law definitions of what constitutes a security, definitions of securities can also be broader in state law systems of securities regulation than the definition of a security on the federal level. For example, a substantial number of jurisdictions have adopted the "risk capital" test.[52] Use of the test varies with some jurisdictions employing the test as a means of determining the existence of an investment contract and others employing

---

[47] Report of Investigation Pursuant to Section 21(a) of the Securities Exchange Act of 1934, Exchange Act Release No. 81207, 2017 WL 7184670 (July 25, 2017).

[48] Ibid., 1.

[49] Ibid., 8–10.

[50] Ibid., 14.

[51] *See also* Brian Elzweig & Lawrence J. Trautman, *When Does a Non-Fungible Token (NFT) Become a Security?*, 39 Ga. St. U. L. Rev. 295, 326 (2023) ("Because of the lack of specific guidance related to NFTs and the absence of significant case law regarding when NFTs are regulatable securities, the case law and guidance on cryptocurrency will likely be the basis of analysis in this area").

[52] *See* Joel Seligman, *The New Uniform Securities Act*, 81 Wash. U.L.Q. 243, 250 n.19 (2003) ("A number of states, by statute, rule, or case law have … adopted the 'risk capital' test to find a security when an investment is subject to the risks of an enterprise with the expectation of profit or other valuable benefit and the investor has no direct control over the management of the enterprise").

it as a means of determining the existence of a security generally.[53] Formulations of the risk capital test vary as well.[54] As summarized by one court, common features of the risk capital test include:

(1) An offeree furnishes initial value to an offeror, and
(2) a portion of this initial value is subjected to the risks of the enterprise, and
(3) the furnishing of the initial value is induced by the offeror's promises or representations which give rise to a reasonable understanding that a valuable benefit of some kind, over and above the initial value, will accrue to the offeree as a result of the operation of the enterprise, and
(4) the offeree does not receive the right to exercise practical and actual control over the managerial decisions of the enterprise.[55]

Generally, the risk capital test is viewed as being broader than the *Howey* test because the risk capital test merely requires a "benefit" rather than an "expectation of profits."[56] For example, furnishing capital for purposes of membership in certain organizations likely would not be investment contracts under the *Howey* test, but could qualify as securities under the risk capital test.[57] As a result, the risk capital test broadens the chances that certain types of NFTs are securities in states that apply it.

With that said, the application of state and federal securities law to NFTs should be done cautiously and sparingly for at least three reasons. First, the purpose of state securities laws is unsurprisingly focused on the regulation of business investments.[58] NFTs are a recent creation in contrast to the history of state securities regulation in

---

[53] *See* Elaine A. Welle, *Limited Liability Company Interests as Securities: An Analysis of Federal and State Actions Against Limited Liability Companies under the Securities Laws*, 73 DENV. U. L. REV. 425, 465 (1996) ("In some jurisdictions, the risk capital test is used as an alternative to the *Howey* test to determine what constitutes an 'investment contract.' In other jurisdictions, the risk capital test serves as an independent means of defining a security").

[54] Ibid. Mark A. Sargent, *Are Limited Liability Company Interests Securities?*, 19 PEPP. L. REV. 1069, 1092 (1992) ("[T]here is no single risk capital test. There are different versions in different states. Some take the form of statutory definitions, others were established in case law, and others are largely the creation of administrative decisions").

[55] *State by Commissioner of Sec.* v. *Hawaii Mkt. Ctr.*, 485 P.2d 105, 109 (Haw. 1971).

[56] *See* Welle, Limited Liability Company Interests as Securities, 465–466 ("Regardless of the version used, the risk capital test is considered broader in scope than the *Howey* test. Application of the risk capital test often leads to finding a 'security' where the *Howey* test would hold that no security is present").

[57] *See* ibid., 469 ("[C]ourts and state regulators have found club memberships, hotel reservations, and condominium time-share agreements to involve the sale of a security under risk capital tests. The broader benefit concept means the risk capital tests apply to transactions that the *Howey* test may not cover due to the *Howey* test's more restrictive 'profits' requirement").

[58] *See* Andrew A. Schwartz, *Mandatory Disclosure in Primary Markets*, 2019 UTAH L. REV. 1069, 1078 ("With stock trading … open to the public, the state and then federal governments began to impose mandatory regulations on the practice to protect investors. This imposition began in the 1910s when numerous state governments, led by Kansas and other states far from Wall Street, passed so-called 'Blue Sky' laws").

the United States, which extends back to the 1910s.[59] To date, NFTs have mainly been employed in transactions involving virtual artwork and collectibles.[60] While some uses of NFTs might fall squarely within the definition of a security and the purposes for enacting state securities laws, the regulation of markets in virtual artwork and collectibles do not. As a result, regulators should be cautious in applying existing securities regulation in this realm.

Second, because regulation of markets for NFTs relating to artwork and collectibles was not the intended purpose of the passage of state securities regulation, especially because NFTs have only gained popularity in the past few years, due process concerns exist regarding enforcing state securities laws in matters related to NFTs.[61] The 5th and 14th Amendments to the United States Constitution each contain a due process clause that apply to government action in civil and criminal matters and that prevent the government from depriving any person of "life, liberty, or property, without due process of law."[62] In the United States, notice is a foundational aspect of due process.[63] Additionally, in regard to laws that can be prosecuted criminally, notice and notions of due process generally dovetail with the rule of lenity.[64] The rule of lenity provides that in interpreting ambiguous criminal statutes, courts should construe any ambiguity in favor of the defendant.[65] In regard to state securities regulation of NFTs, due process concerns relating to notice require that state securities law be applied sparingly. This is bolstered by the fact that these laws can be enforced criminally, which means that the rule of lenity also mandates that state securities law be applied cautiously and narrowly as well.[66]

---

[59] *See* Rutheford B. Campbell, Jr., *Federalism Gone Amuck: The Case for Reallocating Governmental Authority over the Capital Formation Activities of Businesses*, 50 WASHBURN L.J. 573, 577 (2011) ("In 1911, Kansas passed the first modern blue sky statute, which included rules prescribing required activities of companies when they attempt to raise external capital. Other states soon followed Kansas' lead and adopted similar regimes governing capital formation activities within their states").

[60] *See* Evans, *De-Gentrified Black Genius*, 677 ("NFTs are currently most associated with digital art and collectibles by means of URL reference to the digital asset stored via a decentralized storage system like the Interplanetary File System (IPFS)").

[61] *See* Houser & Holden, *Navigating the Non-Fungible Token*, 892 ("Although the first so-called non-fungible token (NFT) was created in 2014, worldwide interest in NFTs soared in early 2021").

[62] U.S. CONST. amends. V, XIV.

[63] *See* Richard E. Levy, *The Tweet Hereafter: Social Media and the Free Speech Rights of Kansas Public University Employees*, 24 KAN. J.L. & PUB. POL'Y 78, 95 (2014) ("[D]ue process requires that people be given fair notice of what conduct is permitted and what is prohibited and that laws contain standards that protect against arbitrary and discriminatory enforcement").

[64] *See* William Eskridge, *Public Values in Statutory Interpretation*, 137 U. PA. L. REV. 1007, 1029 (1989) ("The rule of lenity rests upon the due process value that government should not punish people who have no reasonable notice that their activities are criminally culpable").

[65] *See* Glen Staszewski, *Constitutional Dialogue in a Republic of Statutes*, 2010 MICH. ST. L. REV. 837, 857 ("The rule of lenity provides that ambiguous criminal statutes should be interpreted narrowly in favor of the accused based on constitutional principles of fair notice and a desire to limit the scope of discretionary authority that is delegated to prosecutors and judges").

[66] *See* Phillip M. Spector, *The Sentencing Rule of Lenity*, 33 U. TOL. L. REV. 511, 511–512 (2002) ("The rule of lenity counsels that criminal laws should be narrowly interpreted in favor of criminal defendants … [T]he judiciary continues to apply the rule with zest").

Third, the application of state and federal securities law to NFTs should be done cautiously and sparingly for the sake of preserving innovation. NFTs are in the infancy.[67] The best uses of NFTs have likely not yet been discovered and the existing uses of NFTs have not yet been refined.[68] Securities regulation in the United States is commonly viewed as being onerous and cumbersome.[69] Applying this existing body of regulation to new technology, such as NFTs, could hinder innovation.[70] This is especially true because many issues relating to NFTs are merely speculative because of their newness and applying regulation to speculative problems is more likely to inhibit innovation.[71]

IV STATE LAW GOVERNING VIRTUAL CURRENCY AND MONEY TRANSMISSION

If NFTs are not securities under state law, the question then becomes what are they? One logical answer to consider is that they might be cryptocurrencies. If they are cryptocurrencies, then they may be subject to various laws and regulations governing currencies and money transmission. This section will explore these issues.

In regard to whether NFTs are cryptocurrencies, both commonalities and differences exist. Focusing on the commonalities, NFTs and cryptocurrencies are both tokens.[72] The viability of NFTs and cryptocurrencies are both made possible through distributive ledger technology, such as blockchain.[73] In addition, NFTs and cryptocurrencies both can be valuable.[74] As currently employed, however, NFTs depart from

---

[67] *See* above, notes 22–23 and accompanying text (discussing the relatively recent development and rise in popularity of NFTs).

[68] *See* above, note 7 and accompanying text (suggesting that additional uses of NFTs will continue to be discovered).

[69] *See* A. C. Pritchard, *Securities Law in the Roberts Court: Agenda or Indifference?*, 37 J. CORP. L. 105, 106 (2011) ("To outsiders, securities law is not all that interesting. The body of the law consists of an interconnecting web of statutes and regulations that fit together in ways that are decidedly counter-intuitive. Securities law rivals tax law in its reputation for complexity and dreariness").

[70] *See* Daniel F. Spulber & Christopher S. Yoo, *Rethinking Broadband Internet Access*, 22 HARV. J.L. & TECH. 1, 19–20 (2008) ("Blind application of a regulatory regime developed for a different technology and different market conditions can lead to regulation that lacks any theoretical justification and can impede technological innovation and consumer welfare").

[71] *See* J. Howard Beales, III & Timothy J. Muris, *FTC Consumer Protection at 100: 1970s Redux or Protecting Markets to Protect Consumers?*, 83 GEO. WASH. L. REV. 2157, 2223 (2015) ("Regulation based on speculative problems, however, is far more likely to chill useful innovations than it is to prevent real harms").

[72] *See* Brian L. Frye, *After Copyright: Pwning NFTs in a Clout Economy*, 45 COLUM. J.L. & ARTS 341, 345 (2022) ("NFTs are called 'tokens' because they are recorded on the blockchain of a digital currency").

[73] *See* Houser & Holden, *Navigating the Non-Fungible Token*, 893 ("NFTs are often confused with cryptocurrency – likely because NFTs and crypto-coins/tokens are both created using blockchain technology").

[74] *Compare* Michael D. Murray, *Generative and AI Authored Artworks and Copyright Law*, 45 HASTINGS COMM. & ENT L.J. 27, 43 (2023) ("NFTs generally are regarded as valuable because they are unique and you can own them"), *with* David G. Chamberlain, *Forking Belief in Cryptocurrency: A Tax*

cryptocurrencies in at least two significant ways. First, similar to traditional currencies, cryptocurrencies are fungible.[75] For example, one bitcoin is identical and interchangeable with another bitcoin.[76] As currently employed, NFTs are non-fungible because they are unique and not interchangeable, which makes them more similar to collectibles.[77] Second, as currently employed, unlike traditional currencies, people acquire NFTs precisely because of their uniqueness, which is often associated with a work of authorship.[78] NFTs could be used like currency but they are not. One could create a currency in which each unit is unique, for example with unique artwork, which would push the boundaries of the meanings of what is considered fungible and non-fungible, which likely are not entirely clear. Notably, United States dollar bills each contain a unique serial number. With that said, as currently used, NFTs almost certainly have not bridged the gap to becoming currency at this point.

In general, as of the writing of this chapter, federal and state regulators have not spoken directly on whether NFTs are cryptocurrencies for purposes of currency and money transmission regulation.[79] Even if federal and state regulators do eventually declare NFTs or certain uses of NFTs to be cryptocurrencies, the application of existing law will be complicated. Although the federal government has been relatively comfortable applying and adapting existing currency and money transmission regulation to cryptocurrencies, states have taken a wide range of approaches.[80] Some states have applied existing law to the regulation of virtual currencies,[81] and other states have

---

Non-Realization Event, 24 FLA. TAX REV. 651, 653 (2021) ("Like fiat currency, cryptocurrency is only valuable if people believe it is valuable and are willing to use it in transactions").

[75] *See* Michael D. Murray, *NFT Ownership and Copyrights*, 56 IND. L. REV. 367, 369 (2023) ("A perfect example of a fungible token is a unit of cryptocurrency, such as one bitcoin on the Bitcoin blockchain or one unit of ether on the Ethereum blockchain. One bitcoin can be exchanged for any other bitcoin. They are fungible and have the same value").

[76] *See* Eric D. Chason, *Crypto Assets and the Problem of Tax Classifications*, 100 WASH. U. L. REV. 765, 788 (2023) ("Like stock and securities, cryptocurrency units and many tokens are fungible. One unit of Bitcoin is typically no different from another").

[77] *See* Joanne Gelfand, *The How and Why of Crypto Anonymity and the Court Challenges That May Undo It All in the Face of Market Upheaval*, 9 ST. THOMAS J. COMPLEX LITIG. 21, 23 (2023) ("NFTs, or 'non-fungible tokens,' are not an alternative currency … Each NFT has a digital signature that makes it impossible for NFTs to be exchanged for or equal to one another").

[78] *See* Brian L. Frye, *How to Sell NFTs without Really Trying*, 13 HARV. J. SPORTS & ENT. L. 113, 113 (2022) ("NFTs are typically associated with a work of authorship, often a digital image").

[79] *See NFTs: Key U.S. Legal Considerations for an Emerging Asset Class*, JONES DAY (April 2021), www .jonesday.com/en/insights/2021/04/nfts-key-us-legal-considerations-for-an-emerging-asset-class ("To date, no state regulator with oversight of virtual currency or money transmission has issued guidance directly about NFTs. Depending on how a particular state defines money transmission, it is possible that some may try to claim regulatory oversight over certain NFTs or certain business activities related to NFTs").

[80] *See Cryptocurrency Laws and Regulations by State*, BLOOMBERG L. (May 26, 2022), https://pro .bloomberglaw.com/brief/cryptocurrency-laws-and-regulations-by-state (providing a survey of the application of money transmitter laws and regulations to cryptocurrencies by state).

[81] *See* Brian Knight, *Federalism and Federalization on the Fintech Frontier*, 20 VAND. J. ENT. & TECH. L. 129, 165 (2017) ("Certain states have found virtual currency to be fully covered by their existing rules").

enacted legislation to include or exclude virtual currency from the definition of currency under their state laws.[82] In a handful of instances, states' approaches to dealing with virtual currencies have been relatively aggressive. New York, for example, has created a BitLicense for companies engaged in virtual currency activities operating in New York or accepting investors who are New York Residents.[83] Louisiana has adopted a virtual currency business Act as well.[84] In general, approaches have been varied and do not reflect consensus.[85] If NFTs or certain uses of NFTs eventually are classified as cryptocurrencies, they would become subject to this patchwork of state regulation.

At least for now, NFTs should not be pushed into the realm of state currency regulation. This is because, as discussed above, NFTs do not even qualify as virtual currencies since they are non-fungible and currently associated with collectibles.[86] To the extent that NFTs might evolve to be used more similarly to virtual currencies, regulation of NFTs should occur sparingly, and to the extent that it does occur, regulatory experimentation and competition offers the best approach to creating a regulatory scheme. Attempting to enact law and regulation prospectively on the chance that NFTs do evolve in this manner should be avoided because of the risks that such an approach would pose to innovation.

V CONCERNS

This chapter argues that regulation of NFTs should occur sparingly, and to the extent that it does occur, regulatory experimentation and competition among the states offers the best approach to creating a regulatory scheme. Because the uses of NFTs are still emerging and being refined, such an approach is appropriate to prevent hindering innovation.[87] In addition, such a cautious approach is also warranted because prior regulation has not been developed with NFTs in mind,[88] and

---

[82] *See* Carol R. Goforth, *Cinderella's Slipper: A Better Approach to Regulating Cryptoassets as Securities*, 17 HASTINGS BUS. L.J. 271, 325 (2021) ("Some states have issued guidance, opinion letters, or other information from their financial regulatory agencies regarding whether virtual currencies are 'money' under existing state rules, while others have enacted piecemeal legislation amending existing definitions to either specifically include or exclude digital currencies from the definition").

[83] N.Y. COMP. CODES R. & REGS. tit. 23, § 200 (2023).

[84] LA. REV. STATE. ANN. § 6:1384 (2023).

[85] *See* Goforth, Cinderella's Slipper, 325 (discussing the lack of "consensus" regarding whether state currency law does or ought to apply to virtual currencies).

[86] *See* above, notes 75–78 (exploring the reasons why NFTs differ from cryptocurrencies and traditional currencies).

[87] *See* above, notes 67–70 and accompanying text (discussing that law and regulation can hinder innovation when it occurs too quickly).

[88] *See* above, notes 58–60 and accompanying text (explaining that state systems of the securities regulation were developed during the first half of the last century to regulate business investments rather than collectibles, as NFTs are currently used); above, note 79 and accompanying text (explaining that federal and state regulators have not spoken directly on whether NFTs are cryptocurrencies for purposes of currency and money transmission regulation).

because of the due process concerns, especially regarding notice, relating to regulating a new and innovative technology.[89] Such a state-focused approach to regulating NFTs, however, does create some concerns, including that an inefficient and unworkable patchwork of regulation will be created and that NFTs may pose real risks to investors, other market participants, and the public in general. Each of these concerns will be addressed in regard to state securities regulation and the state regulation of virtual currency and money transmission.

First, valid concerns exist about a state-focused system of regulating NFTs potentially creating an inefficient and unworkable patchwork of regulation. Over-regulation is a concern in the United States, and additional time and expense are required to comply when states vary in regulating subject matter that transcends their borders, such as blockchain-based technologies.[90] To the extent that they apply to NFTs, state systems of securities regulation vary substantially,[91] and state systems of virtual currency and money transmission vary significantly as well.[92] All of this can potentially lead to over-regulation and high compliance costs. As a result, this chapter advocates for a cautious and sparing approach to regulating NFTs in these realms generally, until the technology surrounding NFTs can grow, mature, and evolve. With that said, even with a sparing and cautious approach to regulation generally, some regulation is likely needed. Regulatory experimentation offers the best path forward in regard to that regulation because NFTs are new, innovative, and evolving.[93] Some inefficiency will occur but it is worth the cost to preserve innovation.

Second, a sparing and cautious system of regulating NFTs may also pose real risks to investors, other market participants, and the general public. This is a valid concern. With that said, a sparing and cautious approach to regulation does not mean a nonexistent approach to regulation. Certain concerns – for example, issues related to fraud, money laundering, and terrorism financing – should be addressed relatively quickly. Notably, in regard to both securities and virtual currency, the federal government provides a floor for regulation across the United States.[94] With

---

[89] *See* above, notes 61–66 and accompanying text (describing the due process issues created by applying existing regulation to NFTs because NFTs are new and innovative).

[90] *See* Jiang Jiaying, *Technology-Enabled Co-Regulation for Blockchain Implementation*, 83 U. Pitt. L. Rev. 829, 873–874 (2022) ("Regulatory fragmentation – owing to the borderless nature of blockchain – results in ineffective and inefficient law enforcement. The demanding regulatory and supervisory requirements also result in inefficient compliance, reporting, and supervision").

[91] *See* above, notes 26–29 and accompanying text (discussing that state systems of securities regulation can vary significantly).

[92] *See* above, notes 80–85 and accompanying text (explaining that state systems of virtual currency regulation can vary widely).

[93] *See* above, notes 22–23 and accompanying text (providing the brief history of NFTs).

[94] *See* Roberta Romano, *Empowering Investors: A Market Approach to Securities Regulation*, 107 Yale L.J. 2359, 2365 (1998) ("While the federal [securities] laws do not preempt all state regulation, states cannot lower the regulatory standards applicable to firms covered by the federal regime because its requirements are mandatory"); Kevin V. Tu, *Regulating the New Cashless World*, 65 Ala. L. Rev.

that said, states have the opportunity to experiment as NFTs evolve and are refined. Innovative technology deserves innovative regulation. Sparing and cautious regulation is the best approach to prevent hindering or killing innovation.

VI CONCLUSION

The "meteoric" rise of NFTs demonstrates that they have some value.[95] However, all of the uses and applications of NFTs have yet to be discovered and polished.[96] While that occurs, regulation of NFTs should occur sparingly, and to the extent that it does occur, regulatory experimentation and competition offers the best approach to creating a regulatory scheme.[97] This is true in regard to the application of state securities laws and regulation of currency and money transmission, and is true more broadly as well. RegLag in regard to FinTech is not always a bad thing. The gap between regulation and technology is often where innovation exists, and regulation should not be allowed to kill or hinder innovation.[98] Innovative technology requires innovative regulatory solutions and regulatory experimentation is key to finding those solutions. State law in areas such as securities regulation and virtual currency and money transmission regulation offers a venue in which such competition can occur.[99]

77, 85 (2013) ("United States regulation of money transmission employs a dual-system of both state and federal laws. State money transmitter laws vary by jurisdiction and focus on consumer protection concerns").

[95] *See* Seligman, The Rise and Fall of Cryptocurrency, 111 (discussing the "meteoric" rise in popularity of NFTs).

[96] *See* above, note 7 and accompanying text (explaining that all of the potential uses of NFTs have not been determined yet).

[97] *See* above, note 9 and accompanying text (exploring the merits of regulatory competition).

[98] *See* above, note 6 and accompanying text (explaining that RegLag is not necessarily a bad thing because regulation can deter or prevent innovation).

[99] *See* above, note 10 and accompanying text (noting that federalism in the United States creates regulatory competition among the states).

6

New Tax-Reporting Rules for a New Class of Digital Assets?

Sean Stein Smith

I INTRODUCTION

There has rarely been a technological or business advancement that has fundamentally changed the accounting and financial services landscape as much as the rise of digital assets has – and continues – to do so.[1] Even with the rapid proliferation of different types of digital assets, which will be examined in detail below, crypto taxation and in particular the tax classification and treatment of crypto assets has not evolved or kept pace. To facilitate the appropriate level and sophistication of future development related to digital assets, tax policy, and treatment will have to evolve in how it treats digital assets. It is worth pointing out that while tax policy considerations are not usually considered a leading factor in the development of an asset class or economic area, such considerations will play a critical role in the success of future crypto developments.[2] Digital assets, after all, represent a new and innovative

---

[1] Although in general there is a need to update the existing international tax regime, which was developed during the 1920s and 1930s and has been unable to address key problems in today's global, digitalized world, prompting 136 countries to sign the OECD's Base Erosion and Profit Shifting statement for reforming international corporate taxation in the digitalized economy, on October 8, 2021. OECD, OECD/G20 Base Erosion and Profit Shifting Project, Statement on a Two-Pillar Solution to Address the Tax Challenges Arising from the Digitalisation of the Economy (2021), www.oecd.org/tax/beps/statement-on-a-two-pillar-solution-to-address-the-tax-challenges-arising-from-the-digitalisation-of-the-economy-october-2021.pdf. For more on the global, digitalized world that requires new taxation rules, *see* Reuven Avi-Yonah, Young Ran (Christine) Kim, & Karen Sam, *A New Framework for Digital Taxation*, 63 Harv. Int'l L.J. 279 (2022); Andrew Hayashi, Young Ran (Christine) Kim, Taxing Digital Platforms, 26 Va. J.L. & Tech. 1, 3 (2023) (explaining that "[b]y the end of the twentieth century, international tax law was a dinosaur: outdated, outmoded, and inadequate at collecting and allocating the taxing rights to the activities of multinational enterprises (MNEs), particularly activity associated with the digital economy"); Ruth Mason, *The Transformation of International Tax*, 114 Am. J. Int'l L. 353 (2020) (explaining that it took the global recession and financial crisis of 2008 to motivate people to consider changes).

[2] One interesting example of this is the potential impact of tax laws on a different digital product: loot boxes. Indeed, thus far scholars have always relied upon virtual goods' real-world value to determine their real-world significance. However, if this dominant value construct by tailoring the economic principle of perceived value for the virtual world is rejected and replaced with valuing a virtual good based on the perceived benefit it can bring in the virtual world, meaning that consumers are driven

class of financial instruments but they are financial instruments. For any financial asset to achieve wider adoption a clear, consistent, and comparable tax framework is imperative. Non-fungible tokens (NFTs) are a dynamic and rapidly growing subset of the digital asset class, and are no exception to the fundamental rules of financial markets. Although NFTs might have been commonly associated with crypto artwork, the reality is far more nuanced; NFTs have real world applications for artwork, healthcare, real estate, self-sovereign identity, and other economic areas.[3] Prior to diving deeper into potential tax treatments for NFTs, it is imperative to define and examine what digital assets are, how they differ from each other, and how tax treatment and policies should be developed.

II DIGITAL ASSET CLASSIFICATION AND DIFFERENTIATION

NFTs are a high-profile and rapidly developing subset of digital assets, but are just one application of digital assets. In order to develop an appropriate and reasonable tax framework for NFTs, policy-makers and investors alike must be able to define and differentiate certain types of digital assets.[4] This section is neither meant to be an exhaustive listing of the types of crypto nor an all-inclusive categorization. Rather, this section should be used as a starting point to assist policy-makers, investors, academics, and other readers of this text in the development of a robust and flexible tax-focused framework.

Decentralized cryptocurrencies. The type of Digital asset that most commonly occupies the minds of market commentators, investors, and policy-makers alike is decentralized cryptocurrencies. These digital assets are not controlled, governed, or managed by any centralized entity or organization. Furthermore, there is no centralized support structure available to market participants. Examples of digital assets in this category include Bitcoin and Ether, which despite some evidence of "whales" holding large amounts of the individual crypto themselves, are not controlled or overtly managed by any investors.

Semi-centralized cryptocurrencies. Digital assets that exist in this category mainly include stablecoins, which are digital assets that are issued and governed by an issuing organization. Stablecoins, designed and intended to be used for transactional purposes by individuals and entrepreneurs alike, were built to combine the

---

to gamble for virtual goods in loot boxes based on the potential prizes' perceived value, then perhaps loot boxes should be regulated similarly to the gambling industry they resemble, which would in turn impact how consumer perceive them and their popularity. *See* Sheldon A. Evans, *Pandora's Loot Box*, 90 GEO. WASH. L. REV. 376 (2022).

[3] Ashish Kumar Jain, *Future of NFTs: Top NFT Use Cases for 2022 & Beyond*, LINKEDIN (October 7, 2022), www.linkedin.com/pulse/future-nfts-top-nft-use-cases-2022-beyond-ashish-kumar-jain/?trk=pulse-article.

[4] Coryanne Hicks & Michael Adams, *Different Types of Cryptocurrencies: The Ultimate Guide*, FORBES, (September 17, 2021), www.forbes.com/advisor/investing/cryptocurrency/different-types-of-cryptocurrencies/.

best features of existing Fiat currencies (government-issued currencies not directly backed by gold or other commodities) with decentralized cryptocurrencies. Tax questions unique to these digital assets, tend to revolve around the taxation of transactions utilizing these digital assets (should there be a de minims exemption). What potential tax liabilities are associated with an increase in the value of the underlying asset and how should this dual-structure digital asset be treated at large?

Central bank crypto. As the pendulum swings, repeating trends from the past, from decentralized options to more centralized options, digital assets do not seem exempt from this trend. Central bank digital currencies (CBDCs), as the name communicates, represent digital assets that are issued, managed, and governed by a central bank or equivalent entity. Tax implications around such instruments are still emerging as widespread adoption of such instruments remains a hypothetical scenario versus market reality. This trend toward centralization, even in the aftermath of FTX, seems set to continue with nations actively investing in CBDCS and regulation almost guaranteed to benefit larger players versus incumbents.

Governance tokens. Popular amongst decentralized finance (DeFi) protocols,[5] but also amongst decentralized autonomous organizations (DAOs),[6] are governance tokens, which can be thought of as a proxy for voting rights or even potentially "super-voting" shares that exist at some publicly traded organizations. Technical differences aside, the tax treatment and classification of said instruments remains at this point equivalent to the treatment of other coins and tokens. Commonly utilized in decentralized applications such as DAOs, governance tokens also seem to represent a new class of utility tokens that had been previously issued in the marketplace.

Even the terminology that has been utilized during blockchain and digital asset conversations and debates has evolved to reflect the increasing complexity around the crypto space. As the digital asset landscape has evolved and become more differentiated, the tax policies and policy implications should have evolved as well; that has not been the case. NFTs do, by any objective analysis, seem to stand for a differentiated and unique subset of the crypto space. Given that reality, it seems appropriate to both: (i) examine the background and characteristics of NFTs, and (ii) seek to develop and implement NFT-specific tax policies and changes.

III NON-FUNGIBLE TOKENS (NFTS)

NFTs represent perhaps the most purely innovative development in the digital asset space with the initial development and introduction of bitcoin in 2008–2009.

---

[5] For a broad discussion of DeFi apps and protocols, *see* Chris Brummer, *Disclosure, Dapps and DeFi*, 5 STAN. J. BLOCKCHAIN L. & POL'Y 137 (2022).

[6] For more on DAOs, *see* Carla L. Reyes, Nizan Geslevich Packin, & Ben Edwards, *Distributed Governance*, 59 WM. & MARY L. REV. ONLINE (2018); Wulf A. Kaal, *Blockchain-Based Corporate Governance*, 4 STAN. J. BLOCKCHAIN L. & POL'Y 3, 5–7 (2020); Carla L. Reyes, *Autonomous Business Reality*, 21 NEV. L.J. 437, 441 (2021).

Differentiated from other digital assets by their non-fungible characteristics, this opens the door to several other key ways in which NFTs are unique and distinct from other existing digital assets.[7] Let us dive into a few of these core and critical differences below.

NFTs are non-fungible tokens and are therefore a class of digital assets that are specifically neither designed nor intended to be used as a medium of exchange.[8] Virtually every other digital asset, coin, token, or iteration of crypto has been intended to some degree to be leveraged as a replacement for existing payment options.[9] Due to their non-fungible nature, however, NFTs were not intended to be traded on a 1:1 basis as equivalents. This difference in valuations also creates a number of NFT-specific tax questions that will be raised later on. At this moment, it seems logical to highlight another way in which NFTs are unique from other existing digital assets.

NFTs represent a connection between the physical and digital worlds and this is evident in several use cases that have garnered attention from financial and mass media audiences. For instance, when an NFT is used to represent ownership of healthcare information, validation of an existing vaccine passport, or educational credentials, it means that a physical record has a digital twin that has been encrypted and stored on a blockchain.

NFTs also have a versatile array of applications that extends far beyond the price speculation and crypto art use cases that have – to date – dominated the NFT conversation. No matter the specifics of the NFT implementation, however, the tax treatment, classification, and policies that apply to NFTs are consistent. Let us look at some of the specifics.

IV TAX TREATMENT AND POLICIES

As of this writing, the global outlook and treatment of digital assets could be described as inconsistent and murky at best.[10] Different jurisdictions clearly treat digital assets

---

[7] Lisa Andrew, *NFT vs. Crypto: What Is the Difference*, NASDAQ (August 9, 2021), www.nasdaq.com/articles/nft-vs.-crypto%3A-what-is-the-difference.

[8] For more on NFTs, *see, for example*, Kimberly A. Houser & John T. Holden, *Navigating the Non-Fungible Token*, 2022 UTAH L. REV. 891, 902 (2022) (exploring the way NFTs function in industries ranging from fine arts to finance); Juliet M. Moringiello & Christopher K. Odinet, *The Property Law of Tokens*, 74 FLA. L. REV. 607, 631 (2022) ("The choices are art, music, videos, collectibles, sports, and utility."). For a deeper explanation of NFTs and their legal status, *see also* Brian L. Frye, *After Copyright: Pwning NFTs in a Clout Economy*, 45 COLUM. J.L. & ARTS 341, 348 (2022) (focusing on IP rights in connection with NFTs).

[9] Robyn Conti, *What Is an NFT? Non-Fungible Tokens Explained*, FORBES, (March 17, 2023), www.forbes.com/advisor/investing/cryptocurrency/nft-non-fungible-token/.

[10] Sean Stein Smith, *What Crypto Investors Need to Know about NFT Tax Changes*, FORBES (March 2023), www.forbes.com/sites/digital-assets/2023/03/27/what-crypto-investors-need-to-know-about-nft-tax-changes/?sh=c37bf8c53b28.

as unique and differentiated assets depending on the policies of that specific regulatory outlook, but a few salient facts appear to be consistent regardless of whichever jurisdiction or tax authority is consulted.[11] First, there is inconsistency with regards to how the wide array of digital assets should be treated or classified. This directly concerns the rapidly growing and differentiating NFT sector as well as the broader digital asset space. For example, in the US, the Internal Revenue Service (IRS) tends to treat digital assets as taxable personal property without exception, regardless of the use case, functionality, or intended users of these digital assets.[12] This uniformity in tax treatment is applied regardless of the intent, design, implementation, or operation of the cryptoasset in question.[13] Meanwhile, in the very same legal jurisdiction, the Commodity Futures Trading Commission (CFTC) lays claim to several digital assets that its legal team claims are commodities as US regulatory agencies continue to seek ways to regulate the wide-ranging crypto sector.[14] The Securities and Exchange Commission (SEC), meanwhile, seems to be trying to establish jurisdiction over the digital asset space as a whole but is not doing so via comprehensive regulation. Rather, the approach seems to have taken one of regulation by edict and court cases.[15] Evidence of the chilling effect this approach is having on crypto development and investment is already being felt as the number of court cases and lawsuits continues to increase.[16]

One notable exception has been the public commentary published by the SEC Commissioner, Hester Peirce, whose testimony continually centers around the indirect effect – lack of investment – that such a regulatory environment has created.[17] Namely, the primary way in which the tax policy and tax treatment of these

[11] Arthur Teller, *The Essential NFT Tax Guide for 2023*, TOKENTAX (May 5, 2023), https://tokentax.co/blog/nft-tax-guide.

[12] Interestingly enough, Chinese case law has established some property rights for users in virtual worlds. William E. Arnold, IV, *Tax Enforcement in Virtual Worlds – Virtually Impossible?*, 40 SYRACUSE J. INT'L L. & COM. 187, 204 (2012).

[13] Nizan Geslevich Packin & Sean Stein Smith, *ESG, Crypto, and What Has the IRS Got to Do with It?*, 6 STAN. J. BLOCKCHAIN L. & POL'Y 1 (2023).

[14] Hannah Lang & Chris Prentice, *U.S. CFTC Head Urges Congress to Act Fast on Crypto Regulation*, REUTERS (December 2022), www.reuters.com/technology/us-cftc-chair-be-questioned-over-ftx-collapse-by-lawmakers-2022-12-01/.

[15] *See, for example,* Yuliya Guseva, *The SEC, Digital Assets, and Game Theory*, 46 J. OF CORP. L. 629 (2021) (discussing regulation by enforcement in connection with the SEC); Chris Brummer, Yesha Yadav, & David T. Zaring, *Regulation by Enforcement*, U. SOUTH. CAL. L. REV. 1, 2 (forthcoming 2023), https://papers.ssrn.com/sol3/papers.cfm?abstract_id=4405036 (stating that "'regulation by enforcement,' prompted fierce critiques from commentators and the marketplace, often from the standpoint of fairness–and based on an implicit assumption that such regulatory conduct might be illegal, or at the very least, politically motivated").

[16] Jesse Hamilton, *SEC's Shadow Crypto Rule Taking Shape as Enforcement Cases Mount*, COINDESK (February 21, 2023), www.coindesk.com/policy/2023/02/21/secs-shadow-crypto-rule-taking-shape-as-enforcement-cases-mount/.

[17] Sander Lutz, *SEC's Hester Peirce: Regulatory Ambiguity Means That NFT Projects Must Be 'Very Careful,'* DECRYPT (October 2022), https://decrypt.co/113090/sec-hester-peirce-nft-regulation-bored-ape.

differentiated assets has been almost exclusively focused on revenue generation activities.[18] Since the primary implication and market effect of tax policies seems to be either to encourage or discourage certain activities or investments, it seems reasonable to assess both the direct and secondary impact of tax code policies on NFTs and other digital assets.

Another significant consideration in relation to the tax treatment of NFTs is the consistent nature of this treatment across various industry implementations.[19] Whether the NFT in question pertains to crypto art, healthcare information, or any other use case, the tax treatment remains unaltered. The overarching principle can be succinctly summarized: both investors and creators are typically subject to a taxable event arising from the creation, trading, or ownership of these financial instruments.

V CURRENT NFT TAX TREATMENT

The tax categorization and treatment of NFTs at present have tended to mirror those of other digital assets with no distinction made for the reality that NFTs operate differently from other existing digital assets and current IRS pronouncements indicating that NFTs might be taxed at higher rates versus other cryptoassets.[20] These differences are derived both from the non-fungible nature of NFTS versus other crypto and the wider array of applications possible with tokenization via NFTS. For illustrative purposes, a simple example of the creation and trading of an NFT highlights the multiple tax treatments that can be applied to this singular digital asset. Let us walk through and take a look at just how these digital assets can complicate the tax planning scenario around digital assets and crypto planning purposes.

In August 2023, the Biden Administration released a new proposed tax framework for NFTs and other cryptoassets, noteworthy by the fact that it specifically mentioned NFTs as a subset of crypto that would be covered by this proposed rule. This proposed rule (and change) would require a new document, Form 1099-DA, to be submitted. As per Treasury Department statements, this form is meant to assist taxpayers in determining whether taxes are owed and, if so, the amount of taxes due to the IRS. Building on previous discourse in the crypto sector, this proposed regulation further clarifies which organizations would be considered a broker; centralized

---

[18] As Nina Olsen noted in an Annual Report to Congress, "federal income tax consequences of a transaction generally depend on what property rights are created or transferred." *See* 2008 ANNUAL REPORT TO CONGRESS, NAT'L TAXPAYER ADVOC. 217 (DECEMBER 31, 2008), www.irs.gov/pub/irs-utl/08_tas_arc_ intro_toc_msp.pdf.

[19] Miles Fuller, *Understanding the Tax Implications of NFTs, Staking and Yield Farming*, COINDESK, (November 16, 2022), www.coindesk.com/layer2/2022/11/15/key-tax-implications-in-crypto/.

[20] Shehan Chandrasekera, *IRS Guidance Could Expose NFTs to a Higher Tax Rate than Other Digital Assets*, FORBES (March 2023), www.forbes.com/sites/shehanchandrasekera/2023/03/29/irs-guidance-could-expose-nfts-to-a-higher-tax-rate-than-other-digital-assets/?sh=34f19afb494c.

exchanges, decentralized exchanges, crypto payment processors, and certain hot wallet provides would all be considered brokers. Under this proposed rule, all entities classified as brokers would need to, in addition to completing and filing Form 1099-DA, have to modify reporting of transactions over $10,000 and potentially disclose additional information about customers and users. As of publication, the rules are set to be effective for brokers in 2025 for the 2026 tax filing season but remain subject to change/revision during the feedback and public hearing period schedule during Q4 2023.[21]

The sale of an NFT is normally treated as ordinary income related to the individual or enterprise that is involved in the mining operation itself, reflecting the argument that the IRS is not seeking to tax the technology but the economic unit to which the technology gives rise.[22] Such treatment can include a range of market actors from content creators, gamers, athletes, artists, and even large institutions. That said, it is worth pointing out that the impact of this tax treatment can vary quite a great deal depending on the scale of the NFT-minting operations.[23] For an organization or an athlete seeking to simply experiment with digital assets and NFTs, the impact on bottom-line results may be minimal. For individuals, retail creators, or other smaller-scale operators, the impact on financial results might be significant.

Trading NFTs, even though they are unique and differentiated from other digital assets, is treated as ordinary trading income as if the instruments being traded were equity securities instead of digital assets. Again, this follows the current standard tax treatment as equivalent to existing fiat-based instruments, even when such treatment seems to be counter-intuitive and even contradictory to the facts on the ground.[24]

One additional wrinkle that should be included in this analysis is that depending on the specifics of the NFT involved, the tax rate might be assessed at the higher collectible tax rate. Stated simply, the current tax treatment for NFTs is both exactly the same as how other digital assets are categorized and treated and seems to be just as overly simplistic. Lumping together every single type of NFT, not even mentioning the reality that all crypto are categorized similarly, for an identical tax treatment does not seem to make either policy or economic sense. Highlighting this inaccuracy and insufficient treatment is the way in which NFTs continue to evolve and develop far beyond the relatively basic characterization of NFTs are artwork- or

[21] Hannah Lang, *Biden Administration Unveils New Crypto Tax Reporting Rules*, Reuters (August 25, 2023), www.reuters.com/markets/us/biden-administration-unveils-new-crypto-tax-reporting-rules-2023-08-25/.

[22] Marco DeMatteo, *How Will NFTs Be Taxed? Understanding the IRS' New Proposed Guidelines*, CoinDesk (April 2023), www.forbes.com/sites/shehanchandrasekera/2023/03/29/irs-guidance-could-expose-nfts-to-a-higher-tax-rate-than-other-digital-assets/?sh=34f19afb494c.

[23] Walter Effross et al., *Tax Consequences of Nonfungible Tokens (NFTs)*, J. Accountancy, (June 24, 2021), www.journalofaccountancy.com/news/2021/jun/tax-consequences-of-nfts-nonfungible-tokens.html.

[24] Joel Khalili, *The Year the NFT Died and Came Back to Life*, Wired (December 22, 2022), www.wired.com/story/the-year-the-nft-died-and-came-back-to-life/.

art-related. It is worth examining, a few of the other use cases connected to NFTs that both highlight the breadth of use cases as well as the need for a more differentiated tax policy.

VI NFT USE CASES

The use cases for NFTs also continue to complicate the conversation around how to treat these assets from a tax perspective. As use cases continue to expand beyond simply representing control over digital artwork. Although the collectible perspective seems to have captivated the attention of regulators, policy-makers, and users of NFTs alike, they represent a relatively small percentage of the overall potential market and scope for these instruments. Taking a step back, there are several areas within which NFTs can – and increasingly are – play an important role moving forward.

A *NFTs and Virtual Real Estate*

While, thus far, the concepts and applications connected to virtual real estate and virtual ownership or control over information and assets are neither new nor particularly innovative on their own, the literature has focused on orienting the academic consciousness to taxation issues within the context of virtual worlds.[25] However, two factors make NFTs in this sector somewhat unique and arguably different from other previous virtual world applications.[26] First, the direct connection between the NFT and the underlying blockchain creates a potentially unalterable record of ownership that allows holders to effectively monetize said records. Second, and something that has only recently moved to the front burner in the broader policy conversation, are the ramifications of fraudulent NFTs.[27] One potential question that should be effectively evaluated is whether or not there should be a tax-affiliated discount, credit, or other said reduction in price if a certain marketplace is known to be rife with fraudulent goods and services. Such an approach is not as radical as it might seem at first glance, with examples of tax incentives and penalties in existence for multiple areas, but specifically for preferential treatment of capital when invested in either (i) certain projects, or (ii) for a certain period of time.

[25] Byron M. Huang, *Walking the Thirteenth Floor: The Taxation of Virtual Economies*, 17 YALE J. L. & TECH. 224, 227 (2015); Bryan T. Camp, The Play's the Thing: A Theory of Taxing Virtual Worlds, 59 HASTINGS L.J. 1 (2007); Leandra Lederman, *"Stranger than Fiction": Taxing Virtual Worlds*, 82 N.Y.U. L. REV. 1620 (2007); Arnold, *Tax Enforcement in Virtual Worlds*; Adam S. Chodorow, Ability to Pay and the Taxation of Virtual Income, 75 TENN. L. REV. 695 (2008); and Theodore P. Seto, When *Is* a Game Only a Game?: The Taxation of Virtual Worlds, 77 U. CIN. L. REV. 1027 (2009).

[26] Langston Thomas, *Virtual Real Estate: How to Buy Land in the Metaverse*, NFT NOW (March 2, 2022), https://nftnow.com/guides/virtual-real-estate-how-to-buy-land-in-the-metaverse-right-now/.

[27] David Yaffe-Bellany, *Thefts, Fraud, and Lawsuits at the World's Biggest NFT Marketplace*, N.Y. TIMES (June 2022), www.nytimes.com/2022/06/06/technology/nft-opensea-theft-fraud.html.

B *NFT and Healthcare Records*

Healthcare and the pharmaceutical sector at large have certainly been in the news quite a bit since Covid-19 burst into the mainstream, but this recent scrutiny overshadows the importance of the healthcare sector to the US economy at large. Depending on the specific data source that is cited, the healthcare sector accounts for 15–25 percent of the US economy, worth well into the trillions of dollars.[28] Despite the size and heft of this sector, however, there are numerous areas that greater technological integration and more secure records would benefit those market participants. For example, with the number of deaths attributed to medical errors due to incomplete or erroneous paperwork, the opportunity for transparent, traceable, and immutable records to improve the record-keeping and data-sharing processes are relatively self-evident.[29]

C *Tangible v. Intangible NFTs*

Attempting to draw a distinction between a tangible NFT and an intangible NFT might seem to be contradictory in nature. This is due to the fact that the vast majority of NFTs that most investors are familiar with, have to do with artwork, collectibles, or other intangible assets. As the NFT sector continues to develop and mature, however, this means that the likelihood of NFTs-linked or otherwise connected real estate, physical assets, or other physical types of information or data is likely to increase. Drilling down into some of the specific implications of tangible or physical NFTs, there are a few considerations that are directly connected to the tax conversation as well as other financial debates that we will address below.

First, *what is the connection between the physical asset itself, and the NFT that has been minted/issued in association with the token itself?* For example, does the NFT also convey ownership rights, control, or other some other type of custody over the asset in question? If so, are these ownership and control rights able to be clearly communicated or delineated in a manner that is understandable, consistent, and comparable? Specifically, if an NFT does convey ownership rights, or some level of control over the physical assets in question, do these NFTs also qualify as a security? Classification as a security might strike some as merely a technical factor, but would bring with it a bevy of reporting, disclosure, and other communication obligations on the part of the issuer, any exchanges involved, or any investors involved in this ownership chain.

---

[28] Munira Z. Gunja, Evan D. Gumas, & Reginald D. Williams II, *U.S. Health Care from a Global Perspective, 2022: Accelerating Spending, Worsening Outcomes*, The Commonwealth Fund (January 2023), www.commonwealthfund.org/publications/issue-briefs/2023/jan/us-health-care-global-perspective-2022#:~:text=Since%20then%2C%20spending%20has%20slowed,as%20the%20average%20OECD%20country.

[29] Sara Harrison, *Some Medical Ethicists Endorse NFTs – Here's Why*, Sci. Am. (April 13, 2022), www.scientificamerican.com/article/some-medical-ethicists-endorse-nfts-heres-why/.

Second, *is the NFT actually a security?* This basic question remains unanswered to some extent by any regulatory authority in the US, yet it continues to be integral to the future of the digital asset space.[30] NFTs, especially those that are connected to physical assets, may actually be the equivalent to equity securities, even if some of the characteristics of these instruments are different.

Third, *does the NFT, which in and of itself is a virtual asset, convey any rights, duties, or obligations to the holder of this NFT in the physical world?* An example of this might be an NFT that is either linked to real estate titles or records, or an NFT that is uniquely connected to higher education records. Such an arrangement represents a unique situation in which the NFT itself might have market value, and the rights and information that are connected to the NFT also convey value to the holders.

Given the multitude of questions and considerations surrounding NFTs, it increasingly appears logical to develop NFT-specific tax and reporting policies, which would incorporate these key points.

VII CREATING NFTS-SPECIFIC TAX POLICIES

Developing and implementing specific tax policies connected to any one specific financial instrument is virtually almost always rife with controversy and second-guessing, as a balance must be struck between the revenue-generating needs of the tax authority and the innovation forces of the free market. Stated another way, the complexity of tax policy is further complicated by the simple fact that attempting to regulate – via edit and court cases – a fast-growing asset class such as a digital asset, is bound to generate unforeseen consequences.[31] Specifically, care must be taken in order not to stifle or otherwise suppress innovation or the creativity that spurred the creation of these digital assets in the first place.[32] That said, there are several ways in which tax policies, rules, and frameworks can be built out that can help regulate the NFT landscape as well as enable creativity to continue to flourish. These ways are not meant to be an all-inclusive list of factors, nor an exhaustive assemblage of the methods through which policy-makers might seek to influence this rapidly growing asset class.

Differentiated tax treatment depends on the digital asset in question. Treating separate assets differently and separately from one another is not an inherently unique or innovative idea but is a concept that might be able to be applied effectively to NFTs.

---

[30] Gary Silverman, *Why US Regulation Is Failing the Cryptocurrency Test*, Fin. Times (July 2021), www.ft.com/content/e196014a-c5bc-4b2e-8455-5b5b8d878209.

[31] Tom Wilson & Elizabeth Howcroft, *Crypto Firms Will Develop 'Offshore' without Clear US Rules, Coinbase Chief Says*, Reuters (April 18, 2023), www.reuters.com/technology/coinbase-ceo-crypto-firms-will-develop-offshore-without-clear-regulations-2023-04-18/.

[32] Camomile Shumba, *OECD Releases New Global Tax Reporting Framework for Digital Assets*, CoinDesk, (October 10, 2022), www.coindesk.com/policy/2022/10/10/oecd-releases-new-global-tax-reporting-framework-for-crypto-assets/.

The effect of tax policy might vary dramatically, depending on the way in which NFTs have been created, which member of the creation team is involved in the tax assessment conversation, and the valuations assigned to these NFTs. Establishing and enforcing a level and consistently applied tax rate to NFTs makes business sense as well as attempting to create an innovative environment supportive of the financial creativity inherent in many blockchain and digital asset applications.

The first place to start assessing the potential for a customized tax outlook and framework for NFTs would seem to be the economic reasoning as to why policy-makers should be bothered constructing a customized framework. With digital assets in the middle of crypto winter and interest in NFTs (as well as other digital assets) tempered when compared to previous all-time highs, it might seem contradictory to focus on one subset of digital assets, but that misses the wider point. As virtual assets, information, and financial instruments continue to become integrated into different aspects of the economy, NFTs will have an integral role to play. Building on the different categories and types of NFTs outlined above and acknowledging the breadth of use cases that are currently under development creates an environment where more specific tax treatment and policies make sense.

VIII TAX POLICY DIRECTIVES FOR NFTS

At their core, tax policies and frameworks serve as instruments for policy-makers, guiding behavior either through incentives or deterrents. Since digital assets gained mainstream recognition, they have been at the center of regulatory and tax discussions. The challenge arises in determining the appropriate tax treatment for assets that neither resemble conventional assets nor function like them in the market.[33] When it comes to establishing tax policies for digital assets, especially for nuanced categories like NFTs, a meticulous approach is paramount. Here are several crucial considerations:

First, the nature and character of the NFTs should be analyzed. Is the NFT tangible or intangible? The foundational asset, from which the NFT garners its value, should decisively influence how it is classified and subsequently taxed.[34]

Second, the tax treatment might need to account for the lifecycle stage of the NFT. Much like how equity securities are subject to fluctuating tax rates based on the duration they have been held, similar considerations might be appropriate for NFTs.

Third, should the very act of producing (minting) an NFT be taxable or should the tax event be triggered only upon its sale? This perspective is in line with how self-created assets, such as art, are treated within the current US tax framework. It is

---

[33] Riley Adams, *Your Crypto Tax Guide*, TurboTax, Miguel Burgos (February 28, 2023), https://turbotax.intuit.com/tax-tips/investments-and-taxes/your-cryptocurrency-tax-guide/L4k3xiFjB.
[34] Ibid.

worth noting that the inherent economic value of an NFT for its creator comes to the fore only upon an external transaction or sale.[35]

Fourth, one must ponder whether specific types of NFTs warrant preferential tax treatments due to their societal or economic implications. For instance, an NFT symbolizing the ownership of tangible real estate stands distinct from one related to celebrities or creative pursuits. Such disparities should ideally influence tax policies.

Fifth, could the ownership modality of an NFT influence its tax treatment? Drawing parallels to the world of traditional investments, assets held in tax-deferred accounts like retirement savings often enjoy favorable tax treatments.

In the evolving digital asset landscape, these pivotal factors could very well shape a tax framework that is both robust and adaptive, especially as tax directives typically seek either to discourage or encourage activities, investments, and other business activities.

IX OTHER TAX-RELATED EFFECTS

Digital assets universally offer the potential to democratize the wealth creation process. This promise extends to NFTs and associated tax policies should align with this objective.[36] Let us consider two external factors that could shape NFT tax policies and simultaneously offer ancillary advantages for the broader digital asset ecosystem.

First, consider NFTs in the context of decentralized security. A fundamental characteristic of blockchain and other digital assets is the decentralized and distributed encryption and security they bring. Introducing digital assets specifically tailored to secure information, whether financial or otherwise, could justify preferential tax treatments.

Second, there is the intersection of NFTs and the Internet of Things (IoT). A clear, consistent, and transparent tax framework for NFTs could bolster the investment and evolution of the IoT. This technology, eagerly anticipated by market players and often envisioned in forms like autonomous vehicles, will necessitate a traceable and transparent data storage and management system to realize its full potential. To reiterate an earlier point, formulating a tax framework that differentiates certain NFTs based on their use case or application is rational. After all, some of these instruments are not designed to function as tradable investment assets.

Considering the myriad benefits that a crypto-specific tax framework can usher in, the next logical progression is to explore taxation structures that could foster and maintain an innovative economic environment for digital assets with a particular emphasis on NFTs.

---

[35] Shalini Nagarajan, *No More Impairment Charges: FASB Weighs Crypto Accounting Standards*, BLOCKWORKS (May 2023), https://blockworks.co/news/crypto-fasb-accounting-standards.

[36] The Cato Institute, *Opening the Door to Cryptocurrency Innovation by Eliminating Unnecessary Regulatory Barriers*, CATO (October 26, 2022), www.cato.org/publications/section-3-opening-door-cryptocurrency-innovation-eliminating-unnecessary-regulatory.

X A FRAMEWORK FOR PRO-INNOVATION NFTS TAX POLICIES

Establishing a comprehensive framework to assess and tax NFTs is economically sensible and promotes the continued development and growth of the asset class. With this in mind, we will delve into proposed tax frameworks and considerations essential for the development and eventual implementation of tax policies.

First, there ought to be differentiated tax treatments for various types of NFTs. These treatments should mirror the differences in the underlying assets that the NFTs represent. Such a tax policy is not a novel or creative approach to taxation. It aligns with the current tax paradigm, much like the treatment of gains from equity trading.

For example, the creation or use of NFTs for purposes linked to higher education or healthcare records should not be taxed in the same manner as NFTs purely created for speculative reasons. As per current tax rules, irrespective of the NFT's intent or use case, every transaction results in a taxable event. The discourse surrounding digital assets and their tax treatments is ongoing, yet NFTs deserve special consideration due to their unique characteristics.

To illustrate, consider an NFT dubbed "NFTedu" issued to students upon completing a degree or certificate. The NFT, verified by the degree-granting institution, can be shared across online platforms without the risk of unauthorized alterations. This ensures the credibility of the credentials. But should every share or post of this NFT trigger a tax liability?

Second, tax policy should be influenced by, and also influence, how NFTs are classified in accounting taxonomy. Specifically, the classification of a financial instrument on the balance sheet will determine how organizations engage with these instruments. This includes considerations like trade frequency, the possibility of rehypothecation, or their use as a basis for derivative instruments.

While accounting standards and technical treatments differ from tax accounting discussions, the two are interrelated. Financial reporting, along with the compliance it demands from organizations, should not be taken lightly. As discussions around crypto and NFT taxation evolve, so too should the financial accounting debates.

A straightforward example underscores the significance of this matter. If every organization aiming to utilize NFTs must classify them as indefinitely lived intangible assets, it implies two main points: (i) the value reported in external financial statements likely does not mirror current market conditions and (ii) the valuation of the given NFT must undergo periodic assessments.

Such a classification means that organizations eager to tap into the potential benefits of NFTs would concurrently grapple with numerous technical accounting challenges. Of particular note in this scenario is the fact that the reported valuations are not only inaccurate but also offer minimal value to users of external financial statements.[37]

---

[37] *See* Nagarajan, *No More Impairment Charges.*

Third, if there are NFTs associated with projects that are connected to Environmental, Social, and Governance (ESG) initiatives, there might be an opportunity to enact preferential tax treatment and policies connected to these specific digital assets.[38] Examples of such initiatives encompass tax credits for solar panels, incentives for producing electric vehicles, and generous government funding for the research and development of alternative energy sources. One significant challenge in the current ESG discourse is the absence of standardization and comparability within the ESG sector. Moreover, there are prevalent concerns about how best to verify and ensure the transparency and accuracy of the information contained within ESG datasets. NFTs could play a crucial role in establishing a transparent and traceable record of information and unequivocally linking this information to the projects in question.

In light of this, one must ponder: What would be the most appropriate tax treatment for such NFTs? It is evident that these tokens are not designed for trading or investment. Instead, they aim to harness the record-keeping capabilities inherent in all blockchain-based instruments. Given this context, it appears incongruous to tax and treat NFTs like cryptocurrencies such as bitcoin, which are taxable upon creation or transfer. This approach seems misaligned from both accounting and economic viewpoints.

Fourth, the volatility of the NFT in question should not influence the tax and other regulatory treatment of these assets. For example, a common statement that has been put forward by the SEC, is that bitcoin and other crypto are simply too volatile to form the basis of an exchanged traded fund (ETF) or other similar security.[39] Volatility exists in all asset classes, and both the market and regulatory bodies have found ways to appropriately contend with this volatility without crashing entire asset classes.

Lastly, there should be a wider debate around what (if any) specific types of crypto-related activities regulators are seeking to encourage. Decentralized and distributed ownership and control over digital information should not be something that is actively discouraged. Especially as the metaverse, virtual reality, and augmented reality continue to become more mainstream, the implications of NFT taxation via these use cases and applications will continue to be felt throughout the crypto economy.[40] Indeed, several scholars have already argued that "[c]urrently, the biggest hurdle standing in the way of governments taxing

---

[38] *See* Packin & Smith, *ESG, Crypto.*

[39] Maggie Fitzgerald & Thomas Franck, *SEC Delays Decision on Approving Bitcoin ETF*, CNBC (April 28, 2021), www.cnbc.com/2021/04/28/sec-delays-decision-on-approving-bitcoin-etf.html.

[40] Fernando R. Lopez, *The Metaverse and NFT Taxation*, PRAGER METIS (November 2, 2022), https://pragermetis.com/insights/metaverse-nft-taxation/; Noor Al Sibai, *Uh Oh: The Metaverse Is Already Being Slammed by Sales Tax*, FUTURISM (March 2, 2022), https://futurism.com/the-byte/metaverse-taxes; Gail Cole, *Taxing the Metaverse: The Basics*, AVALARA (January 25, 2022), www.avalara.com/blog/en/north-america/2022/01/taxing-the-metaverse-the-basics.html.

metaverse transactions is a lack of knowledge concerning what the metaverse is."[41] Therefore, sorting and understanding the type of data management and analysis should be actively encouraged, developed, and supported from a regulatory perspective. Notably, as increasing amounts of personal and business data are created, stored, and managed in an online environment, it makes logical sense to create a way of tracking and monitoring said information that can keep pace with this rapid rate of change.

XI BENEFITS OF SPECIALIZED TAX TREATMENT

Currently, an entrepreneur aiming to utilize the NFT space would be subject to taxes, incurring tax liabilities, and would be obligated to pay income taxes on almost every transaction and transfer involving NFTs. With a tax framework tailored for cryptocurrency, one that recognizes the distinct nature of both NFTs and broader digital assets, consider the following scenario.

Under this treatment, every individual or organization minting NFTs, regardless of scale, would invariably owe income taxes during this phase of the NFT procedure. For those minting NFTs backed by larger entities or not relying exclusively on the proceeds from this endeavor, such taxation is a minor concern. However, at the other end are smaller, often more innovative or creative, NFT minters. To elucidate, let us review a quantitative example.

Suppose an independent content creator, regardless of the medium, boasts a revenue stream yielding $100,000 in annual recurring revenue. Eager to leverage the allure of cryptocurrency, micro-transactions, and the broader NFT market, the creator mints 1,000 NFTs corresponding to various content items. This implies that even if these NFTs lack a market valuation at this juncture, the taxpayer now faces 1,000 taxable events requiring documentation, reporting, valuation, and assessment. An objective economic evaluation should reveal the unsuitability of prevailing tax regulations to situations of this nature.

Let us delve into another illustrative case. Imagine a modest non-profit in a medium-sized US town with, say, 40,000 residents, which recently relaunched a local community museum spotlighting the history of a nearby pond. This organization, albeit not particularly tech-savvy, learns about the rising enthusiasm for cryptocurrency. Hoping to draw a younger demographic to their events, they decide to mint and auction off NFTs associated with the museum's artwork and even photographs

---

[41] Beckett Cantley & Geoffrey Dietrich, *The Metaverse: A Virtual World with Real World Legal Consequences*, 49 Rutgers Computer & Tech. L.J. 1, 23 (2022). For a similar approach, *see* Steven Chung, *Real Taxation of Virtual Commerce*, 28 Va. Tax Rev. 733 (2009) ("As more people are reportedly earning real money through their virtual-world activities, governments are looking into whether virtual-world transactions are subject to real taxes, even if the participants do not convert their virtual income into cash").

of the venue. Would it be constructive to burden this small non-profit, which likely does not employ a dedicated accountant, with intricate and multi-dimensional tax compliance tasks? This would be the consequence under the existing tax system, a situation benefiting no one, especially not the entrepreneurial spirit that the US market depends upon.

Education, setting aside all other aspects of the conversation related to this field, is an economic sector valued in the hundreds of billions in the US alone. As education continues to digitize and transition towards a continuous process,[42] rather than a one-time event that typically concludes before the age of twenty-five for most individuals, the ancillary effects of tokenization must be evaluated. Reflecting this shift from a single event to continuous learning and relearning, there will be a growing need for both individuals and institutions to track and verify the credentials earned and maintained by respective parties. NFTs appear to offer a solution, though not a flawless one, to this challenge.

Given that minting NFTs does not immediately generate wealth or income for those involved, the following process would be logical: first, the minting process itself should be categorized as a non-taxable event. Rather than paying income taxes, individuals involved should merely file a report of this event. This approach would enhance the transparency and traceability associated with NFT transactions and bolster the capability of market participants to disclose the outcomes of minting and related activities comprehensively and accurately.

By now, it should be evident that the tax classification and treatment of various digital assets should, at least partially, be determined by the functionality and use cases for which these NFTs are employed in the marketplace.[43] This stance is neither radical nor uncommon, especially considering that both cash and equity securities receive different tax treatments based on holding periods, investment strategies, and other factors. Beyond the specific tax advantages that can be gained from a more streamlined tax approach to NFTs, there exist broader business opportunities that only impartial tax treatment can unveil.

---

[42] For more on this, *see, for example,* James Fallows Tierney, *Investment Games,* 72 Duke L.J. 353, 405 (2022) (focused on financial education, discussing the techno-optimist vision of gamification – that it will promote education); Rosemary Queenan, *Amplifying Their Voices: Equity and Assistive Technology for Children with Disabilities,* 127 Dick. L. Rev. 1 (2022) (explaining how assistive technology devices are critical for the educational development of children with disabilities); Nizan Geslevich Packin, *Financial Inclusion Gone Wrong: Securities and Cryptoassets Trading for Children,* 74 Hastings L.J. 349 (2023) (discussing the likelihood of the gamification of finance being a tool for financial education); Stephanie Kimbro, *What We Know and Need to Know about Gamification and Online Engagement,* 67 S. C. L. Rev. 345 (2016).

[43] Indeed, US regulators appear to recognize this need and seem to consider and analyze different activities involving cryptoassets separately. *See, for example,* the IRS's recent ruling on staking: Rev. Rul. 2023–14, 2023–33 I.R.B. 484 (holding that cash-method taxpayer receiving additional units of cryptocurrency as rewards for validating transactions on proof-of-stake blockchains must recognize the validation rewards as income).

XII BENEFITS OF NFT SPECIALIZED TAX TREATMENT FOR NFTS

Lobbying for preferential tax treatment and policies is not new for any specific industry or group, but there are several distinct benefits that can – and will – be generated from creating a specialized and customized framework reflecting the unique nature of NFTs. Digital assets, or at least the augmentation of existing payments and banking systems with aspects of blockchain technology, is a fundamental trend that has already arrived in the marketplace. Stablecoins, CBDCs, and other forms of digital assets have already achieved market capitalizations worth hundreds of billions, and the pace of adoption by large institutions is only accelerating. As these digital assets continue to achieve mainstream understanding and adoption, it is inevitable that tax policies and treatment will need to also evolve going forward. Let us examine some of the benefits that will be achieved via a more customized and crypto-specific tax position.

First, greater clarity will lead to more sustainable and consistent investing options. Even as the trend toward institutional adoption and integration of crypto continues, virtually unabated, the regulatory ambiguity and punitive tax treatment continue to provide significant obstacles to growing investment. Second, tax simplicity will allow more innovation and creativity in the use cases surrounding NFTs. Put simply, if the investments and funds allocated to projects in the NFT space are treated well, there will be more opportunities for creative use cases, implementations, and opportunities for non-speculative use. Third, cutting down on tax complexity can also create an environment and landscape more hospitable to capital, intellectual and financial, coming to the US. It is no secret that the global business landscape, especially financial markets, is increasingly interconnected. To attract and retain the financial capital, and intellectual capacity, to construct a robust digital asset sector, the US will need to have a common-sense crypto tax policy.

The trend and overall direction toward digitization, virtual information, and the embedding of these virtual assets onto digital ledgers is not a fad, nor is it a direction that seems destined to fizzle out in the short term. Payments, educational records, real estate transactions, industrial information, and a wide array of other data are increasingly shared, analyzed, and accessed by a wide range of external stakeholders. There is a disconnect between current data storage and security methods and what the marketplace will require to continue to grow. While blockchain and NFTs are by no means a guarantee of success, nor are they a panacea for organizational problems, NFTs represent a powerful tool in the toolkit of management.

XIII CONCLUSION AND FUTURE DIRECTIONS

One aspect of the digital asset tax conversation, particularly concerning NFTs, is that these debates need to address both the current needs of the marketplace and potential future developments of these assets. The evolution of the digital asset landscape will continue to differentiate as investment and interest in new digital assets grow. Globally, both individuals and institutions will increasingly require secure, transparent, and verifiable records. The rise in digitization, and the subsequent growth in online interactions, commerce, and information sharing, underscores the need for better ways to manage the expanding volume of digital information.

While NFTs are not a perfect solution to challenges in data management, custody, and security, they offer a significant contribution to this rapidly evolving discussion. To fully harness the potential of these innovations, certain fundamental business issues must be addressed. Specifically, a proactive resolution regarding the tax treatment and classification of NFTs is essential to promote their broader adoption beyond just speculative investment. The exact path forward remains uncertain but classifying all digital assets identically – from a tax, legal, or economic standpoint – appears misguided. Taxes and tax planning might not be the most riveting parts of the crypto conversation but they are crucial for the continued development and mainstreaming of digital assets and NFTs.

PART III

Capital Markets, Community, and Marketing

7

Non-Investment Finance in an NFT World

Joan MacLeod Heminway

I INTRODUCTION

Non-fungible tokens (NFTs) – the secure, digital assets minted, sold, and acquired on a blockchain that are the subject matter of this Handbook – have grown in prominence and have received much attention in recent years. Ongoing efforts to modernize investment and other finance transactions have been a motivator of this trend. The deemed efficiencies in and other putative benefits of decentralized, automated funding transactions certainly have superficial appeal. However, the overall efficacy of blockchain finance remains questionable – in part because of unsettled policy and law.

Some of the other chapters in this Handbook focus on the use of NFTs in investment finance – one piece of the NFT finance puzzle – an investment sector that invokes, perhaps most prominently, federal and state securities regulation as an actual or possible constraining force. Although some NFTs may be securities,[1] this chapter addresses the use of NFTs in financing transactions that do not involve the offer or sale of securities. Specifically, the ensuing pages address the use of NFTs in the context of non-profit,[2] as well as political fundraising – financing environments governed by their own distinctive laws and regulations (in addition to more generally applicable transactional laws).

There are several ways in which NFTs can be used to provide non-investment funding for nonprofits or political undertakings. NFTs can be sold to generate

---

[1] *See, for example, Friel v. Dapper Labs, Inc.*, No. 21 CIV. 5837 (VM), 2023 WL 2162747, at *22 (S.D.N.Y. Feb. 22, 2023). ("Plaintiffs adequately allege that Dapper Labs's offer of the NFT, Moments, was an offer of an 'investment contract' and therefore a 'security,' required to be registered with the SEC").

[2] The chapter uses the term "nonprofit" in a broad sense for ease of reference to denote an enterprise organized as a nonprofit business association under state law, most of which would also be qualified as exempt from federal income tax under Section 501(a) of the Internal Revenue Code of 1986, as amended (the "IRC"). 26 U.S.C. § 501(a) (2018). However, the contents of this chapter are most likely to be relevant to organizations exempt from federal income taxes under Section 501(c)(3) of the IRC because they are operated exclusively for charitable or other qualified statutory purposes. 26 U.S.C. § 501(c)(3). References to "charitable" organizations may be read as references to all organizations operated for tax-exempt purposes enumerated in IRC § 501(c)(3).

proceeds that can then be donated or contributed, or NFTs themselves can be donated if the nonprofit or campaign is willing to accept them. But other financing options – ones in which NFTs are more integral to the funding model for a nonprofit or campaign – are being employed with increasing frequency. Many of us have crowdfunded a project or cause in exchange for preferential access to a product or service, or for limited-edition merchandise or unique amenities. NFTs can serve as funding incentives in a similar manner.

With that in mind, this chapter focuses most closely on NFT offerings used to fund nonprofit organizations – especially charitable ventures – and political committees and campaigns. A fund-seeking entity or individual may create their own NFTs for this purpose. However, in current practice, it is more typical for a third-party NFT creator to generate an NFT or series of NFTs for the benefit of an enterprise seeking funding (selling or donating the NFTs to the enterprise for use in fundraising) or for an NFT creator to arrange with the enterprise to designate all or a portion of the proceeds of NFT sales (potentially proceeds from both the minting/initial sale and resale royalties) to the enterprise.

Ultimately, this chapter undertakes to offer a practical and applied legal context for, and related reflections on, this innovative use of NFTs as a matter of finance and law. To accomplish its purposes in the short order this format demands, the chapter begins with a brief précis of non-investment Internet finance – providing relevant background and regulatory context. The chapter then explains the use of NFTs in nonprofit and political fundraising. Finally, before concluding, the chapter offers observations on current legal and regulatory approaches to non-investment finance using NFTs.

II NON-INVESTMENT INTERNET FINANCE

The world of finance is deceptively broad. Individuals and entities require funding for many different types of endeavors, for personal or more broad-based benefit. Funders may be motivated to finance these endeavors in many ways. Taxonomies of the field take many different forms, based on the reference point of the observer. This chapter focuses on finance in the context of initiatives that do not exist to generate profit distributions – or even necessarily value appreciation – for funders. Rather, the finance settings addressed in this chapter relate to mission-focused financial support in the form of non-profit donations and political campaign contributions.

Not all financing of these undertakings occur in the personal, negotiated contexts that exemplify traditional nonprofit and political fundraising. Non-investment finance using NFTs occur in digital environments and may therefore be characterized as a type of Internet finance. A brief review of foundational Internet finance concepts provides useful background.

A Internet Fundraising for Projects and Causes

Not all promoters of endeavors have deep private networks of funders sufficient, when aggregated with other funding sources, to enable their enterprises to take shape, gain traction, and move forward operationally. Accordingly, promoters often seek funding from backers outside their existing networks. Those funders may not be realistically or practically financial institutions. They may be individuals.

Making connections with interested, engaged individual funders is not always easy, especially for start-up or early-stage ventures or for more narrowly focused projects or causes. As a result, intermediaries may be essential to making necessary connections. But finding the right intermediary can also be challenging and the cost of securing the intermediary's services may be prohibitive.

With the World Wide Web's second generation, which is generally referred to as Web 2.0,[3] came the possibility and practicability of raising funds efficiently and effectively online. By combining social media and Internet commerce technologies (including online payment systems), entrepreneurs created online platforms that allow fund-seekers to connect with investors looking for funding opportunities by pointing and clicking. Internet finance – the solicitation of funding through these online platforms – was born and has rapidly increased in popularity since the early years of the twenty-first century.

B Crowdfunding as a Key Touchstone

Internet finance is exemplified by crowdfunding. Crowdfunding can be defined in many ways. For this chapter, crowdfunding is defined as the broad-based solicitation of pecuniary backing from an undifferentiated mass of individuals, typically in small per-investor increments through an Internet-based platform. The fundraisers and funders may identify each other online or offline (although commonly the former) but the funding transaction takes place online.

Crowdfunding encompasses several different kinds of financing: investment (securities), presale, reward-based, and donative.[4] Nonprofit and political fundraising

---

[3] *See, for example,* Margaret Chon, *The Romantic Collective Author,* 14 VAND. J. ENT. & TECH. L. 829, 849 (2012) ("Web 2.0 refers primarily to a collection of digital network technologies that facilitate user-based interaction, in contrast to Web 1.0, which consists mostly of websites that do not allow or promote interactivity of content creation among decentralized Internet user-authors" (citing Roggio, *Will Web3 Change Ecommerce?,* following)); Armando Roggio, *Will Web3 Change Ecommerce?,* PRACTICALECOMMERCE (December 24, 2021), www.practicalecommerce.com/will-web3-change-ecommerce ("Web 2.0 added interactivity and social media. It allowed just about anyone to create and share content. Web2 is what we use now for everything from Facebook to ecommerce. It is the 'read-write' web."); Cecilia Ziniti, *The Optimal Liability System for Online Service Providers: How Zeran v. America Online Got It Right and Web 2.0 Proves It,* 23 BERKELEY TECH. L.J. 583, 591 (2008) (explaining that "[l]oosely defined, Web 2.0 embodies interactive service providers that leverage users' collective intelligence and make the web, not the PC, 'the platform that matters'").

[4] *See, for example,* Steven Bradford, *The New Federal Crowdfunding Exemption: Promise Unfulfilled,* 40 SEC'S REG. L. J. 195, (2012) (describing these forms of crowdfunding); Joan MacLeod Heminway,

using NFTs has specific roots in donative and reward-based crowdfunding, respectively. Donative crowdfunding encompasses the solicitation of financing for a project or undertaking that the funder desires to support with a more altruistic intent. While the donor may be incentivized to give by a specific award (a T-shirt or a hat, for example), their primary desired return is merely the warm glow that they have provided financial backing to a worthy cause. Reward-based crowdfunding involves the solicitation of funding with the promise of a specific non-financial reward in return. For example, a backer may provide financial support to a nascent rock band to fund a set of marketable recordings of its music in return for front-row seats to a local appearance. Both types of crowdfunding operate in similar ways and in ways analogous to NFT finance in the nonprofit and political contexts.

1 Key Practical Aspects and Processes of Crowdfunding

Crowdfunding is relatively simple in operation. Internet platforms are used to match prospective funders with those seeking funding.[5] Promotion typically occurs through a dedicated webpage on the platform (offering information about the entity or individual seeking funding and the nature of the project or cause), and the funding operates much like e-commerce: the platform accepts currency from funders and (after taking a cut for itself) the platform passes along the remaining funds to the fundraiser. The conditions and terms of the exchange are explained on the platform, including in lengthy, standardized terms of use. Back-end payment systems (e.g., PayPal) handle the currency processing.

Non-investment crowdfunding platforms may specialize in particular types of financing. For example, GoFundMe (www.gofundme.com) is a well-established US donative crowdfunding site. Similarly, Kickstarter (www.kickstarter.com) is a well-known US crowdfunding platform that has been a long-standing player in pre-purchase and reward-based crowdfunding.

2 Bedrock Regulation of Crowdfunding

US platforms engaged in interstate investment crowdfunding (multistate crowdfunding involving financial instruments defined as securities) are regulated at

---

Securities Crowdfunding and Investor Protection, 14 CESifo DICE Report 11, 12 (2016), www.cesifo-group.de/ifoHome/publications/docbase/details.html?docId=19235734; Joan MacLeod Heminway, *The Legal Regulation of U.S. Crowdfunding: An Organically Evolving Patchwork*, in Legal Aspects of Crowdfunding 271, 272–275 (C. Kleiner, ed., 2018) (offering a slightly different taxonomy that covers the same types of financing, ordered in accordance with their regulatory context).

5   *See generally* Joan MacLeod Heminway, *Intermediating Crowdfunding: A Foundational Assessment*, in Strategic Approaches to Successful Crowdfunding 34, 34–56 (Djamchid Assadi, ed., 2016) (explaining and categorizing crowdfunding intermediation, including by platforms).

the federal level by the US Securities and Exchange Commission (SEC) and the Financial Industry Regulatory Authority (FINRA). Their activities are constrained by federal securities law. Moreover, they are bound to federal disclosure rules and subject to legal actions and liabilities defined in and under federal securities law.

However, the online intermediation that facilitates non-investment crowdfunding is not regulated by any specific authority. Instead, depending on the type of financing, the platform itself and the activities conducted through it may be regulated under tax and other laws governing charitable solicitations and donations or contracts and other laws relating to commercial transactions. Donative crowdfunding is more typically associated with eleemosynary fundraising that may implicate tax and charitable solicitation regulation, while reward-based crowdfunding is more centrally commercial and primarily engages contract and other commercial regulation (although donative crowdfunding also engages contract law, for example).[6]

III NFTS AND NON-INVESTMENT FINANCE

NFTs are most widely used in non-investment crowdfunding as a funding incentive. In this way, they are much like the T-shirt or hat or event ticket that one may get for donating to a nonprofit or contributing to a political committee or campaign outside the blockchain context. They are a premium or reward for providing financing for the fund-seeking project or cause.

One might logically ask why an NFT has value as a reward for funding. The answer is the same in non-investment finance as it is in other contexts. NFTs have value because the person acquiring them believes they have value. Brian Frye offers some relevant observations:

> The value of an NFT seems to depend primarily on the popularity of the brand it represents. NFT collectors want to own NFTs associated with popular brands and want to associate themselves with those brands. That's why the most popular NFT collections are designed to be used as profile pictures or 'PFPs.' NFT collectors crave the clout of owning a popular NFT and PFP NFTs make it easy to show off.[7]

Frye also suggests that the creator of the NFT matters in valuation because authorship is the basis for legitimacy and legitimacy creates value.[8]

---

[6] *See* Heminway, *The Legal Regulation*, 275–280.
[7] Brian L. Frye, *NFTmarks*, ALTI FORUM (August 15, 2022), https://alti.amsterdam/frye-nftmarks/.
[8] Ibid. ("NFTs collectors value NFTs based on the works of art they represent. However, NFT collectors only value NFTs they consider legitimate, and the perceived legitimacy of an NFT usually depends on who created it").

Similarly, observers note that NFTs, as an avowed Web 3.0 application,[9] create and exemplify a sense of community,[10] which may be especially important in non-investment finance. Those who are attracted by NFT offerings to funding nonprofits and campaigns may be seeking a community of like-minded financial contributors – people who, like them, support a specific kind of project or cause. Discord, a server-based social-connection tool,[11] but also other similar application, may be used to facilitate NFT communities for a variety of purposes.[12] For example:

> NFT projects that want to make a charitable donation will hold a vote among their fans and supporters to choose which nonprofit organization(s) to support. Conversations like these usually happen in digital spaces like Discord or Twitter, where project leaders can engage in a direct dialogue and users easily participate in the discussions.[13]

[9] *See* JoHanna Cox, *Money's Future in Web 3.0*, 19 ABA SciTech Law 12, 13 (2023) ("The Web 3.0 era … incorporates more cryptocurrencies, NFTs, and related items … [U]sers and a broader network of people will direct content and information available on the web"); Orly Lobel, *The Law of the Platform*, 101 Minn. L. Rev. 87, 96 (2016) ("[T]he rise of the platform signifies the third generation of the Internet, Web 3.0, in which technology is transforming the service economy, allowing greater access to offline exchanges for lower prices. In turn, the physical infrastructure of offline markets is itself transformed by the technological infrastructure." (Footnote omitted)).

[10] *See* Joshua A.T. Fairfield, *Making Virtual Things*, 64 Wm. & Mary L. Rev. 1057, 1077–1078 (2023) ("People get involved with cryptocurrency or NFTs, they do not merely invest. And most NFTs find meaning within a community that generates interest in their value." (Footnote omitted)); Stacey M. Lantagne, *Of Disaster Girl and Everydays: How NFTs Invite Challenging Copyright Assumptions Around Creator Support*, 13 Harv. J. Sports & Ent. L. 265, 291 (2022) ("The community aspect drives people to purchase your NFTs out of a desire to support you and belong to your digital community"); Kevin McCoy, *Art and NFTs: Past and Future*, 45 Colum. J.L. & Arts 353, 358 (2022) ("Community is another important aspect of the NFT phenomenon's future. NFTs are going to drive community participation as markers of common interests and common goals"); Mark Radcliffe & Katherine M. Imp, *Top Billing for NFTs*, L.A. Law. 20, 22 (May 2022) ("NFT communities … enable community members to collaborate with the lead artist or other community members, share ideas, provide guidance about a project's 'roadmap,' introduce community members to other projects, and encourage purchases of new works, either of the leading artist or other projects").

[11] *See What Is Discord?*, Discord (May 2022), https://discord.com/safety/360044149331-What-is-Discord; *see also Community Building 101: Curating and Cultivating a Space Using Discord*, Tiltify (August 5, 2021), https://blog.tiltify.com/community-building-101-curating-and-cultivating-a-space-using-discord-6f37b0bc6aaa ("Discord is a free voice, video, and text chat app used by thousands of streamers and organizations worldwide to arrange meet-ups, build communities, exchange ideas, or afford people a space to gather and collaborate. It functions similar to Microsoft Teams, Cisco Jabber, Slack or, AOL Instant Messenger … where people type and share into a chat room real time." (Hypertext link removed)).

[12] Wee Min, *Put on the Spot: Damien Hirst's the Currency and the Future of NFTs*, 26 Va. J.L. & Tech. 1, 20 (2022) ("[T]he ownership of NFTs can create relationships between the NFT owner and the artist as well as among the community of NFT owners through Discord servers."); Michael D. Murray, *NFTs and the Art World – What's Real, and What's Not*, 29 UCLA Ent. L. Rev. 25, 57 n.187 (2022) ("Discord is a social media messaging app that has become popular with the crypto and NFT community in part because it is decentralized and therefore matches the ethos of the blockchain world").

[13] The Giving Block, The Rise of NFT Fundraising 12, https://thegivingblock.com/nft-fundraising-report/ [hereinafter NFT Fundraising].

A blog post affiliated with Numero (https://numero.ai/), an Internet-based tool for campaign fundraising, notes more generally that "one of the less obvious – but more powerful – benefits of using NFTs for campaign fundraising is to help build stronger grassroots communities."[14]

Based on the foregoing, it is clear that the use of NFTs (rather than tangible goods or experiences) as rewards in non-investment Internet finance is designed to attract specific – and likely new – funding audiences.[15] Those audiences may include fans of the artist, NFT collectors more generally, or millennials, for example.[16] As a result, enterprises considering the use of NFTs as financing perks should want to understand relevant facts about their target demographics.

A *The Role of NFTs in Non-Investment Finance*

NFTs can be used to generate donations for nonprofits and political campaigns in several different ways. Among the models observed in (or anticipated based on) research conducted for this chapter, several methods emerged as popular. The models identified are distinguishable primarily based on the relationship between the NFT creator and the nonprofit or campaign seeking funding.

For example, staff of the nonprofit or campaign may create their own NFTs for the enterprise as works-for-hire.[17] The nonprofit or campaign may also commission the creation of NFTs by third parties. The nonprofit or campaign would own the NFTs in either such case and be able to offer them to donors or contributors as a premium or, if and as legally permissible, sell them outright to collectors.

More commonly, nonprofits and campaigns will partner with related or unrelated third parties that create, mint, and sell the NFTs as a funding incentive. A nonprofit or campaign may join with an NFT creator to promote the sale of dedicated NFTs or to conduct an auction on an NFT platform. Alternatively, a platform used by a nonprofit to raise funds through cryptocurrency donations may partner with an

---

14 Brian Forde, *How NFTs Can Help Political Campaigns Build Stronger Communities*, NUMERO (March 16, 2022), https://numero.ai/blog/how-nfts-can-help-political-campaigns-build-stronger-communities/ (hypertext link removed); *see also* Laura Romero & Soo Rin Kim, *Not Just for Artwork, NFTs Are Being Used by Political Candidates to Raise Money, Attract Young Supporters*, ABC NEWS (January 26, 2022), https://abcnews.go.com/Politics/artwork-nfts-political-candidates-raise-money-attract-young/story?id=82445596 (quoting Vanderbilt University Finance Professor Joshua White: "NFTs can build a community where there's this positive feedback loop").

15 THE GIVING BLOCK, NFT FUNDRAISING, 6 ("[C]rypto and NFT donors are a distinct audience from their cash-donating peers, with their own set of values when it comes to personal finance and philanthropy").

16 *See* Nest, *Political Fund Raising and the Use of NFTs*, MEDIUM (May 16, 2023), https://nes-tech.medium.com/political-fund-raising-and-the-use-of-nfts-a5ee2579d313 ("NFTs can potentially attract young voters in the context of political fundraising").

17 One might imagine that few nonprofits or campaigns have NFT artists on staff. Accordingly, this self-generated-NFT model may more likely feature photographic or other graphic images related to the mission or operations of the fund-seeking nonprofit or associated with the campaign candidate.

NFT artist to create, mint, and sell NFTs for the financial benefit of the nonprofit, acting as a relational intermediary.

NFT creators or projects may also independently mint and sell NFTs and establish smart contracts to make donations of sale or royalty proceeds to one or more recipients.[18] Similarly, a collector of NFTs may sell an NFT and designate all or a portion of the cryptocurrency proceeds received to a nonprofit or campaign.[19] Alternatively, a collector may donate an NFT directly to a nonprofit or campaign (assuming the donee will accept an NFT donation).[20] These donative asset transfers are comparable to asset transfers occurring outside the NFT context. However, blockchain technology facilitates the execution of the aggregate transactions necessary to convert the asset into a donation or contribution.

A review of the use of NFTs in nonprofit and campaign finance reveals that nonprofit funding initiatives are more prevalent, more innovative, and more diverse. Although NFTs were used to help generate funding for Texas Democrats and New Jersey Republicans generally,[21] published reports indicate that as few as five political candidates may have used NFTs in their fundraising campaigns. To better illustrate how NFTs have been used to date in non-investment financings, examples of actual fundraising campaigns involving nonprofits and political campaigns may be beneficial.

B *Nonprofit NFT Fundraising*

Fundraising using NFTs has been a growing finance market for nonprofits.[22] "Minting new NFTs can serve as an additional stream for regular ol' fundraising.

---

[18] *See* ibid. ("Artists Matthew Weitzman and David Fugit, together with photographer Jon Luvelli, are partnering on canine NFT collectibles in order to donate proceeds to animal rescue groups such as New York Bully Crew, a charity that rescues pit bulls and other animals in need").

[19] *See* Gary P. Kohn, *NFTs and the Law*, L.A. Law. 18, 21 (Nov. 2021)

   ("New York Mets slugger Pete Alonzo sold an NFT and donated the proceeds to More Than Baseball, a nonprofit supporting minor league baseball players in need of housing, equipment, and nutrition, and to his own charity, Homers for Heroes, whose mission is 'to recognize the outstanding work of our heroes and inspire others to be a hero in others' lives.'" (Footnotes omitted)).

[20] Cryptocurrency donative crowdfunding platform The Giving Block notes in a recent report that "[n]onprofits should be cautious when accepting NFTs themselves as donations, because many organizations have restrictions on accepting property-like assets." The Giving Block, NFT Fundraising, 33; *see also* ibid., 15 ("Accepting an NFT is very different from accepting a typical fiat or cryptocurrency donation").

[21] Gopal Ratnam, *Nonfungible Tokens the New Fad for Campaign Fundraising*, Roll Call (January 4, 2022), https://rollcall.com/2022/01/04/non-fungible-tokens-the-new-fad-for-campaign-fundraising/ ("In October, a group of Democratic fundraisers banded together to launch politically themed NFTs through a marketplace called Front Row to raise money for Texas Democrats."); Fred Snowflack, *The Reason for Laura Ali's Confidence*, Insider NJ (January 24, 2022), www.insidernj.com/reason-laura-alis-confidence/ (describing the forthcoming Morris County Republican Committee NFT fundraising campaign in January 2022).

[22] *See* The Giving Block, Crypto Philanthropy Data, Trends & Predictions 22 (2023), https://go.thegivingblock.com/hubfs/Annual%20Report/2023%20Annual%20Report%20on%20

Someone buys an NFT from your nonprofit – or an NFT artist you've partnered with – and your org receives a donation."[23] Exemplar campaigns illustrate more specifically the ways in which this type of a nonprofit fundraising is conducted.

Corporations may sell NFTs and donate the proceeds of those sales to their associated charitable foundations. For example, through its website www .worldofverabradley.com, Vera Bradley marketed and sold two series of NFTs: The Heritage Pass ("a standardized token featuring dynamic imagery of the iconic Jilly Bag in four heritage prints") and The 1982 Collection ("hand-drawn layers of art that share the same hallmarks as Vera Bradley's prints: optimism, happiness, charm, energy and joy").[24] The website indicates that, through its VB Cares initiative, Vera Bradley, Inc. – a for-profit corporation – was to donate all of the primary net proceeds from the two NFT series to the Vera Bradley Foundation for Breast Cancer, a charitable foundation associated with Vera Bradley Inc.[25] The creators of the NFTs are not disclosed but the NFTs feature images and digital art based on Vera Bradley products and textiles.

Similarly, a year earlier, Taco Bell, a division of for-profit YUM! Brands, Inc., commissioned the creation of five NFTs with fast-food themes.[26] Minted and sold on the Rarible platform (https://rarible.com/tacobell), the Taco Bell NFTs were offered at a price of $1.00 each and sold out in 30 minutes,[27] with proceeds to be donated to the Taco Bell Foundation to support young adults' education initiatives and career-readiness.[28]

The Giving Block (https://thegivingblock.com/), a cryptocurrency fundraising platform for nonprofits, labels financing initiatives like those used by Vera Bradley and Taco Bell "corporate giving partnerships."[29] The Vera Bradley and Taco Bell campaigns were both designed to fund nonprofits associated with those for-profit

---

Crypto%20Philanthropy.pdf? ("In 2021, NFT fundraisers emerged as a trend, and we helped raise tens of millions of dollars for charities via creators auctioning off their web3 artwork … In 2022, NFT philanthropy remained a multimillion dollar philanthropic channel for charities on our platform").

[23] Emily Kostic, *What Could NFTs Mean for Nonprofits?*, Ad Council (March 2, 2022), www .adcouncil.org/all-articles/what-could-nfts-mean-for-nonprofits?.

[24] *Explore the World of Vera Bradley*, Vera Bradley (2022), https://worldofverabradley.com/.

[25] Ibid.

[26] *See, for example*, Mitchell Clark, *The Brands Are at It Again – Taco Bell Is Hopping on the NFT Train*, The Verge (March 8, 2021), www.theverge.com/2021/3/8/22319868/taco-bell-nfts-gif-tacos-sell; Jamie Crawley, *Taco Bell Just Sold a Collection of 5 Fast-Food-Themed NFTs*, CoinDesk (March 9, 2021), www.coindesk.com/business/2021/03/09/taco-bell-just-sold-a-collection-of-5-fast-food-themed-nfts/; David Gianatasio, Taco Bell Draws on the NFT Craze for Digital Art Sale, Muse by Clio (March 11, 2021), https://musebycl.io/art/taco-bell-draws-nft-craze-digital-art-sale.

[27] *See* Clark, *The Brands Are at It Again*; Gianatasio, *Taco Bell Draws on the NFT Craze*.

[28] *See* Clark, *The Brands Are at It Again*; Jamie Crawley, *Taco Bell Just Sold a Collection of 5 Fast-Food-Themed NFTs*, CoinDesk (Mar. 9, 2021, 9:27 AM), www.coindesk.com/business/2021/03/09/taco-bell-just-sold-a-collection-of-5-fast-food-themed-nfts/.

[29] *Nonprofits & NFTs Explained: A New Vision for Charitable Fundraising*, The Giving Block (October 12, 2021), https://thegivingblock.com/resources/nonprofits-nfts-explained-a-new-vision-for-charitable-fundraising/.

businesses. However, The Giving Block notes that corporate donors may also employ this strategy for unrelated nonprofits, offering the Coca-Cola Company's NFT-based fundraising campaign benefitting the Special Olympics as an example.[30] In all of these cases, the corporate partner sells NFTs and donates the proceeds to the nonprofit.

The Coca-Cola campaign was structured as an online auction. NFT auctions are a specific way that nonprofits use the Internet and blockchains to incentivize fundraising. Third parties may conduct auctions on NFT platforms to benefit nonprofits, or nonprofits may conduct their own auctions through NFT platforms if they are legally permitted to sell the NFTs being offered.

The Giving Block offers NFT auction services to nonprofits. An online article explains the concept:

> The most common way of using NFTs for fundraising is no different than how we auction off pieces of art today. The only difference is that these pieces of art live on the blockchain as NFTs. For example, Nifty Gateway sold eight unique pieces donated by artists, and over $6.6 million was raised for the Open Earth Foundation. The new owners of those pieces can prove their ownership via the blockchain.[31]

Thus, NFT auctions for the benefit of nonprofits work much the same way as charitable auctions of nondigital assets. In describing the general process of establishing an NFT auction of this kind, The Giving Block asserts that "[a]n NFT charity auction is one of the most exciting ways to fundraise with NFTs. It requires extensive planning, but the results can often be well worth the effort."[32]

Blockchain-engaged crowdfunding platforms also have been a key partner for nonprofits in their NFT fundraising campaigns. For example, the Panxpan platform (www.panxpan.com) promotes its NFT fundraising services to nonprofits by directly linking them to both traditional nonprofit fundraising and non-NFT Internet financing activities for nonprofits. On its website, Panxpan encourages nonprofits to sign up for its services by noting the expense of traditional giveaways in relation to the generated funds.[33] Later on the homepage, under the heading "Digital Collectible," Panxpan explained how campaigns are executed:

> Give your fundraising participants a digital collectible (NFT) based on their donation tier. Its [sp] something real they can keep, transfer or sell. It also enables all the NFT token gated experiences that you can offer participants.[34]

---

[30] Ibid. ("Recently, Coca-Cola partnered with the 3D artists at Tafi to auction off special-edition NFT 'loot boxes,' resulting in $575,883.61 donated to the Special Olympics." (Emphasis removed)).

[31] *Opinion: 3 Reasons Why NFTs Will Shape the Future of Nonprofit Fundraising*, THE GIVING BLOCK (October 6, 2022), https://thegivingblock.com/resources/opinion-3-reasons-why-nfts-will-shape-the-future-of-nonprofit-fundraising/.

[32] THE GIVING BLOCK, NFT FUNDRAISING, 16.

[33] *Fundraise Using NFTs*, PANXPAN (2023), www.panxpan.com/ ("Many of us have tried chocolates, t-shirts and hats. There are a lot of giveways you can try but they usually take most of the funds raised. Consider using NFTs and access to drive engagement and keep 100% of your funds raised." (Emphasis removed.))

[34] Ibid.

Panxpan's services to nonprofits include establishing a fundraising webpage and creating and managing the NFTs.[35] Panxpan's services, taken together, effectively constitute reward-based crowdfunding using NFTs as the reward.

Nonprofit fundraising using NFTs is not all sunshine and rainbows,[36] however. The World Wildlife Fund (WWF) in the UK discontinued an NFT offering (the "Tokens for Nature" collection) in response to public outcry about the negative environmental effects of the offering.[37] Although the WWF in Germany nevertheless continues to offer its Non-Fungible Animals NFTs,[38] the criticism of that offering is much the same.[39]

C NFT Political Campaign and Committee Finance

Typically, the use of NFTs in political campaign finance is quite straightforward. The campaign uses pre-existing art (or other content), generates NFT content on its own, or contracts for content and creates or purchases the related NFT. The NFT is then offered to campaign contributors at a fixed price or through bidding or another pricing process.

A summary of the five political campaigns identified in the research conducted for this chapter offers a quick snapshot of political campaign finance efforts (Table 7.1).[40]

[35] *See* ibid.

[36] *See Life Isn't All Sunshine and Rainbows*, FREE DICTIONARY (2024), https://idioms .thefreedictionary.com/life+isn%27t+all+sunshine+and+rainbows ("Real life does not just consist of innocent, carefree happiness; there is more hardship or suffering in reality than one realizes").

[37] *See* Justine Calma, *How the World Wildlife Fund Tried – and Failed – to Create an Eco-Friendly NFT*, VERGE (February 8, 2022), www.theverge.com/2022/2/8/22923530/world-wildlife-fund-nft-polygon-layer-2-blockchain-energy-emissions; Rosie Frost, *WWF Decision to Sell NFTs Labelled 'Astonishingly Stupid' by Environmentalists*, EURONEWS (March 20, 2022), www.euronews.com/green/2022/02/03/ wwf-decision-to-sell-nfts-labelled-astonishingly-stupid-by-environmentalists; Adam Hunt, *The World Wildlife Fund Has Canceled Its NFT Project after Only a Day*, TWEAKTOWN (February 10, 2022, updated March 8, 2022), www.tweaktown.com/news/84503/the-world-wildlife-fund-has-canceled-its-nft-project-after-only-day/index.html.

[38] *NFA Non-Fungible Animals – The NFT Campaign by WWF* (2023), https://worldwildlife.net/nft/.

[39] *See* Calma, *How the World Wildlife Fund Tried*; Hunt, *The World Wildlife Fund*.

[40] Information included in the chart was obtained from various news media sources. *See, for example*, Marvelous Akpere, *NFTs to Fund US Election*, CRYPTOTVPLUS (June 21, 222), https:// cryptotvplus.com/2022/06/nfts-to-fund-us-election/; Teresa Mettela, *Political Hopefuls Turn to NFTs to Raise Funds for Midterm Elections*, WALL ST. J. (May 14, 2022), www.wsj.com/articles/political-hopefuls-turn-to-nfts-to-raise-funds-for-midterm-elections-11652520603; Reethu Ravi, *Shrina Kurani is Running for Congress to Teach Average Americans about Web3*, NFTEVENING (December 26, 2021, updated February 1, 2023), https://nftevening.com/shrina-kurani-is-running-for-congress-to-teach-average-americans-about-web3; Felix Salmon, *Exclusive: Colorado Governor Jared Polis Fundraises with NFTs*, AXIOS DENVER (June 13, 2022), www.axios.com/local/denver/2022/06/13/ colorado-governor-jared-polis-fundraises-nfts; Ben Strack, *Congressional Candidate Uses NFTs to Raise Awareness, Funds*, BLOCKWORKS (March 14, 2022), https://blockworks.co/news/congressional-candidate-uses-nfts-to-raise-awareness-funds; Eli Tan, *Candidate for Minnesota Governor Releases Campaign NFTs*, COINDESK (September 1, 2021, updated May 11, 2023), www.coindesk.com/ business/2021/09/01/candidate-for-minnesota-governor-releases-campaign-nfts/; David Thomas, *NFTs Gaining Popularity as Fundraising Method in Election Campaigns*, BEINCRYPTO (January 10, 2022), https://beincrypto.com/nfts-gaining-popularity-as-fundraising-method-in-election-campaigns/.

TABLE 7.1 *NFT political campaigns*

Candidate	State	Party	Office	NFT Offering	Price/NFT	Launch Date
Scott Jensen	Minnesota	Republicans	Governor	Digital images of Jensen at the state fair eating a corn dog or carrying a cow	$5	August 2021
Shrina Kurani (two NFT offerings)	California	Democratic	US House of Representatives	Digital representations of Kurani's crypto policy agenda, including "vision and concept statements"; access to free digital assets from crypto and climate projects, communications with climate experts, and a metaverse Earth Day party	Minimum bid of $200, maximum of $5,800; $1,250 and $5,800	December 2021; March 2022
Blake Masters	Arizona	Republicans	US Senate	Limited edition digital images of early cover art for Masters' coauthored book (with Peter Thiel), *Zero to One*	$5,800	December 2021
Steven Olikara	Wisconsin	Democratic	US Senate	Tokenized portraits of Olikara	$50	March 2022
Jared Polis	Colorado	Democrat	Governor	Digital images of a variety of objects relevant to Polis's candidacy or the state (including sneakers, a chili pepper, mountains, and his dog, Gia, depicted with lasers coming from her eyes)	$52.80	June 2022

The NFTs offered in these campaigns vary in content and price. Some "also come with real-life perks and exclusive access to events, which makes them attractive as campaign offerings."[41]

Political committees also have been experimenting with NFT offerings. In the fall of 2021, NFT platform Front Row sold NFTs for the benefit of the Texas Democratic Party (the Lonestar Collection).[42] In New Jersey, the Morris County GOP has been offering and selling NFTs since the last week of January in 2022.[43] Despite initial optimism about sell-throughs,[44] few NFTs have been sold (although the sales reportedly made a total of $17,500).[45] NFT political donation platforms like Electables, which is a platform that was created "specifically for Democratic campaign grassroots fundraising,"[46] are emerging that are designed to deliver comprehensive NFT fundraising services to campaigns. However, overall, campaign finance NFT platforms and sites have been slow to develop.

There are discernible advantages to using NFTs to encourage donations to political campaigns.[47] Nevertheless, NFT campaign finance is not for everyone.

[41] Laura Romero & Soo Rin Kim, *Not Just for Artwork, NFTs Are Being Used by Political Candidates to Raise Money, Attract Young Supporters*, ABC NEWS (January 26, 2022), https://abcnews.go.com/Politics/artwork-nfts-political-candidates-raise-money-attract-young/story?id=82445596; *see, for example*, ibid. ("[F]or those who purchased Masters' digital tokens, the perks included receiving a signed copy of his book and the opportunity to meet him and his co-author, tech billionaire Peter Thiel, who helped develop the NFT collection." (Hypertext link removed)); Salmon, *Exclusive* ("Polis' NFTs will act as tickets to get donors into events, Brian Forde, CEO of Democratic fundraiser Numero, tells Axios." (Emphasis removed)); Tan, *Candidate for Minnesota Governor* ("Purchasing one of the [Jensen] NFTs unlocks access to a rewards program of prizes throughout the campaign, such as the opportunity to meet Jensen and watch a Minnesota Vikings football game with former Viking Matt Birk").

[42] *See* Ben Davis, *Beeple Is Probably Right That NFTs Will Change Politics. So Far, That Change Is for the Worse*, ARTNET NEWS (February 10, 2022), https://news.artnet.com/opinion/political-nfts-blake-masters-zero-to-one-2070585; Savannah Fortis, *Democratic Party Politicians Turning to NFTs to Raise Funds*, BEINCRYPTO (October 11, 2021), https://beincrypto.com/democratic-party-politicians-turning-nfts-raise-funds/; Rachel Janfaza, *Goodbye Campaign Buttons, Hello NFTs: Democrats Turn to Internet Phenomenon to Raise Money*, CNN (October 15, 2021), www.cnn.com/2021/10/15/politics/democrats-fundraising-nfts-cryptocurrency/index.html#.

[43] *See* Snowflack, *The Reason for Laura Ali's Confidence* (indicating that the NFT fundraising campaign began on Thursday, January 27, 2022); *The First Political Committee to Reward Donors with Limited Edition Digital NFT Collectibles*, MORRIS COUNTY GOP NFTs (2022), https://nft.morrisgop.org/ (Morris County's NFT fundraising site, showing the current status of Morris County's NFT sales).

[44] *See* Snowflack, *The Reason for Laura Ali's Confidence* ("Ali is brimming with confidence. She said she expects all the tokens to be sold by the end of this week").

[45] *See First Political Committee* (substantiating the sale of 11 of 39 MCRC Platinum Club tokens for $1000 each, 16 of 199 MCRC Gold Club tokens for $300 each, 5 of 100 Turn New Jersey Red tokens for $100 each, and 24 of 500 Take Back New Jersey tokens for $50 each, evidencing donations totaling $17,500).

[46] *Grassroots Fundraising with NFTs*, ELECTABLES (2022), www.electables.com/ (*see* Frequently Asked Questions: What is Electables).

[47] *See* ibid. (*see* Frequently Asked Questions: Why Should I Buy an NFT Instead of Making a Regular Donation?: "NFTs … are verifiable proof that you were early and right in your support. They give you access and insight into campaigns … They also are a platform for you to raise with your friends and the results of your collective action"); Nest, *Political Fund Raising* ("NFTs have the potential to revolutionize political fundraising, offering benefits like better perks, easy access, lower costs, and the ability to attract younger voters").

Cautionary notes include regulatory ambiguities, skepticism about NFTs among campaign donors, uncertain connections between candidates and the NFT/crypto community, and distractions from more profitable, efficient campaign fundraising tactics.[48] Although one commentator offers tips for using crypto and NFTs in political campaign finance, he also advises that "most campaigns should not try this."[49]

IV THE LEGAL AND REGULATORY ENVIRONMENT FOR NON-INVESTMENT FINANCE USING NFTS

The law governing NFTs and transactions involving them is contextual and multifaceted. While the use of NFTs in non-investment finance does not (as simply employed) engage the application of federal or state securities law, other general and specialized areas of law may be applicable to NFT offerings based on the nature of the NFT being offered and the circumstances in which the NFT is offered. Nevertheless, there are some basic legal and regulatory systems that impact all non-investment finance conducted through NFT offerings.

The acquisition and disposition of NFTs is, at base, a commercial transaction, as are the accompanying arrangements (including through website terms of use) made by and among the NFT artists, platforms, payment system providers, and others involved in NFT offerings. Accordingly, contract law, commercial law, consumer protection law, federal and state anti-fraud laws of various kinds, and other laws governing asset transfers may apply in regulating conduct and resolving controversies. Because "[a]n NFT represents ... typically 'ownership' of a digital image"[50] or another underlying asset, legal issues, and disputes may also arise under property law, most commonly intellectual property law. Much of this general legal and regulatory ground has been trodden to some extent by those involved with non-investment finance accomplished through donative and reward-based crowdfunding, although the application of these foundational areas of law and regulation in the NFT context may not be straightforward.[51]

US federal and state income tax and election law and regulation also play foundational roles in nonprofit and political finance involving NFTs. The application of state income tax and election laws involves a fifty-state analysis that is beyond the scope of this chapter. Many (but by no means all) state income tax and election laws have similar policy reference points and, therefore, may follow principles established in or under federal law. In some cases, federal law preempts state law.

---

[48] Joe Fuld, *Crypto for Political Campaigns and NFTs for Fundraising*, CAMPAIGN WORKSHOP (April 11, 2022), www.thecampaignworkshop.com/blog/political-campaign/crypto-political-campaigns.
[49] Ibid.
[50] Frye, *NFTmarks*.
[51] *See* Heminway, *Legal Regulations*, 275–80; Lloyd Hitoshi Mayer, *Regulating Charitable Crowdfunding*, 97 IND. L.J. 1375, 1399–1419 (2022) (describing laws currently applicable to charitable crowdfunding).

From a federal income tax perspective, NFTs (as digital representations of rights to various types of assets) are treated as property. Accordingly, the minting, sale, and resale of NFTs may result in taxable income, gain, or loss to the creator or reseller.[52] NFTs may be goods or capital assets, depending on the holder and the context.[53] The US Internal Revenue Service (IRS) has also recently identified NFTs as potential collectibles.[54] Among other things, the sale or exchange of property designated as a collectible under federal tax law and IRS guidance "that is a capital asset held for more than one year is subject to a maximum 28 percent capital gains tax rate (while an asset that is not a collectible is generally subject to a lower maximum long-term capital gains tax rate)."[55]

Although NFT transactions can be executed for cash, they are more typically conducted using cryptocurrencies. Convertible cryptocurrencies typically are considered investment property (and therefore capital assets) under applied IRS guidance:

> A taxpayer generally realizes capital gain or loss on the sale or exchange of virtual currency that is a capital asset in the hands of the taxpayer. For example, stocks, bonds, and other investment property are generally capital assets. A taxpayer generally realizes ordinary gain or loss on the sale or exchange of virtual currency that is not a capital asset in the hands of the taxpayer. Inventory and other property held mainly for sale to customers in a trade or business are examples of property that is not a capital asset.[56]

Thus, if a donor to a nonprofit or contributor to a political campaign or committee is required to convert cryptocurrency into dollars before donating or contributing, the donor will be engaging in a taxable transaction and will be required to pay taxes on any gain, decreasing the probability or value of the donation or contribution. Accordingly, it may behoove nonprofits and political campaigns or committees to position themselves to accept cryptocurrencies as well as dollars if they intend to raise funds through NFT sales or royalty proceeds.

Taxpayers must report the receipt, sale, exchange, gift, or other disposition of digital assets (including NFTs and cryptocurrencies) as well as any income, gain, or

---

[52] *See Digital Assets*, IRS (2023), www.irs.gov/businesses/small-businesses-self-employed/digital-assets.

[53] *See* McDermott Will & Emery, *Taxation of the Purchase and Sale of NFTs* (January 11, 2022), www .mwe.com/insights/taxation-of-the-purchase-and-sale-of-nfts/ ("In the hands of creators of and dealers in NFTs, NFTs are ordinary assets. Such taxpayers have ordinary income and loss on their NFT transactions"); ibid. ("NFTs held by traders, investors, collectors and personal users are treated as capital assets. Short-term capital assets are those that are held for one year or less, while long-term capital assets are held for more than one year").

[54] *See* I.R.S. Notice 2023–27, I.R.B. 634, Treatment of certain nonfungible tokens as collectibles; *IR-2023–50, IRS Issues Guidance, Seeks Comments on Nonfungible Tokens*, IRS (March 21, 2023), www.irs.gov/newsroom/irs-issues-guidance-seeks-comments-on-nonfungible-tokens.

[55] I.R.S. Notice 2023-27, 2023-15 I.R.B. 634.

[56] I.R.S. Notice 2014–16, I.R.B. 938 (*modified in other respects by* I.R.S. Notice 2023-34 I.R.B. 837).

loss from those transactions to the IRS.[57] Separate IRS reporting may be required in connection with certain types of transactions. For example, the transfer of an NFT that constitutes a gift for federal income tax purposes must be reported if the fair market value of the NFT exceeds the then current amount of the donor's applicable annual gift exclusion.[58]

In addition to these generally applicable legal and regulatory principles, there are certain distinctive legal and regulatory regimes impacting NFT fundraising for nonprofits and political campaigns or committees, respectively, that deserve individualized treatment. Summaries of the most significant of these applicable laws and regulations are included below. Because NFT fundraising in these contexts is a relatively recent phenomenon, there is some legal and regulatory uncertainty in this environment.[59] As these and other markets for non-investment NFT finance mature, the legal and regulatory landscape will no doubt become clearer.

A *The Legal Regulation of Nonprofit Fundraising Using NFTs*

The legal regulation of nonprofits is principally a matter of concern under federal and state income tax laws and regulations, state entity laws (which offer nonprofits reliable structure and governance rules through which they may conduct their operations), and for charitable nonprofits, state charitable solicitation laws and regulations. In each case, the nature and role of NFTs in the fundraising drives the application of law and the resulting legal conclusions or questions. Because NFT offerings are linked to nonprofit fundraising in multiple ways, several different types of issues arise, some affecting the donor and others affecting the donee nonprofit.

Federal income tax law, specifically IRC § 501(a),[60] offers the opportunity for nonprofits to qualify for an exemption from the payment of income taxes under specified conditions. Although the precise policy and theory underlying the federal tax exemption are difficult to discern,[61] the law establishes specific types of organizations – based on their essential purpose or function – that qualify for the

---

[57] See *IR-2023-12, IRS: Updates to Question on Digital Assets; Taxpayers Should Continue to Report All Digital Asset Income*, IRS (January 24, 2023), www.irs.gov/newsroom/ irs-updates-to-question-on-digital-assets-taxpayers-should-continue-to-report-all-digital-asset-income.

[58] See *Digital Assets*, IRS, www.irs.gov/businesses/small-businesses-self-employed/digital-assets ("[T]he transfer of property, including a digital asset, as a bona fide gift, requires the filing of Form 709, United States Gift (and Generation-Skipping Transfer) Tax Return if the fair market value of the property, at the time of the transfer, exceeds the donor's annual gift exclusion amount available at the time of the transfer").

[59] See *Taxation of Cryptocurrency and Other Digital Assets*, Bloomberg Tax (April 3, 2023), https:// pro.bloombergtax.com/brief/cryptocurrency-taxation-regulations/ ("Not all digital asset transactions are taxed equally").

[60] 26 U.S.C. § 501(a) (2018).

[61] See, for example, Michael Fricke, *The Case against Income Tax Exemption for Nonprofits*, 89 St. John's L. Rev. 1129, 1138–1153 (2015) (describing the development of the exemption and various theories justifying it).

exemption. Charitable organizations can qualify for the exemption under IRC § 501(c)(3).[62] This body of regulation is separate from, but works in coordination with, state business associations laws governing the organization of nonprofit business entities.

A nonprofit exempt from income taxation under IRC § 501(a) as an organization qualified under IRC § 501(c)(3) that desires to create NFTs and offer them to donors must ensure that this activity is consistent with its tax-qualified purpose or function, which is typically embodied in its organizational chartering document.[63] More broadly, regardless of its federal income tax status, a nonprofit organized as a corporation or other business entity under state statutory law must ensure that its activities relating to NFTs (e.g., creating, minting, offering, selling, transferring, or delivering NFTs) are consistent with its chartered purpose under the state law of its organization.[64] Having said that, absent the constraints of, for example, federal income tax law, nonprofit corporate charters – like those of for-profit corporations – can and sometimes do state a very broad corporate purpose, up to and including any lawful purpose.[65]

Supporters of a charitable organization have a tax incentive to donate NFTs that have appreciated in value to a charitable organization because that donation of appreciated assets, although reportable, would result in no gain realized by the donor under federal income tax law.[66] The donor should be able to take a

---

[62] 26 U.S.C. § 501(c)(3).

[63] *See* 26 C.F.R. § 1.501(c)(3)-1(b)

> ("An organization is organized exclusively for one or more exempt purposes only if its articles of organization …: (a) Limit the purposes of such organization to one or more exempt purposes; and
>
> (b) Do not expressly empower the organization to engage, otherwise than as an insubstantial part of its activities, in activities which in themselves are not in furtherance of one or more exempt purposes.");

THE GIVING BLOCK, NFT FUNDRAISING, 34.

[64] *See* Johnny Rex Buckles, *Curbing (or Not) Foreign Influence on U.S. Politics and Policies through the Federal Taxation of Charities*, 79 MD. L. REV. 590, 622–623 (2020) ("[D]irectors of a nonprofit charitable corporation must not cause the entity to act contrary to its corporate purposes (i.e., directors must obey corporate charters), but amendments to corporate charters, including purposes clauses, are often permitted through compliance with specified internal procedures").

[65] *See* Michael Haber, *The New Activist Non-Profits: Four Models Breaking from the Non-Profit Industrial Complex*, 73 U. MIAMI L. REV. 863, 943 (2019) ("[A]lthough corporations are still not permitted to operate outside of the corporate purposes listed in their charters, it has become increasingly common for state non-profit statutes to permit the incorporation of a non-profit for any lawful purpose, raising the issue of whether anything lawful could ever be ultra vires for an entity with such a broad corporate purpose").

[66] *See generally* McDermott Will & Emery, *NFTs and Charitable Fundraising: Navigating Tax Hurdles* (January 11, 2022), www.mwe.com/insights/nfts-and-charitable-fundraising-navigating-tax-hurdles/ ("Donors who can meet IRS reporting requirements can avoid paying tax on the amount of gain they would otherwise incur if they had sold the appreciated NFT in the market and donated cash to the charity.").

deduction equal to the full value of the NFT, up to any maximum values applicable to the particular.[67] The valuation of NFTs for tax (and other) purposes can, however, be challenging because of volatility in the markets for digital assets.[68]

Given that volatility, a charitable organization that receives an NFT as a direct donation likely would want to sell it rather than hold it.[69] Importantly, all transactions in cryptocurrency are required to be reported to the IRS in US dollars, necessitating a conversion requiring a fair market value assessment, in most cases (since NFTs typically are sold for cryptocurrency).[70] Because the process of receiving and reselling an NFT and converting the proceeds to dollars may be more trouble than it is worth, few nonprofits may decide to accept direct donations of NFTs. They may, however, determine to accept digital asset donations through a third-party provider or donor-advised fund that processes transactions for them.[71]

State charitable solicitation laws may also apply to the use of NFTs in charitable nonprofit fundraising. Although specific requirements vary from state to state, they typically fall into two regulatory types: registration and financial reporting.[72] The application of these laws in the context of charitable nonprofit NFT finance is uncertain. An analogy to donative crowdfunding for charitable organizations is instructive.

Based on state charitable solicitation laws in the US generally applicable to donative crowdfunding for charitable nonprofits, NFT fundraising campaigns conducted by the charitable nonprofit for its own benefit would be most likely to trigger the application of charitable solicitation law.[73] Those conducted by

---

[67] *See* ibid. ("Donors [who are not creators] can receive a deduction for an appreciated NFT's full value up to the percentage cap of their adjusted gross income."); Jennifer Galstad-Lee & Patrick Crosby, *Tax Considerations on Charitable Giving of Cryptoassets*, THE TAX ADVISOR (December 1, 2022), www.thetaxadviser.com/issues/2022/dec/tax-considerations-on-charitable-giving-of-cryptoassets.html ("[T]he donor may claim a deduction if the donation is made to a qualifying charity ... The donor's charitable contribution deduction is subject to certain limitation rules ... depending on the character of the contributed property and the donee charity's use of the donated property, among other things").

[68] *See* Galstad-Lee & Crosby, *Tax Considerations on Charitable Giving* ("[F]iguring out the FMV of cryptoassets can be difficult, depending on the circumstances."); McDermott Will & Emery, *NFTs and Charitable Fundraising* (asking about, e.g., valuation methods and appraisals).

[69] *See, for example,* McDermott Will & Emery, *NFTs and Charitable Fundraising* ("[M]ost charities would want to immediately convert an NFT to cash").

[70] *See* Galstad-Lee & Crosby, *Tax Considerations on Charitable Giving* ("[F]or tax purposes, transactions involving virtual currency must be reported in U.S. dollars. Therefore, taxpayers will be required to determine the FMV of virtual currency in U.S. dollars as of the date of payment or receipt").

[71] *See* ibid.

[72] *See, for example, Charitable Solicitation – Periodic State Reporting,* IRS, www.irs.gov/charities-non-profits/charitable-organizations/charitable-solicitation-periodic-state-reporting; *Charitable Solicitation – State Requirements,* IRS, www.irs.gov/charities-non-profits/charitable-organizations/charitable-solicitation-state-requirements.

[73] *See* Mayer, *Regulating Charitable Crowdfunding,* 1408; *see also* ibid., 1422 ("The easiest case for regulating is when a charity uses crowdfunding to benefit itself").

a compensated third party (including an Internet fundraising platform and its related payment service provider) may also be regulated under these laws.[74] NFT offerings conducted for the benefit of charitable organizations by individuals who are uncompensated for their efforts are least likely to trigger the application of these legal requirements.[75] Overall, "while the definitions of the for-profit participants that are subject to charitable solicitation laws tend to be broad, it is still generally unclear whether either the … platforms or their third-party payment processors fall within them."[76] This is a key area for further regulatory development and attention.

B *The Legal Regulation of Campaign Finance Using NFTs*

Among other things, federal campaign finance laws limit the source and dollar amount of contributions to political campaigns and committees. In a series of decisions over the years, the US Supreme Court has expressed its understanding that these limitations exist, in significant part, to prevent corruption or the appearance of corruption through the exchange of contributions for political influence.[77] The application of campaign finance regulation to NFT fundraising for political campaigns and committees has not yet been fully clarified. The Federal Election Commission (FEC) has issued two relevant advisory opinions but unaddressed concerns remain.

Under a 2014 advisory opinion issued by the FEC, cryptocurrency contributions – the likely scenario in most NFT political fundraising situations – may be lawfully accepted as contributions.[78] Specifically, the FEC determined that bitcoins are "money or anything of value" within the meaning of the Federal Election Campaign Act of 1971, as amended.[79] The FEC concluded that bitcoin contributions may be accepted as proposed in the accompanying request and filings "subject to valuation and reporting procedures similar to those that the Commission has previously

---

[74] *See* ibid., 1409–1410; *see also* ibid., 1423 ("Platforms and third-party payment processors may also be reached by those rules if they apply to for-profit participants in charitable solicitation and the activities engaged in by these parties trigger those rules").

[75] *See* ibid., 1409.

[76] Ibid., 1410–1411; *see also* Perlman & Perlman, *What Nonprofits Should Be Asking about Virtual Currency Regulation and Fundraising*, PERLMAN & PERLMAN (October 11, 2021), https://perlmanandperlman.com/nonprofits-asking-virtual-currency-regulation-fundraising/ (advising charitable organizations that are considering accepting cryptocurrency to ask fundraising platforms whether they are registered as professional fundraisers).

[77] *See Citizens United* v. *Fed. Election Comm'n*, 558 U.S. 310, 345 (2010) ("The *Buckley* Court recognized a 'sufficiently important' governmental interest in 'the prevention of corruption and the appearance of corruption.' This followed from the Court's concern that large contributions could be given 'to secure a political *quid pro quo*'").

[78] F.E.C. Advisory Opinion 2014-02, May 8, 2014, www.fec.gov/files/legal/aos/2014-02/2014-02.pdf.

[79] *See* ibid.; 52 U.S.C. § 30101(8)(A)(i) (2018); 11 C.F.R. § 100.52(a) (2023).

recognized in analogous circumstances."[80] Because the concept of value is important to the application of campaign finance regulation, valuation issues (including market volatility) may arise in applying the law to campaign contributions made in cryptocurrencies or NFTs.[81]

The regulation of third-party service providers also has been a cause for concern addressed in an FEC advisory opinion. NFT-focused political committees and candidates that do not have the wherewithal to create and mint their own NFTs would need to arrange with third parties to provide those services. In December 2022, DataVault Holdings, Inc., a firm that designs and markets NFTs for use by third parties, received an advisory opinion from the FEC confirming the legality under federal election finance law of two business models for selling NFTs to political committees.[82] The question at issue was whether DataVault's proposed conduct of business with political committees resulted in it making unlawful contributions to those political committees.[83] Under both models, DataVault would transfer the NFTs to a political committee to allow it to offer the NFTs to contributors, but it would not be compensated for the NFTs by the political committee until the NFTs are transferred to contributors.[84] "The Commission concludes that DataVault's proposals to provide political committees with NFTs on the same terms that it regularly offers its non-political clients would be a permissible extension of credit by DataVault in the ordinary course of business."[85]

Other legal and regulatory questions about NFT campaign finance stem from the nontransparent nature of blockchain transactions. Concerns include potential foreign influence on politics and illicit contributions made by proxies.[86] Contributions by minors may also be harder to discern or track. Federal law prohibits foreign nationals from contributing to federal, state, or local elections, prohibits one person contributing in the name of another to influence any election for federal office, and prohibits individuals aged seventeen and under from contributing to candidates and donating to political party committees.[87] Effective, standardized compliance processes in these areas are still evolving. Additionally, the mechanics of public enforcement of campaign finance rules in the blockchain context present unique challenges.[88]

---

[80] F.E.C. Advisory Opinion 2014-02, *above*, note 78.

[81] *See, for example*, Noah Briggs, *Does the FEC Have a Plan to Deal with Crypto?*, WHOWHATWHY (April 27, 2023), https://whowhatwhy.org/politics/elections/does-the-fec-have-a-plan-to-deal-with-crypto/.

[82] F.E.C. Advisory Opinion 2022-22, Dec. 15, 2022, www.fec.gov/files/legal/aos/2022-22/2022-22.pdf.

[83] *See* ibid.

[84] *See* ibid.

[85] Ibid.

[86] *See* ibid.

[87] 52 U.S.C. §§ 30121, 30122 & 30126 (2018).

[88] *See* Briggs, *Does the FEC Have a Plan?* ("Cryptocurrency and NFTs have so far outpaced the FEC's rulings on their use by campaigns and political donors making enforcement … difficult").

V CONCLUSION

NFTs are here – perhaps to stay. Nonprofits, political candidates, and political committees have begun using NFTs in financings. NFT-fueled funding in the nonprofit sector is developing and growing faster than NFT usage in campaign finance, with specialized funding platforms emerging. Though the IRS and FEC have begun addressing NFT-related issues, many remain unresolved. For example, NFT valuation difficulties in volatile digital asset markets present challenges to the accurate and complete financial reporting required by both nonprofit and campaign finance regulation. Moreover, the faceless nature of blockchain transactions, including NFT-based financings, complicates adherence to laws requiring transparency in value transfers.[89]

Although efforts currently are underway to look at digital asset regulation more holistically, it is not evident where those efforts might lead. President Biden signed the *Executive Order on Ensuring Responsible Development of Digital Assets* in March 2022 that sets forth related policy (supportive of innovation and risk management) and objectives and directs coordinated executive branch action in response.[90] The executive order notes concerns about transparency, among other things, but not valuation.[91] Six months after release of the executive order, the White House published a fact sheet summarizing progress made to date – the output reflected in nine reports outlining frameworks and policy recommendations.[92] The fact sheet, like the executive order, is general in application overall, but it indicates that "the President will evaluate whether to call upon Congress to amend the Bank Secrecy Act (BSA), anti-tip-off statutes, and laws against unlicensed money transmitting to apply explicitly to digital asset service providers – including digital asset exchanges and NFT platforms."[93] Additionally, both the executive order and the fact sheet mention the importance of private and public enforcement numerous times. Hence, the gross parameters of a legal regulatory path forward are being developed but the precise shape and direction of the path remain to be seen.

---

[89] Daniel Castro, *NFTs: US Policies and Priorities in 2023*, INFO. TECH. & INNOVATION FDN. (April 24, 2023), https://itif.org/publications/2023/04/24/nfts-us-policies-and-priorities-in-2023/.

[90] Exec. Order No. 14067, 87 F.R. 14143 (March 9, 2022), *available at* www.whitehouse.gov/briefing-room/presidential-actions/2022/03/09/executive-order-on-ensuring-responsible-development-of-digital-assets/.

[91] Ibid. ("The United States must ensure appropriate controls and accountability for current and future digital assets systems to promote high standards for transparency, privacy, and security – including through regulatory, governance, and technological measures – that counter illicit activities and preserve or enhance the efficacy of our national security tools").

[92] The White House, *Fact Sheet: White House Releases First-Ever Comprehensive Framework for Responsible Development of Digital Assets* (September 16, 2022), www.whitehouse.gov/briefing-room/statements-releases/2022/09/16/fact-sheet-white-house-releases-first-ever-comprehensive-framework-for-responsible-development-of-digital-assets/.

[93] Ibid.

Despite areas of legal and regulatory uncertainty, nonprofits, political candidates, and political committees may be adopters of NFT fundraising campaigns in greater numbers as time moves forward. Unless and until additional legal frameworks are developed to address the uncertainties, however, compliance and enforcement challenges will persist. These challenges may slow the rate of growth of NFT usage in non-investment finance in the short term as fund seekers, funders, and other market participants test the limits of existing regulation.

8

Asymmetric Information in Blockchain-Based Fundraising

From ICOs to INOs

Ido Sadeh and Moran Ofir

I INTRODUCTION

Blockchain has emerged as a transformative force that has redefined numerous industries. Among its myriad applications, one of the most promising and disruptive is blockchain-based fundraising. Blockchain-based fundraising can be defined broadly as the use of smart contracts and distributed ledger technology (DLT) to raise external capital by issuing cryptoassets. Remarkably, this method is gradually gaining popularity and becoming central in our financial system. While the first blockchain-based fundraising mechanism was conducted in 2013,[1] by 2018, over $21 billion was raised by over 3,000 firms and this number keeps growing at a rapid pace.[2] Similarly, while the first blockchain-based fundraising took the form of an Initial Coin Offering (ICO), over time, new methods of fundraising emerged, ranging from Security Token Offerings (STOs) to Initial Exchange Offerings (IEOs) to fundraising events involving non-fungible tokens (NFTs), often referred to as Initial NFT Offerings (INOs).

Despite offering significant benefits in terms of broader access to finance, reduced transaction costs, and innovative ways to engage with investors, blockchain-based finance has, unfortunately, been extensively exploited by fraudulent issuers engaging in scams.[3] The chapter argues that one of the major enablers of blockchain-based fundraising scams is the substantial asymmetric information present in this market. Issuers tend to publish poor and misleading disclosure documents before their offerings and the quality and integrity of these documents often have little to

---

[1] *See* Laura Shin, *Here's the Man Who Created ICOs and This Is the New Token He's Backing*, FORBES (September 21, 2017), www.forbes.com/sites/laurashin/2017/09/21/heres-the-man-who-created-icos-and-this-is-the-new-token-hes-backing/.

[2] *See generally* Moran Ofir & Ido Sadeh, *ICO vs. IPO: Empirical Findings, Information Asymmetry, and the Appropriate Regulatory Framework*, 53 VAND. L. REV. 525, 527 (2021).

[3] Solidus Labs, *The 2022 Rug Pull Report: Everything You Need to Know about Crypto and DeFi Scams* (December 2022), www.soliduslabs.com/reports/rug-pull-report.

no effect on the success of the fundraising event.[4] Potential reasons for this severe asymmetric information are the absence of standardized disclosure requirements, the lack of traditional information intermediaries (e.g., underwriters), the relatively low technical competence of investors, and the early stage of development at which many blockchain-based ventures are launched.[5]

Against this background, this chapter explores the effectiveness of two mechanisms that can potentially be used to address asymmetric information: signaling and analysts. In well-functioning financial markets, this asymmetric information problem can be overcome, to some extent, through signaling. By disclosing information that signals the quality of their projects, issuers can attract investment from investors who expect the highest net present value. However, this mechanism faces significant limitations in the blockchain finance market.[6] First, investors are often unable to verify signals before investing. Second, signals can be easily produced and replicated at low cost based on the issuer's ideas and visions, rather than on a functioning product or service. Third, signals can be widely disseminated through social media at little cost. Finally, there are currently insufficient legal institutions to penalize biased signals in the blockchain finance market. Combined, these limitations of signaling in the context of blockchain-based finance hinder investors' ability to distinguish between low- and high-quality projects.

Another potential mechanism that can be used is analysts. Given the severe asymmetric information associated with blockchain finance and the limited effectiveness of signaling by issuers, analysts play a particularly important information asymmetric reduction role. They can gather and analyze new information that may not be available to or may be too costly for retail investors to obtain about blockchain-based projects. Additionally, they can verify and interpret issuer disclosures, making the information more accessible to retail investors who may lack the time or expertise required to conduct due diligence on each project. And indeed, consistent with this view, ample evidence from the ICO literature suggests that ratings provided by analysts for blockchain-based projects are significantly and positively associated with various determinants of fundraising success, including the amount raised, quick fundraising, liquidity, and subsequent listing.[7] However, despite their vital role, analysts in the blockchain finance market currently exhibit substantial problems in terms of conflicts of interest, lack of transparency, and competence and expertise.[8] These problems can potentially result in analysts contributing to, rather than reducing, information asymmetry in the market.

---

[4]   *See generally* Ofir & Sadeh, *ICO vs. IPO.*
[5]   *See below,* Section III.A.
[6]   *See below,* subsection III.B; Paul P. Momtaz, *Entrepreneurial Finance and Moral Hazard: Evidence from Token Offerings,* 36 J. Bus. Venturing 1, 5(2022).
[7]   Ofir & Sadeh, *ICO vs. IPO,* 605–609.
[8]   *See below,* subsection III.C.

Against this background – of the severe asymmetric information in the market and the limited effectiveness of signaling, and analysts in reducing this asymmetry – the chapter discusses some high-level policy considerations. These include mandating disclosure requirements, enhancing educational initiatives, and adopting a robust enforcement approach against fraudulent issuers and analysts. These policy considerations play a crucial role in fostering the safe growth of this emerging market and harnessing its potential benefits to investors, issuers, and the market.

The remainder of this chapter is organized as follows. Section II provides a brief overview of the blockchain-based finance market. Section III discusses asymmetric information in this market and signaling and analysts as asymmetric information reduction mechanisms. Section IV discusses policy implications. The chapter ends with a conclusion.

II BLOCKCHAIN-BASED FUNDRAISING

Blockchain-based fundraising involves ventures raising public capital through a crowdfunding event where investors can contribute fiat money or cryptoassets in exchange for newly issued digital tokens. These tokens can represent various rights, such as voting, profit, and consumptive rights (and any combination thereof), and the token sale typically runs for a predefined period set by the issuer. After the initial offerings, the tokens are typically listed on crypto exchanges, such as Binance and Coinbase, where they can be traded on the secondary market for fiat currencies or different types of cryptoassets.[9] This section outlines different methods of blockchain-based fundraising, the general process of issuing cryptoassets, and the promises associated with this method.

A Methods

Blockchain-based fundraising mechanisms can generally be subdivided based on the token type and the degree of involvement of different intermediaries. Tokens issued via blockchain-based fundraising can be either fungible or non-fungible. Fungible tokens are equivalent and indistinguishable. Illustrative examples are Bitcoin and Ether. NFTs, by contrast, are unique and their value is determined by their individual characteristics. NFTs can represent ownership over assets, such as art, songs, and in-game items.[10]

Fundraising events involving NFTs, often referred to as INOs, can take the form of game developers offering tokens that will grant access to specific features in the

---

[9] *See generally* Ofir & Sadeh, *ICO vs. IPO*, 547–551.

[10] *See* Qin Wang et al., *Non-Fungible Token (NFT): Overview, Evaluation, Opportunities and Challenges*, ARXIV 2 (October 25, 2021), https://arxiv.org/abs/2105.07447 (explaining fungible tokens and NFTs).

game or to conversations with developers to provide ongoing inputs on the development of the game.[11] INOs can also be used for non-investment purposes to generate donations for nonprofits and political campaigns.[12] For example, an artist may create and sell a collection of NFTs and designate the proceeds received to a nonprofit organization. The use of NFTs in fundraising is, in a way, distinguishable from traditional fundraising methods in that it offers innovative ways to incentivize engagement among investors and users.

Fundraising events involving fungible tokens more typically resemble traditional fundraisings but can vary based on the rights associated with the issued tokens. For example, offerings of tokens that represent security-like rights or whose value is pegged to traditional securities (e.g., equity) are typically referred to as STOs. Substantively, these offerings are similar to Initial Public Offerings (IPOs) and are typically subject to US federal securities regulations.[13] However, tokens can also represent a right to perform work on the platform and be compensated in exchange for this work (work tokens) or grant access to a service/platform that the issuer will provide (usage tokens). These tokens are often referred to as utility tokens and their offerings as ICOs. Tokens can also come in hybrid forms, representing a combination of security- and consumptive-like rights.[14] Additionally, fungible tokens can represent a fractional ownership of non-fungible assets, such as art. Tokens like these are typically referred to as fractionalized-NFTs.[15]

Blockchain-based fundraising methods can be further classified according to the involvement of intermediaries in the token sale event. ICOs and STOs are typically conducted by a group of founders without the participation of intermediaries. The founders create a smart contract that generates the new token and establishes the fundraising rules, and they manage the token offering themselves. A different method from this is called IEO. IEOs are similar to ICOs in that the creation and distribution of the tokens are codified and governed by smart contracts. However, they differ from ICOs in that the sale of the tokens is managed and governed by a third-party exchange (normally for a fee). IEOs may provide benefits in terms of

---

[11] On INOs, *see generally Only1 Initial NFT Offering*, CoinMarketCap (2022), https://coinmarketcap.com/earn/videos/only1-initial-nft-offering. For a specific example, *see* the NFTs issued by Impact Theory, Founders Key: *What Are the Founders Keys?*, Impact Theory (2024), https://wiki.founderskey.io/impact-theory-founders-keys/what-are-the-founders-keys ("The Founders Keys enhance holders' experiences with many aspects of our ecosystem. Depending on your key tier, that could be access to ad-free content, free or discounted access to our online school Impact Theory University, [and] free or discounted digital collectables").

[12] *See* Chapter 7 of this Handbook.

[13] There are still major differences, however, between these two methods. *See* Ofir & Sadeh, *ICO vs. IPO*.

[14] Ofir & Sadeh, *ICO vs. IPO*, 539–544 (discussing classifications of tokens).

[15] While NFTs are not likely to be deemed as securities, fractionalized-NFTs are fungible and can therefore be considered securities, depending on the facts and circumstances. *See generally* Brian Elzweig & Lawrence J. Trautman, *When Does a Nonfungible Token (NFT) Become a Security?*, 39 Ga. St. U. L. Rev. 295 (2023). (discussing whether and when f-NFTs can be considered securities).

quicker listing and lower operational costs and can potentially reduce asymmetric information, as exchanges would normally conduct due diligence before allowing founders to launch a token using their platform.

Combined, these differences in the token type and involvement of intermediaries in the offerings are important as they determine the applicable regulatory framework and the degree of asymmetric information.

B *Process*

Blockchain-based fundraising mechanisms vary in structure and architecture but generally share a similar process. This section provides a brief overview of the process, covering the steps taken by issuers before, during, and after the fundraising event.

Pre-fundraising. The process begins with the founders or project team conceptualizing their idea or business plan. They then create a detailed white paper that outlines the project's goals, objectives, technical specifications, and the problem it aims to solve. This white paper serves as the primary document for potential investors to understand the project's potential and the terms of the fundraising campaign, analogous to a prospectus.

The next step involves smart contract development. The project team develops a smart contract to govern the issuance and distribution of the tokens. The smart contract defines the rules for token sales, the token price, the total supply, and other relevant parameters. For example, issuers can design smart contracts such that if an investor sends X amount of money (usually in the form of Ether) to the issuer then the investor will automatically receive Y newly issued tokens from the issuer in exchange, where X/Y is the exchange rate that has been fixed *ex ante* in the smart contract.[16]

In parallel, the project team normally engages in marketing and promotional activities to generate interest in their blockchain-based fundraising project. Unlike traditional securities offerings, in blockchain-based fundraising projects, the issuers usually approach potential investors directly, without the involvement of underwriters, by announcing their upcoming offerings on social media platforms. Additionally, it is common for these projects to pay for listings on websites such as ICOBench and Coinschedule – which provide details about upcoming blockchain-based fundraising events – to increase awareness for their projects.

The fundraising event. The fundraising event is when issuers collect contributions from investors. The issuers typically predefine the contribution period: a hard

---

[16] *See* Paul P. Momtaz, Kathrin Rennertseder, & Henning Schröder, *Token Offerings: A Revolution in Corporate Finance?*, 49 Capco Inst. J. Fin. Transformation 32, 33 (2019). Once programmed, the smart contract is deployed on a blockchain system, which tracks and records ownership of the issued tokens, that usually represent ownership in the project or offer specific utilities within the project's ecosystem.

cap, which is the maximum amount of capital the project aims to collect, and a soft cap, which is the minimum amount of funds required for the project to process as planned. The contribution by investors is normally made through the project website. Investors are required to transfer money (either crypto or fiat currencies) to a smart contract address, which in return transfers a predefined amount of tokens to the sender.

Post-fundraising. After the fundraising is complete, the project team may list the tokens on crypto exchanges where investors can buy and sell them freely. In the case of IEO, where the token sale is conducted on a crypto exchange, the tokens typically become tradeable on the secondary market automatically after the conclusion of the fundraising period. Having raised the funds, the project team proceeds with the development and implementation of their project, aligning with the promises made in the white paper. This may include refining the underlying blockchain technology, developing smart contracts to enable new utilities and applications, improving the project's infrastructure and security, and the communication and management of and with stakeholders and token holders.

C *Promises*

Utilizing blockchain and smart contracts for fundraising may appeal to firms for a number of reasons. First, there is a reduction in transaction costs. Creating a new token is a simple and inexpensive process using standard, customizable smart contracts like the ERC20. Issuers can use customizable smart contracts to facilitate fundraising, setting only a few simple parameters such as the exchange rate and accepted currencies. Second, blockchain networks have a global reach, enabling issuers to access a worldwide audience. Third, there is potential for achieving a large user base at an early stage. Tokens can incorporate a combination of profit and consumptive rights, which allows token holders to become consumers, helping the issuer attain a large user base during the financing stage.[17]

Blockchain-based mechanisms offer some benefits to investors, too. First, investors may enjoy liquidity in the early stages of the company. Most blockchain-based projects are in the idea stage.[18] These projects' tokens usually become tradeable within less than three months after the conclusion of the fundraising.[19] This means that investors can easily sell their holdings in the early stages of the firm. Second, investing in blockchain-based projects is easy and cheap. In order to invest

---

[17] Ofir & Sadeh, *ICO vs. IPO*, 544–545 (discussing classifications of tokens).

[18] Ernst & Young, *EY Research: Initial Coin Offerings (ICOs)* 16 (December 2017), *available at* www .ey.com/Publication/vwLUAssets/ey-research-initial-coin-offerings-icos/$File/ey-research-initial-coin-offerings-icos.pdf.

[19] Ofir & Sadeh, *ICO vs. IPO*, 577–579.

in a foreign company through an IPO, a potential investor will probably need to use the services of a broker. In contrast, potential investors in blockchain-based projects only need access to the Internet, making the investment process more accessible and cost-effective.[20]

Combined, these perceived benefits, coupled with the astronomical returns for early investors, with ROIs exceeding 50,000 percent,[21] have let this market grow at a rapid pace. While it is hard to estimate the accurate size of the market due to the lack of reliable data sources, various estimates suggest that blockchain-based finance has already been used by thousands of firms to raise billions of funds.[22]

III ASYMMETRIC INFORMATION IN BLOCKCHAIN-BASED FUNDRAISING

Having understood the concept of blockchain-based fundraising and its potential benefits, this section turns to discuss the problem of asymmetric information in this market. Asymmetric information is a condition associated with financial markets wherein potential investors lack the information required to assess the true quality of the financial product.[23] This condition can potentially create a market for lemons where high-quality companies will be deterred from entering the market.[24] The section begins by emphasizing the significance of asymmetric information within the context of blockchain finance and explores the causes of this asymmetry. It then examines whether and to what extent signaling and analysts can be used to mitigate asymmetric information and emphasizes the limitations of these devices in the blockchain finance context.

---

[20] *ICOs vs. STOs vs. IPOs in crypto: Key differences explained*, COINTELEGRAPH (2024), https:// cointelegraph.com/learn/icos-vs-stos-vs-ipos-in-crypto-key-differences-explained. For a more general discussion of the promises and perils brought by fintech, including blockchain, *see* Moran Ofir & Ido Sadeh, *The Rise of FinTech: Promises, Perils, and Challenges, in* LEADING LEGAL DISRUPTION: ARTIFICIAL INTELLIGENCE AND A TOOLKIT FOR LAWYERS AND THE LAW 267 (Giuseppina D'Agostin et al., eds., 2021); Moran Ofir & Ido Sadeh, *More of the Same or Real Transformation: Does FinTech Warrant New Regulation?*, 21 HOUS. BUS. & TAX L.J. 101 (2021).

[21] *Top 10 ICOs with the Biggest ROI*, COINTELEGRAPH (2023), cointelegraph.com/ico-101/top-10-icos-with-the-biggest-roi#10-qtum–9225-roi; Coin and Crypto, *Early Investors Are Making 50,000% Returns on ICOs*, HACKER NOON (December 5, 2017), hackernoon.com/investors-are-making-50-000-returns-on-icos-32432bc741d1.

[22] *See* Ofir & Sadeh, *ICO vs. IPO*, 553–554.

[23] *See* George A. Akerlof, *The Market for "Lemons": Quality Uncertainty and the Market Mechanism*, 84 Q. J. ECON. 488 (1970).

[24] Asymmetric information is often used as a framework for analyzing fundraising mechanisms in various contexts ranging from Initial Public Offerings to Crowdfunding. *See, for example,* Boyd D. Cohen & Thomas J. Dean, *Information Asymmetry and Investor Valuation of IPOs: Top Management Team Legitimacy As a Capital Market Signal*, 26 STRATEGIC MGMT. J. 683 (2005); Gerrit K.C. Ahlers, Douglas Cumming, Christina Gunther, & Denis Schweizer, *Signaling in Equity Crowdfunding*, 39 ENTREPRENEURSHIP THEORY & PRAC. 955 (2015).

A *Sources of Uncertainty*

The problem of asymmetric information in blockchain-based fundraising is more acute than in traditional financial markets (e.g., the IPO market) for three main reasons.[25] First, the absence of standard and tailored disclosure requirements. While securities issuers are subject to disclosure requirements (e.g., prospectus), issuers of non-security cryptoassets are normally not subject to standard disclosure requirements and tend to publish white papers that appear to be overwhelmingly poor and misleading.[26] Even when cryptoassets issuers are subject to disclosure requirements pursuant to securities regulation (i.e., when the issued cryptoassets are securities), the asymmetric information still remains relatively high due to limited relevance of existing disclosure requirements to the nature of blockchain-based fundraising. Cryptoasset projects rely on different types of business models than security issuers, are launched at different degrees of maturity, introduce new risks and concerns not necessarily involved in security offerings, and the valuation of cryptoassets relies on factors not necessarily captured by existing disclosure regulations (e.g., network effect).[27]

Second, investors often lack the technological competence required to assess the quality of blockchain-based projects. To assess the quality and feasibility of blockchain-based projects, investors need to be able to evaluate the quality and integrity of the underlying source codes of these projects. However, evidence suggests they are normally unable to do so. For example, one empirical study found that mismatches between the promises made in ICOs' white papers and the actual software code with regard to the implementation of lock-up mechanisms and the ability of the founders to create new cryptoassets in the future did not significantly affect ICO success, implying that investors were unable to identify such mismatches.[28] Another piece of evidence that supports this assertion is the 2022 Rug Pull Report, by Solidus Labs, which finds that hard rug pull (where the issuer programs the issued cryptoassets to enable them to steal from investors, for example, by allowing them to mint unlimited cryptoassets or hide the change in the

---

[25] *See* Christian Fisch, *Initial Coin Offerings (ICOs) to Finance New Ventures*, 34 J. Bus. Venturing 1, 6 (2019) (discussing sources of asymmetric information in ICOs).

[26] Ofir & Sadeh, *ICO vs. IPO*, at 562–564 (reviewing empirical studies that document poor and misleading disclosure by ICO issuers and that such inefficiencies often do not correlate with ICO success). While in most jurisdictions issuers of non-security cryptoassets are not regulated, it is worth noting that the EU Regulation on Markets in Crypto-Assets, and amending Directive (EU) 2019/1937 (MiCA) contains a tailored disclosure regime that applies to such issuers.

[27] Yuliya Guseva, *When the Means Undermine the End: The Leviathan of Securities Law and Enforcement in Digital-Asset Markets*, 5 Stan. J. Blockchain L. & Pol'y 1, 51 (2022). For a more general analysis of regulatory arbitrage, *see* Ronit Levine-Schnur & Moran Ofir, *Who Shares the Sharing Economy?* 32 S. Cal. Interdisc. L.J. 593 (2023).

[28]   Shaanan Cohney, David Hoffman, Jeremy Sklaroff, & David Wishnick, *Coin-Operated Capitalism*, 119 Colum. L. Rev. 591 (2019).

transaction fees) is highly prevalent in the crypto finance industry and in most cases goes undetected.[29] Instead of assessing the quality of the code, it seems that investors tend to rely on low impact, easy-to-extract signals, such as the mere disclosure of the source code of the project prior to the fundraising.[30]

Third, cryptoassets projects are usually launched at very early stages when there is essentially nothing but an idea, a white paper, and a group of founders.[31] This means that, in contrast to companies launching securities through IPOs, issuers of cryptoassets normally do not have financial records and operational tracks that can be analyzed by investors. Consequently, the information asymmetric and uncertainty in blockchain-based fundraising tend to be higher relative to traditional fundraising methods, such as IPOs.

Fourth, is the absence of traditional intermediaries, such as underwriters, which are used to reduce asymmetric information in traditional finance markets. In an IPO, underwriters reduce asymmetric information by reducing the cost of verifying information produced by issuers and by renting their reputation to issuers. Unlike issuers, underwriters are repeated players in the market, which means they have a vested interest in maintaining their reputation and credibility with investors and thus have a stronger incentive than issuers to ensure that the information provided by issuers they support is accurate and unbiased.[32]

While the level of asymmetric information in blockchain-based fundraising is generally higher than in traditional fundraising methods, it can vary between different types of blockchain-based fundraising mechanisms. For example, security token issuances are subject to heavy disclosure requirements by securities regulators and hence would likely involve a lower degree of asymmetric information relative to issuances of non-security tokens. Similarly, tokens issued through IEO, with the involvement of crypto exchanges that conduct due diligence prior to the offering, are also likely to involve a relatively low degree of asymmetric information.

---

[29] Solidus Labs, *The 2022 Rug Pull Report: Everything You Need to Know about Crypto and DeFi Scams* (December 2022), www.soliduslabs.com/reports/rug-pull-report.

[30] Ofir & Sadeh, *ICO vs. IPO*, 562–564 (reviewing empirical studies that find that the disclosure of the source code prior to the fundraising is associated with success); Shaanan Cohney, David Hoffman, Jeremy Sklaroff, & David Wishnick, *Coin-Operated Capitalism*, 119 COLUM. L. REV. 591 (2019) (comparing the promises made in the disclosure documents with the actual functionality of the digital tokens for the top fifty ICOs that raised the most capital in 2017 and finding that many have failed to meet their promises).

[31] For example, a 2017 study found that most ICOs are in the idea stage, and their platforms/services are expected to be launched in a year or more after the ICO. *See* ERNST & YOUNG, EY RESEARCH: INITIAL COIN OFFERINGS16 (December 2017), https://assets.ey.com/content/dam/ey-sites/ey-com/en_gl/topics/banking-and-capital-markets/ey-research-initial-coin-offerings-icos.pdf. *See* Ofir & Sadeh, *ICO vs. IPO*, 546–547.

[32] Momtaz, *Entrepreneurial Finance*, 4.

B *Mitigating Asymmetric Information through Signaling*

Signaling theory was originally developed in the context of labor markets to examine how high-quality job candidates can distinguish themselves from low-quality candidates.[33] In the context of financial markets, signaling theory examines how high-quality ventures can distinguish themselves from low-quality firms by sending signals about the venture's true quality.[34]

For signaling to be effective in reducing asymmetric information, two conditions must be met: the signal needs to be observable and costly to realize and imitate. Under the assumption that equivalent signals incur different costs for ventures of different quality, high-quality signalers (firms) would be able to produce signals that would be too costly for low-quality signalers to convey, enabling high-quality signalers to distinguish themselves from low-quality signalers.[35]

Given the high asymmetric information in blockchain-based fundraising and the great variation in the quality of the project, signaling appears to be a promising device to mitigate asymmetric information in blockchain-based finance. And indeed, there are some anecdotal pieces of evidence that suggest that signaling can be useful, at least to some extent, in this context. For example, evidence from the ICO literature suggests that the quality and informativeness of white papers are generally associated with determinants of success, such as the amount raised in the fundraising and liquidity of the issued tokens.[36] Similarly, empirical papers from the ICO literature find that the fraction of tokens retained by issuers is positively associated with fundraising success, suggesting that signaling through risk-bearing can be effective in this context.[37]

Despite this anecdotal evidence, which suggests that signaling through informative disclosure and risk bearing is associated with success in the fundraising event, signaling in the context of blockchain finance faces some substantial limitations and it is unclear to what extent it actually helps investors distinguish between low- and high-quality projects.

---

[33] *See* Michael Spence, *Job Market Signaling*, 87 Q.J. ECON. 355, 355–361 (1973) (outlining the signaling theory as it applies to labor markets).

[34] *See, for example,* Trevis Certo, Catherine M. Daily & Dan R. Dalton, *Signaling Firm Value through Board Structure: An Investigation of Initial Public Offerings*, 26 ENTREPRENEURSHIP: THEORY & PRAC. 33, 36 (2001) (explaining the application of signaling theory to the incentives a firm's board of directors has at the IPO stage). In the context of crowdfunding, *see* Ahlers et al., *Signaling in Equity Crowdfunding*, 956–964 (describing how signaling theory works in crowdfunding ventures). In the context of ICOs, *see* Fisch, *Initial Coin Offerings*, 5–8 (discussing how signaling theory can apply to the ICO market).

[35] See generally Brian L. Connelly et al., *Signaling Theory: A Review and Assessment*, 37 J. MGMT. 37, 43–45 (2011). In the context of ICOs, *see* Fisch, *Initial Coin Offerings*, 5.

[36] Ofir & Sadeh, *ICO vs. IPO*, 557–558.

[37] Ofir & Sadeh, *ICO vs. IPO*, 559–560. In the context of IPO, *see also* Richard Brealey, Hayne E. Leland, & David H. Pyle, *Informational Asymmetries, Financial Structure, and Financial Intermediation*, 32 J. FIN. 371 (1977). In the context of ICO, see Jiri Chod & Evgeny Lyandres, *A Theory of ICOs: Diversification, Agency, and Information Failure*, 67 MGMT. SCI. 5969 (2021).

The first limitation is that investors appear to be unable to verify signals *ex ante*.[38] For example, evidence from the ICO literature suggests that the disclosure of information that should, in theory, signal quality – for example, the disclosure of the applicable laws, the jurisdiction where the founders operate, the project's risk, and the use of proceeds – tend to have little to no effect on ICO success.[39] Other relevant evidence here comes from a paper by Cohney et al.[40] Based on a sample of the largest 50 ICO in 2017, they show that issuers make false promises in their white papers – promising to implement lock-up mechanisms and a restriction on the ability to create new tokens in the future but fail to code it – and that these mismatches have little to no effect on ICO success.[41] Relatedly, a more recent study analyzes ICO white papers using text-mining algorithms and finds that issuers tend to exaggerate the information disclosed in white papers and that exaggerated projects raise more funds in significantly less time.[42] Combined, this evidence suggests that the ability of investors in blockchain-based fundraising to verify signals *ex ante* is highly limited.

There are many potential explanations for this observation. One could be that, as noted above, retail investors may not possess the technological competence required to evaluate cryptoasset offerings. Furthermore, due to the high number of offerings that occurred each day, with more than three offerings taking place at times, retail investors may not have sufficient time to acquire enough knowledge about each offering.[43] Another potential reason is that the astronomical returns for early investors, with ROIs exceeding 50,000 percent,[44] have created a Fear Of Missing Out ("FOMO") and led investors to irrationally ignore red flags.[45]

The second limitation is that it is relatively inexpensive to produce (and thus imitate) and disseminate signals in the blockchain finance context.[46] As noted, blockchain-based ventures are normally launched at a very early stage when they have nothing but an idea and a team. Producing signals about the quality of an idea is easier and cheaper relative to producing signals about the quality of a product or service. On top of that, signals in the blockchain finance context are disseminated exclusively through social media, making the distribution of signals inexpensive.[47]

---

[38] *See* Momtaz, *Entrepreneurial Finance*, 5.

[39] Ofir & Sadeh, *ICO vs. IPO*, 585.

[40] Shaanan Cohney et al., *Coin-Operated Capitalism*, 119 COLUM. L. REV. 591 (2019).

[41] Ibid.

[42] *See* Momtaz, Entrepreneurial Finance (it is worth noting, however, that this study also finds that the biased signals backfire once investors learn about the bias when the tokens become tradeable on the secondary market).

[43] Ibid., 20.

[44] *See Top 10 ICOs with the Biggest ROI.*

[45] Momtaz, Entrepreneurial Finance, 20.

[46] Ibid.

[47] Ibid.

The third limitation is that biased signals often go unpunished.[48] The regulation of blockchain-based fundraising is yet unsettled. Some tokens may be considered securities and subject to securities regulations, while others may combine utility and share-like rights, or solely have utility rights, resulting in their public offerings being largely unregulated. Furthermore, even when legal action is possible, the anonymity provided by blockchain and jurisdictional challenges stemming from the global nature of the blockchain-based finance market can make it difficult to hold issuers accountable for sending biased signals. Finally, while the market can punish issuers for sending biased signals – and indeed, anecdotal evidence suggests that, in some cases, biased signals backfire once investors learn about the bias when the tokens become tradeable on the secondary market – issuers who are not repeated players and are solely motivated by fraudulent fundraising and subsequent disappearance are unlikely to be dissuaded by these consequences.

Combined – the limited ability of investors to verify signals *ex ante*, the relative ease of imitating signals (as most signals are based on the issuers' idea and visions, rather than a functioning product or services), the rather low costs of disseminating signals (e.g., through social media), and the current limited ability of legal institutions to penalize biased signals – create a moral hazard problem. Issuers are incentivized to engage in opportunistic behavior and use biased signals to their advantage. This theory is supported by evidence that suggests that cryptoasset issuers tend to exaggerate the information disclosed in their white papers and that exaggerated projects attract substantially more funding in significantly less time.[49]

C *Mitigating Asymmetric Information through Analysts*

Another mechanism that can potentially help to mitigate the asymmetric information in the blockchain ecosystem is intermediaries, such as rating websites and aggregators. These websites usually list upcoming blockchain-based fundraising events on their websites and frequently also assign a rating and/or an analysis of these projects.[50] They do so in exchange for fees paid by the issuers. Considering the high asymmetric information in the market, the limited effectiveness of signaling, and the absence of traditional asymmetric information reduction intermediaries (e.g., underwriters), these websites can play a vital intermediary role in the market. They can reduce asymmetric information by screening the information disclosure of blockchain projects and signaling and making it more accessible to unsophisticated investors, for whom conducting

---

[48] Ibid.

[49] Momtaz, Entrepreneurial Finance (however, the study also finds that exaggerating information ultimately results in negative long-term outcomes such as price reduction and increased volatility during the first month of trading).

[50] Dmitri Boreiko & Gioia Vidusso, *New Blockchain Intermediaries: Do ICO Rating Websites Do Their Job Well?*, 21 J. ALTERNATIVE INV. 67 (2019).

due diligence on each project might be too costly. And indeed, ample evidence from the ICO literature suggests that analysts' rating is significantly and positively associated with fundraising success.[51]

That being said, there are currently several problems with these websites that hinder their ability to efficiently reduce asymmetric information. First are biased ratings and the popularity of the pay-to-play business model. Commentators suggest that it is uncommon for analysts to accept payment for better ratings without conducting serious due diligence, and that analysts likely produce biased ratings for self-serving reasons (e.g., to subsequently get hired as advisors in such projects).[52] Consistent with this view, one empirical study found that analysts' rating is only associated with fundraising success but not with future performance (e.g., liquidity).[53] Second is the (low) quality of the due diligence. To start, evidence suggests that analysts tend to over-rely on easy-to-extract variables (e.g., team size and number of social media channels) and overlook the actual content and quality of the white paper.[54] Relatedly, evidence suggests that analysts systematically disregard the technological aspects of the projects (e.g., the quality of the source code or the underlying blockchain).[55] These pieces of evidence can be explained, at least in part, by the lack of formal expert accreditation in this space, which means that the ratings and analyses the rating websites provide can be done by analysts with little to no competence and expertise.[56] Finally, rating websites are often not transparent about their evaluation process. For example, an empirical study that analyzed twenty-eight rating websites found that only six provided information about their evaluation process.[57]

Despite these flaws, investors appear to value the ratings and information provided by these websites and evidence suggests that these ratings tend to be significantly and positively associated with fundraising success.[58] This means that, despite

---

[51] For an overview of the evidence, see Ofir & Sadeh, *ICO vs. IPO*, 587–588.

[52] *See, for example*, Markus Hartmann, *This Is How Easy It Is to Buy ICO Ratings – An Investigation*, MEDIUM (June 14, 2018), medium.com/alethena/this-is-how-easy-it-is-to-buy-ico-ratings-an-investigation-13d07e987394; David Florysiak & Alexander Schandlbauer, *Experts or Charlatans? ICO Analysts and White Paper Informativeness*, 139 J. BANK. FIN. 1 (2022) (claiming that analysts are likely to produce positive biased reviews to increase their chances of getting hired as advisors in successful projects).

[53] Ibid.

[54] *See* David Florysiak & Alexander Schandlbauer, *The Information Content of ICO White Papers* (June 21, 2019) (unpublished manuscript), https://papers.ssrn.com/sol3/papers.cfm?abstract_id=3265007.

[55] For example, a study that analyzed twenty-eight websites that offered ICO evaluations found that none of them provided "technical information regarding the underlying blockchain infrastructure that a startup project builds upon." *See* Felix Hartmann, Xiaofeng Wang, & Maria Ilaria Lunesu, *Evaluation of Initial Cryptoasset Offerings: The State of the Practice*, 1 2018 INT'L WORKSHOP ON BLOCKCHAIN ORIENTED SOFTWARE ENGINEERING 33, 36 (2018).

[56] David Florysiak & Alexander Schandlbauer, *Experts or Charlatans? ICO Analysts and White Paper Informativeness*, 139 J. BANK. FIN. 1, 2 (2022).

[57] Felix Hartmann, Xiaofeng Wang, & Maria Ilaria Lunesu, *Evaluation of Initial Cryptoasset Offerings: The State of the Practice*, 1 2018 INT'L WORKSHOP ON BLOCKCHAIN ORIENTED SOFTWARE ENGINEERING 33, 36 (2018).

[58] For an overview of the evidence, *see* Ofir & Sadeh, *ICO vs. IPO*, 587–588.

their potential, the rating websites can actually hinder information asymmetric reduction by distracting from non-biased, informative signals, such as white paper informativeness.[59]

To summarize, this section argues that rating websites play a vital intermediary role in the blockchain finance market, but their effectiveness in mitigating asymmetric information is limited. These websites reduce informational asymmetry to some extent, by processing easy-to-extract information about blockchain-based projects and making it more accessible to investors. However, they appear to overlook complex, technical information, and in some cases be biased, incompetent, and not transparent.

IV POLICY

Overall, our analysis suggests that asymmetric information, and related moral hazard problems, are acute market frictions in the blockchain-based fundraising market and that the effectiveness of singling and analysts in mitigating these problems is limited. This section discusses the high-level policy implications of these observations.

A Mandating Tailored Disclosure Requirements

As a starting point, a promising way to increase the effectiveness of both signaling and analysts in reducing asymmetric information in the blockchain finance market is to mandate and tailor disclosure requirements for issuers of cryptoassets. Mandating tailored disclosure requirements may increase the effectiveness of signaling, by making it more expensive for issuers to produce and disseminate signals, and for analysts, by reducing the costs of obtaining, comparing, and analyzing information produced by issuers.[60] It could also help to reduce asymmetric information by signaling to both issuers and analysts as to what are the important factors that should be disclosed to investors.

To illustrate the necessity of this proposal and how it can be implemented, it is useful to use the US market and the regulation of disclosure of cryptoassets offerings by the US Securities and Exchange Commission (SEC) as an example. The US regime faces two main problems.

First, most cryptoasset issuers are either not subject to disclosure requirements or manage to avoid disclosure requirements by opting for private placements. Offerings and sales of non-security cryptoassets are not subject to disclosure requirements under federal securities laws. Offerings and sales of security cryptoassets are subject to disclosure requirements under federal securities laws, but

---

[59] David Florysiak & Alexander Schandlbauer, *Experts or Charlatans? ICO Analysts and White Paper Informativeness*, 139 J. BANK. FIN. 1 (2022).

[60] *See generally* John C. Coffee Jr., *Market Failure and the Economic Case for a Mandatory Disclosure System*, 70 VA. L. REV. 717 (1984).

most issuers opt for private placements under which they are subject only to minimal disclosure requirements. An empirical analysis of crypto issuers filing with the SEC between 2017 and 2021 found that crypto issuers are hesitant to pursue public offerings (Form S-1 and Form F-1 filings) or "mini-public" offerings under Regulation A (Form 1-A filings), with only three Form 1-A filings and one Form F-1 being declared effective by the SEC out of a total of 262.[61] Instead, the majority of crypto issuers prefer to pursue private placements, most commonly Reg D.[62] A potential reason for this reluctance is that existing registration regimes may not be well suited for crypto. The financial and opportunity costs associated with registration are often too high for small crypto issuers and the benefits may not justify the investment.[63] Furthermore, in some cases, such as when launching an open-source, decentralized blockchain-based project, ongoing disclosure requirements might make little sense because the issuers would not have superior access to material non-public information following the launch.[64] The consequence of crypto issuers avoiding registration and opting for private placements is that investors and analysts are provided with less information.[65]

Second, even when crypto issuers are subject to mandatory disclosure requirements, these disclosure requirements often fail to capture the novelty of blockchain-based projects. Cryptoassets rely on novel business models, are launched at different degrees of maturity than traditional offerings, introduce new risks and concerns not necessarily involved in security offerings (e.g., code integrity), and their valuation may rely on factors that might already be publicly available and outside the issuers' control, such as network effect, user adoption, and developers activity (in the case of open source projects).[66] Accordingly, the effectiveness and fitness of existing disclosure requirements to cryptoasset sales and offerings are limited.

Mandating tailored disclosure requirements can potentially address these problems and reduce the asymmetric information problem in the market by ensuring both that more issuers are providing disclosure and that issuers are providing more relevant disclosure. The disclosure regime of cryptoasset offerings should be designed in a way that complying with it is more cost-effective for issuers than registering or avoiding registering with the SEC. An example of a regime that goes in this direction is Commissioner Peirce's 2021 Token Safe Harbor Proposal ("Proposal").[67]

---

[61] *See* Guseva, *When the Means Undermine the End.*

[62] Ibid.

[63] Ibid., 21–28; Ofir & Sadeh, *ICO vs. IPO,* 590–592.

[64] *See* Guseva, *When the Means Undermine the End,* 34–36.

[65] *See generally* HESTER M. PEIRCE, REMARKS AT THE SECURITIES REGULATION INSTITUTE, 47TH ANNUAL, SAN DIEGO, CALIFORNIA (January 30, 2020), available at www.sec.gov/news/speech/crenshaw-remarks-securities-regulation-institute-013023.

[66] Guseva, *When the Means Undermine the End,* 51.

[67] Which formed the basis for the Clarity for Digital Tokens Act of 2021. Hester M. Peirce, Comm'r, SEC, Token Safe Harbor Proposal 2.0 (Apr. 13, 2021), www.sec.gov/news/public-statement/peirce-statement-token-safe-harbor-proposal-2.0.

The Proposal sets out a safe harbor exemption from the Securities Act of 1933 for "any offer, sale, or transaction involving a cryptoassets" (including offerings and sales of non-security tokens).[68] The safe harbor would last for three years after the conclusion of the crowdfunding event, during which time issuers "can facilitate participation in, and the continued development of, a functional or decentralized network, exempt from the registration provisions of the federal securities laws so long as certain conditions are met."[69] By the end of this period, if the issuer developed a functional or decentralized network, exempted from the registration provisions of the federal securities laws, the issuer can exit the temporary safe harbor by filing an exit report accompanied by an opinion by outside counsel concerning network maturity.[70] Otherwise, if the issuer failed to do so, it would be required to fully comply with the disclosure requirements applying to securities offerings under federal securities laws.[71]

The Proposal can potentially solve the issue of crypto issuers evading registration and opting for private placements that provide minimal disclosure because complying with the safe harbor requirements is expected to be more cost-effective than registering with the SEC.[72] It may also benefit issuers of non-security tokens by reducing regulatory uncertainty. Due to the lack of clear regulation and an agreed-upon classification of cryptoassets, issuers are currently facing uncertainty as to whether their assets would be considered securities by the SEC. By complying with the safe harbor, issuers can reduce this uncertainty, making it an attractive option for them. This outcome would also be beneficial for investors as it would require such issuers – who are otherwise not required to provide any disclosure – to produce disclosures for a period of three years. Finally, the Proposal also regulates the content of the disclosure and mandates the disclosure of items such as the source code of the project, transaction history, token economics, token supply, and the ability to create new tokens,[73] thereby ensuring that both analysts and investors are provided with more relevant information.

To summarize, this section argues that mandating tailored disclosure on crypto issuers might help to reduce asymmetric information in the market by making signaling more effective and reducing costs for analysts. It uses the US regime as an example to illustrate the necessity of mandatory tailored disclosure, as well as how such a disclosure regime can be implemented. To clarify, the chapter does not aim to provide a throughout analysis of the Proposal or advocate its adoption. Rather, it seeks to illustrate how a mandatory tailored disclosure regime can be implemented in the blockchain finance context, taking into account the frictions identified in this chapter.

---

[68] Ibid., section (a).
[69] Ibid.
[70] Ibid., section (f).
[71] Ibid., section (f)(3)(c).
[72] *See* Guseva, When the Means Undermine the End, 50–51.
[73] *See* Proposal, section (b).

B *Strengthening Enforcement Efforts*

Our analysis reiterates the need for clear regulation and a robust enforcement approach against fraudulent crypto issuers and analysts. In the current state of the market, issuers are incentivized to send biased signals as doing so is associated with attracting more funds in significantly less time. Furthermore, the pay-to-rate structure of crypto analysts creates substantial conflicts of interest problems and it appears that there are currently insufficient market institutions (due to the low competence of retail investors and the limited involvement of institutional actors) to punish analysts who produce biased reviews and analyses. Robust enforcement actions are thus important to punish issuers and analysts who produce biased signals and prevent the market from becoming a market of lemons where high-quality companies will be deterred from entering the market.[74]

C *Enhancing Educational Efforts*

Our analysis highlights the need to enhance educational efforts, especially regarding the roles of analysts. Policy-makers may reduce asymmetric information by publishing insights into best practices and investor warnings about blockchain-based fundraising and analysts. While policy-makers have been actively engaged in the former, only a little attention has been given to crypto analysts. Given the essential asymmetric information reduction role of analysts in the market, regulators should allocate resources to research the market for analysts and provide investors and market practitioners with warnings regarding bad practices and red flags (e.g., lack of transparency, lack of competence and professionalism, and conflicts of interest that arise when analysts run their own projects). Furthermore, they could potentially publish guidance or best practices for analysts operating in this space. The analysis presented in this chapter can serve as a useful starting point for such educational initiatives.

V CONCLUSION

The blockchain finance market is too significant to ignore and its potential benefits are too compelling to disregard. Although the ICO market has slowed down, new methods of blockchain-based fundraising continue to evolve, with INOs being a notable example. These new methods are transforming the way capital is raised, invested, and utilized, promising to reduce transaction costs, broaden access to finance, and reshape the way in which issuers and investors interact.

Despite this disruptive potential, however, the blockchain finance market is currently plagued by significant asymmetric information and is rife with fraudulent and

---

[74] George A. Akerlof, *The Market for "Lemons": Quality Uncertainty and the Market Mechanism*, 84 Q. J. ECON. 488 (1970).

low-quality issuers who take advantage of this situation. Drawing upon the existing literature on ICOs, this chapter explored the acute nature of asymmetric information in blockchain finance and the effectiveness of signaling and analysts as asymmetric information reduction mechanisms in this context. While these mechanisms can effectively reduce asymmetric information in well-functioning financial markets, their effectiveness is limited in the blockchain finance context. With these observations in mind, this chapter discussed how mandating tailored disclosure requirements, strengthening enforcement actions against fraudulent issuers and analysts, and enhancing educational initiatives can both reduce asymmetric information and make signaling and analysts more effective in addressing this friction.

While this chapter and these policy implications primarily focus on blockchain-based fundraising involving fungible tokens, which has dominated the landscape for the past decade, they can provide valuable guidance for regulators as new forms of blockchain finance continue to evolve, such as INOs. The issuance and sale of NFTs pose a similarly significant asymmetric information problem and appropriately and addressing it proportionally is crucial to preventing this market from suffering a fate similar to that of the ICOs. As with the issuance and sale of fungible tokens, regulators and courts should pay attention to the substantial differences between different types of offerings and sales in terms of the issuance process, asset type, degree of asymmetric information, and the potential effectiveness of signaling and analysts.[75] Simply applying existing securities regulations – as previously done by the SEC with respect to offerings of fungible tokens,[76] and more recently in its inaugural enforcement action against Impact Theory's NFT offering[77] – may not be the most suitable approach.

[75] At least some courts appear to recognize some of these differences between traditional offerings and sales of securities and blockchain-based ones, adopting a more deferential approach in the latter cases. An example is the decision of the Southern District of New Your Court to dismiss the proposed class action lawsuit against decentralized crypto exchange Uniswap. The court declined "to stretch the federal securities laws to cover the conduct alleged, and conclude[d] that Plaintiffs' concerns are better addressed to Congress than to this Court." *See Risley* v. *Universal Navigation Inc.*, 1:22-cv-02780, (S.D.N.Y. Aug 29, 2023) ECF No. 90.

[76] For an overview of the SEC's position on fundraising involving the sale of fungible tokens, *see* Lewis Cohen et al., *The Ineluctable Modality of Securities Law: Why Fungible Crypto Assets Are not Securities*, 73–86 (December 13, 2022) (unpublished manuscript), https://papers.ssrn.com/sol3/papers.cfm?abstract_id=4282385.

[77] *See* In the Matter of Impact Theory, LLC Securities Act Rel. No. 11226 (Aug. 28, 2023), www.sec.gov/files/litigation/admin/2023/33-11226.pdf. *See also* the dissent by SEC commissioners Hester M. Peirce and Mark T. Uyeda, which questions the square application of securities regulations to NFT sales: Hester M. Peirce & Mark T. Uyeda, *NFTs & the SEC: Statement on Impact Theory, LLC* (August 28, 2023), www.sec.gov/news/statement/peirce-uyeda-statement-nft-082823#_ftn1

("[T]he NFTs were not shares of a company and did not generate any type of dividend for the purchasers…. We do not routinely bring enforcement actions against people that sell watches, paintings, or collectibles along with vague promises to build the brand and thus increase the resale value of those tangible items. Even if the NFT sales here fit squarely within Howey, is this set of facts one that warrants an enforcement action?").

9

Power to the People

Consumers, NFTs, and Marketing in Pursuit of a Decentralized World

Hamutal Schieber

I INTRODUCTION

Advertising and marketing in the 2020s have undergone a significant transformation compared to the traditional marketing campaigns of the past. In today's digital reality where individuals are not only users but also content generators and potential influencers, new and advanced technologies like cryptocurrencies, social media features, and Artificial Intelligence (AI)-powered products have emerged as crucial marketing tools. These tools have gained relevance in part due to the rise of user-generated content which has fundamentally changed the landscape of marketing and information sharing. Non-fungible tokens (NFTs) have become a part of this evolution, harnessing the power of decentralized technology. The unique features of NFTs and their strong connection to Gen Z (born between 1996 and 2010) and Gen Alpha (born between 2011 and 2025) consumers have propelled them to prominence in the marketing world.[1] NFTs offer numerous opportunities for those who utilize them.

To truly grasp how this phenomenon came about, it is essential to understand the evolution of the marketing world in the Internet-based era. Over the past decade, social platforms have proliferated worldwide giving rise to social movements and political shifts. Digital technology has not only facilitated the dissemination of ideas and the formation of communities but has also given rise to a new generation of influential figures: content creators. These content creators play a significant role in shaping trends, consumer behavior, and the overall marketing landscape. Today, the Creator Economy is a mirror image of the values and ideas shared by many of the new generations of consumers, Gen Z and Gen Alpha. Needing to market in this new economy, companies and platforms are currently working to comprehend the role of new tools in the realm of the blended, interconnected physical and

---

[1]   Rushan Ziatdinov & Juanee Cilliers, *Generation Alpha: Understanding the Next Cohort of University Students*, 10 Eur. J. Contemporary Edu. 783 (2021).

virtual existence era, which some think might evolve into a full blown metaverse at some point.

In this new economy, NFTs have garnered significant attention in connection with marketing, as brands worldwide continue to seek avenues to engage with digital natives and content creators. However, within a relatively short span of less than a year, many of these brands have withdrawn their investment in NFTs due to a luke-warm reception from consumers and limited return on investment.[2]

The underperformance of NFTs in meeting marketers' expectations, despite being a tool that seemingly caters to the demands of new consumers for identity, creativity, and creator-led commerce, raises the question of why this is the case. Furthermore, it prompts an exploration of the future and potential of NFTs.

While making precise predictions about the future can be challenging, particularly given the rapid disruption of existing technologies in recent years, a valuable approach to understanding the potential of NFTs in the marketing world involves examining the consumers they are meant to serve, the environment in which they are active, and the benefits they can derive from this tool. By gaining insights into these factors, we can have a clearer understanding of the trajectory and possibilities for NFTs within the marketing landscape.

II THE NEW CONSUMERS

One common trait shared by the world's most successful companies is a strong focus on the consumer. Understanding who the consumer is, what they desire, and how to better serve them is paramount. Technology, as emphasized by accomplished founders like Steve Jobs of Apple and Jeff Bezos of Amazon, is not an end in itself but a means to enhance the consumer experience.[3]

Generation Z (Gen Z) consumers, in particular, exhibit open-mindedness and diversity that surpass previous generations. A report by Meta's Facebook IQ discovered that people are finding joy in aspects of their identity that were once concealed, such as bisexual pride or cultural heritage. Globally, 47 percent of respondents believe that society has become more inclusive over the past year, with Gen Z and Millennials leading this perception. These consumers expect brands and influencers to align with their values and perspectives, reflecting their own uniqueness and diversity. They actively seek opportunities for self-expression and inclusion, reclaiming their power and asserting their place in the world using any available means – and even creating new tools as they see fit.[4]

---

[2] Reto Hofstetter et al., *Crypto-Marketing: How Non-Fungible Tokens (NFTs) Challenge Traditional Marketing*, 33 MKTG. LETTERS 705 (2022).

[3] Vasilios Priporas, Nikolas Stylos, & Anesits K. Foriadis, *Generation Z Consumers' Expectations of Interactions in Smart Retailing: A Future Agenda*, 77 COMPUTERS IN HUMAN BEHAVIOR, 374 (2017).

[4] Facebook IQ, *Culture Rising: 2022 Trends Report*, META (2022), www.facebook.com/business/news/insights/culture-rising-2022-trends-report.

A study conducted by Ernst and Young highlights that Gen Z will continue to be early adopters of technology and play a pivotal role in pushing new technologies into the mainstream. To effectively cater to the digitally native Gen Z, businesses must embrace digital transformation and disruptive technologies. Gen Z strongly gravitates towards brands that align with their values, emphasizing the significance of purpose and cause in marketing efforts.

The study further reveals that Gen Z has a keen ability to detect inauthenticity. They have a low tolerance for anything they perceive as "fake" and are quick to disconnect from individuals or brands that they deem disingenuous. They possess the capability to silently block someone or dismiss a brand from their lives, both literally and figuratively. This underscores the importance of genuine and authentic engagement when targeting Gen Z consumers.[5]

It is impossible to consider Gen Z and Gen Alpha without discussing digital technology. These consumers are digital natives: they grew up with smartphones in their hands and social media as their main means of communication.[6] Gen Z is considered the most connected generation to date, with 99.6 percent of this cohort in the US expected to become regular Internet users by 2026.[7] The younger generations, namely Gen Z and Gen Alpha, have grown up in a digital era where information, product discovery, purchases, and deliveries can be accessed instantaneously. This efficiency grants them more time for content consumption and gaming. Moreover, these generations exhibit a higher comfort level with crypto technologies and blockchain-based products like NFTs. They seamlessly incorporate these technologies into various aspects of their lives, such as playing video games, creating art, sharing recommendations on social media, and more.

Importantly, Gen Z and Gen Alpha do not adhere to the same societal norms and conventions as older generations. They engage in activities like creating content, upcycling clothes, carpooling, and working remotely, effectively redefining the traditional boundaries of consumption and production. This generation views their online, virtual life as equally significant as their physical, "in real life" (IRL) existence. A recent survey revealed how connected to technology Gen Z consumers are, spending hours per day on different social media platforms, with a significant portion of American Gen Z and Millennials claimed to "live online" in a survey conducted by Coefficient. Capital.[8] These findings highlight the profound

---

[5] Lizzie McWilliams, *EY Releases Gen Z Survey Revealing Businesses Must Rethink Their 'Plan Z,'* ERNST & YOUNG (November 4, 2021), www.ey.com/en_us/news/2021/11/ey-releases-gen-z-survey-revealing-businesses-must-rethink-their-plan-z.

[6] Stacy Wood, *Generation Z As Consumers: Trends and Innovation*, 119 INST. FOR EMERGING ISSUES: NC STATE UNIVERSITY 7767 (2013).

[7] Melanie Larsen, *WGSN – US & UK Gen Z: New Status Symbols*, WGSN (February 12, 2022), https://tinyurl.com/45fkbe7u.

[8] Dan Frommer, "THE NEW CONSUMER" REPORT 2023, CONSUMER TRENDS SURVEY, POWERED BY COEFFICIENT CAPITAL (2023), https://newconsumer.com/wp-content/uploads/2022/12/Consumer-Trends-2023.pdf.

integration of digital platforms and virtual experiences in the lives of younger generations.[9] Relatedly an interesting statistic reveals that 65 percent of Gen Z consumers interact more with their peers through video games than at school or work. This highlights the increasing significance of video games as a crucial component of the metaverse, the blended physical and virtual world. Moreover, this preference for socializing within the gaming realm is now becoming an expectation for Gen Z consumers. It underscores the growing importance of video games as a social platform and a means of connecting and engaging with peers for this generation.[10]

Gen Z represents a socially and environmentally conscious generation. They are incredibly diverse in terms of ethnicity, gender, and sexual identity, making them the most diverse generation to date. The widespread distribution of ideas through various individuals, rather than being limited to a few corporations or officials, has fostered a heightened awareness of ethics, morals, and pressing issues like global warming, social injustice, and financial inequality.

Gen Z's interconnectedness and exposure to diverse perspectives have fueled their passion for social causes and their drive for positive change. They actively seek out brands businesses and organizations that align with their values and are dedicated to making a meaningful impact. This generation holds a strong belief in the importance of sustainability, inclusivity, and social responsibility. They are vocal advocates for change and actively support initiatives that address these critical issues.[11] Gen Z prioritizes values and attributes that go beyond mere technological innovation. They place greater importance on companies and influencers who are committed to making a positive impact and engaging in meaningful social endeavors. While technology serves as an enabler it is not the ultimate goal or the sole determining factor of value. However, it is undeniable that technological innovation, particularly in the realm of the web, has played a pivotal role in driving major movements in both marketing and society. Technological advancements have revolutionized the way businesses operate and how people connect and communicate. The rise of social media, digital platforms, and other web-based technologies has provided avenues for widespread dissemination of ideas, fostering movements and facilitating engagement on a global scale. These innovations have had a profound impact on marketing strategies, consumer behavior, and the overall fabric of society. While the attributes that matter most to Gen Z extend beyond technology, it is crucial to acknowledge that technological innovation has played a significant role in shaping the marketing landscape and driving societal change. It is the combination of values, purpose-driven actions, and technological advancements that resonates most with this generation.[12]

---

[9]　Ellyn Briggs, *Gen Z Is Extremely Online*, MORNING CONSULT (December 12, 2022), https://morningconsult.com/2022/12/12/gen-z-social-media-usage/.

[10]　*See* ibid.

[11]　*See* Wood, *Generation Z As Consumers*, 1.

[12]　Priporas, Stylos & Foriadis, *Generation Z*, 375.

III THE WEB POWER SHIFT

In the book *Sapiens: A Brief History of Humankind* by Yuval Noah Harari, it is argued that the progress and evolution of the human race can be attributed to its ability to create and embrace shared myths.[13] Whether it is through religion, human rights, corporations, or the concept of money, humans have been able to collectively accept abstract ideas and imagined narratives. This capacity has given rise to a continuous trend of clustering and community formation, from families and tribes to settlements, metropolises, states, and countries. Harari asserts that communities are defined by the shared values, beliefs, and religions that bind their members together. He argues these shared belief systems amount to what can be considered shared "myths" that unite communities. These myths create a sense of communal identity and purpose that have played a vital role in shaping human history and our social structures.

Nowadays, it seems that a new wave of consumer-generated stories is created in an ever-growing number as consumers have immediate access to social media, data, and ideas distributed by other people. The result is a reversal of the clustering trend we have been witnessing for hundreds of years: communities are becoming nuanced, with one person identifying as a member of multiple communities of like-minded people. In the contemporary landscape, our virtual presence and activities hold equal if not greater significance than our physical location. This shift has been facilitated by various digital technologies, including the Internet, smart digital devices, artificial intelligence, blockchain technology, and social media platforms. These advancements have fundamentally altered the distribution and narration of stories.[14]

The Internet has opened up new avenues for sharing different points of view (POVs) and narratives, allowing information and stories to reach global audiences instantaneously. Smart devices have made it possible for individuals to engage with digital content and connect with others regardless of their physical location. Artificial intelligence has enhanced the personalization and customization of storytelling experiences. Blockchain technology has enabled decentralized and transparent distribution of digital assets, including stories and creative works. Social media platforms have provided a platform for individuals to share their own stories and engage with others on a massive scale. Together, these digital technologies have transformed the way stories are disseminated, consumed, and participated in, shaping our identities and experiences in the virtual world. They have expanded our storytelling capabilities, allowing for new forms of expression, interaction, and connection.

During the 1990s, the content available on the World Wide Web was primarily read-only, commonly referred to as Web 1.0 (or Web1). This era resembled the experience

---

[13] Yuval Noah Harari, Sapiens: A Brief History of Humankind (2015).

[14] Barry Wellman, *Physical Place and Cyberplace: The Rise of Personalized Networking*, 25 Int'l J. Urb. & Reg. Res. 227 (2001).

of reading a digital version of a newspaper, where content was predominantly produced by a limited number of creators. In this format, there was little to no opportunity for users to provide feedback or engage in correspondence with content creators,
let alone with the content itself. Users were largely passive consumers of information
with limited avenues for active participation or interaction.[15] People could, of course,
have opinions about what they read – but their opinions would be shared with people
they knew in real life. For established businesses, this centralized reality worked well:
it enabled control over the message and the information and created a barrier to entry
stemming from the need for a big media and advertising budget.

Largely due to Section 230 of the Communications Decency Act (CDA),[16] a
unique law[17] which provides immunity from liability for online service providers for
content created by third parties,[18] Web 1.0 evolved into Web 2.0 (or Web2). The reason for this evolution was that the section, which was enacted in 1996 – a time when
Web 1.0 was in its infancy – enabled the Internet to develop into what we know
it to be today.[19] It permitted online service providers to host a wide range of User-
Generated Content without fearing legal liability, provided that they do not create
or develop the content themselves.[20] Section 230's broad protections have enabled
tech platforms to become central features of the modern Internet,[21] facilitating users'
content,[22] ranging from videos to NFTs featuring bored apes or yachts, which contributed to modern advertising practices and consumer-targeting practices.[23]

In the 2000s, the Internet witnessed a significant rise in the number of individuals actively sharing their own content. This shift provided businesses with a new
source of data and opportunities. Companies could now listen to what consumers were saying they wanted and needed, regardless of whether they were directly

---

[15] Neha Choudhury, *World Wide Web and Its Journey from Web 1.0 to Web 4.0*, 5 INT'L J. COMP. SCI.
      & INFO. TECH. 8096 (2014).

[16] 47 U.S.C. § 230.

[17] *See, for example*, Eric Goldman, *The Third Wave of Internet Exceptionalism*, TECH & MKTG. L.
      BLOG (March 11, 2009), https://bit.ly/2KGhOkP.

[18] *See, for example*, Michal Lavi, *Publish, Share, Re-Tweet, and Repeat*, 54 U. MICH. J. L. REF. 441, 446
      (2021).

[19] *See* JEFF KOSSEFF, THE TWENTY-SIX WORDS THAT CREATED THE INTERNET 77–78 (2019);
      Eric Goldman, *Why Section 230 Is Better than the First Amendment*, 95 NOTRE DAME L. REV.
      REFLECTION 33 (2019).

[20] Cecilia Ziniti, *The Optimal Liability System for Online Service Providers: How Zeran v. America
      Online Got it Right and Web 2.0 Proves It*, 23 BERKELEY TECH. L.J. 583, 585 (2008) ("Almost uni-
      formly, courts have interpreted § 230's safe harbor broadly").

[21] *See generally* Anupam Chander, *How Law Made Silicon Valley*, 63 EMORY L. J. 639 (2014).

[22] *See* Abbey Stemler, *The Myth of the Sharing Economy and Its Implications for Regulating Innovation*,
      67 EMORY L.J. 197, 216 (2017) (describing how the section has been very broadly interpreted).

[23] In *Gonzalez* v. *Google*, the US Supreme Court will consider Section 230's scope in con-
      nection with targeting certain content to users based on their online activities. *See* Lydia
      Wheeler & Kimberly Strawbridge Robinson, *Top Five US Supreme Court Cases to Watch in
      the New Year*, BLOOMBERG (January 3, 2023), https://news.bloomberglaw.com/us-law-week/
      top-five-us-supreme-court-cases-to-watch-in-the-new-year.

communicating with the brand. Online forums, groups, and social media platforms became platforms where certain individuals gained prominence as content creators, trendsetters, and movement leaders.

Simultaneously, people could directly connect with their favorite celebrities, key opinion leaders, businesses and organizations, politicians and tastemakers for the first time ever. These celebrities accumulated millions, and even tens of millions, of followers and were able to monetize their influence by collaborating with brands, recommending products, and effectively becoming media platforms themselves. Brands saw the potential in utilizing these influencers as brand ambassadors, allowing them to distribute messages from companies to the public through the intermediary of these mega-influencers. This new landscape created a more direct and influential communication channel between brands and consumers.[24]

However, with the influx in information and influencers came a decline in consumers' trust. People increasingly reported that they trust people they know more than they do mega-influencers and brands. According to Edelman, Gen Z trusts "regular" people they can relate to more than celebrities (including social celebrities).[25] And 62 percent of consumers say celebrity-founded brands only make sense if the celebrity has expertise in the products they are selling according to *"The New Consumer" Report*.[26]

Consequently, people are favoring content creators whom they viewed as "authentic" – here to create, not here to sell. In turn, these creators became influential and gained a larger following, driving their followers to once again search for authentic "regular people" creators.[27] Social media platforms like TikTok and Instagram recognized the trend and placed a greater emphasis on "discovery" and personalized "for you" pages to let anyone have their "15 minutes of fame."[28]

Web 2.0 gave rise to a new layer of "super consumers" who are the pinnacle of their community: trendsetters, distributors of ideas, content, art, and games. These creators depend on social platforms – social media, gaming, and social commerce platforms but at the same time, platforms depend on them: people use content to discover brands, goods, and services, and the best content wins.[29] A growing preference for YouTube over Netflix in Gen Z is a further proof that people would rather have access to a multitude of creators rather than an expensive production. And so gradually platforms became more dependent on creators: in fact, many of the changes

---

[24] Ibid.

[25] Corey Martin, *The Rise of Trusted Influence: 3 Key Gen Z Trends to Act On*, EDELMAN (June 14, 2022), www.edelman.com/insights/rise-trusted-influence-3-key-gen-z-trends-act.

[26] *See* "THE NEW CONSUMER" REPORT.

[27] Douglas B. Holt & Mona Srivastava, *The 'Real Thing': Branding Authenticity in the Luxury Wine Trade*, 58 J. BUS. RES. 1343 (2005).

[28] Danni Zheng, Shasha Liu, & Wei Lu, *Do You Trust Digital Health Pass? Understanding Tourists' Responses toward Using Health QR Codes in Pandemic Travel*, 19 J. CHINA TOURISM RES. 31 (2023).

[29] Kate Klonick, *The Law of the Platform*, 106 CAL. L. REV. 683 (2018).

deployed by the platforms in recent years are responding to the Creator Economy and the massive opportunity it brings with it. Creators are becoming a source of revenue for platforms, and monetizing the relationship between a creator and its followers allows social platforms to ignite commerce directly on the platforms, rather than relying on marketers' budget, competing with various other media channels.[30]

This influx in tastemakers is a game changer for the business and marketing communities and is at the core of what is now called "Web 3.0" (or "Web3"): a futuristic decentralized, peer-based network in a world where identity, sustainability, democratization, and inclusion matter to consumers more than a vast media budget.[31]

To understand the profound shift in power and how disruptive grassroots-based, social-media driven movements can be, we can look at the #MeToo movement as an example. Today, no one entity has control over the media or the message. Forbes' David Blum says: "Mass communication is no longer largely top-down, wielded by a relatively few, oligarchic gatekeepers. Rather, it's as likely to be a peer-to-peer massively parallel conversation coalescing out of the online ether in a few hours."[32]

The concept of decentralization, which already started taking place in Web 2.0, is key to understanding the future of business as it correlates with Gen-Z's values and meets enabling technology like social commerce, blockchain, and NFT. Web 3.0 would allow consumers to reclaim their power, reshuffle norms, resell goods, and celebrate self-expression over conformity, opening the era of "many to many."

According to the World Economic Forum, in a Web 3.0 world, "activities and data would be hosted on a network of computers using blockchain rather than corporate servers. The internet would likely have the same look and feel, at least initially, but your internet activities would be represented by your crypto-wallet and websites hosted through decentralized applications (dapps), digital applications run on a blockchain network."[33]

Trend researcher, Mary Madden, explains:

> The practices of today's youth are potentially more seismic. Contrary to the goals of Big Tech's investments, young people are shifting their time, content, and data away from mainstream social apps to a much more fragmented and less public kaleidoscope of communications and communities. More than previous generations, young people are now explicitly and thoughtfully controlling their boundaries of in-groups and out-groups.[34]

---

[30] Ibid.

[31] Richard Florida, *The Rise of the Creator Economy*, CREATIVE CLASS GROUP (November 2022), https://creativeclass.com/reports/The_Rise_of_the_Creator_Economy.pdf.

[32] David Bloom, *How Gen Z and Millennials Are Reshaping What Power Is, and What It Means for Brands*, FORBES (September 12, 2019), www.forbes.com/sites/dbloom/2019/09/12/how-gen-z-and-millennials-are-reshaping-what-power-is-and-what-it-means-for-brands/?sh=674bbe146d9f.

[33] Rebecca King, *Web3: The Hype and How It Can Transform the Internet*, WORLD ECON. FORUM (February 1, 2022), www.weforum.org/agenda/2022/02/web3-transform-the-internet/.

[34] Mary Madden., *Gen Z Refuses to Be Locked In*, NEW_ PUBLIC (September 23, 2021), https://newpublic.org/article/1654/gen-z-refuses-to-be-locked-in.

The growing availability of smaller, like-minded communities overrides central-ized sources of power and information such as governments and large leading insti-tutions that for the past centuries determined what people thought and did.

IV THE CREATOR ECONOMY

The evolving trends have given rise to a new sub-economy of creators who collaborate with companies, establishing themselves as trusted tastemakers and key opinion lead-ers. These creators have become hubs of information due to their perceived insider knowledge, ultimately serving as the primary source of information and opinions for many people. Over the past two decades, influencers have transitioned from being mere messengers to being the central focus, allowing smaller brands to increase their visibility. Interestingly, many of these smaller brands have themselves become influ-encers through the strategic use of content and user engagement, challenging the previous dominance of larger corporations with substantial media accounts.

Influencers, for their part, are deeply passionate about their content. A recent survey conducted revealed that 51 percent of influencers favor the term "creator," while 32 percent prefer "influencer."[35] The same influencers overwhelmingly agree that the quality of their content is the most crucial factor for their success. According to a report from Morning Consult, 70 percent of Gen Y and Gen Z consumers fre-quently or occasionally learn about products they are interested in through social media. Additionally, 56 percent have made a purchase after seeing a post from someone they follow and 50 percent claim that social media is their primary source for discovering new products to purchase.[36]

In response to this virtuous cycle, new monetization tools are rapidly emerging. If a platform helps a creator earn more money, the creator is likely to continue favor-ing that platform over others. This in turn leads to more active followers on the plat-form, which draws more attention from marketers, consequently generating more revenue for the creator.

With a wider array of commerce options available, creator-to-consumer com-merce has seen significant growth, as has "fandom." This phenomenon represents a reversal of the typical creator–consumer relationship wherein consumers produce merchandise inspired by content that they or others might admire.[37]

Gen Z, naturally more digitally adept than any other generation, view them-selves as entrepreneurial. They have grown up in a world where it is easier than

---

[35] Hamutal Schieber, *The Next Generation of Influencer Marketing: Creator Collaborations and Peer-to-Peer Platforms*, FORBES (January 7, 2020), www.forbes.com/sites/forbesagencycouncil/2020/01/07/the-next-generation-of-influencer-marketing-creator-collaborations-and-peer-to-peer-platforms/?sh=2296248018b5.

[36] Briggs, *Gen Z Is Extremely Online*.

[37] Regina Weber et al., *A European Mind? Europeanisation of Football Fan Discussions in Online Message Boards*, 19 EUR. J. FOR SPORT & SOC'Y 323 (2022).

ever to call out injustice and where ethnic and gender diversity are on the rise. Consequently, these consumers are taking matters into their own hands. Among Gen Z, and expectedly among the following Gen Alpha, an increasing number of individuals are embracing both the roles of follower and creator, rather than confining themselves to just one. For instance, as sustainability is a key concern for Gen Z, over half of this demographic plans to "DIY their clothes" in 2023, as per the Trends Report by Instagram and WGSN.[38] Furthermore, the report found that 50 percent of the surveyed participants view secondhand items as a status symbol.[39]

Now that consumers have more tools to exchange ideas, goods, and services, virtually anyone can become a creator or an ambassador. This is further democratizing and decentralizing the Internet, paving the way for the emergence of Web 3.0. Global awareness of the metaverse is growing. Approximately half (52 percent) of adults across twenty-nine countries, especially among the younger generations, claim familiarity with the metaverse. There is a widespread expectation that this new realm will significantly transform our entertainment, learning, and work experiences over the next decade.[40]

A report by Edelman estimates that globally, 100 million people or more have a following of over 10,000 on one or more social media accounts.[41] In 2020, eMarketer found that 50 million people identified as "content creators" – but Mavrck, a marketing company, predicts that by 2027 an estimated 1 billion people worldwide will identify as content creators. Influencer Marketing Hub found that in 2022, the Creator Economy has reached $104.2 billion.[42]

According to General Catalyst, "the same way that Silicon Valley became a mindset and millennials from all over the world realized that tech entrepreneurship can be a career option, Gen Z'ers for the very first time can now earn a living from their ingenuity online."[43]

To comprehend the potential disruption in the economy, let us consider the music industry as an example. In past generations, listeners would only be exposed to musicians if these artists were able to meet the criteria set by a handful of gatekeepers – namely, radio broadcasters and record companies.[44] In the past, many stations reliant on advertising dollars had to cater to mainstream tastes. At the same

---

[38] Larsen, *WGSN*.

[39] Ibid.

[40] Nokia & IPSOS, Gen Z and the Metaverse (September 2022), ipsos.com/sites/default/files/ct/publication/documents/2022-10/Gen-z-and-the-metaverse-2022.pdf.

[41] Martin, *The Rise of Trusted Influence*.

[42] Werner Geyser, *22 Influencer Marketing Experts Give Their Predictions for 2022*, eMarketer, (January 2023), https://influencermarketinghub.com/influencer-marketing-predictions-2022/.

[43] Ollie Forsyth, *The New Creator Economy: A Guide on Web3 Creator Platforms*, Antler (March 30, 2022), www.antler.co/blog/the-new-creator-economy-a-guide-on-web3-creator-platforms.

[44] Gary Graham et al., *The Transformation of the Music Industry Supply Chain: A Major Label Perspective*, 24 Int'l J. Operations & Prod. Mgmt. 1087 (2004).

time, the lack of access to alternative channels meant the music they chose defined what was considered mainstream. Thus, up until the 2000s, individuals interested in discovering new or underground music had to rely on niche stations, clubs, or other tastemakers. This group included record stores where knowledgeable staff could recommend music based on the customer's taste or their own preferences. However, as streaming services became more widely available, people gained access to a multitude of artists. Tastemakers were to some extent replaced by algorithms. Spotify, a leader in music streaming, has become a go-to resource for new music discovery. But it is not all about the algorithm or AI. Spotify also serves as a social network, enabling people worldwide to discover others who share their musical tastes. In this way, it empowers anyone to potentially become an influencer, trendsetter, or tastemaker.[45]

The implications are huge: artists who might never have made a living through their music are able to gain a large following, infiltrate into other platforms like TikTok and Instagram, and earn a living from their art. With fewer people depending on radio stations, marketing dollars shifted toward the aforementioned streaming and social media platforms. This is a process of decentralization that involves access to information, creating a network of reciprocal knowledge exchange hubs rather than a one-way or even two-way idea stream.

In today's era, consumers lead highly curated lives, with their chosen sources of information, commerce, and entertainment taking center stage, all thanks to the influence of social media. Each individual who has access to social platforms holds the power to influence, sell, and create, while also being influenced by others, making purchases, and following content creators. This dynamic results in a significant power shift from the few to the many, compelling companies to reconsider their marketing strategies, product development, and go-to-market approaches.[46]

V NFT: LOYALTY, MARKETING, CREATIVITY

At first glance, NFTs provide creators with fresh avenues for monetization, allowing fans to purchase directly from their favorite creators. This gives consumers the opportunity to become stakeholders in the creative process, elevating their status as loyal followers and potentially gaining recognition through their purchases. The reclamation of power and the pursuit of technological innovation are key factors that make NFTs an intriguing concept. On the one hand, NFTs empower Gen Z consumers-creators to monetize their talents and influence, completing the circle of

---

[45] Varvara Andreeva, *The Impact of the Digital Era on Marketing in the Music Business Industry*, (2021) (unpublished MA thesis, LAB University of Applied Sciences), www.theseus.fi/bitstream/handle/10024/509842/final%20thesis.pdf?sequence=2.

[46] Ibid.

the Creator Economy. In fact, some envision NFTs as the cornerstone of the future Creator Economy.[47]

However, it is important to consider the opposing perspective. Some argue that creators and consumers are increasingly moving away from a society that equates big brands with affluence or success. The indoctrination of money as the ultimate goal and the key to happiness may persist for the foreseeable future but the younger generations, particularly Gen Z and Gen Alpha, are challenging the status quo. They prioritize their genuine, authentic identities over the worship of brands, emphasizing mental well-being and happiness. Consequently, the current focus on the financial value and the ostentatious display of wealth and social inequality in relation to NFTs may hold little relevance for most Gen Z and Gen Alpha consumers. In fact, this emphasis on financial aspects could potentially hinder the growth of this emerging technology. Supporting this perspective and further reinforcing this insight is a 2022 survey by Nokia and IPSOS titled "Gen Z and the Metaverse."[48]

Indeed, according to the survey, Gen Z generally displays a lack of interest in NFTs as they currently exist. The initial appeal of NFT collectibles lies in their novelty but consumer interest tends to wane once that novelty wears off. However, this does not imply that we are approaching the demise of this influential tool. Companies have been exploring fresh approaches to leveraging NFTs, aiming to provide greater value to consumers and empower them. Rather than solely focusing on the technological aspect itself, attention is shifting toward the possibilities it enables. By emphasizing what NFTs can accomplish rather than what they are, companies are seeking to enhance their appeal and resonate more effectively with consumers.

One driving force behind the Creator Economy and consumer-to-consumer (C2C)[49] commerce, as previously discussed, is Gen Z's pursuit of inclusion and democratization. They prioritize self-expression over commercialization. While some brands have achieved limited success with NFTs, this success is largely attributed to the novelty factor rather than the actual value provided to consumers at present. The rising sales of avatars and skins demonstrate a strong demand for self-expression tools in the metaverse.

---

[47] Brett Hemenway Falk, Gerry Tsoukalas, & Niuniu Zhang, *Economics of NFTs: The Value of Creator Royalties* (November 22, 2022) (unpublished manuscript), https://papers.ssrn.com/sol3/papers.cfm?abstract_id=4284776.

[48] *See* Nokia & IPSOS, Gen Z and the Metaverse.

[49] For more on C2C, *see* Godwin C. Ariguzo, Efrem G. Mallach, and D. Steven White, *The First Decade of E-Commerce*, 1 Int. J. Bus. Information Systems 239, 242 (2006); Ivonnely Colón-Fung, *Protecting the New Face of Entrepreneurship: Online Appropriate Dispute Resolution and International Consumer-to-Consumer Online Transactions*, 12 Fordham J. Corp. & Fin. L. 233, 235 (2007)(explaining that "[t]he C2C category relates primarily to electronic retailing between merchant-consumers and traditional purchaser-consumers, which has expanded significantly with the growth of the Internet. Although the volume of C2C virtual transactions has grown slowly in comparison to B2B transactions, the impact of this area of commerce should not be underestimated.")

Rather than using NFTs as a direct source of revenue, brands can benefit by empowering consumers through this technology. Microsoft, the owner of the popular game Minecraft, often considered the original and currently most popular metaverse for Gen Z and Gen Alpha, has taken a stance against NFTs. They have stated that NFTs and other blockchain technologies create digital ownership based on scarcity and exclusion, which contradicts Minecraft's values of creative inclusion and playing together. NFTs are seen as exclusive and can lead to a division between "haves" and "have nots." The speculative pricing and investment mentality surrounding NFTs also divert attention away from playing the game and encourage profiteering, which Microsoft believes is not in line with the long-term enjoyment and success of their players.[50]

To put it simply, establishing financial-based hierarchies in the metaverse and providing consumers with tools to purchase status rather than earning it through engaging content and talent goes against the evolution of Web 3.0 and contradicts the beliefs and values of Gen Z and Gen Alpha.

Today, brands are developing NFTs that offer access to reward programs, membership benefits, and digital twins of physical products.[51] An NFT can be seen as a modern-day, lightweight version of a company share, granting holders special privileges such as exclusive access to limited releases, exclusive sales, and even direct communication with the brand or creator. According to the *Harvard Business Review*, owning an NFT essentially makes you an investor, a member of a club, a brand shareholder, and a participant in a loyalty program all at once. Moreover, the programmability of NFTs supports new business and profit models. For instance, NFTs have facilitated the implementation of royalty contracts, where a portion of the proceeds from each resale goes back to the original creator.[52]

---

[50] *Minecraft and NFTs*, MINECRAFT (July 20, 2022), www.minecraft.net/en-us/article/minecraft-and-nfts.

[51] Janine S. Hiller, Gerlinde Berger-Walliser & Aaron F. Brantly, *Critical Protection for the Network of Persons*, 25 U. PA. J.L. & SOC. CHANGE 115, 121–122 (2021) (explaining that "[u]sing dynamic data collection, a 'digital twin' of a person – a simulated and constantly updated digital version of the actual person – is created virtually. Creating a digital twin of an individual by collecting and combining very personal information can be used, for example, to predict illness and for medical treatment. Retail industries are not far away from using digital twins to create a replica of each consumer, using both purchase and non-purchase data in order to make predictions about individual consumer behavior in order to 'cross-sell and up-sell'"); "While the concept has been floated for years, it is only since the introduction of IoT – and all the sensors, networking, and Big Data that may be included – that the Digital Twin has become a financially viable concept to implement." Charlie Osborne, *Digital Twin Initiatives Set to Take Enterprise Center Stage: Gartner*, ZD NET (March 13, 2018), www.zdnet.com/article/digital-twin-initiatives-set-to-take-center-stage-in-the-enterprise-gartner [https://perma.cc/RNW6-8LF9]; *see also* Daniel Newman, *Digital Twins: The Business Imperative You Might Not Know About*, FORBES (May 30, 2017), www.forbes.com/sites/danielnewman/2017/05/30/digital-twins-the-business-imperative-you-might-not-know-about/#12052a0693c3 (describing how digital twins can result in partnerships and various collaborations).

[52] Steve Kaczynski & Scott Duke Kominers, *How NFTs Create Value*, HARV. BUS. REV. (November 10, 2021).

In May 2022, luxury fashion brand Prada incorporated NFTs into its monthly releases of new apparel through the "Timecapsule NFT Collection."[53] This initiative offered exclusive perks and experiences to owners of these NFTs. Similarly, in June 2022, fashion brand Puma collaborated with creator Wagmi-san to introduce wearables based on NFT collections, while also providing physical merchandise inspired by NFT collectibles, such as shoes and sporting goods.[54]

In July 2022, Diageo's spirits brand Johnnie Walker launched a new NFT program, which enables customers to buy a token for a physical bottle, in addition to an art piece and a virtual storytelling experience from a master blender.[55]

Starbucks, known for its highly successful loyalty programs,[56] has ventured into Web 3.0 loyalty programs, facing scrutiny from competitors. Their NFT-based loyalty program enables members to engage in interactive games and quizzes and earn "stamps" in the form of NFTs. These limited edition stamps can be purchased through the program's web app marketplace without the need for cryptocurrency. Each stamp is assigned a point value based on its rarity, and Starbucks Rewards members have the option to trade these points on the marketplace. The rewards associated with these stamps are exclusive to NFT holders. Notably, the stamps will showcase artwork created through collaborations with both Starbucks employees and external artists.[57]

Somewhat similarly, Nike unveiled "Dot Swoosh," a platform to house its Web 3.0 activations and enable fans to buy and sell virtual or physical items.[58] According to research conducted by eMarketer, the hype surrounding cryptocurrencies and

[53] *Prada Timecapsule*, PRADA (May 2022), www.prada.com/eu/en/pradasphere/special-projects/2022/prada-timecapsule.html.

[54] Shlomik Sen Bhattacharjee & David Delima, *Puma's First Metaverse Experience Lets You Redeem Nfts as Real Sneakers*, GADGETS 360 (February 10, 2023), www.gadgets360.com/cryptocurrency/news/puma-metaverse-website-nft-redeem-sneaker-new-york-fashion-week-web3-3331792.

[55] Jessica Lis & Yoram Wurmser, *Tech Trends to Watch for 2023: Brands Look Beyond Hype to Build Value*, EMARKETER (December 2022), www.insiderintelligence.com/content/tech-trends-watch-2023.

[56] Natalie M. Banta, *Inherit the Cloud: The Role of Private Contracts in Distributing or Deleting Digital Assets at Death*, 83 FORDHAM L. REV. 799, 854 (2014) (explaining that "[l]oyalty programs also could be considered a form of digital asset and are controlled by private contracts. Loyalty programs give customers who are loyal to certain service providers or retail stores 'points' or 'miles.' These points or miles can then be redeemed for free flights, merchandise, or nights at resorts."); Xavier Dreze & Joseph C. Nunes, *Using Combined-Currency Prices to Lower Consumers' Perceived Cost*, 41 J. MKTG. RES. 59, 59–60 (2004) (tracing the rise and implication of loyalty programs); Knowledge@Wharton, *The Lowdown on Customer Loyalty Programs*, FORBES (January 2, 2007, 2:30 PM), www.forbes.com/2007/01/02/frequent-flyer-miles-ent-sales-cx_kw_ 0102whartonloyalty.html (describing how it is the case that loyalty programs have been around for more than a century and how more than 75 percent of consumers nowadays have at least one loyalty card that they keep or use or maintain).

[57] *Starbucks Brewing Revolutionary Web3 Experience for Its Starbucks Rewards Members*, STARBUCKS (September 2022), https://stories.starbucks.com/press/2022/starbucks-brewing-revolutionary-web3-experience-for-its-starbucks-rewards-members/.

[58] *See Nike Has Unveiled Its New "Dot Swoosh" Platform for Hosting Web3 Projects*, NFTCULTURE (November 2022), www.nftculture.com/nft-news/nike-has-unveiled-its-new-dot-swoosh-platform-for-hosting-web3-projects/.

NFTs has often overshadowed the genuine advancements in Web 3.0. However, the study highlights that blockchain technologies have the potential to facilitate assets that can be easily activated and controlled by individuals. As a recommendation, eMarketer suggests that companies leverage Web 3.0 to enhance loyalty programs by offering benefits such as individual ownership of rewards, introducing novel methods for registration or activation of rewards, providing virtual goods or experiences, and fostering the creation of a community environment.[59]

But what might just be one of the most significant opportunities for brands with NFTs lies in utilizing them as a means to support and empower consumers and creators in values that hold importance to them, such as creativity, inclusivity, and self-expression. Avatars and skins have long served as a way for consumers to express themselves within online games. Considering the significance of identity and authenticity to Gen Z it becomes evident why companies recognize the immense potential in this domain.

A 2022 Instagram & WGSN Trends Report revealed that 67 percent of Gen Z users expressed the desire for avatars to better reflect diverse body types, clothing, and skin tones in the coming year. This finding underscores the importance of inclusivity and representation, indicating a strong demand for NFTs that align with the diverse identities of consumers. By embracing these aspects, brands can foster a stronger connection with their target audience and tap into the immense creative and expressive potential of NFTs.[60]

Undoubtedly, innovations like NFTs and the concept of digital twins hold immense potential for individuals to express themselves and embrace their uniqueness. The ability to create virtual copies of purchased physical products, and vice versa, provides a platform for self-expression. However, it is crucial to recognize that focusing solely on these innovations as the primary topic of business discussions would be a mistake.

The true driving forces behind Gen Z's behavior are their quest for trust and democratization, which ultimately leads to decentralization, as we have previously explored. Platforms such as Discord and Reddit, designed to cater to Gen Z's social and gaming habits, serve as prime examples of the new landscape where marketers must adapt by unlearning conventional practices to secure a place in the conversation. In this evolving environment, marketers must embrace new approaches and strategies to effectively engage with Gen Z and participate in their digital communities.[61] On these platforms, users engage in anonymous sharing of experiences and recommendations. In this environment, social status, demographics, fame, or affluence are detached from status, influence, and power. Users are not interested in

[59] Lis & Wurmser, *Tech Trends to Watch for 2023*.
[60] Larsen, WGSN.
[61] Jegg Fromm & Angie Read, Marketing to Gen Z: The Rules for Reaching This Vast – and Very Different Generation of Influencers (2018).

divulging their private thoughts and data to mega corporations like Meta, Alphabet, or Google, only to be targeted with promotional offers. They prioritize their own agency and refuse to serve as tools for corporations that profit from selling their data to marketers. This shift represents a reclamation of power and autonomy.

Even Reddit, a prominent platform, has introduced an NFT marketplace where users can purchase avatars for use within the platform. Interestingly, Reddit refers to these items as "blockchain-backed collectible avatars," distinguishing them from traditional NFTs.[62] The platform does not accept cryptocurrency as payment and places emphasis on equality and affordability. The prices of these avatars cannot be artificially inflated through trading. Furthermore, the avatars are designed by artists who receive the funds, with Reddit collecting fees for its services. This approach is seen as fair and supportive of creators, rather than driven by greed, serving as an example of how consumers perceive fairness and the promotion of creative individuals.[63]

Another notable instance of utilizing NFTs in a socially conscious manner, rather than solely focusing on status symbols, is the collaboration between WPP and the New York-based artist, Shawna X. The artist dedicated her NFT collection to the fight for racial equality. In a unique approach, WPP decided to give away the NFTs and encouraged recipients to trade them. Sellers would receive a percentage of the proceeds, while the rest of the profits would be directed towards supporting the emerging artist and WPP's racial equality program. This initiative demonstrates how NFTs can be used as a tool for promoting important social causes and supporting talented artists.[64]

VI CONCLUSION

The C2C economy is poised to succeed the creator-led economy. With the advent of new tools, more and more individuals can now become trendsetters, followers, sellers, buyers, storytellers, and viewers. In this economy, breaking through the noise becomes increasingly challenging. Companies have an opportunity to empower consumers-as-creators by offering exclusive tokens, merchandise, and limited drops to foster ambassadorship.

Furthermore, treating NFTs as a stake in the company and granting consumers a seat at the table becomes crucial for future consumers, particularly Gen Alpha. It is worth noting that soon enough, brands themselves may need to seek a seat at the table.

---

[62] Ivan Mehta, *Reddit Is Launching a New NFT Avatar Marketplace*, TECHCRUNCH (July 7, 2022), https://techcrunch.com/2022/07/07/reddit-is-launching-a-new-nft-avatar-marketplace.

[63] Ibid.

[64] *See NFT Shawna X Sign up*, WPP (July 2022), www.wpp.com/events/2022/the-wpp-beach-at-the-cannes-lions-festival-of-creativity-2022/NFT-Shawna-X-sign-up.

However, companies cannot solely rely on the novelty factor of NFTs, nor should they expect Web 3.0 to have a single, predetermined form. Web 3.0 represents an era of decentralized information, identity, and self-expression. It revolves around chosen communities and curated experiences. It is highly personalized and controlled by users, leaving little room for inauthenticity.

In summary, NFTs can serve as an enabling technology for marketing in the Web 3.0 era by fostering creator–consumer relationships and empowering communities and individuals. Nevertheless, to achieve this, a mindset transformation is necessary to relinquish control and empower the people.

10

The Nexus of Gaming and NFTs

A Deep Dive into the Future of Digital Interaction

Nizan Geslevich Packin

I INTRODUCTION

Gaming is a big deal. In a world where nearly two-fifths (39 percent) of the global population immerses themselves in the virtual realms of video games, equating to over 3 billion souls, the integration of new technology and gaming cannot be ignored.[1] In terms of economic impact, the sheer number of gamers means there is a vast market potential, and the global gaming industry has already eclipsed other entertainment sectors and is likely to see further expansion,[2] which is also likely to result in more employment opportunities and contribute significantly to global economies. But gaming is not just about entertainment anymore. For many, it is a primary form of social interaction, especially in online multiplayer environments.[3] Technologies like virtual, augmented, and extended reality (VR, AR, and XR) can redefine these social interactions, creating deeper connections and more immersive experiences. Likewise, as more diverse populations engage in gaming, there is potential for cross-cultural interactions and understanding.

Focusing on gaming as a preferred activity which draws engagements from users, private and public sector entities started utilizing it in various additional contexts. One such application is educational settings for both children and adults,[4] and entities operating

---

[1] Diane-Laure Arjaliès & Samuel Compain-Eglin, *Trying to Sell the Crow Queen in Web 3.0.: On the Resistance of Video Gamers to Cryptocurrencies, NFTs and Their Financial Logic*, CRYPTOCARNIVAL (April 5, 2023), https://cryptocarnival.wtf/index.

[2] Newzoo, *Global Games Market Report 2022* (2022), https://newzoo.com/resources/trend-reports/newzoo-global-games-market-report-2022-free-version.

[3] *See for example*, Leon Anidjar, Nizan Geslevich Packin, & Argyri Panezi, *The Matrix of Privacy: Data Infrastructure in the AI-Powered Metaverse* (forthcoming, 2023 HARVARD LAW & POLICY REVIEW), https://papers.ssrn.com/sol3/papers.cfm?abstract_id=4363208 (discussing the future usages of the metaverse and online gaming, including as a social form of interaction).

[4] *See generally*, Nizan Geslevich Packin, *Financial Inclusion Gone Wrong: Securities and Cryptoassets Trading for Children*, 74 HASTINGS L.J. 349 (2023) (discussing the gamification of the financial markets using crypto and fintech apps offering game-like products and services and whether these products and services should be used as a financial literacy tool).

in this space integrate new technologies, which can arguably make educational games effective. Illustrative examples include games utilizing artificial intelligence (AI)-driven personalized learning paths and tailored virtual shopping experiences. This integration of novel technologies not only expands gaming's utility but also gradually integrates it into the fabric of everyday life, offering new and diverse applications.[5]

Another noteworthy development in gaming involves the integration of blockchain technology and smart contracts, which results in new types of business models and utilities. Particularly, this integration creates the possibility of providing users with full control over their in-game assets and enabling them to tokenize, sell, and transfer these assets outside the boundaries of a specific game.

This possibility is enabled by a combination of two pillars. One pillar is cryptoassets, such as non-fungible tokens (NFTs), which allow users to tokenize and own assets like in-game assets, experiences, or even pieces of land in specific games.[6] The second is decentralized finance (DeFi) protocols, which allow independent parties to engage in traditional financial activities, such as asset swapping, in an online manner and without the involvement of a centralized authority.[7] By combining DeFi protocols and NFTs, decentralized applications (dApps),[8] which offer consumers control over their digital lives, allow them to create and tokenize in-game assets and then transfer these assets to other games, or sell them for fiat money or other digital assets in the secondary market.[9] To put it in context, in contrast to traditional games, where users' information is stored on centralized servers and in-games assets can normally be used only within the confines of a specific game, blockchain-based games in the form of dApps enable users to keep full control over their in-game assets and information and to trade and sell these assets externally.[10]

---

[5] Anders Drachen et al., *Guns, Swords and Data: Clustering of Player Behavior in Computer Games in the Wild*, in 2012 IEEE Conference on Computational Intelligence and Games 163, 163–170 (IEEE 2012).

[6] NFTs are digital assets that represent real-world objects such as art, music, in-game items, and videos. *See* Juliet M. Moringiello & Christopher K. Odinet, *The Property Law of Tokens*, 74 Fla. L. Rev. 607, 631 (2022) ("The choices are art, music, videos, collectibles, sports, and utility"). For a deeper explanation of NFTs and their legal status, *see* Brian L. Frye, *After Copyright: Pwning NFTs in a Clout Economy*, 45 Colum. J.L. & Arts 341, 348 (2022); *see also* Mike Isaac & Kellen Browning, *Crypto Enthusiasts Meet Their Match: Angry Gamers*, N.Y. Times (January 19, 2022), www.nytimes.com/2022/01/15/technology/cryptocurrency-nft-gamers.html?searchResultPosition=1 ("For more than a year, crypto mania has been at a fever pitch. Cryptocurrencies such as Bitcoin and Ethereum have soared in value. Crypto-based assets like NFTs have taken off. Jack Dorsey, a Twitter founder, recently renamed one of his companies Block in honor of the blockchain, the distributed ledger system that powers digital currencies").

[7] *See generally* Harvey R. Campbell et al., DeFi and the Future of Finance (2021).

[8] *See generally* Chris Brummer, *Disclosure, Dapps and Defi*, 5 Stan. J. Blockchain L. & Pol'y 137, (2022) (providing an overview of decentralized finance and a brief overview of blockchains, protocols, and smart contracts).

[9] *See Introduction to dApps*, Ethereum, https://ethereum.org/en/developers/docs/dapps/.

[10] For an analysis of this in the context of banking apps and consumers' inability to manage their banking data, *see generally* Nizan Geslevich Packin, *Show Me the (Data About the) Money!*, 2020 Utah L. Rev. 1277 (2020).

This chapter analyzes the integration of blockchain, NFTs, and DeFi into gaming. Section II analyzes the interaction of gaming and society and situates the integration of blockchain and NFTs within this context. Section III discusses the ongoing shift in the gaming industry from a focus on pure enjoyment to a focus on the monetization of in-game assets and the financialization of gaming. In particular, it explains how the integration of blockchain and NFTs in gaming affects this shift. Section IV provides a high-level overview of the legal and ethical issues stemming from this integration, with a focus on the potential adverse consequence of the exposure of children and minors to digital gaming, as well as the application of securities regulation and gambling laws.

II DIGITAL GAMING AND SOCIETY

NFTs in gaming are more than just a fleeting trend. It is a representation of how intertwined digital art, creativity, finance, and commerce have become. However, from its inception, gaming has always been central to building communities, shaping cultural and psychological perspectives, and offering a platform for shared experiences. The historical roots of gaming reveal a profound journey.[11]

Some believe that games in general and video games in particular offer an escape, a realm where the ordinary can become extraordinary and players can embody heroes, live epic narratives, or even just forge deep social connections.[12] This sentiment is captured perfectly by making each user feel as if he or she is "the hero in this world. And not just one human among millions. You are the hero of the story."[13] This declaration speaks to the core of why millions dive into games daily. These are not just games; they are experiences, a tapestry of emotions, challenges, and stories that resonate deeply.[14]

However, it is not just about playing; it is also about creation. The immense following that those engaged in digital gaming now have for their work, with many followers tuning in to learn things about individual characters, underscores the profound impact gaming has had on contemporary culture. From a business standpoint, the video game industry has evolved from being just about entertainment to being all about engagement, community, and artistry.[15] In terms of numbers, by 2026, the worldwide gaming market is projected to reach a value of $321 billion.[16]

---

[11] Arjaliès & Compain-Eglin, *Trying to Sell the Crow Queen*.
[12] Ibid. Data supporting these claims also includes an explanation about how "Morgan Stanley's recent survey found that more than a quarter of those under 35 gamers believe gaming is a better social connection platform than social media platforms." *See* ibid., 7.
[13] Ibid., 5.
[14] Ibid.
[15] Ibid., 7–8.
[16] Simon Read, *Gaming Is Booming and Is Expected to Keep Growing. This Chart Tells You All You Need to Know*, WORLD ECON. FORUM (July 28, 2022), www.weforum.org/agenda/2022/07/gaming-pandemic-lockdowns-pwc-growth/.

Among the segments, social and casual gaming leads the charge, anticipated to bring in a staggering US$242.7 billion. This is trailed by PC games at US$42.2 billion, console games at US$31.5 billion, and revenue from integrated video game advertising rounding it off at US$4.7 billion.[17]

In terms of digital games' development, in recent years, a new kind of immersive digital gaming space started becoming very popular. It could be a virtual world that resembles a video game, such as Roblox,[18] which has about 57 million daily active users,[19] with environments representing physical ones and avatars representing users and digital objects, or XR and AR situations, where virtual elements are overlaid on top of the real world in real-time.[20] And while gaming was the initial AR application that reached a broad audience, it is not the only one.[21] Immersive digital environments could potentially be accessed through a variety of devices, including AR glasses and other wearable technology and VR equipment that big tech companies have focused on in recent years.[22] In 2020, Facebook introduced Project Aria, a project that uses AR glasses to map the world and objects within it,[23] and in 2021, the company's Oculus Quest 2 VR headset became extremely popular.[24] But the interest in innovative new technologies has expanded beyond VR, AR, and XR to cover more broadly various prospects, and other big tech companies have started investing in creating places for people to play, work, and hang out.[25]

---

[17] Ibid.

[18] Beckett Cantley & Geoffrey Dietrich, *The Metaverse: A Virtual World with Real World Legal Consequences*, 49 RUTGERS COMPUTER & TECH. L.J. 1, 3 (2022) (defining Roblox as the "largest online game creation platform").

[19] Sofia Pitt, *Roblox Closes Down More than 15% after November Update Shows Slowing Growth*, CNBC (December 15, 2022), www.cnbc.com/2022/12/15/roblox-stock-sinks-after-november-update-shows-slowing-growth.html.

[20] Many first encountered AR through the game Pokémon GO. AR technology overlays digital content in the real world. Users can view the world with digital images appearing by using devices/special glasses. *See* Mark Lemley & Eugene Volokh, *Law, Virtual Reality, and Augmented Reality*, 166 U. PA. L. REV. 1051, 1054 (2018).

[21] Ibid.

[22] For example, Meta (formerly known as Facebook), which started pursuing its interest in VR in 2014, purchased back then the VR company, Oculus, for $2 billion, gaining the ability to track and influence behavior in both real and virtual three-dimensional environments. *See* Josh Constine, *Facebook's $2 Billion Acquisition of Oculus Closes, Now Official*, TECHCRUNCH (July 21, 2014), https://techcrunch.com/2014/07/21/facebooks-acquisition-of-oculus-closes-now-official/.

[23] *See* S. A. Applin, *Why Facebook Is Using Ray-Ban to Stake a Claim to Our Faces*, MIT TECH. REV. (September 15, 2021), www.technologyreview.com/2021/09/15/1035785/why-facebook-ray-ban-stories-metaverse/.

[24] Will Greenwald, *The Best VR Headsets for 2021*, PC MAG. (October 21, 2021), [https://perma.cc/WJ2U-68V7]. Mark Zuckerberg, Facebook's founder and CEO, referred to it as "an embodied Internet that you're inside of." *See* Kyle Chyka, *Facebook Wants Us to Live in the Metaverse*, NEW YORKER (August 5, 2021), www.newyorker.com/culture/infinite-scroll/facebook-wants-us-to-live-in-the-metaverse.

[25] This led Facebook in 2020 to rename Oculus as "Reality Labs" and in 2021 to rebrand itself as "Meta." *See* Andrew Ross Sorkin et al., *Could a New Name Help Facebook After All?*, N.Y. TIMES (October 29, 2021), www.nytimes.com/2021/10/29/business/dealbook/facebook-meta-rebranding.html; Shirin

Similarly, as mentioned above, upon delving into the realm of Web 3.0 games,[26] dApps have also started getting more attention once industry members realized their potential when integrated into the sophisticated immersive digital gaming spaces. Illustrations of dApps, which were created to be used in the immersive digital space, include the following: (i) Decentraland,[27] which is a virtual reality platform built on the Ethereum blockchain that permits users to create, experience, and monetize data, content and applications.[28] (ii) Somnium Space, built on blockchain technology, and enables users to buy, sell, and build on virtual land, create and monetize 3D content, and interact with others in decentralized virtual worlds.[29] (iii) The Sandbox, a blockchain-based virtual world game where players can create, share, and monetize their own 3D pixel gaming experiences using NFTs.[30] (iv) Axie Infinity, Binemon, Blankos Block Party, My Crypto Heroes, and Lost Relics, which are all blockchain-based role playing games (RPG) that have proven somewhat popular and provide cool interactive, art and history and culture-related offerings.[31]

Ghaffary, *Facebook's Name Change Plan Reflects Its Real Priorities*, VOX (October 20, 2021), www .vox.com/recode/2021/10/20/22737168/facebook-name-change-metaverse-zuckerberg-frances-haugen-whistleblower. In doing so, Zuckerberg, Facebook's founder and CEO, as noted above, has connected the new name to his strategic plan to develop a metaverse social network. Ibid.

26 Designed to address Web 2.0's failings, Web 3.0 (or Web3, Semantic Web, Web of Data, or Web of Intelligence) has been used to describe a futuristic Web in which the Internet would be more intelligent, semantically rich, and interconnected. Sean B. Palmer, *The Semantic Web: An Introduction* (2001), http://infomesh.net/2001/swintro/Arguably. *See also Web 1.0 vs Web 2.0 vs Web 3.0 vs Web 4.0 vs Web 5.0 – A Bird's Eye on the Evolution and Definition*, Flat World Bus., https:// flatworldbusiness.wordpress.com/flat-education/previously/web-1-0-vs-web-2-0-vs-web-3-0-a-bird-eye-on-the-definition; Sareh Aghaei, Mohammad Ali Nematbakhsh, & Hadi Khosravi Farsani, *Evolution of the World Wide Web: from Web 1.0 to Web 4.0*, 3 Intl' J. of Web & Semantic Technology 1 (2012); Norasak Suphakorntanakit, *WEB 3.0* (2008), https://webuser.hs-furtwangen.de/~heindl/ ebte-08ss-web-20-Suphakorntanakit.pdf.

27 James Ross, *Web3 Was Meant to Be Integral to the Metaverse – It Isn't Yet*, Forbes (January 5, 2023), www .forbes.com/sites/forbesagencycouncil/2023/01/05/web3-was-meant-to-be-integral-to-the-metaverse-it-isnt-yet/?sh=1c6d99da624f.

28 Elizabeth Howcroft, *Virtual Real Estate Plot Sells for Record $2.4 Million*, Reuters (November 24, 2021), www.reuters.com/markets/currencies/virtual-real-estate-plot-sells-record-24-million-2021-11-23/.

29 Elizabeth Howcroft, *Metaverse Pioneers Unimpressed by Facebook Rebrand*, Reuters (November 1, 2021), www.reuters.com/technology/metaverse-pioneers-unimpressed-by-facebook-rebrand-2021-11-01/.

30 Sheila Dang, *Gaming Platforms FlickPlay, The Sandbox Take Steps toward Metaverse*, Reuters (April 18, 2022), www.thestar.com.my/tech/tech-news/2022/04/18/gaming-platforms-flickplay-the-sandbox-take-steps-toward-metaverse.

31 *Blockchain Gaming Market Report 2022: Shift from Traditional Games to Blockchain-Based Games Bolsters Sector*, Yahoo! Fin. (December 26, 2022), www.yahoo.com/now/blockchain-gaming-market-report-2022-113300103.html. RPG is a type of game in which players assume the roles of characters in a fictional setting and take responsibility for acting out these roles within a narrative. RPGs can be differentiated by the method of narrative delivery, but they typically prioritize character development, complex storylines, and interaction with the game world and its inhabitants. *See* Esther MacCallum-Stewart & Justin Parsler, *Role-Play vs. Gameplay: The Difficulties of Playing a Role in World of Warcraft, in* Digital Culture, Play, and Identity: A World of Warcraft Reader, 226 (Hilde G. Corneliussen & Jill Walker Rettberg, eds., 2008) (quoting the *Oxford English Dictionary*) ("a game in which players take on the roles of imaginary characters, usually in a setting created by a referee, and thereby vicariously experience the imagined adventures of these characters"); Jaime E.

III NFTS, DIGITAL GAMING, AND NEW REVENUE BUSINESS MODELS

Among the new blockchain-based business models and revenue opportunities is GameFi,[32] which refers to "video games with decentralized financial components that are backed by blockchain technology."[33] GameFi has become very popular in both the gaming and blockchain industries,[34] and enables players, via the usage of digital assets such as NFTs, to do unique and relatively cutting-edge things such as owning different virtual elements of games, like skins, characters, objects, and even certain areas of the actual game itself.[35]

A *Playing, Earning, and Owning*

Traditionally, games have sourced revenue through either pay-to-play (P2P) or free-to-play (F2P). In the F2P model, users have free access to the game and developers generate revenues primarily through channels such as advertisements, subscriptions, and in-game purchases.[36] In F2P games, users can normally purchase in-game assets – for example, to customize the look of their characters or accelerate their progress more quickly – but can only use such assets inside the game and cannot sell them off for fiat money.[37] P2P games follow a similar pattern but in such games, developers also generate revenue by users for game access.

Muscar, *A Winner Is Who? Fair Use and the Online Distribution of Manga and Video Game Fan Translations*, 9 Vand. J. Ent. & Tech. L. 223, 233 (2006) (describing RPGs and explaining they

> feature interactive narratives in which the player's choices shape the story's outcome. RPGs are often compared to interactive novels or films, because the story and the characters are an integral part of the experience. Thus, translating RPGs from Japanese to English presents many of the problems of translating a film or a novel, and this is reflected in the official translations of these games).

[32] Ojash Yadav, *What Is GameFi and Can You Really Earn Money Playing Video Games?*, Make Tech Easier (February 9, 2022), www.maketecheasier.com/what-is-gamefi

> (The term GameFi comes from joining two words: games and decentralized finance (DeFi). It was first coined in a 2020 tweet by Andre Cronje, the CEO of Yearn Finance.... But the roots actually go back to 2013. Some early initiatives in this field included bitcoin integrations in Minecraft servers and other games like Bombermine that rewarded players with real Bitcoins).

[33] Ibid.

[34] *See, for example,* Paul Tassi, *Reddit Cofounder Says 90% of Games in 5 Years Will Be Blockchain 'Play-To-Earn' Titles*, Forbes (January 17, 2022), www.forbes.com/sites/paultassi/2022/01/17/reddit-cofounder-says-90-of-games-in-5-years-will-be-blockchain-play-to-earn-titles/?sh=415c803914b1 (describing how Reddit's cofounder believes that "in five years, 90 percent of gamers will be playing games on the blockchain that allow them to 'earn' value by their loot/currency having some sort of token equivalent that has actual value").

[35] *See also* Isaac & Browning, *Crypto Enthusiasts*.

[36] *See* Juliane Proelss, Stéphane Sévigny & Denis Schweizer, *GameFi: The Perfect Symbiosis of Blockchain, Tokens, DeFi, and NFTs?* 5 (January 2, 2023) (unpublished manuscript), https://papers.ssrn.com/sol3/papers.cfm?abstract_id=4316073.

[37] Ibid.

Recent decades have witnessed a subtle shift in the gaming landscape with the emergence of the play-to-earn (P2E) model.[38] Under this model, users can acquire in-game assets, not only through purchasing, but also through gameplay. This model focuses on the monetization of in-game purchase opportunities and on encouraging micro-transactions and in-game purchases as an additional source of revenue for developers.[39] In these games, users' in-game purchases can normally be utilized or traded with other players but exclusively within the confines of the game. The growing prominence of this model holds significance for at least two reasons. First, it underscores am emphasis on micro-transactions and in-game purchases and trading as important revenue streams. Second, it brings a new type of participant to the gaming industry: speculative investors who may not actively engage in gameplay but instead invest in in-game assets, speculating on the game's success and popularity.[40]

The integration of blockchain, NFTs, and DeFi protocols introduces an additional layer to the realm of P2E games. While P2E games enable users to monetize their in-game assets, the scope typically remains confined to a single game, with the assets typically stored on the developers' servers. The integration of NFTs and DeFi protocols in gaming change these very two aspects.[41] First, NFTs allow users to truly own their in-game assets detached from developers' influence (e.g., developers cannot unilaterally revoke ownership, such as by shutting down the game). Second, DeFi protocols allow users to transfer their in-game assets outside the confines of a single game, to be utilized in other games, or to be sold or traded on secondary markets for fiat money or other digital assets.

Some commentators describe the growing prevalence of this model of blockchain-based P2E games as a "symptom of a long-developing problem in modern Western economies – 'the financialization of everything.'"[42] This model represents a paradigm shift, focusing on generating value for users and allowing them to better capture the utility and value of the in-game assets they deal with through gameplay and in-game purchases.[43] While in the "traditional" models, the utility of users' in-game purchases is limited to the confines of a specific game (e.g., enhancing gameplay experience), in blockchain-based P2E games with NFTs in-game assets can

---

[38] *See* Udonis, *Play-to-Earn Games 101: How Do They Work?*, Medium (January 25, 2022), https:// medium.com/udonis/play-to-earn-games-101-how-do-they-work-56b07ad2117c.

[39] Ibid.; Daniel L. King et al., *Unfair Play? Video Games as Exploitative Monetized Services: An Examination of Game Patents from a Consumer Protection Perspective*, 10 Comp. in Human Behav. 131, 140 (2019) (noting that "in-game purchasing [is] becoming an increasingly central part of some video games").

[40] Ibid.

[41] *See* Isaac & Browning, *Crypto Enthusiasts* ("One such game was CryptoKitties, a 2017 hit where players collected digital cats, some of which sold for more than $100,000. In the pandemic, blockchain-based games like Axie Infinity, where players make money by earning and selling NFTs, also became popular").

[42] Clive Thompson, *The Untold Story of the NFT Boom*, N.Y. Times (May 12, 2021), www.nytimes .com/2021/05/12/magazine/nft-art-crypto.html?searchResultPosition=1.

[43] *See* Udonis, *Play-to-Earn Games 101*.

be tokenized into transferable assets that can prove useful in other, interconnected games and be exchanged for different digital assets or even money.[44]

The integration of blockchain, NFTs, and DeFi protocols into P2E games introduces a new intersection between gaming and finance that entirely undermines the way society views financial participation and wealth creation. More than banking the unbanked, blockchain-based P2E games are fun, game-based systems that reward time and skill rather than privilege, financial means, and even maturity and legal age.[45]

This innovative ecosystem facilitates the creation of new types of business models and attracts new participants to the gaming industry. An illustrative example is associated with the business of Yield Guild Games (YGG). YGG invests across the blockchain "metaverse" space in order to look to "farm" gaming assets and land parcels. For example, in the digital game Axie Infinity, YGG buys up Axies (in-game fantasy creatures) and then recruits potential players to play Axie Infinity using these Axies, which are lent to the players. By doing so, YGG takes care of the upfront cost of the Axies, lowering the barrier of entry for players and, in return, making players split their earnings with it.[46]

These financial possibilities have made other game studios and companies express interest in P2E as well but not everyone – young gamers included – is happy with this trend; certain critics have even compared P2E to a Ponzi scheme.[47] Yet, despite this divergence of opinions, experts are fairly certain that the industry is changing and that these trends are part of its natural evolution. As Steven Walters, CEO and founder of Gallant Token, puts it:

[R]egular gaming could go the way of the dinosaur due to the play-to-earn gaming model. After all, there are opportunities for parents to create a wallet and allow their children or teenagers to play these games in the future, which would give them the opportunity to do things they couldn't do after playing an Xbox. For example,

---

44 Roger W. Dorsey, Kyleen Prewett, & Gaurav Kumar, *Taxation of NFTs*, 136 J. TAX'N 3, 5 (2022) ("The P2E movement has attracted millions of users across several blockchains. The P2E sector attracted 754,000 daily Unique Active Wallets (UAW) on average during the third quarter of 2021").

45 Beryl Li, *A Play-to-Earn Account Beats a Bank Account*, COINDESK (September 14, 2021), www.coindesk.com/markets/2021/07/29/a-play-to-earn-account-beats-a-bank-account/.

46 Jillian Godsil, *Blockchain Games Take on the Mainstream: Here's How They Can Win*, COINTELEGRAPH (May 3, 2022), https://cointelegraph.com/magazine/2022/05/03/can-p2e-gaming-grind-away-market-share-from-mainstream-games.

47 *See* Isaac & Browning, *Crypto Enthusiasts* (detailing the story of eighteen-year-old high schooler Christian Lantz, who for years played S.T.A.L.K.E.R. and was upset by the "transformative step" toward cryptoassets, joining thousands of other young fans on Twitter and Reddit who raged against this trend); *see also* Leeor Shimron, *Axie Infinity: Pernicious Pyramid Scheme or Gaming Breakthrough?*, FORBES (August 13, 2022), www.forbes.com/sites/leeorshimron/2022/08/13/axie-infinity-pernicious-pyramid-scheme-or-gaming-breakthrough/?sh=21e0e12674b3 ("Since players are required to purchase the in-game assets to participate … analysts have begun to question whether the entire GameFi model is truly an innovative user acquisition strategy or just a plain vanilla pyramid scheme fueled by speculative hype").

they could earn money to spend on real-world items, save for college, or save for the future.[48]

In 2021–2022, echoing this sentiment and the fear of missing out, mainstream news outlets greatly featured the trend of blockchain-based P2E games, expressing much interest in it. Some have focused on how these new trends can contribute to, and have already resulted in, children's financial success and possible educational learning.[49] Others have expressed concerns about ethical and legal concerns that can be associated with these new, innovative, and cutting-edge models.[50]

B *Loots Boxes, NFTs, and Gambling*

In the evolving digital landscape, the concept of loot boxes has emerged as a pivotal element, especially within the realm of gaming and digital assets.[51] Loot boxes are virtual in-game treasure chests that refer to any items, currency, or content that players can buy within a video game. These can include cosmetic items (like character skins or outfits), power-ups, virtual currency, expansions, and more. However, not all in-game purchases are loot boxes – only the ones that when unlocked, yield random items.[52] Therefore, a key aspect of loot boxes is that they provide randomized rewards. When players buy a loot box, they do not know exactly what they will get and the contents might range from common items to rare and valuable ones.

The use of loot boxes in games is a subject of controversy due to their resemblance to gambling: purchasing a stake in an outcome determined by chance.[53] And indeed, studies have shown that those purchasing loot boxes in games tend to score higher on problem gambling assessments.[54] This reported connection between gambling and loot boxes has prompted concerns regarding the exposure of children

---

[48] Robert Farrington, *Play-to-Earn Gaming Is Driving NFT and Crypto Growth*, FORBES (December 13, 2021), www.forbes.com/sites/robertfarrington/2021/12/13/play-to-earn-gaming-is-driving-nft-and-crypto-growth/?sh=600e1e7fc2dc.

[49] *See, for example*, Joe Cortez, *How to Pick the Right Play-to-Earn Game for You*, COINDESK (March 10, 2022), www.coindesk.com/learn/how-to-pick-the-right-play-to-earn-game-for-you/.

[50] *See* Packin, *Financial Inclusion Gone Wrong*, 368–369.

[51] On the financial success of loot boxes, *see* Michael Baggs, *Genshin Impact Earns $2 Billion After 'Unheard Of' Success in First Year*, BBC (September 30, 2021), www.bbc.com/news/newsbeat-58707297.

[52] Edwin Hong, *Loot Boxes: Gambling for the Next Generation*, 46 W. ST. L. REV. 61 (2019) (describing loot boxes and their gambling-like features). The loot boxes phenomenon is a global one. In terms of origin, "[o]ne of the earliest forms of loot boxes began in Japan, known there as "kompu gacha," or "complete gacha." The word itself was derived from the word "gachapon," which is a toy capsule vending machine. The concept was identical to that of loot boxes: players would exchange currency for a random chance at prizes, some more valuable than others. Perhaps even more predatory is the kompu gacha's mechanism that requires the player to win several specific prizes in order to ultimately combine into an even rarer and valuable item." Ibid., 69.

[53] Paul Delfabbro, Amelia Delic, & Daniel L. King, Understanding the Mechanics and Consumer Risks Associated with Play-to-Earn (P2E) Gaming, 11 J. BEHAV. ADDICTIONS 716, 717 (2022).

[54] For an overview of the empirical research in this area, *see* ibid.

under the age of eighteen to these gambling-like elements in games and the potential for loot boxes to cause financial harm to these children.[55]

The integration of NFTs and DeFi protocols into games adds an additional layer to loot boxes and their associated concerns. Normally, the value obtained from a video game loot box cannot be used or transferred outside the confines of the specific game in which the loot box was acquired and the obtained item is normally stored on a third-party's server. By integrating NFTs and DeFi protocols into loot boxes, developers can offer users more control over the acquired items and expand the ways in which these items can be utilized, including the possibility of trading them externally on NFT marketplaces.

This potential for external trading has led developers to increasingly integrate NFTs within loot boxes. One prominent example of such integration comes from Boxed.gg, a platform that offers loot boxes that can contain a variety of digital collectibles in the form of NFTs.[56] Another example of this combination comes from Atari. For its fiftieth anniversary, the company teamed up with NFT developer Republic Realm to create a collection of what they call "GFTs," or NFTs designed for gifting.[57] Each GFT contains an NFT based on Atari gaming and the content of the GFT – the NFT – will be revealed at a specific date in the future.[58] Each GFT contains an NFT based on Atari gaming and the content of the GFT – the NFT – will be revealed on a specific date in the future. Essentially, these GFTs combine the elements of loot boxes and NFTs, with the distinction that they are free. An additional illustration is MEMEbox, which offers loot boxes containing meme coins, such as Dogecoin.[59] And as the NFT and gaming markets continue to grow, it is highly plausible that more games will use NFTs in combination with loot boxes.

Despite the increasing popularity of loot boxes in general and NFT-based ones in particular, US regulators have not yet given sufficient attention to the concerns associated with the use of such instruments. Indeed, in 2020, the Federal Trade Commission (FTC) issued a report, titled "Staff Perspective on Its Workshop, Inside the Game: Unlocking the Consumer Issues Surrounding Loot Boxes,"[60] which discussed a workshop the agency held concerning this issue.[61] The report focused on

---

[55] Ibid. With this in mind, it is also worth noting that, it is also possible that loot boxes were attractive to those who were already interested in gambling. *See* ibid.

[56] *See* Thomas Wilde, *VideoGame Loot Box Platform That Uses NFTs Raises $1.5M*, GEEKWIRE (May 25, 2023), www.geekwire.com/2023/video-game-loot-box-platform-that-uses-nfts-raises-1-5m/.

[57] *See The Atari Collection*, GFT Shoppe (2022), https://gftshoppe.com/atari.

[58] *See* Sean Murray, *Atari Celebrates 50th Birthday with Every Gamer's Nightmare: NFT Lootboxes*, THE GAMER (January 27, 2022), www.thegamer.com/atari-50th-anniversary-lootbox-nft/.

[59] See MEMEBOX (2024), https://thememebox.io/.

[60] Lesley Fair, *Loot Boxes: What's in Play?*, FED. TRADE COMM'N (August 14, 2020), www.ftc.gov/business-guidance/blog/2020/08/loot-boxes-whats-play.

[61] *Inside the Game: Unlocking the Consumer Issues Surrounding Loot Boxes*, FED. TRADE COMM'N (August 7, 2019), www.ftc.gov/news-events/events-calendar/inside-game-unlocking-consumer-issues-surrounding-loot-boxes.

the impact of loot boxes on video gamers, particularly children. It also explored the financial impact paid loot boxes have on revenue streams and consumers,[62] including a pay-to-progress and pay-to-win scenarios, where child gamers find themselves in "grinding gameplay loops unless they buy loot boxes."[63] It stressed that these aspects are critical as many of the consumers purchasing loot boxes are children who do not fully understand the cost of loot box transactions, they are susceptible to marketing tactics that lure them to buy more loot boxes or engage in problematic digital media use.[64] However, while the FTC has paid attention to learning some of the relevant concerns, it has refrained from implementing regulations or continuing the work they started doing on these issues. Specifically, the FTC pointed to the varied opinions of commenters and panelists on the need for government intervention and advocated for "industry self-regulation," noting the need to do "continued research and public education."[65] Therefore, the FTC has left loot boxes to be, at least for now. Similarly, it has not tackled topics related to GameFi, or emerging and related business models like the integration of DeFi protocols and NFTs into P2E games.

Contrastingly, other governments have been taking action. In early 2023, the European Parliament advocated for harmonized EU rules to bolster protection for online video game players, with a significant focus on loot boxes.[66] There has been a push to understand and regulate how these in-game randomized purchases operate, emphasizing transparency from game developers and potential restrictions to protect consumers, particularly minors. In fact, studies, like the one backed by twenty consumer organizations from a Norwegian Consumer Council report in 2022, have highlighted deceptive practices within the industry.[67] Some nations, like Belgium and the Netherlands, had already initiated strict measures against loot boxes. Belgium, for instance, classified loot boxes purchased with real money as gambling.[68] The Netherlands, after a series of legal battles with game developers like Electronic Arts, started moves towards a complete ban on loot boxes in 2022, citing their connection to gambling through microtransactions, responding to commentators' concerns and arguments that loot boxes could lead to gambling addictions as players may

---

[62] Fair, *Loot Boxes.*

[63] Ibid.

[64] Ibid.

[65] Ibid.

[66] European Parliament resolution of January 18, 2023, On Consumer Protection in Online Video Games: A European Single Market Approach (2022/2014(INI)).

[67] Forbrukerrådet (Norwegian Consumer Council), Insert Coin: How the gaming industry exploits consumers using loot boxes (May 31, 2022), available at https://storage.forbrukerradet.no/media/2022/05/2022-05-31-insert-coin-publish.pdf.

[68] Chris Scullion, *18 European Countries' Consumer Groups Have Joined the Fight against Loot Boxes,* Video Games Chronicle (June 1, 2022), www.videogameschronicle.com/news/18-european-country-groups-have-joined-the-fight-against-loot-boxes/.

be tempted to keep buying loot boxes in the hopes of getting a rare or valuable item or NFT.[69]

Meanwhile, the UK emphasized improved industry self-regulation rather than outright bans or reclassification of loot boxes as gambling. The UK Government's response was to call for better protection mechanisms, mainly for young individuals.[70] Then, in July 2023, the UK government published an update on improvements to industry-led protections in the form of a guidance in connection with loot boxes in video games.[71] Germany updated its age-rating criteria to include loot box considerations, while Spain proposed comprehensive regulation of loot boxes in 2022.[72] Austria's courts and Finland's legislature are examining how loot boxes fit within existing gambling regulations.[73] Poland, at present, views loot boxes outside the purview of its Gambling Law Act.[74]

In conclusion, the discourse around loot box regulation in the EU is gaining momentum. The shared concerns revolve around the potentially exploitative nature of loot boxes, drawing parallels with gambling, and the urgent need to protect vulnerable populations, especially minors. Incorporating blockchain and NFTs into loot boxes may amplify these concerns, increasing the appeal of the "prizes" within these boxes by granting users greater control over the prizes and enabling external trading of them. While it remains to be seen how the use of NFTs in loot boxes will evolve in the future, as the digital frontier continues to expand, the intricate dance between these two concepts will undeniably shape the future of gaming economies.

C *Differing Financial Needs and Perceptions of Monetization of Gaming*

The integration of blockchain, NFTs, and DeFi protocols into gaming creates unique opportunities for both users and developers. Users can have greater control over tokenized in-game assets and can more easily transfer and trade them on secondary markets. Developers are provided with an additional potential revenue

---

[69] *Loot Boxes Likely to Be Banned in the Netherlands Due to Gambling Links*, USA TODAY: FOR THE WIN (July 4, 2022), https://ftw.usatoday.com/2022/07/loot-box-ban-the-netherlands.

[70] UK Government, Department for Digital, Culture, Media & Sport, Government Response to the Call for Evidence on Loot Boxes in Video Games (July 18, 2022), www.gov.uk/government/consultations/loot-boxes-in-video-games-call-for-evidence/outcome/government-response-to-the-call-for-evidence-on-loot-boxes-in-video-games.

[71] UK Government, Department for Digital, Culture, Media & Sport, Guidance: Loot Boxes in Video Games: Update on Improvements to Industry-Led Protections (July 2018, 2023), www.gov.uk/guidance/loot-boxes-in-video-games-update-on-improvements-to-industry-led-protections.

[72] *Loot Box Regulation in the EU: Loading Status*, DENTONS LAW FIRM (June 28, 2023), www.dentons.com/en/insights/guides-reports-and-whitepapers/2023/june/28/loot-box-regulation-in-the-eu-loading-status (explaining that "the German age rating board, has expanded its test criteria and will now include loot boxes, other in-game transactions and online chat features within the "possible online risks" category when classifying a game. The new rules came into effect on January 1, 2023").

[73] Ibid.

[74] Ibid.

stream – one that goes beyond merely selling games and embedding in-game purchase features, such as micro-transactions and loot boxes. This alternative revenue stream involves creating blockchain marketplaces for in-game assets and other types of NFTs and generating revenue through transaction fees.

Despite this promising potential, the reception to the integration of blockchain and NFTs into gaming has been polarizing. For example, Ubisoft's ambitious introduction of NFTs in "Ghost Recon Breakpoint" ended up underwhelming.[75] Similarly, Steam, one of the largest gaming platforms in the world, banned the use of cryptocurrencies and NFTs on its platform, revising its developers' guidelines to state to include "[a]pplications built on blockchain technology that issue or allow exchange of cryptocurrencies or NFTs" in the list of things developers should not "publish on stream."[76] One potential reason for this adverse attitude is that the users see the integration of NFTs as a prioritization of financial gains over genuinely needed gameplay improvement.[77]

Interestingly, however, the perception of the integration of NFTs in gaming is not uniform in the global context and appears to differ between users from North America and those originating in the Asia-Pacific region.[78] North American and European users, who primarily play for entertainment, tend to resist the integration of NFTs more than Asian Pacific users, seeing the integration of NFTs in gaming as a mere profit-driven move that does not enhance the actual gaming experience.[79] By contrast, users from Asia-Pacific regions seem to embrace the integration of NFTs. For many in countries like Vietnam, Indonesia, and the Philippines, the potential to earn from playing games is a game-changer.[80] Given the relative strength of cryptocurrencies against local currencies, playing crypto games can result in substantial earnings and so for many in these regions, crypto gaming is not just a pastime, it's an alternative source of income.[81]

To put it simply, there is a geographical divergence in opinions about NFTs in gaming that is rooted in differing financial needs and perceptions. Players from Western countries, who primarily play for entertainment, view the monetization through NFTs mainly as an intrusion into their fun time or even an escape from

---

[75] Diane-Laure Arjaliès, Harsheen Anand, & Lakshay Kumar, *Blockchain, Cryptos and NFTs in the Gaming Industry: A Tale of Two Worlds*, U. Western Ont. Research Report (2023), https://ir.lib.uwo.ca/iveypub/64/.

[76] *See Onboarding*, Steam (2023), https://partner.steamgames.com/doc/gettingstarted/onboarding; Mitchell Clark, *Valve Bans Blockchain Games and NFTs on Steam, Epic Will Try to Make It Work*, The Verge (October 15, 2021), www.theverge.com/2021/10/15/22728425/valve-steam-blockchain-nft-crypto-ban-games-age-of-rust.

[77] Arjaliès, Anand, & Kumar, *Blockchain, Cryptos and NFTs*, 8–9.

[78] Ibid.

[79] Ibid., 7–8.

[80] Ibid., 9–10.

[81] Ibid.

reality. In contrast, players from Asia-Pacific regions embrace it as a livelihood opportunity.

IV LEGAL AND ETHICAL ISSUES ASSOCIATED WITH NFTS AND GAMEFI

Digital gaming, especially with the integration of blockchain and NFTs, raises various legal and ethical issues, ranging from the exposure of children to gambling-like and addictive features to the application of securities regulation to products whose primary focus might be non-financial (e.g., entertainment). This part provides a high-level overview of some of these major issues.

A *Children and Digital Gaming*

The digital gaming industry targets both children and adults but the representation of children and minors among gamers is clearly high. As a result, any conversation about the target audience for digital games must include a focus on children and adolescents. This emphasis is crucial because minors, especially children, differ significantly from adults in many ways. These differences span developmental, biological, social, intellectual, and legal dimensions, to name a few.

One particular concern regarding the involvement of children in digital gaming is the exposure to gaming-like activities and elements. Digital games may involve activities such as esports bets, which appeal to children and adults[82] and can result in gambling addictions.[83] The integration of loot boxes in games – which essentially allow users, including minors, to purchase a stake in an outcome determined by chance – creates similar concerns. Studies have shown that those purchasing loot boxes in games tend to score higher on problem gambling assessments,[84] creating concerns that the exposure of minors to these gambling-like elements in games may increase the interest of children in gambling and cause financial harm to children.[85] These concerns are amplified by the integration of blockchain and NFTs, which makes it easier to participate in gambling-like activities by spending money (e.g., purchasing NFTs on NFT marketplaces)

---

[82] *See, for example*, Raffaello Rossi & Agnes Nairn, *How Children Are Being Targeted with Hidden Ads on Social Media*, Yahoo! Fin. (November 3, 2021), https://uk.news.yahoo.com/children-being-targeted-hidden-ads-122439705.

[83] Raffaello Rossi & Agnes Nairn, *Esports Could Be Quietly Spawning a Whole New Generation of Problem Gamblers*, The Conversation (October 1, 2020), https://theconversation.com/esports-could-be-quietly-spawning-a-whole-new-generation-of-problem-gamblers-147124.

[84] For an overview of the empirical research in this area, *see* Delfabbro, Delic, & King, *Understanding the Mechanics and Consumer Risks*, 717.

[85] Ibid.

rather than earning these rewards through game-play,[86] and because the rewards within loot boxes become more valuable as users can trade externally.

Another concern is the addictive nature of digital games, especially for minors. With the unique characteristics and susceptibilities of minors in mind, studies identified digital gaming as an addictive activity for children,[87] one that is associated with non-ideal consequences.[88] Due to their design, social digital platforms, including digital games, can function like casinos, in that they are structured in a way that makes users lose their sense of time with videos that start automatically and content feeds that can scroll on to infinity, in an attempt to keep children glued to their devices.[89] This is reflected, for example, by the integration of interactive "game-like" features, such as point scoring, competitions among players, and rules of play.[90] Put in simpler terms, digital platforms – including digital games – can function like "hard drugs" for children.[91] Being online, predominantly by web-surfing or playing in interactive platforms, "acts like a stimulant," like caffeine or cocaine.[92] The surge of dopamine triggered by electronic stimuli impacts children and teens more intensely as their underdeveloped cerebral cortexes hinder them from feeling content with minimal exposure or effectively self-regulating.[93] Thus, it is very difficult for everyone, but children in particular, to simply stop and turn off their digital devices.

This concern is significantly exacerbated by the monetization of in-game assets and the integration of NFTs. Some commentators suggest that the increasing monetization of games may shift the motivation behind playing digital games from pure enjoyment to a focus on the monetary outcome.[94] This shift in motivation has been found to be associated with poorer self-control, maladaptive gaming behaviors, and greater risk of excessive gaming.[95] The integration of NFTs, which provides users with greater control over in-game assets and enable external trading beyond the confines of a particular game, may elevate the monetary incentive associated with gaming, and thus exacerbate these concerns.

[86] Ibid.
[87] *Saving Children from Digital Gaming Addiction*, EDUCATIONWORLD (2023), www.educationworld.in/saving-children-from-digital-gaming-addiction/.
[88] *See* Anya Kamenetz, *Is 'Gaming Disorder' an Illness? WHO Says Yes, Adding It to Its List of Diseases*, NPR (May 28, 2019), www.npr.org/2019/05/28/727585904/is-gaming-disorder-an-illness-the-who-says-yes-adding-it-to-its-list-of-diseases.
[89] *Why Social Media Apps Are Like Casinos for Children*, DOT.LA (March 21, 2022), https://dot.la/social-media-addiction-2657010894.html (citing Ed Howard, senior counsel at the University of San Diego School of Law's Children's Advocacy Institute).
[90] Melanie Waddell, *FINRA Targets 'Game-Like' Digital Platforms*, THINKADVISOR (February 3, 2021), www.thinkadvisor.com/2021/02/03/finra-examiners-eye-game-like-digital-platforms/.
[91] Marika Lindholm, *Parenting in the Era of Addictive Electronics*, PSYCH. TODAY (July 13, 2017), www.psychologytoday.com/us/blog/more-women-s-work/201707/parenting-in-the-era-addictive-electronics.
[92] Ibid.
[93] Ibid.
[94] Delfabbro, Delic, & King, *Understanding the Mechanics and Consumer Risks*, 723 (for an overview of this line of literature).
[95] Ibid.

Finally, digital gaming raises concerns with regard to the exploitation of data on minors. Although numerous children and young adults perceive digital games and social media apps as harmless leisure, these platforms can significantly jeopardize user data and privacy,[96] specifically when used by young, naïve, and inexperienced people. In fact, these users frequently find themselves monitored, with their decisions, data, and even vulnerabilities being capitalized upon, whether by entities seeking to exploit naive minors or by conventional business strategies.[97]

Combined, these legal issues raise various novel questions and considerations. For example, how many hours a day and starting at what age should children be permitted to play with the intention to earn a significant income? Likewise, how can the authorities monitor this information in an effective way and know which children are involved in such labor activities? Similarly, educational aspects beyond the obvious financial ones should be considered. One such consideration is children's exposure to adult content like M-rated video games.[98] Another is children's exposure to gambling-like activities. Finally, privacy law issues that go far beyond the scope of this chapter and relate to the engagement with digital and online platforms should be considered.[99]

---

[96] *See* Jacob Leon Kröger et al., Surveilling the Gamers: Privacy Impacts of the Video Game Industry, 44 ENT. COMPUTING (January 2023)

> (Since the workings of data collection and data mining are completely invisible to ordinary video game users, it can be impossible for them to understand and control what information is revealed. Sophisticated surveillance and assessment mechanisms can be imperceptibly woven into the fabric of game environments and storylines. The immersive and distractive nature of video games may further impede a reasonable reflection on the staggering scope of the data harvesting taking place and on potential data misuses. Considering the immense and growing popularity of video gaming, consumer education in this field is urgently needed, along with effective technical and legal safeguards).

[97] *See, for example*, Matt Levine, *People Are Worried about Payment for Order Flow*, BLOOMBERG (February 5, 2021), www.bloomberg.com/opinion/articles/2021-02-05/robinhood-gamestop-saga-pressures-payment-for-order-flow; Divya Seth, *Payment-for-Order-Flow Implications for Robinhood Users* 1 (2020) (unpublished manuscript), https://ssrn.com/abstract=3779648 (highlighting problems associated with payment for order flow (PFOF), assessing policies allowing it, and exploring policy alternatives); David Easley, Nicholas M. Kiefer, & Maureen O'Hara, *Cream-Skimming or Profit-Sharing? The Curious Role of Purchased Order Flow*, 51 J. FIN. 811, 812–813 (1996).

[98] *See also* Sam Reynolds, *GameFi Faces Regulatory Headwinds in Major Asian Markets*, COINDESK (February 1, 2022), www.coindesk.com/policy/2022/02/01/gamefi-faces-regulatory-headwinds-in-major-asian-markets/ (detailing how, appreciating the importance of some of these issues, Asian regulators have recently expressed concerns over the GameFi trend).

[99] *See for example*, Michal Gilad et al., *Science for Policy to Protect Children in Cyberspace*, SCI. (March 31, 2023) (advocating for presenting scientifically informed approaches or evidence to shape policy decisions); Nizan Geslevich Packin, *Protecting Our Children In Cyberspace: What Are We Missing?*, FORBES (November 10, 2022), www.forbes.com/sites/nizangpackin/2022/11/10/protecting-our-children-in-cyberspace-what-are-we-missing/?sh=7bbb2a572c42 (explaining why we need to devote more attention to the protection of children in cyberspace).

B *Securities Regulation*

Another issue worth exploring in this context is the application of securities regulation, which plays a significant role in the offering and selling of cryptocurrencies in
general and NFTs in particular.[100] Under US federal securities laws, the definition
of "security" is broad and includes transactions that are "investment contracts." An
investment contract may be formed when users pay money for a tokenized in-game
asset based on an expectation of profit and the expectation of profits is derived from
the managerial efforts of others (e.g., the issuer of the tokenized asset).[101] With this
in mind, game developers must be cautious about not inadvertently creating investment schemes that could be classified as securities. Relatedly, developers must also
exercise caution regarding the potential applicability of the provisions applying
to securities exchanges, which could apply to any platform permitting the sale of
tokenized in-game assets that are securities. The integration of DeFi protocols and
NFTs in digital gaming may arguably increase the potential application of securities regulation to digital games as it enables users to trade and sell their in-game
assets in the secondary markets and thus realize financial gains from them more
easily.[102]

An illustration of this point can be found in the 64-page judgment in the case of
Friel v. *Dapper Labs*.[103] In the case, Dapper Labs, the defendant, was recognized
for its creation of a sought-after NFT series, "Moments," produced in collaboration
with the NBA. These NFTs were distinctive video highlights of NBA matches, each
uniquely serialized and stored on the proprietary flow blockchain by Dapper Labs.
In a groundbreaking verdict, the Court declined Dapper Labs' request to dismiss the
case. It determined that the plaintiffs had sufficiently claimed that Moments were
not merely akin to sports trading cards but potentially operated as securities and
should have been registered accordingly. Notably, the Court did not generalize that
all NFTs are "securities." Instead, it indicated that, based on the plaintiffs' claims,

---

[100] For an analysis of the applicability of the federal securities laws to cryptoassets and crypto exchanges,
see, for example, Yuliya Guseva, *The SEC, Digital Assets, and Game Theory*, 46 J. Corp. L. 629, 641
(2021); Thomas Lee Hazen, *Tulips, Oranges, Worms, and Coins – Virtual, Digital, or Crypto Currency
and the Securities Laws*, 20 N.C. J.L. & Tech. 493, 499 (2019); Carol R. Goforth, *Cinderella's Slipper:
A Better Approach to Regulating Cryptoassets as Securities*, 17 Hastings Bus. L.J. 271, 271 (2021).
[101] The term "investment contracts" is defined in Howey Test. *SEC* v. *W.J. Howey* Co., 328 U.S. 293, 301
(1946). Under the *Howey* test, a transaction is an investment contract, and hence a security, if (i) it
involves an investment of money; (ii) in a common enterprise; (iii) with a reasonable expectation of
profits from the investment; and (iv) the profits are to be derived from the entrepreneurial or managerial efforts of others.
[102] *See, for example*, Strategic Hub for Innovation & Fin. Tech., *Framework for "Investment Contract"
Analysis of Digital Assets*, Sec. & Exch. Comm'n (April 3, 2019), www.sec.gov/files/dlt-framework
.pdf (noting, with regard to the reasonable expectation of profits prong, that "[a] purchaser may expect
to realize a return through participating in distributions or through other methods of realizing appreciation on the asset, such as selling at a gain in a secondary market").
[103] *Friel* v. *Dapper Labs, Inc.*, No. 21 CIV. 5837 (VM), ECF No. 43 (S.D.N.Y. Feb. 22, 2023).

Moments displayed security-like attributes. Key aspects of the ruling, including Dapper Labs' exclusive control over Moments' secondary market and promotional tweets containing emojis suggesting investment returns, serve as a crucial lesson for NFT vendors aiming to reduce potential pitfalls.

C Gambling

Another key legal issue in this context concerns the application of gambling laws. In the US, gambling activities are primarily governed by state laws. In most states, an activity is considered gambling if it involves (i) some degree of chance, (ii) a prize that constitutes something of value, and (iii) the payment of some consideration.[104]

The integration of NFTs into digital games, and especially into loot boxes, can affect the analysis of the prize element. While there appears to be a consensus that prizes of value do not have to be monetary winnings and can include different forms, such as cars and vacations, it is still unclear whether and when virtual items – especially in-game virtual items – can be considered something of value.[105] In particular, courts seem to be split as to whether virtual items that cannot be cashed out outside a game (e.g., virtual tokens that can only be used to play the game again or accelerate progress in the game) can fulfill the prize of value element.[106]

This argument – that in-game virtual assets that cannot be cashed out outside the boundaries of the game do not qualify as something of value for the purpose of state gambling law – is commonly being used by game developers.[107] This argument can arguably hold in "traditional" digital games where the transfer of the in-game assets outside the boundaries of the game is, indeed, typically prohibited or impossible. However, in the context of blockchain-based games that allow external trading of tokenized in-game assets and operate marketplaces for buying and selling such assets, this argument may be less likely to hold. In this way, the integration of blockchain and NFTs can have a significant impact in this context.

V CONCLUSION

The concepts of playfulness and gamification hold central positions in our societal fabric. In recent years, the digital gaming industry has experienced an exponential surge and has gradually shifted its focus toward the monetization of in-game assets. This transformation has been accelerated by the integration of blockchain, DeFi

---

[104] See Kimberly A. Houser & John T. Holden, *Navigating the Non-Fungible Token*, 2022 UTAH L. REV. 891, 904 (2022); James Gatto, *Legal Issues with Blockchain-Based Crypto Games and Collectibles*, SHEPPARD MULLIN (May 2018), www.sheppardmullin.com/media/publication/1718_Blockchain-Issues-for-Interactive-Entertainment-Companies-Article-0518.pdf.

[105] See Sheldon Evans, *Pandora's Loot Box*, 90 GEO. WASH. L. REV. 376, 405–406 (2022).

[106] Ibid., 408–409.

[107] Gatto, *Legal Issues.*

protocols, and NFTs that enable external trading of in-game assets and provide users with more control over their in-game assets.

This transformation, however, has not been smooth sailing. A sizable faction of gamers vocalizes their discontent over the amalgamation of NFTs and crypto-currencies within gaming, perceiving these primarily financial-driven inclusions as contaminating the genuine spirit of gaming. Interestingly, these voices appear to come mainly from American European users, whereas users from Asia Pacific regions seem to embrace the financialization of gaming, embracing it as a live-lihood opportunity. Furthermore, commentators raised concerns that the mone-tization of in-game assets and the inclusion of gambling-like activities (e.g., loot boxes) – particularly when combined with NFTs – may create risks to minors in terms of excessive play, exposure to gambling activities that may lead to future inter-est in such activities, and potential financial harm.

Against this background, policy-makers are faced with major challenges. One challenge is to balance business ethics and consumer protection principles, includ-ing those related to children, with the advancement of innovation in the gaming and financial industry. Indeed, digital platforms and developers find themselves at the crossroads of artistic integrity, gaming experience, and financial viability. Therefore, they need to find ways to incorporate NFTs without alienating or even harming their core player base, while also complying with various legal requirements and laws relating to privacy, financial regulation, gambling, deception, advertising, and much more. Another challenge is to adjust the existing legal frameworks to appro-priately accommodate the innovative features of NFTs and GameFi. As players and developers continue to develop and examine new and innovative models, the line between gaming and tangible assets will likely continue to blur, forging new fron-tiers in the gaming realm. Regulators and policy-makers should pay close attention to these developments and assess whether and how existing frameworks can, and should, accommodate these new business models.

PART IV

Intellectual Property and Ownership Rights

11

NFTs and Copyright Law

Tyler T. Ochoa

I INTRODUCTION

The concept of using non-fungible tokens (NFTs) to facilitate and authenticate sales of digital art dates back to 2014,[1] but it took several years before the it really captured public attention. The market for NFTs began to grow in 2017, with the release of two large-scale NFT projects, CryptoPunks,[2] and CryptoKitties.[3] By October 2020, when the National Basketball Association (NBA) paired with Dapper Labs to launch Top Shot, collectible NFT-based digital trading cards,[4] a speculative bubble had begun to build in the market for NFTs. The NFT craze exploded in March 2021, when auction house Christie's sold an NFT of a collage of 5,000 images by digital artist Mike Winkelman, known professionally as Beeple, to a Singaporean investor for $69 million.[5] Suddenly it seemed like NFTs were everywhere.

Shortly after the sale, Winkelman described the NFT market as "extremely speculative" and he warned: "This is for people who are looking to take some risks, because a lot of this stuff will absolutely go to zero … And I believe it's absolutely in an irrational exuberance bubble."[6] Winkelman was prescient: in May 2022, the *Wall*

---

[1] *See below*, Section III.

[2] CryptoPunks is a collection of NFTs of 10,000 unique, algorithmically generated images. It was released on the Ethereum blockchain in June 2017. For details, *see* Brian L. Frye, *Are CryptoPunks Copyrightable?*, 2021 PEPP. L. REV. 105, 108–110 (2022).

[3] CryptoKitties is a blockchain-based game in which buyers purchase, "breed" and sell NFTs of cartoon kittens. It was released on the Ethereum blockchain in November 2017, but is now hosted on Dapper Labs' Flow blockchain. *See* Nellie Bowles, *CryptoKitties, Explained … Mostly*, N.Y. TIMES (December 28, 2017), www.nytimes.com/2017/12/28/style/cryptokitties-want-a-blockchain-snuggle.html.

[4] *See* David Gerard & Amy Castor, *NBA Top Shot: A Short History of the Largest Mainstream NFT Project*, DAVID GERARD (April 17, 2020), https://davidgerard.co.uk/blockchain/2022/04/17/nba-top-shot-a-short-history-of-the-largest-mainstream-nft-project/.

[5] *See* Scott Reyburn, *JPG File Sells for $69 Million, as 'NFT Mania' Gathers Pace*, N.Y. TIMES (March 11, 2021) www.nytimes.com/2021/03/11/arts/design/nft-auction-christies-beeple.html.

[6] *See* Anthony Cuthbertson, *NFT Millionaire Beeple Says Crypto Art Is Bubble and Will 'Absolutely go to Zero,'* THE INDEPENDENT (March 24, 2021) www.independent.co.uk/tech/nft-beeple-cryptocurrency-art-b1821314.html.

Street Journal reported that "[t]he NFT market is collapsing."[7] Average daily sales of NFTs had fallen 92 percent from September 2021 and the number of active "wallets" (active buyers) had fallen 88 percent from November 2021.[8] By October 2022, "NFT sales were down by more than 90 percent in nearly every metric – including volume and price – compared to the year before."[9] This negative trend has persisted into 2023, as sales and trading volume continued to undergo a sharp decline.[10]

Anytime people are making or losing large amounts of money, lawsuits are inevitable; so it is hardly surprising that 2021 and 2022 also saw the first wave of lawsuits concerning NFTs. Many of those lawsuits either alleged copyright infringement or sought a declaration of copyright ownership. Since copyright law governs the reproduction of works of art, including digital images, the connection to NFTs seems obvious. Yet, as this chapter will explain, copyright law is only tangentially related to NFTs, for two reasons. First, buying an NFT does *not*, by itself, convey *any* rights to reproduce or display the work associated with that token. Instead, those rights are governed entirely by the contract that accompanies the sale. Second, minting and selling an NFT, by itself, likely does *not* violate any of the exclusive rights provided by copyright. As a result, although copyright may provide a useful tool for artists seeking to monetize their art, it is probable that its usefulness will be limited in lawsuits concerning NFTs. Instead, as this chapter notes, trademark law may emerge as a more promising legal strategy.

II BACKGROUND: COPYRIGHT LAW

Copyright law governs the rights of authors, publishers, and users in literary and artistic works, including paintings, drawings, and digital art.[11] In the US, it grants to the author the exclusive rights to reproduce and distribute copies of the work, to publicly perform or display the work, and to prepare derivative works based on the

---

[7] *See* Paul Vigna, *NFT Sales Are Flatlining*, Wall. St. J. (May 3, 2022), www.wsj.com/articles/nft-sales-are-flatlining-11651552616.

[8] Ibid.

[9] *See* Danny Parisi, 2022 *Was the Year of the NFT Reality Check*, Glossy (December 27, 2022), www.glossy.co/fashion/2022-was-the-year-of-the-nft-reality-check/.

[10] *See, for example*, Jacquelyn Melinek, *Monthly NFT Sales Fell for Fifth Consecutive Month to $495M in July*, TechCrunch (August 23, 2023), https://techcrunch.com/2023/08/03/monthly-nft-sales-fell-for-fifth-consecutive-month-to-495m-in-july/; Leeor Shimron, *NFT Market Meltdown: How Can Investors Best Position Themselves?*, Forbes (July 11, 2023), www.forbes.com/sites/leeorshimron/2023/07/11/nft-market-meltdown-how-can-investors-best-position-themselves/?sh=10aef2905821.

[11] In the US, copyright is governed by the Copyright Act of 1976, as amended. The subject matter of copyright includes "pictorial, graphic, and sculptural works," 17 U.S.C. §102(a)(5), the definition of which includes "two-dimensional and three-dimensional works of fine, graphic, and applied art." 17 U.S.C. §101. In the UK, copyright is governed by the Copyright, Designs and Patents Act 1988, as amended [hereinafter CDPA 1988]. The subject matter of copyright includes "artistic works," CDPA 1988, § 1(1)(a), the definition of which includes "a graphic work [or] photograph." CDPA 1988, § 4(1)(a). A "graphic work" is defined to include "any painting [or] drawing." CDPA 1988, § 4(2)(a).

work.[12] In the UK, copyright grants the exclusive rights to copy the work, to issue copies to the public, to rent or lend the work to the public, to perform, show, or play the work in public, to communicate the work to the public (by broadcasting or electronic transmission), and to make an adaptation of the work.[13] Member states of the EU are required to provide authors the exclusive rights of reproduction, public distribution, communication to the public (by wire or wireless means), and making the work available to the public, so that members of the public may access the work from a time and place individually chosen by them.[14] Although phrased somewhat differently, these rights are largely the same in each of the three jurisdictions.[15]

US copyright law carefully distinguishes between the work (an intangible selection and arrangement of words, images, or pixels) and the tangible embodiments of the work (which are either copies or phonorecords).[16] For example, a literary work is a sequence of words that is fixed initially in a manuscript (if handwritten or typed) or hard drive (if written on a computer) and can be reproduced in the form of books or manuscripts (copies) or as an audiobook in the form of CDs or cassettes (phonorecords).[17] An audiovisual work is a series of related images, together with any accompanying sounds, that can be fixed or reproduced in the form of film, videotapes, or DVDs (copies).[18] A musical work is a selection and arrangement of notes (with or without words) that is fixed initially in a manuscript or master recording and can be reproduced in the form of sheet music (copies) or vinyl discs, CDs, or cassettes (phonorecords).[19] A pictorial or graphic work is a selection and arrangement of lines and shapes or pixels that is fixed initially in a tangible medium (such as oil on canvas, pencil on paper) and can be reproduced in the form of posters, greeting

---

[12] 17 U.S.C. §106.

[13] CDPA 1988, §16.

[14] Directive 2001/29/EC of the European Parliament and of the Council of 22 May 2001 on the Harmonisation of Certain Aspects of Copyright and Related Rights in the Information Society, 2001 O.J. (L 167/10) [hereinafter Directive 2001/29/EC], arts. 2, 3 & 4. These are augmented by Directive 2006/115/EC of 12 Dec. 2006, on rental right and lending right and on certain rights related to copyright in the field of intellectual property, 2006 O.J. (L 376/28), art. 3; Directive 2001/84/EC of 27 Sept. 2001, on the resale right for the benefit of the author of an original work of art, art. 1; and Directive 93/83/EEC of 27 Sept. 1983, as amended, on the coordination of certain rules concerning copyright and rights related to copyright applicable to satellite broadcasting and cable retransmission, arts. 2 & 8.

[15] *See below*, Sections V.A–B.

[16] "The Copyright Act establishes a 'fundamental distinction' between the original work of authorship and the material object in which that work is 'fixed.'" *Matthew Bender & Co. v. West Publishing Co.*, 158 F.3d 693, 702 (2d Cir. 1998). "Phonorecords" are material objects in which only sounds are fixed, while "copies" are material objects in which any other type of work is fixed. 17 U.S.C. §101. Both terms include the material object in which the work is first fixed (the tangible original). Ibid.

[17] 17 U.S.C. §101 (defining literary works).

[18] 17 U.S.C. §101 (defining audiovisual works).

[19] Compendium of Copyright Office Practices §802.1 (3d ed. 2021) [hereinafter Compendium III] (defining musical works); ibid., §802.4(A) ("Copies of musical works" include sheet music and non-audio digital files); ibid., §802.4(B) ("Phonorecords of musical works" include "compact discs, vinyl records, and tapes" and "Digital audio files embodying recorded sound").

cards, or other tangible objects.[20] Thanks to digital encoding, any of these works can be represented as a sequence of 1s and 0s (a work) and can be fixed initially and/or reproduced in an electronic storage medium (such as a hard drive or flash drive).[21]

A fundamental principle of copyright law is that "[o]wnership of a copyright, or of any of the exclusive rights under a copyright, is distinct from ownership of any material object in which the work is embodied."[22] As a result:

> [t]ransfer of ownership of any material object, including the copy or phonorecord in which the work is first fixed, does not of itself convey any rights in the copyrighted work embodied in the object; nor, in the absence of an agreement, does transfer of ownership of a copyright or of any exclusive rights under a copyright convey property rights in any material object.[23]

Thus, if a person writes and mails a letter, the recipient owns the letter itself (a manuscript) but the author owns the right to reproduce the letter (the copyright).[24] Similarly, if an artist makes and sells a painting, the buyer owns the painting itself (the canvas) but the artist owns the right to reproduce the painting.[25] This principle was not without controversy; in 1942, the New York Court of Appeals held that the unconditional sale of a painting, without reservation of the copyright, included the right to reproduce the painting.[26] But the legislative history of the 1976 Copyright Act specifically explains that it was the intent of Congress to overrule that decision.[27] This was accomplished in part by requiring that any transfer of copyright ownership, in whole or in part, must be memorialized in a signed writing.[28]

III USING NFTS TO CERTIFY "OWNERSHIP"

In the market for fine art, a tangible original work of art has an economic value that far exceeds the value of any reproductions. The scarcity of original works helps

---

[20] 17 U.S.C. §101 (defining "pictorial, graphic, and sculptural works"); Compendium III §903.1 (listing examples of pictorial, graphic, and sculptural works); ibid. §904 (listing examples of fixation of visual art works, including canvas, paper, prints, and photographic film).

[21] Compendium III, §§ 705 (literary works fixed in "a computer file"), 802.4(A), (B) (musical works), 807.4 (audiovisual works), 904 (pictorial or graphic works) ("digital files").

[22] 17 U.S.C. §202.

[23] Ibid.

[24] *See, for example, Werckmeister v. American Lithographic Co.*, 142 F. 827, 830 (S.D.N.Y. 1905), *aff'd mem.*, 148 F. 1022 (2d Cir. 1906).

[25] Ibid.

[26] *Pushman v. New York Graphic Soc'y, Inc.*, 287 N.Y. 302, 39 N.E.2d 249 (1942).

[27] H.R. Rep. 94–1476, at 124 (1976)

> ("Under [*Pushman*], authors or artists are generally presumed to transfer common law literary property rights when they sell their manuscript or work of art, unless those rights are specifically reserved. This presumption would be reversed under the [Act], since a specific written conveyance of rights would be required in order for a sale of any material object to carry with it a transfer of copyright").

[28] 17 U.S.C. §204(a).

create value and people also value the status of owning an original work of art and its connection to the artist. To maintain that value, an original work of art must be recognized as genuine by art experts. Usually, this requires a careful documentation of the work's provenance or history of ownership. Original works that are recognized as genuine are often compiled in a *catalogue raisonné*, a comprehensive, annotated listing of all of the known artworks of an artist.

With works of art created in a digital medium, however, the distinction between the original and reproductions vanishes because the original work (a collection of 1s and 0s fixed in an electronic storage medium) is identical to every other copy. In other words, an original digital artwork and each of its copies are completely fungible. This limitation meant that digital artists and works typically could not achieve the status and value associated with traditional artists and their original paintings and sculptures.[29]

To try to create and capture the value of scarcity that comes with owning an original work of art, in 2014 artist Kevin McCoy and consultant Anil Dash hit upon the idea of using a unique digital identifier, stored in a blockchain, to certify authenticity and "ownership" of a digital work.[30] They called their idea "monetized graphics" but in time such digital identifiers came to be known as NFTs.[31]

An NFT is simply an encoded digital file that contains specified types of information. It is a "token" because it is a digital record that represents something else; and it is "non-fungible" because it is unique and cannot be copied, substituted, or subdivided. It comprises a unique combination of two numbers: a tokenID (a number generated when the NFT is created, or minted) and a contract address (an address for the transaction protocol (code) that is stored and can be viewed on the blockchain).[32] Optional elements that usually are also included are the wallet address of the creator (which "authenticates" the token), a hash value (a unique hexadecimal number generated by applying an algorithm to the digital data representing the work) and a link to a URL (a web address) where the digital work is stored.[33] In addition, an NFT may contain other information, such as the title of the work, the name of the author or artist, the copyright status of the work, and perhaps even legal terms and conditions.[34] The most

---

[29] *See* Anil Dash, *NFTs Weren't Supposed to End Like This*, THE ATLANTIC (April 2, 2021), www .theatlantic.com/ideas/archive/2021/04/nfts-werent-supposed-end-like/618488/ ("By default, copies of a digital image or video are perfect replicas–indistinguishable from the original down to its bits and bytes. Being able to separate an artist's initial creation from mere copies confers power").

[30] *See* ibid.

[31] *Merriam-Webster Dictionary* defines NFT as "a unique digital identifier … that is recorded in a blockchain, and that is used to certify authenticity and ownership." *See NFT*, MERRIAM-WEBSTER (2024), www.merriam-webster.com/dictionary/NFT.

[32] *See* Andres Guadamuz, *The Treachery of Images: Non-Fungible Tokens and Copyright*, 16 J. INTELL. PROP. LAW & PRACTICE 1367, 1370 (2021).

[33] Ibid.

[34] Ibid., 1370–1371.

commonly used NFT standard is ERC-721, and NFTs generated using this standard are stored on the Ethereum blockchain.[35]

Importantly, a copy of the digital work itself is *not* one of the components of the typical NFT.[36] As Dash later observed:

> This means that when someone buys an NFT, they're not buying the actual digital artwork; they're buying a link to it. And worse, they're buying a link that, in many cases, lives on the website of a new start-up that's likely to fail within a few years. Decades from now, how will anyone verify whether the linked artwork is the original?
>
> All common NFT platforms today share some of these weaknesses … They still depend on the old-fashioned pre-blockchain internet, where an artwork [will] suddenly vanish if someone [forgets] to renew a domain name.[37]

"The idea behind NFTs was, and is, profound[:] … enabling [digital] artists to exercise control over their work, to more easily sell it, [and] to more strongly protect against others appropriating it without permission."[38] Unfortunately, NFTs have utterly failed to achieve these goals. There is nothing that prevents someone from minting and selling an NFT to a work they did not create and do not own. Moreover, anyone can mint and sell multiple NFTs of the same work, depriving them of the scarcity that was supposed to give them value. The result was a speculative market for NFTs that many commentators condemned as a Ponzi scheme.[39]

IV COPYRIGHT, "OWNERSHIP," AND NFTS

As noted above, a fundamental principle of copyright law is that "[o]wnership of a copyright, or of any of the exclusive rights under a copyright, is distinct from ownership of any material object in which the work is embodied."[40] Thus, under copyright law, the traditional art market must keep track of ownership of three different things: ownership of the tangible original artwork (as a piece of tangible personal property);[41]

---

[35] *See ERC-721*, ETHEREUM, https://ethereum.org/en/developers/docs/standards/tokens/erc-721/ (2023). The technical specifications for the ERC-721 standard are set forth in William Entriken, et al., *EIP-721: Non-Fungible Token Standard*, ETHEREUM IMPROVEMENT PROPOSALS (January 2018), available at https://eips.ethereum.org/EIPS/eip-721 (*See* proposal no. 721).

[36] Guadamuz, *The Treachery of Images*, 1371. Although one *can* store the digital work itself as part of the NFT (and there are a few examples of such "on-chain works"), in practice this is very rarely done because it is prohibitively expensive to do so. Ibid., 1371–1372. *See also* Dash, *supra* note 29.

[37] Dash, *NFTs Weren't Supposed to End Like This*.

[38] Ibid.

[39] *See, for example*, Shanti Escalante-De Mattei, *Bloomberg's Massive Crypto Article Derides NFTs as Nothing More than a Ponzi Scheme*, ARTNEWS (October 25, 2022), www.artnews.com/art-news/news/bloomberg-crypto-nfts-matt-levine-1234644343/.

[40] 17 U.S.C. §202.

[41] Ibid. ("Transfer of ownership of any material object … does not of itself convey any rights in the copyrighted work embodied in the object; nor, in the absence of an agreement, does transfer of ownership of a copyright … convey property rights in any material object"). Because single original artworks

ownership of any reproductions or copies of the work;[42] and ownership of the copyright (as a piece of intangible personal property).[43] The copyright, in turn, is a bundle of exclusive rights that can be subdivided in any way the copyright owner chooses and each stick in the bundle can be transferred and owned separately.[44]

Which of these things do you get when you buy an NFT? All too often, the answer is "none of the above." As one cynical-but-accurate commentator explained:

> An NFT is a crypto-token on a blockchain. The token is virtual – the thing you own is a cryptographic key to a particular address on the blockchain – but legally, it's property that you can buy, own or sell like any other property …
>
> When I buy an NFT, what do I get? The art itself is not in the blockchain – the NFT is just a pointer to a piece of art on a website. You're buying the key to a crypto-token. You're not buying anything else. An NFT doesn't convey copyright, usage rights, moral rights, or any other rights, unless there's an explicit licence saying so …
>
> Without a specific contract saying otherwise, an NFT *does not* grant ownership of the artwork it points to in any meaningful sense. All implications otherwise are lies to get your money.[45]

In other words, an NFT is like a digital "Certificate of Authenticity" that can be transferred and owned separately from the thing that it supposedly authenticates. That means in the digital art market, one must now potentially keep track of ownership of *four* different things: ownership of the tangible original artwork (if any exists); ownership of any digital reproductions or copies of the work; ownership of the copyright; and ownership of any NFTs (tokens) associated with the artwork.

One supposed benefit of NFTs is that ownership of the token itself is easily verified: every transaction in which the NFT changes hands is recorded permanently on the blockchain, so one can easily determine current ownership simply by ascertaining the owner of the digital "wallet" who was the most recent purchaser of the token. Even this benefit, however, turns out to be illusory. Although blockchain

are often quite valuable, they are usually transferred with formal contracts and ownership is typically recorded in the artist's *catalogue raisonné*.

[42] Copies are defined as material objects in which a reproduction of a work is fixed. 17 U.S.C. §101. Because most copies (other than the original) have only a small monetary value, ownership of such copies is typically transferred merely by transfer of possession. Under the first-sale doctrine, also known as the doctrine of exhaustion, the owner of a lawfully made copy has the right to redistribute and to publicly display *that copy* only. 17 U.S.C. § 109(a), (c).

[43] 17 U.S.C. §201(d)(1) ("The ownership of a copyright may be transferred in whole or in part by any means of conveyance or by operation of law, and may be bequeathed by will or pass as personal property by the applicable laws of intestate succession").

[44] 17 U.S.C. §201(d)(2) ("Any of the exclusive rights comprised in a copyright, including any subdivision of any of the [exclusive] rights specified by section 106, may be transferred … and owned separately"). To be valid, however, a transfer of copyright ownership must be made in a signed writing. 17 U.S.C. §204(a).

[45] *See* David Gerard, *NFTs: Crypto Grifters Try to Scam Artists, Again,* DAVID GERARD (March 11, 2021), https://davidgerard.co.uk/blockchain/2021/03/11/nfts-crypto-grifters-try-to-scam-artists-again/.

technology frequently is touted as being "unhackable," that is not entirely the case.[46] In the most prominent example, on May 17, 2022, actor Seth Green announced on Twitter that he had four NFTs "stolen" by a scam artist who used a phishing attack to gain control of his cryptographic wallet.[47] The scammer immediately "flipped" one of the NFTs (Bored Ape #8393) to a pseudonymous buyer, Mr. Cheese, known by his Twitter handle @DarkWing84, for $200,000.[48] Although Green initially threatened litigation, he ended up repurchasing his Bored Ape (which he had named Fred the Simian) from @DarkWing84 for $297,000, almost $100,000 more than the buyer had paid to the scammer for it.[49]

Similarly, in February 2022, a British citizen named Lavinia Osbourne alleged that two NFTs from the "Boss Beauties" collection were stolen from her online wallet by unknown persons. She successfully obtained an *ex parte* order from the High Court of England and Wales requiring Ozone Networks, Inc., the US-based owner of the NFT marketplace OpenSea, to freeze the NFTs (preventing their further transfer) and to disclose information concerning the identity of the alleged wrongdoers.[50] The High Court subsequently permitted the plaintiff to effect service of the amended complaint and interim injunction on the defendants by depositing NFTs comprising hyperlinks to the legal documents into their cryptographic wallets.[51] This was "the first occasion on which service by NFT had been approved by a court in England and Wales as the sole method of service of documents."[52]

Disputes have also arisen about the meaning of ownership of an NFT. The very first artwork for which Kevin McCoy minted an NFT (Token ID: 0) was a 5-second animated Graphic Interchange Format (GIF) of colored octagonal patterns titled *Quantum*, created by Kevin McCoy and his wife Jennifer.[53] As McCoy publicly

[46] *See* Werner Vermaak, *Crypto Basics: Why Nobody Can Hack a Blockchain*, CoinMarketCap (2022), https://coinmarketcap.com/alexandria/article/why-nobody-can-hack-a-blockchain; Mike Orcutt, *Once Hailed as Unhackable, Blockchains Are Now Getting Hacked*, MIT Tech. Rev. (February 19, 2019), www.technologyreview.com/2019/02/19/239592/once-hailed-as-unhackable-blockchains-are-now-getting-hacked/.

[47] *See* Seth Green, Twitter (May 17, 2022), https://twitter.com/SethGreen/status/1526583358859759617; Daniel Van Boom, *Seth Green Loses $200K Bored Ape Yacht Club NFT in Phishing Scam*, CNET (May 18, 2022),www.cnet.com/personal-finance/seth-green-loses-200k-bored-ape-yacht-club-nft-in-phishing-scam/.

[48] *See* Jessica Rizzo, *A Bored Ape Lawsuit Won't Set the NFT Precedent Seth Green Wants*, Wired (May 26, 2022), www.wired.com/story/seth-green-bored-ape-nft-stolen/; Sarah Emerson, *Seth Green's Stolen Bored Ape Is Back Home*, BuzzFeed News (June 9, 2022), www.buzzfeednews.com/article/sarahemerson/seth-green-bored-ape-nft-returned.

[49] *See* Emerson, *Seth Green's Stolen Bored Ape*.

[50] *Osbourne* v. *Persons Unknown*, [2022] EWHC 1021 (Comm) (10 March 2022).

[51] *Osbourne* v. *Persons Unknown Category A*, [2023] EWHC 39 (K.B.) (13 Jan. 2023), at ¶¶ 12, 23, 47.

[52] Ibid. at ¶¶ 48. *See also Osbourne* v. *Persons Unknown Category A*, [2023] EWHC 340 (K.B.) (22 Feb. 2023) (extending interim injunction and confirming service by NFT).

[53] *See Quantum*, McCoy Space (2014), http://static.mccoyspace.com/gifs/quantum.gif. Contrary to many reports, however, Quantum was *not* the GIF that was sold to Anil Dash for $4 at the demonstration in May 2014. That GIF (created by Kevin McCoy from a video shot by Jennifer McCoy) was

stated in 2021, *Quantum* was "[o]riginally minted on May 3, 2014 on [the] Namecoin blockchain," and was later "preserved on a token minted on May 28, 2021 by the artist."[54] Why was the *Quantum* NFT "re-minted" on the Ethereum blockchain in 2021? It seems that entries in the Namecoin blockchain had to be renewed periodically to keep them current and McCoy had never renewed the original entry in the Namecoin blockchain.[55] According to the "Condition Report" commissioned by Sotheby's in 2021, "this specific Namecoin entry was removed from the system after not being renewed, and was effectively burned from the chain."[56] Since then, the Ethereum blockchain had become the most popular location for new NFTs, so McCoy apparently hoped to capitalize on the speculative bubble in NFTs by re-minting and selling the "first-ever" NFT at auction.[57]

On June 10, 2021, the *Quantum* NFT on the Ethereum blockchain was sold at auction by Sotheby's for $1.47 million to Alex Amsel, known by his Twitter handle @sillytuna.[58] Two months earlier, however, a Canadian corporation named Free Holdings, Inc. (owned by an anonymous user with the Twitter handle @EarlyNFT) allegedly had "claimed the Quantum blockchain record on Namecoin."[59] Eight months after the auction, Free Holdings sued McCoy and Sotheby's for slander of title, deceptive trade practices, and commercial disparagement, seeking damages and an injunction prohibiting defendants from "advertising, marketing, or otherwise promoting the sale of the New Quantum NFT as the Original Quantum NFT," and "requiring [them] to engage in corrective advertising."[60] In an amended complaint, it added a claim for false advertising under section 43(a) of the Lanham Act.[61]

According to one commentator, Free Holdings' claim can be analogized to re-registering a domain name that was not renewed by its previous owner:

---

a short video of cars in a parking lot. *See Cars*, McCoy Space (2014), at www.mccoyspace.com/project/126/. This is documented in a video recording of the May 2014 demonstration. *See Seven on Seven 2014: Kevin McCoy & Anil Dash*, Vimeo (2014), https://vimeo.com/96131398 (*see* time 20:02).

54 *See Quantum: Condition Report*, Sotheby's (2021), www.sothebys.com/en/buy/auction/2021/natively-digital-a-curated-nft-sale-2/quantum.

55 *See Sotheby's Sued over Quantum NFT Auction*, Ledger Insights (February 4, 2022), www.ledgerinsights.com/sothebys-sued-over-quantum-nft-auction/.

56 *See Quantum: Condition Report*. The Condition Report was later withdrawn by its author, the Nameless Corporation. *See below*, note 60.

57 *See* Felix Salmon, *Exclusive: The First-Ever NFT from 2014 Is on Sale for $7 Million Plus*, Axios (March 25, 2021), www.axios.com/2021/03/25/nft-sale-art-blockchain-millions.

58 *See* Felix Salmon, *First-Ever NFT Sold for $1.47 Million*, Axios (June 10, 2021), www.axios.com/2021/06/10/first-nft-sold; Complaint, ¶¶ 54–55, *Free Holdings, Inc.* v. *McCoy*, Case No. 1:22-cv-00881-LGS (S.D.N.Y. filed Feb. 1, 2022) [hereinafter Free Holdings Complaint].

59 Ibid., ¶ 24.

60 Ibid., ¶ 101. The complaint also originally named the buyer Amsel and the Nameless Corporation, which had prepared the "Condition Report" for the Sotheby's auction. Free Holdings later dismissed its claims against both of those defendants after Nameless retracted its condition report. *Free Holdings, Inc.* v. *McCoy*, 2023 WL 2561576, at *7 (S.D.N.Y. Mar. 17, 2023), *appeal pending*, No. 23–644 (2d Cir. filed Apr. 19, 2023).

61 *Free Holdings, Inc.* v. *McCoy*, 2023 WL 2561576, at *7.

If you look at the blockchain entries, when EarlyNFT registered the name in 2021, it [was registered] as a 'new' name. He subsequently updated the entry contents (the metadata) to copy the exact text as the original entry, which points to the McCoy art. Compare this to acquiring a domain name. If a domain name lapses, someone else can claim it. But they can't claim the contents of the old website because the domain [name] and the website are not the same things.

EarlyNFT currently owns the NameCoin 'name'. It's not-very-user-friendly: 'd41b8540cbacdf1467cdc5d17316dcb672c8b43235fa16cde98e79825b68709a'. But the question is whether he has rights to the original metadata associated [with that name] when the 'name' was first registered.[62]

In March 2023, the district court granted the defendant's motion to dismiss the action, reasoning that the original NFT on the Namecoin blockchain and the new NFT on the Ethereum blockchain were two "different NFTs" (two separate items of property).[63] Free Holdings has filed an appeal with the US Court of Appeals for the Second Circuit.[64]

The *Quantum* NFT lawsuit is a cautionary tale. NFTs were designed to avoid ownership disputes by keeping a permanent record of all transactions concerning the token on a blockchain, avoiding the need for art experts to opine on authenticity and provenance. But the design of the Namecoin blockchain was not conducive to that purpose; and it was not until 2017, when the popular ERC-721 standard was created on the Ethereum blockchain, that the NFT market really took off. It is undisputed by the parties that *Quantum* was the first artwork to have an NFT minted for it.[65] But whether that NFT still exists, who has "control" of that NFT, who has "title" to the "work," and exactly what any of those statements actually means, still must be mediated by artistic and technical experts and resolved in a court of law.

V DOES COPYRIGHT GRANT THE EXCLUSIVE RIGHT TO "MINT" AN NFT?

As noted above, there is nothing in the technical specifications that prevents someone from minting and selling an NFT to a work they did not create and do not own. Indeed there are numerous news reports of sellers (usually scammers) who have attempted to do just that.[66] Such conduct naturally raises the question: is it a copyright violation to

---

[62] Ibid. The "name" referred to in the quote is the hash value of the digital file of *Quantum*, generated using the SHA256 hash algorithm.

[63] *Free Holdings, Inc.* v. *McCoy*, 2023 WL 2561576, at *10–11.

[64] *Free Holdings, Inc.* v. *McCoy*, No. 23–644 (2d Cir. filed Apr. 19, 2023).

[65] Again, however, it should be noted that the first transfer of ownership of an NFT from one person to another, as documented in the first public demonstration of the idea that would later be named NFTs, involved a different artwork: a GIF derived from a video of cars in a parking lot. *See above*, note 53 and accompanying text.

[66] *See, for example*, Kevin Collier, *NFT Art Sales Are Booming. Just without Some Artists' Permission*, NBC News (January 10, 2022), www.nbcnews.com/tech/security/nft-art-sales-are-booming-just-artists-permission-

mint an NFT of an artwork without the authorization of the copyright owner? This section discusses this question from a comparative perspective, analyzing it under US, EU, and UK laws, while Chapter 12 of this Handbook offers a normative discussion of whether copyright law *should* forbid unauthorized minting of NFTs.[67]

A United States

Copyright gives the owner the right to reproduce the copyrighted work and to distribute copies of the copyrighted work.[68] If the work itself is stored in digital form with the NFT on the blockchain, this constitutes a reproduction of the work,[69] which means that the sale of the NFT would be a "distribution" of the work.[70] As noted above, however, the typical NFT does *not* contain a copy of the copyrighted work. Instead, the typical NFT contains only a link (or pointer) to the digital work, along with a hash value that is generated from the original work.[71] Are either of those things a "reproduction" of a copyrighted work?

A hash value is an alphanumeric sequence that is generated by applying an algorithm to a digital copy of a work.[72] The hash value itself does not meet the definition of a "copy." In the US, a "copy" is defined as a "material object ... in which a work is

---

rcna10798; Edward Ongweso, Jr., *Site Sells Famous Songs as NFTs without Permission, Sparks Global Outrage*, VICE (February 2, 2022), www.vice.com/en/article/pkpqyy/site-sells-famous-songs-as-nfts-without-permission-sparks-global-outrage.

[67] *See* Chapter 12 of this Handbook.

[68] 17 U.S.C. § 106(1) (exclusive right "to reproduce the copyrighted work in copies or phonorecords"); §106(3) (exclusive right "to distribute copies or phonorecords of the copyrighted work to the public, by sale or other transfer of ownership, or by rental, lease, or lending").

[69] A digital file stored on an electronic storage medium is a copy or a phonorecord. *Matthew Bender & Co. v. West Publishing Co.*, 158 F.3d 693, 703 (2d Cir. 1998) ("the definition of 'copies' ... include[s] material objects that embody works capable of being perceived with the aid of a machine ... [such as] reproductions of copyrighted works contained on media such as floppy disks, hard drives, and magnetic tapes"); *London-Sire Records, Inc. v. Doe 1*, 542 F. Supp. 2d 153, 171 (D. Mass. 2008) ("The electronic file (or, perhaps more accurately, the appropriate segment of the hard disk) is therefore a ['copy' or] 'phonorecord' within the meaning of the statute"). *Cf. New York Times Co. v. Tasini*, 533 U.S. 483, 498 (2001) ("It is clear" that computer databases and CD-ROMs "reproduce ... copies" of news articles).

[70] Transmission of a digital file from one person to another constitutes a distribution. *See London-Sire Records*, 542 F. Supp. 2d at 172–74. *Cf. Tasini*, 533 U.S. at 498 (2001) ("It is clear" that by selling CD-ROMs and access to computer databases containing copies of news articles, defendants "distribute copies" of the articles "to the public by sale").

[71] Guadamuz, *The Treachery of Images*, 1371.

[72] *See United States v. Reddick*, 900 F.3d 636, 637 (5th Cir. 2018) ("a hash value is a string of characters obtained by processing the contents of a given computer file ... us[ing] a complex mathematical algorithm to generate a relatively compact numerical identifier (the hash value) unique to that data") (internal quotes omitted); *United States v. Stevenson*, 727 F.3d 826, 828 (8th Cir. 2013) ("A hash value is an algorithmic calculation that yields an alphanumeric value for a file."); 2017 Advisory Committee Note to Fed. R. Evid. 902(14) ("A hash value is a number that is often represented as a sequence of characters and is produced by an algorithm based upon the digital contents of a drive, medium, or file").

fixed by any method now known or later developed, and *from which the work can be perceived, reproduced, or otherwise communicated,* either directly or with the aid of a machine or device."[73] A hash value is *not* reversible: even if one knows the algorithm used to derive the hash value, one *cannot* "perceive, reproduce, or otherwise communicate" the original work from the hash value.[74] Thus, a hash value is different from encoding,[75] which is also different from encryption,[76] with the latter two being reversible and are therefore reproductions (or derivative works) of the copyrighted work.

Copyright also grants the copyright owner the exclusive right to prepare derivative works. A derivative work is defined as "a work based upon one or more preexisting works, such as a translation[,] ... art reproduction, abridgment, condensation, or any other form in which a work may be recast, transformed, or adapted."[77] One could plausibly argue that a hash value is "based upon" a preexisting work, and that it is an "abridgement [or] condensation" of a work. Ordinarily, however, we think of an "abridgement [or] condensation" of a work as containing some of the original expression of the work, which a hash value does not. This is consistent with case law in the US, which indicates that an infringing work must be "substantially similar to protected expression" in the original work.[78] A hash value does not consist of or comprise any original expression; it is meaningless gibberish. Nor can any of the original expression from the original work be "perceived, reproduced, or otherwise communicated" from

---

[73] 17 U.S.C. § 101 (definition of copies) (emphasis added).

[74] *See Surety Technologies, Inc. v. Entrust Technologies, Inc.,* 74 F. Supp. 2d 632, 634 (E.D. Va. 1999). *Cf. Unwired Planet, LLC v. Apple, Inc.,* 829 F.3d 1353, 1361 (Fed. Cir. 2016) ("'[A] hash is designed so that the original input into the hash function cannot be derived from the hash value, and thus [it] can be used for validation only'").

[75] "Encode" means "to convert data into code according to a specified coding scheme," while "decode" means "to convert data by reversing the effect of some previous encoding." *Network Appliance, Inc. v. Bluearc Corp.,* 2004 WL 5651036, at *8 (N.D. Cal. Nov. 30, 2004). By definition, all digital data is "encoded," because it has been converted from words or images into 1s and 0s, and it must be "decoded" from 1s and 0s back into words or images using a known algorithm. ASCII, JPEG, and MP3 formats are all examples of digital encoding.

[76] "Encryption" means "an operation performed on digital data in conjunction with an associated algorithm and digital key to render the digital data unintelligible or unusable," while "decryption" means "a method that uses a digital key in conjunction with an associated algorithm to decipher (render intelligible or usable) digital data." *Personalized Media Comms., LLC v. Apple, Inc.,* 2016 WL 6247054, at *9–10 (E.D. Tex. Oct. 25, 2016). *See also Junger v. Daley,* 209 F.3d 481, 482 (6th Cir. 2000) (defining "encryption"); *Bernstein v. U.S. Dept. of State,* 974 F. Supp. 1288, 1292 (N.D. Cal. 1997) (defining "encryption" and "decryption"), *aff'd,* 176 F.3d 1132, 1137 (9th Cir. 1999) (adopting District Court's definitions), *reh'g granted and opinion withdrawn,* 192 F.3d 1308 (9th Cir. 1999). According to the docket, the *Bernstein* appeal was later dismissed without prejudice and the case was remanded to the district court.

[77] 17 U.S.C. §101.

[78] *See Rentmeester v. Nike, Inc.,* 883 F.3d 1111, 1117 (9th Cir. 2018) ("To infringe, the defendant must also copy enough of the plaintiff's expression ... to render the two works 'substantially similar.'"); *Blehm v. Jacobs,* 702 F.3d 1193, 1202 (10th Cir. 2012) (A court "must determine whether the protected elements [in the copyrighted work] are substantially similar to the accused work"); *Tufenkian Export/ Import Ventures, Inc. v. Einstein Moomjy, Inc.,* 338 F.3d 127, 131 (2d Cir. 2003) (Plaintiff "must establish 'substantial similarity' ... [including] that it was protected expression in the earlier work that was copied").

the hash value.[79] Thus, if this case law is taken seriously, a hash value cannot be considered a reproduction or a derivative work based upon the copyrighted work.

Likewise, a "link" is not itself a reproduction of a copyrighted work. A link is a pointer to a location where the digital data representing the copyrighted work is stored. The digital data is a copy of the work but the link itself is not. Depending on the type of link, however, a link may enable, or even cause, a copy to be reproduced. A hyperlink, for example, requires the active participation of a user: when the user clicks on a hyperlink, the user's browser software will retrieve the digital data from the linked location and download it into to the Random Access Memory (RAM) of the user's computer. In such a case, the user is making a copy, although courts disagree whether it is an infringing copy.[80] If it is an infringing copy, the provider of the link may be held liable for contributory infringement if that person has knowledge of the infringement.[81] By contrast, an "embedded" link will cause the user's browser software to download the digital data into to the RAM of the user's computer *automatically*, without any additional action by the user.[82]

In the US, the copyright owner has the exclusive right to publicly display the copyrighted work,[83] and there is an active debate on whether providing an "embedded" link to a copy of a work is a public display of that work. In *Perfect 10 v. Amazon.com*, Inc., the US Court of Appeals for the Ninth Circuit held that in order to publicly display a work, one must have a copy of the work in one's possession.[84] Providing a link to a copy in someone else's possession is not a direct infringement.[85] Many district courts in the Second Circuit, however, have distinguished the Perfect 10 case on the ground that it involved search engines and that users had to click on a link to access the full-size images.[86] Those courts have held that because providing an "embedded" link automatically causes the user's browser to display the work, the

---

[79] *See above* note 74 and accompanying text.

[80] Compare *Perfect 10, Inc. v. Amazon.com, Inc.*, 508 F.3d 1146, 1169 (9th Cir. 2007) (assuming that automatic "cache" copies of linked images could constitute direct infringement, making such copies facilitates browsing the internet and is a fair use) with *Intellectual Reserve, Inc. v. Utah Lighthouse Ministry, Inc.*, 75 F. Supp. 2d 1290, 1294 (D. Utah 1999) (browsing an infringing website makes a temporary RAM copy that is infringing).

[81] *Perfect 10 v. Amazon.com, Inc.*, 508 F.3d at 1172; Intellectual Reserve, 75 F. Supp. 2d at 1293, 1294–1295. Note, however, that "referring or linking users to an online location containing infringing material or infringing activity" is subject to the statutory safe harbor for online service providers, if the service provider complies with the statutory conditions, including the notice-and-takedown procedure. 17 U.S.C. § 512(d).

[82] *See, for example, Goldman v. Breitbart News Network*, 302 F. Supp. 3d 585, 587 (S.D.N.Y. 2018).

[83] 17 U.S.C. § 106(5).

[84] *Perfect 10, Inc. v. Amazon.com, Inc.*, 508 F.3d 1146, 1160–1161 (9th Cir. 2007). According to this test, known as the "server test," ibid. at 1159, the only person who is directly liable for public display is the person who controls the server on which the data representing the copyrighted work resides.

[85] Ibid. at 1160–1161. The Ninth Circuit recently reaffirmed its "server test," even as applied to embedded images. *See Hunley v. Instagram, LLC*, 73 F.4th 1060, 1070–1071 (9th Cir. 2023).

[86] *See, for example, Goldman v. Breitbart News Network, LLC*, 302 F. Supp. 3d 585, 595–596 (S.D.N.Y. 2018); *Nicklen v. Sinclair Broadcast Group, Inc.*, 551 F. Supp. 3d 188, 194–195 (S.D.N.Y. 2021).

provider of the link directly infringes the public display right, even if the copy that is displayed resides on someone else's server.[87]

It is not necessary to resolve this conflict to apply the public display right to NFTs because it is clear that the link that is incorporated into an NFT is *not* the kind of link that automatically causes the underlying work to be displayed. Instead, a user must actively find and use the link in order to display the work.[88] Thus, the person who mints and sells a typical NFT is *not* directly infringing any of the exclusive rights provided by US copyright law.

B United Kingdom and European Union

The EU requires its member states to grant authors "the exclusive right to authorise or prohibit direct or indirect, temporary or permanent reproduction by any means and in any form, in whole or in part."[89] The EU also requires its member states to grant authors "the exclusive right to authorise or prohibit any form of distribution to the public by sale or otherwise."[90] Although it is no longer a member state, the UK provides to authors "the exclusive right ... to copy the work,"[91] "to issue copies of the work to the public,"[92] and "to rent or lend the work to the public."[93] "Copying in relation to a literary, dramatic, musical or artistic work means reproducing the work *in any material form*," including "storing the work in any medium by electronic means."[94] Again, however, except in the rare case where the work itself is encoded and stored on the blockchain, an NFT "is *not* a reproduction of the work in any sense of the word: there is no literal embodiment of anything resembling the original in the NFT."[95]

The Berne Convention requires that member states provide to authors "the exclusive right of authorizing adaptations, arrangements and other alterations of their works,"[96] including "the translation of their works."[97] In the UK, "[t]he making of

---

[87] *See, for example, Goldman,* 302 F. Supp. 3d at 593–594; *Nicklen,* 551 F. Supp. 3d at 193–94.

[88] *See* Guadamuz, *The Treachery of Images,* 1381 ("In order to extract the link, one has to have some knowledge of the technology, and sometimes one may require knowing both the unique token ID and the smart contract address").

[89] Directive 2001/29/EC, art. 2.

[90] Ibid., art. 4(1).

[91] CDPA 1988, §16(1)(a).

[92] Ibid., §16(1)(b).

[93] Ibid., §16(1)(ba).

[94] Ibid., §17(2) (emphasis added). "Copying" also "includes the making of copies which are transient or are incidental to some other use of the work." Ibid., §17(6). The requirement of a "material form" appears to correspond to the "fixation" requirement in the US. Such a requirement does not appear in the law of most EU countries.

[95] Guadamuz, *The Treachery of Images,* 1379 (emphasis added).

[96] Berne Convention for the Protection of Literary and Artistic Works, 1971 Paris Text, as amended, art. 12 [hereinafter Berne Convention]. Directive 2001/29/EC does not attempt to harmonize the national laws of the EU member states concerning the adaptation right.

[97] Berne Convention, art. 8.

an adaptation of the work is an act restricted by the copyright."[98] The British statute, however, defines "adaptation" more narrowly than does the corresponding derivative work concept in US law.[99] As with derivative works in the US, moreover, "[i]n most cases where there is some form of transformation of a work into another format or medium, there is often a recognizable element of the original work," an element that is lacking in a typical NFT.[100] Finally, the British adaptation right applies only to "a literary, dramatic or musical work,"[101] so it does not apply to an artistic work.

In the UK, there is no "public display" right as such. Instead, the copyright owner has the exclusive right "to communicate the work to the public,"[102] including "making [the work] available to the public … in such a way that members of the public may access it from a place and at a time individually chosen by them."[103] The case law of the Court of Justice of the EU has been somewhat inconsistent on whether providing a link constitutes a "communication to the public." Where the copyright owner has made the work available to the public, providing a link to an authorized copy is *not* a "communication to the public," unless it makes the work available to a "new public," that is, a public that was not already taken into account by the copyright holder when it authorized the initial communication to the public of its work.[104] Providing a link to an unauthorized copy *is* a "communication to the public," unless the person providing the link did not know, and could not reasonably have known, that the copy to which it linked is infringing.[105] If the person providing the link has a profit motive in doing so, there is a rebuttable presumption that the person has the requisite knowledge.[106]

Although the UK is no longer a member of the EU, its courts have ruled that the preexisting case law of the Court of Justice still has precedential effect.[107] Since NFTs are sold for profit, there is a rebuttable presumption that minting and selling an NFT that contains a link to an unauthorized copy of a work violates the public communication right.[108] If the NFT contains a link to an authorized copy, however,

---

[98] CDPA 1988, §§21(1), §16(1)(e).

[99] *See* ibid., §21(3); Patrick R. Goold, *Why the U.K. Adaptation Right is Superior to the U.S. Derivative Work Right*, 92 NEB. L. REV. 843, 871–874, 878–881 (2013).

[100] Guadamuz, *The Treachery of Images*, 1379.

[101] CDPA 1988, §21(1).

[102] Ibid., §16(1)(d).

[103] Ibid., §20(2)(b).

[104] *Svensson* v. *Retriever Sverige AB*, Case C-466/12 (ECJ 2014). Making a work available to a "new public" could occur if, for example, the link bypasses technical measures used by the copyright owner to prevent "framing" or to otherwise limit access to the work. *VG Bild-Kunst* v. *Stiftung Preußischer Kulturbesitz*, Case C-392/19 (ECJ2021).

[105] *GS Media DV* v. *Sanoma Media Netherlands BV*, Case C-160/15 (ECJ 2016).

[106] Ibid.

[107] *TuneIn, Inc.* v. *Warner Music UK, Ltd.*, [2021] EWCA Civ 441, at ¶¶ 89, 184, 197.

[108] One scholar questions that result, however, pointing out that the link embedded in an NFT is not an ordinary hyperlink; instead, it is code that a user must deliberately find and extract in order to use, so it is accessible only to "a small number of technical enthusiasts" rather than to "the public." *See* Guadamuz, *The Treachery of Images*, 1381.

or if it contains a link to a copy that no longer exists (a phenomenon known as "link rot"), it is doubtful that the link violates the public communication right.

Finally, one should note that the EU's concept of "the exclusive right to authorise or prohibit *any form of distribution* to the public *by sale or otherwise*" is limited by the clause, "in respect of the original of their works or of copies thereof."[109] Similarly, the UK's implementation of that right grants the rights "to issue copies of the work to the public,"[110] and also "to rent or lend the work to the public."[111] The Court of Justice has indicated that the distribution right refers only to physical or electronic copies of the work.[112] It does *not* include allowing the public to use a copy of the work or to publicly display the work.[113] The distribution right *does* include advertising or offering a copy of the work for sale, even if no sale is actually consummated.[114] The Court of Justice has defined a "sale" as "an agreement by which a person, in return for payment, transfers to another person his rights of ownership in an item of tangible or intangible property belonging to him."[115] Likewise, a British court has indicated that NFTs should be treated as "property" under English law.[116] However, although the commercial nature of an NFT transaction might tempt the court to read the distribution right broadly, a typical NFT simply cannot be considered a copy of the work, for the reasons discussed above.

C Ancillary Copyright Violations

Even assuming that minting and selling an NFT is not itself an infringing act, there may still be ancillary violations of the copyright owner's exclusive rights.[117] One must have access to a digital copy of a work to mint an NFT or to generate a

---

[109] Directive 2001/29/EC, art. 4(1) (emphasis added).

[110] CDPA 1988, §16(1)(b).

[111] Ibid. §16(1)(ba). Note that although this section refers to renting or lending the *work*, the explication of this right refers to "rental or lending of *copies* of the work" (emphasis added). CDPA 1988, §18A(1).

[112] *See Peek & Cloppenburg KG v. Cassina SpA*, Case No. C-456/06 (ECJ 2008) ("The concept of distribution to the public … of the original of a work or a copy thereof … applies only where there is a transfer of the ownership of that object") [hereinafter *Peek & Cloppenburg KG*]. *See also UsedSoft GmbH v. Oracle Int'l Corp.*, Case No. C-128/11 (ECJ 2012) (electronic copies of computer programs under both Directive 2001/29/EC, art. 4(1) and Directive 2009/24/EC of 23 April 2009 on the legal protection of computer programs, O.J. 2009 (L. 111), art. 4(1)(c)).

[113] *Peek & Cloppenburg KG, see previous note* 112 ("As a result, neither granting to the public the right to use reproductions of a work protected by copyright nor exhibiting to the public those reproductions without actually granting a right to use them can constitute such a form of distribution").

[114] *Dimensione Direct Sales Srl v. Knoll Int'l SpA*, Case No. C-516/13 (ECJ 2015).

[115] *UsedSoft GmbH v. Oracle Int'l Corp.*, Case No. C-128/11 (ECJ 2012), at ¶ 42.

[116] *Osbourne v. Persons Unknown*, [2022] EWHC 1021 (Comm), at ¶ 13 ("as to whether non-fungible tokens constitute property for the purposes of the law of England and Wales, … I am satisfied … that there is at least a realistically arguable case that such tokens are to be treated as property as a matter of English law").

[117] In the US, if there are ancillary copyright violations involved in minting and selling the NFT, it gives the aggrieved party a basis for having the entire dispute between the parties heard in federal

hash value.[118] In addition, it is difficult to sell an NFT without displaying the under-lying work of art in some way. After all, purchasers will want to see the image asso-ciated with the NFT that they are buying. If the seller makes an unauthorized copy and publicly displays it in order to market the NFT, that action will be infringing, even if the act of minting and selling the NFT itself is not. If instead the seller uses a link to someone else's copy of the work (authorized or not) to display the work, then liability would depend on the resolution of the conflicting case law on the public display right in the US or the right of communication to the public in the UK and the EU. It is plausible to assume that players will adjust their practices if courts attach copyright liability to platforms or to NFT sellers based on these ancil-lary functions.[119]

VI OTHER COPYRIGHT IMPLICATIONS

A *Disputes Regarding Copyright Ownership*

Copyright owners, of course, will take the position that minting and selling an NFT *is* one of the exclusive rights of the copyright owner. Indeed, if two or more parties claim an interest in the copyright, the legal question might be *which* of those parties has the legal right to mint and sell NFTs concerning a particular work. Two of the first lawsuits in the US involving NFTs concerned ownership disputes of this type.

In 1996, rapper Jay-Z (Shawn Carter), together with Damon Dash and Kareem Burke, incorporated Roc-a-Fella Records, Inc. (RAF, Inc.).[120] In 1996, RAF, Inc. released Jay-Z's first album, *Reasonable Doubt*, which became a best-selling album.[121] In June 2001, Dash announced plans to sell his "ownership of the copy-right to Jay-Z's first album" as an NFT.[122] RAF, Inc. sued Dash for conversion, breach of fiduciary duty, and a declaratory judgment of copyright ownership; and the district court issued a preliminary injunction prohibiting Dash from "in any way disposing of any property interest in *Reasonable Doubt*, including its copyright."[123] In June 2022, the parties announced a settlement, clarifying that "RAF, Inc. owns all

court rather than state court. Federal courts have exclusive subject-matter jurisdiction over any claims "arising under" the copyright laws, and if there is a federal claim, any state-law claims that are closely related may be heard in federal court as well. *See* 28 U.S.C. §§ 1338(a), (b), 1367(c).

[118] Guadamuz, *The Treachery of Images*, 1378.

[119] *See* Chapter 12 of this Handbook.

[120] *See Complaint in Roc-a-Fella Records, Inc. v. Dash*, ¶19–20, No. 1:21-cv-5411 (S.D.N.Y. filed June 18, 2021) (hereinafter *RAF v. Dash Complaint*).

[121] *See Reasonable Doubt*, Wikipedia (last edited: December 2023), https://en.wikipedia.org/wiki/Reasonable_Doubt_(album).

[122] *RAF v. Dash Complaint*, ¶¶ 23–26 & Exhibit B.

[123] *See Joint Stipulation in Roc-a-Fella Records, Inc. v. Dash*, at *2, No. 1:21-cv-5411 (S.D.N.Y. filed June 24, 2022).

rights to the album *Reasonable Doubt*, including its copyright," but that Dash could sell his 1/3 ownership interest in RAF, Inc., if he chose.[124]

In 1993, filmmaker Quentin Tarantino wrote the screenplay for the movie *Pulp Fiction*. To get the movie produced, Tarantino granted to Miramax "all rights (including all copyrights and trademarks) in and to the Film (and all elements thereof in all stages of development and production) now or hereafter known."[125] However, Tarantino reserved certain rights to himself, including "print publication (including without limitation screenplay publication ... and novelization, in audio and electronic formats)" and "interactive media."[126] The movie was released in 1994 and it won the Palme d'Or at the Cannes Film Festival.[127] In November 2001, Tarantino announced that he would sell seven NFTs based on parts of the *Pulp Fiction* screenplay.[128] Two weeks later, Miramax filed a lawsuit against Tarantino alleging copyright infringement, trademark infringement, unfair competition, and breach of contract.[129] Despite the legal action, Tarantino sold the first NFT in January 2022 for $1.1 million.[130] Nine months later, the parties announced that they had settled the case.[131] No further NFTs were issued, presumably because the market for NFTs had collapsed.[132]

B Notice and Takedown Procedure

Although the person who mints an NFT can sell it directly to the public, in practice most NFTs are offered for sale on various "platforms" that act as marketplaces for NFT transactions, such as Foundation or OpenSea. These platforms typically host and publicly display images (or embedded links to images) of the works associated with those NFTs. To avoid liability to the copyright owners of any such images, such platforms will comply with the notice-and-takedown provisions of the Digital Millennium Copyright Act (DMCA) in the US,[133] or its counterpart in the

---

[124] *See Final Judgment in Roc-a-Fella Records, Inc. v. Dash*, at *2, No. 1:21-cv-5411 (S.D.N.Y. approved June 27, 2022).

[125] *See Complaint in Miramax, LLC v. Tarantino*, at ¶20, No. 2:21-cv-08979 (C.D. Cal. filed Nov. 16, 2021).

[126] Ibid., ¶ 21.

[127] Ibid., ¶¶ 16–17.

[128] Ibid., ¶¶ 35–41.

[129] Ibid., ¶¶ 51–72.

[130] *See Royale with Cheese*, TARANTINO NFTs (2022), https://tarantinonfts.com/nft/1.

[131] *See* Gene Maddaus, *Quentin Tarantino Settles with Miramax over "Pulp Fiction" NFT Auction*, VARIETY (September 8, 2022), https://variety.com/2022/film/news/quentin-tarantino-miramax-pulp-fiction-nft-settlement-1235365550/.

[132] Ibid. ("[T]he remaining six auctions were canceled due to 'extreme market volatility'").

[133] 17 U.S.C. § 512(c). This section provides a "safe harbor" exemption from monetary liability if "upon notification of claimed infringement ... [the service provider] responds expeditiously to remove, or disable access to, the material that is claimed to be infringing or to be the subject of infringing activity," § 512(c)(1)(C), among numerous other conditions.

E-Commerce Directive of the EU.[134] Consequently, as a practical matter, the copyright owner of the underlying work only has to *plausibly allege* that the sale of the NFT violates its exclusive rights and the platform operator will respond by removing or disabling access to the listing.

Digital artists complain that the notice-and-takedown procedure is insufficient because it requires them to constantly search the internet for unauthorized copies or NFTs of their images in order to serve takedown notices. But the same thing is true for ordinary copyright violations (reproducing digital images is easily accomplished with the click of a mouse), and it would continue to be true even if it was clear that minting and selling NFTs without authorization was a copyright infringement. The notice-and-takedown system is imperfect but is currently the best tool that copyright owners have for policing and preventing unauthorized uses of digital works.

C Trademark as an Alternative

As for other legal tools, trademark law may be more promising than copyright. In the US, the Lanham Act prohibits any person from conduct that "is likely to cause confusion, or to cause mistake, or to deceive as to the affiliation, connection, or association of such person with another person, or as to the origin, sponsorship, or approval of his or her goods, services, or commercial activities by another person."[135] The equivalent action in the UK is a common-law action for "passing off."[136] If the unauthorized minting and sale of an NFT creates the false impression in the public mind that the NFT is authorized or endorsed by the artist (or anyone else), then these causes of action can provide relief (usually an injunction, and sometimes damages).

In the US, the Lanham Act was the basis of a complaint filed by Hermès International, "a luxury fashion company known for ... designing and producing the Birkin handbag," against Martin Rothschild, a digital artist who "designed and marketed a collection of digital images depicting faux-fur-covered Birkin handbags titled 'MetaBirkins'" and sold NFTs of his images.[137] The district court denied Rothschild's motion to dismiss, holding that "the amended complaint includes sufficient allegations that Rothschild ... intended to associate the 'MetaBirkins' mark with the popularity and goodwill of Hermès's Birkin mark."[138] After a trial, the jury

---

[134] Directive 2000/31/EC of 8 June 2000 on certain legal aspects of information society services, in particular electronic commerce, in the Internal Market, O.J. 2000 (L. 178), art. 14. In the UK, the Directive was implemented by regulation, instead of by statute. *See* Electronic Commerce (EC Directive) Regulations 2002, art. 19(a)(ii).

[135] 15 U.S.C. § 1125(a)(1)(A). This statute is known as Section 43(a) of the Lanham Act, after the section number in the original legislation, even though it has been amended since.

[136] *See, for example, Irvine* v. *Talksport, Ltd.*, [2002] EWHC 367 (Ch).

[137] *Hermès Int'l* v. *Rothschild*, 590 F. Supp. 3d 647, 650 (S.D.N.Y. 2022).

[138] Ibid., 5. The court later denied Rothschild's motion to certify an interlocutory appeal to the U.S. Court of Appeals for the Second Circuit. *Hermès Int'l* v. *Rothschild*, 590 F. Supp. 3d at 650, 657. On the motion for summary judgment, the district court found there were triable issues of fact on both

found Rothschild liable for trademark infringement and awarded $133,000 in damages.[139] The court enjoined Rothschild "from using the Birkin marks or otherwise misleading the public about the source of the MetaBirkins NFTs."[140] However, it declined to order him to "transfer any MetaBirkins NFTs in his possession, including the smart contract, to Hermès (in order to be destroyed)."[141]

Similarly, Yuga Labs, Inc., the creator of the popular Bored Ape Yacht Club series of NFTs, relied on the Lanham Act to pursue trademark claims against conceptual artist Ryder Ripps, who created a different series of NFTs that pointed to the same digital images.[142] The court granted partial summary judgment to Yuga Labs, holding that the "[d]efendants used Yuga's BAYC Marks to make their competing product look identical to Yuga's product and ensure that the consumer will be explicitly misled."[143]

VII CONCLUSION

Although the speculative bubble in NFTs burst in 2022, NFTs will continue to challenge the legal system. Copyright law is one of the tools that artists and others can use in trying to ensure that the profits from this technological development go to those who created the works with which the NFTs are associated. But artists and investors should exercise caution for two reasons. First, buying an NFT does *not*, by itself, convey *any* rights to reproduce or display the work associated with that token. Instead, those rights are governed entirely by the contract that accompanies the sale, which should be drafted and agreed to with care. Second, careful analysis demonstrates that minting and selling an NFT, by itself, is *not* a violation of any of the exclusive rights provided by copyright. Copyright law may nonetheless provide a useful tool in policing any ancillary violations that occur when unauthorized NFTs are offered for sale.

prongs of the *Rogers* test. *Hermès Int'l* v. *Rothschild*, 2023 WL 1458126, at *8–9 (S.D.N.Y. Feb. 2, 2023). *But see Jack Daniel's Properties, Inc.* v. *VIP Products, LLC*, 599 U.S. 140, 153 (2023) (holding *Rogers* "does not [apply] when an alleged infringer uses a trademark … as a designation of source for the infringer's own goods.").

[139] *Hermès Int'l* v. *Rothschild*, No. 22-cv-384, at *1, 7 (S.D.N.Y. Jun. 23, 2023).

[140] Ibid., 12. The court also ordered Rothschild to transfer the metabirkins.com domain name to Hermès, and to disgorge any additional profits he had earned since the beginning of the trial. Ibid., 12–13.

[141] Ibid., 12.

[142] *See Yuga Labs, Inc.* v. *Ripps*, 2023 WL 3316478, at *1–2 (C.D. Cal. Apr. 21, 2023). There are likely three reasons why Yuga Labs chose not to rely on copyright. First, it had not yet registered any copyrights in its images, a precondition to filing a lawsuit for "United States works." 17 U.S.C. § 411(a); *see Fourth Estate Public Benefit Corp.* v. *Wall-Street.com*, LLC, 139 S. Ct. 881, 887–888 (2019). Second, there is at least a serious legal question whether algorithmically generated images are entitled to copyright protection. *See* Frye, *Are CryptoPunks Copyrightable?*, 121–126; *Thaler* v. *Perlmutter*, No. 22-cv-01564 (D.D.C. Aug. 18, 2023) (affirming denial of registration to an AI-generated work). Third, as explained above, minting and selling NFTs of images created by others likely is not a copyright infringement under US law.

[143] *Yuga Labs, Inc.* v. *Ripps*, 2023 WL 3316478, at *17.

Legislative clarification would be welcome; but in the meantime, we can expect that copyright law will remain on the margins in disputes between artists and investors concerning NFTs. The primary advantages of copyright law are that it helps artists get into federal court, and that the major NFT platforms have adopted notice-and-takedown policies that can assist artists who are vigilant in monitoring and sending notices to those platforms. Ultimately, however, other legal tools (such as trademark law) may provide better relief when litigation concerning NFTs becomes necessary.

12

Unauthorized Minting and NFTs

Lital Helman and Ofer Tur-Sinai

I INTRODUCTION

Minting of non-fungible tokens (NFTs) without the authorization of the authors of the underlying works is notoriously prevalent.[1] Unauthorized minting of NFTs is commonly acknowledged as a concern, yet it is in fact uncertain whether authors possess the exclusive right to mint or authorize minting of NFTs of their works.[2] Establishing clear rules on this matter is imperative in order for the NFT technology to fulfill its potential in the market for creative works.

This chapter aims to provide theoretical underpinnings for legal systems around the world that endeavor to tackle this issue. Towards this aim, the chapter offers a comprehensive analysis of the three primary theoretical constructs that undergird copyright law. These include the utilitarian theory, which maintains that copyright law provides incentives to produce creative works; the labor theory, which accords property rights to creators based on the effort invested in creating works; and the personality theory, which holds that works are reflective of their authors' individuality and autonomy, and therefore authors ought to have control over their works.[3]

This chapter concludes that the three theoretical frameworks examined, the utilitarian, labor, and personality theories, all support the proposition that authors ought to possess exclusive rights over the minting of NFTs of their works. This conclusion

For helpful comments, suggestions, and discussions, the authors are grateful to Orly Lobel, Hanan Mandel, Gideon Parchomovsky and Michal Shur-Ofry, as well as the participants of the Smart Compliance Workshop of the Israel Science Foundation (2022) and the Israeli IP Scholars Annual Workshop (2022). For superb research assistance, the authors are grateful to Alon Aviram and Yarden Haltovsky.

[1] *See below*, Section II.
[2] Copyright laws' default rule regarding ownership grants the initial copyrights to authors in most cases. Exceptions include inter alia the work for hire doctrine in the US and employment contexts around the world. Authors can also transfer rights to third parties. Because copyright is mostly bestowed upon authors as a default, for the purposes of this chapter, we use the terms "authors" and "copyright holders" interchangeably, although distinguishing between the two may be needed for various policy decisions. *See also* note 10.
[3] *See below*, Section III.

is relatively natural under both the labor and personality theories, which tend to favor broader grants of rights to authors. As is detailed in the chapter, the labor theory would authorize the grant of NFT minting rights to authors as a means to avail to authors new markets that open for their works. The personality theory would advocate for exclusive minting rights on the basis that authors should be able to exert control over the usage and monetization of their works. Perhaps unexpectedly, the utilitarian theory also lends support to the grant of exclusive minting rights to authors. The reason for this is that NFTs hold the potential to restore the scarcity of creative works online, which was lost in the digital revolution, and thus boost the incentive to create in the digital sphere.

The award of minting rights to authors would further two additional principles that are central to contemporary copyright policy: distributive justice and the cultural diversity of authorship. Indeed, a robust market for NFTs with exclusive minting rights to authors can reduce access barriers to art markets and alleviate the dependency on intermediaries who act as gatekeepers.

It is noteworthy that NFTs, which initially emerged in the market for creative works, have since expanded to various other domains.[4] Yet, while the analysis in this chapter may offer insights for NFT policy in other industries, this chapter focuses on NFTs in the markets for digital art.

The chapter unfolds as follows. In Section II, we discuss unauthorized minting through the prism of copyright law. In Section III, we discuss the theoretical justifications for copyright law and show that these justifications support the award of exclusive minting rights to authors. Section IV is the concluding part.

II UNAUTHORIZED MINTING

Unauthorized minting of NFTs refers to the creation and circulation of NFTs without the permission of the copyright holders of the underlying works. No empirical data on the scope of unauthorized minting exists but this phenomenon is assumed to be quite widespread.[5] The presumed broad scope of unauthorized minting should not come as a surprise. First, there is no technical restriction on unauthorized minting. The minting process involves locating (or uploading) a digital file on (or to) a server and creating a blockchain token that contains a link to that file. NFT marketplaces

---

4 *See, for example*, EUROPEAN PARLIAMENT, INTELLECTUAL PROPERTY RIGHTS AND DISTRIBUTED LEDGER TECHNOLOGY WITH A FOCUS ON ART NFTS AND TOKENIZED ART 18 www.europarl .europa.eu/RegData/etudes/STUD/2022/737709/IPOL_STU(2022)737709_EN.pdf ("not only digital artworks can be tokenized, but any digital content. Such digital content may include memes, GIFs, literary works, music, videogames, trademarks/logos, inventions, but also unexpected content like a tweet on twitter").

5 *See, for example*, Othmane Zizi, *Why These 10 Artists Hate NFTs*, THE BUSINESS OF BUSINESS (December 13, 2021) www.businessofbusiness.com/articles/nfts-turning-artists-into-millionaires-overnight-these10-creators-are-against-the-hype/ (reporting that many artists have protested the unauthorized minting of NFTs of their works).

are not obligated to check NFTs that were put up for sale for proper authorization.[6] This means that technically, anyone can mint an NFT of any digital file.

But the issue is deeper than just technical. Contrary to popular belief,[7] it is not at all evident on what legal basis mining of NFT requires the consent of the owner of the underlying work. Understandably, minting NFTs of works simply to piggy-back on authors' creative efforts, skill, or reputation *feels* wrong.[8] But unauthorized minting can occur in a variety of ways and is not necessarily spiteful. For example, a buyer of an artwork may believe that they possess the right to mint an NFT of that work.[9] Similarly, copyright licensees and licensors may debate who has minting rights under the license. Disputes over the right to mint NFTs may also arise in cases where the author has transferred the copyright to a third party who wishes to control the minting of NFTs of the work.[10] Likewise, Internet users may innocently mint NFTs of works that they come across, believing that they are not harming the market of the work or even the ability of the author to mint NFTs herself. In these cases, the appropriate legal outcome is not obvious and copyright laws around the world lack clear answers.[11]

---

[6] NFT platforms usually address unauthorized minting through notice and takedown policies. *See* European Parliament, *above*, note 4, at 18 ("most NFT marketplaces pragmatically provide for a notice-and-take-down functionality"). For examples, *see* Andrew Hayward, *Pepe the Frog Meme NFTs Removed from OpenSea after Copyright Dispute*, DECRYPT (August 17, 2021), https://decrypt.co/78788/ pepe-the-frog-meme-nfts-opensea-copyright-dmca (Reporting that OpenSea has removed NFT project Sad Frogs District from its marketplace following a Digital Millennium Copyright Act (DMCA) takedown notice); Daniel Kuhn, *OpenSea Once again Delists CryptoPunks v1 As Legal Battle Heats Up*, COINTELEGRAPH (February 8, 2022), https://cointelegraph.com/news/opensea-once-again-delists-cryptopunks-v1-as-legal-battle-heats-up (Reporting that OpenSea delisted the CryptoPunks v1 collection, allegedly due to a DMCA takedown notice issued by CryptoPunks v2 developers Larva Labs).

[7] *See, for example*, Gregory Chinlund and Kelley S. Gordon, *What Are the Copyright Implications of NFTs?*, REUTERS (October 29, 2021) www.reuters.com/legal/transactional/what-are-copyrightimplications-nfts-2021-10-29/ (warning NFT minters that the unauthorized minting of an NFT will expose creators to copyright liability); Harsch Khandelwal, *Minting, Distributing and Selling NFTs Must Involve Copyright Law*, https://cointelegraph.com/news/minting-distributing-and-selling-nfts-must-involve-copyright-law (August 22, 2021) ("Minting an NFT typically involves storing a copy of the digital file on a server, but only the owner of the copyright in the underlying work can make copies of that work. So, unless an NFT is minted by the copyright owner (or someone operating with their permission), the act of minting the NFT is an infringement of copyright").

[8] *See, for example*, Andrés Guandamuz, *The Treachery of Images*, 16(12) J. INTL.PROP.L. & PRAC., 1367, 1380 (discussing "sleepminting," a practice where "a third party can mint a work without authorisation making it appear as if it came from the author").

[9] *See, for example*, Artforum, *Basquiat NFT Pulled from Auction after Sparking* Controversy (April 28, 2021), www.artforum.com/news/basquiat-nft-pulled-from-auction-after-sparking-controversy-85640 (reporting that the owner of a physical drawing by Jean-Michel Basquiat was prevented from minting an NFT of the drawing by the Basquiat estate, who owned the underlying copyright).

[10] *See, for example*, Complaint, *Miramax LLC* v. *Quentin Tarantino et al.*, 2:21-cv-08979 (C.C. Dist. Ct. Nov. 16, 2021) (a copyright and trademark lawsuit filed by production company Miramax against Quentin Tarantino over his Pulp Fiction NFTs. Tarantino is the author of the files underlying the NFTs but not their copyright owner. The case has been settled).

[11] *See also generally* Emily Behzadi, *The Fiction of NFTs and Copyright Infringement*, PENN. L. REV. ONLINE (2021).

Copyright confers upon authors numerated exclusive rights. While the specifics may differ among jurisdictions, there is a high degree of similarity as to the rights that copyright laws comprise. The set of rights may include, for example, the right to *reproduce* a work, to *display* the work, to *distribute* the work, and to make *derivative works*.[12] Using one or more of the exclusive rights without the copyright holder's consent is considered infringing, provided that no relevant exception applies, while any other uses of the works are considered non-infringing.[13]

Thus, for unauthorized minting to constitute copyright infringement, the minting process must interfere with the numerated exclusive rights. Remarkably, at least literally, it does not. Clearly, NFT minting is too recent and specific to be numerated as a separate exclusive right, and indeed – no copyright statute in the world to date has been amended to add minting rights to the copyright holder's bundle of rights. More interestingly, as others have pointed out and as we shortly discuss below, minting NFTs also does not interfere with rights that *are* typically numerated in copyright statutes. The most basic right in copyright, which gave copyright its name, is the *reproduction right*.[14] This right means that copyright owners solely can copy (or authorize copying of) their works. The minting of NFTs does not violate the *reproduction* right because the minting process does not technically reproduce the work.[15] NFTs contain a link to a digital copy of the associated work and some metadata, such as information on the creator of the NFT, the date of minting, and contractual terms that follow the NFT. But NFTs do not comprise nor embody the work itself.

For the same reason, minting NFTs probably does not, at least literally, violate other exclusive rights of copyright owners. An NFT cannot be considered a *derivative work* of the associated work because the NFT does not constitute a "work" at all.[16]

---

[12] *Cf.* 17 U.S.C. §106 (detailing the exclusive rights in the USA); CDPA 1988, §16 (detailing the exclusive rights in the UK); Directive 2001/29/EC of 22 May 2001, on the harmonization of certain aspects of copyright and related rights in the information society 2001 O.J. (L 167/10), arts. 2, 3 & 4 (detailing some of the exclusive rights in the EU).

[13] In some jurisdictions, authors also enjoy moral rights, which denote rights such as the right of attribution and the right to the integrity of the work.

[14] *See, for example,* 17 USC §101. *See also Mazer* v. *Stein,* 347 US 201, 218 (1954) ("without copying there can be no infringement").

[15] *See generally* Chapter 11 of this Handbook (analyzing NFT minting under EU, US, and UK laws and suggesting that an NFT typically does not violate the reproduction right, constitute a derivative work, and display the associated work). Notably, underlying works are not copied to the blockchain due to technical limitations. It is simply too costly to store creative works on the blockchain, hence the use of linking. The storage of NFTs' associated works outside of the blockchain causes problems, including the risk that the host of the work would change the URL or remove it altogether, and the NFT would comprise a broken link. If this technological hurdle is overcome and underlying works are copied to the blockchain as part of the minting process, the copyright obstacle would become material because minting would inherently consist of copying.

[16] *See, for example,* 17 USC §106(2) (defining a "derivative work" as "a work based upon one or more preexisting works, such as a translation, musical arrangement, dramatization, fictionalization, motion picture version, sound recording, art reproduction, abridgment, condensation, or any other form in

NFTs also do not *distribute* the works nor *display* them. NFTs only link to works that are distributed and displayed elsewhere.[17]

It may be possible to interpret copyright law broadly – for example, through a particularly broad definition of the right to display, distribute, or make derivative works – in order to "catch" unauthorized NFT minting. But expanding copyrights through interpretation in response to new technologies may have undesired consequences and could stifle innovation or distort incentives of market players.[18]

It may also be possible to rely on ancillary functions of the NFT process that *do* violate copyrights in order to effectively save minting rights to authors. Indeed, while at its core, NFT minting may be beyond the confines of copyright law, related NFT practices typically require reproduction, display, and distribution of the underlying work. After all, a potential NFT trader needs to advertise it, offer it for sale and of course brag about owning it. It is also rather common for NFT sellers to copy the underlying work to a different location on the web in order to better control the URL. But all of these functions are not essential to the minting process. Players may shift their practices accordingly if courts attach copyright liability to platforms or to NFT sellers based on these ancillary functions. It is easy to imagine NFT platforms that avoid all these ancillary functions and rely on linking alone. Conceptually, regulation through ancillary activities is often destructive. Such regulation is not only likely to be ineffective in curbing infringement. It also represents waste, opportunity costs and inefficient use of innovative resources, which are directed towards avoiding liability.[19]

The inevitable conclusion of this discussion is that copyright law does not, for now, forbid unauthorized minting of NFTs. But is this the preferred normative conclusion? The remainder of this chapter sets forth a theoretical account *against* unauthorized minting. We analyze the three main theories that underlie copyright law and show that all three support the conclusion that minting rights should be granted to copyright owners exclusively. We also show that exclusive minting rights can produce additional advantages in the world of creativity and diversity.

which a work may be recast, transformed, or adapted"). *See also Mirage Editions, Inc. v. Albuquerque A.R.T. Co.*, 856 F.2d 1341 (9th Cir. 1988); *Midway Mfg. Co. v. Artic Int'l, Inc.*, 704 F.2d 1009 (7th Cir. 1983); *Twin Peaks Prods. v. Publ'ns Int'l, Ltd.*, 996 F.2d 1366 (2d Cir. 1993); *Lewis Galoob Toys, Inc. v. Nintendo of America, Inc.*, 5 964 F.2d 965 (9th Cir. 1992) (finding no infringement due to lack of copy or modification of the work). H.R. Report. No 94–1476, 94th Cong., 2nd Sess. 62 (1976) (explaining that "the infringing work must incorporate a portion of the copyrighted work in some form"); Michael K Erickson, *Emphasizing the Copy in Copyright: Why Noncopying Alterations Do Not Prepare Infringing Derivative Works*, BYU L. REV. 1261 (2005).

[17] Generally, linking to a work, particularly a non-infringing work, does not give rise to copyright violation claims. *See, for example, Ticketmaster Corp. v. Tickets.Com, Inc.*, 2000 U.S. Dist. LEXIS 12987, at *7 (C.D. Cal. Aug. 10, 2000).

[18] *See generally* Lital Helman, *Pull Too Hard and the Rope May Break: On the Secondary Liability of Technology Providers for Copyright Infringement*, 19 TEX. INTELL. PROP. L.J. 111 (2010) (analyzing the effects of applying copyrights to the file-sharing technology).

[19] *See* Helman, ibid., 40–41.

III THEORETICAL PERSPECTIVES

Copyright law is justified on utilitarian foundations in addition to certain non-utilitarian theories, including the labor and personality theories. In Sections III.A, III.B, and III.C, we survey each of these theoretical perspectives and show that all three point towards granting exclusive minting rights to authors. In Section III.D, we show that support for this conclusion can be drawn from two additional principles that copyright law strives for: distributive justice and cultural diversity.

A Utilitarian Theory

Under the utilitarian account, copyright law is designed to encourage creativity for the benefit of society.[20] The idea behind the utilitarian rationale is that by providing authors with exclusive rights over their works *ex post*, the system incentivizes authors to produce creative works *ex ante*.[21] Without such an incentive, the theory goes, authors would be discouraged from creating new works.[22] This is so due to the public goods nature of creative works, which are both non-excludable – as once created and distributed, it is impossible to exclude people from consuming them – and non-rivalrous, as many can access them without harming the enjoyment of others to do the same.[23] As a result, there is no scarcity in creative works. Copyright law tackles this market failure by generating artificial scarcity through a set of exclusive rights that forbid the copying and sharing of creative works. Artificial scarcity creates a market around creative works, which in turn allows authors to recoup the investment in creating the work and make a profit and thus incentivizes them to engage in creative processes.[24]

---

[20] *See* Abraham Bell & Gideon Parchomovsky, *Reconfiguring Property in Three Dimensions*, 75 U. CHI. L. REV. 1015, 1047 (2008) ("Because the initial production of intellectual goods often necessitates considerable investment and once produced they can be copied at a very low cost, there is a serious risk that not enough intellectual goods would be created without legal protection"); Julie E. Cohen, *Lochner in Cyberspace: The New Economic Orthodoxy of "Rights Management,"* 97 MICH. L. REV. 462, 471 (1998) ("By guaranteeing authors certain exclusive rights in their creative products, copyright seeks to furnish authors and publishers, respectively, with incentives to invest the effort necessary to create works and distribute them to the public"); Neil W. Netanel, *Copyright and a Democratic Civil Society*, 106 YALE L.J. 283, 285 (1996) ("To encourage authors to create and disseminate original expression, copyright law accords them a bundle of proprietary rights in their works").

[21] *See* Shyamkrishna Balganesh, *Foreseeability and Copyright Incentives*, 122 HARV. L. REV. 1569, 1577 (2009).

[22] Granted, authors may well be driven by intrinsic motivations. But if they are unable to make a living off art, they will have to devote less time to creativity. *See, for example*, Diane L. Zimmerman, *Authorship without Ownership: Reconsidering Incentives in a Digital Age*, 52 DEPAUL L. REV. 1121, 1137 (2003) ("Having made the point that artistic production is not only, and perhaps not even primarily, about money, it is nevertheless unlikely that writers will devote themselves as fully to authorship as a profession if they cannot profit from the value that others place on their work").

[23] *See, for example*, Ofer Tur-Sinai, *The Endowment Effect in IP Transactions*, 18 MICH. TEL. & TECH. L.J. 117, 129–130.

[24] The utilitarian theory is the predominant rationale for copyright law in the USA, where the Constitution justifies the copyright regime solely by protecting authors' incentives. *See* U.S. CONST.

Would the utilitarian theory support exclusive minting rights to authors? Notably, the analysis cannot be simplistic. It cannot merely be argued that minting rights would expand authors' profit forecasts, that this effect would boost the incentive to create, and that minting rights are therefore desired. The utilitarian theory does not by any means support expanding copyright to *all* markets. Any expansion needs to be justified by showing that it is likely to have beneficial effects on authors' incentives. Moreover, such benefits must outweigh the costs of greater protection, particularly the cost of diminished access to creative works. As the next paragraphs show, in the specific context of minting rights, exclusive rights are likely to significantly enhance authors' incentives to create because of their potential to bring back scarcity and authenticity to the online world. As to the costs side of the equation, while any limitations on uses of works necessarily restrict some freedoms of others, exclusive minting rights do not create additional access barriers to creative works, which is generally the biggest concern arising out of copyright expansion.

As explained, copyright law under the utilitarian theory has a crucial role: to boost the incentive to create by generating scarcity. But this strategy has become futile in the digital world. The Internet has enabled mass duplication and dissemination of digital works without permission or consideration on a scale never before imaginable. Notably, digital copies are identical, perfect copies of the original, to the bit level. It is not only impossible to distinguish between them and the original work, but there is *in fact* no distinction between the two, besides the location of the files.

Copyright law stood weaponless against the digital revolution. While the legal rules remained in place, and even expanded, they were unable to effectuate scarcity anymore. In a state where pirated copies of works are disseminated freely, one cannot distinguish between original and nonoriginal copies and enforcement is cost-prohibitive, copyright can no longer generate scarcity and further the financial incentives of authors. After all, why would someone pay anything for something they can copy for free?

Various laws, enforcement measures and novel business models have attempted to tackle this predicament throughout the years but proved unable to overcome these inherent hurdles and reinstate scarcity in the Internet's free economy.[25] NFTs may pave a way forward. The NFT is an object separate from the work and due to the characteristics of blockchain, it is scarce: NFTs cannot be duplicated and only one person can own them.[26] Unlike the internet's modus operandi, the NFT must leave the seller's wallet in order to move into the buyer's. In essence, owning an NFT is as

---

art. I, § 8, cl. 8 (Authorizing Congress "[t]o promote the Progress of Science and useful Arts, by securing for limited Times to Authors and Inventors the exclusive Right to their respective Writings and Discoveries").

[25] *See* Lital Helman, *Fair Trade Copyright*, Colum. J. L. Arts (2013).

[26] *See* Michael D. Murray, *NFT Ownership and Copyrights* 3–4, 15–16 (July 2, 2022) (unpublished manuscript), https://papers.ssrn.com/sol3/papers.cfm?abstract_id=4152468; Zachary L. Catanzaro, *NFT Tethered Sound Recording*, 4 Harv. J. of Sports & Ent. L. 1, 2–3 (2022); Guandamuz, *The Treachery of Images*, 1371.

scarce as owning a physical asset. The NFT injects scarcity back into the market of creative works by becoming itself an object for the transaction, regardless of how many copies of the associated work exist out there. This way, NFTs provide a way for authors to monetize their works in the digital environment and boost their incentives to create.

Not only are NFTs able to reinstate scarcity online, but they may also be able to recover authenticity. Authenticity is a key concept in traditional markets for creative works, in particular for visual art. Both collectors and investors care very much whether works are original or reproductions and are willing to pay much higher prices for the former. Art markets have developed various means to verify authenticity, including expert analyses, provenance research, and scientific testing. Yet the power of the Internet to create perfectly identical files meant that authenticity has become a meaningless concept online. If all files are precisely the same – what does it even mean that one file is "original" or "authentic"? The concern under the utilitarian theory, of course, is that without authenticity, art markets cannot migrate online and the incentive to create would be stifled. NFTs may be the vehicle to import the authenticity concept online. NFTs generate authenticity by enabling the author to designate one file – the one that they point to – as original, even while copies of the file continue to be copied with no limit. In addition to visual arts, NFTs can introduce authenticity into markets where authenticity has not been as pronounced, such as music and literature. This can create new market opportunities in these areas, thus boosting the incentive to create these types of works too.

The point is that the dual promises of NFTs – reinstating scarcity and reviving authenticity – can only be realized if authors are the only ones allowed to mint their works. The newly emerging authenticity concept enabled by NFTs relies on authors to designate a copy of their works as original among infinite identical copies. And scarcity would also lose its grip if third parties were free to mint NFTs alongside the author.[27]

All in all, the utilitarian account of copyright law seems to offer strong support for treating the unauthorized minting of a copyrighted artwork as copyright infringement. The more prevalent unauthorized minting becomes, the lower buyers' trust in the system turns. Consequently, prices of NFTs will decline and ultimately this market for digital art could lose its potential to incentivize authorship. An exclusive minting right regime, in contrast, can boost artists' incentives to create and disseminate their artwork while enabling buyers to derive more utility from the purchase.

B Labor Theory

One of the principal theories used in support of property rights is the labor theory which is based on the work of John Locke. Locke argued that every person has a right to the fruits of her labor.[28] This is a theory of natural law, which views

---

[27] *See* ibid., 1380.
[28] *See* JOHN LOCKE, TWO TREATISES OF GOVERNMENT 290–291 (Peter Laslett, ed., 1988) (1690).

property rights as preexisting in the state of nature.[29] The starting point for Locke's theory is that God gave the world to men in common;[30] yet, "every man has a property [right] in his own person,"[31] and from such right follows also his right to "[t]he Labor of his Body, and the Work of his Hands."[32] Therefore, whatever a person has removed out of its natural state and mixed her labor therewith belongs to her. Under the labor theory, there are two main limitations to the scope of property rights that a person may acquire in the fruits of her labor:[33] (1) "there is enough, and as good left in common for others";[34] and (2) the laborer does not waste resources by taking more than she needs for her own use, including use by means of exchange with others.[35]

The mere argument that a person owns a right to her own body, hence – to the labor of her body, and therefore – to anything that results from mixing her labor with common resources may be sufficient to justify property rights in the fruits of one's labor. Yet scholars engaging with the labor theory as a justification for property rights often resort to additional reasoning grounded in Locke's writings or elsewhere.[36] One such common explanation for recognizing property rights in the fruits of one's labor is that when labor results in something valuable for society, then the laborer is morally entitled to a just reward in consideration for such value.[37] The labor theory also connects to unjust enrichment principles and corrective justice

---

[29] *See* JEREMY WALDRON, THE RIGHT TO PRIVATE PROPERTY 19 (1988); Daphna Lewinsohn-Zamir, *Compensation for Injuries to Land Caused by Planning Authorities: Towards a Comprehensive Theory*, 46 U. TORONTO L.J. 47, 50 (1996).

[30] *See* LOCKE, TWO TREATISES OF GOVERNMENT, at 286.

[31] Ibid., 287.

[32] Ibid., 287–288.

[33] In addition to these limitations, it can be argued that property acquisition should be limited by the general principle of natural law, pursuant to which one should not cause damage to another, other than in certain instances of extreme necessity. *See* LOCKE, TWO TREATISES OF GOVERNMENT, 271 ("[N]o one ought to harm another in his Life, Health, Liberty, or Possessions"). However, this principle may not be necessary as a separate limitation on the ability to acquire property, as it seems that Locke took it into account while designing the specific rules governing the acquisition of property. First, the principal rule itself, assigning property rights to the laborer, can be justified by the no-harm principle, assuming that taking the fruits of her labor away would cause the laborer harm. *See* Wendy J. Gordon, *A Property Right in Self-Expression: Equality and Individualism in the Natural Law of Intellectual Property*, 102 YALE L.J. 1533, 1544–1545, 1561 (1993); Benjamin G. Damstedt, *Limiting Locke: A Natural Law Justification for the Fair Use Doctrine*, 112 YALE L.J. 1179, 1185–1186 (2003). Second, in order to ensure that no harm is caused to others as a result of the grant of property right to the laborer, Locke set the two specific limitations discussed in the text. *See* Gordon, A Property Right in Self-Expression, 1562; Damstedt, *Limiting Locke*, 1185.

[34] *See* LOCKE, TWO TREATISES OF GOVERNMENT, 288.

[35] Ibid., 290, 295, and 300.

[36] *See, for example*, Wendy Lim, *Towards Developing a Natural Law Jurisprudence in the U.S. Patent System*, 19 SANTA CLARA COMPUTER & HIGH TECH. L.J. 561, 579 (2003).

[37] *See, for example*, Lawrence C. Becker, *Deserving to Own Intellectual Property*, 68 CHI.-KENT L. REV. 609, 624 (1993); Justin Hughes, *The Philosophy of Intellectual Property*, 77 GEO. L.J. 287, 305 (1988). For other justifications for property rights in the fruits of one's labor, *see* Ofer Tur-Sinai, *Beyond Incentives: Expanding the Theoretical Framework for Patent Law Analysis*, 45 AKRON L. REV. 243, 258–59 (2012).

notions. Without property rights over the fruits of one's labor, others could exploit those fruits and unjustly profit at the laborer's expense.[38]

While the labor theory has been criticized on various grounds,[39] it has become one of the main theories for justifying rights in private property.[40] Even though the theory originally focused on property rights in physical assets,[41] it has also been used for the justification and analysis of intellectual property rights, including copyright.[42] Applying the theory to intangibles is quite obvious. When a person creates a work of authorship or develops a technological invention, she invests her labor in the process and therefore – according to the labor theory – she is entitled to rights over the product resulting from such process, provided only that the conditions for the acquisition of property set forth by Locke are met: enough is left for others and there is no waste of resources.[43]

Analyzing the situation of unauthorized minting under the labor theory bolsters the argument for locating exclusive control of minting NFTs of works at the hands of their authors. The author, who has put the labor to create the artwork, is the one who deserves to enjoy the fruits of such labor, including fruits "hanging" in NFT markets. As noted above, due to the difficulty of profiting from selling or licensing digital art in other means, NFTs may become an important source of revenue for digital artists.[44] Exclusive minting rights to authors also prevents free riders from unjustly enriching at the authors' expense.[45] Notably, by giving control to artists over minting their own works, we do not narrow down the opportunities of others

---

[38] *See* LOCKE, TWO TREATISES OF GOVERNMENT, 297 ("He that had as good left for his Improvement, as was already taken up, needed not complain, ought not to meddle with what was already improved by another's Labour: If he did, 'tis plain he desired the benefit of another's Pains, which he had no right to").

[39] *See, for example,* Tur-Sinai, *Beyond Incentives,* 259–260. For one critical argument, *see below,* note 47 and accompanying text.

[40] *See, for example,* J. W. HARRIS, PROPERTY AND JUSTICE 182–212 (1996); STEPHEN R. MUNZER, A THEORY OF PROPERTY 254–91 (1990); Waldron, The Right to Private Property, 137–252.

[41] For an argument that a more thorough examination of Locke's writings reveals that he actually had a solid point of view as to rights in intangibles as well, *see* Lior Zemer, *The Making of a New Copyright Lockean,* 29 HARV. J.L. & PUB. POL'Y 891 (2006).

[42] *See, for example,* Becker, *Deserving;* Hughes, *The Philosophy;* Damstedt, *supra* note 33; Gordon, DESERVING TO OWN INTELLECTUAL PROPERTY; Zemer, *The Making of a New Copyright;* Adam D. Moore, *A Lockean Theory of Intellectual Property,* 21 HAMLINE L. REV. 65 (1997); Stephen M. McJohn, *The Paradoxes of Free Software,* 9 GEO. MASON L. REV. 25, 44 (2000); Caroline Nguyen, *Toward an Incentivized but Just Intellectual Property Practice: The Compensated IP Proposal,* 14 CORNELL J.L. & PUB. POL'Y 113, 119–126 (2004); Molly A. Holman & Stephen R. Munzer, *Intellectual Property Rights in Genes and Gene Fragments: A Registration Solution for Expressed Sequence Tags,* 85 IOWA L. REV. 735, 832–835 (2000); Tur-Sinai, *Beyond Incentives.*

[43] For a discussion of these conditions in connection with intellectual property protection, *see generally* Hughes, *The Philosophy,* 315–329; Nguyen, *Toward an Incentivized,* 119–126; Tur-Sinai, *Beyond Incentives,* 265–272.

[44] *See above,* section III.A.

[45] *See* note 38 and accompanying text for the relevance of unjust enrichment considerations to the labor theory.

to labor, contrary to the first Lockean proviso. In fact, they can even labor in NFT markets as long as they tokenize their own work or negotiate a license to tokenize someone else's work.

One potential counterargument to the argument presented above could be that aside from an artist's labor invested in the creation of an artwork, there are other factors, including the ideas and inspiration behind the work, which contribute to its value. Indeed, a general argument often made against the labor theory is that it is predicated on an unrealistic assumption that labor can be attributed exclusively to a single individual. As work in modern day, so goes the argument, is typically done in teams comprised of numerous individuals and in an environment that provides the laborer with the necessary tools and opportunity to work, granting exclusive rights in an asset to an individual cannot be justified based on the argument that it is the product of her labor.[46] Yet even if we acknowledge that other factors contribute to the value of an artwork, it is fundamentally the artist's labor that is the most central and significant element in its creation.

C Personality Theory

Another theory that is often used to justify property rights is Hegel's personality theory.[47] According to the personality theory, property is necessary as a means for developing and realizing one's personality. Pursuant to Hegel, an individual needs control over external objects in order to exercise their will and achieve self-identity.[48] Property rights provide the freedom of action and sense of security needed for a person to identify herself through her relationship with assets.[49]

This theory was refined by Margaret Jane Radin in the twentieth century.[50] Radin has gone a step further in her attempt to use the personality theory as the basis for detailed recommendations with respect to the appropriate design of property protection. According to Radin, a distinction should be made between various types of objects, based on how closely they are bound up with personhood. At one end of the spectrum there are certain objects that are often part of the way human beings constitute themselves as continuing personal entities in the world ("personal property"),

---

[46] See Morris R. Cohen, *Property and Sovereignty*, Law and the Social Order 41, 51 (1933) (noting that "economic goods are never the result of any one man's unaided labour").

[47] See G. W. F. Hegel, Philosophy of Right (S. W. Dyde trans., 1996) (1821).

[48] See ibid., 51–52.

[49] Ibid., *See also* Margaret Jane Radin, *Property and Personhood*, 34 Stan. L. Rev. 957, 957, 972–973 (1982); Lim, *Towards Developing*, 579; Hughes, *The Philosophy*, 330; Brian M. Hoffstadt, *Dispossession, Intellectual Property, and the Sin of Theoretical Homogeneity*, 80 S. Cal. L. Rev. 909, 934, 948 (2007).

[50] See Margaret Jane Radin, *Market-Inalienability*, 100 Harv. L. Rev. 1849 (1987). For a recent criticism of Radin's version of the personality theory, *see* Jeanne L. Schroeder, *Unnatural Rights: Hegel and Intellectual Property*, 60 U. Miami L. Rev. 453 (2006) (claiming that Radin's version is too remote from the original Hegelian theory to be considered derived from it). For Radin's treatment of the differences between her thesis and Hegel's theory, see Radin, *Property and Personhood*, 977.

such as a wedding ring, a portrait, an heirloom, or a house; while at the other end of the spectrum there are objects held for purely instrumental reasons ("fungible property"), such as money, a share certificate, an automobile in the hands of a dealer, or an undeveloped tract of land in the hands of a contractor.[51] An indicator of an object being "personal" is that its loss cannot be compensated through payment or replacement with another object of a similar market value, due to its unique value to its owner; whereas a "fungible" object, by definition, is perfectly replaceable with other goods of equal market value.[52] Radin thus does not focus on the development process of an object but rather on the relationship formed between the object and whoever holds it; accordingly, the same object can be considered personal or fungible, depending on the identity of its current holder.[53]

On a normative level, Radin's basic argument is that legal rules should be designed with sensitivity to this distinction. In essence, the more a relationship to an object is located toward the personal end of the continuum, the more the entitlement should be protected.[54] Radin suggests that, at least in certain cases, interests in personal property should be protected against invasion by the government and against cancellation by conflicting fungible property claims of other people by property rules as no compensation for their taking could be just.[55]

Radin's personality theory has been criticized from various angles. The theory has nevertheless been used often in discussions of intellectual property law, especially copyright law.[56] The common position in the literature is that intellectual products are closer to the personal end of Radin's continuum of objects. Such assets are not only held by an individual but are also her creation and thus reflect her personality, and the personal bond between the individual and such assets

---

[51] *See* Radin, *Property and Personhood*, 959–960.

[52] For a description of Radin's insight with respect to the distinction between personal objects and fungible objects as part of a broader phenomenon – the existence of a gap between the price at which the holder of an object is willing to sell it and the which buyers are willing to pay for the same object in the market – *see* Abraham Bell & Gideon Parchomovsky, *A Theory of Property*, 90 CORNELL L. REV. 531, 568 (2005). The gap might be due to sentimental causes as Radin points out but it might also be caused by a variety of other reasons, some rational and others affected by cognitive biases, such as the "endowment effect." *See* ibid.

[53] *See* Radin, *Property and Personhood*, 987. *See also* Steven Cherensky, *A Penny for Their Thoughts: Employee-Inventors, Preinvention Assignment Agreements, Property, and Personhood*, 81 CAL. L. REV. 595, 644 (1993).

[54] *See* Radin, *Property and Personhood*, 986.

[55] Ibid., 988, 1005, 1014–1015.

[56] *See generally* Becker, *Deserving*; Amie N. Broder, *Comparing Apples to APPLs: Importing the Doctrine of Adverse Possession in Real Property to Patent Law*, 2 N.Y.U. J.L. & LIBERTY 557, 573 (2007); Cherensky, *A Penny*; Hoffstadt, *Dispossession*; Hughes, *The Philosophy*; Justin Hughes, *The Personality Interest of Artists and Inventors in Intellectual Property*, 16 CARDOZO ARTS & ENT. L.J. 81 (1998); Lim, *Towards Developing*; McJohn, *The Paradoxes*, 45; Nguyen, *Toward an Incentivized*, 126–130; David W. Opderbeck, *Symposium: Closing in on Open Science: Trends in Intellectual Property & Scientific Research: A Virtue-Centered Approach to the Biotechnology Commons (or, the Virtuous Penguin)*, 59 ME. L. REV. 315 (2007).

is particularly strong.[57] Accordingly, various scholars used the personality theory in support of arguments calling for the strengthening of authors' rights and, in particular, their moral rights, including the right of attribution and the right of integrity.[58] It should be noted that this approach, according to which a personhood interest – justifying an increased level of protection – can result from the fact that an object was created by someone whose personality is embedded in it,[59] deviates from Radin's version of the personality theory, which focuses on the attachment created between an object and its holder, while attributing no significance to the development process of the object.[60]

The personality theory strengthens the argument for exclusive minting rights for authors. Commercializing creative works, including via tokenizing it and offering the NFT for sale, may contribute to the development of an artist's personality. By doing so, the artist reveals herself to others (if only by a pseudonym) and may acquire recognition, respect, and appreciation from others.[61]

Remarkably, there is an unobvious connection between the personality theory and the utilitarian theory discussed above. As discussed, unauthorized minting may deprive artists of the opportunity to profit off their work and discourage further creativity. But this can not only affect the availability of works in society, which is the utilitarian theory's concern, but also close a venue for expression for authors and hurt their ability to further develop their personality through creativity.[62]

Further, as the artist is the one whose skills, aesthetic choices, and other aspects of personality are embedded in the work, she should have the right to determine how these personal expressions of hers are shared and distributed. This may be particularly important in this context, considering that the NFTs sphere is new and evolving and various choices are involved in the process: whether to tokenize the work at all, what smart contract to include in it, what platform to use, and many others.

---

[57] See Hughes, *The Philosophy*, 330, 365; Becker, *Deserving*, 610; Hoffstadt, *Dispossession*, 935; McJohn, *The Paradoxes*, 45; Opderbeck, *Symposium*, 319.

[58] See, *for example*, Hughes, *The Philosophy*, 165 (as to the right of attribution); Edward J. Damich, *The Right of Personality: A Common-Law Basis for the Protection of the Moral Rights of Authors*, 23 GA. L. REV. 1, 4 (1988) (as to the right of integrity; though not explicitly mentioning the personality theory as such, the article's thesis is grounded in the notion that artistic works reflect the creative personalities of their authors).

[59] For a discussion of various personality aspects that may come into effect in the process of creating an intellectual product, *see* Hughes, *The Personality*, 82.

[60] *See above*, note 54 and accompanying text. This approach is certainly remote from Hegel's original theory. *See* Schroeder, *Unnatural Rights* (pointing out that Hegel's theory cannot be legitimately used to justify moral rights or other increased rights with respect to intellectual property). Interestingly, the approach described in the text has early roots in the writings of Kant and Fichte, who viewed literally works, specifically, as external expressions of their authors' personalities. *See generally* PETER DRAHOS, A PHILOSOPHY OF INTELLECTUAL PROPERTY 80–81 (1995); DAVID SAUNDERS, AUTHORSHIP AND COPYRIGHT 106–115 (1992).

[61] *Cf.* Hughes, *The Philosophy*, 349–351 (making a similar argument with respect to commercialization of copyrighted works in general).

[62] Ibid.

Relatedly, some authors may wish to resist tokenization altogether. Through the prism of the personality theory, such decisions that are made for authors by others violate their very personality. Interestingly, at least in some cases, artists whose works were minted without permission felt precisely that.[63]

For all of these reasons, the personality theory clearly supports the arguments in favor of granting exclusivity to the artist over tokenization of her works. This conclusion may not come as a surprise. The personality theory may well be the most expansive of all three main theories of copyright law. Yet in the NFT context, this theory offers an even stronger argument. Among other things, the environmental effect of blockchain and the idea that everything and anything can be tokenized, monetized, and sold are two propositions that can create aversion for authors. Forcing them to participate in this market by minting NFTs of their works whether they agree or not can be found rather offensive under the personality theory.

Interestingly, this theory can have intriguing consequences in the area of NFTs, which exceed the scope of this chapter. Mainly, this theory may be hesitant as to the ability of authors to untie the knot with their creative works. This theory may therefore seek to place limitations on the ability to release full control over the use of the work, on the type of smart contracts that can be written, and perhaps on other issues as well.

D Distributive Justice and Cultural Diversity

Support for exclusive minting rights for authors stems from two additional principles: distributive justice and cultural diversity. These principles are not conceived as fundamental underpinnings of copyright, yet contemporary copyright policies endeavor to promote them both. In the NFT context, these principles can be viewed as two sides of the same coin. The idea is to allow more diverse authors in the market and more varied works of authorships. From the prism of distributive justice, this policy aim would correct historical discrimination against authors who were excluded from traditional art markets. From the perspective of cultural diversity, opening the floor to more diverse authorship would produce a kaleidoscope of authorship and enrich society with a variety of artistic expressions.

Exclusive minting rights can promote distributive considerations in three main ways. First, exclusive minting rights would enable a more just distribution of the value that creative works produce. Generally, distributive considerations support policies that enable authors to profit from their work because most authors do not earn a sustainable income from authorship. In fact, authorship and creativity produce much value that authors do not capture. This value is divided between users, distribution platforms, and a plethora of intermediaries that play a role in cultural industries. Exclusive minting rights would prevent additional third parties from

---

[63] *See above*, note 5.

taking a share with authors in the value that their works produce by freely minting NFTs of their works.

The second related way that NFTs promote distributive justice is that the NFT market skips over the need to sell art through traditional intermediaries: galleries and curators, record labels, film production companies, publishers, and various others. Thus, not only would exclusive minting rights prevent new third parties from taking a share in the value that creative works produce but it would also enable authors to seize a larger chunk of sales compared with traditional markets.

Finally, NFT markets have a potential to be more inclusive towards diverse artists. Traditional art markets have benefited from economies of scale. A museum or radio station could not profit from selling works that appealed to small audiences. The NFT market can allow more niche authors to find audiences and, unlike in the pre-NFT Internet, actually sell to these audiences.

For similar reasons, exclusive minting rights for authors can advance cultural diversity. Evidently, the gatekeeping function of intermediaries has adversely affected the variety and diversity of art. The overwhelming control intermediaries have held over the funding and distribution in the creative industries created barriers to entry for artists because authors who were unable to secure recording contracts, publishing contracts or gallery access could not effectively create and disseminate art.[64] Even when the digital age reduced the costs of creation and distribution, intermediaries were much needed for monetization of works because the Internet made it possible to distribute works freely but not to monetize them.[65]

The pre-NFT system, where artists had few opportunities to earn money without the involvement of intermediaries, subjugates the availability of art to the business interests of intermediaries. Intermediaries' profits stem from economies of scale. They thus have an incentive to produce art that fits the mainstream taste and yields maximum profits. The dominance of intermediaries in the art business thus produces a powerful incentive for artists to create works that would fit the dominant taste and appeal to gatekeepers.

Placing the right to mint NFTs in the hands of authors can dramatically improve their independence and, as a result, authorship diversity. The NFT technology offers a simple way for artists to reach diverse audiences and monetize their art without giving up their uniqueness. Granted, intermediaries in the NFT market abound.[66] But while their existence bites into the value that NFT provides for distributive justice, it barely affects cultural diversity because most of these intermediaries do not screen for quality, genre, or taste.

---

[64] See, for example, Raymond Shih Ray Ku, *The Creative Destruction of Copyright: Napster and the New Economics of Digital Technology*, 69 U. Chi. L. Rev. 263, 306 (2002); Lital Helman, *When Your Recording Agency Turns into an Agency Problem: The True Nature of the Peer-to-Peer Debate*, 50 IDEA 49 (2009).

[65] *See* Helman, *Fair Trade*.

[66] Such intermediaries include, for example, NFT marketplaces and sales platforms, payment gateways, such as Ethereum wallets, storage solutions, and others.

IV CONCLUSION

This chapter seeks to show that current copyright laws probably do not cover the practice of unauthorized NFT minting and that this reality produces uncertainties, which potentially tilts the delicate balance that copyright law strives to strike.

While it is imperative that legal systems provide certainty in this area, no thorough analysis thus far has provided policy-makers with the theoretical grounds for decision-making in this realm. The chapter seeks to fill the gap. To do that, we have analyzed the phenomenon of unauthorized minting from the perspective of the three principal theories that underlie copyright law. We concluded that all three primary theoretical accounts complement each other in supporting the same normative conclusion that unauthorized minting should be discouraged or forbidden. Distributive justice and cultural diversity considerations support this conclusion as well.

The long-term value of NFTs for creative works is uncertain and subject to speculation. Some of the factors that would influence the development of NFTs probably concern the legal rules that would be put in place. We hope that our analysis can serve as a basis for policy-makers who seek to regulate this fundamental aspect of the NFT space.

13

Visual Art, Galleries, Collectibles, and NFTs

Lawrence J. Trautman

I INTRODUCTION

Dominating news reports on March 11, 2021, Metakovan, a pseudonym, paid $69 million for a piece of unique digital art titled *Everydays – The First 5000 Days*, and paid for it with cryptocurrency ether.[1] This landmark purchase, fueled in part by wealth recently created from digital currencies, art buyers, creatives, and investors, resulted in an exploding market for unique digital art. The art world and major traditional art dealers such as Christie's and Sotheby's rapidly embraced this new development. The underlying strange brew of cryptography, game theory, interest in art collection, need for the creation of true unique digital ownership interests, and a solid dose of speculative hype quickly fermented into a term that has become one of the driving law and technology stories of recent years: non-fungible tokens (NFTs). Also during 2021, $2.9 million was paid "for the NFT of Twitter founder Jack Dorsey's first tweet, which you can easily see on-line: 'just setting up my twttr.'"[2]

In a very short period of time digital art has been added to the growing list of uses for blockchain technology. In addition, the application of NFTs to art has created a new asset class. While one bitcoin is much like another, an NFT equivalent of the *Mona Lisa* is very different from the NFT equivalent of Action Comics #1. NFT technology leverages digital uniqueness in a way that makes a new social phenomenon possible. While there is only one *Mona Lisa* in the Louvre, owning a copy does not provide the same thrill.

This chapter is substantially influenced by and draws heavily from a prior law journal article, Lawrence J. Trautman, *Virtual Art and Non-Fungible Tokens*, 50 HOFSTRA L. REV. 361 (2022).

[1] Scott Reyburn, *The $69 Million Beeple NFT Was Bought with Cryptocurrency*, N.Y. TIMES (March 12, 2021), www.nytimes.com/2021/03/12/arts/beeple-nft-buyer-ether.html.

[2] Andy Kessler, *Op-Ed: Mark Cuban Known Crypto*, WALL ST. J. (May 23, 2021), www.wsj.com/articles/mark-cuban-knows-crypto-11621785848. However, in less than a year, the value of this tweet plummeted by 99 percent and as of April 2022, bids for the tweet on OpenSea amounted to only $10,000. *See* Jeff Kauflin, *Why Jack Dorsey's First-Tweet NFT Plummeted 99% in Value in a Year*, FORBES (April 14, 2022), www.forbes.com/sites/jeffkauflin/2022/04/14/why-jack-dorseys-first-tweet-nft-plummeted-99-in-value-in-a-year/?sh=1ffcdda165cb.

The demand for one-of-a-kind art seems to have roots as firmly planted online as off and showing that the demand for digital collectibles has long driven economies in online environments and virtual worlds will help ground the inevitable discussion over whether NFTs are merely a fad or a phenomenon.

The thesis for digital art is simple – it is grounded in the belief that humans value uniqueness and rarity, particularly in a social context. The value that humans ascribe to art is based on uniqueness and is tied to the strength and breadth of markets that form around the art, admiring it, valuing it, and providing social value to those who collect, support, and enjoy it. The NFT phenomenon is largely independent of valuation of cryptocurrencies, except to the extent that those who are excited about cryptographic token technologies are more likely to understand and value unique tokens and in a crypto boom, are more likely to pay eye-grabbing sums.

This chapter proceeds in five sections. First, the evolutionary progression of blockchain technology in the form of NFTs is acknowledged. Second, the emergence of the market for digital art is explored. Third, an explanation and historical account of digital art and recent related issues are suggested. Fourth, coverage of the abrupt decline in the market price for many NFTs is provided. And last, a conclusion is offered.

This dramatic extension of blockchain and other digital technology to the world of art represents a new and exciting platform for creative expression. This chapter offers a valuable addition to the literature by providing a readable introduction and overview of what is now known about the likely impact of blockchain technology and NFTs on art and collectibles.

II BLOCKCHAIN AND EVOLUTION OF THE VIRTUAL WORLD

Virtual or crypto art in the form of NFTs is an outgrowth in the evolutionary progression of applications in blockchain technology. Understanding the development of blockchain technology, the technological foundation upon which virtual currencies and NFTs are based, is a necessary building block in acquiring a working knowledge about NFTs. Earlier in this Handbook, Carla L. Reyes provides a chapter discussion of *The Language Landmines Of Blockchain Technology And Cryptocurrency*.[3] She addresses the technical aspects of blockchain technology and differentiates between types of cryptocurrency, tokens, and NFTs.[4] Similarly, Brian L. Frye provides some background and context to the development of digital assets and particularly NFTs.[5] I will not attempt to replicate this material here. Rather, this chapter's discussion starts with the emergence of NFT art that caught my attention on a morning in mid-March 2021.

---

[3] *See* Chapter 2 of this Handbook.
[4] *See* ibid.
[5] *See* Chapter 1 of this Handbook.

III MARKET FOR DIGITAL ART EMERGES

It was on March 13, 2021, when *The Wall Street Journal* reported a first sale of an entirely digital work by auction house Christie's, creating "a frenzy in crypto asset markets by paying a record sum for ... artwork that exists only digitally. Its authenticity is verified primarily because it carries an NFT, or digital proof of purchase that is recorded on a digital ledger known as a blockchain."[6]

A *The NFT Gold Rush*

According to Christie's, "a cryptocurrency investor based in Singapore called Metakovan won Beeple's $69 million digital collage at auction–a sale that smashed records in markets for both art and non-fungible tokens, or NFTs."[7] As reported:

> Metakovan is the founder of Metapurse, a crypto-based investment firm. [A spokesman for Metkovan known as] Twobadour said that their fund outbid dozens of rivals over the course of the 15-day online contest to win Beeple's pixilated amalgamation of irreverent drawings and fantastical landscapes that the artist combined into a single collage called 'Everydays: The First 5000 Days' ...
>
> NFTs are all the rage now, but Twobadour, who spoke on Metakovan's behalf as the fund's steward said he and his partner have spent the past several years focused on amassing what might be the world's biggest collection of tokenized collectibles and art, worth nearly $120 million combined, with Beeple serving as its star. Four months ago, the fund paid $2.2 million for a different set of 20 Beeple works on the online marketplace Nifty Gateway ...
>
> The artist [Beeple], whose real name is Mike Winkelmann, is known for completing a new work each day for the past 13 years and counting ... Metapurse has been able to scoop up Beeple's works at such high prices because Metakovan was an early investor in cryptocurrencies, starting around 2013 ... After buying that previous set of 20 Beeple works in December [2020], they bought land in digital gaming spaces and built museums to display the images before minting tokens off the virtual experience they created. An initial 1.6 million tokens of B.20 were sold at 36 cents apiece. By [March 12, 2021] the cost of one token had risen to $16.35, giving the tokens a collective worth of 163.5 million, according to Coinmarketcap.com.[8]

Speculation grew as reports documented that just a month before, digital art depicting (2018–2022) US President "Donald J. Trump facedown in the grass, covered in words like 'loser,' sold for $6.6 million, a record for a non-fungible token,

---

[6] Kelly Crow & Caitlin Ostroff, *Crypto Investor Won Record Auction of Beeple Digital Art*, WALL St. J. (March 12, 2021), at B12. *See also* Lawrence J. Trautman & Mason J. Molesky, A Primer for Blockchain, 88 UMKC L. REV. 239 (2019); Lawrence J. Trautman & Alvin C. Harrell, Bitcoin Versus Regulated Payment Systems: What Gives?, 38 CARDOZO L. REV., 1041 (2017).

[7] *See* Crow & Ostroff, *Crypto Investor*.

[8] Ibid.

or NFT … Fittingly, the image was paid for in Ethereum, a form of cryptocurrency that, among millennials, is almost as well known as Bitcoin."[9] Although US-centric, *The New York Times* provides a potential explanation for this phenomenon: "Rather than elbowing past one another for reservations at the latest restaurants … or getting into bidding wars for apartments at 740 Park Avenue, they are one-upping one another in online auctions for jewelry, watches, furniture, sports cards, vintage cars, limited-edition Nikes and crypto art."[10] A Christie's spokesperson indicates their shift in strategy "ahead of the NFT boom, but the sudden popularity of the digital medium indicated that the art world was primed for an overhaul. 'People are collecting art differently now, and it's time for some radical changes.'"[11]

It is now evident that, "[t]he art market, coming off a pandemic year marked by sluggish sales, also sees an opportunity to cozy up to a largely untapped audience of crypto-millionaires."[12] Also during March 2021, *The Wall Street Journal* reports:

> Christie's is capitalizing on the momentum by reorganizing its sales in May in part to appeal to millennials and cryptocurrency investors who want more emerging art and NFTs, the house said. Instead of labeling its two biggest sales by their artistic styles–like impressionist-modern and postwar-contemporary–Christie's will slot its offerings by time frame, specifically the 20th century and 21st century.[13]

Bids from more than thirty parties were received, resulting in a winning offer of "350 Ether, or about $560,000."[14] Mr. Roose writes, "[a] few minutes later, after the auction platform had taken its cut, nearly $500,000 in cryptocurrency landed in my digital wallet."[15] Describing the auction process, Mr. Roose notes, "I listed it on Wednesday morning, and before I went to bed that night, the top bid had risen to more than $30,000. When I woke up the next morning, it was $43,000. In the final hour of the auction … a bidding war broke out."[16] Mr. Roose reflects:

> Some NFT collectors believe that owning early, prominent crypto-tokens, will eventually be like owning rare, first-edition books or priceless paintings. [NFT collector] Mr. Ouyang admitted that the value of my NFT was 'still highly speculative and subjective.' But he said he believed that NFTs and other blockchain-based

---

[9] Jacob Bernstein, *Here's How Bored Rich People Are Spending Their Extra Cash*, N.Y. TIMES (March 20, 2021), www.nytimes.com/2021/03/20/style/spending-rich-people.html.

[10] Ibid.

[11] Kelly Crow, *NFT Works Spark Frenzy in Art World*, WALL ST. J. (March 18, 2021), at A12.

[12] *See* ibid.

[13] Ibid.

[14] Kevin Roose, *Why Did Someone Pay $560,000 for a Picture of My Column?*, N.Y. TIMES (March 26, 2021), www.nytimes.com/2021/03/26/technology/nft-sale.html (citing Kevin Roose, *Buy This Column on the Blockchain*, N.Y. TIMES (March 25, 2021), www.nytimes.com/2021/03/24/technology/nft-column-blockchain.html).

[15] Ibid.

[16] Ibid.

technologies would ultimately reshape the entire media landscape, allowing creators to reimagine how they create and monetize their works.

'This particular NFT from The New York Times is one of the answers and will become a historical landmark in this inevitable movement,' he said. 'That's why I think it is valuable.'[17]

On May 28, 2021, we read about historical documents of interest being monetized by the University of California at Berkeley. According to *The New York Times*, University of California, Berkeley's plan is to "auction the first of two digital art … NFTs. The object being offered is based on a document called an invention and technology disclosure. That's the form that researchers at Berkeley fill out to alert the University about discoveries that have the potential to be turned into lucrative patents."[18] Originating in 1996:

> The title of the invention … is 'Blockade of T-Lymphocyte Down-Regulation Associated with CTLA-4 Signaling.' The University hopes that potential bidders will be attracted to an early description of a revolutionary approach to treating cancer developed by James P. Allison, then a professor at Berkeley. He found a way to turn off the immune system's aversion to attacking tumors and he showed that it worked in mice.
>
> That advance eventually led to the creation of Yervoy, a drug for the treatment of metastatic melanoma, and Dr. Allison, who is now at the MD Anderson Cancer Center at the University of Texas, shared the Nobel Prize in Medicine in 2018. Thus, the Berkeley disclosure form could be thought of as the scientific equivalent of Mickey Mantle's rookie baseball card – a memento of the beginnings of greatness. 'I think of it almost as a history of science artifact,' said Richard K. Lyons, the chief innovation and entrepreneurship officer at Berkeley. 'Imagine somebody saying, 'I want to own the NFTs for the 10 most important scientific discoveries of my lifetime.' A 24-hour auction of the NFT of Dr. Allison's invention disclosure will take place as early as June 2 [2021] using Foundation, an NFT auction marketplace that uses Ethereum, the cryptocurrency network of choice for NFT collectors.[19]

IV HISTORY OF DIGITAL ART AND RELEVANT ISSUES

Christie's provides a history of digital art, "dating back to the 1960s. But the ease of duplication traditionally made it near-impossible to assign provenance and value to the medium." During November 2018, Christie's first transaction of this type took place "when it registered the entire 42-lot Barney A. Ebsworth Collection of twentieth-century American Art on the Artory blockchain. The collection totaled more than $322 million and marked the first time an art auction at this price level

---

[17] Ibid.
[18] Kenneth Chang, *University to Auction NFTs of Early Nobel Prize Work*, N.Y. TIMES (May 28, 2021), at B4.
[19] Ibid.

had been digitally recorded." Robert Alice's Block 21 was offered by Christie's during October 2020, "as part of its Post War & Contemporary Art Day sale … The first work of art with an embedded NFT to be offered at a traditional auction house, the lot attracted non-traditional bidders and crypto enthusiasts alike—and sold for almost 11 times its low estimate."[20] Christie's states:

> The recent introduction of Non-fungible tokens (NFTs) and blockchain technology has enabled collectors and artists alike to verify the rightful owner and authenticity of digital artworks. *EVERYDAYS: THE FIRST 5000 DAYS* will be delivered directly from Beeple to the buyer, accompanied by a unique NFT encrypted with the artist's unforgeable signature and uniquely identified on the blockchain.[21]

Additional transactions taking place before the Christie's $69 million Beeple's sale are reported by financial journalist Jason Zweig who notes, "In February [2021], an NFT representing the Nyan Cat video meme, which looks like a feline Pop-Tart dragging a rainbow through outer space, sold for more than $500,000. A video NFT of LeBron James dunking a basketball sold for $208,000."[22]

Rapid technological changes brought about by significant product developments such as the Gutenberg Press often help facilitate Renaissance-like artistic creativity. The Gutenberg "formation of the printing press in the fifteenth century paved the way for mass production of texts and images. With new communication capacity being enabled by this technological advancement, the widespread of material and intellectual exchange becomes possible."[23] In modern times, "many of the working approaches used by digital artists can be traced back to the early days … of computer development. Since the emergence of the World Wide Web in the 1990s, a diverse variety of opportunities were further opened for visual arts with seemingly infinite permutable dimensions."[24] Bo Xing attributes the emergence of digital art to three primary factors:

> Firstly, it is such a common practice for artists, in particular young professionals, to use a wide range of media arts for creative purposes, producing static/dynamic images, as well as manipulating soundtracks and text scripts;
>
> [S]econdly, digital art is not an isolated practice, divided from other forms of arts. It is essentially a methodology that incorporates all types of interconnections with other art exercises together with other manner of presentations and enquiries,

[20] *Beeple: A Visionary Digital Artist in the Forefront of NFTs*, CHRISTIE'S (2024), www.christies .com/features/Monumental-collage-by-Beeple-is-first-purely-digital-artwork-NFT-to-come-to- auction-11510-7.aspx.

[21] Ibid.

[22] Jason Zweig, *The Method to the Madness of a $69 Million Art Sale*, WALL ST. J. (March 20–21, 2021), at B5.

[23] Bo Xing, *Creativity and Artificial Intelligence: A Digital Art Perspective* 1 (2018) (unpublished manuscript), https://ssrn.com/abstract=3225323.

[24] Ibid.

illustrating that we are witnessing and experiencing a new wave of creative revolution; [and] [L]ast but not the least, it is worth noticing that an army of digital artists are now working in numerous industries shoulder to shoulder with hardware and software practitioners at the forefront of innovation.[25]

Just as in the physical world, so too have the advent and growth of the electronic social spaces, from games like World of Warcraft to blockchain-based environments like Decentraland to the social bubbles of Twitter, fostered a need for online value, both in terms of currency and payment and in terms of unique digital assets to hold that value. Paying fungible currency – dollars – for a unique creation – art – is a loop we have not yet experienced in the present economy. Our economies remain half online, half off. While current laws and the scope of regulations struggle to keep up with rapid technological change, policy-makers and criminal enforcement officials face significant new challenges.

According to Harvard professor Jonathan Zittrain and researcher Will Marks, in sum, an NFT's "first buyer is getting three things: the warm feeling that may accompany financing an artist; the pride that comes with claiming a relationship to a digital artifact and its creator; and perhaps most tangibly, an asset that can be traded."[26] Consider:

In the physical world, if you purchase a candy bar, you can't give someone a piece of it without losing a few bites of your own. That makes your freedom to take a bite valuable, because the bar has only so much chocolate.

By contrast, an NFT buyer is not purchasing a work, but rather a publicly available token that links to a work. For example, for a digital picture, the token may be a unique number and a link to a copy of the picture, hosted on a service such as IPFS. The token itself is visible to all, as is the work to which it points, so anyone else can look at the work and download it. And most NFT transactions don't purport to convey copyright or other intellectual-property interests regarding the work in question, so owning an NFT tied to an animation of, say a flying Pop-Tart cat doesn't put you in a position to use that animation any differently than someone who hadn't bought it. You have only a token that is hosted publicly online, 'registered' as assigned to your digital wallet rather than someone else's. If you orchestrate your wallet through an app, the app might present you with a handsome visual trophy case listing the NFTs that you've purchased. (As you can see, we're having to reach to describe unique value).[27]

---

[25] Ibid. (citing Julian Sefton-Green & V. Reiss, Multimedia Literacies: Developing the Creative Uses of New Technology with Young People, in YOUNG PEOPLE, CREATIVITY AND NEW TECHNOLOGIES: THE CHALLENGE OF DIGITAL ARTS (Julian Sefton-Green, ed., 1999)); ANNA BENTKOWSKA-KAFEL, TRISH CASHEN & HAZEL GARDINER, DIGITAL ART HISTORY: A SUBJECT IN TRANSITION (2005).

[26] Jonathan Zittrain & Will Marks, *What Critics Don't Understand about NFTs*, THE ATLANTIC (April 2021), www.theatlantic.com/ideas/archive/2021/04/nfts-show-value-owning-unownable/618525/.

[27] Ibid. *See also* Caroline Anders, *Finally Impressed? NFT of Side-Eying Toddler Meme Fetches over $74,000 in Cryptocurrency*, WASH. POST (September 25, 2021), www.washingtonpost.com/technology/2021/09/25/chloe-side-eye-meme-nft-sale/.

Christie's announced the sale of works made during the mid-1980s by Andy Warhol that were recovered from obsolete floppy disks during 2014. These five original Andy Warhol works, existing previously only as digital files "will be brought to life again as 1/1 NFTs … They are being offered for sale individually by Christie's on behalf of the Andy Warhol Foundation for the Visual Arts established by Warhol."[28] The online sale ran on Christie's website from May 19 to May 27, 2021.[29]

A *CryptoPunks*

Noah Davis, Post-War and Contemporary art specialist at Christie's, New York states, "[t]he CryptoPunks are the alpha and omega of the CryptoArt movement … This is a historic sale."[30] Accordingly, during Christie's "21st Century Evening Sale" on May 13, 2021, a single lot of nine Punks, courtesy of LarvaLabs, was brought to market. About three years earlier, "two software developers created a quirky art project called CryptoPunks that posed a serious and provocative question: Could a few lines of code translate to a feeling of meaningful ownership? It was a crazy idea that would require, in their words, 'a conceptual leap.'"[31] Christie's contends that CryptoPunks is now regarded as the genesis of the CryptoArt movement of today. The experiment begins when, according to Christie's:

> In 2017, Matt Hall and John Watkinson, founders of New York-based software company Larva Labs, created a software program that would generate thousands of different, strange-looking characters. At first, they thought they might have had the makings of a smartphone app or game … [However, as we have seen, their creation] was a paradigm-altering model for the digital art market and a challenge to the concept of 'ownership' itself.
>
> Larva Labs launched CryptoPunks on June 23, 2017. The CryptoPunks are a collection of 24x24, 8-bit-style pixel art images of misfits and eccentrics. There are exactly 10,000 of them, each with their own ostensible personality and unique combination of distinctive, randomly generated features. Each Punk has its own personality, thanks to distinct, randomly generated features, from glasses to caps to hoodies.[32]

In sum, "[t]here are 6,039 male Punks and 3,840 female Punks. A total of 696 wear hot lipstick, while 303 have muttonchops. There are 286 Punks with 3-D glasses, 128 rosy-cheeked Punks, 94 Punks with pigtails, 78 Punks with buck teeth and 44

[28] Press Release, *Christie's Presents Proof of Sovereignty: A Curated NFT Sale by Lady PheOnix*, CHRISTIE'S (May 2021), www.christies.com/about-us/press-archive/details?PressReleaseID=10079& lid=1.

[29] Ibid.

[30] *See 10 Things to Know about CryptoPunks, the Original NFTs*, CHRISTIE'S (2021), www.christies .com/features/10-things-to-know-about-CryptoPunks-11569-1.aspx.

[31] Ibid.

[32] Ibid.

beanie-wearing Punks."[33] In addition, "eight Punks with no distinctive features at all – sometimes referred to as Genesis Punks – and only one with seven attributes: CryptoPunk 8348 a big bearded, bucktoothed, cigarette-smoking Punk with an ear-ring and a mole, wearing classic shades and a top hat."[34]

To be expected, some CryptoPunks are rarer than others. In an homage to popu-lar culture archetypes, by tweaking software algorithms, Hall and Watkinson created both human CryptoPunks and "a scarcer number of fantastical, non-human works, adding 88 green-skinned zombie Punks, 24 hirsute ape Punks and nine light-blue-skinned alien Punks to the series. Like their human counterparts, the non-human Punks have different combinations of accessories: one alien is smoking a pipe … and has been dubbed the 'wise alien.'"[35] Christie's writes:

> CryptoPunk 635, one of only nine alien Punks and the only one with a sub-1,000 series number, is the highlight of the nine works featured in Larva Labs' single lot offered … at Christie's in New York. 'The core of the idea was that every character should be unique,' says Larva Labs. 'The advantage of generative art is that the process, once set in motion, can produce results that are even surprising to us. We ran the generator hundreds of times, reviewed the results, and made adjustments. Then, with little fanfare, we ran it one last time, linked it to the Ethereum smart contract that we deployed, after which the CryptoPunks were completely set in stone.' The collection of 10,000 Cryptopunks is definitive and unalterable … Once minted, Hall and Watkinson offered the CryptoPunks for free, not forgetting to claim 1,000 for themselves, 'just in case it becomes a thing,' as Hall put it … But before too long, Punks were selling for thousands of dollars. 'For fans of collectibles, it's clearly a version of trading cards or something similar. However, generative art fans see it as an interesting example in that category. We like that its perception is flexible and brings together several of these worlds into a single project.'[36]

Christie's describes the CryptoPunks market as "extremely active," observing that "[a]s of early April 2021, over 8,000 sales had been recorded in the previous 12 months, with an average sale price of 15.45 ether ($30,412.40). The total value of all sales is 127,360 ether ($251,620,000) – and that value grows daily."[37] Noteworthy other sales include, "In February, CryptoPunk 6965, a fedora-wearing ape Punk, sold for 800 ether – equivalent to $1.5 million … on 11 March 2021, CryptoPunk 7804, the previously mentioned pipe-smoking 'wise alien,' was sold for the equiva-lent of $7.5 million – the highest amount ever paid for a Punk at the time."[38]

---

[33] Ibid.
[34] Ibid.
[35] Ibid.
[36] Ibid. *See also* Lawrence J. Trautman, Scott Shackelford, & W. Gregory Voss, *How We Learned to Stop Worrying and Love AI: Analyzing the Rapid Evolution of Generative Pre-Trained Transformer (GPT) and Its Impacts on Law, Business, and Society* (July 22, 2023) (unpublished manuscript), http://ssrn .com/abstract=4516154.
[37] *See 10 Things to Know*, CHRISTIE'S.
[38] Ibid.

According to *The Wall Street Journal*, Sarah Meyohas's art "places her at the vanguard of this art-world revolution. She will be relaunching an early project, Bitchcoin, on the Ethereum network, with a public presale at Phillips auction house on May 25 [2021]. Her 2015 project sold tokens entitling investors to portions of her photographic prints."[39] Ms. Meyohas reports, "[t]he new Bitchcoins will be backed by flower petals from a previous work called 'Cloud of Petals ... many of the artists who have been doing well financially tend to release 'drops' of hundreds of the same image."[40]

In retrospect, "Bitchcoin functioned as a sort of proto-NFT, and the boom in digital tokens has brought a niche of tech-focused artists into the mainstream ... Ms. Meyohas revived Bitchcoin to mark her place in the NFT boom."[41] According to proponents, "NFTs empower artists to sell their own work online, by-passing traditional auction houses ... solv[ing] a key problem in the digital age: how to verify the authenticity of an infinitely replicable artifact that exists as computer code."[42] *The Wall Street Journal* writes, "Sales of CryptoPunks – early NFTs of pixilated digital images of humans, aliens and other creatures – peaked in mid-March at about $21 million in one day, according to data-tracking site NonFungible.com."[43]

B Nifty Gateway

Twins Griffin and Duncan Cock Foster "started Nifty Gateway to mainstream what had been a highly technical subculture by, among other things, allowing civilians to buy nifties (on the Nifty Gateway website) with credit cards."[44] During 2019, they sold the less-than-a-year-old company to another set of twins, the Winklevosses (of Facebook start-up fame). Now, the Winklevoss-led company called Gemini has big plans for Nifties:

> 'The brothers' stated mission is to have 1 billion people collecting them. They talk about how nifties could one day be paired with physical assets, so you could use a digital token to prove your ownership of say, real estate. But in these early days, the use cases can seem generationally exclusionary. The first nifty to go viral was *CryptoKitties*, a game featuring a digital feline you can collect and breed. A single CryptoKitty has sold for a record $170,000, and venture capitalists including Union Square Ventures and Andressen Horowitz have put money into the

[39] Bourree Lam, *Finance Meets Crypto Art*, WALL ST. J. (May 24, 2021), at B7.
[40] Ibid.
[41] Ibid.
[42] Ibid.
[43] *See 10 Things to Know*, CHRISTIE'S.
[44] Benjamin Wallace, *The Twin Blockchain Entrepreneurs Who Dream of "Digital Air Jordans" Forecasting the Future of Art Collecting with Duncan and Griffin Cock Foster*, NY MAG. (March 4, 2020), https://nymag.com/intelligencer/2020/03/duncan-and-griffin-cock-foster-nifty-gateway-gemini.html.

company behind the game. 'CryptoKitties was the thing that got my attention,' Duncan said. 'The amount of money people were spending on CryptoKitties was remarkable.'[45]

More recently, journalist Benjamin Wallace writes that Nifty Gateway 2.0 provides "a marketplace to buy and sell nifties along with several nifties by noted artists with whom they've partnered. The brothers sketch a vision of a fully niftified world: 'We want Supreme making nifties,' Duncan said. 'We want some CryptoPunks in the permanent collection of MoMA.'"[46]

C NFTs and Energy Consumption

With a population of 1.41 billion and an important global economy and trading partner to other countries, Chinese policy regarding cryptocurrencies and NFTs is important. *The Wall Street Journal* reports, "[c]rypto-related activities have posed two serious issues in China,' namely financial stability and energy consumption, said Shen Wenhao, a Beijing based partner at JunZeJun Law Offices."[47]

In their compelling article about NFT energy consumption, WIRED magazine reports, "[t]wo years ago, Joanie Lemercier, a French artist known for his perception-bending light sculptures, took on a new role as climate activist. He attended protests against coal mining ... and began a campaign demanding Autodesk stop selling its design software to fossil fuel operations."[48] Artist Lemercier "also took a closer look at his own energy use, which included a hefty heating bill for his studio in Brussels, electricity for the high-end computers to render his creations, and dozens of flights each year to exhibitions around the world."[49] And:

> Then, a few months ago, in the course of a few minutes, his progress was erased. The culprit was Lemercier's first blockchain 'drop.' The event involved the sale of six ... NFTs, which took the form of short videos inspired by the concept of platonic solids. In the clips, dark metallic polyhedrons rotate on loop and glisten – a reference to Lemercier's installations in the physical world. The works were placed on a website called Nifty Gateway, where they sold out in 10 seconds for thousands of dollars. The sale also consumed 8.7 megawatt-hours of energy, as he later learned from a website called cryptoartWTF. That figure was equivalent to two years of energy use in Lemercier's studio. Since then, the art has been resold, requiring another year's worth of energy. The tally was still climbing. The problem, as Lemercier saw it, went well beyond himself. His fellow artists were becoming millionaires overnight as the cryptoart world exploded. But so was their

---

[45] Ibid.
[46] Ibid.
[47] Ibid.
[48] Gregory Barber, *NFTs Are Hot. So Is Their Effect on the Earth's Climate*, WIRED (March 6, 2021), www.wired.com/story/nfts-hot-effect-earth-climate/.
[49] Ibid.

role in admitting carbon. Artists didn't seem to understand the scope of this problem – Lemercier himself hadn't – and the platforms making the sales didn't seem interested in clarifying.[50]

D Eden Fine Art Gallery

A particularly thoughtful and informative source of NFT information, Eden Gallery writes, "[c]rypto art can take many forms, from digital graphics to music, VR dreamscapes, or programmable art. These digital assets can have a collector's value and can represent items, including still graphic images, photography, GIFs, videos, music, and much more."[51] In sum, "[t]he crypto art concept revolves around the idea of digital scarcity … you treat digital art like physical goods and buy, sell, trade and collect it. Like traditional art, crypto art exists in limited quantities, and in some cases, buyers can purchase the rights to partial royalties and reproduction."[52]

While discussing the art of Alec Monopoly, Eden Fine Art Gallery observes that his works draw "the viewer in with its vibrant color schemes and iconic characters, that he uses to portray the lifestyles of the rich and famous. Apropos to the Miami scene Monopoly sets his painted characters atop yachts, flying helicopters, or coming out of the bank with overflowing bags of money."[53] Further:

> Alec Monopoly entertains his audience with his brightly colored embodiments of the wealthy one percent in his graffiti-styled art. Represented by the 'Monopoly Gang,' embodying the wealthy elite, epitomize the lifestyle of the rich and famous. As detached from our own world as they may be, these characters still remain relatable as they are the ones that we grew up watching on television and read about in our comic strips. Richie Rich, the world's richest kid, Scrooge McDuck, a duck that enjoys swimming in his fortune, and everyone's favorite family, The Simpsons, are some of Monopoly's favorite characters to illustrate the story of luxury living.[54]

Eden Gallery writes, "[i]t can be difficult to wrap your head around the idea of buying digital art that can be copied. You can certainly copy a digital file, including art sold with an NFT. In some cases, the owner can buy the rights to reproduction, although artists usually retain this."[55] While the original version of any artwork can

---

[50] Lawrence J. Trautman & Neal Newman, The Environmental, Social and Governance (ESG) Debate Emerges from the Soil of Climate Denial, 53 U. MEMPHIS L. REV. 67 (2022).

[51] *Monop$ in Miami*, EDEN GALLERY (November 28, 2019), www.eden-gallery.com/news/monops-in-miami/.

[52] Ibid.

[53] Ibid.

[54] *Contemporary Comics: How American Comic Art Stays Relevant in 2020*, EDEN GALLERY (April 20, 2020), www.eden-gallery.com/news/contemporary-comics-how-american-comic-art-stays-relevant-in-2020/.

[55] *What Is Crypto Art and How Does It Work?*, EDEN GALLERY (May 19, 2021), www.eden-gallery.com/news/what-is-crypto-art/.

only have one owner, "[a]n NFT grants … ownership of the work, but it can be copied with permission or illegally. This is not actually that different from the reproductions we see all the time of traditional artwork. Just as the Mona Lisa has been reproduced countless times in print and digital."[56] Regarding crypto art platforms, "[w]ith no less than 20+ individual marketplaces available on Ethereum, it is currently the most extensive network for crypto art."[57] Consider:

> Each marketplace on Ethereum caters to its own specific artistic style, so you can find something that suits your niche or style. Some marketplaces like Raible and Mintable offer a complete range of digital art. Others like Ephemera cater mainly to photographers. The digital art marketplace is a constantly changing world, with new entries popping up almost weekly. Most, but not all, crypto art marketplaces require a portfolio review to gain entry. The ones who do are quite obvious upon inspection of the site. So, make sure you are working with the most reputable and focused marketplace for each artistic medium.
>
> Sites like … Raible, Mintable, and Ephemera are older and more established in the crypto marketplace world, so they are highly regarded. But don't let that stop you from searching out other marketplaces like … ArtOlin; Crypto.com NFT; Ethereum; EOSIO; Flow; Hive; Near; Phantasm; Tezos; Waves; Zilliqa; [and] VeChain Thor.[58]

E Crypto Art in Sports

Worldwide, in just a short period of time NFTs have become wildly popular and a significant revenue source for sports teams.[59] In just one recent example, journalist Patrick Murray writes, "[t]he Golden State Warriors today launched a new NFT … collection, becoming the first team in U.S. professional sports to release their own officially licensed NFTs."[60] *Forbes* reports:

> NFTs have exploded onto the scene over the past few months, and nowhere has that explosion been more visible than on NBA Top Shot, the marketplace where basketball fans and collectors can buy, sell and trade NFTs … NBA Top Shot alone was responsible for a third of the $1.5 billion NFT trading volume seen in the first quarter.[61]

The global sports market for NFTs is well represented by the world's most popular sport, football (known as soccer in the United States). To better understand the relationship between avid soccer fans and the market for NFTs, we offer the

---

[56] Ibid.
[57] Ibid.
[58] Ibid.
[59] Patrick Murray, *Golden State Warriors Launch NFT Collection, Becoming First U.S. Sports Team to Release Own NFTs*, FORBES (April 27, 2021), www.forbes.com/sites/patrickmurray/2021/04/27/golden-state-warriors-launch-nft-collection-become-1st-sports-team-to-create-own-nfts/?sh=626a00921d94.
[60] Ibid.
[61] Ibid.

following courtesy of Coinbase. For background, consider the following event taking place on the evening of December 5, 2020: "[I]n a soccer stadium just north of Moscow, a football club called Spartak, of the Russian Premier League, played FC Tambov. It was a cold night. The few fans in attendance, bundled in heavy jackets, cheered as the home team routed Tambov 5–1."[62] In brief, "[t]he hero of the match was Ezequiel Ponce, a 24-year-old Spaniard who scored two goals. It was a forgettable game. Most of the world ignored this random match, one of hundreds played around the globe every day."[63] Here is where the example of the connection to NFTs takes place. We learn that "[w]ith traditional NFL fantasy football, you plunk down some money at the beginning of the year and then you hope to win a small weekly purse or a bigger payout in the playoffs."[64] Of the niche crypto sports platforms, "Sorare and Socios are both blockchain projects involving soccer [and are] 'crossover' use cases, bringing non-crypto people into the world of blockchain … Blue-chip teams like Manchester City, AC Milan and Juventus now use Socios tokens as a way to engage their fans."[65] In terms of rapid growth, "Nonfungible.com ranks Sorare as the third-most active NFT project, trailing only CryptoPunks and SuperRare. Twenty thousand soccer fans played it in February and this exploded to 120,000 in March. When Sorare launched in January 2020, it had $70,000 in trading volume. [During March 2021] it topped $27 million."[66]

F Topps Ventures into NFTs

The Topps Company announced on April 12, 2021 "the release of 2021 Topps Series 1 Baseball NFT … collectibles, ushering in a new era of baseball card collecting in partnership with Major League Baseball and MLB Players, Inc."[67] Topps says, "[l]aunching Tuesday, April 20 … Topps will build on its legacy as an innovator of digital collectibles by releasing its flagship yearly baseball card collection for the first time as NFTs."[68] Evan Kaplan, the managing director of MLB Players, Inc. states, "[a]s collectibles enjoy a breakout moment with NFTs and blockchain technology, we can't think of a better way to honor the legendary players from years past … today's stars and breakout rookies … offer[ing] a new innovative way for today's collectors and fans to connect with their favorite stars."[69]

---

[62] *See* Jeff Wilser, *In Europe, Football NFTs and Tokens Are No Fantasy*, COINDESK (April 6, 2021), www.coindesk.com/europe-football-nfts-tokens-fantasy-socios-sorare.

[63] Ibid.

[64] Ibid.

[65] Ibid.

[66] Ibid.

[67] *Topps Debuts Its First MLB Baseball Card NFT Collection with Topps Series 1 Baseball Launch*, TOPPS NEWS (April 12, 2021), www.topps.com/blog/topps-debuts-its-first-mlb-baseball-card-nft-collection-with-topps-series-1-baseball-launch-.html.

[68] Ibid.

[69] Ibid.

Topps describes itself as "a global consumer products company that entertains … consumers through a diversified, engaging, multi-platform product portfolio that includes physical and digital collectibles, trading cards, trading card games, sticker and album collections, memorabilia, curated experiential events, gift cards and novelty confections."[70] Evolving from a family-owned Brooklyn, New York-based chewing-gum company founded in 1938, Topps is now "a global sports and entertainment, digital/media and confections company."[71]

Topps describes its new technology business model as "undergoing significant innovation and continued transition to utilize various digital ecosystems. In addition to mobile digital applications, we are focused on developing digital collectibles that utilize blockchain technology and non-fungible tokens ('NFT'), and we successfully released several products in 2020, with more planned in the near-term."[72] Accordingly, Topps "successfully released Garbage Pail Kids collections using a blockchain platform in 2020, and … see further opportunity to expand into other properties with this and other digital platforms that protect the authenticity of our consumers' digital product purchases while providing … incremental net sales generated through … [asset] secondary trading."[73]

G *Threat of Data Breach*

Data breach negatively impact many aspects of modern life and remains a threat to individuals,[74] business enterprises,[75] and all nation-state actors.[76] While the integrity of blockchain-distributed ledger technology seems to hold at this point, several entities actually holding blockchain assets have been breached. One example of

---

[70] MUDRICK CAP. ACQUISITION CORP. II, PROXY STATEMENT TO SECTION 14A 167 (2021), www
 .sec.gov/Archives/edgar/data/1820727/000119312521160680/d161477dprer14a.htm#rom161477_20.

[71] Ibid.

[72] Ibid., 56.

[73] Ibid. *See also* Neal F. Newman & Lawrence J. Trautman, Special Purpose Acquisition Companies
 (SPACs) and the SEC, 24 U. PA. J. BUS. L. 639 (2022).

[74] Lawrence J. Trautman et al., Posted: No Phishing, 8 EMORY CORP. GOV. & ACCT. REV. (2021).

[75] Kenneth A. Bamberger et al., Verification Dilemmas, Law, and the Promise of Zero-Knowledge
 Proofs, 37 BERKELEY TECH. L.J. 1 (2022); Michael Mendelson, From Initial Coin Offerings
 to Security Tokens: A U.S. Federal Securities Law Analysis, 22 STAN. TECH. L. REV. 52 (2019);
 Lawrence J. Trautman et al., Corporate Directors: Who They Are, What They Do, Cyber and Other
 Contemporary Challenges, 70 BUFF. L. REV. 459 (2022); Neal Newman & Lawrence J. Trautman,
 Securities Law: Overview and Contemporary Issues, 16 OH. ST. BUS. L.J. 149 (2021); Lawrence J.
 Trautman & Peter C. Ormerod, Corporate Directors' and Officers' Cybersecurity Standard of Care:
 The Yahoo Data Breach, 66 AM. U. L. REV. 1231 (2017); Lawrence J. Trautman & Peter C. Ormerod,
 WannaCry, Ransomware, and the Emerging Threat to Corporations, 86 TENN. L. REV. 503 (2019).

[76] Lawrence J. Trautman, Is Cyberattack the Next Pearl Harbor?, 18 N.C. J.L. & TECH. 232 (2016);
 Lawrence J. Trautman, Managing Cyberthreat, 33 SANTA CLARA HIGH TECH. L.J. 230 (2016);
 Lawrence J. Trautman, Congressional Cybersecurity Oversight: Who's Who & How It Works, 5 J.L.
 & CYBER WARFARE 147 (2016); Lawrence J. Trautman, Cybersecurity: What About U.S. Policy?,
 2015 U. ILL. J.L. TECH. & POL'Y 341 (2015).

"a smart-contract-based attack happened on Ethereum in June 2016, when about $60 million was stolen."[77] More recently, customers of cryptocurrency company Coinbase suffered from a similar hack, resulting in "drained accounts."[78]

Theft of virtual currencies and other digital assets from data breaches takes place in several ways. As Andrew Balthazor describes, "[c]rypto-theft occurs when a person dispossesses the rightful owner of the address's bitcoin without the true owner's consent. This may happen because the private key (which controls the bitcoin address) was compromised, which is what occurred in the Mt. Gox hack."[79] Discussing possession and security issues, Balthazor further observe that "[p]rivate keys are stored in any number of ways: digitally, online, offline, encoded into devices, or written down on paper.[80] Crypto-thieves acquire an address's private key by hacking, malware, social engineering, coercion, or any other manner of taking the private key from a person."[81] Others in this volume have provided coverage about this topic and I will not replicate their findings here.

H Future Regulatory Compliance Issues

Rapid adoption of novel technologies such as NFTs vividly illustrates the struggle for our laws and regulations to keep pace.[82] The failure of FTX has caused increased focus by Congress on cybersecurity and crypto risk to financial services, investors, and national security.[83]

---

[77] *See* Valentina Gatteschi et al., To Blockchain or Not to Blockchain: That Is the Question, 20 IT PRO. 62, 68 (2018). *See also* Adam J. Kolber, Not-S-Smart Blockchain Contracts and Artificial Responsibility, 21 STAN. TECH. L. REV. 198 (2018).

[78] Kellen Browning, *Coinbase Users Got Hacked*, N.Y. TIMES (March 27, 2021), at B1.

[79] Andrew Balthazor, The Bona Fide Acquisition Rule Applied to Cryptocurrency, 3 GEO. L. TECH. REV. 402, 407 (2019) (citing Robert McMillan, *The Inside Story of Mt. Gox, Bitcoin's $460 Million Disaster*, WIRED (March 3, 2014), www.wired.com/2014/03/bitcoin-exchange/). *See also* Lawrence J. Trautman, Virtual Currencies: Bitcoin & What Now after Liberty Reserve, Silk Road, and Mt. Gox?, 20 RICH. J. L. & TECH. 13 (2014).

[80] Balthazor, *The Bona Fide Acquisition Rule* (citing Max I. Raskin, Realm of the Coin: Bitcoin and Civil Procedure, 20 FORDHAM J. CORP. & FIN. L. 969, 989 (2015)).

[81] Balthazor, *The Bona Fide Acquisition Rule*, 407 (citing Mariella Moon, *Cryptocurrency Expert Kidnapped for $1 Million Bitcoin Ransom*, ENGADGET (December 30, 2017), www.yahoo.com/now/2017-12-30-cryptocurrency-expert-kidnap-1-million-bitcoin.html).

[82] Lawrence J. Trautman, Bitcoin, Virtual Currencies and the Struggle of Law and Regulation to Keep Pace, 102 MARQ. L. REV. 447 (2018); Lawrence J. Trautman, Governance of the Facebook Privacy Crisis, 20 PITT. J. TECH. L. & POL'Y 41 (2020) (Facebook struggling with privacy issues); Lawrence J. Trautman, How Google Perceives Customer Privacy, Cyber, E-Commerce, Political and Regulatory Compliance Risks, 10 WM. & MARY BUS. L. REV. 1 (2018); Lawrence J. Trautman, E-Commerce and Electronic Payment System Risks: Lessons from PayPal, 17 U.C. DAVIS BUS. L.J. 261 (2016); Lawrence J. Trautman, Rapid Technological Change and U.S. Entrepreneurial Risk in International Markets: Focus on Data Security, Information Privacy, Bribery and Corruption, 49 CAPITAL U. L. REV. 67 (2021).

[83] Michael J. Conklin, Brian Elzweig, & Lawrence J. Trautman, Legal Recourse for Victims of Blockchain and Cyber Breach Attacks, 23 U.C. DAVIS BUS. L.J. 135 (2023); Brian Elzweig & Lawrence J. Trautman,

I The Business of NFTs

The business environment of NFTs is an amalgam of various areas of law and enter-prise and may encompass issues involving: art, copyright, cybersecurity, entertain-ment, intellectual property, music, performance, technology, and video editing, just to name a few.[84] In just a matter of months, "[i]n new online marketplaces such as Nifty Gateway, SuperRare, and Foundation, artists can upload, or 'mint,' their works as unique N.F.T.s, then sell them."[85] As an informative case study of just one example, journalist Kyle Chayka writes:

> On October 30th [2020], Winkelmann [Beeple] launched his first 'drop' of three art works on the N.F.T marketplace Nifty Gateway, to test his salability. One was a piece called 'Politics Is Bullshit,' featuring a diarrheic bull half-daubed in an American flag pattern amid a rain of dollar bills. The work came in an edition of a hundred, at a cost of one dollar each. A core feature of blockchain technology is 'immutabil-ity': all transactions recorded are permanent and transparent, which means that any N.F.T. purchase or sale is visible to the public. As of March, 2021, the editions had resold for as much as six hundred thousand dollars. (In N.F.T. marketplaces, artists receive a percentage of resale prices, typically around ten percent).[86]

In sum, "NFTs and the related concept of the blockchain hold the promise to, in part, give people ways to make their work more valuable by creating scarcity. There is promise in letting creators rely less on middlemen including social media com-panies, art dealers and streaming music companies."[87] For example, on March 31, 2021, we learn, "Michael Jordan and Kevin Durant are among those betting that the company behind NBA Top Shot is poised to build on the craze over digital collect-ibles. Dabber Labs Inc. said … it raised $305 million from investors … [valuing] the company at $2.6 billion."[88] *The Wall Street Journal* reports, "[t]he sums reflect an

---

When Does *a* Nonfungible Token (NFT) Become *a* Security?, 39 GA. ST. U. L. REV. 295 (2023); H. Justin Pace & Lawrence J. Trautman, Mission Critical: Caremark, Blue Bell, and Director Responsibility for Cybersecurity Governance, 2022 WISC. L. REV. 887 (2022); David D. Schein & Lawrence J. Trautman, The Dark Web and Employer Liability, 18 COLO. TECH. L.J. 49 (2020); Lawrence J. Trautman & Neal Newman, A Proposed SEC Cyber Data Disclosure Advisory Commission, 50 SEC. REG. L.J. 199 (2022); Lawrence J. Trautman, Following the Money: Lessons from the "Panama Papers," Part 1: Tip of the Iceberg, 121 PENN ST. L. REV. 807 (2017); Lawrence J. Trautman et al., *Cyber Threats to Business: Identifying and Responding to Digital Attacks* (November 2022) (unpublished manuscript), https://ssrn.com/abstract=4262971; Lawrence J. Trautman et al., Governance of *the* Internet of Things (IoT), 60 JURIMETRICS 315 (2020).

[84] Lawrence J. Trautman, *Anthony "Tony" Luppino & Malika S. Simmons*, Some Key Things U.S. Entrepreneurs Need to Know about the Law and Lawyers, 46 TEX. J. BUS. L. 155 (2016).

[85] Kyle Chayka, *How Beeple Crashed the Art World*, NEWYORKER (March 22, 2021), www.newyorker .com/tech/annals-of-technology/how-beeple-crashed-the-art-world.

[86] Ibid.

[87] Shira Ovide, *Some Straight Talk on NFTs*, N.Y. TIMES (March 29, 2021), at B3.

[88] Sebastian Pellejero, *Starts Help Raise $305 Million for Basketball NFT Site*, WALL ST. J. (March 31, 2021), at B4.

exploding interest in non-fungible tokens, or NFTs … The market for NFTs grew to at least $338 million in 2020, according to a report from NonFungible.com and research firm L'Atelier, from around $41 million in 2018."[89]

J Payments for Artistic Endeavors

Financial journalist Jason Zweig suggests that NFTs provide an opportunity for artists to gain a greater payback for their labors by providing "an ownership stake they've never had before."[90] He presents the example of, "Josei Bellini, an artist based in Chicago who majored in finance in college and worked briefly at an investment-advisory firm. Since late 2018, she has sold about 300 of her paintings this way."[91]

V MARKET FOR NFTS PLUMMETS

During 2022, the value of many NFTs softened and in many cases declined significantly.[92] As 2023 began, the implosion of cryptocurrency platform FTX that took place at the end of 2022 resulted in contagion and loss of value among many participants in the crypto markets impacting various associated products and services.[93]

A The FTX Bankruptcy

It was during November 2022, that "[i]n less than a week, the cryptocurrency billionaire Sam Bankman-Fried went from industry leader to industry villain, lost most of his fortune, saw his $32 billion company plunge into bankruptcy and became the target of investigations by the Securities and Exchange Commission and the Justice

---

[89] Ibid.

[90] Zweig, *The Method.*

[91] *Id.*

[92] Shanti Escalante De Mattei, *NFT Trading Volume Is Reportedly Down 97 Percent since January,* ARTNEWS (September 29, 2022), www.artnews.com/art-news/news/nft-trading-volume-down-97-since-january-artnews-1234641141/; Andrew Hayward, *Bored Ape Yacht Club NFT Prices Fall after NFT Sinks Crypto Market,* DECRYPT (November 10, 2022), https://decrypt.co/114158/bored-ape-yacht-club-nft-prices-fall-after-ftx-sinks-crypto-market. This negative trend has persisted into 2023, as sales and trading volume continue to undergo a sharp decline. *See* Jacquelyn Melinek, *Monthly NFT Sales Fell for Fifth Consecutive Month to $495M in July,* TECHCRUNCH (August 23, 2023), https://techcrunch.com/2023/08/03/monthly-nft-sales-fell-for-fifth-consecutive-month-to-495m-in-july/; Leeor Shimron, *NFT Market Meltdown: How Can Investors Best Position Themselves?,* FORBES (July 11, 2023), www.forbes.com/sites/leeorshimron/2023/07/11/nft-market-meltdown-how-can-investors-best-position-themselves/?sh=10aef2905821.

[93] George Kaloudis, *Crypto Markets Are Suffering – But Is It Really 'Contagion'?,* COINDESK (November 21, 2022), www.coindesk.com/business/2022/11/20/crypto-markets-are-suffering-but-is-it-really-contagion/.

Department."[94] Just days later, Bankman-Fried was extradited from the Bahamas, posted a $250 million bond in New York, and released pending his later court appearances.[95] Among the immediate questions raised in the FTX demise and failure of other crypto entities around the same time period is "where were the auditors and board audit committees?"[96] One NFT-oriented blog estimated that "NFT losses are estimated at around $25 trillion since it all came crashing down."[97] These losses continued to grow in 2023, resulting in more and more angry investors and consumers that felt frustrated with prior expensive purchases of NFTs, which have sharply fallen in value.[98] Eventually, some of this outrage resulted in lawsuits, which were filed against various parties involved or associated with NFTs sales.[99] Among those getting sued was the auction house Sotheby's, which has been accused of allegedly misleading price manipulation of Bored Ape Yacht Club (BAYC) NFT sales.[100]

[94] Lawrence J. Trautman, *The FTX Crypto Debacle: Largest Fraud Since Madoff?*, U. Mem. L. Rev. (forthcoming 2023), http://ssrn.com/abstract=4290093 (citing David Yaffe-Bellany, *FTX Founder Says He Expanded Too Fast and Missed Warnings*, N.Y. Times (November 15, 2022, at A1)).

[95] Corrine Ramey & James Fanelli, *FTX Founder Bankman-Fried Released on $250 Million Bond*, Wall St. J. (December 23, 2022), at A1.

[96] Hon. Bernice Donald et al., *Crisis at the Audit Committee: Challenges of a Post-Pandemic World*, Rev. Banking & Fin. L. (forthcoming 2023), http://ssrn.com/abstract=4240080; Lawrence J. Trautman, The Board's Responsibility for Crisis Governance, 13 Hastings Bus. L.J. 275 (2017); Lawrence J. Trautman & Kara Altenbaumer-Price, The Board's Responsibility for Information Technology Governance, 28 J. Marshall J. Computer & Info. L. 313 (2011).

[97] *How to Use Worthless NFTs to Slash Your Crypto Tax Bill*, Koinly.io (December 11, 2022), https://koinly.io/blog/nft-tax-loss-harvesting/.

[98] *See, for example*, Arijit Sarkar, *Popular NFT Collections Take Massive Price Hit in 2023*, CoinTelegraph (May 30, 2023), https://cointelegraph.com/news/popular-nft-investments-take-a-massive-hit-in-2023 ("Investments in top NFT projects such as Doodles, Invisible Friends, Moonbirds and Goblintown have lost up to 95 percent of their value in Ether"); Shimron, *NFT Market Meltdown* (noting that as of July 2023, the floor price of Yuga Labs' Bored Apes sits "at $62,000, an 83 percent decline from its all-time high of $370,000 in April 2022").

[99] An illustrative notable example is the lawsuit against Yuga Labs and others. On December 10, 2022, investors of the Board Ape Yacht Club NFTs "filed a class-action lawsuit against over 40 defendants, including Yuga Labs [the creator of the NFTs] and celebrities like Post Malone, Justin Bieber and Paris Hilton. The lawsuit alleged that Yuga Labs and the celebrities were able to 'artificially increase' the prices of the NFTs through celebrity promotions." Later, the lawsuit was amended to include Sotheby's Holdings Inc., alleging that it colluded with creator Yuga Labs to artificially inflate the prices of the NFTs. *See* Ezra Reguerra, *Sotheby's and Yuga Labs Respond to Lawsuit from Bored Ape Investors*, CoinTelegraph (August 17, 2023), https://cointelegraph.com/news/nft-bored-ape-sotheby-s-and-yuga-labs-respond-to-lawsuit-from-bored-ape-investors. Christy Choi, *'Bored Apes' Investors Sue Sotheby's, Paris Hilton and Others as NFT Prices Collapse*, CNN (August 17, 2023), www.cnn.com/style/article/bored-apes-sothebys-lawsuit/index.html.

[100] Ibid.; Wahid Pessarlay, *Sotheby's Faces Lawsuit over Alleged Misleading, Price Manipulation of BAYC NFT Sales*, CoinGeek (August 18, 2023), https://coingeek.com/sothebys-faces-lawsuit-over-alleged-misleading-price-manipulation-of-bayc-nft-sales/#:~:text=Specifically%2C%20the%20plaintiffs%20point%20to,for%20the%20increase%20in%20valuation ("[T]he plaintiffs point to the famous sale of the NFTs at Sotheby's in September that netted over $24 million in sales. The aggrieved investors say that the sale of 101 BAYC NFTs exceeded presale estimates by up to $10 million, blaming the auction house for the increase in valuation").

Targeting Sotheby's as an expert participant in the art world, the plaintiffs claimed that the art dealers artificially inflated the prices of the sold NFTs by engaging in shill bidding, a practice where fake bids are used to drive up prices.[101] The plaintiffs have argued that this manipulation resulted in an unjustified increase in the NFTs' valuations. The lawsuit raises questions about the transparency and integrity of NFT auctions conducted by major institutions in the art industry and in general like Sotheby's.

B Donald Trump NFT Issuance

Just weeks after the FTX implosion, Donald Trump digital cards were sold, "[f]eaturing cartoon depictions of the former president including as a superhero, golfer, race car driver and Old West sheriff."[102] Purchasers of cards automatically entered into a "sweepstakes" to receive experiences with Trump, ranging from a Zoom call to a cocktail hour at Mar-a-Lago.[103] Reports emerge that "[f]orty-five thousand cards were produced, all but 1,000 of which were offered for sale … at $99 each … That would mean at least $4.3 million was raised."[104]

Donald Trump digital cards gathered significant attention and received widespread mockery and criticism.[105] Despite the success of the initial sale, the value of the cards has been highly volatile over the past year. After a sharp increase post-launch in December 2022, they dropped by over 50 percent in January 2023, and then rebounded in February as Trump re-emerged into the mainstream and returned to social media.[106] A few months later, in April 2023, the release of a second series of Trump Digital Trading Cards, featuring 47,000 NFTs sold at $99 each, resulted in another sharp decline in the value of the first series.[107] Over the next months, prices continued to swing sharply in responses to news related to Trump.[108] As of August 2023, Trump reportedly earned "$4.87 million in licensing fees from the Trump NFT collection."[109]

---

[101] Ibid.

[102] Alex Leary, *Trump Digital Cards Mocked, but Sell Out*, WALL ST. J. (December 17–18, 2022), at A5.

[103] Cam Thompson, *Donald Trump Announces $99 Digital Trading Card NFTs*, COINDESK (August 15, 2022), www.coindesk.com/web3/2022/12/15/trump-announces-99-digital-trading-card-nfts/.

[104] Leary, *Trump Digital Cards*.

[105] *See, for example,* Andrew Hayward, *Trump Drops More NFTs – And Now the First Batch Is Plummeting in Price*, DECRYPT (December 15, 2022), https://decrypt.co/117317/donald-trump-nft-collection-crypto-cant-even.

[106] Andrew Hayward, *Trump NFTs Are Mooning Again – Here's What's Going On*, DECRYPT (February 13, 2023), https://decrypt.co/121228/trump-nfts-mooning-again-here-whats-going-on.

[107] Cam Thompson, *Trump's Second NFT Collection Sells Out While Prices on First Collection Plunge*, COINDESK (April 19, 2023), www.coindesk.com/web3/2023/04/19/trumps-second-nft-collection-sells-out-while-prices-on-first-collection-plunge/.

[108] Shaurya Malwa, *Donald Trump NFTs Surge after Tucker Carlson Interview*, COINDESK (August 23, 2023), www.coindesk.com/web3/2023/08/24/donald-trump-nfts-surge-after-tucker-carlson-interview/.

[109] Ibid.

C *This Time It Is Different?*

Is the value of NFTs as modern art pieces significantly different from that of other tangible assets that have been highly valued at various points in history due to subjective factors or hype? The value of tangible assets has long been a testament to the subjectivity of human perception and faith in their worth. History provides us with intriguing examples, such as the Dutch Tulip Mania in the seventeenth century, where tulip bulbs became astonishingly valuable commodities, not due to any intrinsic utility but solely because of the collective belief in their worth. The Tulip Mania serves as a vivid illustration of how market values can be driven by perception, speculation, and human emotions, rather than concrete utility. Similarly, in the modern era, diamonds, both natural and lab-grown, present an intriguing case study in subjective value. Natural diamonds have been revered for their rarity, yet their value has been heavily influenced by the perception of scarcity, despite the existence of abundant diamond supplies. Lab-grown diamonds, chemically identical to natural ones, challenge these traditional perceptions. The perceived value of lab-grown diamonds is shaped by factors like ethical sourcing and sustainability, highlighting how shifts in societal values can redefine the worth of tangible assets.

In both the case of tulips and diamonds, tangible objects have showcased the malleability of their value, driven not solely by objective characteristics but by the beliefs, emotions, and changing societal priorities of those who value them. These historical and contemporary examples remind us that the value of tangibles remains a fascinating interplay of economics, psychology, and cultural context.

VI CONCLUSION

The dramatic extension of blockchain and other digital technology to the world of art represents a new and exciting platform for creative expression. This chapter offers a valuable addition to the literature by providing a readable introduction and overview of what is now known about the likely impact of blockchain technology and NFTs to art. This important development should have a significant impact on the future of innovation and property law.

14

NFTs, Property Rights, and Realty

Juliet M. Moringiello and Christopher K. Odinet

I INTRODUCTION

For over a decade now,[1] the promise of distributed ledger technologies (often referred to merely as "blockchains") has filled the minds of policy-makers, politicians, investors, corporate giants, and even the general public.[2] Articles have proclaimed that "Blockchain is transforming the investment and asset management market,"[3] while others have argued that it will "revolutionize the world economy."[4] Of late, the rise of non-fungible tokens (NFTs) has added fuel to the fire, further enhancing the rhetoric around what crypto can do to change the world.[5] And perhaps nowhere have these promises had more resonance than in the case of property rights.[6] Blockchain technologies have been touted as a mechanism to track and resolve disputes over property, ranging from intellectual property to personality and even to real estate.[7] It is with this final asset class – *real property* – that this chapter

---

[1] Paulina Likos & Coyranne Hicks, *The History of Bitcoin, the First Cryptocurrency*, U.S. News (February 4, 2022), https://money.usnews.com/investing/articles/the-history-of-bitcoin.

[2] Bobby Lee, The Promise of Bitcoin: The Future of Money and How It Can Work for You (2021); Harnessing the Promise of Blockchain to Change Lives, UNCTAD (March 2, 2021), https://unctad.org/news/harnessing-promise-blockchain-change-lives.

[3] *Time for Trust*, PWC (October 2020), www.pwc.com.cy/en/issues/assets/blockchain-time-for-trust.pdf.

[4] *How Blockchains Can Change the World*, McKinsey & Company (May 6, 2016), www.mckinsey.com/industries/technology-media-and-telecommunications/our-insights/how-blockchains-could-change-the-world.

[5] Clive Thompson, *The Untold Story of the NFT Boom*, N.Y. Times (May 12, 2021), www.nytimes.com/2021/05/12/magazine/nft-art-crypto.html.

[6] Desiree Daniel & Chinew Ifejika Speranza, *The Role of Blockchain in Documenting Land Users' Rights: The Canonical Case of Farmers in the Vernacular Land Market*, Front. Blockchain (May 12, 2020), www.frontiersin.org/articles/10.3389/fbloc.2020.00019/full; Rosa M. Garcia-Teruel & Héctor Simón-Moreno, *The Digital Tokenization of Property Rights. A Comparative Perspective*, Computer Law & Security Review, Vol. 41 (July 2021), www.sciencedirect.com/science/article/pii/S0267364921000169.

[7] *See* Gabriel Khoury & Jared A. Wachtler, *Blockchain Technology Is Changing the Real Estate Industry*, Nat'l L. Rev. (February 24, 2022); *Blockchain and Property Rights*, New America, www.newamerica.org/future-land-housing/reports/proprightstech-primers/blockchain-and-property-rights/.

concerns itself. In these pages, we question the use of blockchain networks and NFTs in real property transactions by interrogating how the existing technologies work against the backdrop of the realities of real property transfers. Moving beyond the hype, we explain that a blockchain system would provide few if any benefits to our system of real estate transactions.

The real estate recording system in the US is quite old and has, at least histori-cally, been based on paper records.[8] Additionally, the system is almost exclusively one of notice, which aims to convey information to parties that may or may not be accurate.[9] Rather than be definitive, record information serves as a basis for further investigation.[10] One may find a cloud on title to property, only to then discover that the basis for the ostensible claim is invalid.[11] In other cases, the claim revealed in the record may require additional acts to cure the title.[12] All of this, plus the very paper-based nature of the system, has given rise to numerous objections over the years – primarily that the system is antiquated and inefficient.[13] Surely blockchain systems, with their distributed networks and immutable record-keeping all operating seamlessly through smart contracts and tokenized assets rather than through paper deeds and filings, would vastly improve land transfers.

But we are incredulous as to these claims. While many aspects of the existing land recording system are old and, at least in many parts of the country, are still paper-based, not all components are bad. Indeed, for all its inefficiency, land trans-actions abound in the US – and have done so even during the Covid-19 pandemic.[14] In other words, for all its flaws and ripe old age, the US land recording system seems to be working quite fine. Moreover, moving to a blockchain-based system would be a significant undertaking. Not only would it involve changes to numer-ous laws – indeed, it would involve fundamentally moving to a land registration system,[15] which would mean leaving the notice recording system behind – it would also require that changes be made to property law itself.[16] Specifically, current law does not allow one to tokenize rights in real property.[17] In other words, one cannot

---

[8] *See* P. H. Marshall, *A Historical Sketch of the American Recording Acts*, 4 Clev. Mar. L. Rev. 56 (1955).
[9] Dale Whitman, Ann Burkhart, R. Wilson Freyermuth, & Troy Rule, The Law of Property 819 (2019).
[10] *See* Lawrence M. Dudek, *Common Issues Regarding the Validity, Enforcement and Priority of Construction Liens*, 47 Mich. Real Prop. Rev. 32 (2020).
[11] *See* ibid., 32.
[12] *See* 3 Patton and Palomar on Land Titles § 604 (3d ed. 2003).
[13] *See generally* Dale Whitman, *Optimizing Land Title Assurance Systems*, 42 Geo. Wash. L. Rev. 40 (1973).
[14] Peter Grant, *Covid-19 Fuels Best-Ever Commercial Real-Estate Sales*, Wall St. J. (January 25, 2022), www.wsj.com/articles/covid-19-fuels-best-ever-commercial-real-estate-sales-11643115601.
[15] 66 Am. Jur. 2d *Registration of Land Titles* § 1 (2021) (describing the Torrens system of land registra-tion, rather than recordation).
[16] *See* Section III.A.
[17] Juliet M. Moringiello & Christopher K. Odinet, *The Property Law of Tokens*, 74 Fl. L. Rev. 607 (2022).

merely through contract or some other private law mechanism create a digital asset (an NFT) and have it embody ownership or any other rights in real estate.[18]

But putting aside the legal obstacles, there are also systemic barriers – some of which are bound up in basic political economy. First, to change the system of recording from the way it is now to one that involves a blockchain as contemporarily conceived would be expensive and present issues of public trust, as it might seem to require the introduction of private firms as central nodes in the system to substitute for accountable government officials.[19] Indeed, as we explain below, efforts in at least two states to use blockchain technology in corporate record-keeping and in land transfers have largely come to nothing.[20]

Yet we think there is indeed a potential use case for blockchains and crypto technology when it comes to property rights. However, it is not in the world of real property – which our existing system has largely shown itself to be sufficient – but rather for *intangible property*.[21] American law developed to deal with tangible assets – whether personal or real. This makes sense because these asset types represented the primary forms of wealth for most of history.[22] But tracking and transferring rights in intangible property – particularly *purely intangible personal property* – has always been underdeveloped.[23] It is here, so we argue, that blockchain technology and NFTs might have the highest utility.

In order to make all of these arguments, this chapter proceeds in three sections. First, we question whether the hype of blockchains and crypto have a meaningfully useful role to play in real estate transactions. We do this by describing the various uses proffered by crypto enthusiasts and the companies experimenting with various crypto offerings – ranging from NFT land transfers to crypto mortgages and more. Our main contribution comes to the fore in Section III where we problematize the use of blockchains and NFTs in real property transactions to show how current property and commercial law, as well as considerations of political economy and pure costs, make the crypto promise quite hollow. Section IV concludes, however, with some crypto optimism – arguing that blockchains and attendant technologies can play a useful role in how we deal with rights in certain kinds of intangible property.

---

[18] Ibid.
[19] *See below* Section III.B.
[20] *See below* Section III.B.
[21] *See below* Section IV.
[22] *See* CLAIRE PRIEST, CREDIT NATION: PROPERTY LAWS AND INSTITUTIONS IN EARLY AMERICA (2021); H. W. BRANDS, THE AGE OF GOLD: THE CALIFORNIA GOLD RUSH AND THE NEW AMERICAN DREAM (2003).
[23] *See generally* Juliet M. Moringiello, *False Categories in Commercial Law: The (Ir)relevance of (in) tangibility*, 35 FLA. ST. U. L. REV. 119 (2007); Christopher K. Odinet, *Bitproperty and Commercial Credit*, 94 WASH. U.L. REV. 649 (2017); Joshua A.T. Fairfield, *Bitproperty*, 88 S. CAL. L. REV. 805 (2015); Christopher K. Odinet, *Data and the Social Obligation Norm of Property*, 29 CORNELL J. L. & PUB. POL'Y 643 (2020).

II DO BLOCKCHAIN AND CRYPTOASSETS HAVE A
ROLE IN REAL ESTATE TRANSACTIONS?

In this section of this chapter, we discuss the hype surrounding crypto-enabled land transactions. We then explain several models that companies are promoting. In doing so, we explore possible roles for the blockchain in land transfers.

A *The Hype*

The promise of faster, cheaper, frictionless, inclusive, and reliable real estate transactions has lured numerous companies into the world of blockchain and crypto-enabled land transfers. In this section, we discuss products whose promoters claim to improve the real estate closing process by transacting on a blockchain, as well as products that enable holders of crypto to buy land without liquidating their cryptoasset holdings.

Speed is an often promoted benefit of both blockchain and crypto-enabled real estate closings. The CEO of Propy, which offers "[a]utomated [t]ransactions from the [l]eading [r]eal [e]state [i]nnovator,"[24] claims that it took only 22 minutes to transfer a studio apartment using an NFT.[25] This speed is cited as particularly desirable to members of certain demographic groups, such as millennials and Gen Zers, who "are already purchasing high-value assets … online [and] expect the same ease and transparency when buying real estate."[26] A blockchain entrepreneur who auctioned her Florida home as an NFT lauded the ability of NFTs to consummate real estate transactions as quickly as Venmo transactions.[27] The platforms' consumer-facing websites propose to take the boredom out of real estate transactions, with the crypto mortgage company Milo's explicitly stating that: "[w]e deal with the boring stuff like title, insurance, appraisals, all behind the scenes."[28]

In addition to marketing their products as more desirable to younger people, the companies also promote their transaction structure as the gateway to wealth-building for those who have been denied access to traditional financial products.

---

[24] PROPY (2023), https://propy.com/browse/.
[25] Natalia Karayaneva, *Real Estate NFTs: How It Began*, FORBES (November 24, 2021), www.forbes .com/sites/nataliakarayaneva/2021/11/24/real-estate-nfts-how-it-began/?sh=3d7e59353b12.
[26] Ibid. The author also claims that the buyer in the 22-minute transaction had never purchased a home in the Bay Area because traditional real estate transactions were far too complicated.
[27] Bernadette Berdychowski, *This Tampa Bay Home Is Being Sold as an NFT*, TAMPA BAY TIMES (February 5, 2022), www.tampabay.com/news/real-estate/2022/02/04/this-tampa-bay-home-is-being-sold-as-an-nft/.
[28] MILO CREDIT, *Whats's ACrypto-Backed Mortgage?* (2024), www.milocredit.com/crypto/. We note that describing legal necessities as "boring" was also a hallmark of "Web 1.0" transactions, when companies offered their online terms of use behind cleverly labeled links. *See* Walter Effross, *The Legal Architecture of Virtual Stores: World Wide Web Sites and the Uniform Commercial Code*, 34 SAN DIEGO L. REV. 1263, 1378–1379 (1997) (describing the Simon & Schuster SuperStore, which presented its terms with the link "Out lawyers made us put this here," and Kraft's Interactive Kitches, whose terms were behind a link labeled "[A] message from our lawyers").

Milo promotes its Crypto Mortgage product in access to credit terms, justifying its high interest rates for loans by a goal of "expand[ing] access to those with crypto wealth who are currently 'unbanked' in regards to mortgage loans."[29] RealT, which offers investors the opportunity to buy fractionalized, tokenized interests in rental properties, promotes its product as one that allows "the average person" to make "sound real estate investments without any additional financing."[30]

Another type of accessibility might be described as *access parity*. many sellers might be wary of taking bitcoin or any other cryptoasset as payment for real estate. Yet those with large crypto holdings tend not to want to liquidate them because of the tax consequences of doing so. These buyers desire the same ability to use their crypto holdings as collateral for loans in the same way that those with large tax portfolios can do so.[31] The central idea behind all of these crypto real estate efforts is to upend traditional market practices using crypto technologies in an effort, at least nominally, to expand access and democratize both finance and ownership.

B Crypto- and Blockchain-Enabled Real Estate Transactions: The Practice

Actual efforts to implement these crypto real property strategies are still nascent. But that is not to say they do not exist. To better understand how the promise of the hype is being put into practice, the following divides the crypto real property market into three categories (with examples): property transfers, property financing, and property recording-keeping.

1 Land Transfers by NFT

At the time of this writing, companies are offering several different types of crypto and blockchain enabled real property transactions. Propy's product claims to speed up real estate transactions by using blockchain technology from the execution of the contract through the closing. It has been experimenting with the use of blockchain since late 2017, when Propy enabled a buyer of an apartment in Kyiv, Ukraine, to purchase an apartment with crypto and record the transaction on a blockchain ledger.[32]

---

[29] Maxwell Strachan, *VC-Backed Startup Promises Bitcoiners Way to Bypass Taxes While Buying Home*, MOTHERBOARD (February 1, 2022), www.vice.com/en/article/y3vn85/vc-backed-startup-promises-bitcoiners-way-to-bypass-taxes-while-buying-home. This promoter also noted the large percentage of non-white crypto traders, a statistic (coupled with the high percentage of crypto-market participants without a college degree) used by *New York Times* columnist Paul Krugman to christen crypto the "new subprime." Paul Krugman. *How Crypto Became the New Subprime*, N.Y. TIMES (January 28, 2022), www.nytimes.com/2022/01/27/opinion/cryptocurrency-subprimevulnerable.html.

[30] REALT, LEGALLY COMPLIANT OWNERSHIP OF TOKENIZED REAL ESTATE 10 (May 2019), https://realt.co/wp-content/uploads/2019/05/RealToken_White_Paper_US_v03.pdf.

[31] Strachan, *VC-Backed Startup Promises Bitcoiners*.

[32] Peter Grant, *An Entire Real Estate Deal Takes Place Online, Using Cryptocurrency Technology*, WALL ST. J. (September 26, 2017), www.wsj.com/articles/an-entire-real-estate-deal-takes-place-online-using-cryptocurrency-technology-1506462545.

The transaction was not solely on the blockchain, however, it was also recorded in Ukraine's paper land records system. We note that it is not clear what blockchain added to the transaction and the promoter, in a *Wall Street Journal* article, explained that because Ukraine had adopted regulations that integrated the online and offline title recording processes, the paper deed contained the blockchain address of the digital transaction.[33] Four years later, Propy facilitated the sale of that same property, this time in a transaction that used the paper and online systems in a successive rather than a parallel fashion. To facilitate the 2021 transaction, the real property was transferred to a US limited liability company (LLC) and the NFT purportedly transferred ownership in the LLC.[34] This structure eliminates the need for recording each successive sale; the LLC is recorded as the owner of the real estate in the paper land records and the ownership of the LLC changes through transfer of the NFT on the applicable blockchain.

Propy has moved its product stateside, conducting an auction of a home in Florida via an NFT. As it did in the Ukraine sale, Propy first facilitated the transfer of the real estate to an LLC. Then Propy "minted" the property rights into an NFT.[35] According to the Propy website, the NFT equals ownership rights in the home valued at $650,000 and claims that the NFT is "a DeFi asset, that can be borrowed against."[36] The NFT includes "access to the ownership transferred paperwork," a picture of the house, and an NFT mural by a local artist.[37] The NFT business appears to be a miniscule part of Propy's overall operations; the remainder of the business provides a platform for online real estate transactions. For these more traditional transactions, Propy provides a platform for storing the transaction documents on the blockchain. As was the case in the original Ukrainian transaction, the blockchain address is on the recorded deed, now by a QR code.[38]

RealT offers investors the opportunity to buy interests in rental property. RealT's hook is democratization; by using Ethereum tokens to represent fractional interests in real estate, it allows smaller investors to access the markets.[39] As is the case in Propy's structure, the tokens do not actually represent interests in real estate; the tokens represent interests in a business entity. RealT has structured its entity as a Delaware Series LLC and each series owns one real property asset.[40] Each deed evidencing the transfer of the real estate to the series is recorded in the county in which the real estate is

33 Ibid.
34 Karayaneva, *Real Estate NFTs.*
35 Berdychowski, *This Tampa Bay Home.*
36 *Florida – The Home of the First US Real Estate NFT,* Propy (2023), https://propy.com/browse/first-us-real-estate-nft/.
37 Ibid. A news report on the transaction clarifies that the NFT art is a mural that will be painted on a wall of the house. *See* Berdychowski, *This Tampa Bay Home* (solidifying the fact that the NFT is in there just for marketing purposes).
38 *FAQs, Why Does Blockchain Matter to Me?,* Propy (2023), https://propy.com/browse/faq/.
39 RealT, Legally Compliant Ownership 10.
40 Ibid., 11.

located.[41] Investors then buy tokens, known as Real Tokens, that represent units of the series. One benefit of the token structure is the mechanism for disbursing rental payments. The management company collects rent from the tenants and exchanges the rent for stablecoins that are then distributed to the rent contract associated with each property. The rent contract then automatically disburses the rental payments, pro rata, to the digital wallets that hold the Real Tokens.[42] The RealT white paper available on the company's website gives a balanced view of the pros and cons of tokenized real estate ownership, recognizing, for example, that while a homeowner might tokenize her house on the RealT platform, the possibility of using that token as collateral for a loan is "purely hypothetical."[43] RealT also recognizes the importance of "real world" conditions that affect real estate and intends to use Ethereum's Interplanetary File System (IPFS) to give token holders access to their property's inspection reports, maintenance histories, and repair and renovation histories.[44]

2 Crypto-Enabled Loans

Two companies, Milo and LoanSnap, are offering crypto mortgage loans. Both are claiming to offer the world's first crypto mortgage, using different structures. Milo makes loans to customers who hold bitcoin, which they must transfer to a third-party wallet custodian for Milo's benefit. Milo then advances the purchase price (in US dollars) to the seller and the customer pays the purchase price over time. If the customer misses a payment, Milo withdraws the customer's crypto and liquidates it to make the payment (ostensibly, by selling it on the open market). The benefit of the Milo loan is that the borrower does not have to liquidate the bitcoin to buy the house. It is not clear from the Milo website how their loans are structured but they do not appear to be mortgage loans. That said, the founder of Milo told one news outlet that customers have an incentive to pay because he (the lender) has a lien on the house and the buyer's bitcoin.[45]

LoanSnap's product is more clearly a mortgage. LoanSnap is a mortgage lender and it claims to have minted the first NFT mortgages using its Bacon Protocol. According to LoanSnap, NFTs can improve the mortgage lending process because the blockchain can permanently record information that lenders take into account in making lending decisions, such as the applicant's credit score.[46] On the other

[41] Ibid., 10.
[42] Ibid., 19.
[43] Ibid., 20.
[44] Ibid., 23.
[45] Maxwell Strachan, *VC-Backed Startup Promises Bitcoiners*; CNBC Squawk Box Interview with Josip Rupena, CEO of Milo, March 25, 2022, at www.youtube.com/watch?v=LjJskQqcRzw.
[46] Kamran Rosen, *This Company Wants to Turn Your Mortgage into an NFT*, Forbes (November 18, 2021), www.forbes.com/sites/kamranrosen/2021/11/18/this-company-wants-to-turn-your-mortgage-into-an-nft/?sh=3216278c37fe.

end, LoanSnap, through the Bacon Protocol, enables anyone with a wallet to act as a lender by purchasing LoanSnap's "Stable +" coin, that will be backed by the NFT mortgages.[47] Like the other projects that involve real estate transfers, this one begins with a signed mortgage recorded in the county in which the land is located. The "wrap" works as follows: a loan originator (who must be a licensed lender) enters into a traditional mortgage transaction with the property owner. The originator then mints an "Egg" NFT (get it, Bacon and Egg?) and transfers the Egg to the mortgagor. From that point, the originator acts as a loan servicer and the mortgagor uses the Egg to borrow money from the Pan (staying with breakfast), which is a smart contract that pools funds, mints the Stable + coin, and funds the loans.[48] Like the proponents of other crypto-enabled real estate transactions, LoanSnap claims that its product will make real estate transactions (in this case, mortgages) "cheaper, faster, and more flexible for homeowners."[49] In reality, LoanSnap's Bacon-enabled loans cannot exist without the traditional real estate transfer and recording system and the value added by the Bacon, Egg, and Pan seems to be that it gives homeowners the ability to borrow money secured by their homes quickly.[50]

3 Moving Recording to the Blockchain

Some companies have proposed transferring local land records to a blockchain. Propy, mentioned above, has entered a partnership with the city of South Burlington, Vermont, to test blockchain as a recording system.[51] Propy's goal is to become South Burlington's recording system, but it will take several steps to get there.[52] The city received its first "blockchain deed" in early 2018,[53] which was a paper deed, recorded in the city's land records, that contained a blockchain address and QR code that points to the deed's location on the public Ethereum blockchain.[54] This is according to plan; in the next level of the Propy-South Burlington collaboration the recording office would enter onto the blockchain an acknowledgment that it has received the deed and the necessary fees. Level three required the city recording office to

---

[47] Allan Carroll & Karl Jacob, *HomeCoin Whitepaper*, BaᴄᴏɴCᴏɪɴ (July 25, 2022), https://files .baconcoin.finance/bacon-protocol-whitepaper.pdf.

[48] Ibid.

[49] Ibid.

[50] *See* Cʜʀɪsᴛᴏᴘʜᴇʀ K. Oᴅɪɴᴇᴛ, Fᴏʀᴇᴄʟᴏsᴇᴅ: Mᴏʀᴛɢᴀɢᴇ Sᴇʀᴠɪᴄɪɴɢ ᴀɴᴅ ᴛʜᴇ Hɪᴅᴅᴇɴ Aʀᴄʜɪᴛᴇᴄᴛᴜʀᴇ ᴏꜰ Hᴏᴍᴇᴏᴡɴᴇʀsʜɪᴘ ɪɴ Aᴍᴇʀɪᴄᴀ (2019).

[51] Ben Miller, *Vermont City, Real Estate Startup Try Out Blockchain for Recording Property Transactions*, Gᴏᴠ. Tᴇᴄʜ. (undated), www.govtech.com/biz/vermont-city-real-estate-startup-try-out-blockchain-for-recording-property-transactions.html.

[52] Ibid.

[53] Jonathan Wolf, *Will Blockchain Technology Really Ever Supplant the Humber Title Search?*, Aʙᴏᴠᴇ ᴛʜᴇ Lᴀᴡ (February 2, 2022), https://abovethelaw.com/2022/02/will-blockchain-technology-really-ever-supplant-the-humble-title-search/.

[54] Miller, *Vermont City*.

link its records with Propy's system to enable Propy to record deeds within the city's system electronically, and the last level – level four – would be achieved when Propy becomes South Burlington's land records software.[55] In late 2019, Propy and the city launched a six-week trial during which Propy's blockchain registry system ran in parallel to the city's recording office.[56] As of this writing in 2023, the project has not progressed any further than the six-week trial.[57]

C *Crypto, Blockchain, and Real Estate Transactions: The Reality*

The debates over the role of electronic technologies in real estate transactions are not new. The paper-based land recording system exposes some flaws that might be solved by a system in which records are created and stored electronically. Even before the emergence of electronic technologies, critics of the existing system proposed title registration, such as the Torrens system, as a solution for flaws in the recording system.[58] As various transactional technologies, such as electronic signatures, developed and were enabled by legislation, commentators proposed technology-enabled improvements to the land transfer system.[59]

The difference between today's crypto transaction promoters and the commentators of the recent and distant past is that the former advocate for transforming the land transfer system in its entirety and the latter proposed targeted improvements to harness technologies. We take a more targeted approach in the discussion that follows, recognizing both the flaws and strengths of the existing system. We discuss problems that might be solved by electronic recording and then explain impediments to the implementation of a blockchain-based system. We close this section by discussing off-record claims to land and noting that ownership interests in land, which straddle the border between the tangible and intangible, are already signaled by existing practices and institutions that the blockchain will not likely replace.

Calls to modernize real estate transactions and the systems that enable them are not new. It is no surprise that a recording system that was developed more than 300 years ago would adapt imperfectly to today's society. In 1999, Dale Whitman recognized that the emerging technology of the time could be harnessed to make recording "easier, faster, and less costly."[60]

---

[55] *See* ibid.
[56] *Propy Trials Blockchain for Land Registry in Vermont*, LEDGER INSIGHTS (January 8, 2020), www .ledgerinsights.com/propy-blockchain-real-estate-title-registry-vermont/.
[57] Wolf, *Will Blockchain Technology*.
[58] *See generally* Ted J. Fiflis, *Land Transfers Improvement: The Basic Facts and Two Hypotheses for Reform*, 38 U. COLO. L. REV. 431 (1966).
[59] *See, for example*, Tanya Marsh, *Foreclosures and the Failure of the American Land Title Recording System*, 111 COLUM. L. REV. SIDEBAR 19, 24–25 (2011); Dale A. Whitman, *Digital Recording of Real Estate Conveyances*, 32 J. MARSHALL L. REV. 227, 228 (1999); Dean Arthur R. Gaudio, *Electronic Real Estate Records: A Model for Action*, 24 W. NEW. ENG. L. REV. 271, 271 (2002).
[60] Whitman, *Digital Recording*, 228.

The calls to modernize real estate transaction systems were notable at two points in the past twenty-five years: after the promulgation and enactment of the Uniform Electronic Transactions Act (UETA) and its federal counterpart, the Electronic Signature in Global and National Commerce Act (E-Sign), and after the havoc wreaked by the 2008 mortgage crisis.[61] Indexing was identified by several authors as a problem with a system in which humans deliver paper documents to other humans who are responsible for ensuring that those documents can be found by anyone searching for information about real property.[62] In 1999, Dale Whitman recognized that UETA and E-Sign, by providing that a record could not be denied legal effect solely because it is in electronic form,[63] could facilitate improvements to the recording system. Whitman proposed that electronic documents with standard fields could make real estate documents "self-indexing," thus removing the problem of human error from the indexing system.[64] Tanya Marsh suggested more than twenty years later that recording offices could harness more sophisticated technology to create completely searchable documents that could include what she described as "limitless data," including tax records, prior conveyances, and subdivision plats.[65]

To be sure, electronic recording has made some progress. Thirty-nine US jurisdictions have enacted the Uniform Real Property Electronic Recording Act, promulgated by the Uniform Law Commission in 2004.[66] The Act establishes that any legal requirement that a document be original or on paper and manually signed is deemed to be satisfied by an electronic document. It also establishes in enacting states an Electronic Recording Commission to set statewide electronic recording standards and gives local offices the authority to automate recording procedures.[67]

The takeaway is that most if not all of the problems identified by real estate experts with the current land recording (and related transfer) system can be solved by any number of secure electronic systems and managed by a government entity. But making a blockchain network the secure electronic system of choice is not the way. As we describe in Section III, the impediments to implementing a blockchain system for real estate transactions likely outweigh any benefits that such technology might offer.

---

[61] *See, for example*, Marsh, *Foreclosures*, 19; Gaudio, *Electronic Real Estate Records*, 273–274.
[62] *See* Marsh, *Foreclosures*, 21–22; Whitman, *Digital Recording*, 240.
[63] Unif. Elec. Trans. Act. § 7 (a) (1999); 15 U.S.C. § 7001 (a)(1).
[64] Whitman, *Digital Recording*, 240.
[65] Marsh, *Foreclosures*, 24–25.
[66] *See Project Page for Uniform Real Property Electronic Recording Act*, Unif. L. Comm'n, www .uniformlaws.org/committees/community-home?communitykey=643c99ad-6abf-4046-9da4-0a6367da00cc.
[67] Unif. L. Comm'n, The Uniform Real Property Electronic Recording Act: A Summary, www.uniformlaws.org/HigherLogic/System/DownloadDocumentFile.ashx?Document FileKey=3be821b4-d463-170c-000d-ae0bd9ee5e6d&forceDialog=0.

III PROBLEMATIZING CRYPTO IN PROPERTY AND COMMERCIAL LAW

To better understand the barriers to blockchain's promise, this section identifies the major obstacles standing in the way – namely, existing law and existing systems. We also argue that these difficulties are not merely theoretical nor are they easily solved. Rather, recent efforts to effectuate blockchain's promise have fallen short. Additionally, we describe how the speed promoted by those developing crypto-enabled real estate transactions is undesirable given the uses to which buyers put land. We close this section by discussing off-record claims to land and noting that ownership interests in land, which straddle the border between the tangible and intangible, are already signaled by existing practices and institutions that the blockchain will not likely replace.

A *Impediment # 1: Overhauling the Law*

Crypto land transaction promoters tend to overestimate the utility of blockchain tokens in facilitating real estate transactions. For example, the Propy CEO wrote that when real property becomes an NFT, "the NFT will become collateral in the crypto world which unlocks crypto-enabled mortgages."[68]

There is just one problem: both the Uniform Commercial Code (UCC) and real property law stand in the way of the veracity of that claim.

As explained above, the Propy model of crypto real estate transactions requires that the real property first be transferred to an LLC. The LLC rights are represented by an NFT (to the degree such a tokenization is even legally possible).[69] In the above-described sales transactions, the cryptoasset transfers an interest in a business entity, not an interest in land. The crypto-enabled mortgage that Propy claims to be made possible by NFTs is not a real estate mortgage at all; it is a loan secured by an interest in a business entity that is the owner of real estate. Milo's mortgage may not be a mortgage at all and LoanSnap's mortgage lending scheme seems to be a complicated way to fund mortgages. Current commercial and real estate law explains some of the complexity because there is nothing in either set of laws that enables an NFT real estate transaction. The open question that we address in this chapter is whether the law should enable such transactions. Below we explain what the law is now and for the foreseeable future.

1 The UCC Today and Tomorrow

The current UCC does not facilitate the transactions that the crypto land transfer companies are promoting. Under Article 9, both cryptocurrency and NFTs fall into the

---

[68] Karayaneva, *Real Estate NFTs*.

[69] We do not address in this chapter whether it is legally possible to tokenize an interest in an LLC such that the holder of the NFT is the holder of the interest (with the NFT and the interest being one and the same). Whether this is possible will depend upon the limited liability company law of the

category of "general intangibles."[70] This classification produces several undesirable results for companies that promote blockchain and cryptocurrency enabled real estate transactions. One is that a person with a security interest in a general intangible can perfect that interest only by filing a financing statement.[71] This is significant because the proponents of crypto real estate transactions purport to perfect their interests in crypto collateral by taking possession or control of it. Such a method is preferable to those who deal in crypto in that it allows them to liquidate the collateral easily, something that they cannot do if their security interest in the crypto collateral is non-possessory.

The other problem for the crypto community is that transferees of neither cryptoassets broadly nor NFTs specifically benefit from the same take free rules that the UCC grants other financial instruments. For example, although a creditor can perfect a security interest in a promissory note by filing a financing statement,[72] the UCC makes such perfection less desirable than perfection by possession. A transferee who takes possession of a promissory note takes free of all competing property claims of which it has no knowledge. Recognizing that promissory notes are routinely transferred in commerce by negotiation, which includes the transfer of possession, the UCC provides that a filed financing statement does not give knowledge of a competing property claim to a promissory note.[73] The absence of such a rule for cryptoassets, including NFTs, means that anyone who takes a transfer of these digital assets would take them subject to a blanket security interest that encumbers all "general intangibles."

The crypto industry has pushed for laws to remove the above described barriers to using cryptoassets in commerce. Some states, notably Wyoming,[74] have passed laws to facilitate such use and other states have followed Wyoming's lead.[75] However, even in these "crypto-forward" statutes, NFTs do not transfer interests in other assets in the way that those promoting the use of NFTs in real estate transactions would like.[76]

The sponsoring bodies of the UCC, the Uniform Law Commission and the American Law Institute, recognizing the growing use of cryptoassets in commerce

---

applicable jurisdiction. *See* R. Wilson Freyermuth, Christopher K. Odinet, & Andrea Tosato, *Crypto in Real Estate Finance*, 75 Ala. L. Rev. (2023).

[70] UCC § 9-102 (a) (42).

[71] UCC § 9-310 (a).

[72] UCC §§ 9-310 (a), (b)(6) (providing that all security interests must be perfected by filing, except for those perfected by possession); 9-313 (allowing a secured party to perfect its interest in instruments by possession).

[73] UCC § 9-330 (f).

[74] Wyo. Stat. §§ 34-29-101 to 34-29-106.

[75] *See, for example,* Idaho Code §§ 23-5301 to 23-5306 (amending the Uniform Commercial Code by adding a definition of "digital asset," allowing a secured creditor to perfect its security interest in a digital asset by possession or control, and providing that perfection by possession or control is a better method of perfection than filing a financing statement); Tex. Bus. & Com. Code §§ 9.314, 9.331, 12.001 to 12.004 (amending the Uniform Commercial Code to provide for perfection by control of virtual currency and providing that a person with control over virtual currency takes the virtual currency free from competing property claims).

[76] Moringiello & Odinet, *The Property Law of Tokens*.

and the desire in various states for crypto-friendly legislation, have completed revisions to the UCC that will facilitate and clarify the rules regarding transactions in these assets.[77] The Amendments create a new collateral category, the "controllable electronic record."[78] The drafters intended that this category include assets that purport to link to other assets, such as NFTs.[79] But even those amendments, when enacted in the states, will not facilitate transactions that purport to transfer real estate by an NFT representing the real estate. The reason for this is that non-UCC law does not recognize a link between an NFT and any underlying real or personal property.[80] In other words, a transfer of an NFT transfers only the NFT, not the underlying asset.[81] Although the 2022 Amendments to the UCC allow a secured party to perfect a security interest in an NFT by control and provide that a good faith transferee of that NFT takes it free from competing property claims to the NFT,[82] those rules govern the NFT, not the underlying asset.

2 Real Estate Law

One might say that real property is already tokenized and has been for centuries. As explained above,[83] property law requires the delivery of a deed to transfer ownership of the land. The deed delivery requirement evolved from the requirement in preliterate England that a transferor of land show intent to transfer by handing a clod of dirt to the grantee.[84] Dirt gave way to paper and it may be desirable that paper give way to documents that are electronically created and stored.[85] Indeed, a system that enables the electronic creation, transfer, and storage of deeds might eliminate disputes over lost deeds, mis-recording, and failure of delivery.

Deed transfer requirements should not be an impediment to electronic real estate transactions. Just as the paper deed delivery requirement emerged from preliterate practices, an electronic substitute for a deed could certainly emerge. As we explained in earlier work,[86] deeds serve a tokenization function and could be

---

[77] *See UCC, 2022 Amendments to,* Unif. L. Comm'n (2022), www.uniformlaws.org/committees/community-home?CommunityKey=1457c422-ddb7-40b0-8c76-39a1991651ac [hereinafter *2022 Amendments to the UCC*].

[78] Ibid., § 12–102 (a)(1).

[79] Ibid., Prefatory Note to Article 12.

[80] Moringiello & Odinet, *The Property Law of Tokens.*

[81] The amendments make an exception for tokens that represent certain payment rights, giving those tokens treatment that makes them the equivalent of electronic negotiable instruments. *See 2022 Amendments to the UCC, see above* note 77, §§ 12–104 (b), (f).

[82] Ibid., §§ 9–314; 9–331; 12–104.

[83] *See* Sheldon F. Kurtz, Herbert Hovenkamp, Carol Necole Brown, & Christopher K. Odinet, Cases and Materials on American Property Law (7th ed. 2019).

[84] John G. Sprankling & Raymond R. Coletta, Property: A Contemporary Approach 539 (5th ed. 2021).

[85] Contract law is far ahead in this respect, with the UETA and E-Sign granting validity to electronically created and signed contracts for statute of frauds purposes.

[86] *See* Moringiello & Odinet, *The Property Law of Tokens.*

replaced or supplemented by electronic deeds if the law supported such a practice. A deed serves several functions: it facilitates the transfer of land, it describes the land and the state of title to the land, and it serves as a document that can be placed on the public record to establish a chain of title. An electronic equivalent of a deed could perform all of the same functions.

Current real estate financing practices and law, however, do not enable NFT real estate transactions. Real estate financing is effectuated by the use of mortgage documents that grant the lender an interest in the land as security for a loan. When the buyer misses a payment or otherwise defaults on a mortgage obligation, the mortgage document and state law provide the procedures for obtaining the land to satisfy the debt. Substituting this document with an interest in an NFT raises a host of issues, ranging from the right of redemption, to foreclosure waiting periods, notice requirements, and sundry equitable principles that have long attended mortgage law.[87]

Various consumer laws protect individuals when they finance their homes using a mortgage. Such protection may be lost if the financing used does not qualify as mortgage financing under the relevant laws, such as when the collateral is an NFT and not the home.[88] For example, in a residential mortgage transaction, federal laws such as the Truth and Lending Act (TILA)[89] and the Real Estate Settlement Procedures Act (RESPA)[90] provide a host of special protections for home buyers. Lenders cannot even make a residential mortgage loan without first assessing whether the borrower has the ability to repay it.[91] Additionally, the TILA-RESPA Integrated Disclosure requires that consumers be given a preliminary and then a final statement of information as to the loan's key terms, including pricing.[92] TILA also grants to the mortgage borrower the right to rescind the entire financing transaction for three business days after it is consummated.[93] This right is often referred to as a cooling-off period that affords the borrower some time to think through whether the deal was in the individual's best interest outside the pressures of a mortgage lender's sales pitch.[94] But even after the mortgage loan is made and the cooling-off period expires, federal mortgage law continues to furnish the borrower with special

---

[87] *See* Freyermuth, Odinet, & Tosato, *Crypto in Real Estate Finance*.

[88] Notably, federal law ties various residential mortgage borrower protections to there being a "residential mortgage loan." *See, for example*, 15 USC § 1639c(a)(1). The definition of a residential mortgage loan requires that there be "a mortgage, deed of trust, or other equivalent consensual security interest on a dwelling or on residential real property that includes a dwelling." If the lien is on the NFT, rather than on real property, then the credit transaction would not be one involving a residential mortgage loan. *See* 15 USC § 1602(dd)(5).

[89] 12 USC §§ 1601–16.

[90] 12 USC §§ 2601–17.

[91] 15 USC § 1639c(a)(1) (applies only to a residential mortgage loan).

[92] 12 CFR §§ 1024.5(d), 1026.19(e), 1026.37, 1026.38. Notably, these provisions only apply to a loan secured by real property.

[93] 15 USC § 1635.

[94] Adam J. Levitin, Consumer Finance Law: Markets and Regulation 603 (2018).

protections and benefits. This is particularly true in the context of mortgage servicing, where, for instance, servicers have obligations to help borrowers work through loan defaults[95] and are obligated to answer qualitied written requests within certain set deadlines.[96] Indeed, federal intervention in the residential mortgage market even requires that lenders give borrowers a fifteen-day grace period to make late payments without a penalty and another fifteen days before the loan is considered delinquent.[97] There is also likely no more cherished tax advantage to individuals than the mortgage interest tax deduction, which may also be lost if the financing is not mortgage financing. But again, all of these depend upon the transaction being or involving a mortgage over real property – not taking a security interest in an NFT that forms the basis of an interest in a real estate holding company.

B Impediment # 2: Overhauling the System

The other major roadblock involves the realities of changing the system of land recording itself. Setting aside changes to the law, changes to the system pose their own unique set of considerations – and indeed, these may be the most significant of them all. These problems involve factors tied to any governmental change (the expense of the change and the public's trust in what the change brings). And then there is always the chance that the overhaul will be half-hearted, with the partial implantation of a new system and concurrent maintenance of the old, thereby creating more complexity and inefficiency in real property transactions.

1 The Problems of Cost and Trust

More than twenty years ago, commentators recognized the substantial financial costs that would be involved in moving real estate records to an electronic system. In 2002, Sam Stonefield wrote that the cost of moving one county in Iowa to an electronic system would cost the local government $75,000.[98] Relatedly, Arthur Gaudio recognized that the realities of state and local government financing would likely delay the goal of implementing electronic recording systems nationwide.[99]

In addition to the cost of moving systems is the threat of lost revenue. Counties rely on recording fees generated by their Recorder of Deeds offices. The controversies

---

[95] 12 CFR §§ 1024.41(a); 1024.39(a)-(b), 1024.40, 1024.41(b)(2)(i).

[96] 12 USC § 2605(e).

[97] Ann M. Burkhart, R. Wilson Freyermuth, Christopher K. Odinet, Grant S. Nelson, & Dale A. Whitman, Real Estate Transfer, Finance, and Development, Cases and Materials (2021).

[98] Sam Stonefield, *The Use and Recording of Electronic Real Estate Instruments: Context, Unresolved Cost-Benefit Issues, and a Recommended Decisional Process*, 24 W. New Eng. L. Rev. 205, 233 (2002).

[99] Gaudio, *Electronic Real Estate Records*, 299; *see also* Stonefield, *The Use and Recording*, 237 (noting the political impediments to allocating funds to move recording systems from a paper format to an electronic system).

over the Mortgage Electronic Registration System (MERS) illustrate how jealously the counties guard those fees.[100] MERS established an independent system for tracking mortgage assignments. There have been myriad complaints about the effect of MERS on the property recording system but the counties had a specific concern: the loss of recording fees. As a result, several counties sued MERS to recover unpaid recording fees, claiming that the failure to pay such fees upon the assignment of a mortgage violated state law. Although every county that challenged MERS ultimately lost,[101] which happened because no statutes require mortgage recording, the litigation illustrates how fervently counties protect their fees, which, in turn, introduces yet another political economy barrier.

Issues of trust compound the cost problem. Twenty years ago, there was low consumer trust when it came to electronic transactions.[102] To maintain trust in the recording system, it must be transparent and public. Tanya Marsh emphasized that for these reasons, establishing and maintaining land records must remain an essential government function.[103] It is hard to imagine that the average person trusts a blockchain system whereby anonymous nodes and related parties work to maintain the ledger through incentives and mechanisms that often mystify the public.[104] The examples below suggest that the mainstream trust of blockchain system has yet to surface.

2 The Delaware Corporations Example

Before blockchain was promoted as the answer to problems in the real estate world, it was touted as a better way to maintain corporate records. And Delaware, the paper home of 68 percent of Fortune 500 companies, took the bait.[105] Delaware's story provides an example of some of the practical impediments to replacing a well-established, if sometimes creaky, system with a new one.

Blockchain promoters went to Delaware raising a host of issues that could be solved by an automated system housed on a blockchain. According to the proponents,

---

[100] MERS (Mortgage Electronic Registration Systems, Inc.) is a national database that tracks the holders of mortgage servicing rights and beneficial ownership interests in loans secured by real estate mortgages. To participate in the system, the borrower and lender agree to name MERS as the mortgagee on the mortgage, which is recorded in the applicable county land records. The information about the mortgage is then recorded on the MERS system and servicing rights and ownership of the promissory notes associated with the mortgage are tracked on the system. *See* MERSINC (2023), www.mersinc.org/products-services/mers-system.

[101] Some trial courts sided with the counties but were reversed on appeal. *See, for example, Montgomery City v. MERSCORP Inc.*, 795 F. 3d 372, 375–76 (3rd Cir. 2015) (explaining lower court rulings and ruling in favor of MERS, stating that Pennsylvania law does not require that land transfers be recorded).

[102] Stonefield, *The Use and Recording*.

[103] *See* Marsh, *Foreclosures*, at 24.

[104] Dawn Allcot, *Crypto Comprehension Study: 98% of People Don't Grasp Basics of Bitcoin, Stablecoins or NFTs*, YAHOO! (November 2, 2021), www.yahoo.com/video/crypto-comprehension-study-98-people-190349019.html.

[105] Holly Quinn, *What Ever Happened to the Delaware Blockchain Initiative?*, TECHNICAL.LY (March 31, 2022), https://technical.ly/civic-news/delaware-blockchain-initiative/.

blockchain could solve issues with the secured loan filing system and disputes over corporate share ownership.[106]

Delaware responded positively to the blockchain lobbyists. The state established the Delaware Blockchain Initiative and appointed a state blockchain ombudsman.[107] Even the legislature moved to recognize blockchain as a method of maintaining corporate records, passing a law that allows corporate records to be maintained on "[one] or more electronic networks or databases (including [one] or more distributed electronic networks or databases)" so long as the records can be converted to paper records within a reasonable time.[108]

Even with legislative facilitation, the Delaware Blockchain Initiative went nowhere.[109] We believe the lessons from Delaware are instructive for those who promote blockchain for real estate transactions. Most importantly, despite the Delaware law allowing blockchain corporate records and the state's support of the Delaware Blockchain Initiative, the state itself never developed any blockchain infrastructure. Traditionally, corporations maintain physical ledgers of stock ownership.[110] The blockchain initiative envisioned a state-sponsored blockchain to replace such ledgers. Yet in the absence of this blockchain, few companies took advantage of the new law allowing them to maintain stock ledgers on the blockchain. One explanation is that companies did not find an unregulated blockchain to be an attractive place to maintain corporate records – said another way: they did not trust them.[111] Another is that there is already an established corporate registration and record-keeping business in Delaware. Even though a physical location for a corporate agent may seem antiquated to some, people who deal with Delaware corporations are comfortable with the existing system.[112] Moreover, the current system creates jobs in Delaware – for registered corporate agents, for lawyers, and for other service providers, and the state did not want to risk losing those jobs if a public blockchain were implemented.[113] The jobs concern is closely related to the revenue concern

---

[106] Karl Baker, *Delaware Eases Off Early Blockchain Zeal after Concerns Over Disruption to Business*, DEL. ONLINE (February. 2, 2018), www.delawareonline.com/story/news/2018/02/02/delaware-eases-off-early-blockchain-zeal-after-concerns-over-concerns-over-disruption-business/1082536001/. The Delaware blockchain ombudsman and the president of the software company working with Delaware to develop its blockchain promoted the idea of a smart Uniform Commercial Code filing system which would, in theory, lower the costs of searches and filings and reduce mistakes and fraud. Andrea Tinianow & Caitlin Long, *Delaware Blockchain Initiative: Transforming the Foundational Infrastructure of Corporate Finance*, HARV. L. SCH. FORUM ON CORP. GOVERNANCE (March 16, 2017), https://corpgov.law.harvard.edu/2017/03/16/delaware-blockchain-initiative-transforming-the-foundational-infrastructure-of-corporate-finance/.

[107] Quinn, *What Ever Happened*.

[108] 8 DEL. C. § 224.

[109] *See generally* Quinn, *What Ever Happened*.

[110] Moringiello & Odinet, *The Property Law of Tokens*.

[111] Quinn, *What Ever Happened*.

[112] Ibid.

[113] Baker, *Delaware Eases Off*.

generally; although blockchain advocates claimed that adoption of a public block-chain for corporate records could bring more money into the state, the Secretary of State's office was uneasy about the impact of a move to the blockchain on other revenue sources.[114]

3 Back to Vermont

We described above South Burlington's experiment with Propy. Last anyone heard of it, the city and Propy were maintaining parallel systems for recording. That is the worst possible outcome – for all its failures, county land records provide some level of certainty in that everyone knows where to find information about land located in that county. Two places to search means the possibility of errors and mismatches in information, not to mention adding additional information-gathering to the trans-action due diligence.

C *The Problem of the Recording System as a Repository of a Variety of Interests in Land*

Lastly, the proponents of blockchain-based real estate transactions seem to assume that all interests in land are created in consensual transactions involving one per-son conveying the entire interest in the land to another. Real estate transactions are messier than that.

For example, judgment liens can attach to real property.[115] It is not clear how a judgment lien creditor can add its interest to a blockchain-based system.[116] There is also the issue of materialmen and mechanic's liens, which sometimes require a filing to be made by a claimant into the land records.[117] We wonder what would happen when these filings need to be canceled (such as when they create an invalid cloud on title). Additionally, land often transfers by will or intestacy. Again, it is not clear how to integrate those facts into the smart contracts that are said to so seam-lessly guide these transactions.

IV THE INTANGIBLE CASE FOR BLOCKCHAIN PROPERTY REGISTRIES

We described above the existing system for verifying rights in real estate. Real estate rights straddle the line between the intangible and the tangible. Title is an intangible

---

[114] Ibid.

[115] *See, for example*, Thomas J. Mitchell, *Perpetuating the Force of Judgments and Judgment Liens in Texas*, 29 TEX. L. REV. 530 (1951).

[116] *See, for example*, 5AP2 NICHOLS CYC. LEGAL FORMS § 113:37.

[117] *See Bob DeGeorge Assocs., Inc. v. Hawthorn Bank*, 377 S.W.3d 592, 598 (Mo. 2012) (describing the lien and the filing requirements in Missouri); *see also* MO. ANN. STAT. § 429.010 (West).

concept; no one can determine the title rights in a parcel of land solely by looking at it.[118] A parcel of land can be physically possessed and possession is a fact that is visually verifiable. In this section, we provide our final analysis as to why the attributes of contemporary blockchain technology do not actually address all the facets of real property transactions, but we conclude on a high note by offering a way that crypto and its attendant technologies can serve a useful purpose when it comes to tracking and verifying rights in purely intangible property.

A *Signals, Recording Systems, and Property Rights*

The real estate system signals ownership rights in two ways. First, the recording system provides signals regarding the intangible rights, or *title*. However imperfect, it is a system that would be difficult to dismantle and dismantling the system would require time-consuming law reform. The recording system provides a method of publicizing tokens representing rights to real estate (such as deeds, mortgages, and easements) and it is difficult to find a benefit in replacing today's system for tracking rights with one that incorporates NFTs and blockchain. Second, because the real estate is tangible, physical possession can also signal title in the same way possession signals title in all other tangible assets. Possession by someone who did not initially have rights in the real or personal property can ripen into title if the possession persists uninterrupted for a long enough time.[119] Moreover, certain conditions on a parcel of land might provide inquiry notice of a competing title claim, such as an easement. For these reasons, a real estate buyer's title due diligence includes not only a record search but also a visual search of the land. As a result, even if all a buyer cared about was the title to real estate, a search of the real estate records without a visual inspection of the property would be inadequate title due diligence.

It is important to note that title is only part of what makes a house or any other unit of real estate attractive to a buyer. A buyer of real estate will want to know the condition of the real estate before buying it, and many buyers insist that their obligation to buy be contingent on a satisfactory physical inspection of the premises.[120] A frictionless real estate transaction that is as quick as a Venmo payment would not allow the inspections that buyers (and their lenders) view as critical. In addition to an inspection showing whether the roof is leakproof and that the heating system works, a buyer will want to know whether a home suits her personal preferences and needs. A buyer of a four-bedroom house will want to see the house to assess whether the size and placement of the four bedrooms matches her family's needs.

---

[118] Hernando de Soto, The Mystery of Capital: Why Capitalism Triumphs in the West and Fails Everywhere Else (2003).

[119] *See generally* John Lovett, *Disseisin, Doubt, and Debate: Adverse Possession Scholarship in the United States (1881–1986)*, 5 Tex. A&M L. Rev. 1, 2 (2017) (providing an exhaustive discussion of the theories of adverse possession).

[120] Kurtz, Hovenkamp, Brown, & Odinet, Cases and Materials.

This physical assessment is part of why the Venmo analogy is inapposite. No one needs to inspect funds before accepting a Venmo payment. But a physical inspection of real estate is an important part of the purchasing process.

We also note that frictionless transactions are not always good. This is especially true when individuals enter into sales and financing transactions. The law recognizes the importance of friction by, as we described above, mandating a three-day "cooling off" period in certain consumer credit transactions.[121] As we noted, the effect of this rule is to give an individual three days after receiving required disclosures to rescind a loan transaction.[122] The goal of these consumer protection laws is to encourage consumers to compare loan products and to promote informed decision-making.[123] This is because we recognize consumers make hasty decisions.[124] So having some friction in such a major transaction (real estate is typically someone's most valuable asset) can be a good thing. This is what underpins the idea of forcing mortgage creditors to wait before foreclosing on residential property – friction in foreclosure is good because it can result in saving a home if the borrower can refinance or make up missed payments or else gives the borrower more time for negotiation.

B The Intangible Case(s) for Tokenizing Property Rights and Tracking Them on a Blockchain: The Case of Visual Art

Although moving real property title to a blockchain might be impractical and expensive and would provide little improvement to real estate transactions, the use case for blockchain as a property registry is more compelling for tracking *purely* intangible property rights. Commentators writing about intellectual property, specifically as applied to fine art, have explored this use case and we summarize some of their arguments below, concluding that if there is a use case for tracking property rights on a blockchain and through the use of NFTs, that use case is to track property rights for which there is no clear signal of possessory rights to an original.

As we discussed above changes in technology that enabled electronic creation and storage of legal documents created benefits in commercial transactions, including real estate transactions. The opposite holds true for rights in digital creative works; the Internet enabled the perfect copying of such works and such perfect copying is anathema to copyright holders.[125]

---

[121] *See above*, Section III.

[122] 15 U.S.C. § 1635.

[123] Christopher L. Peterson, *Predatory Structured Finance*, 28 Cardozo L. Rev. 2185, 2226 (2007).

[124] *See* Levitin, Consumer Finance Law, 247.

[125] *See* Tonya M. Evans, *Cryptokitties, Cryptography, and Copyright*, 47 AIPLA Q. J. 219, 228 (2019). The Internet was not the first technology to raise concerns about "perfect copying." Almost a hundred years ago commentators expressed the same concerns about photography. *See* Stefan Bechtold & Christopher Jon Sprigman, *Intellectual Property and the Manufacture of Aura* 9–10, (NYU L. Sch. Pub. L. Research Paper, Paper No. 22–09, 2022) https://papers.ssrn.com/sol3/papers.cfm?abstract_id=4002717.

That said, there are some who argue that copyright is an imperfect mechanism for protecting the rights of creators. Amy Adler wrote that rather than encouraging creativity on the part of creators of visual art, copyright may do the opposite. According to Adler, it is the "norm of authenticity" that protects the rights of artists because authenticity provides the foundation for the art market.[126] Where visual art is concerned, the value is not in the tangible – the sculpture, painting, or photograph – it is in the intangible quality of authenticity. A work by a known artist will sell for far more than an exact copy by someone else.[127]

Art law scholars have observed that ownership stripped of possessory rights might be sufficient for participants in the art market. Stefan Bechtold and Christopher Sprigman have explained how many creators develop an "aura" around their works and that it is the aura that is valuable to buyers. This aura is valuable despite the fact that the works to which the aura pertains are not unique originals, rather, they are identical copies of works.[128] Bechtold and Sprigman use Thomas Kinkade as an example of an artist whose manufactured aura provided his mass-produced works with an aura of provenance and authenticity.[129] Brian L. Frye, the author of the first chapter in this Handbook, also promotes the idea of "bare" ownership, arguing that authenticity is merely a proxy for the clout that accompanies ownership.[130] If the intangible ideas of ownership, aura, and authenticity drive the art market, then perhaps NFTs and blockchain registries have a place in the digital art world.

Others have promoted blockchain as a method of providing scarcity for digital works of art. According to Tonya Evans, blockchain technology enables ownership of digitally scarce assets.[131] Evans analyzes blockchain's benefits from a creator's point of view and posits that blockchain technology protect an artist against counterfeiting.[132] Moreover, he also suggests that blockchain technology also grants creators new ways to monetize and enforce their copyrights. As an example of the latter benefit, she explains that NFTs, combined with smart contracts, might enable an artist to profit from each transfer of a digital work of art.[133]

We explain in another paper that an NFT grants no property rights in an underlying asset.[134] Yet as the discussion above illustrates, in the art market the proof of ownership represented by the NFT might be more important than any exclusive rights to a digital work of art. Rather, it is the status granted by a verifiable claim

[126] Amy Adler, *Why Art Does Not Need Copyright*, 86 GEO. WASH. L. REV. 313, 323 (2018).
[127] Ibid., 346 (explaining that the designation of a work as inauthentic is "the equivalent of an economic death sentence").
[128] *See* Bechtold & Sprigman, *Intellectual Property*, 21–24.
[129] Ibid.
[130] Brian L. Frye, *After Copyright: Pwning NFTs in a Clout Economy*, 45 COLUM. J.L. & ARTS 341, 348 (2022).
[131] Evans, *Cryptokitties*, 249.
[132] Ibid., 254.
[133] Ibid., 265.
[134] Moringiello & Odinet, *The Property Law. See also* Frye, *After Copyright*, 346.

of ownership that matters and that a blockchain registry can enable such a status. NFTs might provide an aura of exclusive ownership even though they grant no exclusive ownership rights in any work of art.[135] Doing so would protect both the creator of the work, who, by bestowing authenticity, could earn more for the work, and the buyer, who, by proving authenticity, could maximize her investment.

V CONCLUSION

Amidst the hype surrounding the use of blockchains and NFTs in the context of property rights, a measure of true potential does exist. This potential, however, is not in the context of real property, where the American existing legal system has largely shown itself to be sufficient. Rather, blockchain's potential lies in tracking and transferring rights in intangible property – particularly purely intangible personal property – a longstanding legal challenge demanding resolution.

The American system for transferring and recording interests in real property might be imperfect but the potential of blockchain and NFTs to improve it is arguably limited. The recording system provides signals regarding the intangible rights, the title, and dismantling the system to incorporate blockchains and NFTs would require time-consuming law reform. Furthermore, the tangible aspects of real estate, such as the physical condition of the property, are verified by signals such as physical possession.

Things are different when it comes to intangible property. The American legal system governing the tracking and transfers of these rights is largely undeveloped and unlike real property, the ownership of intangible assets cannot be possessed in a way that easily gives a signal to the entire world. This is where blockchains and NFTs can prove useful. They can confer a verifiable claim of ownership and enhance an artwork's perceived exclusivity. Even if NFTs do not grant direct property rights, they strengthen the bond of ownership, benefiting both artists and buyers through assured originality.

---

[135] Bechtold & Sprigman, *Intellectual Property*, 25.

PART V

Data Protection, Privacy, Cybersecurity, and NFTs

15

Fungibility, Information Flow, and Privacy

Jamiel Sheikh and Jiaying Jiang

I INTRODUCTION

In popular culture, the term "non-fungible token" (NFT) is associated with owner-ship of digital collectibles or digital art, such as CryptoKitties or Bored Ape Yacht Club, a set of tradeable images, each enshrined in stories or provenance of the creators or communities behind the art.[1] While the association of an NFT with dig-ital art is the use case that has gained the most popularity, NFTs are a method of representation that encompass a much larger number of current and potential use cases. Understanding the components and mechanisms of how an NFT comes into existence and is traded can be instructive in understanding what its potentials are and what the challenges, such as privacy and fees, may be.

A slew of technologies, components, and techniques are employed in the minting, or issuance, and trading of an NFT. The designer of an NFT, whether an artist and/ or a software developer, selects from a myriad of an ever-growing set of options, each option offering a set of tradeoffs or benefits and compromising that need to be taken into careful consideration. For example, how much and what information about the tokenized asset should be stored on a blockchain as opposed to an external repository? What smart contract standard best fits the use case? Should a platform, like OpenSea, be used to mint and sell the NFT? What is gained or lost by doing so? Can the token be burned or destroyed, if desired? How is the token uniquely identified? Can issu-ance be paused? Should the NFT be minted on Layer 1 or Layer 2 blockchain?

At the most fundamental level, an NFT is a token that represents an asset that is typically not mergeable or divisible into any other asset of its kind. Much like it is not possible to take the *Mona Lisa* and physically merge it into another paint-ing, short of turning both paintings into powder, an NFT represents an asset that is unique. A discussion around the nuances of fungibility and non-fungibility is out of scope for this chapter and can better be addressed not by merely the two categories

The authors thank research assistants, Cara Shelhamer and Hanley Gibbons, for their hard work on this project.

[1] *See generally* Elizabeth Ferrill, Soniya Shah, & Michael Young, *Demystifying NFTs and Intellectual Property: What You Need to Know*, 29 No. 05 WESTLAW J. INTELLECTUAL PROP. 02 (2022).

of fungible or non-fungible, but by an information model.[2] It should be made clear that a token's fungibility and an asset's fungibility are two separate matters, although often and practically speaking, a non-fungible token represents a non-fungible asset. It is also possible for a set of fungible tokens to represent shares in a non-fungible asset or a non-fungible token to represent a pool of fungible assets.

The NFT, a token by definition, is a digital placeholder stored on a blockchain, most commonly on Ethereum, which is a decentralized, open-source blockchain system that features smart contract functionality. But NFTs can also be stored on other blockchains that are not derivatives of Ethereum and are therefore not compatible with the same underlying principles or technology as the Ethereum blockchain's computational component.[3] These include Algorand, Stellar, or Corda,[4] which all can store NFTs but vary in how they implement the placeholder. We explore the variations in the interest of demonstrating the flexibility with which a token can be implemented and not with the intent of being exhaustive in the coverage of the variation and divergences. We then continue by discussing technical details on minting and using NFTs, move on to analyze information collection in NFT transactions and processes, advance to explain information flow of NFT lifecycle, and then focus on breaking down and describing the privacy implications of all of these issues, diving into privacy legal theories and their application.

II TECHNICAL DETAILS: SMART CONTRACTS, ALLOCATION TABLES, AND MINTING NFTS

This section provides a detailed and technical overview of NFT transactions. It begins in Section II.A by demonstrating the varying ways in which NFTs are created and represented in smart contracts. Section II.B, using the context of a digital art NFT, outlines the process of storing NFT files and metadata off-chain. In Section II.C, two common methods of NFT minting are discussed, one using Ethereum and the other using Corda. Finally, Section II.D turns to a discussion of NFT processes and the ways in which personal information can be collected in NFT transactions.

A *Allocation Tables*

On Ethereum, the most common way a token is represented in a smart contract is analogous to an allocation table or, technically speaking, a hash map, which associates a key to a value, as seen in Table 15.1. The key is an arbitrary and unique integer

---

[2]   One such information model is presented by JAMIEL SHEIKH, FINANCE 3.0 (forthcoming 2023).

[3]   In the blockchain industry, this is typically referred to as Ethereum Virtual Machine (EVM)-based or not. Hence, when something is referred to as "EVM-based," it means that it operates on or is compatible with Ethereum and its native cryptocurrency, Ether (ETH).

[4]   For a detailed explanation of non-fungible tokens on such other systems, *see for example*, Corda DLT, *see* JAMIEL SHEIKH, MASTERING CORDA (2020).

TABLE 15.1 *Representation of tokens in a smart contract*

Token ID	Owner
1	address1
2	address2
3	address1
4	address4

of the token, think of it as a serial number, and the address of the owner, think bank account number, if you will. The token ID can be manually set or automatically incremented by the smart contract. In Table 15.1, four NFTs exist, each NFT with an arbitrary and unique token identifier and an owner of that token. The existence of the entry in the allocation table represents the existence of the NFT or token.[5]

In Table 15.1, we see the existence of four NFTs, owned by three parties or addresses. Token ID 1 and 3 are owned by the same address. An address is effectively a beautified hash of a public key. The allocation table stores who the owner is for each token minted. If a token ID does not exist, then that token has not been minted. The maximum number of tokens per smart contract instance is $2^{256} - 1$, a number that is 78 digits long and there is no theoretical limit to the number of smart contract instances that can exist on a blockchain. It is possible to pre-allocate token IDs as a strategy to save on gas fees,[6] for example minting token ID 1 through 100 before those tokens actually point to any asset.

The code that creates a blank allocation table in Solidity, the programming language used most commonly, in the design of smart contracts looks like the below:

$$mapping(uint256 => address) \ private \_ owners$$

The minting of a new NFT is simply a new entry into the allocation table. Interaction with the allocation table, via methods or functions, allows for the modification of owners and addresses. For example, the transfer of an NFT is simply the atomic change of address to the new owner's address in the allocation table.

1 ERC-721

The above approach of an allocation table is the most common but by no means necessarily the only way to represent tokens on Ethereum. The approach, used by many

---

[5] *See What is Mapping in Solidity?*, ALCHEMY (October 4, 2022), www.alchemy.com/overviews/solidity-mapping ("Mapping is a hash table in Solidity that stores data as key-value pairs, where the key can be any of the built-in data types, excluding reference types, and the value of the data type can be any type. Mappings are most typically used in Solidity and the Ethereum blockchain to connect a unique Ethereum address to a corresponding value type").

[6] *See* INSTAMINT (2023), https://instamint.com/.

NFT smart contracts, has been canonicalized by OpenZeppelin in their implementation of the ERC-721 standard for non-fungible tokens.[7] The ERC-721 standard, under which most NFTs were originally issued on the Ethereum blockchain,[8] codifies a set of methods or functions that smart contracts must implement to be considered ERC-721 compliant. The software developer decides how the smart contract follows the standard. For instance, the balanceOf method checks how many tokens a given address owns. The ownerOf method identifies the owner of a provided token ID. Meanwhile, transfer methods let you change the current owner's address to a new one.[9]

2 Lazy Minting

Lazy minting is a popular strategy where NFTs are created only when needed for an on-chain transfer. With this method, a central database holds the potential token ID for the NFT. When a transfer occurs, the NFT is minted and its ID and transfer are processed in one, single transaction.[10]

3 ERC-1155

The ERC-721 set of functions and the OpenZeppelin implementation of that standard is the gold standard of the NFT world and the most prevalent. Other standards,

---

[7] OpenZeppelin is a leading blockchain infrastructure security provider. It audits smart contracts, monitors digital and online vulnerabilities, and alerts for potential threats applicable to smart contracts, and even metaverse operations and frameworks. *See, for example*, Cam Thompson, *The Sandbox Onboards Security Firm OpenZeppelin to Protect Its Platform from Attacks*, CoinDesk (December 15, 2022), www.coindesk.com/web3/2022/12/15/the-sandbox-onboards-security-firm-openzeppelin-to-protect-its-platform-from-attacks/.

[8] *See* William Entriken et al., *ERC-721 Non-Fungible Token Standard*, Github: Ethereum (January 24, 2018), https://github.com/ethereum/EIPs/blob/master/EIPS/eip-721.md. It was initially introduced by AxiomZen to support its CryptoKitties application and also in order to encourage the development of other uses); *ERC-721 Non-Fungible Token Standard*, Ethereum (April 16, 2022), https://ethereum.org/en/developers/docs/standards/tokens/ERC-721. For more on this standard, *see* Tonya M. Evans, *Cryptokitties, Cryptography, and Copyright*, 47 AIPLA Q.J. 219, 248 (2019) (explaining the inspiration for the standard and comparing it to others); and Michael D. Murray, *Nfts and the Art World – What's Real, and What's Not*, 29 UCLA Ent. L. Rev. 25, 50–51 (2022) (describing how it "allowed NFTs to be created as 'non-fungible' (i.e., unique) bundles of data").

[9] For more on this, *see* Shaanan Cohney & David A. Hoffman, *Transactional Scripts in Contract Stacks*, 105 Minn. L. Rev. 319 (2020). The authors explain that:

> [w]hile any human can manually inspect the ledger, an Ethereum script can only access the balances via the balanceOf() function which outputs the balance for a given address. This includes the token script itself, which uses balanceOf within the transfer function to check if there is sufficient balance available to debit, before subtracting that amount from one address and crediting to another. (ibid., 349.)

[10] Mariyah S. Wakhariya, *New Frontiers in Technology: Can Traditional Intellectual Property Rights Laws Be Adapted and Applied to NFT?*, 31 Cath. U.J.L. & Tech. 173, 215 (2023); Alex Atallah, *Create NFTs for Free on OpenSea*, OpenSea (December 29, 2020), https://opensea.io/blog/announcements/introducing-the-collection-manager/ (defining lazy minting as a process allowing creation of NFTs without upfront costs which are generally charged by miners at a fluctuating rate).

TABLE 15.2 *The ERC-1155 Example*

Token ID	Owner	Balance
1	address1	1
2	address2	1
3	address1	5
4	address4	1

including ERC-1155 – which allows both NFTs and fungible tokens within the same contract and supports other features and possibilities – do exist but are not necessarily that common.[11] The ERC-1155 extends the allocation table to include a balance or quantity for each token ID and allows batch modifications to the allocation table, significantly reducing gas fees on transactions that would have otherwise been done one by one on the ERC-721 (Table 15.2).

In the ERC-1155 paradigm, if a token ID has a total quantity of one, then it is a non-fungible token. A quantity greater than one renders that token fungible. As such, the ERC-1155 smart contract standard allows for the existence of non-fungible and fungible tokens within the same allocation table. Before the introduction of the ERC-1155 standard, NFTs were created using ERC-721 smart contracts, while fungible tokens used the ERC-20 standard.[12] However, despite the advantages that ERC-1155 provides, the market continues to view the ERC-721 as more "genuine" NFTs than those minted on any other standard. Platforms like OpenSea support both standards, leaving the decision of which type of smart contracts to mint to the designer.

It is important to note that ERC-721-compliant smart contracts are not necessarily created equal. Compliance only refers to the minimum set of known functions that must be available. The precise behavior of how those functions achieve their objectives can differ between different ERC-721 implementations and potentially create non-uniform behaviors or outcomes, despite being labeled as an ERC-721.

B Off-Chain Storage

The process of minting an NFT includes more than merely creating an entry in an allocation table. In fact, the entry into the allocation table may be the last step in a multi-step issuance process. In the case of, say, digital art, a number of steps need to be taken, including making the digital art accessible to the token.

---

[11] Kimberly A. Houser & John T. Holden, *Navigating the Non-Fungible Token*, 2022 UTAH L. REV. 891, 901 (2022) (explaining that "Ethereum creates other standards with different functionality, such as ERC-1155, which permits the creation of semi-fungible tokens").

[12] For more on this, *see* James J. Park & Howard H. Park, *Regulation by Selective Enforcement: The SEC and Initial Coin Offerings*, 61 WASH. U. J. L & POL'Y 99, 109 (2020) ("The ERC20 standard is governed by several mandatory rules. It has a standardized method for token creators to set their token's names and symbols … When an ERC20 token is transferred, such 'transfer events' must be

1 Storage of File Represented by NFT

Due to the inherent cost structure of blockchains, storing more than a small amount of data on-chain can be very expensive. For instance, storing a LMB file on Ethereum might cost thousands of dollars, depending on current gas fees. Consequently, most digital art is kept on external, often decentralized, storage systems where costs are much lower or almost negligible.

This is possible to do as in general, there are two primary storage options for digital items: on-chain and off-chain. Off-chain storage places the digital item on a centralized server, with the token acting as a record or "deed" of ownership. However, items stored off-chain risk deletion if the hosting company shuts down or faces other issues.[13] On-chain storage, on the other hand, embeds the digital item directly into the token, ensuring its existence even if the hosting company disappears. This offers better security for owners. The drawback of on-chain storage is its limited space.[14]

The most common of these decentralized storage systems is the Interplanetary File System (IPFS).[15] IPFS can be thought of as being analogous to a free decentralized cloud storage system, although there are significant differences.[16] Users can store binary objects, like a PDF or a JPEG and then retrieve them later via a URL and the object's unique identifier. Any upload to IPFS returns a content ID, or content identifier (CID), a unique identifier to the content.[17] Using the CID and a browser, the digital content can be retrieved and viewed.[18] IPFS does not provide reliability guarantees and can often perform slow and alternatives like Filecoin, Arweave and Pinata are fee-based solutions that offer alternatives to or value-add services on top of IPFS.

---

broadcasted to other users of the network … When the ICO is ready to launch, another smart contract can govern the process by which the token is sold").

[13] Joshua A.T. Fairfield, *Tokenized: The Law of Non-Fungible Tokens and Unique Digital Property*, 97 Ind. L.J. 1261, 1283 (2022).

[14] Ibid. *See also* Devin Finzer, *The Non-Fungible Token Bible: Everything You Need to Know about NFTs*, OpenSea (January 10, 2020), https://blog.opensea.io/guides/non-fungible-tokens/.

[15] Megan E. Noh, Sarah C. Odenkirk, & Yayoi Shionoiri, *Gm! Time to Wake Up and Address Copyright and Other Legal Issues Impacting Visual Art NFTs*, 45 Colum. J.L. & Arts 315, 340 (2022) (providing that "[m]ost commonly, the visual asset associated with an NFT – be that a JPEG, GIF, or other digital file format – will be separately hosted on the InterPlanetary File System (IPFS), a distributed file system and peer-to-peer network, or arweave, a decentralized blockchain data-storage protocol"). *See* Interplanetary File System (2024), https://ipfs.io/; Arweave (2023), www.arweave.org/.

[16] Noh, Odenkirk, & Shionoiri, *Gm!*, 340 ("NFT-associated asset(s) may also be hosted by a cloud-computing platform like Amazon Web Services, or by any secure server that can reliably store content linked to the NFT").

[17] Lauren Au, *Fractionalization to Securitization: How the Sec May Regulate the Emerging Asset of NFTs*, 96 S. Cal. L. Rev. 253, 260 (2022) (explaining that:

"when housing an NFT on IPFS, the NFT gets assigned a unique content identifier ('CID') hash that links to the data in the IPFS network. Using an IPFS CID hash, as opposed to an HTTP URL, allows someone to find the NFT based on its content rather than by its location on a server. Thus, if the content of the NFT is changed, the original CID link would break and create a new one").

[18] Ibid.

2 Storage of Metadata

Missing from the allocation table and in the ERC-721 or ERC-1155 smart contract is detailed information about the asset the token represents. For example, for digital art that information includes what the title of the artwork is, who created it, and any description of the art. Given that this information, known as metadata, can be fairly extensive, it is also typically not stored on-chain.

Manifold, an NFT publishing platform, takes a stab at moving the creators name into an ERC-721 smart contract.[19] ASCII-based art is also embedded in the smart contract as comments. When the smart contract is deployed, all commentary is stripped, but platforms like Etherscan, which is a blockchain viewer with additional data, maintain and display the commentary.[20] As such, Etherscan can be a repository for creator information extracted from sources that exist either on-chain or in the metadata.

Metadata, encoded in JavaScript Object Notation (JSON) format,[21] is also typically stored on IPFS and has canonicalized standards themselves, such as the ERC-721, ERC-1155, Enjin, or OpenSea standards and recommendations. This means that for a typical NFT, two components are stored off-chain, namely the digital art (if it is art that the NFT represents) and the metadata that describes the art. ERC-721 and ERC-1155 smart contracts provide the linkage, via a URL, between a token ID and the URL that retrieves the metadata. However, this approach has been used by platforms to inject a centralized dependency on the platform. See below for an illustration:

```
{
    "description": "My Selfie",
    "external_url": "https://api.instamint.com/3",
    "image": "https://ipfs.io/CID,"
    "name": "Joe Shmo",
    "attributes": [ ... ]
}
```

C Minting Process

The next stage is the process of minting an NFT, which generally involves a number of steps: (i) uploading the digital art to IPFS and retrieving its CID; (ii) generating metadata and inserting into it a URL that points to the digital art on IPFS; (iii) uploading the metadata and retrieving its CID; and (iv) allocating a token and having it point to the metadata on IPFS.

---

[19] MAINFOLD (2023), https://manifold.xyz/.
[20] ETHERSCAN (2024), https://etherscan.io/.
[21] *See* Gabriel Nicholas, *Taking It with You: Platform Barriers to Entry and the Limits of Data Portability*, 27 MICH. TECH. L. REV. 263, 298 (2021) (JSON is a machine-readable format as opposed to the more human-readable HTML format).

1 Minting on Ethereum

Typically, modification to the allocation table can be only done by the party that created the smart contract. This means that an artist creating an NFT on a smart contract created by OpenSea and wishing to move it to another platform will need to allow the new platform the right to make the move. ERC-721 and ERC-1155 have delegated mechanisms where token owners can approve an account to act on its behalf for transfers.

NFT smart contracts are also responsible for generating a URL that points to an online resource, typically the metadata. This is often a point of central control since the URI of an NFT is an offset of a static URL, for example api.instamint. com/INSTA/1 and api.instamint.com/INSTA/2. These centralized URLs, typically served by centralized platforms, potentially redirect to the decentralized IPFS URL that points to the metadata of the asset. Given that it is centralized, it has been and can continue to be a source of manipulation (i.e., switching what assets a token ID points to) and other shenanigans.[22]

Ethereum tracks token owners in its unique way but other blockchains have different methods. For example, Stellar uses its currency, Lumens (XLM), and its smallest unit, called a Stroop, to represent NFTs. When you transfer a Stroop, you are transferring an NFT.[23] While you can theoretically make NFTs on bitcoin using special units called colored coins, this method might not be practical. Other projects, like Stacks and Rootstock (RSK), are exploring ways to integrate NFTs with bitcoin.[24]

2 Minting on Corda

Corda, a private permissioned system, relies on the Bitcoin-inspired Unspent Transaction Outputs, or UTXO, model. In the UTXO model, a token is a thing itself, a reified placeholder and not an entry in an allocation table. A non-fungible token in Corda can potentially have all of the metadata embedded into the token because transaction and storage fees are non-existent by default on the distributed ledger technology (DLT). The only

---

[22] *See, for example,* Jacob Kastrenakes, *Your Million-Dollar NFT Can Break Tomorrow If You're Not Careful,* THE VERGE (March 25, 2021), www.theverge.com/2021/3/25/22349242/nft-metadata-explained-art-crypto-urls-links-ipfs ("Traditional URLs pose real problems for NFTs. The owner of the domain could redirect the URL to point to something else (leaving you with, perhaps, a million-dollar Rickroll), or the owner of the domain could just forget to pay their hosting bill, and the whole thing disappears").

[23] *See generally* Frederic Kyung-Jin Rezeau, *Best Practices for Creating NFTs on Stellar,* MEDIUM (February 16, 2022), https://medium.com/stellar-community/best-practices-for-creating-nfts-on-stellar-5c91e53e9eb9.

[24] *See* IshanOnTech, *RSK Brings NFTs to the Bitcoin Blockchain,* HACKERNOON (March 24, 2023), https://hackernoon.com/rsk-brings-nfts-to-the-bitcoin-blockchain; *Features,* STACKS, www.stacks.co/learn/features ("Bringing NFTs to Bitcoin: As with fungible tokens, NFTs on the Stacks blockchain are created with Clarity smart contracts. Because of the relationship between Stacks and Bitcoin, NFTs created on Stacks settle to and are secured by Bitcoin").

constant in a non-fungible token on Corda is a UUID,[25] a randomly generated set of characters and numbers that is guaranteed to be unique across space and time, assigned to each NFT when the token is first created. On Corda, a token can potentially be created but not necessarily issued as of yet, if such a design was desired.[26]

Because Corda relies on Kotlin,[27] Java, and the JVM for designing its tokens and both languages are statically typed, meaning the structure of an NFT and its data elements can be difficult to change and changes require careful migration strategies. On Ethereum, newer NFT tokens can point to new JSON schemas that reflect changing business requirements more easily than an NFT on Corda can be redesigned to accommodate additional fields, for example. Tight coupling and decoupling have costs and benefits associated with them.

An NFT on Corda can represent the entire description of the token and even, if designed so, hold the digital art in the token or Corda node itself, although this approach may not necessarily be ideal. Whether Corda is an ideal platform for publicly tradable art is debatable, but an NFT that represents a credit default swap and traded interbank is a better DLT use case. In the scenario where an NFT represents a credit default swap, the Corda NFT would hold embedded in the token the public key of the issuer, current owner, and counterparties, including any financial information (notional amount, rate, etc.). ERC-721 and ERC-1155, with just allocation tables, do not have this capability currently, although designing similar on Ethereum is not difficult and standards like ERC-1400, ERC-777 and others help address some of these limitations.

On DLTs, like Corda, that have no gas fees, the notion of metadata seems redundant, especially where information is intrinsic to the asset and the token and asset are potentially one and the same on UTXO-based systems, the trading of the token is the trading of the asset, whereas on Ethereum the trading of the token is the trading of a pointer to the asset that is housed externally. Much like the columns of a spreadsheet constitute that spreadsheet, the fields of an NFT on Corda constitute many, if not all, of the parameters of that asset.

D *Information Collection in NFT Transactions and Processes*

The transactions involving an NFT require the interaction of at least two software processes, each often located on different computers. The first process submits

---

[25] For more details on UUIDs, *see* Network Working Group, A *Universally Unique Identifier (UUID) URN Namespace*, IETF (July 2005), www.ietf.org/rfc/rfc4122.txt.

[26] For more on this, *see* Sheikh, Mastering Corda.

[27] Louis F. Del Duca, Josias N. Dewey & Michael D. Emerson, *Beyond Bitcoin: How Distributed Ledger Technology Has Evolved to Overcome Impediments under the Uniform Commercial Code*, 47 UCC L.J. 2, Art. 1 (2017) (stating that: "Kotlin is a relatively new programming language that was derived from the popular Java programming language, but with certain changes intended to make it easier to use. Notwithstanding its modified syntax, it is completely interchangeable with Java and will run on any computer with JVM (Java Virtual Machine) installed – or in programming jargon, it is said to

transactions and we can refer to this as the client. The second software process, the blockchain server processing entity or node, processes the request and responds on the success or failure of the attempted transaction to the client.

Additional processes can be involved for various reasons, including creating convenience, repeatability, and modularity, and these processes introduce centralization and dependencies, often intermediating between the client and the node. For instance, frameworks like Web3.js for Ethereum are used pervasively by clients to communicate with nodes. Examples for transactions and actions that are associated with information collection in NFT transaction include the following.

1 Remote Procedure Call (RPC) Mechanisms

An NFT can be issued directly from a local machine to the blockchain using the most basic tools, such as private key generators and command line-based (like CURL) invocation of blockchain node functionality. This approach reveals the least amount of information but is the least robust and requires significant technical capabilities. Complicating things further, an NFT can be minted to either a local node (or a node one controls) or remote node (a node someone else runs) via RPC mechanisms, which are protocols that allow one program to request services from other programs located on another computer in a network. RPCs are powerful tools for developers because they simplify the process of making the program logic available across multiple network locations, and can potentially be enhanced to collect additional information beyond performing blockchain work.[28]

2 Dummy Nodes

Even if a clean untampered local node is used to mint an NFT, once the node has successfully processed the transaction, it will initiate the consensus portion of the transaction and propagate information to peer nodes. Peer nodes can be augmented with additional capabilities to collect the probable geographical location of where the request to mint the NFT has come from given the location of the dispatching node. Certain companies are known to set up these types of dummy nodes to obtain such information.[29]

'compile to the JVM.' The Corda protocol itself was coded in Kotlin, but since Java and Kotlin are interchangeable, smart contracts for Corda can be written in either language").

[28] Rebecca Helene Sussman, *The Reusable Bomb: Exploring How the Law of Armed Conflict Applies in Cyberspace*, 23 B.U. J. SCI. & TECH. L. 481, 497 n.117 (2017) (explaining RPC to be "a service that allows two computers to talk to each other to perform a command. By replacing dedicated protocols and communication methods with a robust and standardized interface, RPC is designed to facilitate communication between client and server processes. The functions contained within RPC are accessible by any program that must communicate using a client/server methodology").

[29] A "dummy node" is a term that can be used in various contexts in computer science. Generally, a dummy node is a placeholder or fictitious node introduced into a data structure or system to simplify the handling of boundary conditions or special cases.

3 Service Providers

Services providers, which provide business application programming interfaces (APIs) that in turn call RPC on nodes hosted by the service provider, can be used in the process as well.[30] An example of such a service provider is Infura, which hosts Ethereum, IPFS, Filecoin, and NEAR nodes or Purestake for Algorand nodes. These service providers often, if not always, collect IP address information and usage statistics (i.e., how many NFTs did you mint this month across any and all blockchains they service). A large number of tools that exist on the market route blockchain transactions through these service providers, including most popular wallets like MetaMask.

4 Platforms

Another path is the use of a platform, like OpenSea, which provides a comfortable user experience but is able to collect a significant amount of additional information that is typically collected by Web 2.0 and social media applications by leveraging IP address and cookie techniques.

E Information Flow of NFT Lifecycle

At different points of the life of an NFT, different types of information shift from being less accessible (private) to being more accessible (public). We can categorize the business lifecycle of an NFT into three broad phases – issuance, transfer, and burning of a token. Out of the three phases, the first one, issuance, is where most information around an NFT becomes public. Differently, the second phase, transfer, is when the most change in the information model takes place. Finally, the third phase, burning of the token, is where further action with the token is no longer possible.

1 Issuance

At issuance, multiple pieces of information become exposed. Exactly what is exposed when and where can be complicated by how the issuance is accomplished, as discussed in the previous section. Indeed, the mechanics of minting can involve tools and off-chain platforms that capture additional information beyond what is strictly required for the issuance.

2 Smart Contract Deployment

The life of an NFT can only start if the smart contract that holds the NFT is deployed to a blockchain. When a smart contract, say an ERC-721 compliant one,

---

[30] For more on APIs and how they work, *see* Nizan Geslevich Packin, *Show Me the (Data about the) Money!*, 2020 UTAH L. REV. 1277 (2020) (focusing on APIs in open banking).

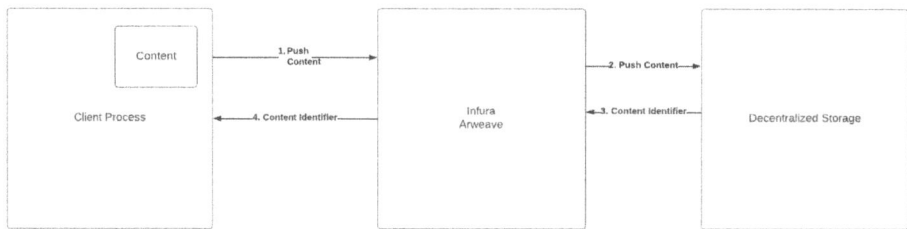

FIGURE 15.1 Push content to storage

is deployed, it is empty and contains no set of NFTs initially. An NFT contract can hold the NFTs of a single creator or any number of creators, depending on the implementation of the smart contract. Manifold allows this 1:1 correlation between NFTs belonging to a creator and being hosted in a smart contract dedicated to the creator. Platforms like OpenSea allow multiple creators to mint into the same smart contract while Instamint offers both options.[31]

The deployment of a smart contract incurs gas fees and is possibly one of the reasons, besides being technically involved, that many creators and artists choose to mint existing smart contracts and co-mingle their NFTs with other creators. A single smart contract can host trillions of NFTs and thus is an economical means to host multiple tenants.

When a smart contract is deployed, it is identified by a contract address. Even if the same smart contract code is deployed twice, two different instances of the contract with unique smart contract addresses will exist on-chain.

Once a smart contract exists on-chain, it is now possible to mint NFTs into the smart contract. The smart contract acts like a registry for a set of NFTs, managing the minting of the NFT and query of the NFTs it holds. However, the process of minting, or issuing, an NFT generally requires a number of steps. We can break these into three major steps.[32]

Step 1: Push content to storage. In the first step, any content the NFT represents must first be published (Figure 15.1). For example, if an NFT represents digital art, then the art must be published and located in a publicly accessible repository. The most popular repository is IPFS and communication from the publishing

---

[31] *See* Vineet, *Manifold Studio Guide: From No-Code NFTs to Open Edition NFT Minting*, NFTEVENING (May 30, 2023), https://nftevening.com/manifold-studio-guide-from-no-code-nfts-to-open-edition-nft-minting/ (explaining that Manifold enables artists to easily create and mint their own NFTs while retaining full ownership and control of the smart contract that defines the NFT, whereas "many existing NFT marketplaces, such as OpenSea, use third-party smart contracts for NFT minting on behalf of artists, which means that ownership of the smart contract is shared between the artist and the marketplace").

[32] For a similar breakdown of the process of minting and issuing an NFT, *see* Sumi Mudgil, *How to Mint an NFT (Part 2/3 of NFT Tutorial Series)*, ETHEREUM (April 21, 2021), https://ethereum.org/en/developers/tutorials/how-to-mint-an-nft/.

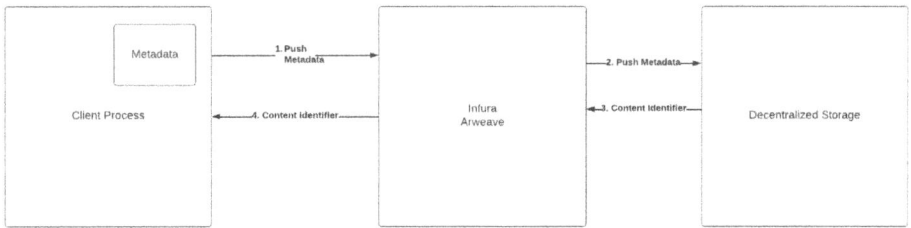

FIGURE 15.2 Push metadata to storage

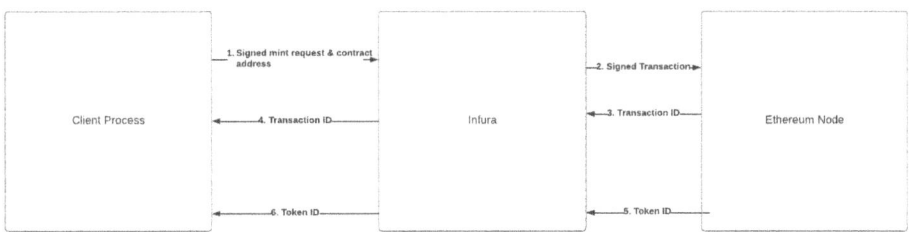

FIGURE 15.3 Mint token and store URL

software to the repository can occur via an intermediary service provider, like Infura or Arweave,[33] or directly to a hosted IPFS node. Once the content is published off-chain, the repository returns a content ID or CID that uniquely identifies the content published.

Step 2: Push metadata to storage. The second step involves the generation of a metadata file, a file that contains details about the content (Figure 15.2). For example, the file will contain the name of the artist or creator, description of the art, and any other pieces of information. Given the metadata is lengthy and often verbose, and just like the content, it is not stored on-chain due to the significant storage costs the size can incur. The metadata file has embedded in it CID of the content published in step 1, linking the metadata to the content. The metadata file is then also published to a storage platform, again most commonly IPFS. Publication of the metadata file generates a second CID that uniquely identifies the metadata file.

Step 3: Mint token and store URL. The final step is the actual minting of the NFT and the association of the NFT to the metadata file (Figure 15.3). IPFS allows access to the metadata via a URL that contains the CID, and this URL is embedded in the smart contract when the NFT is created. The creation of an NFT allocates a newly incremented token ID and the token ID is associated with a URL that points, either directly or ultimately, to the metadata file which in turn points to the content image.

---

[33] *See, for example,* INFURA (2024), www.infura.io/faq/general, (explaining also how Infura can be used as an intermediary in such contexts). *See also above,* n. 15.

3 Transfer

An NFT smart contract maintains a registry or allocation table correlating owner accounts to token IDs. To find all of the tokens an account owns, an individual can search the registry for the account. The search results will display a list of token IDs identifying the owner's portfolio from a given smart contract. Conversely, a smart contract can accept a token ID in a search query and return back the owner's address. The transfer of ownership of an NFT involves a transaction where the current owner of an NFT modifies the registry, updating the owner to the new owner's account address.[34]

4 Burning

An NFT can be burned or destroyed if the new owner is set to the null address (0x0 0000000000000000000000000000000000000000 on Ethereum), an address deemed inaccessible. By transferring ownership to an account that no one controls, the token is considered burned and is no longer transferable to anyone else.

III PRIVACY IMPLICATIONS OF NFTS

After delving into the processes and mechanisms in which information can be collected and transferred in the context of NFTs, in this section we move into the privacy aspects associated with these processes. Section III.A begins the analysis by presenting current discussions of NFTs and privacy law. In Section III.B, the privacy theory of contextual integrity is briefly introduced alongside historical theories of privacy. Historical theories of privacy are then applied to NFT information flows, demonstrating the inability of these theories to properly address the needs and concerns of NFT technology. Then in Section III.C, the four parameters of contextual integrity are introduced and then applied to NFT information flows. The chapter concludes that contextual integrity is the most apt theory of privacy for NFT information flows. Finally, the chapter suggests that while privacy is an important societal concern, in some situations society may benefit from data transparency.

A *Privacy Literature of NFTs*

The intersection of NFTs and privacy law is an area filled with uncertainty. Practicing attorneys, legal scholars, and the Congressional Research Service have written about and researched the topic in an effort to figure out how NFTs will fit into the current

---

[34] *See* Julia Martin & Carrie Hay Kellar, A *Technical Deep Dive into and Implementation of Non-Fungible Tokens in a Practical Setting* 3–4 (December 2021) (unpublished manuscript), https://timroughgarden.github.io/fob21/reports/r8.pdf (discussing transfers of NFTs on Ethereum and explaining that transfers may only be initiated by parties which are currently associated with the NFT, such as the owner or other approved addresses).

landscape of privacy law. These articles examine characteristics of NFT technology and assess the potential impacts that may result from its widespread use.

1 Potential Downsides of NFT Technology

The immutability and public nature of the blockchain raises a number of potential privacy issues. The Congressional report titled *Non-Fungible Tokens (NFTs)* explains that an online alias could potentially be linked to a real-world identity, exposing that person's NFT transactions.[35] A user can partially hide their identity if there is no link between their online addresses and real identity; otherwise, all the activities of users under the exposed address are observable.[36] In *NFT for Eternity*, Jabotinsky and Lavi assert that the combination of immutability and public availability of the blockchain could be weaponized against third parties.[37] If an individual's sensitive data or private photos were tokenized, the data would remain on the record indefinitely.[38] For example, an individual could store the social security number of another in an NFT's data where it would remain permanently and be viewed publicly on the blockchain.[39] The chapter calls for "ex ante" methods of preventing this type of NFT use.[40]

The permanency of the record can also cause NFTs to conflict with regulatory requirements. Some privacy regulations require that data be deleted at regular intervals or upon request of the subject of the data, which is incompatible with the blockchain's immutable nature. A number of articles address this issue. Both *NFTs and Personal Data Protection* by KP Law and *NFTs Privacy and Data Protection* by law firm Versteeg Wigman Sprey explain that NFTs are incompatible with the European Data Protection Legislation's (GDPR's) requirement that data be destroyed.[41] Specifically, article 17 of the GDPR states that a "data subject shall have the right to obtain … the erasure of personal data concerning him or her" – a requirement that the blockchain cannot fulfill.[42]

The Congressional Research Service discusses the potential need for Congress to step in and regulate NFTs to address concerns regarding content moderation and

---

[35] *Non-Fungible Tokens (NFTs)*, Congressional Research Service 1 (July 20, 2022), https://crsreports.congress.gov/product/pdf/R/R47189 [hereinafter CRS].

[36] Ibid.; *see also* Erin Ravenscraft, *NFTs are a Privacy Nightmare*, Wired (April 5, 2022), www.wired.com/story/nfts-privacy-security-nightmare/; Qin Wang et al., *Non-Fungible Token (NFT): Overview, Evaluation, Opportunities and Challenges*, S.U. Sci. & Tech. (2021).

[37] Hadar Y. Jabotinsky & Michal Lavi, *NFT for Eternity*, 56 U. Mich. J. L. Reform 827, 832–834 (2023).

[38] Ibid.

[39] Ibid.

[40] Ibid.

[41] Onur Küçük & Melodi Özer, *NFTs and Personal Data Protection*, KP Law (May 30, 2022), https://ceelegalmatters.com/briefings/20089-nfts-and-personal-data-protection; Jetse Sprey, *NFTs: Privacy and Data Protection*, Versteeg Wigman Sprey (June 2021), www.vwsadvocaten.nl/en/nfts-privacy-and-data-protection/.

[42] Ibid.

privacy on a federal level.[43] In deciding whether regulation is needed, the Research Service posited that Congress may want to consider the following questions: whether current privacy laws sufficiently address NFT use; whether moderating NFT content will implicate the First Amendment's Free Speech Clause; and whether concerns about NFTs and privacy harm the well-being of the public to a degree high enough to warrant legislative action.[44]

2 Potential Benefits of NFT Technology

The availability of only partial anonymity on the blockchain is beneficial in some situations. *The New Use Case for NFTs – Solving Online Identity Identification* asserts that NFT's lack of anonymity may solve issues with enforcing data privacy laws. The lack of anonymity may lead to increased enforcement of data rights and privacy issues because movement of NFT data is tracked so bad actors cannot hide from law enforcement behind online anonymity.[45]

In *Blockchain, and Artwork Registries: Consensus Between Constraints*, Yujia Zheng argues that the partial anonymity maintains a balance of privacy and transparency that could be useful in the context of blockchain-based artwork registries.[46] Current art registries are kept in databases that do not allow potential purchasers of art to see other transactions. Purchasers of art enjoy the anonymity that the current database provides, but the anonymity hinders potential purchasers from entering the market. Zheng argues that a blockchain based registry would be the best solution for both parties. Purchasers can also use public and private keys, which allow them to share the information they want with the public and keep private the information they do not want to share.

The authors of *The Impact of Blockchains for Human Rights, Democracy, and the Rule of Law* posit that the blockchain can allow individuals to control their own identities and data.[47] The immutable nature of the blockchain, if used as a self-sovereign identity, could securely store documentation and proof of identification for vulnerable populations. The blockchain would also give individuals power over whom to release their information to. The authors acknowledge many of the critiques regarding the lack of full anonymity on public blockchains, but ultimately frames pseudo-anonymity as a guarantee of partial privacy. Partial privacy is an improvement for individuals, like refugees and other vulnerable groups, who might normally have no expectations of privacy with their personal information.

---

[43] CRS.

[44] Ibid.

[45] Zachary Ignoffo, *The New Use Case for NFTs – Solving Online Identity Verification*, PRIVACY AFFAIRS (April 29, 2023), www.privacyaffairs.com/nft-identity-verification/.

[46] Yujia Zheng, *Blockchain, Privacy and Artwork Registries: Consensus between Constraints*, N.Y. UNIV. STEINHARDT SCH. OF CULTURE, EDUC. AND HUM. DEV., 1, 13 (Spring 2021).

[47] Florence G'Sell, et al., The Impact of Blockchains for Human Rights, Democracy, and the Rule of Law, COUNCIL OF EUR. 24–5 (2022).

NFTs use of smart contracts can solve privacy issues in some fields. In Florence G'Sell, et al., *Non-Fungible Token (NFT): Overview, Evaluation, Opportunities and Challenges*, the authors offer as a solution the use of privacy-preserving contracts instead of plain smart contracts to protect user privacy by only permitting disclosure of information to authorized users.[48] Compounding this idea in their book, *Privacy Laws, Genomic Data and Non-Fungible Tokens*, Daniel Uribe and Gisele Waters examine how NFTs and smart contracts can solve the privacy issues surrounding genetic testing.[49] This chapter posits that data privacy laws, such as the GDPR, California Consumer Privacy Act (CCPA), and Consumer Online Privacy Act (COPRA), can be programmed into NFT smart contracts to prohibit actions that would not comply with regulations.

B Contextual Integrity

Helen Nissenbaum's privacy framework of contextual integrity can be instrumental in evaluating privacy implications of NFTs. Contextual integrity determines whether privacy has been maintained by evaluating whether a transmission has reflected the *appropriate* flow of information within specific contexts.[50] We adopt contextual integrity for two reasons. First, other approaches to understanding privacy have yet to capture the characteristics of NFTs that evolve over time at different stages of NFT lifecycles. Second, contextual integrity recognizes the complexity and variability in the privacy constraints people expect to hold in the NFT context and enables an understanding of privacy through information flow.

The existing approaches to understanding privacy can be dealt with under six general headings, which include:

> (1) the right to be let alone – Samuel Warren and Louis Brandeis's famous formulation for the right to privacy; (2) limited access to the self – the ability to shield oneself from unwanted access by others; (3) secrecy – the concealment of certain matters from others; (4) control over personal information – the ability to exercise control over information about oneself; (5) personhood – the protection of one's personality, individuality, and dignity; and (6) intimacy – control over, or limited access to, one's intimate relationships or aspects of life.[51]

However, many scholars have criticized these theories of privacy for being either too narrow or too broad.[52] Take the conception of the right to be let alone as an example. Samiel Warren and Louis Brandeis, in their famous article, *The Right*

---

[48] Qin Wang et al., *Non-Fungible Token*.
[49] Daniel Uribe & Gisele Waters, *Privacy Laws, Genomic Data and Non-Fungible Tokens*, JBBA (May 30, 2020), https://jbba.scholasticahq.com/article/13164-privacy-laws-genomic-data-and-non-fungible-tokens.
[50] HELEN NISSENBAUM, PRIVACY IN CONTEXT: TECHNOLOGY, POLICY, AND THE INTEGRITY OF SOCIAL LIFE, 127–128 (2010).
[51] Daniel J. Solove, *Conceptualizing Privacy*, 90 CALIF. L. REV. 1087, 1087–1088 (2002).
[52] *See* ibid., 1094 (critiquing all six categories of conceptions and explaining why each conception is either too broad or too narrow or both).

to Privacy,[53] inspired significant attention to privacy and framed the discussion of privacy in the United States throughout the twentieth century.[54] But their conception of privacy as being let alone fails to provide much guidance about how privacy should be valued with regards to other interests, such as free speech, effective law enforcement, and other values.[55] Being let alone does not inform us about the matters in which we should be let alone.[56] Therefore, many commentators argue that defining privacy as the right to be let alone is too broad.[57]

In the context of NFTs, it seems all conceptions are relevant, but they are either too broad or too narrow when applying to NFTs. Take the conception of "limited access to the self" as an example. Yes, privacy in the context of NFTs is about one's ability to shield oneself from unwanted access by others. An owner of a digital art NFT may want to allow the general public to access the digital art associated with the NFT while prohibiting access to their personal data. The owner may also take some measures to shield themselves from unwanted access. However, "unwanted" access can be a very subjective standard – some are highly concerned about any unauthorized access by any unauthorized person(s) or by an authorized person(s) in an unauthorized manner, whereas some allow for a greater extent of access by others in various manners. The NFT system would by default allow for access by others because the information is published on the blockchain regardless of whether the access is "unwanted" or "wanted." In some cases, preference does not matter. Various parties, including developers and vendors, require access to some types of information to create an NFT. Therefore, the "limited access to the self" conception of privacy fails to consider this situation in the NFT context.

The examples can go on and on under each of the headings of the current privacy conceptions, such as the right to be let alone, secrecy, control over personal information, personhood, and intimacy. All of these traditional conceptions are too broad and abstract to capture all aspects of privacy in the NFT context. Therefore, we need an alternative to understanding privacy.

---

[53] Warren and Brandeis defined privacy as the "right to be let alone," a phrase adopted from Judge Thomas Cooley's treatise on torts in 1880. Cooley's right to be let alone was, in fact, a way of explaining that attempted physical touching was a tort injury; he was not defining a right to privacy. Samuel D. Warren & Louis D. Brandeis, *The Right to Privacy*, 4 HARV. L. REV. 193, 195 (1890); *See* Robert E. Smith, BEN FRANKLIN'S WEB SITE: PRIVACY AND CURIOSITY FROM PLYMOUTH ROCK TO THE INTERNET 128 (Chisheng Li, ed., 2000).

[54] Solove, *Conceptualizing Privacy*, 1100; *See also* Irwin P. Kramer, *The Birth of Privacy Law: A Century Since Warren and Brandeis*, 39 CATH. U. L. REV. 703, 704 (1990); Harry Kalven has even hailed it as the "most influential law review article of all." Harry Kalven, Jr., *Privacy in Tort Law – Were Warren and Brandeis Wrong?*, 31 LAW & CONTEMP. PROBS. 326, 327 (1966); Richard C. Turkington, *Legacy of the Warren and Brandeis Article: The Emerging Unencumbered Constitutional Right to Informational Privacy*, 10 N. ILL. U. L. REV. 479, 481–82 (1990).

[55] Solove, *Conceptualizing Privacy*, 1101.

[56] Ibid.

[57] Ibid., 1102; *See also* David M. O'Brien, PRIVACY, LAW, AND PUBLIC POLICY 5, 16 (1979); Tom Gerety, *Redefining Privacy*, 12 HARV. C.R-C.L. L. REV. 233, 234, 263 (1977).

Contextual integrity provides an alternative because the framework is not only broad enough to catch the evolving characteristics of an NFT lifecycle but also sufficiently recognizes the complexity and variability in the privacy constraints people expect to hold over the flow of information.

Contextual integrity requires analysis of four parameters: (1) the context in which an information transmission occurs, (2) the actors involved, (3) the attributes of the conveyed information, and (4) the principle facilitating the transmission of the data.[58]

Context refers to the situation in which information is transmitted, which provide the means to determine the informational norms associated with the activity being evaluated.[59] Actors are the parties involved in an information exchange and are divided into three categories: the sender, the receiver, and the subject of the information.[60] Actors may be individuals or groups. Additionally, each actor may fill multiple roles simultaneously, such as being both the information sender and subject. Attributes are the characteristics and content of the information being transmitted.[61] Transmission principles are constraints on the flow of information from one actor to another in a specific context and determine what information norms apply within that context.[62] A change in any of these parameters will alter the subject's perception of privacy, which may lead to a different response about whether their privacy has been maintained. Context, actors, and attributes are all objective descriptions, but transmission principles involve normative assessment.

C Applying Contextual Integrity to NFT Creation

As an example of how contextual integrity may be applied to NFTs, consider the following example of the issuance stage of an image NFT's lifecycle. We analyze four parameters (i.e., context, actors, attributes, and transmission principles) of the issuance stage. As described in the previous section, the issuance stage involves several steps and actors, with new attributes added for each step.

1 Context

Context is straightforward and remains largely the same at each step: a party is providing the information necessary to enable tokenized ownership via a smart contract that updates the hosting blockchain.

2 Actors

In the first step, the content creator (or their technologically-savvy agent) must push the main content that is to be tokenized into decentralized storage (*see* Figure 15.1).

---

[58] Nissenbaum, Privacy in Context, 140–147.
[59] Ibid., 141.
[60] Ibid.
[61] Ibid., 143–144.
[62] Ibid. 144–145.

To do this, the creator sends the content to an IPFS node where it is assigned a CID to enable later retrieval and is then sent to a decentralized network of storage hosts. During this step, the creator is the sender of the content, the receiver of the CID, and data subject; the IPFS node, as an intermediary, is both the recipient and sender of the content and the sender of the CID; the decentralized storage hosts are the recipients of both the content and the CID. If the creator opts to use a service to push data to the IPFS node, the service provider becomes an additional intermediary actor; one that is receiving the information from the creator, translating the creator's request to a remote procedure call (RPC), and sending the information out to the IPFS network.

3 Attributes

The attributes of the data include the content itself (e.g., a JPG file of digital art), the content's exchangeable image file format (Exif) data,[63] and the sender's IP address (which may be maintained or discarded by the IPFS node after the transmission is complete). If an intermediary service provider is used, they may require additional attributes to be included such as information about the creator so that they can track usage statistics.

4 Transmission Principle: Minimum Necessary Standard

The transmission principle is the only subjective parameter because NFTs have been a new development in the last two years and the NFT space still lacks norms. No agreements have been made on what principles or norms should govern the transmission of information from one party to another. For instance, in this first step, if an intermediary service provider is used, the service provider may require additional attributes to be included. But are these additional attributes necessary to create an NFT? If it is not necessary, how can one justify adding additional attributes? Will such additional attributes increase the risks of exposing the creator's personal information?

To determine what terms and conditions under which transfers of information ought (or ought not) to occur, we propose a minimum necessary standard. The standard would require actors to restrict the transfer of attributes to the minimum amount necessary to achieve the purpose for which it is being used. If an actor included any additional attributes, the actor would violate transmission principles and thus violate contextual integrity.

The application of this standard involves three steps, as described below.

Step 1: If we apply the minimum necessary standard to the first step, first consider the purpose for which the attributes are being used. The purpose of this step

---

[63] Exif files enable interoperability in editing, viewing, and displaying images among different devices such as computers, digital photo frames, servers, etc. *See Exchangeable Image File Format for Digital Still Cameras: Exif Version 2.3,* STANDARD OF THE CAMERA & IMAGING PRODS. ASS'N 5 (December 2012), www.cipa.jp/std/documents/e/DC-008-2012_E.pdf.

is to publish the digital art by pushing the content directly to a hosted IPFS node, assuming no intermediary is used. The minimum necessary attributes would be the digital art itself, the content's exchangeable image file format data, and the sender's IP address. Attributes such as the artist's name, address, date of birth, price of the digital art, and previous owners are not necessary to publish the digital art. If the sender includes any unnecessary attributes to publish the digital art, then the sender violates the transmission principle.

Step 2: The second step, pushing metadata to storage, involves the same context and actors as step one (*see* Figure 15.2). However, the attributes of the information have changed; the creator's IP address is still possibly transmitted, but the creator is now sending metadata that describes characteristics of the content that was pushed to storage in step one. This can include the creator's name or pseudonym, a description of the art, and other information that the creator wishes to include. The IPFS node receives the metadata and sends back a second CID to the creator. As in step one, an intermediary service provider may be used and facilitates the transmission by acting as both a sender and receiver of the metadata and CID.

We follow the same framework to analyze the transmission principle: first, identify the purpose for which the attributes are being used then decide the minimum necessary attributes to meet the goal. In the second step, the purpose is to publish metadata by pushing the metadata file to the IPFS. The minimum necessary attributes could vary because different platforms have different standards. Take OpenSea as an example, the attributes would be the name, description, external link, and traits.[64]

Step 3: The final step of issuance is the minting of the token and storage URL. Here the context differs slightly because the information transmitted in steps one and two are now being published and disseminated to the general public (e.g., anyone viewing a marketplace like OpenSea). At this point a new set of actors becomes involved because, in addition to the creator, the public become the recipients of the transaction ID and token ID. This enables the public to see the transaction minting the NFT on the relevant blockchain and view the NFT itself. With the exception of the smart contract itself, each piece of information in this step has similar attributes in that each is functional rather than substantive. No new information from the creator is transmitted other than the signed mint request.

The final step is a functional one that enables the public to see the transaction ID and token ID. What attributes should or should not be disclosed is determined in the first two steps before the creation of the transaction ID and token ID. Transmission principles, therefore, apply to the first two steps.

Exception to the Minimum Necessary Standard. One exception to the minimum necessary standard is that the sender must include additional attributes for the greater good after evaluating conflicting values. The rationale for the minimum

---

[64] *Metadata Standards: How to Add Rich Metadata to Your ERC721 or ERC1155 NFTs*, OPENSEA (2023), https://docs.opensea.io/docs/metadata-standards.

necessary standard is that society values privacy. That is why we enact laws and create norms to protect privacy and do not expect to disclose too much unnecessary information for certain matters. But the law should weigh the value of keeping certain things, places, or affairs private against other values that may be in conflict.

For instance, keeping one's online photos and text messages private is valuable because it would protect one's safety, dignity, and autonomy, as well as the ability to control and live one's life as one desires. Any disclosure of those photos and messages could create enormous psychological stress and pain and/or physical threat and harm to the person. However, assuming these photos and text messages involve human trafficking, government (even the general public) obtaining access to photos and messages would benefit many families suffering from losing their children or other loved ones. Society would be better off if such information were public (in other words, one person's state of being private is violated or destroyed). The law should weigh up these conflicting values to decide if certain matters should be private.

In the case of NFT creation, it could be argued that society would be better off if the names of NFT creators were included in the NFTs' attributes rather than discarded., Although names are not a necessary attribute to create an NFT, including names would be valuable for ownership protection, intellectual property protection, or tracking illegal transactions.

Barring new developments in the process of issuing NFTs, the context, actors, and transmission principles remain relatively constant in each scenario, so the attributes of the NFT will determine whether a party feels as if their privacy has been maintained. If the content or metadata includes sensitive personal information such as the creator's social security number as hypothesized above, the creator will not feel that their privacy has been maintained. The public nature of NFTs means that information that would normally be kept confidential and used in one context is now public and being used as a commodity to facilitate transactions.

IV CONCLUSION

The adoption of NFTs, while possibly signifying an advancement in the world of digital representation and ownership, has unveiled considerable privacy concerns. NFTs, through their inherent design, expose creators and users to potential vulnerabilities surrounding their personal data. As this chapter revealed, present privacy frameworks are out of step with the nuanced intricacies of NFTs. Helen Nissenbaum's "contextual integrity" emerges as a potentially fitting approach, emphasizing the adaptability that our privacy paradigms desperately require in the face of such technological innovations. As society grapples with the dual imperatives of data protection and the collective good, it is paramount that our legal and policy mechanisms evolve. Striking the right balance between privacy interests and the need for transparency in the realm of NFTs will be a formidable, yet indispensable challenge, as we forge ahead in this digital frontier.

16

The Cybersecurity of NFTs and Digital Assets

Scott J. Shackelford and Esfan Haghverdi

I INTRODUCTION

Blockchain technology is no panacea but its potential for disruption is nevertheless high, including as it pertains to so-called non-fungible tokens (NFTs). Yet, as these volatile assets see-saw in value, security concerns have come to the fore. This chapter surveys the literature to date both in regards to the law and policy, as well as the technical aspects of the cybersecurity of NFTs and other digital assets. We begin with a brief primer on the topic of blockchain and NFTs for the uninitiated before moving on to discuss pressing technical concerns involving NFTs and how state and federal law and policy in the United States have responded to date. Policy implications are then discussed along with a research agenda for future work at this intersection.

II BLOCKCHAIN AND NFT PRIMER

There has been increasing interest in the transformative power of not only cryptocurrencies like bitcoin,[1] but also the technology underlying them – namely blockchain.[2] Though bitcoin gets most of the press, blockchains arguably enjoy the far greater potential to transform business and potentially revolutionize cybersecurity; simply put, according to Goldman Sachs, it could "change 'everything.'"[3] To the uninitiated, a blockchain is a sophisticated, distributed online ledger. From making

---

An earlier version of this research was published as Scott J. Shackelford & Steve Myers, *Block-by-Block: Leveraging the Power of Blockchain Technology to Build Trust and Promote Cyber Peace*, 19 YALE J.L. & TECH. 334 (2017).

[1] *See, for example,* Luke Graham, *India's Rupee Restrictions Are Boosting Demand for Bitcoin*, CNBC (November 15, 2016), www.cnbc.com/2016/11/15/india-rupee-restriction-boost-Bitcoin-digital-currency.html.

[2] *See* Naomi Lachance, *Not Just Bitcoin: Why the Blockchain Is a Seductive Technology to Many Industries*, NPR (May 4, 2016), www.npr.org/sections/alltechconsidered/2016/05/04/476597296/not-just-Bitcoin-why-blockchain-is-a-seductive-technology-to-many-industries.

[3] Ibid.

businesses more efficient to recording property deeds to engendering the growth of "smart" contracts and even securing medical devices,[4] blockchain technology is being investigated by a huge range of organizations and is attracting billions in venture funding.[5] Even the US Defense Advanced Research Projects Agency (DARPA) is investigating blockchain technology to "create an unhackable messaging system,"[6] as are IBM and Disney.[7] Yet, as is discussed in Section III, blockchains are in fact very hackable. For example, Ronin Network had a developer fall victim to a spear-phishing attack in which they were sent a fake offer letter as an attached file. By clicking on this attachment, attackers – allegedly from North Korea – were able to steal $622 million in "the largest cryptocurrency heist to date."[8] Indeed, the immutability of blockchain makes it tougher and more cumbersome to patch than traditional software. This, coupled with basic failings like dollar limits on fund transfers without preapproval, contributes to the scope of the problem. The situation has been exacerbated by the fall of crypto asset prices in 2022 and the broader "crypto winter" that risks becoming an ice age.[9]

At its root, a blockchain is a "shared, trusted, distributed ledger that everyone can inspect, but which no single user controls."[10] The participants in a given blockchain system work together to keep the ledger updated; it may be amended only by strict rules and consensus.[11] For example, bitcoin's blockchain ledger "prevents double-spending and keeps track of transactions continuously," which is "what makes possible a currency without a central bank."[12] It has also been said that blockchains are "the latest example of the unexpected fruits of cryptography."[13] This has come

---

[4] *See, for example*, Suliman Mulhem, *Four Ways Blockchain Can Make Businesses More Efficient and Profitable*, FORBES (July 12, 2023), www.forbes.com/sites/forbesbusinesscouncil/2023/07/12/four-ways-blockchain-can-make-businesses-more-efficient-and-profitable/?sh=61c2b7e069f3; Justin Malonson, *Blockchain Technology Is Revolutionizing the Real Estate Industry*, ENTREPRENEUR (May 19, 2022), www.entrepreneur.com/money-finance/blockchain-technology-is-revolutionizing-the-real-estate/424715; Asha McLean, *ASX Argues Medical Records Are Ripe for Blockchain*, ZDNET (November 16, 2016), www.zdnet.com/article/asx-argues-medical-records-are-ripe-for-blockchain/.

[5] *See* Kyle Torpey, *Prediction: $10 Billion Will Be Invested in Blockchain Projects in 2016*, COIN J. (January 22, 2016), http://coinjournal.net/prediction-10-billion-will-be-invested-in-blockchain-startups-in-2016/.

[6] *See* Lachance, *Not Just Bitcoin*.

[7] Don Tapscott & Alex Tapscott, *Here's Why Blockchains Will Change the World*, FORTUNE (May 8, 2016), http://fortune.com/2016/05/08/why-blockchains-will-change-the-world.

[8] Rob Pegoraro, *Why Is Web3 Security Such a Garbage Fire? Let Us Count the Ways*, PC MAG. (August 12, 2022), www.pcmag.com/news/why-is-web3-security-such-a-garbage-fire-let-us-count-the-ways.

[9] *See* Julian Mark & Gerrit De Vynck, *'Crypto Winter' Has Come. And It's Looking More Like an Ice Age*, WASH. POST (December 18, 2022), www.washingtonpost.com/business/2022/12/18/crypto-winter-ftx-collapse-bitcoin-prices/.

[10] *The Trust Machine*, ECONOMIST (October 31, 2015), www.economist.com/leaders/2015/10/31/the-trust-machine.

[11] Ibid.

[12] Ibid.

[13] Ibid.

to fruition particularly in the context of smart contracts, which are integral to NFT creation and distribution.

Smart contracts were originally introduced by Szabo, aiming to accelerate, verify, or execute digital negotiation.[14] Ethereum, an open-source, blockchain-based platform that was proposed and launched by Vitalik Buterin, further integrated smart contracts in the blockchain system,[15] enabling Szabo's smart contracts to be executed. Blockchain-based smart contracts achieve complicated functionalities and execute thorough state transition replication over consensus algorithms to realize final consistency. Smart contracts enable unfamiliar parties and decentralized participants to conduct fair exchanges without a trusted third party and further propose a unified method to build applications across a wide range of industries. Most NFT solutions rely on smart contract-based blockchain platforms to ensure their order-sensitive executions.[16]

III TECHNICAL CONCERNS OF NFTS AND OTHER DIGITAL ASSETS

NFTs were first proposed in the Ethereum Improvement Proposal (EIP)-721 as a use case for smart contracts that depend on tracking distinguishable assets.[17] The proposal lists LAND in Decentraland, the eponymous punks in CryptoPunks, and in-game items using systems like DMarket or EnjinCoin as existing examples of NFTs and predicts future uses like tracking real-world assets. It also emphasizes that in each of these cases these items should not be "lumped together" as numbers in a ledger, but instead each asset must have its ownership individually and atomically tracked.

The choice of the name "NFT" appears to have been satisfactory to nearly everyone and applicable to distinguishable digital assets. These ideas were further developed in EIP-1155.[18] Even though NFTS were introduced on the Ethereum network,

---

[14] Nick Szabo first introduced the concept of "smart contracts" in 1994, proposing a computer code that could automatically implement the terms of an agreement. Nick Szabo, *Smart Contracts: Building Blocks for Digital Markets*, 16 J. OF TRANSHUMANIST THOUGHT 18 (1996). It was not until 2015, however, when smart contracts were executed using blockchain technology. *See* Florian Martin-Bariteau & Marco Pontello, *Hashing out Agreements: An Overview of "Smart" Contracts under Canadian Law* 10 (July 9, 2020) (unpublished manuscript), https://papers.ssrn.com/sol3/papers.cfm?abstract_id=3592986.

[15] For more on this, *see, for example*, Kristin N. Johnson, *Decentralized Finance: Regulating Cryptocurrency Exchanges*, 62 WM. & MARY L. REV. 1911 (2021); Peterson K. Ozili, *Decentralized Finance Research and Developments Around the World*, 6 J. BANKING & FIN. TECH. 117 (2022).

[16] *See* Kimberly A. Houser & John T. Holden, *Navigating the Non-Fungible Token*, 2022 UTAH L. REV. 891, 900 (2022) (explaining how NFTs are created and noting that the Ethereum blockchain "functionality enabled NFT marketplaces to run ... guaranteeing security and anonymity without centralized oversight").

[17] *EIP-721: Non-Fungible Token Standard*, ETHEREUM IMPROVEMENT PROPOSALS (January 2018), https://eips.ethereum.org/EIPS/eip-721.

[18] *EIP-1155: Multi Token Standard*, ETHEREUM IMPROVEMENT PROPOSALS (June 2018), https://eips.ethereum.org/EIPS/eip-1155.

TABLE 16.1 *All-time trades and volumes for the top five (ranked by trade volume) NFT markets as of December 2022*

Marketplaces	Traders	Volume $
OpenSea	2,459,795	33.09B
Axie Marketplace	2,175,552	4.26B
CryptoPunks	7,283	2.98B
Magic Eden	1,380,780	1.93B
LooksRare	112,522	1.64B

they can be housed on other blockchains as well. The non-fungibility of NFTs implies that they cannot be altered or changed and have a unique property that can be preserved. Even though they are like cryptocurrencies and tokens that live on blockchains they are also very different from these latter products in that NFTs can store more data of various formats, anyone can develop them and trade them.[19]

According to Cointelegraph, Verified Market Research (VMR), the global research and consulting firm, valued the global NFT market at $11.3 billion in 2021 as part of a 202-page deep dive into the burgeoning space. Due to the ongoing crypto winter as of this writing, NFT valuation plummeted to some $3 billion globally in 2022, and is projected to reach $7.6 billion by 2027.[20] A key driver of demand for NFTs is their proliferation across multiple industries and walks of life, including music, films, and sports. The report highlights some key areas of interest and use cases that have helped drive NFT sales.[21] NFTs can be created and traded on marketplaces like OpenSea, which is perhaps the most popular – and, by far, the largest – NFT marketplace nowadays, CryptoPunks/Larva Labs, Rarible, SuperRare, and Known Origin, among others.

The trade volume of NFTs in 2021 was $24.9 billion, according to DappRadar, which is up from $95 million in 2020.[22] Overall, NFT transaction volume in 2022 slowed dramatically. From January 2022 to September 2022, NFT trading volume collapsed by 97 percent, from $17 billion in value to just $466 million.[23] Table 16.1 summarizes the all-time trades and volumes for the top five (ranked by trade volume) NFT markets as of December 2022.[24]

[19] Yash Gupta & Jayanth Kumar, *Identifying Security Risks in NFT Platforms*, COMPUTERS & SEC. (2022), https://arxiv.org/abs/2204.01487.
[20] *Global Non-Fungible Token (NFT) Market Size, Status and Forecast 2022–2028*, MARKET RES. (2022), www.marketresearch.com/QYResearch-Group-v3531/Global-Non-Fungible-Token-NFT-30956108/.
[21] Gupta & Kumar, *Identifying Security Risks*.
[22] Ibid.
[23] Josh Wilson, *With the Decrease in NFT Trading Volumes, Where Does the Sector Go from Here*, BLOOMBERG (December 12, 2022), www.forbes.com/sites/joshwilson/2022/12/12/with-the-decrease-in-nft-trading-volumes-where-does-the-sector-go-from-here/?sh=1c0219969fef.
[24] DAPPRADAR (2024), https://dappradar.com/.

TABLE 16.2 *A taxonomy of risks in the NFT landscape*

Layer 8 Risks	Missing or Failing Processes	External Risks
Inadvertent	Process controls	Regulatory risk
Malicious attacks	Partnerships	Disasters
Scams	Platform bugs	Geopolitical risk

Despite this amazing growth, the security of NFTs has not been studied extensively in the literature. We shall review some recent publications.

Security concerns and attack types. One of the core security concerns with NFTs is proper assignment, protection, and validation of ownership.[25] In particular, this problem needs to be solved in a decentralized context which is the main rationale for the excitement and enthusiasm about Web 3.0, blockchains, and NFTs. Moreover, in practice we are dealing with a mixture of centralized and decentralized environments that further confound the security problems.

ERC-721 offers a solution to verification of ownership using a single token ID that can verify different attributes of a unique NFT.[26] However, the safe and reliable storage issue still remains. Note that even though NFTs live on blockchains, their content and metadata only exist on permanent off-blockchain storage networks, which are centralized servers.[27] In this way, the content is open to all Web 2.0 vulnerabilities, for example, ransomware, data alteration, etc. Gupta and Kumar introduce a taxonomy of risks in the NFT landscape.[28] This taxonomy of risk is summarized in Table 16.2, and below, each item is briefly explained.

- *Inadvertent*: User error related risks especially since such transactions are generally not user-friendly or straightforward for many people.
- *Malicious attacks*: Phishing or social engineering.
- *Scams*: Developers may accept funds and then stop development, stop the project, and run away with the collected funds.
- *Process controls*: The development process is moving very fast and hence there are several gaps in the product development lifecycle that create vulnerabilities.
- *Partnerships*: Lack of industry-wide collaborations.
- *Platform bugs*: Poorly documented and understood bugs or issues on various platforms.
- *Regulatory risks*: Regulation is viewed as one of the significant risks for developing crypto technologies.

---

[25] Gupta & Kumar, *Identifying Security Risks*.
[26] ERC721, https://erc721.org/.
[27] Gupta & Kumar, *Identifying Security Risks*.
[28] Ibid.

TABLE 16.3 *Potential security issues of NFTs*

STRIDE	Security Issues
Spoofing	Attacker may exploit authentication vulnerabilities
	Attacker may steal a user's private key
Tampering	The data stored outside the blockchain may be manipulated
Repudiation	The hash data may bind with an attacker's address
Information disclosure	Attacker can easily exploit the hash and transaction to link a particular NFT buyer or seller
Denial of Service	The NFT data may become unavailable if the asset is stored outside the blockchain
Elevation of Privilege	A poorly designed smart contract may make NFTs lose such properties

- *Disasters*: NFTs need to be protected with appropriate policies related to business continuity.
- *Geopolitical risk*: NFTs are newly emerging technology that may become victims involving geopolitical conflict.

They also offer solution ideas to mitigate such risks that we shall not discuss in this paper and refer the reader to the original work.[29]

Another approach is the STRIDE [Stride] threat and risk evaluation model to investigate security issues.[30] These are listed in Table 16.3.

Wang and co-authors offer security solutions to each of these categories.[31]

Finally, Das and co-authors study security challenges in the NFT ecosystem.[32] They start by identifying the three components of the NFT ecosystems which are subsequently analyzed to discover security, privacy, and usability issues. These components (actors) in an NFT ecosystem consist of *users* who belong in one of the categories of content creator, seller, and buyer; *Marketplaces* that are decentralized app (dApp) platforms where NFTs are traded and consist of two main components: a user-facing web front and a collection of smart contracts that interact with the blockchain. Finally, the third component is *external entities*, external to both NFT marketplaces (NFTMs) and blockchain, these are services and devices that provide the necessary infrastructure for the system.

---

[29] For more details and examples of each case, we refer the reader to Gupta & Kumar, *Identifying Security Risks.*

[30] Qin Wang et al., *Non-Fungible Token (NFT): Overview, Evaluation, Opportunities and Challenges* (2021), https://arxiv.org/abs/2105.07447.

[31] Ibid.

[32] Dipanjan Das et al., *Understanding Security Issues in the NFT Ecosystem*, ACM CONF. ON COMPUTER & COMMUNICATIONS SEC. (CCS) (2022), https://arxiv.org/abs/2111.08893.

Issues arise when these components interact with each other. Below is a brief presentation of the detailed and systematic analysis carried out by Das and co-authors.[33]

User Authentication. (U1) Identity verification: NFTs might make criminal activity easier due to the anonymity of the users and lack of physical artworks. Identity verification is the first step to deter such criminals. (U2) Two-factor authentication: Enabling 2FA (Two-Factor Authentication) greatly enhances the security of a password-based authentication workflow.

Token Minting. (M1) Verifiability of token contracts: A token contract is considered "verifiable" if its source code is submitted to Etherscan. Verifiability of external token contracts is crucial as they can be malicious or buggy. A malicious token contract can be abused to mint more tokens than the rarity threshold, thus dropping the token's price, which hurts the buyers. (M2) Tampering with token metadata: The metadata of a token holds the pointer to the corresponding asset. Hence, if the metadata changes, the token loses its significance.

Token Listing. (L1) Principle of least privilege: While listing an NFT, the NFTM takes control of the token so that when a sale is executed, it can transfer the ownership of the NFT from the seller to the buyer. To this end, the NFTM needs to be (i) the owner of the NFT: that is, the current owner transfers the asset to an escrow account E during listing, (ii) a controller: an Ethereum account C that can manage that specific NFT on behalf of the owner, or (iii) an operator: an Ethereum account O that can manage all the NFTs in that collection.

Invalid caching. (L2) While displaying an NFT on sale, OpenSea and Rarible leverage a local caching layer to avoid repeated requests to fetch the associated images. If the image is updated, or disappears, the cache goes out of sync. This could trick a buyer into purchasing an NFT for which the asset is either nonexistent or different from what the NFTM displays using its stale cache.

Seller and collection verification. (L3) Listings by verified sellers/collections are not only given preferential treatment by the NFTMs, but they also attract greater attention from the buyer community.

Lack of transparency. (T1) NFTs are asset-ownership records that should be stored on the blockchain to allow for public verifiability. Among other things, each transaction includes the following information: (i) address of the seller (current owner), (ii) address of the buyer (new owner), (iii) how much the NFT was sold for, and (iv) time of ownership transfer.

Fairness in bidding. (T2) NFTMs implement bidding either (i) on-chain, through a smart contract that requires the bid amounts to be deposited while placing the bid, or (ii) off-chain, through the NFTM dApp which maintains an orderbook without requiring any upfront payment. Off-chain bidding is unfair as it can be abused by both the NFTM and the users. Since bids are not visible from the blockchain, NFTMs can inflate the bid volume to create hype. Also, placing bids is inexpensive

---

[33] Ibid.

as there is no money transfer involved. Therefore, such NFTMs are more suscepti-ble to bid pollution, a form of abuse where a large number of casual bids are placed on items.

Royalty distribution and marketplace fee evasion. (T3) If a royalty is set, every trade should earn a fee for the creator. However, there are ways in which users can poten-tially abuse the royalty implementations.

Each of these potential vulnerabilities and tactics requires tailored governance interventions, some of which we discuss next in Section IV.

IV NFT CYBERSECURITY LAW AND POLICY

The law and policy literature pertaining to the cybersecurity of NFTs remains, per-haps not surprisingly, nascent as of this writing. Despite the fact that hundreds of law review articles were written on the topic of blockchain, only a scant twenty of these have touched on the specific topic at hand. Indeed, the issue has only gained academic interest quite recently. For example, Carol Goforth explores the growing issues surrounding fraud in NFT trading.[34] Among other things, this article broke new ground by exploring which federal agencies might be most appropriate at addressing harms experienced by consumers trading NFTs, including the Securities and Exchange Commission (SEC), Commodity Futures Trading Commission (CFTC), and the Federal Trade Commission (FTC). Thus far, though, it remains unclear "whether NFTs will be treated as a type of cryptoasset or as something dis-tinct from Bitcoin and other 'virtual currencies'" because NFT functions differently from other fungible cryptoassets and "there are certainly no futures being traded in NFTs at this time."[35] Thus, even though the SEC and the CFTC could potentially oversee NFT frauds, they have been "silent so far."[36] As a result, the burden cur-rently falls heavily on consumers involved in NFT transactions to safeguard them-selves from fraud and other potential risks.[37]

---

[34] *See* Carol R. Goforth, *How Nifty! But Are NFTs Securities Commodities, or Something Else?*, 90 UMKC L. Rev. 775, 776 (2022)

("The reality is that NFT fraudsters are already in the picture. In some cases, artists wake up to find that their art is being packaged and sold as NFTs by unauthorized third parties. Nor is this the only kind of illicit activity. Reports suggest that there are at least five kinds of scams being perpetrated in connection with NFTs: sites that imitate legitimate NFT platforms; NFT platforms that do not really exist; counterfeit or fraudulently created NFTs; fake giveaways or airdrops of NFTs; and impersonation of platforms and brands on social media. These schemes are so prevalent that potential purchasers have been advised to conduct careful research and due diligence, as '[n]obody else is doing that for consumers, so the burden really falls on the individual to protect themselves'").

[35] Ibid., 794.

[36] Ibid., 796–97.

[37] Another related issue that Goforth raises is jurisdiction, given that, for example, the Ethereum block-chain on which many NFT applications are built is based in Switzerland. As a result, it may well prove challenging for consumers to utilize US courts to address fraud or other claims. *See* ibid.

Other authors have lamented the general lack of comprehensive, federal cybersecurity and data privacy laws that has caused consumers in many cases to have to rely on a hodgepodge of state-level data breach notification and other laws to address harms related to NFT transactions.[38] One such incident occurred in March 2021, as has been covered by Jihye Choi in *Fueling the Path Toward the Metaverse*, when an NFT exchange, Nifty Gateway, "suffered a theft in which some of the user accounts were hacked due to a centralized exchange that trades NFTs."[39] Similar concerns surrounding hacks of cryptocurrency exchanges have been similarly prevalent.[40] Specific applications, including the NFT art and music markets, also deserve special consideration as they pertain to cybersecurity, as has been ably discussed by Lawrence Trautman.[41] The remaining law review articles on the topic focus on the intellectual property impact of NFTs,[42] estate and property aspects of NFTs,[43] or utilizing NFT as tools or examples in discussing other areas of regulations.[44] The overall consensus seems to be that there is not enough clarification regarding regulations over NFTs specifically or cryptoassets in general. Indeed, the Congressional Research Service noted in 2022 that the security concerns of blockchain applications including NFT deserve the attention of regulators.[45]

Needless to say, though, just because NFT regulation is not occurring in the United States does not mean that other nations are not acting. For example, the

---

[38] *See, for example*, Scott J. Shackelford, Anne Boustead, & Christos Madrikis, *Defining 'Reasonable' Cybersecurity: Lessons from the States*, 25 YALE J. L. & TECH. 86 (2023). *But see* Anne Toomey McKenna, *A New US Data Privacy Bill Aims to Give You More Control over Information Collected about You – and Make Businesses Change How They Handle Data*, CONVERSATION (August 23, 2022), https://theconversation.com/a-new-us-data-privacy-bill-aims-to-give-you-more-control-over-information-collected-about-you-and-make-businesses-change-how-they-handle-data-188279 (discussing a consumer privacy reform bill with bipartisan support).

[39] *See* Jihye Choi, *Fueling the Path toward the Metaverse*, STAN. J. BLOCKCHAIN L. & POL'Y (2021).

[40] *See, for example*, Elizabeth Napolitano, *ZB Exchange Loses Nearly $5M in Suspected Hack, Pauses Withdrawals*, COINDESK (August 4, 2022), www.coindesk.com/tech/2022/08/04/crypto-exchange-zb-exchange-loses-nearly-5m-in-suspected-hack-pauses-withdrawals/.

[41] *See* Lawrence J. Trautman, *Visual Art and Non-Fungible Tokens*, 50 HOFSTRA L. REV. 361, 422 (2022) ("Crypto-thieves acquire an address's private key by hacking, malware, social engineering, coercion, or any other manner of taking the private key from a person. The thief then uses the stolen private key to send the address' bitcoin to another address under the thief's control, stealing the bitcoin from the true owner").

[42] Katya Fisher, Esq., *Once Upon a Time in Nft: Blockchain, Copyright, and the Right of First Sale Doctrine*, 37 CARDOZO ARTS & ENT. L.J. 629 (2019).

[43] *See* Roee Sarel, *Property Rights in Cryptocurrencies: A Law and Economics Perspective*, 22 N.C. J. L. & TECH. 389 (2021); Richard Ong, *Hard Drive Heritage: Digital Cultural Property in the Law of Armed Conflict*, 53 COLUM. HUM. RTS. L. REV. 247 (2021); *A New Era in Estate Planning for the Digital Age*, PROB. & PROP., March/April 2022, 60.

[44] *See* Jon M. Garon, *When AI Goes to War: Corporate Accountability for Virtual Mass Disinformation, Algorithmic Atrocities, and Synthetic Propaganda*, 49 N. KY. L. REV. 181 (2022); Joshua Fairfield & Niloufer Selvadurai, *Governing the Interface between Natural and Formal Language in Smart Contracts*, 27 UCLA J.L. & TECH. 79 (2022); Chris Brummer, *Disclosure, Dapps and Defi*, 5 STAN. J. BLOCKCHAIN L. & POL'Y 137 (2022).

[45] CRS Report No. R47064, Congressional Research Service (CRS) Reports (Apr. 8, 2022).

National Law Review's most recent regulatory analysis of NFTs, which noted a lack of express binding cybersecurity regulations both in the United States and globally.[46] Some countries such as China have proactively banned all cryptocurrencies, while NFTs may well fall under the scope of existing legislation in nations such as Australia, France, Germany, and Italy.[47] Indeed, given the more comprehensive data governance laws in other jurisdictions, including the European Union's (EU's) General Data Protection Regulation (GDPR), it is likely that Brussels (and perhaps Sacramento) will shape the future of NFTs more than Washington or Beijing. Yet the EU's Markets in Crypto Assets Regulation (MiCA) specifically excludes NFTs from its scope but may still regulate NFT if it is treated as a "security token."[48] Already, conflict of laws cases are emerging, such as a 2022 decision by the Ninth Circuit to upload a French court's determination involving the enforceability of copyrighted material, here photographs of paintings by Pablo Picasso.[49] To date, though, there have been no decided cases on the cybersecurity of NFTs, though we have seen a former employee of the NFT marketplace OpenSea be charged with insider trading.[50]

V IMPLICATIONS

What should "reasonable" cybersecurity resemble for NFTs? The debate has long raged in cybersecurity circles generally across a range of industries and sectors. It is, to put it mildly, a moving target that evolves along with technology and the overall regulatory environment. NFT providers along with small and medium-sized businesses more generally, are rightly confused about what constitutes "reasonable" cybersecurity given the confusion of state-level laws and industry norms.[51] Globally, this is also an area of concern since both California's CCPA and the EU's GDPR call for "reasonable" cybersecurity.[52] Certain European nations, such as Norway, have similar long-standing and well-defined commitments to requiring reasonable cybersecurity practices. For example, Norway's 2019 Security Act requires "that any

---

[46] *See* Sunny J. Kumar, *The NFT Collection: A Brave NFT World – A Regulatory Review of NFTs (Part 2)*, Nat'l L. Rev. (June 30, 2022), www.natlawreview.com/article/nft-collection-brave-nft-world-regulatory-review-nfts-part-2.

[47] Ibid.

[48] Ibid.

[49] Natalie Hanson, *Ninth Circuit Reverses US Judge's Refusal to Enforce French Court's Picasso Copyright Ruling*, Courthouse News Service (July 13, 2022), www.courthousenews.com/appeals-court-reverses-us-judges-refusal-to-enforce-french-courts-picasso-copyright-ruling/.

[50] United States Attorney's Office, U.S. Dep't Justice, Former Employee of NFT Marketplace Charged in First Ever Digital Asset Insider Trading Scheme (June 1, 2022).

[51] *See* Shackelford, Boustead, & Madrikis, Defining 'Reasonable' Cybersecurity.

[52] *See, for example*, Abraham Kang, *What Is "Reasonable Security"? And How to Meet the Requirement*, CSO Online (April 23, 2019), www.csoonline.com/article/3390150/what-is-reasonable-security-and-how-to-meet-the-requirement.html.

sensitive objects, infrastructure information and information systems shall have a 'reasonable' level of security."[53] This marks a departure from previous specific to functional requirements for Norwegian firms, with reasonability being a dynamic concept that will be in constant change based on technological development, innovations, and new threats.[54] As with other jurisdictions including China, though, Norway's classification/grading system will help in this regard with more critical and higher-level threats receiving more stringent security requirements.[55]

More broadly, in the EU, there has been a push to regulate blockchain platforms. For example, in April 2018, twenty-one EU Member States and Norway signed a Declaration that created the European Blockchain Partnership (EBP), which is a cooperation to establish the European Blockchain Services Infrastructure (EBSI) that supports the roll-out of cross-border digital public services with a focus on privacy and security. From that time, eight more countries joined the Partnership bringing the number of partners to thirty as of 2022.[56] Since 2020, EBSI has deployed a peer-to-peer network of distributed nodes across Europe.[57] The nodes support use cases that include critical infrastructure, with each member node creating and broadcasting transactions that update the ledger. In February 2022 alone, the European Commission announced investments in cybersecurity totalling nearly €300 million, though without a focus on NFTs.[58] Still, the EU is ahead of the US government in creating a framework around which innovation can happen, including with regards to privacy and security concerns.

Reasonability, then, is clearly a moving target given technological and regulatory trends as well as the knowledge level of the business in question. For example, in *Patco Construction Co.* v. *People's United Bank*, the First Circuit found that the cybersecurity protections in place were unreasonable under the circumstances because the bank's leadership were aware of ongoing fraud using keyloggers but did not have activity-based monitoring in place to detect such nefarious activity.[59] Thus, bank executives had breached their duty to their customers.[60]

Another related issue here is professionals who hold themselves out as having "specialized skills related to executing a job successfully."[61] Cybersecurity

---

[53] Jeppe Songe-Møller, Erlend W. Holstrøm, & Tore Fjørtoft *The New Security Act*, SCHJØDT (August 30, 2019), www.schjodt.no/news--events/nyhetsbrev/the-new-security-act/.

[54] Kang, *What Is "Reasonable Security"?*.

[55] Møller, Holstrøm, & Fjørtoft, *The New Security Act*.

[56] *See* European Blockchain Partnership, EUR. COMM'N (June 7, 2022), https://digital-strategy.ec .europa.eu/en/policies/blockchain-partnership.

[57] *European Blockchain Services Infrastructure*, EUR. COMM'N (October 2023), https://ec.europa.eu/ digital-building-blocks/wikis/display/EBSI/Home.

[58] Ibid.

[59] *Patco Const. Co.* v. *People's United Bank*, 684 F.3d 197 (1st Cir. 2012).

[60] For other examples of unreasonable cybersecurity practices according to the FTC, *see* Kang, *What Is "Reasonable Security"?*.

[61] Ibid.

professionals, then, would in many cases likely be included under a broad professional standard of care.[62] Further, there is a strong ethical case to be made that business leaders and lawyers should likewise hold themselves up to a higher standard of care given the trust placed in them by their clients and shareholders. This could include an ethical obligation to create a reasonable security-aware culture, as was discussed above.

Hence, a universal baseline standard of "reasonable" cybersecurity is impossible to state for all circumstances. Such a standard, therefore, should be thought of as a sliding scale with certain universal precautions that all businesses, regardless of their size or sophistication, should (i) take into account the sensitivity of the information in question, and (ii) utilize a cost/benefit analysis. With those caveats, it seems clear that given the wide array of cybersecurity frameworks and standards on offer, a safe harbor law, such as Ohio's, has distinct advantages given that it offers businesses a menu of options. Indiana's 2020 attempt fell short, in part due to a rigidity in only permitting the National Institute of Standards and Technology Cybersecurity Framework (NIST CSF). Scott J. Shackelford and co-authors presented data demonstrating that while the NIST CSF is the dominant cybersecurity framework used by most small and medium-sized businesses, many prefer the CIS Top 20, NIST SP 800–53, or other approaches as well as the newer Cybersecurity Maturity Model Certification (CMMC).[63] More can certainly be done to help small business owners by not just developing small business cybersecurity guides for particular frameworks, but highlighting areas of overlap, as was done by the Center for Applied Cybersecurity Research with their Information Security Practice Principles.[64]

The Sedona Conference similarly has made effort in developing a cybersecurity reasonability test to help guide businesses, regulators, and judges.[65] The organizers recognize that while frameworks such as NIST CSF are useful, they are divorced from context, are static, and there is relatively little overlap between diverse approaches – fewer than half of the laws Sedona reviewed, for example, had a common cybersecurity component.[66] Moreover, the guidance that has been offered to help firms interpret these often conflicting and ambiguous definitions is often non-binding, and even where it does have legal force such as with regards to the FTC, oftentimes high-level controls are favored over clear instructions.[67] Without clear guidance, courts are left to determine reasonability, which has

---

[62] Ibid.

[63] *See* Shackelford, Boustead, & Makridis, *Defining 'Reasonable' Cybersecurity. See also About CMMC*, U.S. Dep't Def. (2021), https://dodcio.defense.gov/CMMC/about/.

[64] *See Information Security Practice Principles*, CACR (2024), https://cacr.iu.edu/principles/index.html.

[65] *The Sedona Conference Commentary on a Reasonable Security Test*, 22 Sedona Conf. J. 345 (2021).

[66] Ibid., 353.

[67] Ibid.

been shown to be increasingly essential in data security claims such as those seen in *Dittman* v. *University of Pittsburgh Medical Center*, when the Pennsylvania Supreme Court "affirmed the preexisting, negligence-based duty to safeguard personal information where an employer had required employees to provide personal information and then stored it in a manner that permitted an undetected breach of that information."[68] As such, the Sedona organizers argue for a test for "reasonable" cybersecurity that does not mandate security controls, define "personal information," require that a breach has happened to be actionable, and establish causation, or legal fault.[69] Instead, they opt for an adaptation of the test that Judge Learned Hand famously articulated in *Untied States* v. *Carroll Towing Co.*, which states that $B2 - Bl < (P \times H)1 - (P \times H)2$.[70]

Although the Sedona test is laudable for its utility, reliance on precedent along with industry best practices, and desire not to be either too prescriptive or vague in its terms, there is a concern that the average adjudicator or small business owner – when faced with such a formula – could become even more confused than when reading the list of Top 20 CIS Security Controls. Further, it requires the ability to access quantitative data to fill in values for these variables, which is often not available. This complexity is compounded by the fact that cybersecurity professionals, or software engineers, are not able to implement all of these security controls on their own but instead require an organization-wide effort to include developers, facilities managers, and senior leadership to make and keep cybersecurity fundamental to a firm's operations. Only then could a decision-maker be able to defend their crafting of "a security program that a reasonably prudent security professional would have implemented."[71]

No single checklist or framework will protect at-risk organizations from the wide variety of cyber threats they face. Rather, each decision should be tailored to the particular cybersecurity needs of a given organization, including its functions, footprint, assets, and customer base.[72] Yet the closer we can get to treating cybersecurity as a commodity and enhancing certainty over reasonableness, the more we will help engender economies of scale and drive down costs. Of course, defining "reasonable" cybersecurity for a given organization is just the first step. A potentially even more daunting problem is demonstrating compliance with that framework, or standard, such as in the event of an audit or government investigation, as well as enforcing compliance, and levying penalties when necessary.

---

[68]   Ibid. (citing 196 A.3d 1036 (Pa. 2018)).

[69]   Ibid. at 356–357.

[70]   Ibid. (citing 159 F.2d 169, 173 (2nd Cir. 1947)) ("Where B represents the burden, P represents the probability of harm, H represents the magnitude of harm, subscript 1 represents the controls (or lack thereof) at the time the information steward allegedly had unreasonable security in place, and subscript 2 represents the alternative or supplementary control").

[71]   Kang, *What Is "Reasonable Security"?*.

[72]   Ibid.

VI CONCLUSION

Much has been written in recent years about blockchain technology's promise,[73] given its high potential for disruption.[74] Nevertheless, further research is needed to grapple with both US and global laws and policies related to cybersecurity in the NFT context, potentially making use of novel conceptual tools such as the literature on polycentric governance.

[73] *See for example*, Samuel N. Weinstein, *Blockchain Neutrality*, 55 GA. L. REV. 499, 591 (2021) (describing a strategy that "offers the best chance for blockchain networks to realize their potential to make financial-services markets more competitive and more democratic–an outcome that might reduce the grip of the big banks and big tech in this sector."); Jonathan Rohr & Aaron Wright, *Blockchain-Based Token Sales, Initial Coin Offerings, and the Democratization of Public Capital Markets*, 70 HASTINGS L. J. 463, 523 (2019) (explaining that "[i]n less than a decade, blockchain technology has made fundamental changes to the financial system. Blockchains are supporting alternative currencies and reduce the need for intermediaries to perform certain financial services. When combined with smart contract technology, blockchains hold out the potential to alter traditional methods"); Mark Fenwick & Erik P.M. Vermeulen, *Technology and Corporate Governance Blockchain, Crypto, and Artificial Intelligence*, 48 TEX. J. BUS. L. 1, 16 (2019) (stating that: "artificial intelligence and distributed ledger technologies, including blockchain, are increasingly viewed as offering a superior and more radical long-term alternative. These technologies have the potential to create a genuinely level playing field, transparency and 'applications that run exactly as programmed without any possibility of downtime, censorship, fraud or third-party interference'"); Stephen Stonberg, *Cryptocurrencies Are Democratizing the Financial World. Here's How*, WORLD ECON. FORUM (January 22, 2021), www .weforum.org/agenda/2021/01/cryptocurrencies-are-democratising-the-financial-world-heres-how/.

[74] Aaron Wright and Primavera De Filippi explain that blockchain technology can achieve unique functions by "combining peer-to-peer networks, cryptographic algorithms, distributed data storage, and … decentralized consensus mechanisms." Aaron Wright & Primavera De Filippi, *Decentralized Blockchain Technology and the Rise of Lex Cryptographia* 4–5 (March 12, 2015) (unpublished manuscript), https://papers.ssrn.com/sol3/papers.cfm?abstract_id=2580664.

17

NFTs within the Commercial Supply Chain

Data and Compliance at the Heart of the Value

Anjanette H. Raymond and Chris Draper

I INTRODUCTION

In the usual tech-hype, non-fungible tokens (NFTs)[1] have proven fascinating – and headline-grabbing – experiments in the world of gaming and digital art. Yet more interesting are the practical, real-world uses for NFTs that can exist in everything from titles to supply chains. Moreover, these broader applications are serving as foundational elements in the development of the new Web 3.0[2] that has been

---

The opinions expressed in this chapter are those of the authors.

[1] In the blockchain context, "fungibility" refers to the ability of an item to be interchanged with other items of the same type. However, NFTs are "non-fungible" as they are unique tokens (representing digital assets) that cannot be interchanged with other tokens. As such, when an NFT is minted it is recorded onto the blockchain. Due to the nature of blockchain, NFTs contain immutable data stored across a distributed ledger. This means that no one can unilaterally modify the record of ownership associated with an NFT, nor can anyone make another copy of an NFT.

[2] *See, for example,* Paul Drexler, *Token Wars: How the SEC Can Learn to Embrace Utility Tokens*, 72 DUKE L.J. 5 (2023) (explaining that "the new internet would allow users to … transact through decentralized platforms that use consensus-based mechanisms to verify users' exchanges. And rather than rely on fiat money, users would use the platforms' native currencies,"); Zoe Niesel, *#personaljurisdiction: A New Age of Internet Contacts*, 94 IND. L.J. 103, 137 (2019) (describing the goal of Web 3.0 applications as "immersion with an ecosystem that understands itself and is able to freely correct and publish information through the use of artificial intelligence."); Leon Yehuda Anidja, Nizan Geslevich Packin, & Argyri Panezi. *The Matrix of Privacy: Data Infrastructure in the AI-Powered Metaverse*, HARV. L. & POL'Y REV. (forthcoming 2023), SSRN: https://ssrn.com/abstract=4363208 (explaining that while it is still unclear what Web 3.0 would look like, and how blockchain-dependent it would be, "some envision it to offer a decentralized digital experience that would allow users to take back control over their data by operating without intermediaries thereby enhancing their autonomy and privacy."); *Web 1.0 vs Web 2.0 vs Web 3.0 vs Web 4.0 vs Web 5.0 – A Bird's Eye on the Evolution and Definition*, FLAT WORLD BUS. (May 2018), https://flatworldbusiness.wordpress.com/flat-education/previously/web-1-0-vs-web-2-0-vs-web-3-0-a-bird-eye-on-the-definition (discussing the evolution of the web). In addition, certain commentators believe that the seeds of Web 3.0 were realistically planted in 2009 when Bitcoin was initially introduced and first launched. *See, for example,* Balázs Bodó & Alexandra Giannopoulou, *The Logics of Technology Decentralization – The Case of Distributed Ledger Technologies, in* BLOCKCHAIN AND WEB 3.0: SOCIAL, ECONOMIC, AND TECHNOLOGICAL CHALLENGES 114 (Massimo Ragnedda and Giuseppe Destefanis, eds., 2019) ("The Nakamoto paper describes a technology that can be applied without needing established, centralized, and trusted intermediaries"); Mary C. Lacity and Steven C. Lupien, BLOCKCHAIN FUNDAMENTALS FOR WEB 3.0 99–152 (2022).

described as a futuristic web and is of particular interest for the design of domains
and other web addresses such as emails. However, as with so many other forms of
blockchain-derived tokens,[3] domain and mail addresses can be performed by any
number of other functions – and as such, the question is, why use an NFT or other
blockchain-based solutions? Despite the uncertainty of wide-scale adoption, numerous websites and digital communication channels are full of early adopters that are
actively buying up addresses on these new networks. Thus, the question is when and
why should we use the newest technology. The answer might surprise you!

II NFTS IN THE SUPPLY CHAIN

In the context of a supply chain,[4] using NFTs make sense because companies
are concerned with maintaining trustworthy digital data related to their physical
world assets. In situations such as this, companies can benefit by using NFTs to
represent their physical assets digitally. For example, as will be discussed in greater
detail below, in the context of the supply chain, NFTs can assist in tracing products
throughout the supply chains, can confirm ownership, and can verify any product
certifications or compliance driven requirements.

Because NFTs are digital representations of real-world objects, supply chains can
use NFTs to track a variety of products, materials, and services.[5] For example, NFTs
can allow warehouse companies to create digital representations for packages and
other types of "goods" for delivery and/or service. In all cases, the shipment moves
through stages of the delivery or other processes, with the process of transportation

---

[3] For more on blockchain-derived tokens *see, for example,* Sean Kwon, *Regulation of Defi Lending:
Agency Supervision on Decentralization,* 24 Col. Sci. & Law J. 379, 394–395 (2023) (explaining how
DeFi relies on a standalone peer-to-peer flow of funds that is facilitated via tokenization and smart
contracts operating); Jonathan Rohr & Aaron Wright, *Blockchain-Based Token Sales, Initial Coin
Offerings, and the Democratization of Public Capital Markets,* 70 Hastings L. J. 463, 523 (2019)
(explaining how in less than a decade, blockchain technology and the tokens it powers have offered
various fundamental changes to various industries, including the financial one, as it reduces "the
need for intermediaries to perform certain … services. When combined with smart contract technology, blockchains hold out the potential to alter traditional methods").

[4] The entire ecosystem of producing and delivering a product or service, from sourcing the raw materials to the final delivery of the product or service to end users.

[5] An example of using blockchain-powered tokens for non-digital assets is in supply chain management,
where it can be used to track inventory from production to point of sale, allowing for improved transparency and traceability. *See Using Blockchain to Drive Supply Chain Transparency,* Deloitte (2024),
www2.deloitte.com/us/en/pages/operations/articles/blockchain-supply-chain-innovation.html.   The
advantages associated with using blockchain technology and specifically blockchain-powered tokens
in this context include the ability to fairly simply track products back to their origin, as well as target
responses to any issues that may arise in connection with these products and their shipment, and make
the data sharing more democratic across different users, all around the world. *See, for example, How
Blockchain Technology Will Lead to Safer Food,* Institute of Food Technologies (February
2018),   www.ift.org/news-and-publications/blog/2018/february/how-blockchain-technology-will-lead-
to-safer-food; Mireille van Hilten, Guido Ongena & Pascal Ravesteijn, *Blockchain for Organic Food
Traceability: Case Studies on Drivers and Challenges,* 3 Frontiers in Blockchain 1 (2020).

and storage and other aspects necessary for successful delivery to be verified and stored in the chain, in real time.[6]

In addition, because blockchain-based activity contains an immutable record of transactions, third parties can easily confirm the origin of a physical world product connected to the NFT as well as current and past owners of the product or service providers connected to the NFT. For instance, the luxury watch brand, Breitling, introduced an NFT passport for each of its watches, which allows customers to receive the physical watch along with a digital version.[7] And, of course, there are currently applications of such technology in the service arena when a particular item/product/commodity moves through various stages of services that result in the final delivery of a refined product.

In the long term, this type of coordinated activity may lead to supply chain collaborations amongst and all along the supply environments. To date, it is cumbersome and oftentimes difficult to fully integrate collaboration across supply chain providers. Supply chain collaboration would allow organizations to work closely together to meet shared objectives, such as cost reduction and overall supply chain performance. The supply chain partnership formed between P&G and Walmart is a well-cited example of collaboration that led to increased profit margins, better decision-making, reduced inventory runs, and a more customer-centric approach.[8] As can be inferred, blockchain-based solutions deployed within the supply chain environment, especially in situations where interoperability and coordination are prioritized will likely increase efficiencies and reduce the costs incurred when the supplier needs to acquire the goods and services.[9]

Moreover, there is growing support for the use of metadata as a mechanism to improve accurate information about the goods themselves.[10] Because

---

[6] *See* Muddassir Ahmed, *NFTs & Supply Chain: What Are the Applications?*, SCMDOJO BLOG (2022), www.scmdojo.com/nfts-supply-chain-what-are-the-applications/.

[7] *See* Stephanie Girod, *Breitling Shows Other Luxury Brands How to Future Proof with Agility*, FORBES (August 27, 2021).

[8] Michael Grean & Michael J. Shaw, *Supply-Chain Partnership between P&G and Wal-Mart*, in E-BUSINESS MANAGEMENT: INTEGRATION OF WEB TECHNOLOGIES WITH BUSINESS MODELS Shaw 155–171 (Michael J. Shaw, ed., 2002).

[9] *See* Nir Kshetri, 1 *Blockchain's Roles in Meeting Key Supply Chain Management Objectives*, 39 INT'L J. INFO. MGMT. 80 (2018).

[10] Xuan-Thao Nguyen, *Blockchain Games and a Disruptive Corporate Business Model*, 6 STAN. J. BLOCKCHAIN L. & POL'Y 43, 51 (2023) (explaining that "[w]ith physical goods, NFTs can be used to tag tangible goods for purposes of origin tracing, ownership, provenance verification, and authenticity certification." This improvement of accurate information about goods can in turn "lead to a reduction of theft, counterfeits, or fraud in sectors dealing with precious gemstones, luxury goods, arts, supply chains, and trade finance"); Judith A. Lee & Shuo (Josh) Zhang, *Non-Financial Applications for Distributed Ledger Technology and Blockchain*, in PAYMENT SYSTEMS AND ELECTRONIC FUND TRANSFERS GUIDE (2021) ("Proof-of-origin applications can also be used for any high-value product, including gemstones, art, and food. Using distributed ledger technology, a gemstone supplier could provide evidence of authenticity (particularly important now, when synthetic diamonds are approaching gem standards) and compliance with international regimes such as the Kimberly

blockchain-based solutions allow for the representation of real-world objects in a digital form, some argue that the digital form can be thought of as the real-world object's "digital twin."[11] The digital twin allows for the real-world metadata about the object, such as its identity, current physical location, responsible party, possession, container temperature, and other metrics, to be attached to this digital twin.[12] This attachment is done in order to yield useful insights about the condition of these objects in the real world and updated as conditions change, which presents an accurate and timely view of the physical object to all involved parties helping the detection of lost, stolen, and counterfeit goods and materials.[13]

Finally, the use of NFTs can provide trusted certifications such as "organic" and "fair trade" and may even be able to produce certifications that serve to provide governmental agencies with compliance documents.[14] To accomplish this, third-party

Process"); Miriam Farhi, Andrew Grant, & Colleen Ganin, *The Digital Opportunities & Issues That Luxury Brands Need to Consider*, THE FASHION LAW (September 29, 2021), www.thefashionlaw .com/from-virtual-fashion-to-big-data-a-look-at-the-emerging-digital-issues-that-luxury-brands-need-to-consider ("NFTs also have touted as promising anti-counterfeiting applications").

[11] The evolution of "digital twin" as a word over the past few years has been quite interesting. Traditionally a digital twin was a physics-based fast-running model that allowed for quickly estimating certain parameters of a physical thing too complicated to accurately model in real work objects like a heat pump or air-conditioning compressor (with "too complicated" often referring to things as conceptually "basic" as fluid). More recently the concept of a digital twin has expanded in scope to incorporate a more "mushy" definition, often referring to a digital archive of qualities versus the traditional predictive model components.

[12] For more on this in the context of Web 3.0 and specifically the metaverse, *see generally* Joshan Abraham et al., *Digital Twins: The Foundation of the Enterprise Metaverse*, MCKINSEY & COMPANY 2 (2022), www.mckinsey.com/capabilities/mckinsey-digital/our-insights/digital-twins-the-foundation-of-the-enterprise-metaverse (explaining how the concept of digital twins refers to creating spaces that encompass an equal digital representation of any physical asset, person, process, or operation using data flows across and beyond the metaverse. The report describes how in the metaverse, AI algorithms are employed in processing real-time data to achieve a highly realistic simulation of physical objects and predict their future development and condition).

[13] *See* Christian Petersson Nielsen, Elias Ribeiro da Silva, & Fei Yu, *Digital Twins and Blockchain – Proof of Concept*, 93 PROCEDIA CIRP 251 (2020).

[14] U.S. DEP'T OF TREASURY, CRYPTO-ASSETS: IMPLICATIONS FOR CONSUMERS, INVESTORS, AND BUSINESSES 24–25 (Sept. 2022), https://home.treasury.gov/system/files/136/CryptoAsset_EO5.pdf ("NFTs have a number of potential future applications, including: (i) enabling the recording and verification of transfers of real estate ownership; (ii) facilitating automatic royalty payments for music and film; (iii) preventing duplication and counterfeits in the titling of other property and consumer goods; (iv) enabling more digital credentials, including identification, licensing, certification; and (v) facilitating financial industry legal compliance"); *see also* Oleg Fonarov, *What Is the Role of NFTs in the Metaverse?*, FORBES (March 11, 2022), www.forbes.com/sites/forbestechcouncil/2022/03/11/what-is-the-role-of-nfts-in-the-metaverse/?sh=e8355b36bb87; Eric L. Sophir, Eugenia Wang & Kathleen E. Wegrzyn, *Not By the Same Token: NFTs in Supply Chain*, FOLEY (November 16, 2021), www.foley .com/en/insights/publications/2021/11/not-by-the-same-token-nfts-in-supply-chain

> ("NFTs work for supply chain purposes because companies are particularly concerned with maintaining trustworthy digital data related to their physical world assets. Therefore, companies can benefit by using NFTs to represent their physical assets digitally. Some ways in which NFTs address supply chain needs are in the areas of tracing products through supply chains, identifying product origin and authenticating ownership, and verifying product certifications").

certifiers for product standards or labor safety requirements could mint an NFT with the appropriate certification onto the blockchain, which supply chain members would pass downstream until it reaches the end user in the supply chain who can ultimately access the certification via a web link.[15]

III DATA INTEGRITY AND SECURITY

Data security and data integrity are two of the largest benefits in the use of NFTs and other blockchain-based solutions. This is especially true in the lifecycle management of and related product-driven data.[16]

Blockchain-based solutions function of connecting multiple chains to digitized products or parts used in manufacturing helps to resolve supply chain integrity issues, including counterfeit goods. In fact, as authors Huang et al. state:

> The blockchain is used for data storage through cryptography that ensur[es] only eligible participators can access the corresponding data. The change sensitive characteristic of blockchain can ensure data authenticity as well. In addition, the concept of smart contract can be used to execute some actions automatically to increase data sharing efficiency.[17]

In this way, blockchain-based technology can enhance overall cybersecurity of the data and permit data sharing amongst and across environments, thereby strengthening identity management and data validation.[18]

IV MONITORING AND COMPLIANCE

As described above, NFTs create a digital identity for every part included in a system. For example, each semiconductor (in fact any part, from a bumper to a steering wheel) could have its own digital identity stored in the system in the automotive industry. And each semiconductor and other electronic connect device could update data automatically via time-stamping and geo-positioning.[19]

As such, NFTs could help identify the product line and manufacturing batch more quickly – allowing tracing and back-tracking of an entire supply chain. As will be described below, an easy example is within the trucking sector in which every tiny detail is fed into one digital ledger.[20] While blockchain is nothing new to the

---

[15] Ricardo Borges dos Santos, Nunzio Marco Torrisi & Rodrigo Palucci Pantoni, *Third Party Certification of Agri-Food Supply Chain Using Smart Contracts and Blockchain Tokens*, 21 SENSORS 5207 (2021).

[16] *See* Sihan Huang, Guoxin Wang, Yan Yan, & Xiongbing Fang, *Blockchain-Based Data Management for Digital Twin of Product*, 54 J. MFG. SYS. (2020).

[17] *See id.*

[18] *See id.*

[19] *See ibid.*

[20] *See* Jack Daleo, *NFTs Are Coming to a Supply Chain Near You*, FREIGHT WAVES (2021), www.freightwaves.com/news/nfts-are-coming-to-a-supply-chain-near-you.

supply chain – companies like Maersk,[21] as well as Amazon,[22] which is the leading U.S. e-commerce platform, have been using blockchain-based solutions to track the movement of their products for years – the technology now allows for more advanced uses. For example, in an ongoing basis trucks undergo repairs and maintenance. While almost every state requires maintenance and upkeep of the fleet, few have a true easy and efficient way of tracking the information. In these situations, non-fungible tokens will be capable of giving the details of every repair made to the truck and can thus have the ability to potentially look out for future breakdowns and maintenance needs.

Yet there is a much more forward-thinking potential. Imagine tracking carbon emissions and having that tracking feed into an automated compliance framework. Internet of Things (IoT) smart meter could (and can) measure power consumption by the companies. These IoT devices provide readings that have the potential to reduce costs in terms of manpower but also have the potential to reduce error and reporting irregularities. Of course, this is a simple use case, in fact the IoT sensor can directly exchange information with the environment and capture carbon emissions either by the company's operations or during transportation. The data collected from these IoT sensors can be stored on the blockchain. As such, as soon as the platform receives the data, smart contracts can be executed and the platform can calculate the carbon footprints. Moreover, as described above, the company's carbon footprint report *will be* stored on a blockchain in a tamper-proof manner. And, of course, all of these carbon credits would be maintained on a blockchain, allowing compliance reporting as well.[23]

Finally, it would be possible to imagine a system in which carbon credits on the blockchain are even traded because any transaction of carbon credits between the companies would be recorded on the digital ledger in a transparent and immutable manner.[24] The technology is not years away. In fact, MintCarbon allows carbon-offset project owners to mint their offsets into NFT,[25] while CarbonABLE[26] links NFTs with offsetting projects based on real natural resources,[27] and Moss[28]

---

[21] See Nye Longman, *Maersk and IBM Are Bringing Blockchain Tech to the Shipping Industry*, Supply Chain (2020), https://supplychaindigital.com/technology/maersk-and-ibm-are-bringing-blockchain-tech-shipping-industry#:~:text=IBM%20and%20Maersk%20have%20just,chain%20pilot%20using%20blockchain%20technology.&text=The%20blockchain%20will%20begin%20scaling,customs%20authorities%20later%20in%202017.

[22] See Linda Baker, *Amazon Looks to Establish Supply Chain Trust with New Blockchain Patent*, Freight Waves (2020), www.freightwaves.com/news/amazon-looks-to-establish-trust-with-new-blockchain-patent.

[23] See, for example, Nagi An, *Using NFTs as Carbon Credits*, NFT News Today (October 5, 2022), https://nftnewstoday.com/2022/10/05/using-nfts-as-carbon-credits/.

[24] See ibid.

[25] See ibid.

[26] CarbonABLE (2024), https://carbonable.io/.

[27] See An, *Using NFTs*.

[28] Moss (2023), https://nft.moss.earth/.

distributes encrypted digital ownership certificates as NFTs.[29] These digital ownership NFTs represent land shares of its Amazon rainforest preservation project.[30] In this way, NFTs are directly linked to a specific high-quality carbon-offset initiative.[31]

V SUPPLY CHAIN USES: A REAL-WORLD EXAMPLE

The permanence and transparency of NFT-based compliance tools are both their greatest strength and challenge.[32] For example, while an NFT can capture every quality a truck manufacturer may want to know about its regulated components, making all the qualities of those components fully transparent to every related party could result in disclosure of valuable company secrets. As an alternative example, calculating the impact of greenhouse gas (GHG) reduction efforts that depends on trees sequestering carbon dioxide relies on digital twins that are continually updating, making permanent project impact valuations nearly impossible. One NFT-based framework introduced in 2021 that addresses these issues is the Regenerative Authentication Credit (RAC).

The RAC framework was designed by renewable fuel feedstock producers and traders to decrease the compliance costs of environmental, social, and governance (ESG) contributors that do not have standardized digital twins, universally accepted input-to-output conversion factors, or centralized compliance authorities.[33] For example, the alternative treatment or reuse of wastewater separated from waste

---

[29] *See* An, *Using NFTs.*

[30] *See* ibid.

[31] *See* ibid.

[32] For more on the permanence of NFTs, *see* Hadar Y. Jabotinsky & Michal Lavi, *NFT for Eternity*, 56 U. MICH. J. L. REFORM 827 (2023) (describing how NFTs offer a unique level of permanence due to their storage on blockchain technology, which ensures that the information associated with each token is unalterable and provides verifiable proof of ownership. The authors argue that while the decentralized technology has the positive potential to serve as an engine for free speech, offering a way to bypass censorship, it also comes with considerable risks. Tokenized speech is permanent and can virtually not be easily deleted or altered, posing significant threats to individual dignity and public interest).

[33] *See, for example,* Elizabeth Pollman, *The Making and Meaning of ESG* (September 12, 2022) (Uni. of Penn, Inst. for Law & Econ Research Paper No. 22–23, European Corporate Governance Institute – Law Working Paper No. 659/2022), https://ssrn.com/abstract=4219857 (stating that: "ESG is one of the most notable trends in corporate governance, management, and investment of the past two decades. It is at the center of the largest and most contentious debates in contemporary corporate and securities law"); Nizan G. Packin & Srinivas Nippani, *Ranking Season: Combating Commercial Banks' Systemic Discrimination of Consumers*, 59 AM. BUS. L. J. 123, 136 (2022) (discussing how ESG has become such a globally significant trend); Stavros Gadinis & Amelia Miazad, *Corporate Law and Social Risk*, 73 VAND. L. REV. 1401 (2020); George S. Georgiev, *The Human Capital Management Movement in U.S. Corporate Law*, 95 TUL. L. REV. 639, 675 (2021) (describing how "a significant number of companies now include ESG metrics in the incentive compensation plans for corporate executives"); Dana Brakman Reiser & Anne Tucker, *Buyer Beware: Variation and Opacity in ESG and ESG Index Funds*, 41 CARDOZO L. REV. 1921, 1924 (2020) (stating that in 2019, global ESG assets under management reached $30 trillion).

products like used cooking oil (UCO) reduces the current burden borne by water treatment facilities or the wider watershed networks impacted. Yet water treatment models and ESG targets for water-quality improvement are still far from standardized. Entities that are implementing wastewater reduction actions that benefit the wider watershed can document the actions taken, tokenize the evidence of those actions, and integrate that evidentiary token into an RAC, with the RAC then being the backing of a tradeable NFT. Entities that have a collective obligation to a wider watershed yet are unable to further reduce their negative contributions can contribute to its improvement in an auditable, transparent manner by purchasing the RACs associated with the originator's positive contributions, thus transferring the intangible value of those actions to the buyer. Since their introduction in the renewable fuel feedstock industry, RACs have also been used more broadly to support efforts ranging from food insecurity reduction to endangered animal habitat protection.

The RAC framework produces customizable contracts that functionally mimic the renewable energy certificate (REC) and renewable identification number (RIN) tools that are overseen by the United States Environmental Protection Agency (EPA) for renewably generated electricity and renewable fuels, respectively. The REC and RIN tools allow the desired intangible benefits (i.e., production of "green energy" and "sustainable fuels") to be separated from the tangible object that created them (i.e., the specific kilowatt hours of electricity and gallons of fuel that are created for consumption) if the origin and chain of custody of those tangible objects can be proven (i.e., auditable documentation can be provided as demanded for all inputs and transactions relevant to producing and consuming the tangible objects). Separating this intangible value using an REC or RIN is vital for facilitating a viable renewable energy economy because those responsible for ensuring the desired intangible value is generated (i.e., more electricity is generated using renewable means) are rarely capable of directly producing or purchasing the tangible product that creates the intangible benefit (e.g., an industry with a renewable electricity requirement may be too far from the windmills that generate the renewable electricity it is required to use). However, the cost of operating the REC and RIN programs in a centralized manner as the EPA does with traditional compliance technologies and auditing strategies is prohibitively costly for smaller entities working with unconventional materials.

The NFT architecture employed by the RAC framework drastically reduces compliance costs and risk in two major ways. First, the ability for an NFT to tokenize any digital file (e.g., identically to how there are no restrictions on the digital art form that can be converted into an NFT) allows a RAC to incorporate a wide range of custom terms or restrictions that can be verified at a later date without ever sharing the original file or its sensitive contents with a central authority. Second, archiving each token on a blockchain provides a chain of custody tracking and auditable certainty that any legal obligations contained in the tokenized file are permanently protected from modification or forgery.

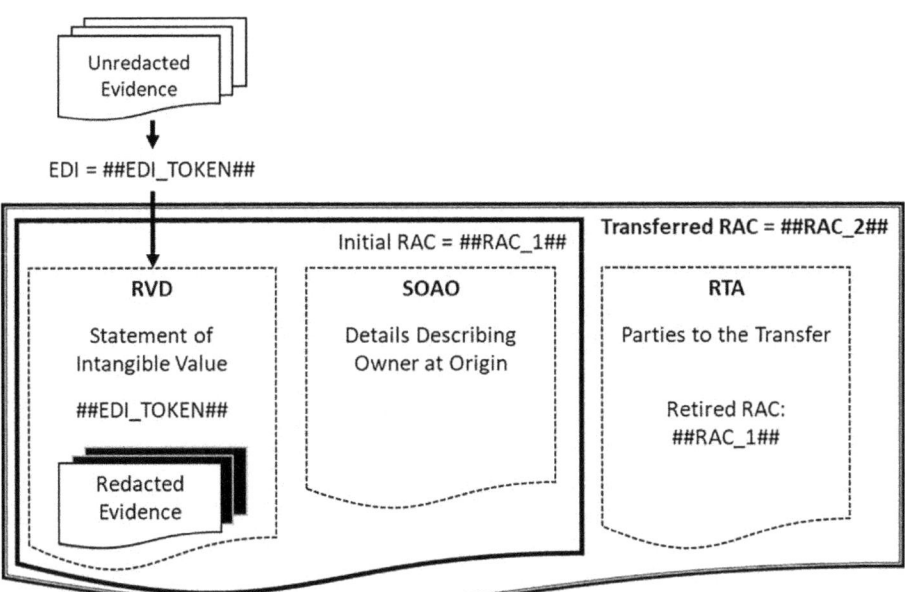

FIGURE 17.1 Relationships between the unredacted evidence, EDI, redacted evidence, RVD, SOAO, RTA, and RTA within the RAC framework.

The first platform for ESG-related RACs is the RAC Clearinghouse, launched in 2021 and built upon the Trokt Neopublic Blockchain network.[34] The contract defining each RAC in the RAC Clearinghouse must be made up of no less than an RAC value definition (RVD) and a statement of ownership at origin (SOAO). If the intangible value of an RAC is transferred from the originator, a new RAC is created that both prepends an RAC transfer agreement (RTA) to the old, previously existing RAC and identifies that the previously existing RAC is now retired. This process of continually creates a new RAC upon each transfer by prepending an RTA and retiring the previously existing RAC is functionally equivalent to traditional property deeds (Figure 17.1).

RAC generation starts with collecting the type and quality of evidence an end purchaser will deem sufficient to prove the intangible value claimed in the RAC. This dependence on market participants to define appropriate evidentiary standards is a core feature of NFT-based Web 3.0 compliance concepts that exist outside structures requiring centralized authorities. For renewable fuels applications, this evidence includes the source of every coproduct or byproduct that was collected or purchased before it was processed and sold to a renewable fuel producer. This

[34] The RAC Clearinghouse is still an invite-only platform as of January 1, 2023. *See* RAC (2023), www .searchracs.com.

evidence can be collected through or use any range of sources, from manual documentation to IoT devices. For renewable fuels applications, this evidence includes items like bills of laden that prove when ownership of a material is transferred, scale tickets that prove the weight of products coming into a facility, pump speeds that indicate how much material has flowed through a particular process, and invoices that show when product was bought or sold at what prices. This type of data is highly sensitive, containing customer or vendor details or trade secrets that would commercially harm the originator if released.

It is reasonable for a counterparty to expect an originator to maintain this type of sensitive compliance evidence in the event the intangible value the purchaser requires is questioned by a future counterparty. Yet traditional methods for ensuring this evidence exists can be commercially risky for the originator. Compliance with renewable fuels regulations like 40 CFR §§ 80.1454(d)-(n) are traditionally interpreted as giving the EPA authority to demand all sensitive collection, processing, and sales data must be turned over in its entirety. Even the least onerous low carbon fuel regulations and requirements, like those of the California Air Resources Board (CARB) or Low Carbon Fuel Standard (LCFS), facilitate risk-based auditing by requiring a regulated entity to give the centralized authority limited access directly to their internal data. Neither of these strategies are reasonable in a Web 3.0 environment where a major objective of the RAC framework is to facilitate transactions between untrusted parties.

The RVD is the component of the RAC framework designed both to protect sensitive data and enable buyer transparency. The RVD is made up of three parts: a statement defining the intangible value covered by the RAC, an evidentiary documentation identifier (EDI), and a redacted version of the sensitive evidence proving intangible value was generated. The statement defining the intangible value covered by the RAC may be all or just a part of the intangible value that may be created. For example, the RAC Clearinghouse held multiple RACs on January 1, 2023, that were owned by Eat Greater Des Moines. Each RAC was associated with an event where Eat Greater Des Moines picked up food that was no longer needed by a donor and redirected it to individuals who were able to accept the food. For each of these food rescues, Eat Greater Des Moines created three different RACs: one that assigned the intangible value of feeding people, one that assigned the intangible value of the food being diverted from the landfill it would have otherwise gone to, and one that assigned the intangible value of the GHG reduction that occurred through the reduced demand for processing and shipping food that would replace that being wasted. Since all of these intangible values were created by a single food rescue event, all three RACs shared the same EDI that was equal to the SHA256 token archived in the Trokt network representing the unredacted compliance documentation, often called the "Trokt thumbprint." Finally, the RVD included a redacted version of the internal compliance documentation that made all sensitive information unreadable (e.g., donor contact details, volunteer names, or other identifying characteristics that could commercially damage any involved party).

Once the SOAO and RTV are prepended to the RVD, this combined contract becomes the RAC, a SHA256 hash of the combined document is generated as its token, and this NFT is stored in the Trokt network. In the RAC Clearinghouse, both this combined document with the redacted evidentiary documentation and the thumbprint of the unredacted RAC can be viewed by anyone with access to the RAC Clearinghouse.

Unlike compliance by centralized authorities, being provided both the redacted documentation and the token for the unredacted RAC allows a Web 3.0-viable level of future compliance. For any future buyer or auditor who has a legal right to force the originator to turn over the sensitive compliance information for a specific RAC, the auditor does not require access to the originator's core systems or any special access that can compromise security in any other part of the originator's systems. Instead, the originator can send or provide access to only the unredacted RAC and its authenticity can be validated by independently hashing and comparing that thumbprint to the EDI contained in the RAC. This use of the NFT-based RAC framework and its implementation in the RAC Clearinghouse allow for communities to collectively invest in unconventional commodities in a traditionally trust-free environment.

VI CRITICISMS

NFTs and other blockchain-based solutions are not without critics and the criticism can be loud and potentially spot on, in at least some instances. First, it is important to acknowledge NFTs have a cult following – and a potential disaster yet to occur – as it relates to NFTs tied to a singular object such as a digital artwork or photograph.[35] There are two primary causes for why an NFT fiasco in the art space is practically unavoidable. First, NFTs are caught up in the same misinformation surrounding the concept of "trustless trust" that makes too many people believe that anything that has been turned into an NFT is free of forgery when the addition of NFT protection only ensures permanence.[36] NFT protection neither prevents art theft nor digital modification that is imperceivable to humans, a fact that has already seen significant confusion in the NFT art space.[37] Second, since a major concept

---

[35] *See* Amanda Yeo, *Think Cryptocurrency Is Bad? NFTs Are Even Worse*, MASHABLE (March 10, 2021), https://mashable.com/article/nft-cryptocurrency-bad-environment-art.

[36] *See, for example*, Will Gottsegen, *NFT Forgeries Aren't Going Away*, COINDESK (December 20, 2021), www.coindesk.com/layer2/2021/12/20/nft-forgeries-arent-going-away/ (quoting digital artist Lois van Baarle, whose artwork was minted as NFTs on the marketplace OpenSea without her permission, stating that: "NFTs are supposedly about authenticity, but these platforms [NFT marketplaces] … do less than the bare minimum when it comes to making sure that the images are being uploaded by their original creators"); Carol R. Goforth, *How Nifty! But Are NFTs Securities Commodities, or Something Else?*, 90 UMKC L. REV. 775, 776 (2022) ("The reality is that NFT fraudsters are already in the picture. In some cases, artists wake up to find that their art is being packaged and sold as NFTs by unauthorized third parties").

[37] Because NFTs are stored on blockchain systems, typically decentralized ones, people might believe that these assets are immune against Web 2.0 vulnerabilities, such as data alteration. However, less known is the fact that the content and metadata associated with an NFT exist only on an off-blockchain,

propelling NFT art creation was ongoing royalties which could only be collected if the NFT remained on its originating chain, there are no NFT art exchanges that are truly decentralized.[38] While all exchanges accept cryptocurrencies as payments that may log their transactions on a distributed ledger, the exchanges themselves are centralized entities exposed to the same risk of fraud or threat seen in the numerous high-profile exchange failures from MT. Gox to FTX.[39] Of course, what is described above relies on the same technology – but it is not the same use, not at all.

Second, NFTs are environmentally irresponsible because they contribute to causing planet-threatening environmental conditions like climate change.[40] Yet the research (and criticism) is mostly directed toward cryptocurrency mining and new technology is changing this conversation, at least for entities willing to make such a commitment. For example, El Salvador is using geothermal energy to create energy for some of their bitcoin mining operations.[41] Moreover, NFTs used in the supply chain will typically depend on proof of stake or hybrid networks that do not require mining – nor do they need to be mined or anything similar.[42] Again, the technology has real potential, without the mining conversation overwhelming the discussion.

Finally, NFTs are unregulated. This may be a real issue for everyone, even those using NFT technology without any mining or digital art component. Why? New regulation is often brutal and done without fully understanding the technology. Examples of regulating to the hype over the reality are already seen in how Wyoming has fundamentally threatened its corporate and commercial code by not carefully reconciling how enforcement of commonly accepted governance norms can possibly be enforced when allowing the existence of distributed autonomous organizations (DAOs).[43] As such, one wonders if the regulation of NFTs and other blockchain-based solutions will not be a bit of a mess – with supply chain type NFTs

---

centralized server, making it vulnerable to the very risks associated with Web 2.0 content, such as theft and digital modification of the content. *See* Yash Gupta & Jayanth Kumar, *Identifying Security Risks in NFT Platforms*, COMPUTERS & SEC. (2022), https://arxiv.org/abs/2204.01487; and Chapter 16 of this Handbook.

[38] *See, for example,* Peter Van Valkenburgh, *There's No Such Thing As a Decentralized Exchange*, THE BLOCK (October 3, 2020), www.theblock.co/post/79768/theres-no-such-thing-as-a-decentralized-exchange; @loudposts, *Are NFT Marketplaces Really Decentralized?*, HACKERNOON (January 9, 2022), https://hackernoon.com/are-nft-marketplaces-really-decentralized.

[39] *See, for example,* David Yaffe-Bellany, *Thefts, Fraud and Lawsuits at the World's Biggest NFT Marketplace*, N.Y. TIMES (June 6, 2022), www.nytimes.com/2022/06/06/technology/nft-opensea-theft-fraud.html.

[40] *See* Andy Storey, *7 Reasons Why Everyone Seems to Hate NFTs*, POSTER GRIND (January 6, 2022), https://postergrind.com/7-reasons-why-everyone-seems-to-hate-nfts/.

[41] *See* Daily Hodl, *El Salvador Begins Bitcoin Mining Operation Using Geothermal Energy from Volcanoes*, DAILY HODL (October 4, 2021), https://dailyhodl.com/2021/10/04/el-salvador-begins-bitcoin-mining-operation-using-geothermal-energy-from-volcanoes/.

[42] *How Do NFTs Impact the Environment?*, COINTELEGRAPH (2023), https://cointelegraph.com/learn/nfts-environmental-impact (noting that mining NFTs using proof of stake mechanisms consumes less energy than mining using proof of work mechanisms).

[43] *See* Jordan Teague, *Starting a DAO in the USA? Steer Clear of DAO Legislation*, THE DEFIANT (2022), https://thedefiant.io/starting-a-dao-in-the-usa-steer-clear-of-dao-legislation.

being caught in the regulation of the "other" blockchain-based uses – such as digital art and cryptocurrency. At the same time, efforts like those in Iowa that defined distributed ledger technology and smart contracts,[44] such that had a deference to their original intent and expansiveness,[45] give hope that NFT legislation could be effectively pared down to the fundamentals of the technology instead of targeting the wider issues of some unavoidable, future FTX-style incident. The absence of well-drafted legislation might be a major issue long term – and is, of course, something everyone should keep an eye on.

VII RECOMMENDATIONS

Implementing NFTs into a supply chain application requires careful consideration of the technology's fundamentals over the hype of its current uses. Those designing an NFT-based solution for their supply chain needs should consider:

  i. *An NFT is just a token of a digital file.* The currently unregulated flexibility around NFTs can allow them to be used as a power validation tool, yet they offer no intrinsic protection outside the technology's limitations.
 ii. *NFT-based smart contracts are not always contracts.* Blockchain-based smart contracts are widely recognized as UETA-compliant electronic agreements, yet there is nothing inherent in an NFT that ensures they will always generate a legal contract.
iii. *An NFT that is used as a security is a security.* A contract that falls within the definition of a security is not exempt from security laws by tokenizing it, so one must be careful to ensure the underlying structure of any deal is not placing unreasonable risk mitigation on an NFT-based vehicle.
 iv. *NFT exchanges are highly specialized.* It is technologically easy to create an NFT exchange, yet difficult to build an efficient marketplace, so one must be careful not to overvalue the NFT demand if NFT sales are factored into any revenue projections.

VIII CONCLUSION

While NFTs have proven themselves to be a headline-grabbing-phenomenon, practical real-world uses are beginning to emerge. The real-world broader uses are being utilized as the building blocks to a new Web 3.0 architecture and are of particular interest for the design of domains and other practical applications, such as integrity, security, and regulatory compliance. Despite the uncertainty of widescale

---

[44] For example, *see* Iowa Code Electronic Transactions – Computer Agreements § 554D.103.
[45] *See* ibid.

adoption, numerous websites and digital communication channels are full of early adopters that are actively buying up addresses on these new networks. And at least one area, the supply chain, might have real-world instances where NFTs and other blockchain-based solutions can and will be used. Yet questions remain as to the definition and regulation to be undertaken. Time will tell if these technologies provide long-term worth and prove effective. As of now, it is worth considering – and planning – for the possibility of this particular real-world utilization.

PART VI

Other Legal Issues with NFTs

18

NFTs, the Metaverse, and Emerging
Technology Governance

Jon M. Garon

I INTRODUCTION

To fully understand the concept of non-fungible token (NFT) and its long-term relevance to digital propertization, the NFT must be understood in the broader context of the Web 3.0 movement and the growth of the metaverse environment. As NFT business and regulation evolve, there will be a myriad of uses for NFTs in both the analog and digital economic systems but their use in the digital economy may be significantly different than that in the analog environment.

Currently, some of the most economically significant uses of NFTs have occurred in analog transactions. For example, one of the most expensive NFTs ever sold was the work "Everydays: The First 5000 Days," by Beeple, through a Christie's online auction in 2021.[1] Although the work is itself a digital image and the auction was conducted online, Christie's is a traditional art and antiquities auction house that primarily caters to physical objects. As an NFT, the ownership of the *Everydays* artwork was recorded on a blockchain operated through MakersPlace, providing unique provenance for the ownership, but it was also recorded in Christie's record-keeping and ledgers as a traditional sale. Hence, this sale was still predominantly conducted in the context of analog record-keeping and marketed through conventional promotional techniques.

At least potentially, the use of NFTs creates a mechanism for digital assets to be uniquely identified with nearly unforgeable provenance and to be available for trading, mainly without the need for large, centralized intermediaries.[2] Such uses go far beyond

---

[1] *Beeple, The First 5000 Days*, CHRISTIE'S (March 11, 2021) (close date), https://onlineonly.christies .com/s/beeple-first-5000-days/beeple-b-1981-1/112924; Langston Thomas, *The 20 Most Expensive NFT Sales of All Time*, NFT NOW (August 4, 2022), https://nftnow.com/features/most-expensive-nft-sales/#beeple-everydays.

[2] *See* Pratin Vallabhaneni, *The Rise of NFTs – Opportunities and Legal Issues*, WHITE & CASE (April 20, 2021), www.whitecase.com/publications/alert/rise-nfts-opportunities-and-legal-issues ("[A]n NFT ... contains a unique identification code and metadata that distinguishes one NFT from any other, and represents items on the blockchain that cannot be replicated ... Moreover, NFTs are composed of software code in the form of 'smart contracts' that can be crafted to provide significant benefits to NFT creators").

the identification and collection of stored digital assets but these benefits will only emerge in a wholly digital environment. These type of environments exist in instances of the emerging metaverse platforms and may emerge as a central component of the Web 3.0 internet architecture, if the early promises of that environment come to fruition.

II WEB 3.0

Web 3.0 is not a technological standard. Instead, it is a metaphor to identify how the next iteration of Internet-based commerce will be organized. Advocates for Web 3.0 point to the consolidation of market power in the present Web 2.0 environment among a small set of Internet intermediaries, including Meta (formerly known as Facebook) and X (formerly known as Twitter), which dominate social media, Amazon, which dominates online sales, and Apple and Google for their control of mobile. These companies collectively control the marketplace for ad spending throughout the rest of the US economy. Since most of the Web 2.0 services provided to the public are funded through this ad-based model then free services can and are provided (in exchange for receiving advertising). To maximize revenue, the permitted advertising techniques are often highly targeted, invasive, and manipulative.[3] Moreover, in the US, the First Amendment limits the regulation of advertising unless the government can prove it is unfair and deceptive.[4]

Web 3.0 proponents identify this model for much of the source of the current unhappiness created by social media platforms and societal harms from the Internet economy. Replacing advertising-based media with consumer-based media would create barriers to many of the harmful activities and promote better content. Paying for a person's social media postings, for example, would probably reduce the likelihood of trolling behavior, since the trolls would have to pay for their content distribution. Payment mechanisms would also provide a filter mechanism to limit bot activity and high-volume trolling behavior. The transaction costs would disincentivize some portion of the online harmful content.

In addition, by using micropayments to reward content creators for their games and videos, the marketplace would support popular content creators. Both content creators and consumers would be more cautious of what they consume because they would be spending money on those services. Although the volume would likely

---

[3] *See, for example, Bringing Dark Patterns to Light*, FTC BUREAU OF CONSUMER PROTECTION (September 15, 2022), www.ftc.gov/news-events/news/press-releases/2022/09/ftc-report-shows-rise-sophisticated-dark-patterns-designed-trick-trap-consumers. *See generally*, Jon M. Garon, *Overcoming Sludge and Dark Patterns: Implications of the Constitutional Limits on Health Information Regulation*, 56 AKRON L. REV. 179 (2023).

[4] 15 U.S.C. § 45 (2022). *See* FTC, A Brief Overview of the Federal Trade Commission's Investigative, Law Enforcement, and Rulemaking Authority, www.ftc.gov/about-ftc/mission/enforcement-authority (*quoting* 15 U.S.C. Sec. 45(n) (unfair); FTC Policy Statement on Deception, in Cliffdale Associates, Inc., 103 F.T.C. 110, 174 (1984) (summarizing deceptive)).

decrease as a result, at least in theory, the choices would become more intentional and the experience would improve. Finally, as the concept goes, the use of cryptocurrencies and NFTs would allow the bulk of these transactions to occur using self-executing software, which has been inaccurately labeled a "smart contract." The Web 3.0 architecture would allow code to execute and recognize when an instruction from a particular user triggers a payment obligation or resource right, enabling the transaction to take place autonomously.

According to those promoting decentralized, token-centric models of digital engagement,[5] Web 3.0 "will democratize everything, reshaping art, commerce and technology; displacing intermediaries; and putting people more directly in control of their destinies."[6] In this way, Web 3.0 differs from Web 1.0 and Web 2.0 because of both the content and interactivity. The first iteration of the Internet, which has now been relabeled as Web 1.0, has been in existence since the 1970s. The origins are tied directly to the launch of the graphical user interface beginning with the Mozilla (Netscape) web browser in 1994.[7] Web 1.0 served as a digital publisher and library. Pre-Internet media companies in the print and broadcast business competed to provide content and organize that content through portal websites.[8]

The regulatory understanding of the Internet was framed by the understanding that this was a very cheap and fast way of distributing the content the public was used to receiving, distributed from the key content producers to the public in the same one-to-many model of content distribution that had emerged with the printing press.[9]

---

[5] Despite the 2022–2023 crypto winter, and some regulatory crackdown on crypto entities and activities, token-centric models are becoming more and more a mainstream concept. For example, in the financial context, in September 2023, the London Stock Exchange Group (LSE) announced that it made plans for a new digital markets business, saying this will make it the first major exchange to offer extensive trading of traditional financial assets on the blockchain technology best known for enabling and powering cryptocurrency. *See LSEG Explores Blockchain for Cross-Asset Digital 'Ecosystem,'* REUTERS (September 4, 2023), www.reuters.com/technology/lse-group-draws-up-plans-blockchain-based-digital-assets-business-ft-2023-09-04/.

[6] *See* Ephrat Livni, *Welcome to 'Web3.' What's That?*, N.Y. TIMES (December 5, 2021), www.nytimes.com/2021/12/05/business/dealbook/what-is-web3.html.

[7] *See* Gilad Edelman, *The Father of Web3 Wants You to Trust Less*, WIRED (November 29, 2021), www.wired.com/story/web3-gavin-wood-interview/ ("Web 1.0, the story goes, was the era of decentralized, open protocols, in which most online activity involved navigating to individual static webpages."); *What Was the First Web Browser?*, STARRY (June 19, 2019), https://starry.com/blog/inside-the-internet/what-was-the-first-web-browser (Netscape launched in October 1994 as Mozilla and set most of the industry standards. Tim Berners-Lee created an earlier browser in 1990. Marc Andreessen and Jamie Zawinski developed the NCSA Mosaic web browser in 1993, which became Microsoft's Internet Explorer in 1995).

[8] *See* Joe Zhou, *A History of Web Portals and Their Development in Libraries*, 22 INFO. TECH. & LIBRARIES, 119 (September 2003), link.gale.com/apps/doc/A109847209/AONE?u=anon~d7e617f&sid=googleScholar&xid=62f95ed5 ("A Web portal is a doorway that can be customized by individual users to automatically filter information from the Web. It typically offers a search engine and links to useful pages such as news, weather, travel, and stock quotes").

[9] *See* ibid.; Nupur Choudhury, *World Wide Web and Its Journey from Web 1.0 to Web 4.0*, 5 INT'L J. COMPUT. SCI. & INFO. TECH. 8096, 8096 (2014).

User-generated content changed the distribution model from one-to-many into many-to-many, upending the centuries-old supply management, content editing, and censorship models that had gone before. "Web 2.0 refers to worldwide websites which highlight user-generated content, usability, and interoperability for end users. Web 2.0 is also called the participative social web."[10] With Web 2.0, search replaced hierarchy as the manner in which the public surfed the net. Media conglomerates became irrelevant to the user experience. Search intersected with social media and the ability of audience members to repost content for free further upending the business model of the content industry.[11]

For those hoping to institute Web 3.0, the democratization anticipated in Web 2.0 lost its promise. The use of automated bots to flood social media, the need by advertisers to psychometrically microtarget and manipulate online participants, and the use of algorithms to promote content for the purpose of stickiness rather than value, have come together to create an often toxic and rarely beneficial user experience.[12] Naval Ravikant tweeted, "Web 2: Users are the data, corporations own the platform, and the code is closed. Web 3: Users own their data, contributors own the platform, and the code is open."[13]

At the heart of the Web 3.0 philosophy is the creation of digital property. These unique digital assets are NFTs, which provide the attributes of permanence and unique identification essential to provide property-like transactions. Through digital property transactions, the owners of the property assets – members of the public – will have power rather than the intermediaries that serve content through algorithms and sell customer data to advertisers. "For Web3, the internet is shifting from ad-based business models to *commerce*-based business models ... As the internet

---

[10] *Web 1.0, Web 2.0 and Web 3.0 with Their Difference*, GEEKSFORGEEKS (November 8, 2021), www.geeksforgeeks.org/web-1-0-web-2-0-and-web-3-0-with-their-difference/. *See* Susannah Fox & Mary Madden, *Riding the Waves of "Web 2.0*," PEW RESEARCH CTR. (October 5, 2006), www .pewresearch.org/internet/2006/10/05/riding-the-waves-of-web-2-0/ (Web 2.0 "provided a useful, if imperfect, conceptual umbrella under which analysts, marketers and other stakeholders in the tech field could huddle the new generation of internet applications and businesses that were emerging to form the 'participatory Web' as we know it today: Think blogs, wikis, social networking, etc.").

[11] *See* Paul Miller, *Web 2.0: Building the New Library*, ARIADNE (October 30, 2005), www.ariadne.ac.uk/ issue/45/miller/; Scott Karp, *What Magazines Still Don't Understand About The Web*, PUBLISHING 2.0 (June 9, 2008), https://publishing2.scottkarp.ai/2008/06/09/what-magazines-still-dont-understand-about-the-web/; Choudhury, *World Wide Web*, 8099.

[12] *See* Jessica Dawson, *Microtargeting as Information Warfare*, CYBER DEFENSE REV. 63 (Winter 2021), https://cyberdefensereview.army.mil/Portals/6/Documents/2021_winter_cdr/04_CDR_V6N1_ Dawson.pdf; Florian Saurwein & Charlotte Spencer-Smith, *Automated Trouble: The Role of Algorithmic Selection in Harms on Social Media Platforms*, 9 MEDIA & COMM. 222 (2021) ("Evidence of harms involving social media algorithms [include] (1) algorithmic errors, undesirable, or disturbing selections; (2) manipulation by users ...; (3) algorithmic reinforcement of pre-existing ... inequalities in society; (4) enablement of harmful practices that are opaque and discriminatory; and (5) strengthening of platform power over users, markets, and society").

[13] Naval Ravikant (@naval), TWITTER (October 12, 2021, 7:52 PM), https://twitter.com/naval/ status/1448089151677603846.

evolves, it becomes more participatory. People move from passive consumers to active creators."[14] Gavin Wood, founder of the Web3 Foundation, has been quoted explaining, "Web3 is actually much more of a larger sociopolitical movement that is moving away from arbitrary authorities into a much more rationally based liberal model. And this is the only way I can see of safeguarding the liberal world."[15]

Of course, the Web 3.0 economy is presently just a theoretical model.[16] History has shown that it is difficult for the public to leave free content and replace it with pay-per-use or subscription content so long as free remains an option.[17] More importantly, a paywall will have a significant impact on access, leaving behind the poor and those with modest means. And since poverty disproportionately impacts communities of color, the Web 3.0 model has a significant risk of racializing the Internet. As a result, it is unclear whether the pay-per-use or subscription model of the Internet will ever fully develop or solve more social problems than they create. Nonetheless, efforts to return control to individual users through a digital property rights regime will continue.

The early indications of the Web 3.0 transformation do not necessarily capture the idealism any more than the earlier phases of Internet commerce.[18] The cryptoassets industry is in consolidation mode,[19] with market volatility forcing investors to seek the most stable leaders in the field. According to the Congressional Research Service (CRS), the bankruptcy of FTX represented "perhaps most consequential of a spate of crypto company failures this year."[20] More broadly, the crypto market fell from a peak of nearly $3 trillion in assets at its high in November 2021 to barely one-third of that value or $1 trillion by summer 2022.[21]

---

[14] Rex Woodbury, *Chain Reactions: How Creators, Web3, and the Metaverse Intersect*, Digital Native (May 5, 2021), https://digitalnative.substack.com/p/chain-reactions-how-creators-web3 ("Most big Web1 and Web2 companies make money through advertising").

[15] Edelman, *The Father of Web3*.

[16] Leon Anidjar, Nizan Geslevich Packin, and Argyri Panezi, *The Matrix of Privacy: Data Infrastructure in the AI-Powered Metaverse* (forthcoming 2024 Harv. L. & Pol. Rev.) (describing Web 3.0, while explaining that no one really knows what it would look like or what its decentralized and automated nature would be like).

[17] In August 2023, it was reported that some of the big tech giants would start offering paid, ad-free services in the EU. It remains to be seen how this would work out. Mike Isaac & Adam Satariano, *Meta May Allow Instagram and Facebook Users in Europe to Pay to Avoid Ads*, N.Y. Times (September 1, 2023), www.nytimes.com/2023/09/01/technology/meta-instagram-facebook-ads-europe.html (explaining that Meta, the parent company of Instagram and Facebook, is considering offering European users the option to pay and avoid advertisements).

[18] *See* Jon M. Garon, *Legal Implications of a Ubiquitous Metaverse and a Web3 Future*, 106 Marquette L. Rev. 106, 178 (2022) ("The question remains whether this vision is different than the vision of earlier Web 1.0 and Web 2.0 advocates … The earlier utopian idea failed and created a vacuum into which U.S. corporations were able to bestride the narrow world, each like a mighty colossus").

[19] *See* Taylor Locke, *Mark Cuban Is Reliving the Internet Boom When He Looks at Crypto. The 'Consolidation Phase' Is Coming, He Says*, Fortune (May 9, 2022), https://fortune.com/2022/05/09/mark-cuban-compares-crypto-to-internet-consolidation-phase-coming/.

[20] Paul Tierno, *What Happened at FTX and What Does It Mean for Crypto?*, Cong. Rsch. Serv. 1 (November 17, 2022), https://crsreports.congress.gov/product/pdf/IN/IN12047.

[21] Ibid., 2.

The FTX collapse highlights the patchwork of regulators and compliance regimes for crypto trading which must provide stability if it is to finance the Web 3.0 micropayment architecture. While all crypto services were required to register with the US Treasury's Financial Crimes Enforcement Network as money transmitters for compliance with anti-money laundering (AML) regulations,[22] these regulations did not address any of the fiscal responsibility obligations inherent in securities regulation, commodities trading regulation, or even currency exchange laws. Moreover, since FTX was not the first crypto fund or exchange to collapse nor were the last regulators aware of, but inattentive to, the risks that allowing unregulated marketplaces may pose to investors in failing funds, and more broadly, to the entire sector.[23]

The collapse of FTX, however, signaled two fundamental shifts in the development of Web 3.0. First, it forced regulators and legislators to understand the importance of acting to impose appropriate fiduciary standards and anti-fraud compliance across the sector. Indeed, the scale of the collapse and the ripple effects of the harm meant that the Wild West era of crypto has come to an end. Second, the failure debunked the naive notion that opaque, unregulated, and widely distributed financial networks can operate without becoming hosts to criminal conduct. And while this understanding is still trickling down across the legal system,[24] many understand the potential risks better than before. Therefore, although micropayments and digital assets can still be the core of the Web 3.0 environment, these attributes will only exist in an ecosystem backed by governmental regulation, stability, business predictability, and compliance.

III THE METAVERSE

These lessons, in turn, provide the basis for understanding the emerging "metaverse" and the role NFTs play inside this digital environment. The term metaverse is merely a label for an online interactive environment, typically featuring game play or similar user experiences that allows for unscripted participant interaction on the platform and may also allow commercial activities. Participants or users are typically represented through avatars, which may approximate the real-world characteristics of the person, may be highly fanciful, or may be anything in between.

---

[22] *See* Eva Su, *Crypto-Asset Exchanges: Current Practices and Policy Issues*, CONG. RSCH. SERV. 1 (July 23, 2021), https://crsreports.congress.gov/product/pdf/IN/IN11708.

[23] *See* Tierno, *What Happened at FTX*, 3.

[24] There are still many questions about risks associated with blockchain and crypto-based entities. For instance, in August 2023, a New York Federal District Court dismissed a potential class action of a group of Investors, which claimed they were scammed by Uniswap, a decentralized protocol that averted potential legal liabilities, due to questions regarding the classification and responsibility of actors behind decentralized platforms. *See, for example,* André Beganski, *Uniswap Ruling Creates Regulatory 'Anomaly' for DeFi: Legal Scholar,* DECRYPT (September 1, 2023), https://decrypt.co/154651/uniswap-ruling-creates-regulatory-anomaly-defi-legal-scholar.

The presumed interface for the metaverse is through virtual reality (VR) headsets or glasses that replace the analog world with an entirely digital environment. Although it is common to refer to "the metaverse" as popularized in movies like *Ready Player 1*, there are many competing metaverse platforms, making the term "multiverse" a more appropriate description. As the platforms develop, some metaverses will be connected to an interoperable multiverse while others will remain stand-alone and independent.

Virtual worlds such as Second Life were early examples of metaverse environments as are massive multiplayer online role-playing games like Halo and World of Warcraft. Games like Roblox, Minecraft, and Fortnite all have the essential characteristics of the metaverse. Pokémon Go, an augmented reality game, is sometimes identified as having many of these aspects as well. Meta operates Meta Horizon Worlds as its metaverse experience. Fortnite, which started as a gaming platform and expanded to include opportunities for players to create their own worlds, allows players to attend virtual concerts.

The metaverse, however, is anticipated to be much more than just a gaming and social platform. As the technology continues to evolve, the quality of VR on headsets will continue to improve, eventually making VR glasses an alternative to a computer screen. Educational environments, work environments, and commercial activities can all be adapted to the metaverse. For example, the current shopping experience on Amazon remains frustrating and sometimes overwhelming. Designers may be able to replicate a better consumer experience using VR to replicate the benefits of walking through a grocery store or sitting in a boutique where virtual models show how possible clothing choices will look on models with body measurements identical to that of the purchaser.

Religion has already begun to find a home in the metaverse as well. For example, the Virtual Reality Church has been in operation since 2016.[25] According to its pastor, D. J. Soto, "the spiritual connection people experience in person in church, is equally accessible in VR. 'We believe God is everywhere, he's in physical dimensions, spiritual dimensions, and virtual reality.'"[26] To participate, congregants wear VR goggles. Their prayer books appear within the VR environment and the accompanying music is created and streamed within the virtual world. From an operational standpoint, this makes the service even more accessible for its members but it also highlights that intellectual property concerns need to be addressed differently in virtual worlds than they do in their real-world counterparts.

---

[25] Chace Beech, *Virtual Reality Church Brings Worship to New Dimensions*, SPECTRUM 1 NEWS (March 15, 2021), https://spectrumnews1.com/ca/la-west/technology/2021/03/14/virtual-reality-church-brings-worship-to-new-dimensions ("VR Church is designed, built, and run entirely online. It was founded in 2016 by D.J. Soto, an ordained Bishop. He was experimenting with virtual reality and realized he could marry this new technology with his religious work").

[26] Ibid. (*quoting* Bishop Soto).

IV METAVERSE ESSENTIALS: UBIQUITY, PERSISTENCE, UNLIMITED CAPACITY, FUNCTIONING ECONOMY, AND INTEROPERABILITY

The success of Roblox, Fortnite, and World of Warcraft along with lessons from physical card games, including the Yu-Gi-Oh! Trading Card Game and Hasbro's Magic: The Gathering, create a blueprint for success in the design of future metaverse environments. As a technological platform, the service must have ubiquity, persistence, and the appearance of unlimited capacity. Ubiquity means that a user can join the subscriber's metaverse from any compatible device and any Internet connection. Persistence requires that it be available essentially on a twenty-four/seven basis with maintenance and upgrades rarely, if ever, making the environment unavailable. And unlimited capacity requires that the system always have excess capacity to accommodate the usage of the subscribers at all times, even peak events like the World Cup or a Taylor Swift concert.[27] These requirements are no different from any successful online game but the scale could be unprecedented.

Next, to be successful and sustainable, the metaverse must operate a stable, functioning economy. An online game economy is entirely artificial but this hides the fact that government-backed fiat currency denominated economies are equally artificial. Value exists in currency, metals, and real property only because society ascribes value to those objects.[28] An object's value in society increases or decreases because of how the community values that object. A neighborhood which was once the most expensive and elite changes into the low-rent district as housing patterns change, while a few blocks away gentrification transforms an inexpensive neighborhood into a city's new hot zip code. A Yu-Gi-Oh! or Magic trading card shoots up in value in response to a company announcement that it will no longer reprint that card, while another card might fall precipitously in value if the company overproduces that card. A card's value may change whenever the publisher bans from gameplay another card that had previously synergized well with the card being traded. Neither the real property nor the collectible card changed in any manner but the context for the value substantially altered the value ascribed by willing buyers and sellers.[29]

Digital assets are more vulnerable to the effects of the market because there is a false, public perception that physical goods have intrinsic value and so tend to

---

[27] *See* Matthew Ball, *The Metaverse: What It Is, Where to Find It, and Who Will Build It*, Matthew Ball. vc (January 13, 2020), www.matthewball.vc/all/themetaverse. *See* Ben Thompson, *Microsoft and the Metaverse*, Stratechery (November 9, 2021), https://stratechery.com/2021/microsoft-and-the-metaverse/ (*quoting* Ball and noting that these attributes describe the Internet as well).

[28] *See generally*, Joshua Fairchild, Owned: Property, Privacy, and the New Digital Serfdom (2017).

[29] *See generally*, Michael J. Zimmerman and Ben Bradley, *Intrinsic vs. Extrinsic Value*, Stan. Encyclopedia of Philosophy (2019 Ed.), https://plato.stanford.edu/entries/value-intrinsic-extrinsic/.

be somewhat overvalued while inchoate rights tend to be undervalued due to the same bias.[30]

These simple economic examples highlight the critical importance of a metaverse to have clear, well-established, and stable economic controls. To be sustainable, a platform must have clear, actively enforced rules about the types of transactions that are permitted and those that are prohibited. Within the metaverse, asset values should only be altered in intentional, incremental steps.

In gaming environments, the in-game economies are usually subject to the control of the game publisher. Metaverse platforms that have contractual publishing controls can follow the same model. If the markets become financially significant to the general economy, however, the need for economic stability might eventually become the subject of governmental regulation. This is even more likely for metaverse platforms that are operated using a decentralized, self-regulating governance.

The final attribute necessary to have a successful metaverse is a compelling reason for the public to engage on that platform. A person's time is a limited, precious commodity. Each form of entertainment must compete with every other form of entertainment to attract and retain its audience. Even if the metaverse becomes useful for work, education, and religion, the providers of that platform will need to compete for attention to that particular platform as the place to go to work, study, or engage spiritually and religiously. The environment must be compelling.

At the moment, most of the focus for metaverse development remains on entertainment. In that context, the metaverse is perceived as a place to do things, so its use is driven by games, concerts, events, and the ability to undertake those activities socially. Where a metaverse feels "empty," the experience is off-putting to most users. Purely social mixers tend to be awkward and uninviting in the real world and do not improve in VR. Only by combining the active experience with the social engagement can the metaverse operator offer a compelling reason for a person to participate.[31]

In addition to these essential attributes for the successful metaverse, Web 3.0 advocates promote the need for interoperability, so that the user can move from one metaverse to another, retaining the user's avatar and digital properties to be used in other marketplaces. One can analogize this to the benefits of the European common market and currency that promotes the ease of movement and payment from one European country to another. Interoperability can also be understood as the difference between the Apple App Store and the Google Play Android marketplace. Within each of the two markets, interoperability and equipment compatibility is essential but the marketplaces themselves can be closed gardens, depending on the software architecture and contractual arrangements.

---

[30] *See* Wanda Thibodeaux, *People Still Value Physical Goods More than Digital Ones, Research Shows,* INC. (December 18, 2017), www.inc.com/wanda-thibodeaux/people-still-value-physical-goods-more-than-digital-ones-research-shows.html.

[31] *See* Ball, *The Metaverse.*

V USING NFTS IN THE METAVERSE AND DIGITAL ENVIRONMENTS

NFTs are essential to the decentralized, interoperable metaverse because they enable participants to hold their digital assets outside the direct control of the platform publisher. This affords the asset owner control over their property and protection from arbitrary decisions by publishers to disable or destroy consumer assets. For example, policies in app stores sometimes trigger publishers to remove content from user's apps. In addition, game publishers and virtual world platforms retain the power to delete user accounts for violating terms of service, which can effectively delete all in-app purchases. And in one instance, Amazon actually deleted purchased copies of George Orwell's 1984 from customer accounts due to a copyright issue.[32]

Beyond the property protection afforded by holding digital assets in NFTs written to blockchains outside the metaverse accounts, the use of third-party data will increase the potential for interoperability of these assets. To illustrate this, assume that a publisher of a metaverse wishes to promote interoperability and asset resilience within its metaverse platform and game. Users of the site can participate in esports as well as engage in commercial transactions from authorized vendors on the platform, including a bookstore named Gutenberg's Fine Books.

A brief visit to fictional Gutenberg's Fine Books illustrates the role of NFTs. The human user enters the broader metaverse environment wearing VR goggles. To those who see and interact with the user, the person presents as a human with feline attributes (including furry, pointy ears, and a long tail) with the username Katia. Katia speaks with an AI-generated salesperson who directs Katia to a shelf of illustrated manuscripts. As Katia opens and browses the books, the book reads itself aloud. A few of the volumes pop up illustrations to accompany the text and audio performance. Since the metaverse is a social environment, other shoppers might stop by to recommend their own favorite books or offer advice on the books Katia is considering. After discussing the options with the store's staff and fellow patrons, Katia selects a book to purchase, pays for the book, drops it into an infinite pocket, and exits the store.

Here are where the NFTs might have been used in the prior scenario. The metaverse software automatically generates a generic avatar for every user on the platform, but this manakin has no attributes or characteristics. Upon entry into the metaverse, the platform software "reads" the participant's user profile to pull the data needed to translate the manakin into the persona of Katia. Katia's persona is kept as an NFT distinct from the platform so that the user can maintain the same persona in every compatible metaverse environment. Depending on the software architecture, the owner of Gutenberg's Fine Books may also include all the shop's attributes in an NFT (or series of NFTs) so that the shop can be integrated into each metaverse in which the shop owner has an account. The artificial intelligence (AI)

---

[32] Brad Stone, *Amazon Erases Orwell Books from Kindle*, N.Y. Times (July 17, 2009), www.nytimes .com/2009/07/18/technology/companies/18amazon.html.

shopkeeper may be generated directly within the metaverse, or this functionality may actually be an Application Programming Interface (API) or a similar input being pulled from a source outside metaverse itself.

There are still more NFTs. Each book being browsed is owned by an author or publisher. It is licensed to the shop with an agreement that allows for limited browsing (much like the "see inside" functionality on Amazon) and a payment process that triggers when a customer chooses to "purchase" a book. The purchase is actually a software-use license that unlocks the book's content for the reader. Each book is stored on the publisher's platform and the purchaser acquires an NFT with a private key to allow the book to be opened. Although copyright law characterizes this as a license agreement, by contract, the parties will likely agree that the NFT that unlocks the book can be loaned out to friends or sold since the NFT has the same attributes as a physical copy of the book.

Each avatar, and perhaps each piece of clothing and accessory for the avatar, will be encoded as a distinct NFT. The NFTs for the bookstore go beyond the individual books. The artwork on the shop's walls, the music playing in the background, and the shop's furniture are all separate digital assets that can be licensed through NFTs. After all, unlike the physical world, the wall treatments and shelves are simply additional animated images, subject to the same copyright protections as the books or the avatar's clothing. In the online environment, there is no functionality to limit the copyright interest in these mundane components like the fixtures in a room. As a result, everything that comprises a virtual space may be subject to a copyright. A platform publisher could choose to build its environment by acquiring NFT usage rights from a massive repository to combine them into an experience. Moreover, the choice of which elements may represent an interaction between the bookstore owner's catalog of possible assets and the individual customer's user preferences. Advertisers already employ psychometric targeting to shape customer responses, so it is likely that the elements that combine to create the dynamic metaverse experience will eventually rely on similar technology to build personalized spaces in real-time.

At present, many of these elements are being created and encoded by each metaverse platform itself. Publishers are still creating video games directly and using proprietary code to build up the games. But this process is evolving, and increasingly game platforms are adopting models that pull self-contained blocks of code to compile the environment. Proprietary software does not need to rely as heavily on NFTs but it also tends to discourage interoperability.

In addition, in the contractual relationship between Katia and the bookstore, Katia's avatar is pseudonymous, meaning that although Katia is always Katia, the metaverse operator and the shop do not necessarily have information about Katia's legal identity. The NFT could, however, provide information about age restrictions and geographic restrictions so that when Katia went to browse the books, only those books to which Katia had the legal right to purchase would be presented. In this way, age limitations and geofencing would ensure that the bookseller had the rights to sell to a person, in that country, and that the consumer was of age if the work was subject to an "adults only" age restriction.

The transaction described at Gutenberg's Fine Books could also have occurred on the Barnes & Noble or Amazon website without the need for the metaverse. The purchaser simply signs on through the avatar account and proceeds using a website or app rather than VR goggles. Alternatively, Katia goes directly to Barnes & Noble's VR site without entering a metaverse to do so. Retailers will want to empower the VR experience but they will not want to be captured by virtual malls when the customers can as easily log directly into their accounts.

VI REGULATION AND GOVERNANCE OF THE NFT AND METAVERSE

As illustrated from the Gutenberg's Fine Books example, making the metaverse work requires complex software and the seamless integration of data from multiple sources to be used and deployed in that software. The integration of the software and data will require very clear contractual relationships among the parties. To make those contractual relationships effective the metaverse environment and NFT transactions will require a clear regulatory environment and governance structure.

The existing online regulatory framework will largely suffice for the introduction of the metaverse and NFT property regime but there will be some updates and changes needed.

A Geofencing

First, as highlighted by the geofencing example at the bookstore, metaverse and NFT regulation will be subject to territorial jurisdictional obligations. The European Union's Digital Services Act and Digital Markets Act will regulate content and transactions that are significantly more prescriptive than those regulated in the US. Other countries have other priorities. Many countries outside the US prohibit certain types of blasphemous content,[33] while only thirty have legalized same-sex marriage.[34] Not only do countries regulate the distribution of content differently but they also may require different disclosures regarding the sale of goods and services. As a result, the operation of each metaverse environment will be designed to respect national borders – though more libertarian architectures may make it simple to thwart geotagging through the use of virtual private networks (VPNs) or other location spoofing technologies.

---

[33] *See* Virginia Villa, *Four-in-Ten Countries and Territories Worldwide Had Blasphemy Laws in 2019*, PEW RSCH. CTR. (January 25, 2019), www.pewresearch.org/fact-tank/2022/01/25/four-in-ten-countries-and-territories-worldwide-had-blasphemy-laws-in-2019-2/.

[34] David Masci, Elizabeth Podrebarac Sciupac, and Michael Lipka, *Same-Sex Marriage Around the World*, PEW RSCH. CTR. (October 28, 2019), www.pewresearch.org/religion/fact-sheet/gay-marriage-around-the-world/.

B Intellectual Property

Within each country, there will be a series of regulatory regimes that exist to frame the private engagement among the NFT and metaverse users. This chapter will largely limit itself to those in the US. Copyright law has already been identified as an area that significantly impacts how NFTs and the metaverse operate.[35] As noted, unlike operating in an analog environment, ordinary objects are not subject to copyright because copyright excludes "useful articles" from the scope of copyright protection.[36] Illustrations of useful articles, however, are pictorial works and are not excluded from copyright. While the depiction of ordinary objects may be fair use or otherwise unobjectionable, producers of unique goods are likely to enforce their intellectual property rights aggressively. This gives owners of physical objects the potential to control some aspects of what is digitized into the metaverse.

For the rights of trademark holders and for individuals protecting their publicity rights (or name, image and likeness rights), the context of the use will also matter a great deal. While simply using a brand's logo in a metaverse is unlikely to infringe on a trademark owner's rights, the trademark owner may have the right to limit commercial exploitation of the mark. For example, a reproduction of a city's Main Street can reasonably be expected to use the names of the actual stores on that street, just as Google Maps depicts the names on its maps today. If, however, the metaverse functionality allowed a consumer to shop in those stores, then directing those consumers to third-party markets would likely create a false impression that the market was owned or endorsed by the brand owner. This commercial use of the store names would likely violate the trademark rights. The same result would likely occur if the outfits worn by avatars featured trademarked goods and clicking onto those goods would open shopping windows not under the control of the trademark owner. Commercial concerns will force metaverse operators to enter into licensing arrangements with goods manufacturers and retailers to ensure that the commercial opportunities do not violate the trademark interests of the parties.[37] The same protections will likely be available to celebrities to ensure that third parties are not creating the false impression to the public that the celebrities are endorsing goods or services.

Similarly, intellectual property ownership is limited by the first sale and exhaustion doctrines.[38] These statutory provisions limit the intellectual property owner's control

---

[35] *See* Chapter 11 of this Handbook.

[36] *See* 17 U.S.C. §101 (2022) ("The design of a useful article, as defined in this section, shall be considered a pictorial, graphic, or sculptural work only if, and only to the extent that, such design incorporates pictorial, graphic, or sculptural features that can be identified separately from, and are capable of existing independently of, the utilitarian aspects of the article").

[37] *See* Jon M. Garon, *Playing in the Virtual Arena: Avatars, Publicity, and Identity Reconceptualized through Virtual Worlds and Computer Games*, 11 Chap. L. Rev 465 (2008), https://nsuworks.nova.edu/law_facarticles/57.

[38] Michael V. Sardina, *Exhaustion and First Sale in Intellectual Property*, 51 Santa Clara L. Rev. 1055 (2011).

over the sale of an object subject to copyright, trademark, or patent rights to the initial sale of that object. Thereafter, the purchaser of that particular object or device is free to resell the object in any manner the owner sees fit. This limit on intellectual property does not translate to the digital world. In a digital transaction, the purchaser does not acquire a lawfully created object. Instead, the consumer acquires the right to download software and access an electronic file. Every download or stream creates a new work but the original object is never actually transferred. From an intellectual property perspective, the requirements for first sale are never met.

As a contractual matter, parties using the unique identifiers inherent in NFTs might agree to treat the transfer of an NFT as if it had the attributes of the sale of an object under the first sale doctrine but US law does not require that result.

C Money Transfers, Anti-Money Laundering, and Know Your Customer Requirements

Since metaverse platforms and NFT exchanges potentially allow for anonymity in transactions and porous geofencing systems, federal regulators will remain very concerned about the potential to use these platforms for illegal money transfers. Cryptocurrencies are clearly a substitute for fungible assets and any mechanism for transferring fungible assets is subject to money transfer laws.[39] Since operating a healthy economy is essential to the operation of a functional metaverse, each metaverse will be required to register as a money services business.[40]

Because NFTs have been associated with unique, expensive individual objects, regulators have not yet demanded that these are also treated as fungible assets but as the metaverse grows, this will likely change. For example, compare NFT versions of Magic: The Gathering cards, Yu-Gi-Oh! cards, or Pokémon cards with their digital equivalents. eBay owns TCGPlayer and other services that create a marketplace for card traders. In print, each card is unique because of its physical condition as well as variations in the set in which the card was created. Nonetheless, purchasers can buy cards in bulk and sell them in other markets, potentially outside the country. In the digital version, even if each card was a unique NFT, the collective marketplace means that a party could buy cards in bulk and then sell them in a foreign market without much difficulty.

If AML laws limit the use of cryptocurrencies, then tradeable NFTs become a ready substitute. As a result, as the metaverse grows and use of NFTs expands, it is highly likely that the Financial Crimes Enforcement Network (FinCEN) will

[39] *See* Currency and Foreign Transactions Reporting Act, Pub. L. No. 91-508, 84 Stat. 1118 (1970), 18 U.S.C § 1956 (2018) (Bank Secrecy Act); *see also* Stan Sater, *Do We Need KYC/AML: The Bank Secrecy Act and Virtual Currency Exchanges*, 73 Ark. L. Rev. 397, 417, 422 (2020).
[40] *See* 18 U.S.C. § 1960(a)(2) ("[T]he term 'money transmitting' includes transferring funds on behalf of the public by any and all means including but not limited to transfers within this country or to locations abroad by wire, check, draft, facsimile, or courier").

include NFTs in its regulations of asset transfers to enforce AML obligations and combating the financing of terrorism (CFT),[41] as discussed in more detail in a different chapter in this Handbook.[42]

One of the key components of AML efforts are know your customer (KYC) banking regulations. In some metaverse use cases, this will not be a problem. For the metaverse environment adopted by employers to allow employees to work remotely or to engage with colleagues virtually across the globe, each employee will need to be individually identified at sign-in and perhaps each time the VR headset is put back on after a break throughout the day. The information required to verify a banking customer is no greater than that for an employee. Any financial transactions over $10,000 or meeting other risk categories would also be tracked but other than these requirements, the obligations would be minor.

For anonymous and pseudonymous metaverse platforms that emphasized gaming and social activities, the KYC obligations would be more significant. Platforms could meet these requirements by having increasingly detailed levels of identity checks. Anonymous users would be limited to modest-sized financial transactions comparable to the ability to purchase a gift card at the grocery store, while those who were involved in large transactions would need to go through identity verification. This could look much like Las Vegas, where one can gamble anonymously but if one wins big, then reports are filed for purposes of both tax obligation reporting and KYC concerns.

D Securities Law and Foreign Investment Regulation

AML is not the only area of federal regulatory interest. In the crypto and finance sector, there has been growing attention on securities regulation. For NFTs and metaverse operations, this should be less of a concern. The individual ownership of an NFT or other digital asset that is privately held should be analogous to any other piece of property. On the other hand, simply because the metaverse promotes social engagement, there is the potential that users of the metaverse will exploit it to violate securities laws. The law gives state and federal authorities broad power to regulate any scheme of investments and if users on a metaverse platform (or organizers of a metaverse platform or NFT exchange) create an investment opportunity, then it will be subject to investment regulation.

In SEC v. *W.J. Howey Co.*, the Supreme Court created a four-part test: (i) an investment of money, (ii) in a common enterprise, (iii) with the expectation of profit,

---

[41] *See Anti-Money Laundering/Combating the Financing of Terrorism (AML/CFT)*, INT'L MONETARY FUND, www.imf.org/external/np/leg/amlcft/eng (2023)/ ("Money laundering and the financing of terrorism are financial crimes with economic effects. Money laundering requires an underlying, primary, profit-making crime (such as corruption, drug trafficking, market manipulation, fraud, tax evasion), along with the intent to conceal the proceeds of the crime or to further the criminal enterprise").

[42] *See* Chapter 4 of this Handbook.

and (iv) to be derived from the efforts of others.[43] In *SEC* v. *Edwards*, the Supreme Court clarified the standard by adding that "when we held that 'profits' must 'come solely from the efforts of others,' we were speaking of the profits that investors seek on their investment, not the profits of the scheme in which they invest."[44] Participating in a metaverse will likely require the payment for services rather than an investment in a common enterprise. Nonetheless, some platforms will likely abound with schemes that violate these rules.[45] Consumers must be mindful of the potential fraud and regulators will be on the lookout for such arrangements.

For the operators of metaverse platforms and NFT exchanges, however, these businesses are likely to come under significant federal scrutiny to ensure that they have fully disclosed the risks associated with these investments.[46] Entertainment companies tend to promote retail investing and individual investors tend to have less sophistication than institutional investors. Regulators will be mindful, therefore, to require detailed public disclosures as part of any public offerings of securities.

Even more important to federal regulators is the potential for sophisticated technologies to be shared internationally through investments and joint ownership schemes. In 2018, the jurisdiction of the Committee on Foreign Investment in the United States (CFIUS) was expanded.[47] CFIUS provides the US president the authority "to block or suspend proposed or pending foreign 'mergers, acquisitions,

---

43 *SEC* v. *W.J. Howey Co.* 328 U.S. 293, 301 (1946) ("the scheme involves an investment of money in a common enterprise with profits to come solely from the efforts of others"). The applications of this to offerings and sales of cryptoassets have been criticized as far-reaching and uncertain. *See, for example*, Carol R. Goforth, *Regulation of Crypto: Who Is the Securities and Exchange Commission Protecting?*, 58 Am. Bus. L.J. 643, 649–653 (2021); Lewis Cohen et al., *The Ineluctable Modality of Securities Law: Why Fungible Crypto Assets Are Not Securities* (2023) (unpublished manuscript), https://papers.ssrn.com/sol3/papers.cfm?abstract_id=4282385; Yuliya Guseva, *The SEC, Digital Assets, and Game Theory*, 46 J. of Corp. L. 629, 632–633 (2021).

44 *SEC* v. *Edwards* 540 U.S. 389, 393–394 (2004).

45 For example, in February 2023, the Southern District of New York Court denied Dapper Labs, Inc.'s motion to dismiss a securities law complaint concerning NFTs called "NBA Top Shot Moments" on the grounds that these NFTs are securities for purposes of federal securities laws. *See Friel* v. *Dapper Labs, Inc.*, 2023 U.S. Dist. LEXIS 29176 (S.D.N.Y. February 22, 2023). *See also* the recent enforcement action against Impact Theory's NFT offering, wherein the SEC asserted that the NFTs that were offered are securities for purposes of federal securities laws. *See* In the Matter of Impact Theory, LLC Securities Act Rel. No. 11226 (August 28, 2023), www.sec.gov/files/litigation/admin/2023/33-11226.pdf.

46 *See, for example*, SEC charges against Coinbase for allegedly operating as an unregistered securities exchange. Press Release, *SEC Charges Coinbase for Operating as an Unregistered Securities Exchange, Broker, and Clearing Agency*, Sec. & Exch. Cmm'n (June 6, 2023), www.sec.gov/news/press-release/2023-102 (noting, among others, that "Coinbase's alleged failures deprive investors of critical protections, including rulebooks that prevent fraud and manipulation, proper disclosure, safeguards against conflicts of interest, and routine inspection by the SEC").

47 Foreign Investment Risk Review Modernization Act of 2018, Pub. L. No. 115-232, 132 Stat. 2173 (2018). *See* 31 Fed. Reg. Parts 800 and 801 (Jan. 17, 2020) ("FIRRMA amended and updated section 721 (section 721) of the Defense Production Act of 1950 (DPA), which delineates the authorities and jurisdiction of the Committee on Foreign Investment in the United States (CFIUS or the Committee)").

or takeovers' of US business that threaten to impair the national security."[48] The revised CFIUS regulations expand authority to "TID U.S. businesses," a new acronym for critical *technologies*, critical *infrastructure*, and personal *data*.[49] AI and blockchain technologies which are central to the metaverse and the use of NFTs are among the most targeted technologies for CFIUS review and control. Also of significant government concern is the extent to which individual personal data is being made available to foreign nations. As a result, aggressive government policies may require stringent control on cross-border data sharing to meet the CFIUS concerns.

E Privacy and Cybersecurity

New state laws and proposed new federal regulations also highlight the ever-expanding need to protect the public from misuse of personal information through unauthorized exploitation of personal information by hackers as well as by the companies that lawfully acquire the data. Given the nearly infinite amount of data that can be gleaned from tracking how a person uses an avatar in a metaverse space, there will necessarily be a need for expanded regulation of how that data is collected, protected, and exploited.

Avatar pseudonymity will not be enough to protect an individual for a number of reasons. First, for activities involving employment and education, verification of identity is essential to protect the operations of the workplace and the integrity of the accredited learning environment. Workplaces must be secure to avoid disruption, to protect the integrity of the work product, and to ensure that no theft of trade secrets or other assets takes place. Teaching and learning, of course, can take place anonymously, but earning high school or college credit requires that the educational institution has confidence that the person engaged in the education was also the person who was evaluated during the courses and who earned any diplomas, degrees or certificates.

Second, all transactions must be verifiable to an actual payment. Even if the payment system is itself anonymous, there must be some ability to assure that the person who used a particular account had the authority over that account, even if the true identity of the person is not known to the other parties in the transaction. From a privacy perspective, it is a short hop to identify the individual from these points of data.

---

[48] *CFIUS Reform Under FIRRMA*, Cong. Res. Service (Feb. 21, 2020), https://sgp.fas.org/crs/natsec/IF10952.pdf ("CFIUS is an interagency body comprised of nine Cabinet members, two ex officio members, and others as appointed that assists the President in overseeing the national security risks of FDI in the U.S. economy").

[49] See Antonia I. Tzinova, *New CFIUS Regulations Finally Take Effect*, Holland & Knight Alert (February 13, 2020), www.hklaw.com/en/insights/publications/2020/02/new-cfius-regulations-finally-take-effect; *Foreign Investment 2020 (Part 3): CFIUS Spotlight on "TID" U.S. Businesses*, Morrison & Foerster (October 15, 2019), www.mofo.com/resources/insights/191015-foreign-investment-2020.html.

Third, even when financial data is not involved, it is not difficult to connect anonymous activity with particular device attributes that uniquely identify every device based on its configuration and operating characteristics. The combination of hardware and software gives every device a unique fingerprint. If the device is used in any transaction tied to a real identity, such as banking, shopping, or accessing health information, then that device can be triangulated to all anonymous activities that also transpire on it. This is also tracked to social networks, so a device's proximity to other devices can reveal information about the relationship among device holders. And this data can be further triangulated to social media networks and other proximity interactions. Almost nothing remains anonymous.

In addition, while blockchain may protect from direct alteration of data on the chain, it has not stopped hackers from stealing the access to those assets in the crypto space. While the protection of blockchain assets should improve with time, history has also shown that any system involving transactions is vulnerable to fraudulent exploitation and the more complex a system, the more likely that vulnerabilities have been introduced.

Security through anonymity is more theoretical than real. Instead, both regulators and operators will understand that there is a need for comprehensive cybersecurity obligations that proscribe administrative, technical, and physical safeguards. Even if some operators resist such regulation, their investors and insurers will require it. Successful metaverse environments will hold vast amounts of personal data and mediate an increasingly large portion of the domestic retail economy. Dangers and risks associated with foreign nations and terrorists, financially motivated criminals, and threats to individuals from stalkers and bullies will make the need for comprehensive regulation a priority.

F The Law of the Deal

Against the backdrop of federal and state regulation will be the contractual relationships that will exist between the metaverse enterprise, its business partners, and its individual account holders. The example of Gutenberg's Fine Books illustrates this relationship. To provide the shopping experience for Katia, the metaverse will have a business-to-business contract with Gutenberg's Fine Books that will address a number of key provisions that set forth three broad categories of rights and obligations: the affirmative undertakings of the store to operate in the metaverse; the limitations on what the vendor can do in the metaverse; and the revenue arrangements.

As metaverse transactions develop, the affirmative obligations may take on many of the attributes of mall leases. Since the stores will be visualized on metaverse world maps, their "size" will likely depend on the price paid for the prominence. Although in theory, a metaverse can choose to appear as infinite, in practice, audience targeting is a much better marketing strategy, so the metaverse may be selective in how many vendors it hosts and what kind of business each vendor operates. Gutenberg's

Fine Books will be required to operate as a bookstore (as defined in the lease) rather than becoming an avatar tattoo parlor or some other business. In the real world, many bookstores also sell music and T-shirts, but the lease will specify the extent to which this is permitted. Provisions can be highly detailed. A lease might allow T-shirts of authors to be sold but not general clothing or musical concert swag.

A metaverse may choose to have aesthetic standards to which every store must adhere in terms of color schemes or thematic designs. The stores may be obligated to participate in metaverse-wide events and campaigns to tie each vendor into holiday celebrations, big social events, promotional strategies, and similar obligations. There may also be some provisions allowing for the cross-promotional use of selected trademarks and copyrighted content to allow for metaverse-wide promotions of the vendors and national advertising campaigns for the vendors that promote their availability in the metaverse. There will also be operational demands to require that the store meet technical specifications so that all the metaverse customers have a high-quality experience, a requirement of 24/7 operations, and compliance with all applicable laws and regulations.

One area where the metaverse differs from the mall is its interoperability.[50] The lease agreement will likely specify the extent to which the operation of each vendor must adhere to the interoperability standards, require the use of NFTs, specify the technological obligations for compliance with interoperability, and prohibit data theft or retentions from these services. These provisions on NFTs and interoperability will likely be coordinated with the NFT blockchain services to ensure a system that is stable and resilient.

The prohibitory license provisions will probably look much like the terms offered by the app stores to app developers. These prohibitions enforce community standards prohibiting a long list of unacceptable activities: child pornography, obscenity, pornography provided to minors, abusive language, harassment, hate speech, sales of counterfeit goods, spoofing, reverse engineering, violations of copyrights, trademarks, trade secrets, rights of publicity, and patents, transfers of protected healthcare data (regulated by the Health Insurance Portability and Accountability Act of 1996 (HIPAA)), health misinformation, sale of prescription drugs (unless separately licensed), sales of illegal drugs, sales of alcohol or tobacco to minors, sales of firearms and ammunition, unlicensed money transfers or lending, unlicensed gambling, use of child labor or slave labor in the production of goods, and general proscriptions on any activity that violates the applicable laws,

---

[50] *See generally* WORLD ECON. F. & ACCENTURE, INTEROPERABILITY IN THE METAVERSE (January 2023), www3.weforum.org/docs/WEF_Interoperability_in_the_Metaverse.pdf. A worth-noting example in this context is Worldcoin, a crypto project founded by OpenAI CEO Sam Altman, which seeks to create an interoperable token ("digital passport") that will provide authentication into multiple different independent services. *See* Anna Tong, *OpenAI's Sam Altman Launches Worldcoin Crypto Project*, REUTERS (July 24, 2023), www.reuters.com/technology/openais-sam-altman-launches-worldcoin-crypto-project-2023-07-24/.

regulations, or rights of third parties. Metaverse operators may also include a more general "morality clause," giving the metaverse operator the ability to walk away from any vendor that becomes toxic as a result of a perception in the marketplace that the vendor has offended the broader public. In an age where CEO tweets can result in losses of significant stock value losses, contracting parties increasingly want the ability to distance themselves from business decisions or leadership that harms brand value.

For agreements within the regulated industries such as pharmaceutical retailers, medical services, lawful gambling, financial services, and sales of alcohol and tobacco, additional contractual provisions will require that the vendor operates within the required state and federal licensing obligations and that the vendor affirms on a regular basis that it continues to operate lawfully within these obligations.

The payment provisions will also include models that likely derive from the present-day app stores. Vendors will likely be asked to pay a fee proportionate to the size of their presence or footprint in the metaverse's maps and promotional advertising. They will also likely be charged a percentage of their sales in the form of a gross sales calculation or through a provision that requires all financial transactions to be conducted through the metaverse's sales system. In the context of the app stores operated by Google and Apple, the market power wielded by these two companies has raised serious regulatory concerns about such pricing, leading to restrictions in some non-US markets and continued antitrust investigations within the US. But there is nothing inherently in violation of antitrust or competition law to charge gross rent, the concern is the market power tied to the proprietary devices. Whether this concern emerges in the metaverse environment remains to be seen.

Finally, the license agreement will include provisions for the metaverse operator to suspend or terminate a vendor account in the event that it fails to meet its obligations regarding payments, affirmative duties, or prohibitions against improper activities. The metaverse operators will want great flexibility to suspend and terminate vendor accounts to respond to problems in the marketplace.

The metaverse and each vendor in the metaverse will have a contractual agreement (end user license agreement (EULA) or terms of service agreement (ToS)) with each customer. Katia will have agreed to a EULA when creating the initial account. Katia will also have entered into a EULA with Gutenberg's Fine Books prior to making a purchase. To make this work, the vendor's EULA is subject to the metaverse agreement and any conflict will be governed by the metaverse agreement.

The EULA will largely mirror the prohibitory obligations listed above for the vendor agreement as well as specify that the user agrees not to participate in any harmful, illegal, or trolling behavior, nor to violate any intellectual property rights of the metaverse, its vendors, or any third parties. The end user agrees to use the account only for the purposes of engaging in metaverse activities and further agrees not to hack, reverse engineer, or use bots or other automations to participate in the metaverse.

This network of contracts provides the mechanism for enforcement of the law of the metaverse. The EULAs and perhaps the vendors' agreements will all provide for alternative dispute resolution and are likely to prohibit, to the greatest extent permitted by law, any attempt to bring class action litigation. These contracts, therefore, serve both to embody the domestic law that governs the metaverse and control the way in which these laws apply to the consumers who participate in the metaverse.

VII CONCLUSION

The metaverse is in its early stages and the potential to develop will be shaped, at least in part, by the emergence of NFT technology that allows for interoperability and consumer confidence in the experience. The emergence of these operations will depend on the customer experience the metaverse platforms offer but the growth of Roblox, Fortnite, and other existing platforms suggests that this will become a significant part of the leisure economy in the years to come and make its way into education, employment, and all aspects of life.

The true value of the NFT phenomenon, however, will only become apparent when they are part of this economic transformation to a world of interoperable and highly dynamic virtual worlds that will augment how the public works, learns, prays, and plays. There are many existing regulatory systems that will help guide the development of NFTs and the metaverse but these regulations will also likely adapt as the scale and relevance of the metaverse expands.

19

Resolving NFT and Smart Contract Disputes

Amy J. Schmitz

I INTRODUCTION

It is no secret that technology is disrupting many industries, including law.[1] Technology is revolutionizing the art of deal-making by leaps and bounds. Gone are the days when most deals were negotiated in person and sealed with a handshake.[2] Instead, we now expect to make most purchases online through e-contracts, sealed with a click on the "accept" button.[3] Even corporate leaders now use emails and text messages to negotiate deals, which they eventually "sign" online through services like Docusign.[4]

Despite our current comfort with e-contracts, smart contracts, and non-fungible tokens (NFTs), on the blockchain, are something different. They push the envelope even further into the digital age and allow parties to codify an asset, performance, or enforcement in computer code.[5] Those with no coding background cannot easily read or interpret a smart contract in its rawest form. Instead, these smart contract enforcement mechanisms are spread across blockchain nodes distributed throughout the world.[6] In other words, they are made up of "nodes" which consist of computer-coded algorithms that live in a decentralized ledger (blockchain).[7] Indeed, even attempting

I thank Cooper A. Karras, Lara do Valle Pereira, Sarah Mader, and Brittany Munn for their research assistance. Note that parts of this chapter come from or build on a prior article I wrote with Colin Rule, *Online Dispute Resolution for Smart Contracts*, 2019 J. Dis. Res 203 (2019). However, this chapter considers ODR in the NFT context, especially as it relates to the underlying smart contract disputes.

[1] *See generally* Richard Susskind, Tomorrow's Lawyers: An Introduction to Your Future (2013).

[2] Amy J. Schmitz & Colin Rule, The New Handshake: Online Dispute Resolution and the Future of Consumer Protection ix (2017).

[3] Ibid.

[4] *Companies Using Verisign*, iDatalabs (2017), https://idatalabs.com/tech/products/verisign.

[5] David Zaslowsky, *What to Expect When Litigating Smart Contract Disputes*, Law360 (April 4, 2018), www.law360.com/articles/1028009/what-to-expect-when-litigating-smart-contract-disputes.

[6] Ibid.

[7] Jakub J. Szczerbowski, *Place of Smart Contracts in Civil Law. A Few Comments on Form and Interpretation* (January 8, 2018) (unpublished manuscript), https://ssrn.com/abstract=3095933.

to summarize an explanation of smart contracts in an introduction seems foolish, and thus, a greater explanation is provided in this Handbook and throughout this chapter.

NFTs usually exist on a blockchain, which is, as noted above, a distributed ledger that records transactions.[8] The main difference between NFTs and smart contracts is that NFTs are digital assets powered through smart contracts, meaning that smart contracts control the transferability and ownership of NFTs. In other words, smart contracts are not the same as NFTs but are vital to their use. Furthermore, both run on the blockchain and so many of the disputes that arise concerning NFTs go back to the smart contracts that control them.[9]

Although NFTs have been around since 2014, they have gained notoriety in recent years because they have become an increasingly popular way to buy and sell digital artwork. NFTs are different from cryptocurrencies and fungible tokens, such as DAI or LINK, in that each individual NFT is completely unique and is not divisible or fungible. When someone creates or mints an NFT, they execute computer code stored in smart contracts. This information is added to the blockchain where the NFT is being managed.

NFTs have unique value because they are generally one of a kind, or at least one of a very limited run, and have unique identifying codes. Powered by smart contracts, they are also fully trackable by using Ethereum's blockchain as a public ledger, for example (although they can exist on another ledger). An NFT's value is tied to its ability to guarantee the authenticity of, for example, digital art, GIFs, collectibles, music, legal documents, signatures, etc. An NFT can only have one owner at a time, generally managed through a smart contract that assigns ownership and manages the transferability.

Smart contracts are therefore a key component for driving transactions and enforcement mechanisms with respect to NFTs. This is important because some argue that smart contracts will create efficiencies and may largely eliminate the need for complicated and costly letters of credit, bonds, and security agreements by digitizing automatic enforcement or payment.[10] The reality, however, is that smart contracts, like most emerging technologies, often generate more issues than they resolve.[11] Inevitably, disagreements will arise regarding the coding and content of smart contracts.[12] Parties to smart contracts may not understand what they agreed to, or there may be disputes about what exactly the smart contract has codified.[13]

---

[8] *Non-Fungible Tokens (NFT)*, ETHEREUM (October 25, 2023), https://ethereum.org/en/nft/.

[9] Robyn Conti, *What Is an NFT*, FORBES (September 9, 2022), www.forbes.com/advisor/investing/cryptocurrency/nft-non-fungible-token/.

[10] Szczerbowski, *Place of Smart Contracts*, 333–37.

[11] *See* ETHAN KATSH & ORNA RABINOVICH-EINY, DIGITAL JUSTICE: TECHNOLOGY AND THE INTERNET OF DISPUTES 1–25 (2017).

[12] Pindar Wong, *Blockchain's Killer App? Making Trade Wars Obsolete*, COINDESK (May 21, 2018), www.coindesk.com/markets/2018/05/21/blockchains-killer-app-making-trade-wars-obsolete/.

[13] Ibid.

Coding errors are also common. A 2016 study revealed that there are 100 errors per 1,000 lines of coding.[14] Extrapolated to smart contracts, this means that many smart contracts may not be accurately coded to encompass the parties' original intentions.[15] Negligent coders may have crafted the smart contracts.[16]

At the same time, there is no articulated and clear system of rules that apply to smart contracts and NFTs.[17] Other chapters in this Handbook address these legal uncertainties and therefore I will not fully explore the myriad of questions that arise around NFTs. But this chapter will be addressing the uncertain classification of smart contracts driving NFTs since it is unclear whether they are in fact "contracts" under civil and common law.[18] Smart contracts do not fit neatly into legal concepts like offer, acceptance, and consideration. Additionally, if a matter falls under the statute of frauds, it is unclear whether a coded transaction will constitute a "writing" and whether the keys to encrypt the smart contracts will constitute signatures of the parties.[19]

Even if one could get past civil and contract law principles in establishing agreements underlying smart contracts, litigation regarding these digital creations is problematic.[20] What remedies exist for the smart contract party who wants to prevent or reverse enforcement? If this were a traditional contract, a party could rescind it in court but enforcement of smart contracts on the blockchain is automatic and the code is immutable. These are not really "contracts" in the traditional sense where individuals have a "meeting of the minds." Thus, users may have different expectations, generating disputes. At the same time, digital art may raise intellectual property claims if parties claim that minting an NFT with respect to a prior physical art piece would infringe on another's rights.[21] However, this chapter will focus on resolving the claims related to the smart contracts controlling NFTs.

Smart contract disputes raise questions, such as: What law will apply and where will parties turn to resolve their smart contract disputes? Litigation seems nonsensical since it is unclear what court would have jurisdiction, as smart contracts are in a distributed ledger. It is also unclear whether or how contract law should apply, what laws govern the transaction, and what evidence could be collected to adjudicate the matter. As one commentator stated: "Given the complexity and technical character of the issues connected with NFTs, it is of the utmost importance that any disputes be resolved by creative and open-minded people."[22]

---

[14] Zaslowsky, *What to Expect.*
[15] Ibid.
[16] Ibid.
[17] Szczerbowski, *Place of Smart Contracts,* 335.
[18] Ibid., 336.
[19] Zaslowsky, *What to Expect.*
[20] Szczerbowski, *Place of Smart Contracts,* 335.
[21] Paweł Bukiel, *NFT-Relate Disputes: How to Resolve Them?,* SCHÖNHERR (January 3, 2022), www .schoenherr.eu/content/nft-related-disputes-how-do-you-resolve-them/.
[22] Ibid.

Even putting aside the jurisdiction and other issues noted above, offline litigation undermines the efficiency and scalability of smart contracts. Especially because the anonymous nature of smart contracts and the fluidity of online identities make it difficult to determine party identity.[23] At the same time, it is difficult to conceptualize how judges could fashion remedies that often consist of developing new code to update a smart contract, especially when the code is append only deployed on a blockchain.[24] Moreover, changing the course of an NFT brings new issues in smart contract execution.

This chapter discusses smart contract NFT disputes, dilemmas to resolving those disputes, and current offerings for blockchain dispute resolution. It also proposes online dispute resolution (ODR) built into smart contracts to efficiently and fairly resolve disputes that arise along the way, including in matters of transferability and governing terms and conditions. And while this chapter will not focus on the intellectual property issues with NFTs, other chapters in this Handbook will examine the intellectual property issues that NFTs have arisen in recent years.

This chapter proceeds from description to prescription in light of the confusion surrounding smart contracts behind most NFTs. Section II of the chapter will take a step back and provide a greater explanation and background on the evolution of smart contracts as drivers for terms and conditions governing NFTs, as well as NFT ownership and transfer. Section III further tackles questions regarding the complexities of smart contracts and their status under current law. Section IV then notes new means for dealing with smart contract issues within the blockchain. Section V will include a discussion of ideas for fashioning ODR to provide fast and fair resolution, noting cautions for policy-makers. The chapter ends with a conclusion.

II SMART CONTRACTS CONTROLLING NFTS

A *Smart Contracts and NFTs*

Other chapters in this Handbook address the rise and fall of NFTs and their potential uses, significance, promise, and pitfalls. The chapter will therefore leave most of this discussion to the other authors. However, it is essential to note that in addition to recording ownership, an NFT may also contain a smart contract that encompass terms and conditions regarding enforcement as well as governance of later sales of the NFT, including royalties for the original creator beyond the first sale. Smart contracts are therefore crucial in tracking the enforcement of rights regarding NFTs. At the same time, most people do not understand what smart contracts are, or assume that they are the same thing as e-contracts. The first

---

[23] Szczerbowski, *Place of Smart Contracts*, 335.
[24] Zaslowsky, *What to Expect*.

challenge is to explain how smart contracts work at a very basic level and how they relate to NFTs.[25]

As noted in the Introduction, smart contracts may not necessarily be legal contracts. The model of making and enforcing agreements is closely tied to the judicial system, with litigation as the endgame. This means parties usually know that they can litigate if one breaches a contract. The traditional contract model is nonetheless changing in the digital age. As one example, parties continually agree to e-contracts each day by clicking a button and "accepting" terms they never read while purchasing goods and services on the Internet.[26] And these e-contracts are legal contracts that are generally enforceable and commonplace for most of us in our daily lives.[27]

In contrast to these e-contracts, smart contracts are a different animal built with the hope of precluding any judicial involvement. Smart contracts are computer codes consisting of "if/then" statements laying out each obligation and eventuality. These computer programs can be self-enforcing, often linked to oracles, which are external algorithms that feed outside data into the smart contracts and gather certain metrics that trigger events. This allows for continuous monitoring of key performance metrics to trigger the "if/then" statements leading to automatic enforcement. An oracle can be linked to any data, such as a commodity price or shipment delivery.[28]

Through auto-enforcement, smart contracts can add efficiencies for many kinds of agreements. This includes financing, shipping, manufacturing, and NFT contracts. Parties need not worry about facing the inefficiencies of litigation or paying lawyers when the terms and enforcement are established in the computer coding per "if/then" rules. *If* event "x" happens (e.g., stock hits a certain price), *then* "y" occurs (e.g., stock purchase occurs). The computer code can replace letters of credit, security agreements, and other mechanisms that provide trust in traditional deals.[29] This can lead to cost savings when properly coded and deployed, even concerning NFTs.

B *Decentralized Ledgers*

Any discussion of NFTs and smart contracts must note the importance of blockchain. Blockchain is a distributed ledger spread across the Internet. It allows for information to be stored in different, redundant locations throughout the world,

---

[25] Amy J. Schmitz & Colin Rule, *Online Dispute Resolution for Smart Contracts*, 2019 J. Dis. Res. 203 (2019).
[26] Zaslowsky, *What to Expect*.
[27] Amy J. Schmitz, *Pizza-Box Contracts: True Tales of Consumer Contracting Culture*, 45 Wake Forest L. Rev. 863 (2010).
[28] For more on oracles, *see, for example*, Nizan Geslevich Packin & Yafit Lev-Aretz, *Decentralized Credit Scoring: Black Box 3.0*, Am. Bus. L.J. (forthcoming 2024), https://papers.ssrn.com/sol3/papers.cfm?abstract_id=4375920.
[29] Szczerbowski, *Place of Smart Contracts*, 333.

making it much more difficult to "hack." When a document or asset is put into the blockchain, it is replicated across every archival node, so it would take over 50 percent to hack:

> Imagine if you had a notepad where everything you wrote in the notepad would be duplicated exactly in other notepads around the world (and everything written in those notepads would appear in your notepad as well). Even if your notepad was destroyed, the other notepads around the world would have everything you wrote in it, so the contents would never be lost. Also, imagine if there were global rules that governed what could be written in the notepads. If someone tried to write something in a notepad that didn't follow the rules, then all the other notepads would reject it.[30]

This structure makes it very difficult to spoof or edit the information placed in the blockchain. And, in the case of NFTs, they are by nature non-fungible and represent digital originals.

This makes smart contracts and NFTs built into the blockchain valuable for particular uses or clientele. As noted above, smart contracts are already self-enforcing computer programs but they become more secure when placed into the blockchain. When smart contracts are driving ownership and transfer of NFTs, the hope is that computer code will prevent any need for lawyers or courts. This new system, built on smart contracts and blockchain, enforces agreements through code instead of judges and jails. Jurisdiction and legal rules become largely irrelevant because the system itself establishes the basis for enforcement.[31]

In this new structure, a computer network manages all contracts across jurisdictions. It means that contract information is not housed in one central location, vulnerable to outages and hackers. This can enhance trust and enforceability while reinforcing privacy and security. The blockchain also provides encryption with public and private keys, which are blockchain-based identification numbers provided by the network.[32] This eliminates the need or reliance on ink signatures, which are more vulnerable to fraudulent duplication.

That said, blockchain is not perfect or impenetrable. It can be "hacked" and has its own problems and risks.[33] Proponents of the blockchain claim that the distributed ledger is "immutable," "secure," and "trustless."[34] However, hackers can manipulate the technology by, for example, using a "hard fork" to essentially manipulate and steal data and assets. A well-executed "hard fork" can even make a blockchain

---

[30] Schmitz and Rule, *Online Dispute Resolution*, 28.
[31] Marco Dell'Erba, *Demystifying Technology. Do Smart Contracts Require a New Legal Framework? Regulatory Fragmentation, Self-Regulation, Public Regulation* 27–28 (August 20, 2018) (unpublished manuscript), https://ssrn.com/abstract=3228445.
[32] Ibid., 9.
[33] Angela Walch, *Blockchain's Treacherous Vocabulary: One More Challenge for Regulators*, 21 J. INTERNET L. 1, 5–7 (2017).
[34] Ibid., 5.

vulnerable to corruption and collapse.[35] At the same time, blockchain is vulnerable to errors and outside manipulations. The idea that code will prevent claims is unfounded.[36]

These risks have not slowed the blockchain boom.[37] In 2017, venture capitalists invested $1 billion in start-up blockchain companies.[38] At the same time, blockchain companies offered $5 billion in initial coin offerings (ICOs), which are now recognized by the Securities and Exchange Commission and regulated as securities.[39] Venture capitalists have continued to invest substantially in cryptocurrency start-up companies well into 2022, despite the volatility of cryptocurrency markets.[40] Cryptocurrency start-ups received over $9.7 billion in VC funds in the first quarter of 2022 and $5.3 billion in the second quarter before a handful of popular crypto companies filed for Chapter 11 bankruptcy protection that resulted in a "crypto winter."[41] Nevertheless, by 2023's second quarter, they were still able to raise $2.34 billion.[42] Additionally, reports in the summer of 2023 indicated that US financial institutions want to use blockchain to speed up trades on Wall Streetkenize by $5 trillion in the next few years.[43]

Other noteworthy initiatives include the "Dubai Blockchain Strategy," which is a multi-pronged initiative by the Dubai Future Foundation and the Smart Dubai Office, to make Dubai the first city run essentially on the blockchain.[44] The aspiration was to move all essential records to the blockchain, including health records, title transfers, identification verification data, wills, and data related to financing and exchanging goods.[45] Blockchain has also created new opportunities in law, as lawyers

---

[35] Ibid., 2–7. Instead of claiming the technology is "tamper-proof," some proponents now call it "tamper-resistant." Ibid.

[36] Ibid.

[37] Brant Carson et al., *Blockchain Beyond the Hype: What is the Strategic Business Value?*, MᴄKɪɴsᴇʏ Dɪɢɪᴛᴀʟ (June 2018), www.mckinsey.com/business-functions/digital-mckinsey/our-insights/blockchain-beyond-the-hype-what-is-the-strategic-business-value.

[38] Ibid.

[39] Ibid.

[40] Hannah Miller, *VCs Are Still Rushing to Back Crypto Startups*, Bʟᴏᴏᴍʙᴇʀɢ (June 1, 2022), www.bloomberg.com/news/newsletters/2022-06-01/in-crypto-downturn-startups-are-still-getting-venture-capital-dollars.

[41] Ibid.

[42] Jacquelyn Melinek, *Crypto Funding Drops for Fifth Straight Quarter As Investors Continue to Pull Back*, TᴇᴄʜCʀᴜɴᴄʜ (July 5, 2023), https://techcrunch.com/2023/07/05/crypto-funding-drops-fifth-straight-quarter/.

[43] Jordan Smith, *Why Big Banks Like JPMorgan and Citi Want to Put Wall Street on a Blockchain*, CNBC (July 26, 2023), www-cnbc-com.cdn.ampproject.org/c/s/www.cnbc.com/amp/2023/07/26/why-big-banks-like-jpmorgan-want-put-wall-street-on-a-blockchain.html.

[44] Saqr Ereiqat, *Blockchain in Dubai: Smart Cities from Concept to Reality*, IBM (April 10, 2017), www.ibm.com/blogs/blockchain/2017/04/blockchain-in-dubai-smart-cities-from-concept-to-reality/.

[45] Ibid. *See also* Samburaj Das, *Opening Shop? Dubai Government Launches Blockchain Business Registry*, CCN (May 5, 2018), www.ccn.com/dubai-government-launches-blockchain-business-registry/. This gave rise to the Global Blockchain Council, bringing together a consortium of government entities, UAE banks, blockchain technology firms, and companies like IBM and Consensys.

are specializing in smart contracts,[46] and business clients have been experimenting with blockchain through venues like the Accord Project consortium.[47] Finally, by 2018, twenty-five governments were already piloting blockchain platforms.[48]

While different sources vary in their estimates regarding NFT market volumes, the continued increase in the use of crypto wallets signals growth in the industry.[49] The drastic increase in the number of people participating in crypto transactions makes it clear that a high volume of transactions would generate a high volume of disputes.

III DISPUTING NFTS AND SMART CONTRACTS

A *Unclear Legal Status*

Despite the hype around NFTs and blockchain's potential, smart contracts raise many unanswered questions. Unforeseen disputes will almost certainly arise regarding contract coding and execution. As noted above, there is even a risk that fake data will improperly trigger or fail to trigger smart contract clauses. Oracles may provide false data and are notoriously prone to compromise. This may result in major financial losses.[50] Computer programmers, or coders, also may face liability for erroneous coding. Coders working in concert with smart contract drafters could face damages for creating improperly structured contracts, while hackers may attempt to manipulate data to the advantage of one or the other party.[51]

There is no articulated and clear system of rules that apply to smart contracts.[52] At the core of "contract law" is the concept of consent. This idea of consent requires some effective communication of an intentional transfer of rights and obligations between parties.[53] Presumably, the parties to a smart contract, like any contract, will have consented to the terms underlying the code.[54] However, smart contracts

---

[46] Roger Aitken, *Accord Project's Consortium Launching First Legal 'Smart Contracts' with Hyperledger*, FORBES (July 26, 2017), www.forbes.com/sites/rogeraitken/2017/07/26/accord-projects-consortium-launching-first-legal-smart-contracts-with-hyperledger/#34781496472c.

[47] Ibid.

[48] *IBM Joins Accord Project Smart Contract Consortium*, ARTIFICIAL LAW. (June 28, 2018), www.artificiallawyer.com/2018/06/28/ibm-joins-accord-project-smart-contract-consortium.

[49] Jacquelyn Melinek, *Top Crypto App Downloads Rise over 15% Following SVB Collapse*, TECHCRUNCH (March 16, 2023), https://techcrunch.com/2023/03/16/top-crypto-app-downloads-rise-over-15-following-svb-collapse/; Grand View Research, Inc., *Crypto Wallet Market to Be Worth $48.27 Billion by 2030: Grand View Research, Inc.*, PR NEWSWIRE (October 27, 2022), www.prnewswire.com/news-releases/crypto-wallet-market-to-be-worth-48-27-billion-by-2030-grand-view-research-inc-301661026.html.

[50] Wong, *Blockchain's Killer App?*.

[51] Zaslowsky, *What to Expect*.

[52] Szczerbowski, *Place of Smart Contracts*, 335.

[53] Meg Leta Jones & Elizabeth Edenberg, *The Legal Roots and Moral Core of Digital Consent* (February 27, 2018) (TPRC 46: The 46th Research Conference on Communication, Information and Internet Policy 2018), https://ssrn.com/abstract=3131392.

[54] *See* Szczerbowski, *Place of Smart Contracts*.

are translated into code without the same pageantry of traditional contracts.[55] This means that it may be difficult for the parties to understand whether the code accurately memorializes their agreement. In this way, smart contracts lack the usual cautionary, evidentiary, and channeling functions of written contracts in the traditional system.[56]

Smart contracts may also codify agreements or dictate actions outside of the legal system. Smart contracts may therefore allow parties to circumvent legal rules. This is why lawyers debate whether smart contracts are "contracts" in the legal sense.[57] In common law, it is unclear that code constitutes true offer, acceptance, and consideration. Civil lawyers then argue whether there is sufficient documentary evidence to support legal enforcement.[58] Moreover, as of the time of the chapter, there is not any robust legal precedent in the courts clarifying the law on blockchain or smart contracts.[59]

Additionally, even if one gets past contract-formation questions by looking back to the originating documents, jurisdiction and other legal questions create hurdles for litigating smart contracts.[60] Smart contracts on a blockchain are generally anonymous and become even more anonymous when they use cryptocurrencies that make it nearly impossible to discover the true identities of the parties or their computers.[61] Without knowing the identity and domicile of the parties, courts are unable to establish jurisdiction using traditional rules based on minimum contacts or physical presence.[62]

Furthermore, even if a court could determine the jurisdiction of the parties, it would be difficult for a court to interpret a smart contract and understand the code behind an NFT. Code is written to be understood by programmers, not lawyers and judges.[63] Similarly, it would be difficult for a court to intervene to prevent or reverse automatic smart contract executions.[64]Another issue is how could a traditional court fill gaps in smart contracts, especially given that blockchain does not generally allow for modifications[65] Moreover, does a generalist judge understand how to do this?

---

[55] Mark Verstraete, *The Stakes of Smart Contracts* (May 17, 2018), https://papers.ssrn.com/sol3/papers.cfm?abstract_id=3178393 (50 Loy. U. Chi. L.J. 743 (2018–2019)).

[56] Duncan Kennedy, *From the Will Theory to the Principle of Private Autonomy: Lon Fuller's "Consideration and Form"* 100 Colum. L. Rev. 94, 103 (2000); Lon L. Fuller, *Consideration and Form*, 41 Colum. L. Rev. 799, 800–01.

[57] Szczerbowski, *Place of Smart Contracts*, 33–35.

[58] Ibid., 33–40.

[59] Ibid.

[60] Wulf A. Kaal & Craig Calcaterra, *Crypto Transaction Dispute Resolution*, 73 Bus. Law. 1, 37–38 (2018).

[61] Ibid., 4.

[62] Ibid., 36.

[63] Ibid., 39.

[64] Ibid., 40.

[65] Usha Rodrigues, *Law and the Blockchain*, SSRN 5 (May 6, 2018), https://ssrn.com/abstract=3127782 (104 Iowa L. Rev. 679 (2019)).

Some argue that governance standards around the blockchain will emerge to promote "confidence in the technology and the legal and regulatory environment."[66] They see government or other standards groups dictating rules that will govern smart contracts. In the US, states are beginning to introduce and pass legislation regarding the enforcement of smart contracts.[67] Some commentators have also proposed that legal rules could be coded into the blockchain contracts themselves.[68]

The problem with these ideas for governmental regulation is that blockchain technology is advancing faster than any law could possibly move. Reactionary legislation is largely meaningless for those creating and using smart contracts and NFTs. Traditional legal systems are notoriously political and slow to act.[69] Among parties of varying nationalities and legal systems, regulations would have to be international and widely accepted because blockchain contracts are cross-jurisdictional and international.[70]

Nonetheless, some US states have begun passing legislation to essentially endorse smart contracts or to otherwise make their state look attractive to technology investors. For example, some states have passed legislation that defines smart contracts per their jurisdiction and incorporates them into their existing legal structure. Different states vary slightly in wording, but many have also passed laws similar to Tennessee's recognition of a cryptographic signature stored on the blockchain as a legitimate electronic signature.[71] Many states also follow Tennessee in allowing the use of smart contracts and stating that no contract relating to a transaction should be denied legal enforceability just because the contract is a smart contract, concluded in code.[72] It is unclear how much these laws mean or what difference they make when it comes to the practicalities of resolving smart contract disputes. The laws seem like window dressing.

Smart contracts and NFTs need their own dispute resolution systems. Interest in them may continue to grow and disputes regarding these new technologies are not going away. Coding for possible breaches of contract can only go so far because there will always be a lack of foresight and information, as well as unpredictable human behavior.[73] There will also be technical problems and mistakes in the coding.[74] Besides, traditional litigation fails to address smart contracts' need for remedies that preserve anonymity and fit within the blockchain.[75] Courts and traditional processes simply will not work for resolving smart contracts and NFT disputes.

---

[66] Joseph J. Bambara & Paul R. Allen, Blockchain: A Practical Guide to Developing Business, Law, and Technology Solutions 84–95 (2018).

[67] Zaslowsky, *What to Expect*, 2.

[68] Kaal & Calcaterra, *Crypto Transaction*, 44.

[69] Ibid., 45.

[70] Ibid., 45–46.

[71] T.C.A § 47-10-202 (2018).

[72] Ibid.

[73] Ibid., 46–47.

[74] Ibid., 47.

[75] Kaal & Calcaterra, *Crypto Transaction*, 47.

B Remedies

Smart contracts are not set up to allow for creative or equitable remedies. A smart contract is "a set of promises specified in digital form" carried out automatically by an algorithm, so an NFT governed by a smart contract either transfers or does not transfer.[76] Once a smart contract is created and put on the blockchain, execution is automated and irrevocable, or at least prohibitively expensive to revoke.[77] As such, smart contracts essentially eliminate "do-overs." They are self-governing and self-executing.[78] This means that creating remedies would be problematic for a court of law dealing with a smart contract dispute.

Many have compared smart contracts to vending machines: the product is delivered once money is received with no ability for human intervention.[79] In other words, the terms are "embedded" in the machine and it performs (delivers a product) in response to receiving the requisite amount of money.[80] The machine cannot refuse to perform and its structure (thick glass face) protects the product from theft or fraud. This means that one cannot make *post hoc* changes to her selections. If one chooses chips, she is stuck with chips. This is very efficient because the self-execution eliminates transaction costs. However, the consumer may grow angry when the chips get stuck and do not fall all the way down to the doorway where they can be retrieved.

Smart contracts are similarly self-executing. As noted above, this automation makes smart contracts very attractive in terms of efficiency and diminished reliance on lawyers and courts – or at least, theoretically.[81] In a perfect world, smart contracts increase efficiency, lower transaction costs, and largely eliminate the need for litigation.[82] For example, a smart contract could allow for the automatic transfer of an NFT while preserving the anonymity of parties and securing originality on the blockchain. Once again, the problem is that coding does not eliminate conflict.

An example of automatic enforcement gone awry is the 2016 DAO (or decentralized autonomous organization) debacle. Blockchain enthusiasts created the 2016 DAO using blockchain and a web of smart contracts as the foundation for what was to be a tamper-proof extra-legal company on the blockchain.[83] The 2016 DAO was a literal autonomous organization that would continue without the need for code

---

[76] Dell'Erba, *Demystifying Technology*, 2–12.
[77] Ibid., 14.
[78] Ibid.
[79] Verstraete, *The Stakes*, 13.
[80] Ibid.
[81] Ibid. Three justifications underlie this belief: 1) smart contracts can be a tool favoring consumers to overcome doctrines that now give an advantage to firms; 2) the transaction costs of forming and enforcing smart contracts are lower than traditional contracts; and 3) smart contracts allow individuals to set the terms of their agreement without state interference. Ibid., 5–20.
[82] Ibid., 7–8.
[83] Rodrigues, *Law and the Blockchain*, 12.

changes once it began its operations.[84] A flaw in the DAO design, however, allowed an individual to withdraw $50 million from the DAO without any real "breach" or fraud. Moreover, the DAO's self-enforcing code and lack of applicable legal rules eliminated means for reversal or traditional remedies.[85] The only recourse was to completely terminate the DAO and admit defeat.[86] There was no allowance for an equitable remedy, as we see in traditional contract law.

Some also raise the "oracle problem" as a hindrance to fair smart contracting. This refers to the lack of a reliable and secure delivery mechanism that exchanges real time information with blockchain data systems.[87] Currently, there is no clearly secure delivery of information among systems.[88] For example, most existing oracles have the same security issues as any traditional data systems that can be biased or "hacked."[89] Smart contracts and NFTs are not immune to disputes and blockchain technology does not "code away" all problems. Moreover, coded enforcement creates problems in fashioning remedies. For example, a judge would have to somehow "code" to reroute a smart contract or provide a remedy other than a "do-over." The questions, therefore, focus on likely remedies and means for smart contract dispute resolution.

IV SYSTEMS FOR RESOLVING SMART CONTRACTS AND NFT DISPUTES

Developers and entrepreneurs are moving quickly to create solutions for resolving smart contract disputes, including those behind NFTs. They realize that these disputes demand non-judicial remedy systems that are cross-jurisdictional, extra-legal, and efficient. Companies are creating ODR systems in the blockchain, with the primary models to date being online arbitration, crowd-sourced dispute resolution, and AI-powered resolutions. Developments in each of those areas are discussed below and further ideas are presented.

A Arbitration

Arbitration "took its rise in the very infancy of Society" as a private and self-contained process, outside of the courts.[90] Communities created arbitration systems designed

---

[84] Id., 29.

[85] Ibid., 33.

[86] Ibid., 36. Of course, the DAO could be resurrected with new coding using a corporate structure to shield liability, but the fact remains that coding is king in blockchain – but there must be means for resolving disputes along the way without dissolving the smart contract at the core.

[87] Mike Orcutt, *Blockchain Smart Contracts Are Finally Good for Something in the Real World*, MIT Tech. Rev. (2018).

[88] Ibid.

[89] Steve Ellis, Ari Juels, & Sergey Nazarov, *ChainLink: A Decentralized Oracle Network*, CHAINLINK (September 4, 2017), https://link.smartcontract.com/whitepaper.

[90] Julius Henry Cohen, Commercial Arbitration and the Law 25 (1918) (quoting John Montgomerie Bell, Treatise on the Law of Arbitration in Scotland 1 (2d ed. 1877)).

to quickly and efficiently determine disputes in accordance with local norms and accepted equitable principles.[91] These self-contained arbitration systems served community needs for efficient, economical, equitable, and private proceedings.[92] By the early twentieth century, nearly every trade or profession had developed its own machinery for arbitration.[93] Indeed, the New York Chamber of Commerce arbitration panels were independent of the judiciary and continued to resolve disputes between American and British merchants during and after the American Revolution of 1775–1783.[94] Given this history of resorting to extra-legal resolutions, it is no surprise that developers have turned to online arbitration for resolving blockchain disputes (what I have termed "OArb" in prior publications).[95]

Such an OArb includes using technology and digital tools to facilitate and execute processes ending in a final determination of a dispute by a neutral third party. For example, OArb may use asynchronous and/or synchronous communications for parties to present their cases to third-party arbitrators in an online forum. Communications may be text-only or virtual hearings and mixtures thereof. OArb's use of technology allows parties to upload and submit supporting documentation to support their claims at times that work their individual schedules since there is no need to travel to a physical office. Online hearings also save time, cost, and stress of traveling to and attending in-person processes. Such OArb systems may even provide more accurate and complete redress for consumers than class actions, which

[91] Ibid., 22–27 (emphasizing special utility of arbitration despite the development of a reputable judicial system in mercantile cases in which arbitrator expertise in technical matters is essential). *See also* James A.R. Nafziger, *Arbitration of Rights and Obligations in the International Sports Arena*, 35 Val. U. L. Rev. 357 (2001) (demonstrating communal concepts of arbitrations); Earl S. Wolaver, *The Historical Background of Commercial Arbitration*, 83 U. Pa. L. Rev. 132, 144 (1934) (quoting Malynes, Lex Mercatoria 303 (1622)).

[92] "Of all mankind's adventure in search of peace and justice, arbitration is among the earliest. Long before law was established, or courts were organized, or judges had formulated principles of law, men had resorted to arbitration for the resolving of discord, the adjustment of differences, and the settlement of disputes." Frances A. Kellor, American Arbitration: Its History, Functions and Achievements 3 (1948). *See also* Paul L. Sayre, *Development of Commercial Arbitration Law*, 37 Yale L. J. 595, 597 (1928); Margit Mantica, *Arbitration in Ancient Egypt*, 12 Arb. J. 155, 155–159 (1957) (noting scarcity of records of early arbitrations because arbitrations generally involved purely private disputes that had little public significance); Will Durant, The Story of Civilization Volume 1: Our Oriental Heritage 645–647, 795–797 (1954) (describing arbitration systems in early Chinese civilization that provided means for "a wholesome compromise" and means for the people to end "minor" disputes in accordance with face-saving compromise).

[93] Harry Baum & Leon Pressman, *The Enforcement of Commercial Arbitration Agreements in the Federal Courts*, 8 N.Y.U. L.Q. Rev. 238, 247 (1930) (reporting many trade associations with active arbitration facilities).

[94] William Catron Jones, *Three Centuries of Commercial Arbitration in New York: A Brief Survey*, 1956 Wash. U. L. Rev. 193, 207 (1956).

[95] Amy J. Schmitz, *'Drive-Thru' Arbitration in the Digital Age: Empowering Consumers through Regulated ODR*, 62 Baylor L. Rev. 178 (2010) (proposing "OArb" as a distinct type of online dispute resolution); Amy J. Schmitz, *Arbitration in the Age of Covid: Examining Arbitration's Move Online*, 22 Cardozo J. Conflict Res. 245 (2021).

have been criticized for providing insufficient and inequitably distributed relief in some cases.[96]

OArb is just one example of ODR, which generally encompasses using technology to assist in preventing and resolving disputes. Most ODR, however, is not OArb because it involves the facilitation of communications to aid voluntary settlement.[97] In contrast, OArb is a distinct subset of ODR because it culminates in a final award rendered by a third-party neutral, which is usually enforceable under the Federal Arbitration Act (FAA) in the US and New York Convention on an international level.

OArb has spiked during the Covid-19 pandemic.[98] Virtual meeting technologies such as Zoom, Skype, Google Meet, WebEx, and Teams have made virtual hearings relatively cheap and easy and it has become a norm.[99] OArb has become among the offerings of traditional dispute resolution institutions, such as the American Arbitration Association (AAA), the Judicial Arbitration and Mediation Service (JAMS), and the International Institute for Conflict Prevention & Resolution (CPR). For example, the AAA offers a secure portal for parties to file claims, upload and manage their claim-related documents, and view and rank potential arbitrators for selection.[100] In addition, the AAA offers virtual hearing capacity and guidance.[101] AAA and others can now provide OArb with expert arbitrators with respect to blockchain and NFTs who may be better equipped to decide related disputes than traditional judges.

Other OArb systems were developing within the blockchain. For example, OpenBazaar was a market platform for the sale of goods and services using bitcoin and requiring online arbitration to ensure that exchanges between parties are conducted with minimal risk.[102] It sought to create an open marketplace for arbitration to "facilitate a polycentric merchant law to accommodate the requirements and preferences of each individual."[103] In particular, OpenBaazar allowed users to

---

[96] *See generally* Linda S. Mullenix, *Ending Class Actions as We Know Them: Rethinking the American Class Action*, 64 EMORY L.J. 39 (2014).

[97] *See generally* SCHMITZ & RULE, THE NEW HANDSHAKE; *See also* Amy J. Schmitz, *Building on OArb Attributes in Pursuit of Justice*, *in* ARBITRATION IN THE DIGITAL AGE: THE BRAVE NEW WORLD OF ARBITRATION (Maud Piers & Christian Aschauer, eds., 2018).

[98] Melody Alger, *Conducting Arbitrations and Mediations Remotely during the Covid-19 Crisis and Beyond*, 68 R.I. B.J. 15 (2020).

[99] *See 2021 International Arbitration Survey: Adapting Arbitration to a Changing World*, WHITE & CASE LLP (MAY 6, 2021), www.whitecase.com/publications/insight/2021-international-arbitration-survey/technology-virtual-reality.

[100] *See AAA-ICDR Technology Services*, AM. ARB. ASSN. (2024), www.adr.org/TechnologyServices/aaa-icdr-software-and-online-tools.

[101] Svetlana Gitman & Amy J. Schmitz, *Arbitration Conversation No. 1-Amy Chats with Svetlana Gitman*, ARBITRATE (July 14, 2020), https://arbitrate.com/arbitration-conversation-episode-1-svetlana-gitman-american-arbitration-association/; *AAA-ICDR Virtual Hearing Guide for Arbitrators and Parties*, AM. ARB. ASSN (2021), https://go.adr.org/rs/294-SFS-516/images/AAA268_AAA%20Virtual%20Hearing%20Guide%20for%20Arbitrators%20and%20Parties.pdf.

[102] *Dispute Resolution in OpenBazaar*, GITHUB GIST (2021), https://gist.github.com/drwasho/405d51bd1b1a32e38145.

[103] Ibid.

decide at the start if they wished to have an anonymous third party decide related cases regarding obligations on the blockchain.[104] Users opting for the service would pay a fee and deposit bitcoin into an escrow.[105] Despite aspirations, however, it appears that OpenBaazar is no longer in operation.[106] Indeed, it seems that a more standard OArb is having more success through traditional providers like the AAA.

B *Crowdsourced Dispute Resolution*

In contrast to simple OArb, crowdsourced dispute resolution allows anonymous users to vote on who they think should "win" a dispute. Crowdsourced dispute resolution is not new. For example, more than twenty years ago iCourthouse pioneered the notion of online crowdsourcing in civil cases, and over ten years ago eBay India's Community Court invited other eBay users to decide whether a contested eBay review should be deleted.[107] Tokenized crowdsourcing goes further to allow for voting on the blockchain. In other words, jurors vote with tokens (generally cryptocurrency) that they lose if they are on the losing side. In contrast, jurors on the winning side generally gain some reward. This process banks on game theory, expecting jurors to strive for accuracy in hopes of "winning."

For example, Kleros is a crowdsourced online arbitration "court" built on Ethereum for the resolution of smart contract disputes.[108] Kleros's quest is to be "[a] fast, inexpensive, transparent, reliable and decentralized" ODR system built on game theory and discovering a "Schelling point" for resolving disputes.[109] This builds on Thomas Schelling's theory that in the absence of communication and trust, people will nonetheless choose "Focal Points" to reach a consensus.[110] Specifically, Kleros enlists "jurors" from around the world based on the number of "Pinakion" tokens (cryptocurrency) they deposit to show their interest in resolving a given dispute.[111] Parties to a dispute present their cases to the jurors, and jurors use tokens to vote with the proviso that they cannot change or reveal their votes before

---

[104] Kaal & Calcaterra, *Crypto Transaction*, 50–52.

[105] Ibid.

[106] Hazel FinTech, *The Shutdown of OpenBazaar or the Failure of Bitcoin as a Currency*, MEDIUM (May 27, 2021), https://hazelfintech.medium.com/the-shutdown-of-openbazaar-or-the-failure-of-bitcoin-as-a-currency-e34d26f869c4.

[107] Colin Rule & Chittu Nagarajan, *Crowdsourcing Dispute Resolution over Mobile Devices*, in MOBILE TECHNOLOGIES FOR CONFLICT MANAGEMENT: ONLINE DISPUTE RESOLUTION, GOVERNANCE, PARTICIPATION 93, 93–100 (Marta Poblet, ed., 2011).

[108] Clement Lesaege, Federico Ast, & William George, *Kleros*, KLEROS WHITE PAPER 1 (September 2019), https://kleros.io/assets/whitepaper.pdf.

[109] Ibid.

[110] Ibid., 2. According to Schelling, the focal points reflect each person's expectation of what another person expects him to do. In this game theoretic model, even people who do not trust one another will decide to work together and be truthful because it is at this focal point that parties reach "win-win" results.

[111] Ibid., 4.

the voting is closed.[112] To combat fraud, jurors are penalized for communicating with each other and must "justify" their votes.[113] After the vote is closed, the party with the most juror support wins.[114]

Jurors benefit from "winning" resolutions by taking the tokens of jurors who sided with the "losing" party.[115] Additionally, jurors are paid from the arbitration fee the parties pay to use the Kleros court.[116] These fees rise as parties appeal jury decisions, and Kleros is continually updating and amending its program in order to combat collusion.[117] For example, attackers would have to buy 51 percent of the staked work tokens in order to "buy" the jury.[118] In addition, Kleros can fork the system if necessary because it controls the tokens.[119] Moreover, Kleros tested the system through a large-scale study.[120] The study asked voters to evaluate pictures featuring cats and/or dogs, and to vote "dog" or "not dog."[121] After tabulating the votes, the researchers found that 70 percent of the cases were resolved in favor of the plaintiff and in the majority of those cases, by a unanimous vote and honest voters substantially prevailed by earning the most through the system.[122]

At least one court has recognized Kleros as a legitimate means for resolving disputes. For example, in September 2020, a disagreement arising from a rental estate leasing agreement in Mexico led to the use of Kleros Protocol to guide the arbitral decision. The parties in the case stipulated in their agreement that if a disagreement arose, it would be referred to an arbitrator who was to use Kleros. Accordingly, the arbitrator in the case compiled all the evidence and digital materials from both parties and submitted it to Kleros, which submitted it to three Kleros jurors. Based on the jurors' unanimous ruling for the landlord, the arbitrator rendered an arbitral award ordering payment of rent. The landlord then took the award and got it confirmed by a Mexican court, which was the first to recognize this type of blockchain platform as a legitimate form of arbitration.[123] Kleros advertises itself as a fast

---

[112] Ibid., 7.

[113] Ibid., 7.

[114] Ibid.

[115] Ibid., 8. Under its proposed governance, Kleros will create subcourts and update and adapt the program as necessary.

[116] Ibid., 7.

[117] Ibid., 8.

[118] Ibid.

[119] Ibid. *See also* Clement Lesaege & William George, *Kleros and Augur – Keeping People Honest on the Blockchain through Game Theory*, MEDIUM (February 11, 2018), https://medium.com/kleros/kleros-and-augur-keeping-people-honest-on-ethereum-through-game-theory-56210457649c (explaining why the Kleros system is more just than over crowdsourced dispute resolution in the founders' estimation).

[120] E-mail from William George, Cryptoeconomist with Kleros, to Amy J. Schmitz, Professor at University of Missouri (October 9, 2018) (on file with author).

[121] *Observations from Doge Pilot* 1 (October 15, 2018), dogeobservations.pdf (on file with author).

[122] Ibid.

[123] *See* Mauricio Virues Carrera, ACCOMMODATING KLEROS AS A DECENTRALIZED DISPUTE RESOLUTION TOOL FOR CIVIL JUSTICE SYSTEMS: THEORETICAL MODEL AND CASE APPLICATION (June 8, 2022).

and affordable alternative to other online dispute resolution platforms.[124] Currently, Kleros is available for small claims, insurance, e-commerce, finance, freelancing, token listing, content moderation, and intellectual property.[125] Having a court officially recognize its ruling for a small claim was also groundbreaking because it originated in the "real world" and not online.[126]

The Kleros homepage displays the number of ongoing disputes being arbitrated on the platform, many of which are related to online blockchain activities. There are several disputes about "Proof of Humanity Registration Protocol" where jurors and judges are establishing their legitimacy as a unique identity not already existing on a platform. For example, Kleros jurors were deciding whether a user is supposedly creating multiple accounts to increase their voting power on a platform.[127] Another example case is an ongoing dispute over a claim from Unslashed Insurance related to losses sustained trading online tokens via the blockchain application Anchor + UST Peg.[128] The dispute contains documentation of the party's losses, their insurance policy, a comprehensive history of their online token trading, and other evidence.[129] Jurors with technical knowledge about the blockchain will vote on the "winner" following the Kleros protocol.[130]

Jur is another blockchain-driven web service that seeks to modernize and revolutionize the governance of online interactions.[131] Jur seeks to decentralize the legal field by providing an online jurisdiction that overcomes the legal challenges that come with traditional courts focused on physical jurisdiction.[132] With this in mind, Jur seeks to create open-source universal standard digital contracts to promote more efficient online business transactions among people on blockchain platforms.[133] In this regard, Jur is developing online mediation, arbitration, adjudication, assessment, technical verification, and expert opinion services for resolving related disputes.[134]

---

[124] *See* KLEROS (2024), https://kleros.io.

[125] Ibid.

[126] *See* ibid.; *see* Mauricio Virues, *How to Enforce Blockchain Dispute Resolution in Court*, KLEROS (June 8, 2022), https://blog.kleros.io/how-to-enforce-blockchain-dispute-resolution-in-court-the-kleros-case-in-mexico.

[127] *Case Details Case #1224*, KLEROS (June 2022), https://court.kleros.io/cases/1224. Case #1224 is a prime example of a case where there was evidence that allegedly showed that one person was controlling more than one account. The suspected "puppeteer," a person creating multiple accounts, uploaded counterarguments and documents in their defense.

[128] *Case Details Case #1226*, KLEROS (June 2022), https://court.kleros.io/cases/1226.

[129] Ibid.

[130] Ibid.; *see* Stuart James, *3 Things to Know about Becoming a Kleros Juror*, KLEROS (January 24, 2019), https://blog.kleros.io/become-a-juror-blockchain-dispute-resolution-on-ethereum/.

[131] *See* JUR (2024), jur.io.

[132] Jur, *The Network State for the Digital Economy*, JUR LIGHTPAPER 1, 3 (May 2022) https://storage.googleapis.com/jur-webiste/1/2022/05/Jur%20Lightpaper.pdf.

[133] Ibid.

[134] Ibid., 9.

It is hard to see where Jur is in this process. Jur does not currently appear to handle arbitration services, although they have established platform procedures and a "network state."[135] Jur's procedure is similar to Kleros in that enforcement seeks to remain "on-chain," with staked assets that one loses as a losing party in a case.[136] Additionally, the platform seeks to work with individual courts to enforce potential court rulings and arbitration awards for "off-chain" enforcement.[137] Jur also attempts to create a semi-democratic voting system as part of "Jur citizenship."[138] Voters use their votes to check representatives and elect officials on the platform, again seeking to create a decentralized governance structure.[139]

C Bot Resolutions

In the era of ChatGPT, it is clear that Artificial Intelligence (AI) is becoming widely used and data analytics have been employed to make automated decisions in many realms. In fact, AI is entering the courtroom and disrupting the law.[140] AI is helping judges set bail and not just lawyers, but also laypersons conduct legal research and even argue in court.[141] Thus, AI or data analytics may assist fair and efficient dispute resolution for smart contract and NFT disputes by providing predictive analysis and quickly suggesting resolutions that may be subsequently entered into the blockchain. Moreover, AI will likely become "smarter" with the infusion of more data over time.

The use of AI can be problematic for legal determinations and potentially worsen the risk of bias in determinations.[142] First, there is evidence that people tend to defer to statistical data instead of using the data to help form an independent judgment.[143] We may hope that a human will remain "in the loop" and only use analytics to assist their decision accuracy, but there is fear that humans will "rubber stamp" AI or algorithmic decisions. There is fear that the use of AI to provide "bot" predictions to

---

[135] Ibid., 10.

[136] Ibid.

[137] Ibid.

[138] Ibid., 11–15.

[139] Ibid.

[140] Matt O'Brien & Dake Kang, *AI in the Court: When Algorithms Rule on Jail Time*, PHYS.ORG (January 31, 2018), https://phys.org/news/2018-01-ai-court-algorithms.html.

[141] *Artificial Intelligence and Lights-Out Court Document Processing*, COMPUTING SYS. INNOVATIONS (November 6, 2017), http://csisoft.com/artificial-intelligence-and-lights-out-court-document-processing; Hal Marcus, *Court Supports eDiscovery Machine Learning, Addresses AI Transparency*, OPENTEXT (December 12, 2017), https://blogs.opentext.com/court-supports-ediscovery-machine-learning-addresses-ai-transparency/; Rachna Manojkumar Dhanrajani, *Can ChatGPT Replace Lawyers? AI-Powered Robot Lawyer is Already Winning Cases and Even Sued for Malpractice*, BUS. TODAY (May 3, 2023), www.businesstoday.in/technology/news/story/can-chatgpt-replace-lawyers-ai-powered-robot-lawyer-is-already-winning-cases-and-even-sued-for-malpractice-379800-2023-05-03.

[142] Stephen Buranyi, *Rise of the Racist Robots – How AI is Learning All Our Worst Impulses*, THE GUARDIAN (August 8, 2017), www.theguardian.com/inequality/2017/aug/08/rise-of-the-racist-robots-how-ai-is-learning-all-our-worst-impulses.

[143] Ibid.

judges or arbitrators could essentially mean bots actually decide cases. This is made worse when AI relies on data that reflects human prejudice or is incomplete or otherwise faulty.[144] This is the "garbage in, garbage out" problem that occurs when AI "learns" from biased information. Some also worry that AI may take on a life of its own, rendering it harder to identify the factors leading to particular outcomes.[145] With the advancements of AI, the day when it is capable of rendering quick and fair resolutions or predictions on how best to resolve disputes and that people are comfortable with this, may come sooner than expected. Therefore, while we are not quite there yet, this may change in the near future or specific cases, when we will have a full sail "bot resolution" solution for smart contract disputes.

D Metaverse Arbitration

The metaverse is a 3D digital world where individuals use virtual avatars to interact with other users to "purchase and sell goods and services, sign and enforce contracts, recruit and train talent, and interact with customers and communities."[146] Said another way, the metaverse is a general descriptor for an interoperable 3D virtual world or platform created by companies where users can interact.[147] Individuals can create avatars and meet, discuss, make purchases, etc. in the metaverse. Hence, these individuals could get into disputes and even resolve those disputes through avatars in the metaverse.

It is therefore no surprise that persons could arbitrate through avatars in the metaverse. Currently, such metaverse arbitration is in its early stages, prompting numerous questions about how the structure of international arbitration can be adapted to a metaverse environment.[148] Some ask: Who should draft rules governing common metaverse-related disputes like crypto-disputes?[149] There are also questions on how to grapple with anonymity, as avatars allow for anonymity in the metaverse.[150] Arbitrators could potentially arbitrate as avatars in the metaverse and remain anonymous in the process, but how would parties then be able to assess partiality? Other questions relate to arbitration law itself, asking how existing arbitral clauses work for crypto company transactions and

---

[144] Ibid.
[145] Ibid.
[146] *See Demystifying the Metaverse*, PWC (2024), www.pwc.com/us/en/tech-effect/emerging-tech/demystifying-the-metaverse.html.
[147] *See* Andrew Mizner, *PAW2022: Blockchain, the Metaverse, and Arbitration*, Int'l. Compar. Legal Guide (April 7, 2022), https://iclg.com/cdr/arbitration-and-adr/17796-paw2022-blockchain-the-metaverse-and-arbitration.
[148] *See* Jalal El Ahdab & Claire Bentley, *Paris Arbitration Week Recap: Blockchain, NFTs, and the Metaverse*, Kluwer Arbitration Blog (May 14, 2022), http://arbitrationblog.kluwerarbitration.com/2022/05/14/paris-arbitration-week-recap-blockchain-nfts-and-the-metaverse/.
[149] *See* Schmitz & Rule, The New Handshake.
[150] *See* Juliette Asso & Laura Azaria, *Arbitration in the Metaverse: How to Anticipate and Resolve Web3 Disputes*, The Fashion Law (May 23, 2022), www.thefashionlaw.com/arbitration-in-the-metaverse-how-to-anticipate-and-resolve-web3-disputes/; Schmitz & Rule, The New Handshake.

mergers.[151] One perspective of metaverse arbitration anticipates that arbitrators themselves will have avatars in these virtual worlds resolving disputes between other users.[152] Another potential issue with conducting traditional arbitrations virtually through avatars in the metaverse could perhaps be such arbitration's efficiency.

The metaverse may also provide means for resolving blockchain-related disputes, including smart contract issues, while maintaining party anonymity. For example, a party to a smart contract could maintain anonymity while submitting their case to an avatar arbitrator in the metaverse and any decision could be immediately implemented through a smart contract. This would avoid any need for courts or revealing party identity (one of the perceived benefits of transacting through smart contracts).[153] Decentralized platforms often automatically draw decision-makers from a pre-constituted "pool" of expert arbitrators, and these decision-makers could occasionally preserve their anonymity while fulfilling their dispute resolution role in the metaverse.[154] Kleros essentially does this same thing through crowdsourced arbitration as noted above.[155] Accordingly, metaverse arbitration for NFT and smart contract disputes is not too far-fetched from what currently exists.

Managing disclosures while upholding anonymity presents challenges for arbitration in the metaverse. While complete anonymity could prevent arbitrator bias, the introduction of evidence could inadvertently reveal parties' identities. For instance, personal nuances in evidence or language can hint at a participant's identity. However, metaverse arbitration might still offer solutions for smart contracts and NFT disagreements. Limited disclosures could strike a balance between bias prevention and identity protection. In essence, while the metaverse promises intriguing prospects for dispute resolution, it is essential to establish best practices now, as traditional methods may fall short for these modern conflicts.

V ENVISIONING A ROBUST ODR SYSTEM FOR SMART CONTRACT AND NFT RESOLUTIONS

Disputes are inevitable and therefore it has become common in traditional contracts to include "dispute resolution clauses" or "arbitration clauses" that specify the redress process that will be utilized if a disagreement arises regarding the

---

[151] *See* SCHMITZ & RULE, THE NEW HANDSHAKE.

[152] *See Avatar v. Avatar: A Look at International Arbitration within the Metaverse*, WASEL&WASEL (February 2022), https://waselandwasel.ca/canada/avatar-v-avatar-a-look-at-international-arbitration-within-the-metaverse/.

[153] *See* Sneha Vijayan, *Autonomous Arbitration in the Era of the Metaverse*, KLUWER ARBITRATION BLOG (March 11, 2022), http://arbitrationblog.kluwerarbitration.com/2022/03/11/autonomous-arbitration-in-the-era-of-the-metaverse/.

[154] Elizabeth Chan et al., *Paris Arbitration Week Recap: Metaverse-Related Sessions*, KLUWER ARBITRATION BLOG (April 24, 2022), http://arbitrationblog.kluwerarbitration.com/2022/04/24/paris-arbitration-week-recap-metaverse-related-sessions/.

[155] *See* KLEROS (2024); *Aragon Court*, ARAGON (undated), https://court.aragon.org/#/dashboard.

contract.[156] Smart contracts should incorporate mechanisms for dispute resolution, given the inevitable complications that might arise, regardless of meticulous planning or coding. Traditional litigation methods are not efficient for blockchain-related issues due to their decentralized nature. Online dispute resolution (ODR) aligns well with the digital framework of smart contracts and NFTs. Users already comfortable with online platforms would likely prefer tech-driven resolution methods. Furthermore, redress procedures can be embedded directly into smart contracts, bypassing jurisdictional complexities. Using technology to create smart contracts should inherently include clauses specifying ODR for potential disputes.

As suggested by this author and Colin Rule in prior work, the ODR clause can operate in the same manner as the *Andon System* in the field of quality control.[157] The Andon System is an element of the Jidoka quality-control method pioneered by Toyota.[158] It allows any worker on a production line to push a button to stop the line if they identify a problem.[159] In the smart contract context, an ODR clause coded into the smart contract could enable both parties to push "pause" on a smart contract's execution when one of the parties identifies an issue. For example, an NFT would not immediately transfer per a smart contract if the buyer thought that the NFT is fraudulent or faulty or if the seller had evidence that the buyer did not have the funds to cover the cost. This would trigger an ODR process.

The ODR process could then enfold according to the parties' previous agreement, which could provide optionality. Parties may choose any one of the ideas noted in Section IV or something different that they craft for their particular issues. Depending on the outcome achieved, the smart contract may then resume operation or it could be recorded for a different outcome. It could even be replaced by an entirely new arrangement. It is apparent that traditional courts are not best suited for resolving smart contract disputes, but different parties may want different processes – and choice is quite important in serving process satisfaction. Coding for ODR that provides process optionality for resolving eventual disputes could help parties find resolutions without resorting to expensive and inefficient, and often ineffective, litigation.

This "Andon" idea should not allow a party to play games or inject delay into the process, as is all too common in traditional litigation. Strict time limits would be imposed and penalties applied against those who misuse the ability to freeze smart

---

[156] Alexander J.S. Colvin, *The Growing Use of Mandatory Arbitration*, Econ. Pol'y Inst. (April 6, 2018), www.epi.org/publication/the-growing-use-of-mandatory-arbitration-access-to-the-courts-is-now-barred-for-more-than-60-million-american-workers/.

[157] Schmitz & Rule, *Online Dispute Resolution*.

[158] *"Andon" – The Definition*, SageClarity (2024), https://sageclarity.com/solutions/andon-system/.

[159] Gwynn Guilford, *GM's Decline Truly Began with Its Quest to Turn People into Machines*, Quartz (December 30, 2018), https://qz.com/1510405/gms-layoffs-can-be-traced-to-its-quest-to-turn-people-into-machines/. The Andon cord is "a sort of emergency brake that would, once pulled, immediately stop the assembly line." Ibid.

contract execution. There could also be limits on when parties are able to pause execution and requirements could be in place for showing "substantial cause" for the pause. For example, the smart contract code could include examples of when a pause is proper, such as where there is an indication that an NFT violates intellectual property rules or a buyer lacks funds to cover a purchase. Other examples could be where there is evidence of faulty code or fraud in the sale.

Enforcement of such ODR can occur via smart contracts as well. For example, "ODR+" has been used to refer to smart contracts that have been used in China's dispute resolution system for e-commerce disputes.[160] The Chinese Ministry of Justice is working to refine online arbitration guidelines for China's Belt and Road Initiative (BRI), a global infrastructure development program. Arbitration for BRI disputes seeks to use ODR+ to use smart contracts and utilize blockchain efficiencies as means for promoting efficient dispute settlement outside of the courts.[161] Furthermore, China is not the only country utilizing similar measures. The United Arab Emirates, Malaysia, Kazakhstan, Pakistan, South Korea, and Singapore are BRI countries that would benefit and might have already begun utilizing some aspects of ODR+.[162] The United States, Netherlands, UK, and India are also introducing aspects of ODR+ and smart contracts to promote efficient and automatic enforcement.[163] Again, smart contracts have the potential to greatly enhance OArb and ODR, although there is a need for more ethical regulation of ODR+.[164]

Creativity is essential as we enter this new realm of dispute resolution. NFTs and smart contracts, as well as the metaverse, all demonstrate how the old confines of what is "real" and what has "value" have changed. We no longer demand that art, for example, be on canvas and framed on a wall. We also have eschewed the idea that an agreement or performance must be a "written contract inked with a wet signature." Indeed, computer-coded avatars can interact in the metaverse as they buy and sell property. Similarly, we have moved into a new era of ODR and have opportunities to reimagine access to remedies and justice.

VI CONCLUSION

Smart contracts and blockchain more generally have gained steam. Of course, there will be fiascos and frauds and it will not be all positive along the way. We have witnessed crypto crises and collapses and inevitably, there will also be abusive smart contracts and poorly constructed ODR issues that emerge. However, it has also become apparent that traditional courts are not the best suited forum for resolving

---

[160] Julien Chaisse & Jamieson Kirkwood, *Smart Courts, Smart Contracts, and the Future of Online Dispute Resolution*, 5 STAN. J. BLOCKCHAIN L. & POL'Y 62, 66–69 (2022).

[161] Ibid., 70.

[162] Ibid., 72.

[163] Ibid.

[164] Id., 89.

smart contract disputes. The jurisdictional issues alone should cause pause. ODR, therefore, provides the most logical means for addressing smart contract issues. Furthermore, user-centric ODR that provides optionality may be best suited for addressing the wide range of parties and disputes we see in the technology space. The key will be to keep our eyes on ethical design, along with creativity, to craft processes that fit not only the forum to the fuss but also the tech to the fuss.

PART VII

Conclusions and Future Directions

20

The Future of NFTs

Kevin Werbach and Kristof Lommers

I INTRODUCTION

Predicting the future of non-fungible tokens (NFTs) is challenging due to the breadth of possible applications. That breadth is, at the same time, a powerful reason to believe that NFTs will have significant and growing impacts, even as early speculative excitement dissipates.

The ERC-721 standard under which most NFTs were originally issued on the Ethereum blockchain was adopted in 2017.[1] The origins of the concept go back several years earlier.[2] Yet it was only in 2021 that the market exploded, largely around NFT collectibles and art. Even now, so many NFT use cases are still exploratory or hypothetical. As the market matures, however, significant broadening of NFT applications is likely. Many will not explicitly present themselves to users as NFT transactions. And speculation will give way to utility as the prime motivator for NFT activity. Through this process, NFTs could be a key element to onboard the next billion users to Web 3.0.

Although NFTs can represent virtually any kind of assets, digital art and collectibles were the main drivers of the NFT boom in 2021–2022. Beeple's sale of an NFT artwork through Christies for $69 million in March 2021 energized market interest.[3]

---

[1] *See* William Entriken et al., *ERC-721 Non-Fungible Token Standard*, Github: Ethereum (January 24, 2018), https://github.com/ethereum/EIPs/blob/master/EIPS/eip-721.md. It was initially introduced by AxiomZen to support its CryptoKitties application and also in order to encourage the development of other uses); *ERC-721 Non-Fungible Token Standard*, Ethereum (April 16, 2022), https://ethereum .org/en/developers/docs/standards/tokens/erc-721. For more on this standard, *see* Tonya M. Evans, *Cryptokitties, Cryptography, and Copyright*, 47 Aipla Q.J. 219, 248 (2019) (explaining the inspiration for the standard and comparing it to others); and Michael D. Murray, *Nfts and the Art World – What's Real, and What's Not*, 29 UCLA Ent. L. Rev. 25, 50–51 (2022) (describing how it "allowed NFTs to be created as 'non-fungible' (i.e., unique) bundles of data").

[2] Anil Dash, *NFTs Weren't Supposed to End Like This*, Atlantic (April 2, 2021), www.theatlantic.com/ ideas/archive/2021/04/nfts-werent-supposed-end-like/618488/.

[3] Scott Reyburn, *JPG File Sells for $69 Million, as 'NFT Mania' Gathers Pace*, N.Y. Times (March 11, 2021), www.nytimes.com/2021/03/11/arts/design/nft-auction-christies-beeple.html.

Bored Ape Yacht Club launched a month later,[4] spiking demand for rare NFTs as profile pictures (PFPs) and markers of access to exclusive clubs. In January 2022, the NFT-based collectible "play to earn" game Axie Infinity peaked at 2.78 million monthly users,[5] and NFT trading markets hit nearly $6 billion in transactions.[6]

By fall 2022, volumes had collapsed by more than 90 percent. Although trading activity picked up again somewhat in 2023, the initial collectible-driven frenzy was in hindsight clearly a speculative bubble. The demand for traditional forms of art and collectibles is quite large, so these markets for NFTs will not go away. However, as the novelty (and opportunities for dramatic short-term price appreciation) wears off, these segments of the NFT space seem likely to converge with those established markets. An investigation of the future of NFTs must therefore look beyond the areas that dominated NFT activity initially.

The advantages of NFTs – which include instant verifiability of authenticity and ownership, transparency of information on-chain, integrability with smart contracts, and the broader Web 3.0 ecosystem – could be employed for a whole variety of use cases. Beyond the digital collectibles narrative, we believe NFT rails can open up a host of new business models which give power and economic returns to a broader range of stakeholders. Already hundreds of new applications are being developed. Speculative activity such as PFP collections initially bootstrapped the NFT ecosystem. The frivolous appearance of many of these NFT projects, however, hides a deep potential for applications that serve serious business and other needs.

As discussed in Hamutal Schieber's chapter, numerous established brands – from a wide range of industries – such as *Time* magazine, Disney, Reddit, Gucci, Instagram, Nike, Porsche, and Starbucks have been openly experimenting with NFTs.[7] Although many of these initial projects are experiments or straightforward extensions of existing consumer brands through NFT collectibles, they often provide the first opportunity for prominent brands and their communities to interact with Web 3.0.

While digital asset trading and DeFi may represent the lion's share of blockchain activity, these uses still appeal to the relatively limited subset of individuals interested in active investing. NFTs, by contrast, call out to the much larger population that engages regularly with brands, creators, celebrities, and athletes. As an illustration, the popular online content site Reddit onboarded 10 million users for its NFT

---

[4] Samatha Hissong, *How Four NFT Novices Created a Billion-Dollar Ecosystem of Cartoon Apes*, ROLLING STONE (November 1, 2021), www.rollingstone.com/culture/culture-news/bayc-bored-ape-yacht-club-nft-interview-1250461/.

[5] Zhiyuan Sun, *Axie Infinity Player Count Falls Back to Jan 2021 Levels*, COINTELEGRAPH (October 12, 2022), https://cointelegraph.com/news/axie-infinity-player-count-falls-back-to-jan-2021-levels.

[6] Julia Ng, *Total Monthly NFT Trading Volume 2023*, COINGECKO (March 13, 2023), www.coingecko.com/research/publications/nft-trading-volume.

[7] Ekin Genc, *Top Brands in Web3, NFTs and the Metaverse*, COINDESK (November 14, 2022), www.coindesk.com/web3/top-brands-in-web3-nfts-and-the-metaverse/.

avatars within eleven months of its mid-2022 launch, during a period when trading of NFT art on exchanges was falling precipitously.[8]

NFTs thus offer an important foundational pattern – what developers call a primitive – for the future of Web 3.0. They could accelerate the onboarding of the next wave of digital asset users, even more so than financial trading and payment uses. And brand-oriented NFTs are only the beginning. There are numerous use cases where NFTs could provide higher efficiency and an improved experience for widespread consumer and business activities. The NFT infrastructure could be applied to the tokenization of physical assets, metaverse assets, gaming, content monetization, memberships and subscriptions, IP and patents, and many more applications. Furthermore, as argued by Kaczynski and Kominers,[9] NFTs are a tool of market design, which allows for new types of transactions. Because NFTs are programmable through smart contracts, they are flexible building blocks that can be incorporated into new market structures.

We divide our discussion into two sections. First, we look at what aspects of the NFT ecosystem are likely to change in the foreseeable future. These technical, business model, and infrastructure developments will reshape the context in which NFT use cases develop. Second, we frame and examine four emergent categories of NFT use cases beyond the currently dominant art and collectibles: assets, relationships, identity, and attestation.

II EVOLUTION OF NFTS

Existing NFT markets around art, collectibles, and PFPs will not disappear, even as other use cases take hold. However, the capabilities of NFTs and the economic activity around them will evolve. The next stage of NFT development will be manifested in three ways: technical capabilities, new business arrangements, and infrastructure-supporting NFT financialization.

A Technical Developments

The ERC-721 standard that dominated early NFT activity has significant limits. The newer ERC-1155 standard allows for dynamic NFTs, which change in response to external events through the execution of smart contracts. ERC-1155 also allows both NFTs and fungible tokens within the same contract and supports batch trading of NFTs.[10]

---

[8] Martin Young, *Reddit Collectible Avatars Onboard Nearly 10M into the Crypto, NFT Space*, COINTELEGRAPH (May 29, 2023), https://cointelegraph.com/news/reddit-collectible-avatars-onboard-millions-crypto-nft.

[9] Steve Kaczynski & Scott Duke Kominers, *How NFTs Create Value*, HARV. BUS. REV. (November 10, 2021), https://hbr.org/2021/11/how-nfts-create-value.

[10] Kimberly A. Houser & John T. Holden, *Navigating the Non-Fungible Token*, 2022 UTAH L. REV. 891, 901 (2022) (explaining that in addition to ERC-721, "Ethereum creates other standards with different functionality, such as ERC-1155, which permits the creation of semi-fungible tokens").

In 2022, several standards were proposed to support "soulbound" tokens, which cannot be moved from their initial owner. The most prominent is ERC-5114, which represents a so-called "soulbound badge" that is attached to a wallet after mint and cannot be transferred afterward.[11]

Development of new NFT capabilities and associated standards continues. For example, ERC-6551, proposed in February 2023, associates each ERC-721 NFT with a smart contract account. This allows the tokens to own assets and interact dynamically with applications.[12] While such tokens could still be transferred, they could accumulate distinctive assets over time, such as a character in a video game that obtains abilities and gear which make it both unique and more valuable. Other examples described in the ERC-6551 proposal include an NFT representing an automated investment portfolio, which is comprised of a set of fungible asset, and an NFT membership card that not only grants access to an establishment or virtual community, but also records the user's history of past interactions.[13]

Beyond standards evolution, one of the most significant developments for NFTs was the late-2022 introduction of ordinals on the bitcoin blockchain. Unlike Ethereum and the other blockchains with significant NFT activity, bitcoin lacks a generalized smart contract execution environment. This was thought to make it impossible to create NFTs, which depend on smart contracts to identify them uniquely. There are systems to add smart contract functionality to bitcoin, most notably the Stacks project, but these generally involve separate Layer 2 or sidechains that anchor to the main bitcoin chain. With the introduction of the Taproot upgrade to bitcoin, a clever developer figured out a way to inscribe NFTs and their associated content directly onto the chain. This system, called Ordinals, quickly led to a spike in bitcoin activity in early 2023, with transactions on the network reaching an all-time high and transaction fees spiking. As a result, Ordinals are a controversial topic in bitcoin circles. Some see them as effectively a "denial of service attack" against bitcoin's intended function of decentralized payments.[14]

So far, most Ordinals NFTs are derivative of major NFT projects on other blockchains. By opening up NFTs functionality to bitcoin, however, Ordinals may pave the way for new innovations. The ethos and community around bitcoin are different than those involved with other major blockchains such as Ethereum. Bitcoin has always been designed for maximal decentralization, trading off functionality for security. If Ordinals provide a pathway for decentralized application ecosystems to develop in the bitcoin environment, it will have a significant impact on the future of Web 3.0.

---

[11] ERC-5114: *Soulbound Badge*, ETHEREUM (May 30, 2022), https://eips.ethereum.org/EIPS/eip-5114.
[12] *ERC-6551: Non-Fungible Token Bound Accounts*, ETHEREUM (February 23, 2023), https://eips .ethereum.org/EIPS/eip-6551.
[13] Ibid.
[14] Brian L. Frye, *Tokenized Brands*, 9 ST. THOMAS J. COMPLEX LITIG. 31, 38 (2023) (describing this innovation and how "the first popular Bitcoin NFT project was Ordinals, which is literally just Bitcoin NFTs of the CryptoPunks images").

NFTs will also be impacted by general forms of technical evolution in blockchains. Already the introduction of Layer 2 scaling solutions, including optimistic and zero-knowledge rollups as well as sidechains, has dramatically reduced gas costs[15] on major smart contract blockchains such as Ethereum. One enduring question is the extent to which general-purpose blockchains will continue to dominate or the market to divide among "appchains" that are optimized for specific needs. For example, Dapper Labs, the creators of Cryptokitties and NBA TopShot, created its own blockchain, Flow, that is optimized for NFT collectible trading.[16] Evolution of scaling solutions, as well as segmentation mechanisms such as Avalanche subnets and Cosmos sovereign chains, could shift the balance in one direction or another. The extent to which NFTs are a feature of virtually all blockchain environments or substantially concentrated into certain areas will depend on which NFT use cases are most prominent.

Developments in blockchain-associated technologies, such as wallets, oracles,[17] data indexing and storage, and analytics, will also impact the NFT space. The user experiences around discovering, acquiring, and using NFTs will need to improve for mass consumer adoption.

B Business Models

The NFT boom of 2021 was driven by trading activity, most notably on the OpenSea exchange. One of the key business models for NFT projects was royalties, in which the original creator received an ongoing revenue stream every time the NFT changed hands. This structure resembled the traditional business arrangements for intellectual property assets such as music. However, because secondary market NFT transactions are generally conducted off-chain, there is no way to enforce royalty arrangements without the participation of the exchanges. The most common NFT standard, ERC-721, does not even include a mechanism for representing royalties; in most cases, royalties were managed as a proprietary service through OpenSea or other trading platforms.[18] Competing NFT exchanges such as X2Y2, LooksRare, and SudoSwap sought to lower purchaser costs by declining to enforce the specified

---

[15] Shaanan Cohney & David A. Hoffman, *Transactional Scripts in Contract Stacks*, 105 Minn. L. Rev. 319, 339 (2020) (explaining that "[g]as costs don't stem from the regular unit cost of storing a chunk of data or performing a computation. They are artifacts of the replicated work and storage used to maintain and validate consensus").

[16] João Marinotti, *Tangibility As Technology*, 37 Ga. St. U. L. Rev. 671, 729 (2021) (detailing the highlights of these offerings by Dapper Labs).

[17] *See, for example*, James Grimmelmann, *All Smart Contracts Are Ambiguous*, 2 J.L. & Innovation 1, 16 (2019) (generally describing smart contracts, and discussing and demonstrating ambiguity in them, including the type that is the result of oracles – algorithms that provide an information that relates to the terms of a smart contract); *Blockchain Oracles Explained: Decentralized Oracles in DeFi*, Cryptopedia (March 15, 2021), www.gemini.com/cryptopedia/crypto-oracle-blockchain-overview.

[18] *See, for example*, Andrew Hayward, *OpenSea Breaks Silence on NFT Royalties, but Creators Don't Like What They Hear*, Decrypt (June 20, 2023), https://decrypt.co/113698/opensea-breaks-silence-on-nft-royalties-but-creators-dont-like-what-they-hear (discussing the royalties issues on trading platforms).

royalties upon resale. Although Blur, which dethroned OpenSea as the top NFT trading venue in 2022 thanks to its zero trading fee business model, has agreed to enforce royalties, it demands that projects block OpenSea in order to receive them.[19]

In addition to the practical issues, royalty-based business models are problematic for other reasons. They can create misaligned incentives between creators and purchasers because creators are rewarded based on the volume of transactions rather than the value they create. Royalties also function as a tax on transactions, reducing liquidity and shifting the balance of power from consumers to producers. Legal scholar Joshua Fairfield argues that royalties are effectively kickbacks, in which creators of assets extend their control in ways that denigrate the bulk of users.[20]

Moreover, because royalty arrangements require intermediaries to collect and remit the royalties, they also can promote centralization of the transaction ecosystem. OpenSea was the dominant NFT transaction platform for some time subsequently joined and surpassed by Blur.[21] While these two players may not be the dominant ones in the future, the degree of market concentration is likely to persist because of the strong network effects around transactional relationships. The vision of NFTs as empowering creators and decentralizing power over intellectual assets is in conflict with a reality in which a small number of intermediaries exercise dominant control. Beyond the transaction platforms, there is also significant concentration of value in the most prominent NFT projects, such as Yuga Labs' Bored Ape Yacht Club and Cryptopunks. High-powered traditional IP holders such as Nike (with its RTFKT project) and the National Basketball Association (with its NBA TopShot partnership with Dapper Labs) were some of the biggest winners of the initial NFT collectible boom. While anyone can create NFT art, that does not necessarily mean disruption of existing markets.

This is not to suggest that royalties are, *per se*, an illegitimate business model. There will likely continue to be segments of the NFT world where royalties remain important. And several newer NFT standards provide mechanisms for enforcing royalties on subsequent transactions directly. However, royalties are likely to be a less prominent feature of art and collectible NFTs in the future than during the 2021 boom.

Moving away from the royalty model would create pressure for arrangements based more around the value generated by the downstream community than purely

---

[19] Cam Thompson, *Blur Escalates Royalty Battle with OpenSea, Recommends Blocking Platform*, COINDESK (February 15, 2023), www.coindesk.com/web3/2023/02/15/blur-escalates-royalty-battle-with-opensea-recommends-blocking-platform/.

[20] Joshua A. T. Fairfield, *Tokenized: The Law of Non-Fungible Tokens and Unique Digital Property*, 97 IND. L. J. 1261 (2022). But *see* Ed Lee, CREATORS TAKE CONTROL: HOW NFTs REVOLUTIONIZE ART, BUSINESS, AND ENTERTAINMENT (2023) (arguing that NFT-based royalties empower content creators and reduce the extractive power of middlemen).

[21] Jamie Crawley, *Blur Surpassed OpenSea in Daily NFT Trading Volume Wednesday, Nansen Shows*, COINDESK (February 16, 2023), www.coindesk.com/web3/2023/02/16/blur-surpassed-opensea-in-daily-nft-trading-volume-wednesday-nansen-shows/.

the original creator or distributor. Fairfield claims that NFTs provide a "grounding example" for courts to treat transactions in unique digital assets as sales of personal property rather than contractual licenses, reversing decades of caselaw that reinforced the power of content distributors.[22] A personal property model expands the scope for purchasers to create derivative works or resell assets. Some major NFT projects, most notably Bored Apes, already grant purchasers full intellectual property control over their NFTs, which incentivizes creative expansion of the ecosystem. Just as artist revenues in the music industry have shifted away from pure sales to concert revenues and merchandising, NFT projects can focus on building communities around their assets rather than just speculative trading. These models are relevant not only to art and collective NFTs. Companies using NFTs for loyalty programs can take advantage of their programmability to build more sophisticated relationships with their customers, for example.

Another developing NFT business model involves tokenomics designs that combine fungible and non-fungible tokens. Many NFT-based gaming projects also include a fungible token, necessary for participation in the game, for example requiring tokens to "breed" new NFT characters. This arrangement is a key element of the "play-to -earn" model pioneered by projects such as Axie Infinity and StepN.[23] Other NFT projects have begun airdropping fungible tokens to NFT holders, enhancing the value of the NFT and more closely tying together the ecosystem. The challenge with such arrangements is that the speculative interest in the fungible tokens can overwhelm the organic interest in the activity. Axie and StepN both saw usage plunge when token prices fell. For the hybrid NFT-fungible token model to be sustainable, the gameplay or other activity needs to be sufficiently engaging absent the artificial boost from inflated token prices driven by rapid user growth. Successful future NFT business models will need to strike this balance more effectively, building demand initially from the product rather than the financial reward for early adopters.

C Financial Infrastructure

Maturation of NFT markets will also lead to further development of the on-chain NFT transactional ecosystem. Just as decentralized finance (DeFi) protocols are creating increasingly sophisticated mechanisms for trading and lending around fungible tokens, the emergent NFT finance (NFTFi) world will provide similar capabilities for unique assets.[24] Significant categories of NFTfi activity include the following.

---

[22] *See* Fairfield, *Tokenized*, 1300.

[23] Ibid., 1277 (describing the model and giving examples for such games); Nizan Geslevich Packin, *Financial Inclusion Gone Wrong: Securities and Cryptoassets Trading for Children*, 74 HASTINGS L.J. 349, 367 (2023) (explaining the model and how it works).

[24] Sal Qadir & Kirill Naumov, *NFTs & DeFi: A Deep Dive into the Financialization of NFTs*, GALAXY DIGITAL RESEARCH (July 18, 2022), www.galaxy.com/research/whitepapers/nfts-and-defi-whitepaper/.

Trading. The initial major NFT trading platforms, such as OpenSea and Blur, are centralized exchanges maintaining off-chain order books. Just as automated market makers (AMMs) for trading fungible tokens were one of the first use cases for DeFi, NFT AMMs are now becoming available for trading NFTs. The value proposition is similar – better efficiency and liquidity through disintermediation.

Lending. Loans of digital assets may be collateralized by locking up NFTs, similar to the way DeFi lending platforms such as Aave and Compound operate with fungible tokens. These borrowing arrangements allow owners of NFTs to obtain liquidity without selling NFTs they believe will appreciate or that they wish to hold on to for their uniqueness. In situations where the holder believes the price of NFTs will drop significantly, liquidation of the loan might still be an advantageous result if the loan-to-value ratio is sufficiently high.

The most prominent NFT lending firm is NFTfi (not to be confused with the general market segment). As of mid-2023, NFTfi had issued over 40,000 NFT loans, representing a cumulative volume of over $400 million over a two-year period, with nearly $30 million in outstanding debt.[25] Although one Cryptopunks holder took out a loan for more than $8 million,[26] the average NFTfi loan is only $10,000 (https://nftfi.com/).

Fractionalization. Just as a single share can be divided, making it "cheaper and easier than ever before for ordinary people to trade securities and financial products,"[27] a single NFT can be split up into a large number of pieces, typically each represented by a fungible token, which are then sold individually. Fractionalization can lower barriers to entry for investors, improving liquidity for high-value assets. The fractionalized assets might represent an individual NFT, or a pool of NFTs, typically from the same collection, with the fungible tokens representing a pro rata claim on the whole pool. Other mechanisms for users to invest in NFT portfolios include indexes (for more passive investment) and investment DAOs (which give investors a voting stake in governance).

Renting. In some situations, users only need to control an NFT for a limited period of time. Play-to-earn games are an example. The necessary NFT-based assets to play the game may be expensive to acquire and only needed when the player is using them to generate token rewards from the game. NFT renting can thus expand access to the game. Other rental scenarios include museums displaying NFTs artwork. With tokenization of high-value physical assets, NFT rentals could expand to leasing arrangements.

Derivatives. In traditional capital markets as well as on centralized digital asset exchanges, transaction volumes for derivatives significantly exceed spot markets.

---

[25] @rchen8, *NFTfi*, DUNE (2023), https://dune.com/rchen8/NFTfi.

[26] Morgan Chittum, *NFT Whale Who Ditched Auction of 104 CryptoPunks Lands $8M Loan*, BLOCKWORKS (April 1, 2022), https://blockworks.co/news/nft-whale-who-ditched-auction-of-104-cryptopunks-lands-8m-loan.

[27] James Fallows Tierney, *Investment Games*, 72 DUKE L.J. 353, 357 (2022).

There are several efforts underway to create derivatives markets in which traders can bet on future behavior of NFT prices. These include prediction markets as well as perpetual futures.

III EMERGING USE CASES

Going forward, we see four major categories of use cases for NFTs beyond art and collectibles. These include representing assets, representing relationships and access rights, representing identity, and facilitating auditing and compliance.

A NFTs for Assets

As previously discussed, NFTs represent a unique digital certificate of an item. As a result, tokenization of existing assets through NFTs could be one of the most significant use cases going forward. In tokenization, an asset is represented on a blockchain in the form of a token, which allows it to be tracked and transacted in digital form. Virtually anything can be tokenized in this way, including traditional financial assets (stocks, bonds, derivatives), intellectual property assets, and physical goods (real estate, precious metals, artworks). Tokenization thus represents an extension of the long-standing process of securitization, where assets ranging from future royalties of popular musicians to bundles of home mortgages are chopped up into tradable securities.

Asset tokenization offers several benefits beyond existing securitization.[28] These include efficiency gains due to the removal of intermediaries and automation of transactions; improved liquidity; faster settlement; global trading; and broader access for retail investors. And for some physical goods, such as precious metals, tokenization avoids the cost of storage management. A 2022 report by the consulting firm BCG and the Asian private market exchange ADDX predicted the total addressable market for asset tokenization in 2030 would be $16 billion, or 10 percent of global GDP.[29] The market for tokenized gold already reached $1 billion in early 2023.[30]

Tokenization can involve a mix of fungible and non-fungible tokens. When the underlying asset is unique, it will be represented on-chain as an NFT. Various opportunities arise within financial assets when the assets are unique or are only limited in number, such as consumer or corporate loans. NFTs have also been proposed

[28] *The Tokenisation of Assets and Potential Implications for Financial Markets*, OECD (2020), www.oecd.org/finance/The-Tokenisation-of-Assets-and-Potential-Implications-for-Financial-Markets.htm.

[29] Sumit Kumar et al., *Relevance of On-Chain Asset Tokenization in 'Crypto Winter,'* BCG & ADDX (August 2022), https://web-assets.bcg.com/1e/a2/5b5f2b7e42dfad2cb3113a291222/on-chain-asset-tokenization.pdf.

[30] Will Canny, *Tokenization of Real-World Assets a Key Driver of Digital Asset Adoption: Bank of America*, COINDESK (April 14, 2023), www.coindesk.com/business/2023/04/14/tokenization-of-real-world-assets-a-key-driver-of-digital-asset-adoption-bank-of-america/.

as an alternative to real estate deeds where the ledger would be effectively on the blockchain. A house has already been traded on the OpenSea NFT marketplace.[31] Such arrangements have the potential to remove significant administrative burdens, protect against fraud of property documents, facilitate the use of real estate as collateral and lending, and remove frictions in trading of real estate. Furthermore, it can also help to facilitate fractional ownership of real estate and thus democratize real estate investments.

Various forms of physical goods face the challenge of combating fraud and counterfeit products, with the most prominent example being luxury goods. Counterfeiting is even becoming more common in the wine industry, with some numbers suggesting that 20 percent of premium wine in some markets is fake.[32] Linking physical goods to NFTs could help with various aspects such as authentication, tracking of provenance, trading, and even financing of production. Furthermore, various physical goods sectors, such as luxury brands, have generally struggled to digitize themselves. NFTs could be seen as a key bridge to digital assets and the virtual world.

One challenge is to properly link NFTs with "real world assets." If assets are already digital, it is easier to link them through to an NFT that is stored on the blockchain. Most financial assets, contracts, etc. are mostly digital so this is a more straightforward use case. For physical assets, however, the NFT itself merely proves uniqueness on-chain. It does not itself confirm that a particular bottle of wine or other real-world item is the one associated with the NFT. To address this problem, mechanisms such as certificates of authenticity can be implemented, including verification of real-world identity. As NFT and tokenization markets mature, such ancillary services will become a more common component. For example, physical art could be put in a museum or a vault while the digital certificate could be put as an NFT. One could argue about the advantages of NFTs in this case as it would basically not be different from a digital certificate. However, NFTs would still provide for instant proof of authenticity, ability to track provenance, and make use of the entire infrastructure that has been and will be built around NFTs.

NFTs will also be used to tokenize assets that are not commonly traded today. For example, Molecule DAO is issuing NFTs linked to intellectual property associated with biopharmaceutical research. As part of the decentralize science (DeSci) movement, it seeks to expand and democratize funding sources for scientific research.[33]

---

[31] Elizabeth Lopatto, *An Actual House Is an NFT Now*, THE VERGE (April 16, 2021), www.theverge .com/2021/4/16/22388177/nft-house-real-estate-opensea-thousand-oaks-california.

[32] Lauren Mowery, *Blockchain Technology, Fraud Prevention and the Future of Wine*, WINE ENTHUSIAST (May 20, 2021), www.wineenthusiast.com/culture/wine/blockchain-wine-fraud/.

[33] Tom Matsuda, *Decentralized Science Platform Molecule Raises $13 Million in Seed Funding*, THE BLOCK (June 13, 2022), www.theblock.co/post/151539/decentralized-science-platform-molecule-raises-13-million-in-seed-funding.

IP markets in general are often opaque and illiquid, with high search costs to find an appropriate buyer. Tokenizing those intellectual assets as NFTs opens up the potential for better liquidity and price discovery, creating markets where previously they did not exist.

B NFTs for Relationships

A second category of NFT is for representing relationships. The relationship could involve access either to an event such as a concert (tickets) or to an online community (tokengating).[34] Or it could involve an ongoing transactional relationship with a band (loyalty programs).

NFTs could disrupt the traditional ticketing industry as they can prevent forgery, decrease third-party distribution costs, reduce the cost and time of issuance, provide additional monetization opportunities for issuers, and lower the chance of loss or damage. Numerous NFT ticket solutions have focused on representing traditional tickets in the form of NFTs. Future innovation lies in the form of mechanism design to align incentives among the various parties in an access relationship. For example, identity-linked NFTs in combination with smart contract-based exchanges could create controlled markets for tickets. This way event organizers could control resale prices for their tickets and transfer wealth back from ticketing intermediaries to the creators and their communities.

NFT-based tickets also allow for improved secondary market liquidity in seasonal tickets. For example, in the case that one cannot make it to the football game on a certain day, one could lease the seat to someone else where a new NFT ticket would be issued. Market makers could buy seasonal tickets and strategically sell or lease parts of them – this will make the market more efficient and allow organizers to sell more seasonal tickets which increases upfront revenues.

Tokengating is a novel approach to restrict access by requiring the user to possess a specific set of NFTs or tokens. The use of NFTs for memberships would be more scalable and decentralized than using centralized personal accounts and whitelisted addresses. For example, the sharing of account information has been a major problem for the likes of Netflix. If there is an identity-linked subscription token one can verify the identity to use the service. This opens the door for more efficient mechanisms and less privacy-preserving measures that are currently used such as geotracking, etc. Businesses could whitelist certain (digital) identities that have been proven to be good customers. This way, for example, access to some exclusive product launches could be done to chosen identities without much administrational hassle. *Time* magazine issued TimePieces NFTs which provide unlimited access to all

---

[34] Ben Plomion, *Tokengated Communities: How Marketers Can Take Advantage of This Web3 Strategy*, FORBES (November 11, 2022), www.forbes.com/sites/forbescommunicationscouncil/2022/11/11/tokengated-communities-how-marketers-can-take-advantage-of-this-web3-strategy/.

Time content and exclusive invitations to events.[35] The NFTs also included digital art from various digital artists. *Time* has also partnered with The Sandbox to provide a location in the metaverse to host various events which could be tokengated by the TimePieces NFTs as well.

Companies could create more personalized tokengated experiences based on the nature of holdings. NFTs or tokens can trigger or unlock further exclusive NFTs, surprise giveaways, merchandise, access to a metaverse, and other unique utilities for customers. For example, true fans could be rewarded for their attendance at previous events with on-chain proof, while diehard fans holding vast collections of relevant on-chain assets can be rewarded for their long-term commitment and support.

A further evolution of this model is for creators to adopt a membership relationship with their communities. As argued by Yang,[36] NFT memberships could help creators to improve their brand and let fans share in the upside as the community grows. NFT memberships can replace and complement subscriptions and other traditional revenue models by segmentation of willingness to pay – here the exchange part as previously discussed is important – and reward early members.

Loyalty programmes today constitute a core part of customer retention and resale strategies for many of the leading consumer-oriented brands. Proprietary loyalty programs tend to be flawed, rarely interoperate with one another, and suffer from administrative overhead. Furthermore, the benefits within customer loyalty programmes tend to belong to the corporation where they are not owned by the customer. In Web 3.0, thanks to NFTs, the relationship is flipped as the loyalty program could be owned by the customer where the corporation is the issuer or given privileged access.

A myriad of opportunities opens up in terms of collaborations targeting a superset of token-holding fans belonging to one or more communities. In Web 2.0, product developers are required to jump through bureaucratic and technical hoops to collaborate with another project. In Web 3.0, developers query the wallet addresses of users belonging to the communities that they would like to target and then launch a collaboration. As argued by Time president Keith Grossman, NFTs allow consumers to go from "online renters" – where companies give access in return for data or attention span – to "online owners" where customers are actual co-owners.[37]

---

[35] *TIME Launches TIMEPieces, a First of Its Kind Initiative and Collection of More than 4,500 Original NFTs from Over 40 Artists Around the World*, TIME (September 22, 2021), https://time.com/6100404/timepieces-nft-collection/.

[36] Peter Yang, *A Practical Guide to NFT Memberships for Creators*, A16Z FUTURE (June 16, 2022), https://future.com/a-practical-guide-to-nft-memberships-for-creators/.

[37] Riley de Leon, *How 99-Year-Old Publisher Time Is Leading Legacy Media into the NFT Future*, CNBC (July 17, 2022), www.cnbc.com/2022/07/17/99-year-old-publisher-time-is-leading-legacy-media-into-the-nft-future.html.

Web 3.0-based identity systems could also be used to facilitate collaborations between organizations more easily. The main bottleneck to more partnerships, especially for smaller brands, is the headache of sharing data with other brands. In most cases, this is too costly for brands even when collaboration can be beneficial and lucrative. However, if both of these chains used on-chain memberships, each chain would be able to verify an individual's membership of the other chain without much effort and especially without needing to change anything about the brands' infrastructures. This entails that the brands would potentially not even need to agree to this deal. For instance, a local restaurant next to one of the gyms might offer discounts on food to members of the gym without any reciprocal deal, simply because this would attract more gym-goers to the restaurant.

Shopify executive Alex Danco has referred to this "wallet-first" approach as "tokengated commerce."[38] Describing collaborations as the lifeblood of creative work, he states: "But online, how do you organize a collab merch drop that's exclusive for a superset of people: my fans plus your fans? There's no conventional way to do this that's both exclusive and not janky. But tokengated commerce makes this so easy." Luxury jewelry firm Tiffany & Co. created 250 NFTs where only CryptoPunk holders are able to mint a physical custom gem-encrusted pendant based on their CryptoPunk.[39] This NFT collection builds on an existing community of wealthy CryptoPunk holders without needing to directly collaborate with CryptoPunk owners Yuga Labs and saving the commercial and legal contractual agreements which would be typically needed in a partnership without NFTs.

Coupons are a handy tool for customer acquisition and engagement; however, coupon fraud is estimated to cost US businesses approximately $300–600 million a year.[40] This can go to fake coupons, reused coupons, and gaming the distribution systems for the coupons. Countering coupon fraud is a large administrative burden for businesses and (identity-linked) NFT coupons can help to prevent fraud.

Businesses could issue tokens to customers. For example, restaurants could issue non-transferable tokens to diners. Over time, diners would create an on-chain record of their dining experience which benefits restaurants as, for example, they can whitelist their regulars and issue them token-based coupons. More broadly, this activity could replace Google Maps and Reviews, or TripAdvisor where the "dining out" history is now on-chain and tokens can be programmed so that data sharing is optional, if enabled token holders can be remunerated for restaurant querying their data or sending them tokens.

---

[38] Alex Danco, *Tokengated Commerce*, ALEX DANCO'S NEWSLETTER (May 2, 2022), https://danco .substack.com/p/tokengated-commerce.

[39] Tanzeel Akhtar, *Jewelry Brand Tiffany & Co. Unveils $50K CryptoPunk Necklaces*, COINDESK (August 1, 2022), www.coindesk.com/business/2022/08/01/jewelry-brand-tiffany-and-co-unveils-50k-cryptopunk-necklaces/.

[40] Dawn Marron, *Coupon Fraud Is Crime, Even If It Feels Harmless: Coupon Counselor*, PENNLIVE (April 26, 2017), www.pennlive.com/life/2017/04/coupon_crime_is_no_joke.html.

C NFTs for Identity

One of the defining features of blockchain has been the ability to transfer tokens in a decentralized, trustless, and non-reversible manner. As blockchains move outside their narrow financial corridor, the optionality to transfer specific tokens outside a set of given rules can become a restricting feature. Numerous upcoming NFT use cases require non-transferability and efficient verification of on-chain identity. Identity-linked NFTs could represent a core primitive for future use cases within the Web 3.0 ecosystem. Some of the major use cases of identity-linked NFTs include identity and credentials, access and memberships, authentication and ownership, customer engagement and loyalty, and attendance.

The two main ways that have so far been explored to tie a wallet to an off-chain identity are to: (1) create a token that represents on-chain some highly identifiable and persistent information about a person, such as an image of their face or private information; or (2) generate the wallet's private key or other secret information from a person's biometric information. The main concern with the first method is that it would take inherently private information about individuals and save them on a public ledger, which would be detrimental to privacy and, more seriously, could lead to identity theft. On the other hand, the principal objection to the second method is that biometric data has been made public by mainstream adoption of fingerprint- and face-scanning as a way to unlock mobile phones. As a result, this would make any private key derived from biometric data easily compromisable.

Esber and Kominers discuss a framework for reputation-based systems and argue that it could help to incentivize higher-quality contributions of community members.[41] More specifically, they make the case for a two-token system where one would be used for reputation-signaling and the other for offering liquidity. For this purpose, you could divide governance into ordinary token-based governance and a non-token mechanism which can be based on reputation within the protocol community. In the latter part, one could implement a reputation-linked governance token system where meaningful contributors would receive more governance rights. This is in line with the view that distributing governance rights to stakeholders who meaningfully contributed to the protocol can improve governance.[42] In this regard you could introduce two-tiered governance structures with ordinary transferable tokens with governance rights and non-transferable governance tokens which are gained through reputation within the protocol community. Productive members could still be rewarded transferable tokens – which have monetary value and could

[41] Jad Esber & Scott Duke Kominers, *A Novel Framework for Reputation-Based Systems*, A16Z CRYPTO (September 30, 2021), https://a16zcrypto.com/posts/article/reputation-based-systems/.

[42] Andrew Hall & Porter Smith, *Lightspeed Democracy: What Web3 Organizations Can Learn from the History of Governance*, A16Z CRYPTO (June 29, 2022), https://a16zcrypto.com/posts/article/lightspeed-democracy-what-web3-organizations-can-learn-from-the-history-of-governance/.

be sold on the open market – but there would be included a non-transferable element as well.

One would be able to present one's identity based on verified information on holdings, credentials, interests, subscriptions, memberships, protocol interactions, on-chain voting behavior, etc. As argued by Kominers and Esber, one of the main selling points in Web 3.0 is that every wallet would represent a unique identifier of a person or entity.[43] These memberships, credentials, interactions, etc. could all be preserved on an NFT where your wallet represents a collection of these NFTs. An identity-linked credential mechanism is applicable to a whole host of use cases such as education, work experience, extracurricular activities, credits score, etc. Furthermore, one could acquire direct on-chain credentials by participating in DAOs or transacting with specific protocols. As the on-chain ecosystem grows, one could verify which books one has read, which articles one has written, which research one has done, etc. It would allow individuals to present a true picture of one's identity without the conventional constraints of the physical world which are typically used to identify people. Furthermore, as argued by a 2022 report by Web 3.0 Studios, digital identity could help bridge the trust gap online and in the metaverse by allowing appropriate verification. Digital identities would allow online engagement within a trustless yet verified context.[44]

An alternate approach proposed by Weyl, Ohlhaver, and Buterin is that wallets holding non-transferable tokens, which they call "souls," would not necessarily correspond to unique individuals.[45] This would avoid the need for biometric linkage between the virtual representation and the individual in the physical world. It would also allow those who wish to operate multiple personas, for example maintaining a professional identity separate from their personal one. In Weyl, Ohlhaver, and Buterin's conception of "soulbound tokens," the wallets would aggregate non-transferable attestations, which, at least in the initiation instantiations, would be publicly readable on-chain. As users acquire more soulbound tokens, their souls would become increasingly unique and difficult to forge. Reputational systems could be generated based on on-chain verified activities, rather than centralized data aggregators.

While the soulbound token idea, like Satoshi Nakamoto's original conception of bitcoin, operates on the principle that transaction histories are public but not tied to individual identities, another approach is to make NFT-based systems that do not reveal any personal information. Using cryptographic techniques, individuals could be able to store data about themselves, such as credentials or attestations, and prove ownership of these pieces of data in a way that reveals little else about their identity. Technologically,

[43] Scott Duke Kominers & Jad Esber, *With Decentralized Identity, Your Reputation Travels with You Across Cyberspace*, Future (November 18, 2021), www.hbs.edu/faculty/Pages/item.aspx?num=61505.

[44] *See Digital Identities: Who Will We Be in the Metaverse?*, web3 Studios (August 2022), https://uploads-ssl.webflow.com/62f4e01684d011324ec127a4/644fe06a76ad649f9ca07369_Digital-Identities-Market-Report-2022%20(1).pdf.

[45] E. Glen Weyl, Puja Ohlhaver, & Vitalik Buterin, *Decentralized Society: Finding Web3's Soul* (May 10, 2022) (unpublished manuscript), https://papers.ssrn.com/sol3/papers.cfm?abstract_id=4105763.

this focus on privacy has been fueled by the research into zero-knowledge proofs and by toolkits that allow proof systems to be built more quickly and efficiently.

On a high level, zero-knowledge proofs use number theory to prove knowledge about a piece of information without revealing that piece of information. Applied to a macroscale, privacy-preserving identity methods of this type could enable the creation of decentralized societies in which members are vetted in a privacy-preserving way, without giving up personal information. Anything that constitutes a verifiable credential can be preserved securely, allowing you to interact with a host of decentralized applications and societies. Data that we would find unthinkable to share can be securely hosted in your wallet and only shared with the access-controlled permissioned and privileged. Credentials could be securely held and verified without fear of data leakage using privacy-preserving tools.

By using NFT-based credentials, employers can securely and easily verify the qualifications and credentials of job applicants without the need for intermediaries. This can also help to reduce the time and resources required for the hiring process and ensure that only qualified individuals are hired. Even more conveniently, job-matching marketplaces would be able to automatically reject applications that do not meet required qualifications or fast-track candidates based on other decision criteria set out by the hiring company. Similarly, this could be used in academia to verify the credentials and qualifications of students, teachers, and researchers. By using a decentralized and immutable ledger, such as the blockchain, academic institutions can securely store and verify qualifications and credentials without the need for intermediaries.

An interesting application is the ability for individuals or organizations to be able to verify the identity of others without needing to rely on an intermediary. This could be particularly useful in industries such as finance, where accurate and reliable identity verification is crucial for preventing fraud and money laundering. By using digital identity systems, individuals and organizations can securely and easily verify the identity of others through the use of verified credentials or zero-knowledge badges. For example, one's age, credit history, or employment status could easily be proven and verified in a way that does not rely on intermediaries, such as banks or governments. This is related to tokengating, which is an approach to restricting access by requiring the user to possess a specific set of NFTs or tokens. The tokens acting as keys can be used to unlock online content, multimedia, software, access to venues or discounts, and much more. With digital identities, tokengating can be combined with proof of humanity/identity and only allow any unique person to access a specific perk once, even when they hold multiple tokens.

D NFTs for Attestation, Audit, and Compliance

Aside from NFT providing proof of authenticity and ownership, additional data can be provided by Web 3.0 data infrastructure that can be used to track the provenance of products. In addition, production information, inventory status, and all relevant events can be linked to the NTF providing the necessary data to make investment decisions when registered by the relevant actors in the wine supply chain. There have been various projects using Web 3.0 for the purpose of supply chainwide applications that offer this data capturing and distribution protocols (e.g., VeChain, a blockchain platform for tracking provenance of products).[46]

Numerous companies within the NFT sphere have been working on NFT pricing and appraisal where we have reached a point in the NFT ecosystem where real-time appraisals are available for most NFTs. Furthermore, one could also issue proof-of-appraisal where community-based appraisal could be performed and an NFT is issued. Numerous organizations (e.g., Lithium Finance) have been working on decentralized valuation protocols which allow on-demand price estimation of assets by a community of market participants utilizing crowd wisdom and crypto-economics. Together with a proof-of-authenticity, one could leverage a valuation protocol where a (preselected) community of valuators present estimates with a market-clearing mechanism aggregating these inputs to produce an appraisal estimate. This way we would allow for an efficient way to provide immediate proof of ownership, authenticity, and appraisal for assets. This has the opportunity to drastically reduce search and transaction costs in illiquid and ambiguous assets such as art. Appraisal and benchmarks can help make more efficient markets – for example, with houses, if you know the appraisal price of one year ago and the market conditions in the past year, you can fairly well estimate the current appraisal price.

Introduced in 2019, POAPs (proof-of-attendance-protocol) are a unique way to reward and verify physical or virtual event attendees and can represent, endorse, or recognize past history through token ownership. Over time, these could verify and document token holders' experiences. Furthermore, POAPs have become status symbols and – due to no restrictions on transferability – tradeable, as POAP owners sometimes receive benefits from event organizers which provide a financial or utility benefit beyond just proving attendance.[47] However, as argued by Buterin,[48] POAP is an excellent example of an NFT use case that would work better if it were identity-linked. Imagine being able to prove that you were actually at Woodstock with your best friends, witnessing Jimi Hendrix play and you had a unique NFT that was only available to a specific set of eventgoers. That memorable experience becomes set in stone (or more specifically, set on-chain) and would cultivate community and a social connection with the group of token holders as well as providing

---

[46] For more on the impact of the company's products, *see* Godfrey Benjamin, *VeChain Leads the Charge against Billion-Dollar Counterfeit Markets with Unparalleled Transparency and Industry-Leading Security*, CRYPTO NEWS FLASH (June 16, 2021), www.crypto-news-flash.com/vechain-leads-the-charge-against-billion-dollar-counterfeit-markets-with-unparalleled-transparency-and-industry-leading-security/.

[47] Maghan McDowell, *Proofs of Attendance Are Web3's New Status Symbol*, VOGUE BUSINESS (May 17, 2022), www.voguebusiness.com/technology/proofs-of-attendance-are-web3s-new-status-symbol.

[48] Vitalik Buterin, *What in the Ethereum Application Ecosystem Excites Me*, VITALIK BUTERIN'S WEBSITE (December 5, 2022), https://vitalik.ca/general/2022/12/05/excited.html.how.

an immutable "proof of experience." This group of token holders could gain further utility by contributing to the next concert's playlist for example – a superfan playlist DAO.

Using a mechanism of access control and permissioning, POAPs could be programmed to include additional conditions, such as identity linking and a combination, presence, or quorum of POAP holders, unlocking further exclusive soulbound tokens, truly verifying personal attendance at events. These enhanced POAPs can act as access badges, discounts, or a whitelist for a super set of identity-linked NFT holders. In some fields, such as medicine, professional development derived from attendance at conferences is considered a core professional requirement where participation is rewarded with continued professional development and continuing medical education points. Proof of attendance could also help to combat fake online reviews as users would have to provide proof that they were actual customers. Finally, businesses could incentivize online reviews where true customers are rewarded with tokens or other perks after posting a (verified) review.

Aside from NFT providing authenticity and ownership, additional data can be provided by Web 3.0 data infrastructure, which can be used to track the provenance of products. In addition, production information, inventory status, and all relevant events can be linked to the NFT providing the necessary data to make investment decisions when registered by the relevant actors in the supply chain.

On-chain accounting will enable a real-time reporting system where the reports could be put on the blockchain in order to have an authentic immutable version readily available on-chain from the moment these are issued. In this case, the reports could be put on-chain through a censorship-resistant file storage system such as Interplanetary File Systems (IPFS). You could issue crypto-native objects (such as an NFT) that act like an on-chain proof of authenticity and token of access where the object would have a pointer to the report in the (secured) centralized database. Companies could ask for a financial report to be issued where the protocol issues an NFT to be sent to relevant parties. Legal scholar Chris Brummer has proposed using NFT-based disclosures as a foundation for reinventing securities regulation on blockchain-based foundations.[49]

IV CONCLUSION

True mass adoption of NFTs will occur when the technology becomes effectively invisible. The pull for users will be the value of the use case, whether for consumers or enterprises, not excitement about the NFT concept. How long it takes for this to happen and which currently nascent uses find large-scale adoption remains to be seen. We cannot predict which of the NFT-based use cases or financial models described here will succeed with any confidence because adoption depends on

---

[49] Chris Brummer, *Disclosure, Dapps and DeFi*, STAN. J. BLOCKCHAIN L. & POL'Y (2022).

many factors beyond maturity of the technology. On the one hand, excitement and investment around NFT art and collectible markets, as we saw in 2021, proves out the interest in NFTs as a concept and stimulates development of other use cases. On the other hand, with so much of NFT activity associated with these speculative uses, it can become difficult for users to see NFTs as means of providing functional benefits.

Those who succeed in employing NFTs for uses such as tokenization, ticketing, reputation systems, and attestation may well not use the term or even discuss the underlying distributed ledger technology. At the same time, there will continue to be increasingly complex trading arrangements built around NFTfi and tokenomics designs to replace royalties for the more sophisticated participants in NFT-based markets.

Index

64 Gallon Toter (Robness), 28–29

action. *See* common-law action
Adler, Amy, 295
advertising. *See* marketing and advertising, for NFTs
AI. *See* artificial intelligence (AI)
Allison, James P., 258
allocation tables, 300–303
  ERC-721 standard, 301–302
  ERC-1155 standard, 302–303
  lazy minting and, 302
  mapping and, 301
  smart contracts, 301
Alphabet, 193–194
Altman, Sam, 369
AML. *See* anti-money laundering (AML), NFT transactions and
AMLDs. *See* Anti-Money Laundering Directives (AMLDs)
ancillary violations, of copyright law, 232–233
Andresen, Gavin, 14
anonymity, in NFT transactions, 90–91
anti-fraud compliance, 356
anti-fraud laws, 66, 152
anti-money laundering (AML), NFT transactions and. *See also* money laundering, NFTs and
  analysis of, 102
  Anti-Money Laundering Directives, 81–82
  Bank Secrecy Act, 84, 159
  Basel Committee, 80
  Caribbean Financial Action Task Force and, 87
  collaborative efforts against, 96–98
  Commodity Futures Trading Commission, 85
  compliance challenges in, 92
    technological advancements, 100–102
  conceptual analysis of, 78–79
  custodial services and, 97–98
  EGMONT, 86, 88
  exchanges in, 97–98

  Financial Action Task Force and, 80, 82–83
    jurisdictions for, 90
    Private Sector Consultative Forum, 88
  Financial Action Task Force on Money Laundering in South America, 87
  Financial Conduct Authority, 85–86
  Financial Crimes and Enforcement Network, 84, 93
  future trends for, 99–102
    anticipated regulatory developments, 99–100
    technological advancements, 100–102
  industry initiatives and, 87–88, 96–98
  International Monetary Fund and, 87
  JMLIT and, 88
  marketplaces for, 97–98
  metaverse and, 364–365
  Office of Foreign Assets Control, 85
  public–private partnerships and, 87–88
  regulation of, 83–84
    anticipated developments in, 99–100
    CDD measures, 83
    cross-border cooperation in, 86–87, 100
    in EU, 81–82
    evolution of, 80–83, 92–96
    expansion of, 80–81
    harmonization efforts in, 86–87
    international standards and guidelines, 86
    for investor protections, 99
    record-keeping and retention, 84
    relevant regulatory authorities, 84–86
    risk-based approaches in, 84
    self-regulatory organizations, 96–97
    through taxation strategies, 99–100
    through transaction monitoring and reporting, 83
  risks in NFT markets, 88–92
    case studies, 93–95
    international organizations' approach to, 95–96
    typologies and, 89

417

Milton Keynes UK
Ingram Content Group UK Ltd.
UKHW012122041124
450750UK00007B/44